D1230153

ARTHURIAN STUDIES LXIX

GEOFFREY OF MONMOUTH

THE HISTORY OF THE KINGS OF BRITAIN

An Edition and Translation of the

De gestis Britonum

[Historia Regum Britanniae]

ARTHURIAN STUDIES

ISSN 0261–9814

General Editor: Norris J. Lacy

Previously published volumes in the series
are listed at the back of this book

GEOFFREY OF MONMOUTH

THE HISTORY OF THE KINGS OF BRITAIN

An Edition and Translation of

De gestis Britonum

[*Historia Regum Britanniae*]

Edition by
Michael D. Reeve

Translation by
Neil Wright

THE BOYDELL PRESS

Editorial matter © Michael D. Reeve 2007
Translation © Neil Wright 2007

All Rights Reserved. Except as permitted under current legislation
no part of this work may be photocopied, stored in a retrieval system,
published, performed in public, adapted, broadcast,
transmitted, recorded or reproduced in any form or by any means,
without the prior permission of the copyright owner

First published 2007
The Boydell Press, Woodbridge

ISBN 978-1-84383-206-5

.

The publishers are grateful to the Vinaver Trust
for generously providing a subvention towards
the production costs of this volume

The Boydell Press is an imprint of Boydell & Brewer Ltd
PO Box 9, Woodbridge, Suffolk IP12 3DF, UK
and of Boydell & Brewer Inc.
668 Mt Hope Avenue, Rochester, NY 14620, USA
website: www.boydellandbrewer.com

A CIP catalogue record for this book is available
from the British Library

This publication is printed on acid-free paper

Printed in Great Britain by
Biddles Ltd, King's Lynn, Norfolk

CONTENTS

INTRODUCTION

Geoffrey, Merlin, and De gestis Britonum

At Oxford from 1129 to 1152 a Galfridus Artur, twice called *magister*, and a Gaufridus bishop elect and then bishop of St Asaph, once called *magister*, witnessed several extant documents, mostly alongside Walter archdeacon of Oxford[1]. The author of the work commonly known as *Historia regum Britanniae* names himself as Galfridus Monemutensis (§§ 3, 110, 177) and says that he has translated an old British book put at his disposal by Walter (§§ 2, 208); and not only do some of the older and better manuscripts call the author in titles and subscriptions Galfridus Artur (or Arturus) Monemutensis, but in its transmitted form the work must have been finished between 1123, when Alexander was consecrated bishop of Lincoln (§ 110)[2], and January 1139, when Robert of Torigni showed Henry of Huntingdon a copy at Bec[3]. Robert, presumably in a position to know, already treated the three bearers of the name as the same person[4].

So great was the success of the work, especially in England and northern France, that 217 manuscripts have been listed, perhaps a third of them written before the end of the century[5]. From their relationships it will emerge below

1 H. E. Salter, 'Geoffrey of Monmouth and Oxford', *E. H. R.* 34 (1919) 382-5. When he illustrates nos. 5 and 2 as nos. 60 and 101 in *Facsimiles of early charters in Oxford muniment rooms* (Oxford 1929), he repeats in his transcription of no. 5 the mistake *Artour* for *Arturo* and treats no. 2 as a forgery. As no. 102 he adds another document witnessed by Geoffrey, but that too he treats as a forgery.

2 *Oxford dictionary of national biography* on line (David M. Smith).

3 R. Howlett, *Chronicles of the reigns of Stephen, Henry II., and Richard I.* IV (London 1889) 64. J. S. P. Tatlock, 'Contemporaneous matters in Geoffrey of Monmouth', *Speculum* 6 (1931) 206-24, at pp. 221-3, and again in *The legendary history of Britain: Geoffrey of Monmouth's* Historia regum Britanniae *and its early vernacular versions* (Berkeley 1950) 117, 435, plausibly suggests that Anacletus in §§ 9-12 owes his rare name to the antipope of 1130-38, who assumed it.

4 *Chronicles* (n. 3) IV 168 *Gaufridus Artur, qui transtulerat historiam de regibus Britonum de Britannico in Latinum, fit episcopus Sancti Asaph in Norgualis* [1152]. On the name and background of Geoffrey see also O. J. Padel, 'Geoffrey of Monmouth and Cornwall', *Cambridge Medieval Celtic Studies* 8 (1984) 1-28.

5 Julia C. Crick, *The Historia regum Britannie of Geoffrey of Monmouth* III: *A summary catalogue of the manuscripts* (Cambridge 1989). In 'Two newly located manuscripts of Geoffrey of Monmouth's *Historia regum Britannie*', *Arthurian Literature* 13 (1995) 151-6, she added as nos. 216 and 217 Halle Univ. Stolberg-Wernigerode Za 38 and Berlin Lat. 4° 941, the latter of which I saw in January 1991 and

that Geoffrey must actually have called the work *De gestis Britonum*, and so that is what I shall call it here.

He had already released a trailer for it. After telling how Merlin outwitted Vortigern's wizards (§ 108), he turns aside to mention that before he reached that point many people who had got wind of Merlin, not least Alexander bishop of Lincoln, pressed him to issue Merlin's prophecies (§ 109). Most manuscripts of *De gestis Britonum* incorporate them (§§ 111-17), introduced either by an address to Alexander or by a statement that he complied with Alexander's request (§ 110); in both versions of the transaction he says that he had intended to finish *De gestis Britonum* before tackling the prophecies. He could indeed have passed straight from § 108 to § 118, because once Merlin has solved Vortigern's immediate problem it would be natural for Vortigern's own prospects to form the subject of his next question to Merlin; without the first sentence of § 118 there would be an acceptable join, though with repetition of Vortigern's *admiratio*, and an even better join could be obtained by removing *Ammirabantur etiam cuncti ... in illo* from the end of § 108 and *Cum igitur ... uaticinia collaudat* from the beginning of § 118. That Geoffrey did issue the prophecies separately is confirmed both directly and indirectly by Orderic Vitalis, who worked at St-Évroul. In his *Historia ecclesiastica* Orderic quotes a section (§§ 113.72-115.108) as from a *Merlini libellus* and interprets the phrase *leo iusticiae* (§ 113.78) as a reference to Henry I, whom he speaks of in the present tense as awaiting his divinely ordained but uncertain destiny[6]; Henry died on December 1st 1135. The indirect evidence that he furnishes lies in the relationship between his text and the text found in separate copies, of which over 80 survive[7]. In principle, these could be either copies of a separate

mentioned in 'The transmission of the *Historia regum Britanniae*', *J. M. L.* 1 (1991) 73-117, at p. 86 n. 26; on her previous but provisional no. 217, Madrid Nac. R 202, see ibid. and n. 11 on p. 155 of her article. Add as no. 218 Schaffhausen Min. 74 (s. xii/xiii), which I saw in March 1998; it is described by R. Gamper, Gaby Knoch-Mund, & Marlis Stähli, *Katalog der mittelalterlichen Handschriften der Ministerialbibliothek Schaffhausen* (Dietikon-Zürich 1994) 180-82. In June 2005 I found what becomes no. 219, Leipzig UB. 3518 (s. xii²), last mentioned, so far as I know, in 'Handschriften und Urkunden in der Bibliothek des Herrn Hofrath und Prof. Dr Gustav Hänel zu Leipzig', *Serapeum 7* (1846) 234-37, at p. 235 no. 8 ('De gestis Britannorum usque ad ann. 766 ... saec. XIV'); he acquired it from Petruzzi at Rome on 6.2.1825.

6 12.47; see Marjorie Chibnall, *The Ecclesiastical History of Orderic Vitalis* VI (Oxford 1978) 380-88. A. Le Prévost in his edition, IV (Paris 1852) 493 n. 1, followed by Faral (n. 20 below) II 9-10, stated that *usque ad tempora Henrici et Gritfridi, qui nunc dubia sub sorte adhuc imminentia praestolantur quae sibi diuinitus ineffabili dispositione ordinantur* must antedate Henry's death. Tatlock, *Legendary history* (n. 3) 418-21, made light of *Merlini libellus*, argued that Orderic had read the larger work and the prophecies as part of it, and took as the antecedent of *qui* not just *Henrici et Gritfridi* but all the kings listed, who begin with Arthur; yet if *historiarum gnari* will be able to interpret prophecies about those kings, can they themselves still be waiting to find out what befell them?

7 Caroline D. Eckhardt, 'The *Prophetia Merlini* of Geoffrey of Monmouth: Latin manuscript copies', *Manuscripta 26* (1982) 167-76; Crick, *Catalogue* (n. 5) 330-32; M. D. R., 'Transmission' (n. 5) 116 n. 63. Add Berlin Phill. 1880 ff. 182-6 (s. xiii¹), reported by J. Hammer, *M. L. Q.* 3 (1942) 238, and Paris B. N. Lat. 14465 ff. 130-36 (s. xii). There are also commentaries, many of them produced before the end of the 12th century; see Eckhardt, *The* Prophetia Merlini *of Geoffrey of Monmouth: a fifteenth-century English commentary* (Cambridge Mass. 1982) 10-15, and Crick, *The Historia regum Britannie of Geoffrey of Monmouth* IV: *Dissemination and reception in the later Middle Ages* (Cambridge 1991) 85-7.

work or excerpts from *De gestis Britonum*, but some agree with him in a few places against the usual text of *De gestis Britonum* and include a prophecy absent from *De gestis Britonum* for no better reason, it seems, than a scribal *saut du même au même* (§ 116.174)[8]. Geoffrey can therefore be taken at his word, and *De gestis Britonum* becomes an early witness to the *Prophetiae*.

There is not much of a case, however, for editing the *Prophetiae* separately, because the differences between the separate version and the version incorporated in *De gestis Britonum* are few in number, slight in substance, and perhaps mostly or even wholly scribal. Nevertheless, the *saut du même au même* creates a dilemma: if an editor of *De gestis Britonum* remedies it so as to restore what Geoffrey presumably intended, a text results that did not exist until medieval readers noticed the missing passage in copies of the *Prophetiae* and transferred it to *De gestis Britonum*[9]. Furthermore, the division between manuscripts of the two works is untidy, as I shall explain below.

The issuing of the *Prophetiae* before *De gestis Britonum* may have made scholars readier to suspect that *De gestis Britonum* itself went through several versions. A still more obvious reason for the suspicion is that the extant manuscripts attest five different forms of dedication: to Robert of Gloucester alone; to Robert and Waleran, count of Meulan; to King Stephen and Robert; to someone nameless; and to no-one at all. Furthermore, instead of quoting Geoffrey's address to Alexander (§ 110) some manuscripts refer to Alexander's request in language nevertheless characteristic of Geoffrey, which includes his designation of himself as a bashful Briton (*pudibundus Brito*); and the oldest of these (O, no. 156) is also the only manuscript to include in the title or subscription the mysterious phrase *secundum Caratonum*.

The dedication to Stephen and Robert, however, is a clumsy adjustment, found in one manuscript (no. 15), of the dedication to Robert and Waleran[10]; the nameless dedication, found in 25 manuscripts, is a corrupt form of the dedication to Robert alone[11]; and the absence of any dedication surely arose when people decided to make the work begin with the description of Britain (§ 5: nos. 1, 4, 5, 67, 68, 70, 106, 110, 143, 163) or the narrative (§ 6: nos. 41, 69, 86, 132, 140, 142, 178, 200)[12]. Either, then, the original dedication was the one to Robert alone (§ 3), found in 129 manuscripts, and Geoffrey augmented it with three sentences addressed to Waleran (§ 4), or it was the joint dedication (§§ 3-4), found in ten manuscripts (nos. 39, 48, 49, 107, 128, 134, 136, 170,

---

8 'Transmission' (n. 5) 93-7.
9 In 'Errori in autografi', in P. Chiesa & L. Pinelli (ed.), *Gli autografi medievali: problemi paleografici e filologici* (Spoleto 1994), 37-60, I ventured into the controversy over how editors should handle authorial intention.
10 A. Griscom, 'The date of composition of Geoffrey of Monmouth's *Historia*: new manuscript evidence', *Speculum* 1 (1926) 129-56, at pp. 149-54; E. Brugger, 'Zu Galfrid von Monmouth's Historia Regum Britanniae', *Zeitschr. für franz. Sprache und Lit.* 57 (1933) 257-312, at pp. 271-6.
11 'Transmission' (n. 5) 81 (from Neil Wright).
12 Brugger (n. 10) 276-7. No. 12 begins after the prophecies at § 118, no. 215, merely excerpts, in § 31. In 29 manuscripts the beginning is lost. No. 108 begins at § 6, but the hand that took over on f. 223v at § 16.303 *premuntur* added §§ 1-3 and 5 at the end with the dedication to Robert. No. 159 is John Leland's digest of the work.

197², 199), and he reduced it by dropping those sentences. The address in § 177 to a single *consul auguste* supports the former alternative[13]. In either event, the main witness to the joint dedication (H, no. 170) has no peculiarities of note in the body of the text[14]. The main witness to the shorter form of § 110 (O, no. 156) has no other peculiarities of note except that it omits the compliment to Walter at § 2.8-9 and in §§ 173-99 lacks many phrases present in the bulk of the tradition; not only, however, is it easier to imagine that a later reader shortened the usual text than that Geoffrey first produced this version and then padded it out, but the abbreviation stops when a new hand takes over at § 200 (f. 181v) and must therefore have been carried out in this very manuscript.

Peculiarities that go beyond the usual range of scribal whim or frailty do occur in two groups of manuscripts. One group begins at § 5, and the other has the dedication to Robert alone.

The text offered by the former of these groups, known as the First Variant Version, has been edited twice[15], more recently from eight manuscripts (nos. 1, 4, 55, 67, 68, 70, 106, 163), though not all of them represent it throughout. The second editor argues that it is a reworking of *De gestis Britonum* by someone else, who introduced new material from the Bible, classical authors, and Geoffrey's other sources. He accepts the view that it was used by Wace in his *Roman de Brut* and so antedates 1155, but none of the manuscripts is older than the 13th century. It remains to place this version in relation to the rest of the tradition, which I shall do below[16].

Plans for editing the text offered by the latter of the two groups, known as the Second Variant Version, have come to nothing[17] – a gap hard to lament. It occurs in 18 witnesses (nos. 17, 22, 35, 47, 50, 54, 66, 80, 85, 91, 95, 102, 108, 114, 138, 202, 207, 209), though again not all of them represent it throughout[18]. Despite the early date of several witnesses, it is easy to see that it too is a

13 E. K. Chambers, 'The date of Geoffrey of Monmouth's history again', *Rev. Eng. Stud.* 3 (1927) 332-3.
14 Brugger (n. 10) 265, 277, 303 n. 67, expressed doubt about whether different dedications introduced different texts, and J. Hammer, 'Remarks on the sources and textual history of Geoffrey of Monmouth's *Historia regum Britanniae*', *Bulletin of the Polish Institute of Arts and Sciences in America* 2 (1943-4) 501-64, at pp. 524-30, 532, first showed that the same dedication did not always introduce the same kind of text. See also D. N. Dumville, 'An early text of Geoffrey of Monmouth's *Historia regum Britanniae* and the circulation of some Latin histories in twelfth-century Normandy', *Arthurian Literature* 4 (1985) 1-36, at p. 1; he goes on to say, p. 29, that 'it is clear, from the evidence of the Bern group, that to classify copies by the presence or absence of dedicatory material or preliminary matter is foolhardy'. The article is reprinted with the same pagination in his *Histories and pseudo-histories of the Insular Middle Ages* (Aldershot 1990).
15 J. Hammer, *Geoffrey of Monmouth, Historia regum Britanniae: a variant version* (Cambridge Mass. 1951); N. Wright, *The Historia regum Britannie of Geoffrey of Monmouth* II: *The First Variant Version: a critical edition* (Cambridge 1988), which I reviewed in *C. M. C. S.* 15 (1988) 123-5.
16 For a brief statement see 'Transmission' (n. 5) 88-9.
17 The Second Variant, like the First, was identified by Hammer, who began an edition but did not live to publish it. H. D. Emanuel took over his material with a view to completing the task; see 'Geoffrey of Monmouth's *Historia regum Britanniae*: a second variant version', *Medium Aevum* 35 (1966) 103-11. The material now belongs to the Geoffrey of Monmouth Research Project, and consultation can be arranged through the Department of Anglo-Saxon Norse and Celtic, Cambridge.
18 Crick, *Dissemination* (n. 7) 15-16, 181. The Second Variant also provided sections of the text in some other manuscripts; see the 'Survey of the manuscripts' below on nos. 4, 57, 61, 113, 121.

reworking by someone else, someone who made few changes until almost the middle of the work (§ 89) and then without introducing new material. I shall place it lower in the tradition than the First Variant[19].

The transmission of De gestis Britonum

Editors up to the 19th century show no sign of qualms about editing the text as though it were unitary. Edmond Faral had met some of the variations just discussed but selected a few manuscripts and in 1929 published another unitary text, though with an apparatus of variants[20]. In the same year, however, Acton Griscom published a transcript of a single manuscript, no. 48, which he considered to be the oldest and best representative of Geoffrey's earliest version[21]. Reviewers objected, and rightly, both to the diagnosis and to the choice of manuscript[22]. In the interest of bringing *De gestis Britonum* quickly back into print, Neil Wright for his edition of 1985 adopted the same policy of transcribing a single manuscript, this time no. 15, which alone transmits the dedication to King Stephen and Robert of Gloucester[23]. My researches in 1989-91 led me to believe that in over 1000 places no. 15 was corrupt, and I identified its already quite corrupt source, H (no. 170)[24]. I went on to sketch the outlines of the tradition and suggest how *De gestis Britonum* should be edited[25]. In August 2004, when I had not heard of editorial plans in any quarter except for the *Prophetiae*[26], I decided to undertake the task myself.

Unavoidably, I have repeated above a certain amount of what I said in 1991, and in order to produce this edition I set about following my own recommendation that eleven manuscripts should be collated in full and six in part. Long before I had finished collating, some relationships became clearer, and so what I have to say from now on will be a mixture of old and new. It will be easier to express and to follow if I repeat the list of 17 manuscripts and use not just the six symbols that I used then, CMOHGS, but a fuller set.

19 For a brief statement see 'Transmission' (n. 5) 86-7.

20 *La légende arthurienne: études et documents* (Paris 1929) III 63-303; at II 1-401 he discusses both *De gestis Britonum* and the *Vita Merlini*. The edition of 'San-Marte' ≈ A. Schulz (Halle 1854) gives readings from previous editions.

21 *The Historia regum Britannie of Geoffrey of Monmouth* (London 1929). He appended variants from nos. 15 and 10 and included plates of nos. 10, 15, 39, 48, 76, 170, 192, 199.

22 E. Faral, *Romania* 55 (1929) 482-527, at pp. 483-503; Brugger (n. 10) 264-70, 302 n. 65. See also N. Wright in the work about to be cited (n. 23), pp. xlviii-xlix.

23 *The Historia regum Britannie of Geoffrey of Monmouth* I: *Bern, Burgerbibliothek, MS. 568* (Cambridge 1985), reviewed by G. Orlandi in *C. M. C. S.* 15 (1988) 96-7. See also Dumville, 'An early text' (n. 14), especially pp. 16-18.

24 'Transmission' (n. 5) 75-7.

25 'Transmission' (n. 5) 108-13. The article escaped Caroline Palmer, *The Arthurian bibliography: III. 1978-1992* (Woodbridge 1998). With offprints I circulated a correction about two readings of M (no. 112) at § 5.39, 47: I inferred them from the silence of my collation when in fact I had somehow failed to collate it, and on p. 78 I should have reported it as reading *moeniis*, on p. 83 as omitting *sub-*.

26 Gabriella La Placa, *Goffredo di Monmouth: La profezia di Merlino* (Genoa 1990), which I finally saw in January 2007 through the kindness of Francesco Santi.

12 (A)	Alençon 12, s. xii (in §§ 118-208)
15	Bern 568, s. xii (in §§ 1-5)
30 (Y)	Cambridge Caius 406/627, s. xii
34	Cambridge Sidney Sussex 75, s. xii/xiii
43 (C)	Cambridge U. L. Dd 6 12, s. xii
48	Cambridge U. L. Ii 1 14, s. xii
54 (K)	Cambridge U. L. Mm 5 29, s. xii (in §§ 118-208)
76	Leiden B. P. L. 20, s. xii (in §§ 109-208)
96	British Library Cotton Titus C XVII, s. xii
112 (M)	British Library Royal 13 D II, s. xii/xiii
124	Lambeth 503, s. xiv (in §§ 118-208)
156 (O)	Oxford Bodl. Rawl. C 152, s. xii
170 (H)	Paris B. N. Lat. 6040, s. xii
185 (Q)	Paris B. N. Lat. 13710, s. xv
191 (G)	Paris Ste-Geneviève 2113, s. xii
199	Vatican Vat. Lat. 2005, s. xii (in §§ 1-5)
203 (S)	Salisbury Cath. 121, s. xii

I shall write much of my exposition as if these were the only manuscripts and then add a 'Survey of the tradition', in which I go through all the manuscripts in numerical order relating them to these. As before, I must divide the text into sections:

§§ 1-5	prologue and description of Britain
§§ 6-108	narrative
§§ 109-10	prologue to Merlin's prophecies
§§ 111-17	Merlin's prophecies
§§ 118-208	narrative

So far as I can judge, the main lines of the tradition split at some of the points indicated here, all of which correspond to physical breaks in at least one manuscript; but many individual manuscripts and many small groups change their behaviour in the middle of sections. I begin with the easiest section, where I nevertheless air the most fundamental problem of the tradition.

§§ 6-108

Numerous variants set YKMQG against COHS, and all manuscripts not corrupt side with one cluster or the other. In 1991 I cited some of the more interesting divergences[27], but it is no less striking that a trivial one recurs: *post haec, postea, postmodum*, or *deinde*, in YKMQG, for *exin* or *exinde* (§§ 45.233, 50.302, 51.335, 65.279, 67.314, 82.234, 85.331). Each cluster of witnesses must have had a common source, and I will call the two sources Φ and Δ. For either cluster to be called a group in the stemmatic sense, however, it must be shown to have errors (more strictly, innovations); in other words, its source must not have been an autograph of Geoffrey's. If, for instance, Δ was an autograph of Geoffrey's

---

27 'Transmission' (n. 5) 87, 90, 103-4.

but Φ not, then Φ could have been a mere descendant of Δ and would have no more authority than any one of COHS.

I argued that in at least one passage, §§ 103-4, where Φ omitted § 104.470-73 *Quorum corpora ... ipsius extiterat* and at § 103.457 read *iuxta coenobium Ambrii* for *in pago Ambrii*, the variants are hard to account for as anything but two stages of composition, the earlier transmitted in Φ and the later in Δ. If variants as substantial as this occurred more often, the idea of producing a unitary edition might have to be abandoned. On the other hand, I cited a reading of Φ that must be an error, § 91.69 *miserandas imminentes<que> poenas*, because Δ agrees with Geoffrey's source, Gildas 19.2[28]. Which of the other variants in Φ or Δ are errors, and whether any or all of those that are were remedied by conjecture in the other, I find it no easier to decide now than in 1991. I shall return to the question, but meanwhile the symbols Φ and Δ will simplify my exposition.

Φ seems to have antedated the summary of *De gestis Britonum* that Henry of Huntingdon sent to Warinus in 1139, because he reflects three of its readings: § 27.86 *lx* against *xxxix*, § 180.101-2 *tercio anno interfectus est a Conano et* against *quarto anno sententia Dei percussus*, and § 182.113 *iii/iiii annis* against *tandem*[29]. I say only 'seems' because none of these readings is obviously an error; even if they all were, Henry could have used an ancestor or relative of Φ. The family of Φ has this structure:

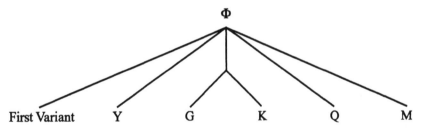

In a stemma with five branches, any one is likely to be editorially dispensable, and I cheerfully dispense with the very idiosyncratic First Variant, except that I treat a few of its adjustments as tantamount to conjectures; for that purpose I cite Wright's text of it as W. YM share the omission of § 28.116 *insistente*, but in the absence of other errors shared against GKΔ the agreement seems likely to be coincidental, especially since the word hardly affects the sense; furthermore, the reading of Q, *insi* or *nisi*, suggests that the scribe of Φ may have written *insi* at the end of a line and neglected to supply the rest.

---

28 The argument goes back to Faral, *Romania* 55 (1929) 498-9.

29 Robert of Torigni included the letter in his chronicle (n. 3), pp. 65-75, but it was edited from manuscripts of Henry's own *Historia Anglorum* by N. Wright, 'The place of Henry of Huntingdon's *Epistola ad Warinum* in the text-history of Geoffrey of Monmouth's *Historia regum Britannie*: a preliminary investigation', in Gillian Jondorf & D. N. Dumville (edd.), *France and the British Isles in the Middle Ages and Renaissance* (Woodbridge 1991), 71-113, at pp. 92-106, before the publication of Diana E. Greenway's edition (Oxford 1996), where see pp. 552-83 for the text and a facing translation. On the connexion with Φ see 'Transmission' (n. 5) 115 n. 59, where I cited observations of Neil Wright's not included in his article.

Y belongs to what Crick dubbed the *tres filios* group, from the variant *<tres> filios* at § 100.367[30]. Several manuscripts that have this variant behave consistently throughout the work and share with Y numerous small omissions and transpositions. I give a selection of words or phrases omitted:

2.8 *multotiens*	75.52 *sibi*	149.165 *iterum*
10.136 *arietibus*	80.191 *copiam*	155.255 *resistere*
28.117 *subito*	82.239 *Hamonis*	158.407 *sancti*
30.130 *homo*	82.270 *accesserunt*	158.413 *et salutato rege*
31.158 *ueritatem*	87.362 *uiriliter*	160.486 *Romam*
31.178 *adhuc*	90.33 *reliquiae*	161.508 *nostratibus*
31.245 *fuisse*	101.381-2 *iuxta murum*	166.140-41 *hoc modo*
31.248 *pristinam*	109.3 *ipsius*	172.364 *modum*
40.111 *puella*	121.81 *Britonibus*	175.450 *colles*
41.132 *quoque*	127.199 *heredes*	186.166 *magno*
45.236 *dira*	132.351 *duo*	189.199 *abbatem*
49.296 *innatae*	136.420 *inquit*	193.296 *stellarum*
50.317 *thalamum suum*	137.448 *praecepit*	194.329 *uos*
54.6 *prosapia*	142.607 *tota*	196.399 *breuiter*
55.18 *Caesar*	145.69 *nemoris*	204.552 *carentem*
56.49 *cum hostibus*	147.113 *lancea*	205.571 *ceterorum*
59.105 *tota*	148.141 *hostes*	207.591 *superbum*

A member or relative of the *tres filios* group was used by Alfred of Beverley in a work usually assigned to 1143[31]. Besides *<tres> filios* at § 100.367 (amidst paraphrase), it shares these errors with Y:

26.71 *Ma<u>lim*
34.328 *celebra<ba>ntur*
34.333 *colon[or]um*
39.79 *est ... nesciebant* for *fuerat ... nesciebatur*
39.82-3 *-siam perducere(n)t* for *-sium litus secaret*
39.90 *historiographus* for *historicus*
49.287 *Gorbodianus* for *Gorbonianus*
51.342 *solio* for *solium*
53.375 *parte ... morabatur* for *tempore ... commanebat*
68.335 *Kaerglau* for *Kaerglou*

70.379 *inscriptis titulis* for *inscriptus titulus*
74.14 *duris* for *diris*
76.96 *Nant<i>gallum*
93.137 *Cirecestriam* for *Silcestriam*
118.9 *Britanni<c>am*
135.397 *<de>ferendum*
158.407 *Thebas* for *Teliaus*
166.140-41 *[hoc modo]*
167.224 *<de> Cad-*
168.262 *post [hos]*
184.136 *ciuitates <combussit>*

G and the Second Variant had a common source, which also gave rise to other manuscripts[32]. It shared a fair number of innovations, for instance these[33]:

---

30 Crick, *Dissemination* (n. 7) 178-9.
31 *Aluredi Beverlacensis annales sive historia de gestis regum Britanniae*, ed. T. Hearne (Oxford 1716) from Bodl. Rawl. B 200 (s. xiv); R. Sharpe, *A handlist of the Latin writers of Great Britain and Ireland before 1540* (Turnhout 1997) 54 no. 105, lists the few manuscripts, of which Hearne's is the earliest that offers more than extracts. On the date of the work see Tatlock, *Legendary history* (n. 3) 210-11.
32 'Transmission (n. 5) 85-7.
33 Emanuel (n. 17) lists others.

15.269 *Peractis <igitur>*

18.376 *rotans* for *rotat*

20.449 *Nec mora* for *Nec plura*

22.496 *[frater]*

24.15 *rumore audito* for *audito rumore*

32.263 *formam* for *famam*

32.274 *[et] dedecus*

36.32 *<in> qua*

39.75 *tota insula* for *totius(que) insulae*

39.87 *omni[que]*

43.205 *consociati<s>*

46.250 *esse uocatos* for *uocatos esse*

49.294 *ammonebat* for *inanimabat*

52.360 *Bleduno* for *Bledudo*

53.389 *etiam* for *autem*

55.25 *qua [in]*

60.114 *reuerti* for *reuertere*

97.243 *patiebatur* for *perpetiebatur*.

By collating K throughout the work I found that the Second Variant, which it represents up to § 117, is serviceable as a witness up to § 88 but then begins to earn its name. Errors or innovations include these:

5.40 *suorum* for *sanctorum*

6.60 *aduenit* for *accessit*

8.88 *itaque Brutus* for *igitur*

9.124 *audacius* for *audaciores*

11.149 *cruciabatur anxietatibus* for *anxietatibus cruciatur*

11.153 *consilio* for *auxilio*

24.27 *[cubilia eius inire] ipsam[que] sibi matrimonio* (for *maritali taeda*) *copulare*

41.121 *uellet* for *affectasset*

41.122-3 *[cum tranquillitate]*

55.20 *[extra orbem positos]*

66.302 *[in duas partes]*

78.135 *Mense ... exacto* for *Emenso ... mense*

89.8 *uocibus postulantes* for *postulationibus poscentes*.

I saw little point, however, in reporting K alongside G when YGQM already represent four lines of descent from Φ. Accordingly, when I cite from it readings attractive as conjectures, I refer to it not by the symbol K but as no. 54. G in §§ 1-108 is written with great clarity and elegance but no great accuracy. It produced a large tribe of descendants, most if not all Continental; they include Leiden B. P. L. 20 (no. 76), written at Bec within about 20 years of composition[34], and the manuscripts that have the nameless dedication. With G they omit for instance these words or phrases[35]:

5.46 *uero*	31.164 *hoc modo*	62.238 *Caesari*
6.48 *filio*	41.148 *cum fletu*	108.563 *sub*
28.111 *urbem*	57.84 *pugnans*	

At § 34.331 Q, though late, has an earlier stage of an innovation shared by M and no. 34: *coram inimico suo* YGK with Δ, *coram inimicorum suo* Q, *coram inimicorum suorum aspectu* M and no. 34. Other innovations shared by M and no. 34 are these:

34 Dumville, 'An early text' (n. 14) 2-6, though the promised Appendix II on the date of the Bec catalogue is missing. The article is reprinted with the same pagination, and still without Appendix II, in his *Histories and pseudo-histories* (n. 14).

35 'Transmission' (n. 5) 81-5.

13.196 *deambul<ab>ant*

15.265 *donec* for *dum*

16.305 *Galli[c]a*

21.475 *[uiuum]*

26.80 *<nomine> genuerat*

31.154 *adquiescere* for *adquieuisse*

31.242 *[omnia]*

35.11 *<saepe> sese*

43.189 *obsederat* for *obsidebat*

44.229 *summa* for *suprema*

48.273 *ipsi[u]s*

50.313 *defleui<sse>t*

56.66 *tenebat* for *tenuerat*

61.176 *morte* for *nece*

62.213 *inuasit* for *inuadit*

63.255 *[tibi]*

66.298 *cum* for *ut*

81.194 *Deinde* for *Denique*

88.397 *uacu[at]am*

107.542 *po[tui]sset*

108.572 *obmutuerunt <et dixit Merlinus>*

In 1991 I assigned Q to the same family as M and no. 34 but cited only evidence to the contrary[36], and full collation has yielded nothing to fill the gap. At § 34.331 *coram inimicorum suo* could easily have been inherited by Q from Φ, corrected in ancestors of Y and GK, and miscorrected in the common source of M and no. 34; and a single passage will not bear enough weight anyway. I therefore treat Q and M as unconnected descendants of Φ and drop no. 34, even though its evidence sheds light on the behaviour of M in passages such as § 19.392-3:

absconditas quoque opes ab eisdem extrahit

quoque opes GKΔ: *quoque* YQM: *-que diuitias* 34
eisdem <opes> M

The readings of YQ and no. 34, together perhaps with *gazas absconditas* in W (the First Variant), suggest that Φ omitted *opes* and M and the common source of GK restored it by conjecture; for M to have inherited it and put it in the wrong place, it would have had to appear in the margin of both Φ and the common source of M and no. 34 and be overlooked by at least three other scribes. Nevertheless, M is by far the most accurate descendant of Φ, and indeed a transcript of M would be a tolerable substitute for an edition. That is almost how 19th-century editors used it for another work that it contains, the *Gesta regum Anglorum*[37]; but the latest editors incline to suspect contamination 'done with discrimination'[38]. Its text of Geoffrey lends colour to the suspicion, because in passages where the descendants of Φ differ it is actually the latest used here, Q, that most often accounts for the behaviour of the rest. As the best examples occur in §§ 118-208, I will hold them over.

In the family of Δ the largest question concerns O, some of whose peculiarities I have already mentioned. In 1991 I seriously misreported it at § 60.110[39], and

36 'Transmission' (n. 5) 88, 110. I may have been unduly influenced by what I thought happened in the prophecies, §§ 111-17, but there too I was under a misapprehension, as I explain below.

37 T. D. Hardy, *Willelmi Malmesbiriensis monachi Gesta regum Anglorum atque Historia novella* (London 1840) I xxii-xxiii; W. Stubbs, *Willelmi Malmesbiriensis monachi De gestis regum Anglorum libri quinque* (Rolls Series 90) I (London 1887) lxxx-lxxxii.

38 R. A. B. Mynors, R. M. Thomson, M. Winterbottom, *William of Malmesbury, Gesta regum Anglorum: The history of the English kings* I (Oxford 1998) xvii-xx.

39 'Transmission' (n. 5) 103.

another passage, § 72.428-31, can be set alongside a revised statement of the evidence:

§ 60.110 [Cassibellaunus puts metal spikes in the bed of the Thames to stop Caesar reaching Trinovantum] ... *Iulius ... mare ingressus est optatam stragem populo qui eum deuicerat inferre affectans. Quam procul dubio ingessisset si illaesa classe tellure potiri <u>quiuisset, quod ad effectum ducere nequiuit</u>; nam dum per Tamensem praedictam ciuitatem peteret, naues eius praefatis palis infixae subitum passae sunt periculum.*

quiuisset Δ: *potuisset* Φ
quod ad effectum ducere nequiuit ΦO: om. CHS

As a scrupulous writer might just as well have avoided *potuisset* after *potiri* as *quiuisset* before *nequiuit*, there is nothing to choose between them; but the ellipse that results from the omission of *quod ad effectum ducere nequiuit* does not seem in Geoffrey's manner, and so the reading of CHS looks like an error – not a simple instance of *saut du même au même* but something akin. A complication is that no. 71, a relative of CHS, agrees with O; but perhaps the contamination visible in its corrections, which look contemporary, also affected its text.

§ 72.428-31 *Confirmatione igitur facta reuersi sunt* [the missionaries] *in Britanniam compluribus aliis comitati, quorum doctrina <u>gens</u> Britonum <u>in fide Christi ex quo uenerunt</u> in breui corroborata fuit.*

gens Φ: om. Δ
in fide Christi OΦ: *fides (fideles* H) *in Christo* CHS
ex quo uenerunt OΦ: om. CHS

At least the first two variants are connected, because they both affect the subject of *corroborata fuit*. If Φ has the oldest reading, then Δ lost *gens* and only O preserves the result unadjusted. If O has the oldest reading, then Φ and CHS made different conjectures. If CHS have the oldest reading, then it is hard to account for the readings of Φ and O, especially their agreement over *in fide Christi*. The easiest way of accounting for the absence of *ex quo uenerunt* from CHS is to suppose that the conjecture *fides in Christo* was misinterpreted as a replacement for the whole of *in fide Christi ex quo uenerunt*. These two passages, then, strongly suggest that CHS descend from a common ancestor that was not an ancestor of O. Whether OCHS all descend from a common ancestor that was not an autograph I leave in suspense.

C, written by several scribes, has lost §§ 5.43-18.364 *Normannis uidelicet ... timorem non*, but in the early part of the work, especially before the change of hand in § 82, it is far more accurate than the rest. Up to that point I have noticed only these errors peculiar to C (on average, less than one every three chapters):

22.494 *Ea* for *Ex* (but see my note
below on the passage)
24.46 *familiaritate* for *-tati*
31.151 *dilig[er]et*
31.218 *mili[t]um*
31.237 *expecta[ba]t*
33.293 *[in] regno*
34.331-2 *[ut] uiae*
35.18 *fugare<s>*
36.33 *[con]socios*
38.67 *illi* for *sibi*

43.187 *sequen<te>s*
44.215 *p[er]arans*
50.300 *infinitos <et infinitos>*
51.337 *alter[a]*
56.45 *insistere[n]t*
61.143 *[in] sacrificiis*
74.11 *Cum[que]*
77.121 *conual-* for *conuola-*
78.126 *dampnum [quod]*
80.166 *ipsos[que]*
81.206 *stabil[itat]em*

O too was written by several scribes, all reasonably accurate; it has lost §§ 190.224-
193.289 *eos fecerunt ... in fugam uersus est arreptoque* and the end after § 203.542
ira Dei deserta quam uos, and some of its original readings were obliterated by
correctors, at least one of whom used an unrelated manuscript; I ignore the correctors
except where the original reading is unavailable, when they show what it was not.
H, a descendant of Δ in §§ 6-108, has numerous corruptions, which reappear in
its own descendants nos. 48 and 15 and therefore in the editions of Griscom and
Wright; I lost patience with no. 48 in collating it from § 147 to the end, but where I
have checked it in §§ 6-108 for errors of H it has them[40]. Of the manuscripts that I
picked out in 1991, the only uninterrupted witnesses to Δ throughout the work are
S and no. 96. Whereas S was written with reasonable accuracy by a single scribe
who took no liberties, an ancestor of no. 96 was carelessly written, and some of
its more unusual readings look like attempts at patching up. It seemed unwise,
though, to use only one uninterrupted witness; but as corrections in no. 96 have
effaced some of its original readings, I substitute its twin no. 23, Cambridge C. C.
C. 281 (s. xii), which I call E.

Repeatable errors, sometimes called 'polygenetic', occasionally make the
relationship of the manuscripts look untidier than I believe it to be. If one descendant
of Δ agrees with Φ against the rest, polygenesis is always the explanation that
should be considered first. After finding several agreements of E with Φ against
OCHS, I checked some of the passages in its fragmentary relative no. 146 (s. xii),
which turned out to agree with OCHS. Even if not polygenesis but contamination
were to blame, which seems unlikely when the variants are as trivial as they are, the
reading of E would still carry no weight. In individual manuscripts the commonest
types of corruption are *saut du même au même*, the omission of dispensable words,
and the substitution of synonyms: *dux/rex, uxor/coniunx, bellum/proelium, urbs/
ciuitas, terra/patria, socii/consocii, coepit/incepit, nomen/uocabulum, perimere/
interficere, uocare/appellare/nuncupare/nominare/dicere*. Substitution especially
affects *is/ille/ipse/idem*, particularly *eius/illius/ipsius/eiusdem/suus*; and since these
words tend to be optional, they are often added or omitted. A similar but more
troublesome phenomenon is the confusion of particles that occupy second position
in the sentence, not just those that bear some resemblance to each other in either

---

40 'Transmission' (n. 5) 76-7.

sense or appearance, such as *autem/uero, itaque/namque, ergo/igitur ($\overset{o}{g}$/$\overset{i}{g}$)*, but any whatsoever; the confusion even involves *ilico*, which Geoffrey often uses in second position. Against *namque* in the other manuscripts, I accept *itaque* at § 103.455 from no. 54 (presumably a conjecture or lucky slip) and at § 142.605 from no. 5.

§§ 1-5

I make this a separate section not just because of the different dedications in §§ 3-4 but also because the First Variant omits §§ 1-4 and in H and no. 15, which augment the usual dedication with another, § 6 begins on a new leaf after a gap. Except for the different dedications, however, the usual division between Φ and Δ recurs, and all manuscripts probably descend from one or other as in §§ 6-108.

No. 199, which like H has the additional dedication to Waleran, betrays in §§ 1-3 and 5 not just descent from Φ by reading § 3.19 *exortum*, § 5.46 *[uero]*, but also kinship with some Continental descendants of G by reading § 1.2 *nimirum*, 6 *aeternitatis laude*, 2.9 *exorticis*, 16 *[in] historia*. The same mixture of readings continues throughout the work. A passage where agreement with H predominates runs from § 39 (between 75 *tota insula* and 87 *omnique*) to § 60 (between 121 *maiorem patiuntur* and 130 *ipsos*), and at § 50.325-6 *quia praedictam pietatem in fratrem habuerat* no. 199 follows a corrector in H, who erased *quia* (or whatever it was), substituted *ob*, and added *quam* at the end of the line after *pietatem*. No. 199 must therefore descend from H, whether or not through an intermediary, and so I dispense with it. In any event, its differences from H in the additional dedication are all errors: *subtilitate, existeres ... esses ... adidisti, edictum, tuae*.

I cite no. 15 for the changes that bring about a dedication to Stephen and Robert, even though I doubt whether Geoffrey himself made them, but ignore it in the rest of the text, because it descends from H in §§ 6-208 and might as well do, whether it does or not, in §§ 1-5. Similarly, I ignore no. 48, which owes most of §§ 6-208 to H and shows no physical or textual sign of owing §§ 1-5 to a different source.

Whatever the precise method by which Geoffrey incorporated the additional dedication, the structure of H and its descent from Δ in §§ 1-3 and 5 suggest that it was incorporated in a descendant ot Δ. As another descendant of Δ is the only independent witness to the alternative version of §§ 109-10, it is tempting to regard Δ as closer than Φ to a text that Geoffrey approved; but all that can safely be said is that when he made the two changes it happened for some reason, perhaps mere availability, to be descendants of Δ that received them.

§§ 118-208

YQM and OC maintain the same relationship here as in §§ 1-108, but the Second Variant has become too idiosyncratic to serve for anything more than consultation where the other descendants of Φ disagree, and G, H, no. 48, and one or other of SE, change their behaviour[41].

41 'Transmission' (n. 5) 84-5, 76-7.

Though it remains a relative of the Second Variant, G, written by a new hand from § 109, is no longer the source of its Continental relatives, but they continue to share errors with it:

125.164 *retinuisset* for *tenuisset*
126.170 *etiam* for *Octam*
127.198 *disposuit regnum suum* for *disponit regno suo*
130.260 *Britonum insulam* for *insulam Britonum*
131.306 *eis* (*ei* G) *iuit* for *perrexit*
133.371 *alter [uero]*
134.373 *existens* for *extans*
137.460 *maritus <suus>*
137.461 *<et> ex*
157.372 *celebrationi <esset>*
160.479 *exorsus* for *iussus*
164.15 *committens* for *permittens*
164.16 *dum [autem]*
165.61 *<namque> recepto*
189.199 *spreuerunt* for *despexerant*
195.357 *solent <perpetrarunt>*
197.421 *perrexit* for *perspexit*

I therefore saw little point in using any of them, even though G is no model of accuracy. Had I decided otherwise, my choice would have fallen on no. 169 (Paris B. N. Lat. 6039, s. xiv, Italian) more honest and accurate than even the best of its earlier relatives.

Somewhere round about § 147 no. 48 switched to a new exemplar, which shared a number of errors with E:

153.212 *adiuit[que]* E *et adiuit* 48
153.221 *GunhỴuar* (uel sim.) for *Gunuasius*
154.230 *transmari<ta>norum*
155.254 *[collegit]*
155.268 *uehementer* after *Frollonis*
156.317 *praepolleba<n>t*
156.334 *quemlibet* for *quemque*
157.369 *processione peracta*
160.488 *<et>enim*
166.143 *suum* for *unum*
168.245 *hostibus proelia* transposed (*proelium* E)

169.280 *Numquid <non>*
170.309 *[nos]*
170.310 *[ipsos]*
171.354 *accepit* for *recepit*
172.371 *horta[ba]tur*
172.384 *fecit* for *facit*
172.385 *renouatis* for *reuocatis*
174.415 *elabora<ba>t*
174.428 *unus* for *ullus*
180.98 *iuuenem Guintoniae* transposed.

Written by a new hand from § 109, E remains a descendant of Δ but now stands closer to S. The change of hand, though, is not enough to prove that E rather than S has changed its behaviour; its twin no. 96 is written by a new hand from a different point, § 114.98-9 *pollex in oleo*. Be that as it may, SE in over a dozen places from

§ 120.57 to § 132.343 substitute *Ambros-* for *Aurel-*[42], and they also have these errors:

122.94 *Glaurerniae* (*Clauserniae* E)	138.517 *socii [sui]*
for *Claudiocestriae*	143.24 *Erat [autem]*
123.106 *Et* for *At*	143.45 *consiliarii [sui]*
123.119 *situm* (+ *sit* E) for *suum*	145.77 *uectigali<bu>s*
126.183 *Erimus [ergo]*	147.109 *clipeo* for *clipeum*
127.193 *urbis illius* for *illius urbis*	150.177 *<in> eodem*
136.432 *eorum [qui]*	150.180 *in eadem* for *eademque*

After the change of behaviour in no. 48, the errors of SE appear there too:

156.342 *Worloit* for *Clofaut*
156.343 *Kimbelin <Edelmuth>*
156.348 *Ho(i)landiae consul* for *consul Boloniae*
157.396 *[cum] saxis*
157.397 *[diei]*
162.519 *quod dicendum erat* for *quae dicenda erant*
162.537 *decreuerunt* for *-rant*
165.50 *cacumine* for *culmine*
165.78 *gladium [suum]*
165.96 *Rethonem* for *Rith-*

The quire of H that contains § 114.104 – 137.505 *Tonantis ... reputaretur adesse*, written by a different scribe, also owes its text to a different source, one that shared errors with Y (though not all the errors of Y):

118.9 *Britanni<c>am*	131.307 *proelium* for *bellum*
119.30 *prius ipsum* for *ipsum prius*	135.397 *sedis <ecclesiae>*
119.36 *huius loci urbes*	136.414 *ubi* for *cum*
122.103 *horta[ba]tur*	136.420 *est opus* for *opus est*
125.163 *[regem]*	137.476 *Vlfin [de]*.
125.167 *ciuitatem* for *urbem*	
128.214 *diffundentes* for *diffid-*	

One or other could be dispensed with, but I hesitate to dispense with Y just in this section, and H makes a suggestive contribution at § 131.306.

To the detriment of both sense and syntax, no descendant of Φ that I use includes § 156.322-3 *Praeterea gimnasium ducentorum philosophorum habebat.* As the omission was caused by *saut du même au même*, it is unsafe to use for stemmatic purposes; but though a manuscript without the passage need not descend from Φ, it does seem that Φ must have omitted it, because as many as five branches would hardly each have omitted it independently (the First Variant repairs the syntax by rephrasing but has nothing that corresponds to *gimnasium*, *ducentorum*, or *philosophorum*).

In the previous section I mentioned that the value of Q best emerges here, and I will now give my evidence.

---

42 Perhaps there was an intermediate stage: abbreviation to the initial, as sometimes happens in E.

§ 130.279-81 ... *cum gaudio in Britanniam reuerti coeperunt. Nec mora, prosperantibus uentis applicant sepulturasque uirorum cum lapidibus petunt*

nec mora Δ: *nec non* M: *et* YHG: *nec* Q
petunt ΔG: *adeunt* YHM: *applicant* Q

For the first set of variants the simplest explanation is that Φ omitted *mora*. The nonsense that resulted survives in Q but has given way in M, YH, and G, to conjectures that would not have taxed anyone's brain; *nec non* is poor, because Geoffrey does not use it for coordinating verbs, and *et* leaves one asking why anyone should have corrupted it to *nec*. For the second set of variants the simplest explanation is that Φ repeated *applicant* from earlier in the sentence (a type of error known as *Perseverationsfehler*) and all its descendants except Q substituted a more suitable verb.

§ 119.36-7 '*Respice, dux nobilis, huius urbis turres et moenia utrum poterint Vortegirnum protegere ...*'

urbis turres et Δ: *urbis* GM: *loci urbes et* YH: *urbes et* Q

Here too, Q has nonsense closer to the truth than the readings of its relatives. As the scene takes place at the *oppidum* Hergign, the conjecture in YH is particularly bad.

§ 151.193-4 *Cumque urbem uisa sacrarum ecclesiarum desolatione condoluit.*

Δ has no verb in the *cum* clause, and Q is the only descendant of Φ that does not supply one: *intrasset* YM, *transisset* G.

§ 155.265-6 *Erat enim ipse magnae staturae et audatiae et fortitudinis*

magnae staturae OHSEY: *mirae magnitudinis* C: *staturae* GM: *staturae staturae* Q

The reading of Q looks like a stage on the way to the omission of *magnae*, which Y could have restored by conjecture.

§ 157.371-2 ... *nec si totus dies celebrationi taedium aliquod ipsis generaret.*

Δ has no verb in the *si* clause, and Q is the only descendant of Φ that does not supply one: *uacaret* YM (a verb that Geoffrey uses only with a personal subject), *esset* G (unconstruable).

§ 171.339-40 ...*agmen illud cui rex Hispaniae et Lucius Catellus praeera(n)t...*

For *rex Hispaniae* YGMQ all have *ex Hispania*, but Q alone leaves the impossible *et* unchanged: G omits it, and before it Y adds *rex*, M *Alifatima*.

§ 174.408-9 *Porro Gualguainus caedendo turmas ut praedictum est inuenit tandem aditum quem optabat*

Only Δ has *caedendo*. Q simply omits it, but before *inuenit* the other descendants of Φ supply an equivalent: *infestans* YM, *inuadens* G. There are further passages where Q is not alone in preserving unchanged an impossible reading due to an omission in Φ, for instance § 34.316-17 *[inter] concurrentes hostium cateruas,* where Y does the same, or § 124.152 *[Aldclud atque eas]* and § 134.388 *tantum regem [decebat]*, where YH do the same, or § 195.383 *[timorem]* (or an equivalent), where Y does the same.

The main difference from §§ 6-108, however, is that not all manuscripts descend from either Φ or Δ. In 1991 I pointed out that in some passages where Φ and Δ diverge some manuscripts have a reading more primitive than at least one of the other two; at § 130.271, for instance, they omit the verb where Φ and Δ have different verbs[43]. For § 204.553-4 *nefandus populus ille* they all read *quaedam nobilissima regina Sexburgis nomine quae uidua fuerat*, and so it is natural to call them the 'Sexburgis' manuscripts; but though they probably had a common source, which I called Σ, my limited collations and samples did not enable me to define Σ adequately or pick out its best representatives. That is one of the chief tasks that I have set myself in preparing this edition.

Among the earliest 'Sexburgis' manuscripts is K, which after the *Prophetiae Merlini* abandons the Second Variant. The next that I collated were A (Alençon 12, s. xii) and no. 210 (Ushaw College 6, s. xii), not just because they too are among the earliest but also because A uniquely contains just §§ 118-208 and in no. 210 §§ 1-109, if not §§ 1-117, were added later. I will call no. 210 U. Corrections in U restore some words or passages omitted by the first hand together with AK, but the first hand shares with AK, or with one of them, many readings absent from ΔΦ:

119.45 *ut <qui>* A²K¹U: *qui* A¹
120.68 *[in]habitandum* AU
120.70 *qui* ΔΦ: *quo* AKU
125.154 *Vt* ΔΦ: *At* AKU
129.250 *[hoc]* AKU
130.258 *didicisse<n>t* AKU
133.366 *subuectauerit* Δ: *subuectet* Φ: *subuectaret* AKU
135.392 *[et]* AU
135.398 *Britanni[c]a* A¹U
147.98 *erunt* ΔΦ: *erit* AKU
147.106 *hilarati* ΔΦ: *hilarata* AU
149.154 *recipit* ΔΦ: *recepit* KU
149.163 *itaque* ΔQYM: *igitur* GAKU
155.264 *ipsi* ΔΦ: *sibi* AKU
156.354 *mirum* ΔΦ: *mora* AU
157.359 *[curam]* AKU
157.383 *praestabant* ΔΦ: *parabant* AU: *praepar-* K
157.401 *praestabant* ΔΦ: *parabant* AKU
158.442 *commacul<ar>et* AKU
162.524 *sex* ΔΦ: *septem* AKU
165.59 *[hic]* AKU
165.75 *tabo* ΔΦ: *tabe* AKU

167.234 *[de tot]* AKU
170.320 *illi <et>* U: *alii et* A: *alii* K
171.341 *<di>stricte* AKU
171.363 *defendendum* ΔΦ: *deferendum (diff-* K) AKU
172.388 *propera<ba>t* AKU
176.469-70 *[Ibi ... positus fuit]* AKU
176.479 *[sub]sequentem* AKU
177.12 *etiam* ΔΦ: *enim* AKU
178.42 *[magis]* AKU
178.67 *<et> uulnerabant* AKU
178.68 *[modum]* AU
180.101 *quarto* Δ: *tertio* Φ: *uigesimo* AKU
181.109 *tertio-* Δ: *secundo-* Φ: *trigesimo* AKU
185.151 *<ir>ruentes* AKU
186.158-9 *Cornubiam ... Gualias* ΔΦ: *Cornubia ... Gualiis* AKU
189.204 *[sui]* AKU
189.209 *primum arma* ΔΦ: *arma primum* KU
191.262 *regno* ΔΦ: *regni* AKU
193.323 *armamenta* ΔΦ: *ornamenta* AKU²

43 'Transmission' (n. 5) 91-3.

196.392 *aquam reginae* ΔΦ: *reginae aquam* AKU
196.395 *dimissa uoce* Δ: *uoce dimissa* Φ: *dimissam* AKU
196.396 *[ipse]* AKU
196.400 *[tunc]* AKU
198.439 *[et]* A¹U
202.517 *[genere]* AKU

202.518-19 *Cad[uallo ... Cad]ualadrum* AKU
204.552 *[gente]* AKU
205.563 *[id]* AKU
205.573 *[ilico]* AKU
206.586 *lxxx* ΔΦ: *lxx* AKU
207.588 *gentem* ΔΦ: *genti* KU

The most striking of these is the omission of § 176.469-70 *Ibi in quodam cimiterio quod in australi parte ciuitatis erat iuxta murum honorifice positus fuit.* There is no obvious reason for it, and it looks unlike a coincidence that the sentence concerns a burial (that of Beduerus at Bayeux), because the passage that Φ lacked at § 104.470-73 also concerns a burial (that of the 460 British dignitaries assassinated by the Saxons). Be that as it may, the omission recurs in all the 'Sexburgis' manuscripts except a few late ones that show other signs of contamination.

The 'Sexburgis' passage and this omission, then, are two striking divergences from the text of ΔΦ. In 1991 I also cited a passage where Δ and Φ differ and the 'Sexburgis' manuscripts have a third reading, § 174.434-6:

> *Duos reges.. infortunium ei obuios fecit, quos abscisis capitibus ad Tartara direxit.*

> *infortunium ei obuios fecit quos* Δ: *infortunium ei obtulit quos* Φ: *ob infortunium ei obuios* Σ

From § 118 to § 173, however, I have found no reading of much consequence that occurs in a majority of the 'Sexburgis' manuscripts and at the same time marks them off from ΔΦ: only § 133.366 *subuectaret* (*-auerit* Δ, *-et* Φ), § 149.163 *igitur* for *itaque*, § 171.341 *<di>stricte.* Instead, Σ has to be defined by the shifting agreements of the 'Sexburgis' manuscripts with Δ or Φ, which in AKU occur roughly in the proportion Δ3:Φ2 (though in §§ 169-71 there is an unusual spate of agreements with Φ). For two reasons, not all the 'Sexburgis' manuscripts display the same pattern: the clearer reason is changes of exemplar, the other contamination. Nos. 98 and 123, for instance, clearly become descendants of Σ when a new hand takes over, in no. 123 (s. xii) with the last syllable of § 127, in no. 98 (s. xiv) on a new quire in § 174; no. 8 (s. xii/xiii) is clearly a *tres filios* manuscript (a relative of Y) up to about § 143 and a descendant of Σ thereafter; and nos. 24 (s. xiii) and 52 (a. 1327) are clearly descendants of Δ up to § 137 and of Σ thereafter. As no. 93 (s. xiii) shares errors from § 118 to § 143 both with no. 8 and with AKU, it must be contaminated; and manuscripts that have passages omitted by AKU and other 'Sexburgis' manuscripts, for instance § 118.22-3 *cum germano suo decem milibus militum comitatus* or the sentence at § 176.469-70 about the burial of Beduerus, seem likely to be contaminated. In order, therefore, to identify 'Sexburgis' manuscripts genuinely independent of AKU and not just contaminated, I looked for any that throughout §§ 118-73, wherever Δ and Φ diverge, share the same pattern of agreements with one or other as AKU. If Σ itself was covered with variants or the later 'Sexburgis' manuscripts were all contaminated relatives of AKU, one would not expect such manuscripts to exist, but four passed the test: no. 132 (Oxford All Souls 35, s. xiii[1]), which I shall call N; no. 118 (London College of Arms Arundel 1, s. xiv); no. 140 (Bodl. Douce 115, s. xiv), which I shall call D; and no. 178 (Paris B. N. Lat. 6233, s. xiii/xiv), P in Faral's edition. They form two pairs: N and no. 118, D and no. 178. There is little point in using both members of each pair, and I have chosen N for its date, D because no. 178 is already reported in Faral's edition[44]. Up to § 174 N and D share no errors with each other and none with AKU except § 133.366 *subuectaret*, § 149.163 *igitur* for *itaque*, and § 171.341 *<di>stricte*, but I do not see how it can be an accident that where Δ and Φ diverge ND always agree with the same one as AKU. In principle, they might do so because the readings in question were all true; but I very much doubt if they are.

Much the most accurate of AKUND is U, but it cannot be the source of AK, because even after correction it has errors absent from AK, among them substantial omissions at §§ 191.257-8 and 200.474-5:

137.497 *tute* for *tuto*	193.304 *dispergunt[que]*
178.61 lac. for *atque*	193.327 *promisit <dicens>*
178.65 *elabor<ar>ant*	194.334 *<com>prouincialium*
185.148 *[tuum]*	194.338 *[re]manserunt*
187.173 *[diadema]*	200.474-5 *[guerram ... filium suum]*
188.178 *delebant* for *deleuerant*	207.594 *patientius* for *sapientius*
190.240 *adeo* for *ab eo*	
191.257-8 *[maestitiae ... Britonum]*	

AK share many errors absent from ΔΦU, for instance these:

118.17 *facies Saxonum* for *Saxonum facies*	159.466 *[quia]*
122.99 *cultellis* for *cultris*	162.535-6 *[tributum ... aditurum]*
127.194-5 *diebus quindecim* for *quindecim diebus*	164.18 *nocte* for *hora noctis*
130.278 *dici* for *credi*	167.233 *repetentes* for *repedantes*
132.335 *[hoc]*	170.320 *alii* for *illi*
132.345 *detestando* for *-da*	172.378 *[et] Marius*
136.414 *tota[que]*	173.405 *eorum[que]*
136.425 *[ergo]*	173.406 *[percuteretur et]*
137.452 *[indulsit]*	174.436 *Britones decertare* for *decertare Britones*
139.551 *dupla* for *dubia*	175.449 *leg<at>ione*
145.75 *immansuros* for *inde mansuros*	191.255 *ratus cecidisse* for *cecidisse ratus*
146.82 *Id[que]*	195.376 *ille* ante *namque*
146.87 *Sumers(et)ensiam* for *Sumersetensem*	195.379 *Caduanum* post *meum*
147.114 *insistebant* for *resistebant*	199.450 *ipse enim* for *enim ipse*
150.178 *et dixit* for *dixitque*	200.459 *imperanti <iam>*
159.463 *qu<i>a*	204.545 *applicatus* for *appulsus*

---

44 Convenience has also played a part. Hammer's material includes two films of N, one better than the other but neither adequate at the end. Even so, the better one is better than the available film of no. 118.

Of the errors peculiar to K, the most damaging is the omission for no obvious reason of § 165.81-2 *tanto conamine percussit quod sonitu ictus et tota littora repleuit*; presumably it formed a line in an ancestor. The omission recurs in no. 5 (s. xiii), a relative of K from about § 149; in no. 123 (s. xii), a fragmentary manuscript related to K from the last syllable of § 127; and in no. 161 (s. xiii), a relative of K from about § 127[45]. The scribe of A fell into many small omissions and transpositions but corrected most of them, probably still in the process of copying; nevertheless, several remain, for instance these omissions:

125.162 *omnes*	165.49 *illud*
126.176 *hoc modo*	166.193 *Parisius*
128.233 *uirorum*	189.212 *obuiam*
133.369 *plagam*	192.283 *sese*
134.374 *prope*	193.286 *sese*
160.499 *omnes*	193.293 *nauigiis*

N and no. 118 share these errors, singly for the most part trivial but collectively significant:

123.120 *se et* for *ipse*	178.36 *<milia> suorum*
138.535 *progenuerunt[que]*	*commilitonum*
159.472 *annis* for *temporibus*	184.133 *auunculo <suo>*
162.528 *[ad]erant*	190.231 *nullatenus ab Edelfrido* for
165.72 *uiriliter <eum>*	*ab Edelfrido nullatenus*
176.457 *[loca]*	190.236 *Caduani <filius>*
	193.300 *delibera<ba>t*

N itself has many peculiarities, among them the omission of these substantial passages:

119.38-9 *nec tibi ... promeruisse*
120.76-7 *destructas ... triumpho*
143.30-31 *inopinum ... Saxonibus*
157.395-6 *in furiales ... saxis*
182-3.111-15 *Vortiporius ... cui successit*

The last of these was restored by a later hand from a descendant of Φ. D and no. 178 each have many errors of their own, especially small transpositions, but they share for instance these omissions:

124.141 *totis*	174.439 *equestres*
125.169 *super corpus*	178.59 *sui*
128.234 *ibi*	190.231 *ab*
134.391 *exequiis*	195.370 *illam*
137.483 *oppidum*	196.409 *iam*
147.114 *uiriliter*	202.518 *rex*
154.228 *sese siue*	203.525 *tantam*
166.192 *autem*	

45 I ignore nos. 80 and 22, certainly descendants of K, and nos. 50 and 114, probably also descendants of K. See below, 'Survey of the manuscripts', no. 80.

My reason for citing only N and D from these two pairs could also be applied to AK, but I am not confident enough of the stemma below Σ to drop one of its few 12th-century descendants[46]. Some other 'Sexburgis' manuscripts, for instance nos. 41 (s. xiv), 113 (s. xiii[1]), and 124 (s. xiv), have so accurate a text that I hoped to find a use for them; but they are variously contaminated and shed no fresh light on Σ. No. 41, for instance, has the sentence at § 176.469-70 about the burial of Beduerus and also at § 168.263-4 a poor variant that connects it with nos. 34 and 103, relatives of M:

> elegit sibi et legioni uni quam sibi adesse affectauerat locum quendam, quo aureum draconem infixit

> et legioni uni ΔΦ, AKUD: legionem unam N, 41, 34, 103
> locum quendam quo ΔΦ, AKUND: et coram se 41, 34, 103

Below, in 'Survey of the tradition', I go further into the classification of the 'Sexburgis' manuscripts; see my remarks on nos. 8, 24, 69, 93, 99.

In my apparatus, Σ stands as usual not for the agreement of UAKND but for their common source. Nevertheless, I refrain from using the symbol where UAKND disagree in such a way that any reconstruction of Σ would prejudice a discussion of its relationship to Δ and Φ.

I now pass to the character of Σ. After § 177 it shows no further agreements with Φ against Δ. These are the last agreements of the kind:

172.371-2 *turmas* <*inanimando*> ... *crebris[que]* ... *[infestare]* **ΦΣ**
174.437 *audaciam* ΔQG: *abundantiam* YMΣ
175.453 *tandem* Δ: *etiam* **ΦΣ**
177.7 *dimisso[que]* **ΦΣ**

After § 177.7 readings shared against ΔΦ not just by UAK but by a majority of the 'Sexburgis' manuscripts become more frequent. Of the 19 listed above from UAK, only five are absent from ND and a fair number of other 'Sexburgis' manuscripts: those at §§ 185.151, 193.323, 196.392, 196.400, 202.518-19. Some of the remaining 14 are plainly errors, one probably a conjecture (§ 186.158-9), none of the rest obviously preferable to the reading of ΔΦ, Δ, or Φ. Has Σ therefore turned into an unremarkable descendant of Δ? Significant errors shared with a descendant of Δ would prove it, but there are none unless UND are contaminated: 182.114 *gubernauit* after *pace* OAK (before *cum* CHSEUNDΦ), 196.387 *[pauperem]* OAK, 196.400 *[tunc]* OUAK (and nos. 93, 99), 200.469 *reges Anglorum* OΣ (*Anglorum reges* CHSEΦ). This outside chance of a link with O reopens a matter that I had taken to be closed. As I mentioned above, O has lost everything after § 203.542 *ira Dei deserta quam uos*, but it has two descendants, nos. 44 (s. xiii[3/3]) and 212 (s. xiv). Unfortunately, no. 44 has lost even more at the end than O itself, but no. 212 (s. xiv) is complete. At § 204.553-4 it has the 'Sexburgis' version, and in §§ 204-6 it shares the errors of Σ just listed. In 1991, before I had noticed the change that comes over Σ in § 177, I inferred that when no. 212 was written O

---

[46] These may include no. 139 (Bodl. Digby 67, s. xii/xiii), a relative of no. 118; but regrettably it is only a short fragment.

had already lost the end, which was supplied from a 'Sexburgis' manuscript[47]; but might O itself not have had the 'Sexburgis' version at § 204.553-4? It has two other notable peculiarities, *secundum Caratonum* in the title and the *pudibundus Brito* version of §§ 109-10: why not a third?

Up to § 177 it is tempting to derive Φ from Σ, because almost all its divergences from Σ could easily be errors. Here are the exceptions:

132.335 *pepigit*	170.320 *duodecim*
132.349 *Haec dum*	171.341 *stricte*
147.98 *erunt*	174.435 *infortunium ei obtulit quos*
149.163 *itaque*	176.469-70 *Ibi ... positus fuit*
156.354 *Nec mirum*	

Though right, the readings of Φ at §§ 132.335, 147.98, 156.354, 170.320, could be conjectures; at § 132.349 there seems to have been a mess in both Δ and Σ; and confusion between *itaque* and *igitur* is so common that at § 149.163 Φ could have corrupted the reading of Σ to the reading of Δ. That leaves just the last three readings, all near what I have been treating as the point beyond which Σ never sides with Φ against Δ; but moving the point back to § 171 in order to rescue the derivation of Φ from Σ would leave unexplained six agreements of ΣΦ in §§ 171-7 (I include *abundantiam* at §174.437, where *audaciam* in QG seems more likely to be a conjecture than to have been corrupted independently by YM). I therefore abandon the idea, at least until I can find a way of rescuing it without special pleading.

As in 1991, however, I still incline to believe that ΣΦ share errors against Δ. Here once again is a passage cited above, this time with the descendants of Σ added to the apparatus in bold type:

130.279-81 ... *cum gaudio in Britanniam reuerti coeperunt. Nec mora, prosperantibus uentis applicant sepulturasque uirorum cum lapidibus petunt*

nec mora Δ: *nec* QU: *nec non* M: *et* **AKDYHG**: *ac* **N**

The absurd *nec* also appears in no. 123, an early but fragmentary relative of K. Plainly Σ as well as Φ simply omitted *mora*. Unless *nec mora* in Δ is a conjecture (a far better one than the descendants of Σ and Φ achieved), the omission links Σ with Φ. The same holds in a more complex passage:

124.151-3 *At Octa filius Hengisti cum maiori multitudine Eboracum adiuit, Eosa uero cognatus suus urbem Aldclud, atque eas innumeris armatis munierunt.*
Aldclud atque eas Δ: *Aldclud adiuit atque eam* U: lac. A: om. NDQYH: *secum* KG (et mox *muniuit* K): *Alclud et sic se* M

From the readings of their descendants it is not immediately clear what Σ or Φ read. To take Φ first, however, the agreement of QYH strongly suggests that it simply omitted *Aldclud atque eas*, leaving *munierunt* with the singular subject *Eosa*; thereupon, someone in the ancestry of K consulted the Second Variant,

47 'Transmission' (n. 5) 93.

its source for § 1-118, and borrowed *secum ... muniuit*, while someone in the ancestry of M either conjectured *Alclud et sic se* or consulted a descendant of Δ but garbled the additional phrase. Two descendants of Σ, namely N and D, agree with QYH, though N repairs the syntax by replacing *Eosa uero* with *eamque ipse et*; but the readings of A and U suggest that rather than an omission Σ had a lacuna, which A left unfilled but U filled by conjecture or contamination. No more than at § 130.279-81 can a conjectural supplement in Δ be ruled out, but again it would be a faultless one. Two phrases present in Δ but absent from ΣΦ, § 119.22-3 *cum germano suo decem milibus militum comitatus* and § 143.41-2 *ac si ex morte resuscitatus esset*, would not have needed to be supplied conjecturally by Δ, because they are dispensable; it is not conjecture, therefore, that would have to be blamed by anyone determined not to treat the omissions as shared errors, but either an afterthought on Geoffrey's part or a common ancestor of ΔΣΦ that left it unclear whether the phrases were meant to be incorporated or not.

§§ 109-10

I have already mentioned that instead of quoting Geoffrey's address to Alexander (§ 110) O has the *pudibundus Brito* version, which summarizes the transaction. Reconstructing Δ therefore becomes impossible, and alongside O I cite CHSE individually.

In § 110 a new witness supervenes: the separate text of the *Prophetiae*, which I shall call Π. Orderic Vitalis, cited in my apparatus as Ord., is an early witness to Π in §§ 113.72-115.108, and for determining which separate copies of the prophecies descend from Π and were not extracted from *De gestis Britonum* I have used two of his readings, § 113.74 *ipsius* for *albi draconis* and § 114.92 *translateralibus* for *collateralibus*. Other readings characteristic of Π include § 112.52-3 *Octo sceptrigeri illius ... glorificabitur* for *Septem sceptrigeri ... sanctificabitur*, § 116.160 *exortus* for *ille*, 162 *puella* for *ipsa*, 170 *[ipsarum]*, 188 *Quattuor* for *Tria*.

Separate manuscripts begin either with Geoffrey's address to Alexander, as might be expected, or with § 111 *Sedente itaque Vortegirno*, of which *itaque* is ineptly reproduced, sensibly omitted, or linked to a new introduction. They either run to the end of the prophecies, and sometimes a short way beyond, or break off in the middle of an episode at § 116.194 *in oculos eius et faciem*. Strangely, the earliest manuscripts break off at § 116.194, and many of them begin with § 111[48]. I have not found a satisfactory antidote to the possibility that some complete manuscripts of the prophecies had an incomplete ancestor later supplemented from *De gestis Britonum*.

This manuscript has the whole of §§ 110-17:

48 Eckhardt's list (n. 7) does not indicate where manuscripts begin or end. Separate manuscripts that do not belong to the separate tradition are too numerous to list here. Most begin at § 111, but they are less disappointing than those that begin at § 110, such as B. L. Arundel 66 (a. 1490), because I start with higher expectations of these. The text in B. L. Add. 25014 (s. xii) runs only to § 110.19 *insulae* (the rest is missing), but its reading *tot doctiores tot ditiores* suggests that despite its early date it was extracted from the *Historia*.

Cambridge U. L. Gg 6 42 (s. xiii[1])

These begin with § 111:

British Library Cotton Titus D VII (s. xv)
Bodl. Bodley 91 (s. xiii[2])
Vatican Reg. Lat. 1534 (s. xv)

These break off at § 116.194 *in oculos eius et faciem*:

Bourges Mun. 367 (s. xiii)
Lincoln Cath. 214 (s. xii)
Paris B. N. Lat. 2599 (s. xiv) ff. 263r-266r
Paris B. N. Lat. 6274 (s. xii)
Vatican Reg. Lat. 807 (s. xii)

These break off at the same point and do not include § 110:

Boulogne 180 ff. 72v-74v + 139 f. 2r (s. xiii)
Oxford Linc. Lat. 27 (s. xii)
Paris B. N. Lat. 2935 (s. xii)
Paris B. N. Lat. 6237 (s. xii)
Paris B. N. Lat. 15172 (s. xii), extended to the end of § 117 by another hand
Vatican Vat. Lat. 3820 (s. xv)

Two include § 110 and break off at other points:

Bruges 428 (s. xiii) ff. 48v-51r, to § 116.237 *uenenatus interibit*
Liège Univ. 369C (s. xii) ff. 143-5, to § 116.192-3 *et aprum*

The former ends in mid column, where another text follows in the same hand. As a bifolium seems to have been cut out of the latter after f. 145, the text surely continued, even if only with the 15 words that would have brought it to *in oculos eius et faciem*; perhaps indeed the bifolium was cut out because so little had been written on it[49]. One manuscript continues to the end of § 118 and then, under the heading *Causa prophetationis Merlini uel modus agnitionis eius et generationis eiusdem*, adds the chapters that precede the *Prophecies* from § 105.489 *Vt igitur nefandum praeceptum* to the end of § 108:

Paris B. N. Lat. 14465 (s. xii)

For no obvious reason most of these manuscripts omit § 112.45 *Sublimabit ... comitabuntur*, and Reg. Lat. 807 places it after 49 *induetur*.

With various levels of unease I use Cambridge U. L. Gg 6 42, Lincoln Cath. 214, Bruges 428, Paris Lat. 14465. In the next section I list manuscripts of *De gestis Britonum* that apparently owe the *Prophecies* to Π, and I use one of them, no. 124 (Lambeth 503, s. xiv).

---

49 B. Meehan, 'Geoffrey of Monmouth, *Prophecies of Merlin*: new manuscript evidence', *Bulletin of the Board of Celtic Studies* 28 (1978-80) 37-46, and Caroline D. Eckhardt, 'Geoffrey of Monmouth's *Prophetia Merlini* and the construction of Liège University MS 369C', *Manuscripta* 32 (1988) 176-84, agree about the bifolium even though they disagree about the original composition of the mutilated quire. Neither draws my conclusions.

Π already differed from manuscripts of *De gestis Britonum* in § 110, and another manuscript of *De gestis Britonum* besides O steps out of line: Y. But for the evidence of Π, one reading of Y would be dismissed as a corruption, and so I cite all variants of Y in §§ 109-10. Φ can still be reconstructed, however, from QGM.

§§ 111-17

I have assumed that descendants of Π are available throughout the prophecies, but see my remarks on §§ 109-10.

Here too realignments occur in the manuscripts of *De gestis Britonum*. As O returns to general agreement with CHSE, Δ can be reconstructed again, but I have already mentioned in connexion with §§ 118-208 that H changed its exemplar at § 114.104. Q now descends from O or at least shares all its errors, for instance these:

111.26 *alter uero* for *et alius*
114.100 *subuertet* for *mutabit*
116.188 *nidifica-* for *procrea-*
116.206-7 *[Bos montanus ... dealbabit]*
116.214 *conglutinent* for *deglutient*
116.217 *igitur* for *iterum*
116.218 *[Vrbes uicinas ... subuertet]*
116.225 *[patriae]*
116.239 *serpentem* for *saeuientem*
116.284 *humo* for *uino*

I therefore dispense with Q here. M sometimes agrees not just with Δ against YG but also with Π against ΔYG. The First Variant (W) can be added, because it does not recast the text; but as the witnesses to it sometimes have the same variants as the rest of the tradition, I cite it only where they agree (a lazy substitute, I admit, for working out which reading to treat as primary). Despite the agreement of WYG in a few passages, I have thought it better not to assume that their common source was Φ.

There are two complications: some manuscripts of *De gestis Britonum* that I do not use (nos. 6, 33, 69, 74, 84, 115, 124, 202) have the text of Π, perhaps because they or an ancestor originally skipped the *Prophetiae* and someone restored them later from a separate manuscript; and in some passages the same variants occur in descendants of Π as in manuscripts of *De gestis Britonum*, notably § 115.116 *exercebit/exacuet*.

Survey of the tradition

Rather than leave my choice of manuscripts to be taken completely on trust, I give here, in numerical order, at least a brief indication of how the rest behave. Most readers, though, will prefer to skip this section.

The numbers and most of the dates are those of Julia Crick's *Summary catalogue* (n. 5), with the addition of 216-19 (n. 5). *Dissem.* is her other work (n. 7), 'Transm.' my article (n. 5). Chapter VIII of *Dissem.*, 'Towards a textual history', combines two kinds of ordering, numerical and genealogical. It starts, for instance, with no. 1, but this represents the First Variant, and so its other representatives are listed in numerical order after no. 1; they do not reappear under their own numbers, which have to be looked up in the 'Index of manuscripts'.

< indicates descent, ≏ a relationship evident from shared errors. I report shared errors only when I can go beyond *Dissem.* and 'Transm.'. I have paid most attention to manuscripts that change their allegiance, because almost nothing is said in *Dissem.* about such changes except when they coincide with breaks in structure. Where I do not know the exact point of transition, I add '(c.)'.

For the large family that descends from G in §§ 1-108 and shares errors with it in the rest of the work I use the notation '≏ 7'; for its large subfamily of 'nameless dedication' manuscripts, '≏ 2'. I pick 2 and 7 not because they are important representatives of their families but merely because they come first in the numerical sequence.

About the diffusion of the text I have nothing to say beyond what Crick said in *Dissem.* and I myself in 'Transm.' 114-17.

1   xviii   Aberystwyth 2005 (Panton 37)
First Variant.

2   xii   Aberystwyth 11611 (Clumber 46)
≏ 7, 'nameless dedication'; see 'Transm.' pp. 81-5.

3   xiii   Aberystwyth 13052 (Phillipps 32)
≏ 2.

4   xiii   Aberystwyth 13210 (Phillipps 26233)
First Variant. In his edition, pp. lxxix, cxv, Wright speaks of conflation with the Second Variant but gives no details; I have not checked, because the matter is of no consequence for the present edition. The text of §§ 1-3 added in a 16th-century hand thought likely to be Matthew Parker's came from another manuscript that he owned, no. 35.

5   xiii   Aberystwyth 21552
Up to § 149(c.) ≏ M with heavy contamination from Δ, then ≏ K.

6   xiii   Aberystwyth Llanstephan 176 (Phillipps 9162)
≏ 69 but with heavy contamination from Δ; §§ 1-5 and 109-10 < Φ.

7   xv   Aberystwyth Llanstephan 196
§§ 1-108 < G, rest ≏ G.

8   xii/xiii Aberystwyth Peniarth 42
§§ 1-143(c.) ≃ Y, then < Σ. See on 93.

9   xiv   Aberystwyth Peniarth 43
[§§ 1-3], §§ 5-95(c.) ≃ Y, 95(c.)-110 ≃ O with contamination (the two versions
of §§ 109-10 are conflated); it passes from there to § 118, of which it rewrites
the opening in the same way as N, and puts §§ 111-17 (up to 301 *Pliades*) after
§ 118; §§ 118-208 ≃ N with contamination from a descendant of Δ (doubtless its
O-like source). See *Dissem.* pp. 110-11, though the conflation in §§ 109-10 is
overlooked. In short, it seems to descend from a relative of N (N in its original
state) supplemented and corrected from O or a relative; errors shared with N
include the rewriting of § 37.44-6 *cum ... mandauitque* as *cumque notificaretur
puellam suam raptam sibi et regem Daciae in carceribus detineri missis nuntiis
mandauit fratri* (with minor variations), 121.82-5 *milia [non procederet ...
milia] armatorum <non excessit>*, 147.101 *contra istos congressum* for *mortem*,
190.228-9 *quod cum illa nullam dignabatur (-aretur* N) *habere cohabitationem*
for *ut ... expelleret.* 143 is very close throughout, 93 a relative up to § 117.

10   xiii   Aberystwyth Porkington 17
≃ Y except that §§ 109-17 < Δ; contaminated.

11   xv   Aberystwyth Wynnstay 14
≃ 7.

12   xii   Alençon 12
A in §§ 118-208 of this edition.

13   xiii   Arras 583 (871)
≃ 21.

14   xii/xiii Auxerre 91 (85)
≃ 2.

15   xii   Bern 568
< H; see above, p. xix. With 86, 100, and 215, it omits § 116.208 *potando*, 272
in before *ferro*, 117.293 *Phoebus*. 86 has many errors absent from 15 and 200,
such as § 120.56 *ceterisque Saxonibus* for *Saxonibusque suis*, but cannot descend
from either, because at § 179.94, where they all omit *grauatus ... Malgone rege*, 15
and 200 restore sense with *mortuus*, and 15 and 200 but not 86 omit § 100.358-9
amauit ... cor suum; contamination might be blamed for the latter difference but
hardly can for the former. I have found no reason why 200, which has errors absent
from 15 such as § 120.62 *[Tales]*, should not descend from 15.

16   xiii   Boulogne 180
≃ 21.

17   xiii   Bruges 428
§§ 1-63 (c.) < Δ, §§ 63(c.)-109 Second Variant, [§§ 110-17], §§ 118-208 Second Variant; §§ 110-17 at end < Π. The text of §§ 23-24.29 *ducturum*, added on a slip, descends from H, probably by way of 48 or a relative, because corrections in the hand that wrote the passage include § 149.151 *dimicantes <et ab ipso superati>*. Cf. 207, 202.

18   xii/xiii Brussels 8495-8505
Fragment < Δ.

19   xii   Brussels 8536-43
≃ 2.

20   xii/xiii Brussels 9871-4
≃ 2.

21   xii   Brussels II 1020 (Phillipps 11603)
≃ 7. It forms a family with 13, 16, 190, 206, 211. See also on 59, 60, 217.

22   xiii   Cambridge Clare 27 (N 1 5)
≃ 54; see on 80.

23   xii   Cambridge C. C. C. 281
E in this edition.

24   xiii   Cambridge C. C. C. 292
§§ 1-31.169 *maritem illud* < the ed. Paris. 1517, §§ 31.169 *autem affirmo* - 137 < Δ, rest < Σ. The change in § 137 occurs between 486 *astitisset* (Δ: -*es* ΣΦ) and 511 *[uirum]* (ΣΦ: hab. Δ), and it may not be an accident that the deviant quire of H ends between these points, with 505 *reputaretur adesse*. Cf. 52, with which 24 shares e. g. § 62.220-21 *[turmas ... ascendentes]*, 236 *[non est diligendus]*, 158.419 *[senatum]*, 196.414 *[uniuersis]*. Cf. also 64, 74, 87.

25   xiv   Cambridge C. C. C. 414
≃ G.

26   xiii   Cambridge Fitzwilliam Mus. 302 (Phillipps 203)
≃ G.

27   xv   Cambridge Fitzwilliam Mus. 346
? < 51; see 'Transm.' p. 86.

28   xii   Cambridge Caius 103/55
§§ 1-178(c.) ≃ Y, then < Σ. See on 69.

29   xv   Cambridge Caius 249/277
≂ G.

30   xii/xiii Cambridge Caius 406/627
Y in this edition.

31   xvii   Cambridge Caius 450/391
< 113, doubtless a direct copy. Corrections made to 113 in erasure recur, together
with such errors as § 130.264 *[quia]*, 268 *[in fugam]*.

32   xiv   Cambridge St John's G 16 (184)
≂ Y, with some contamination.

33   xv   Cambridge St John's S 6 (254)
≂ 69, though with §§ 1-3 < Φ, [§ 5], and §§ 109-10 < Π.

34   xii/xiii Cambridge Sidney Sussex 75 (Δ.4.13)
≂ M; see above, p. xvi. It has two interpolations of interest: § 119.33 *in natione
Hergign <quae modo Hurchenefeld uocatur>*, § 151.196 ... *cessabant <nam
beatus Sampson incursionibus praedonii* [a slip for *praedonum*] *cum .vii.
episcopis illius patriae expulsus Dolensem metropolim petiit ibique honorifice
receptus usque ad extremum diem religiose deguit>*. Another distinctive reading
is § 168.263 *legionem unam ... et coram se* for *et legioni uni ... locum quendem
quo*. See also on 152, 125, 103, 46, 88, 41. The abbreviated version on ff. 75v-
93v of Vat. Reg. Lat. 1534 (s. xv) shares errors with 34, at least near the end:
§ 203.524 *[quam uero]*, 204.546 *[tota]*, 205.561 *[roboratus]*, *[iam]*.

35   xv   Cambridge Trinity R 5 34 (725)
Second Variant.

36   xiii   Cambridge Trinity R 7 6 (744)
≂ 2.

37   xiii   Cambridge Trinity R 7 28 (770)
§§ 1-31.158 *celare nitatur* largely < Φ, though after § 22 several diagnostic
passages are missing; rest (new quire) ≂ G.

38   xiv   Cambridge Trinity O 1 17 (1041)
§§ 1-92(c.) ≂ Y, §§ 92(c.)-108 < Φ (≂ G with contamination?), §§ 118.2
Vortegirnus uero - 208 < Σ, §§ 111-17 (added at the end) ≂ G with contamination.
131 is very similar.

39   xiii/xiv Cambridge Trinity O 2 21 (1125)
§§ 1-4 < H, §§ 5-68(c.) < Δ, §§ 68(c.)-208 ≂ Y. The second change may well
occur after § 68.339 *aedificata igitur*, where a new quire begins (f. 41r).

40   xiv   Cambridge U. L. Dd 1 17
≏ 111. See *Dissem.* pp. 50, 74.

41   xiv   Cambridge U. L. Dd 4 34
[§§ 1-5], §§ 6-23(c.) < Φ, §§ 23(c.)-117 ≏ O, §§ 118-208 < Σ with contamination;
see above, p. xxvii.

42   xv   Cambridge U. L. Dd 6 7 + Bodl. 585
§§ 1-117 ≏ O, §§ 118-208 < Σ; contaminated throughout, most obviously in
§§ 109-10, where it has the usual version but shares § 110.12 *minus sufficeret*
with O and appends *Venia <ergo> ... persono* from the version of O.

43   xii   Cambridge U. L. Dd 6 12
C in this edition.

44   xiii²   Cambridge U. L. Dd 10 31
< O.

45   xiv   Cambridge U. L. Dd 10 32
≏ Y.

46   xv   Cambridge U. L. Ee 1 24
§§ 1-127(c.) < Δ, rest ≏ 103. The point of transition falls between § 127.208
et motus and § 128.217 *praeceptum [tuum]*. The first source shared with O
against CHSEΦ a number of errors but not e. g. its version of §§ 109-10; was it
a contaminated descendant of O or a relative? Cf. 161, 88. Like 103, the second
source shared errors with 34 up to about § 199 and with M in the few remaining
chapters, but it was not 103 itself, which e. g. has § 199.448-9 *in commune* (om.
34, 46).

47   xiv   Cambridge U. L. Ff 1 25
Second Variant.

48   xii   Cambridge U. L. Ii 1 14
§§ 1-147(c.) < H, rest ≏ SE. Many conjectures.

49   xii   Cambridge U. L. Ii 4 4
< H.

50   xiv   Cambridge U. L. Ii 4 12
≏ 54; see on 80.

51   xv   Cambridge U. L. Ii 4 17
? < 26; see 'Transm.' p. 86.

52   a. 1327 Cambridge U. L. Kk 6 16
≈ 24.

53   xii/xiii Cambridge U. L. Mm 1 34
≈ 2.

54   xii   Cambridge U. L. Mm 5 29
K in §§ 118-208 of this edition; §§ 1-117 Second Variant. See also on 80.

55   xiii/xiv Cardiff 2.611
§§ 1-5 <Φ (≈37, 64), §§ 6-108 First Variant (with contamination < Δ), §§ 109-10
< Φ, §§ 111-17 < Δ (≈ O?), §§ 118-177(c.) conflation of Σ and Δ, rest conflation
of Δ and First Variant.

56   xii   Colmar 448 (14)
≈ 2. Very corrupt.

57   xv   Cologny Bodm. 70
§§ 1-110 ≈ G with contamination, §§ 111-149(c.) ≈ 66, §§ 149(c.)-165(c.) ≈ G,
rest < Δ with much abbreviation.

58   xiii   Dôle 348+349
≈ 2.

59   xii   Douai 880 (835)
≈ 7. It shares some errors with 21 and its relatives.

60   xii   Douai 882 (838)
≈ 7; fundamentally a relative of 21 but full of transpositions and expansions.

61   xiv   Dublin Trin. 172 (B 2 7)
§§ 1-91(c.) Second Variant, rest ≈ Y.

62   xiii   Dublin Trin. 493 (E 2 24)
≈ 7; contaminated throughout; variants in the margin.

63   xii/xiii Dublin Trin. 494 (E 5 7)
≈ S.

64   xiv   Dublin Trin. 495 (E 4 30)
≈ 87.

65   xiv   Dublin Trin. 496 (E 6 2)
≈ G.

66 xiv Dublin Trin. 514 (E 5 3)
§§ 1-109 Second Variant, § 110 < Π, §§ 111-17 ≃ O, §§ 118-31(c.) < Σ, rest
Second Variant. Cf. 138, 57. What I said in 'Transm.', p. 86, was inaccurate.

67 xiii/xiv Dublin Trin. 515 (E 5 12)
First Variant.

68 xiv Edinburgh Adv. 18.4.5
First Variant.

69 xiii Eton 246 (Phillipps 25145)
[§§ 1-5], §§ 6-19 (c.) < Φ with contamination, §§ 20-31(c.) ≃ O, §§ 31(c.)-108
≃ G, [§§ 109-10], §§ 111-17 < Π, §§ 118-208 < Σ with contamination at least up
to § 138.517 *peremptus* (Δ: *interfectus* ΣΦ). In §§ 118-208 several errors, e. g.
§§ 149.160 *[tanta]*, 193.303 *[uela]*, 195.366 *[cuncta]*, connect it with such parts
of 6, 28, 64, 84, 87, 100, 109, 115, 124, 134, as descend from Σ. Closest to 69
are 6 and 115: § 119.51 *prius in istum* for *uos in istum prius*, 129.239 *in risum
Aurelius* for *Aurelius in risum*, 149.166 *prout reperiebatur nulli* for *nulli prout
reperiebatur*, 174-5 *petitioni acquiescens* ∼, 155.265 *facerent* for *inissent*.

70 xiii Exeter Cath. 3514
First Variant, with §§ 1-3 and §§ 109-10 ≃ S.

71 xii Florence Laur. S. Croce 17 dextr. 6
< Δ, with rubrics and corrections ≃ 76 (< 76 itself?). It shares the errors of SE listed
above, pp. xx-xxi.

72 xiv Florence Naz. B. R. 55
§§ 1-100 ≃ O, §§ 101-129(c.) ≃ Y, rest ≃ K; contaminated throughout. Cf. 133.

73 xiii Glasgow Univ. U 7 25 (331)
≃ Y up to § 200.470 *solus aberat*, rest (new quire and hand, to § 202.518 *rex
Caduallo*; no more written) ≃ 34.

74 xiv Glasgow Univ. U 7 26 (332)
§§ 1-110 < Δ, §§ 111-17 < Π, §§ 118-37(c.) < Δ, §§ 137(c.)-172(c.) < Σ ≃ 24,
rest ≃ G. Cf. 24, 64, 87.

75 xiii Heidelberg Univ. 9.31
≃ 2; close to 218.

76 xii Leiden B. P. L. 20
≃ 7.

77   xiii/xiv Leiden Voss. Lat. F 77
< G.

78   xv   Leningrad Lat. F IV 76
Not seen.

79   xii   Lille 533
≃ 7. See 'Transm.' pp. 82-3.

80   xii   Lincoln Cath. 98 (A 4 6)
< 54; see *Dissem.* pp. 26-7, 29-30, 34, 42-3, 55, 73, 88. Corrections in 80 taken from a manuscript like 28, e. g. § 5.34 *irrigant* for *irritant,* 44 *ceteros <annos>,* 76.89-90 *sine intermissione interfici* for *interfici sine intermissione* in the supplement, recur in the text of 22, 50, and 114, but the details of those at §§ 76.89-90 and 159.470 are hard to reconcile with straightforward descent from 80. 22 has errors of its own, e. g. § 33.292-3 *[nuncupabatur ... Porrex],* and 50 and 114 share errors, e. g. § 120.61 *[et] super,* 157.397 *ceterorum[que],* 207.587 *cum [autem],* 208.607 *[sermonem].* Like 54, 80 and 22 omit § 165.81-2 *tanto ... repleuit,* present in the text of 50 and 114; 50 and 114 also have § 124.152 *Alclud atque eam,* essentially the reading of Δ, whereas K has *secum,* the reading of G and the Second Variant. Despite the complications, it seems very likely that not just 80 but 22, 50, and 114, descend from 54. The secondary source of 50 and 114 may have a connexion with 99 and its relatives: at § 130.271 all these manuscripts supply *uideatis* ('Transm.' p. 91).

81   xiii/xiv B. L. Add. 11702
≃ 2.

82   xii   B. L. Add. 15732
< G. As G also lies behind the 15th-century section at the end (from § 166.195 *Beduerumque pincernam),* the original end probably served as the exemplar.

83   xii   B. L. Add. 33371
Fragments, ≃ 2; § 26.71-3 *[quo defuncto ... aestuabat]* with 173.

84   xv   B. L. Add. 35295
≃ 69, with §§ 1-5 and 109-10 < Φ.

85   xii   B. L. Arundel 10
Second Variant.

86   xiii   B. L. Arundel 237
≃ 15.

87   xiii   B. L. Arundel 319+409
§§ 1-137(c.) < Δ, rest < Σ. See on 69. Cf. 24, 64, 74.

88   xiii/xiv   B. L. Arundel 326
§§ 1-108 < Δ, [§§ 109-10], §§ 111-17 < Δ with contamination < Π, §§ 118-27
(c.) < Δ, rest ≑ 103. Cf. 116. If, as the pattern of affiliation suggests, 88 and 116
descend from the same source as 46, they represent it less faithfully.

89   xii   B. L. Arundel 403
Fragment, < Δ but not closely related to any of OCHSE. With 160, of which the
same is true, it shares the transposition of § 124.153 *munierunt* before *innumeris*.

90   xiv/xv   B. L. Cotton Cleo. D VIII
≑ M, e. g. § 23.8 *[postmodum]*, 186.165 *[instanti]*. Cf. 137; see *Dissem.* pp. 35,
73-4.

91   xiv   B. L. Cotton Galba E XI
Second Variant.

92   xii/xiii   B. L. Cotton Nero D VIII
< 76. See *Dissem.* pp. 23-4, 74.

93   xiv   B. L. Cotton Titus A XVIII
§§ 1-95(c.) ≑ Y, §§ 96(c.)-117 ≑ O, §§ 118-208 < Σ; see above, p. xxiv. At § 202.518-
19, where UAK omit *Caduallo ... accepit et*, it restores sense in the same way as 8,
by adding *habuit uxorem et*. For its text up to § 117 cf. 132, 9, 210.

94   xiii/xiv   B. L. Cotton Titus A XXV
Fragment < Δ.

95   xii/xiii   B. L. Cotton Titus A XXVII
Second Variant.

96   xii   B. L. Cotton Titus C XVII
Twin of 23. See above, p. xviii.

97   xiv   B. L. Cotton Vesp. A XXIII
< 76.

98   xiii-xiv   B. L. Cotton Vesp. E X
§§ 1-174.431 *diffugie-* ≑ Y, rest (new quire and hand) < Σ ≑ 118, 132.

99   xiii/xiv   B. L. Egerton 3142 (Clumber 47)
§§ 1-117 ≑ G, §§ 118-208 < Σ.

100   xii   B. L. Harl. 225
≃ 28; very corrupt.

101   xii   B. L. Harl. 536
Fragment ≃ C; neither descends from the other.

102   xii/xiii B. L. Harl. 3773
Second Variant.

103   xiii   B. L. Harl. 4003
≃ 34 and M. It shares neither interpolation reported above from 34 but does share § 168.263-4 *legionem unam ... et coram se* and also e. g. § 193.324 *aequora sulcant* for *aequoreum iter aggrediuntur*. From § 200 it shares errors instead with M: 200.486 *adhaeret* for *eam debet*, 500 *adeptus est <Oswi>*, 202.517 *[tantum matre]*, 203.536 *Saxones* after *quiuerunt*, 205.563 *id* after *rege*. As the same change occurs in 46 and 88, the likeliest explanation is that 34 deviated.

104   a. 1349 B. L. Harl. 4123
≃ 7; see on 194.

105   xiv/xv B. L. Harl. 5115
< 125. See also *Dissem.* p. 22.

106   xii/xiii B. L. Harl. 6358
First Variant up to § 149.155 *rupes ma-*, rest (new quire and hand) ≃ G.

107   xii/xiii B. L. Lansdowne 732
< H, probably through 136, because it has in the text some readings that occur as corrections in 136, e. g. §§ 31.150 *exprimere <posse>*, 52.362 *<superabat> et in modulis*, 191.247 *rogauit <Edwinus>*.

108   xii   B. L. Royal 4 C XI
Second Variant.

109   xiv/xv B. L. Royal 13 A III
§§ 1-5 ≃ Y, 6-20(c.) < Φ, §§ 20(c.)-31(c.) ≃ O, §§ 31(c.)-117 ≃ Y, §§ 118-208 ≃ Σ with contamination. The points of transition suggest a connexion with 69, but where they descend from Φ 69 is connected with G, not Y.

110   xiv   B. L. Royal 13 A V
≃ 48 except for [§§ 1-4], §§ 92(c)-108 ≃ G, §§ 178-end (new hand and quire) ≃ Y, contamination (doubtless of the second source with the first or third) in §§ 109-10 and at the beginning of the *Prophecies*.

111   xiv/xv B. L. Royal 13 D I
≏ 2; [§§ 109-10]; very corrupt, with some contamination and much trivial rewriting. Cf. 40.

112   xii/xiii B. L. Royal 13 D II
M in this edition.

113   xiii¹   B. L. Royal 13 D V
§§ 1-23(c.) Second Variant, §§ 23(c.)-117 ≏ O, §§ 118-208 < Σ. Contaminated throughout, and not just where corrections are neatly made in erasure.

114   xiv   B. L. Royal 14 C I
+ Cotton Nero C V ≏ 54; see on 80.

115   xiv/xv B. L. Royal 15 C XVI
≏ 69.

116   xv   B. L. Sloane 289
≏ 88. See *Dissem.* pp. 31-2, 34, 42, 71-2, 73, 88.

117   xii   B. L. Stowe 56
≏ 7.

118   xiv   London College of Arms Arundel 1
§§ 1-23(c.) ≏ G, §§ 23(c.)-117 ≏ O, §§ 118-208 ≏ 132. See above, p. xxv.

119   xiii   London Lambeth 188
≏ Y.

120   xii   London Lambeth 379+357
≏ S.

121   xiv   London Lambeth 401
≏ G, but specifically with 54 (Second Variant) it shares § 5.40 *suorum* for *sanctorum*, § 6.60 *aduenit* for *accessit*, 11.153 *auxilio <uel consilio>*, 164 *po<tui>sse*, 12.172 *cum<que>*. For contamination in §§ 111-17 see 'Transm.' p. 87.

122   xiii/xiv London Lambeth 454 ff. 28r-123r
≏ 99.

123   xii   London Lambeth 454 ff. 124r-204v
§§ 1-109 ≏ Y, §§ 110-127.211 *protege-* (new quire and hand) < Δ with corrections (? < 148), rest (change of ink and perhaps hand) ≏ K.

124   xiv   London Lambeth 503
§§ 1-110 ≃ G, §§ 111-17 < Π, §§ 118-208 < Σ. See on 69.

125   xii   Madrid Nac. 6319 (R 202)
≃ 2 except in §§ 109-17, where ≃ M. Corrections ≃ 34. Cf. *Dissem.* p. 60.

126   xii   Montpellier 92
≃ 2.

127   xii   Montpellier 378
≃ 2.

128   xii   New Haven Yale 590 (Phillipps 2324)
≃ (? <) 48.

129   xiii   New Haven Yale 598
≃ 7; see on 217.

130   xv   Notre Dame 40
≃ 2. Not seen. See *Dissem.* p. 22.

131   xv   Olomouc 411
§§ 1-92(c.) ≃ Y, §§ 92(c.)-110 < Φ, §§ 111-17 ≃ G, §§ 118-208 < Σ. Close to
38.

132   xiii¹   Oxford All Souls 35
N in §§ 118-208 of this edition; §§ 1-5 (later) ≃ 2, §§ 6-95(c.) ≃ Y, §§ 95(c.)-110
≃ O, §§ 111-17 (later) ≃ 2. Cf. 9.

133   xiv   Oxford All Souls 39
§§ 1-108 < Δ with contamination, §§ 109-17 ≃ Y, §§ 118-25(c.) < Φ, §§ 125(c.)-
197.419 *militum quos ex* ≃ K, rest modern but not taken from any of the 16th-
century editions. Cf. 72.

134   xiii   Oxford Bodl. Add. A 61
§§ 1-94(c.) < H, rest ≃ 100.

135   xiv   Oxford Bodl. Bodl. 233
≃ 7.

136   xii   Oxford Bodl. Bodl. 514
< H.

137   xiv   Oxford Bodl. Bodl. 622
≃ M. Cf. 90: see *Dissem.* p. 35.

138   xiv   Oxford Bodl. Bodl. 977
≐ 66 but omits (f. 95r/v) § 108.577 *tantam ... in illo* and § 109.

139   xii/xiii Oxford Bodl. Digby 67
Fragments ≐ 118, with which it shares e. g. § 166.175 *tenuit* for *amplectitur*.

140   xiv   Oxford Bodl. Douce 115
D in §§ 118-208 of this edition; [§§ 1-5], §§ 6-23(c.) < Φ, §§ 23(c.)-117 ≐ O.

141   xii   Oxford Bodl. Fairfax 28
≐ Y and indeed very close to Y itself.

142   xv   Oxford (Bodl.) Jesus 2
< Δ to § 63, rest ≐ Y; contaminated and much interpolated, especially with chronological glossing.

143   xiv   Oxford Bodl. Jones 48
≐ 9.

144   xiv/xv Oxford Bodl. Lat. hist. b 1 fr. 2
Fragment, < Φ.

145   xii   Oxford Bodl. Lat. misc. b 17 f. 10
Fragment, ≐ G.

146   xii   Oxford Bodl. Lat. misc. e 42
≐ E.

147   xv   Oxford Bodl. Laud misc. 579
≐ 103.

148   xii   Oxford Bodl. Laud misc. 592
Fragment, < Δ but with corrections and some readings in §§ 111-17 < Π. Source of 123?

149   xiv   Oxford Bodl. Laud misc. 664
< Δ with light contamination, probably from the relative of UAK that supplied *Merlinus iste ...* after § 117.

150   xiii   Oxford Bodl. Laud misc. 720
≐ 93.

151   xii   Oxford (Bodl.) New Coll. 276
≐ 2.

152   xv   Oxford (Bodl.) Oriel 16
≃ 34 (? <).

153   xiii   Oxford Bodl. Rawl. B 148
≃ Y. See *Dissem.* pp. 87-8.

154   xiii   Oxford Bodl. Rawl. B 168
§§ 1-189.206 *cum Brocmail* < 125, rest (a. 1730) ≃ Y.

155   xiv   Oxford Bodl. Rawl. B 189
≃ 7.

156   xii   Oxford Bodl. Rawl. C 152
O in this edition.

157   xiii   Oxford Bodl. Rawl. D 893
Fragment, ≃ 7/2.

158   xiv   Oxford Bodl. Tanner 195
< Δ.

159   xvi   Oxford Bodl. Top. Gen. c 2
Extracts of Leland's from an *impressus codex* (Paris 1508 or 1517), with occasional variants and a reference to an *exemplar manu scriptum* that *non habebat divisiones librorum*. The heading 'Lelandus' distinguishes summaries from quotations.

160   xiii   Oxford Ch. Ch. 99
§§ 1-199(c.) < Δ, rest ≃ K. See on 89.

161   xii/xiii   Oxford Magd. 170
§§ 1-127(c.) ≃ O, rest ≃ K. Cf. 46, 88.

162   xii   Oxford Magd. 171
≃ G. *Prophecies* cut out.

163   xiv   Paris Ars. 982
First Variant.

164   xiv   Paris B. N. Lat. 4126
§§ 1-24(c.) < Φ, §§ 24(c.)-54(c.) ≃ Y, rest < Δ; in §§ 111-17 some readings < Π. In §§ 1-24(c.) it shares with Q § 11.156 *[fideliter]*, § 16.290 *libamina dederunt* ~, § 24.35 *huic inerit* ~.

165   xiii/xiv Paris B. N. Lat. 4999A + Manchester Ryl. 216
≃ Y. See *Dissem.* pp. 87-8.

166   xii   Paris B. N. Lat. 5233
≃ 2.

167   xii   Paris B. N. Lat. 5234
≃ 7.

168   xv   Paris B. N. Lat. 5697
≃ 2.

169   xiv   Paris B. N. Lat. 6039
≃ 7.

170   xii   Paris B. N. Lat. 6040
H in this edition.

171   xiii/xiv Paris B. N. Lat. 6041
≃ 2.

172   xiv   Paris B. N. Lat. 6041A
≃ 7.

173   xii   Paris B. N. Lat. 6041B
≃ 2.

174   xv   Paris B. N. Lat. 6041C
≃ 7.

175   xii   Paris B. N. Lat. 6230
≃ 2.

176   xii   Paris B. N. Lat. 6231
≃ 2.

177   xii   Paris B.N. Lat. 6232
§§ 1-15.269 *argento donatur* (later) ≃ G, §§ 15.269 *-ro et argento donatur* -
132(c.) < Δ, §§ 132(c.)-177(c.) ≃ G, §§ 177(c.)-194.331 *amisisse nec* < Δ, rest
(later) ≃ G.

178   xiii/xiv Paris B. N. Lat. 6233
[§§ 1-5], §§ 6-23(c.) < Φ, §§ 23(c.)-117 ≃ O, §§ 118-208 ≃ D. See above, p.
xxvii.

179   xii   Paris B. N. Lat. 6275
≃ 2.

180   xii   Paris B. N. Lat. 6432
≃ (? <) 125.

181   xiv/xv Paris B. N. Lat. 6815
< 71, doubtless a direct copy.

182   xiv   Paris B. N. Lat. 7531
≃ 2.

183   xii   Paris B. N. Lat. 8501A
≃ 2.

184   xii   Paris B. N. Lat. 12943
≃ 2.

185   xv   Paris B. N. Lat. 13710
Q in §§ 1-110 and 118-208 of this edition. §§ 111-17 ≃ O; see above, pp. xvi, xxi-xxiii, xxxi.

186   xiv   Paris B. N. Lat. 13935 + 5508
≃ 7; see on 217.

187   xvi   Paris B. N. Lat. 15073
≃ S. Perhaps to be identified with the manuscript described in the *editio princeps* as commissioned by the abbot of St-Victor, Paris; see below, p. lxii.

188   xii/xiii Paris B. N. Lat. 17569
≃ 7.

189   xii   Paris B. N. Lat. 18271
≃ 2.

190   xiv   Paris B. N. Nouv. Acq. Lat. 1001
≃ 21. See also below, p. lxiii.

191   xii   Paris Ste-Gen. 2113
G in this edition. 77 and 82 descend from it throughout. At § 112.54, where ΔYMΠ have *secabuntur* and most of the rest *truncabuntur*, G has *obtruncabuntur*, also found in 25, 26, 38 and 131, 65, 99. At § 206.586 G omits *a contagione carnis solutus caelestis regni*.

192   xii   Philadelphia Free Library E 247
≍ Y, with much trivial rewriting.

193   xii/xiii Reims 1430
≍ 7. See 'Transm.' pp. 82-3.

194   xiii   Rome Vatican. Ottob. Lat. 1472
≍ 7; with 104 it shares § 118.16 *refugium* for *diffugium*, 120.56 *re<ue>latum*, 121.85 *[omnes]*, 87 *impetum facere* ~, 122.103 *[socios]*, 123.112 *semper Eldol* ~, 126 *cesserunt [ei]*, 124.141 *[ipsum]*.

195   xii   Rome Vatican. Pal. Lat. 956
≍ 7.

196   xiii   Rome Vatican. Pal. Lat. 962
≍ 2. Once St-Victor **B** 7 ff. 56-95; see below, pp. lxii-lxiii.

197   xii   Rome Vatican. Reg. Lat. 692
≍ 7; corrections ≍ H.

198   xv   Rome Vatican. Reg. Lat. 825
≍ 7.

199   xii   Rome Vatican. Vat. Lat. 2005
Mixture of ≍ H and ≍ 7; see above, p. xix.

200   xii   Rouen U 74 (1177)
≍ (? <) 15.

201   xviii   Rouen 3069
Collation of 93 against the *editio princeps*.

202   xiv   Saint-Omer 710
§§ 1-63(c.) < Δ, §§ 63(c.)-109 Second Variant, [§ 110], §§ 111-17 < Π, §§ 118-208 Second Variant. Cf. 17, 207.

203   xii   Salisbury Cath. 121
S in this edition.

204   xv   San Marino Huntington EL 34 C 9 (1121)
≍ C.

205   xiii   St Gallen Stiftsbibl. 633
≍ 2; very corrupt.

206   xv   Seville Colomb. 7.3.19
≏ 190.

207   xii/xiii Stockholm Holm. D 1311
§§ 1-63(c.) < Δ, §§ 63(c.)-108 Second Variant, §§ 109-10 < Π, §§ 111-17 ≏ G,
§§ 118-208 Second Variant. Cf. 17, 202.

208   xii/xiii Troyes 273 bis
< 127. Corrections to 127 are incorporated in the text of 208.

209   xiv   Troyes 1531
Second Variant.

210   xii   Ushaw Coll. 6
U in §§ 118-208 of this edition. §§ 1-95(c.) ≏ Y, §§ 95(c.)-117 < Δ. Other
manuscripts that ≏ Y up to § 95(c.) are 93, 132, 9.

211   xiv   Valenciennes 792
≏ 21.

212   xiv   Winchester Cath. 9
< O but not by way of 44, which e. g. at § 32.262 has *coniunctae erant* for *coniugatae
fuerant ambo*. On the behaviour of 212 at the end of the work see above, pp. xxvii-
xxviii. There are a few corrections, especially supplements, from a different source.

213   xvi   Würzburg Univ. M. ch. f. 140
≏ 7.

214   xv   Phillipps 3117
≏ 2. Not seen. See *Dissem.* p. 22.

215   xiv$^{3/4}$ Rome Vat. Ottob. Lat. 3025
Extracts < H by way of 15. See *Dissem.* pp. 40-41, 76, and add that in the *Prophecies*
they share § 112.38 *patebit<ur>*, 116.144 *<.xx.> necem*, both absent from 86 and
200. Ff. 7-36, which include the extracts, were once St-Victor MMM 10 ff. 139-
168[50].

216   xv   Halle Univ. Stolberg-Wernigerode Za 38
Nothing is missing in the last quire: f. 88 should precede f. 87. §§ 1-3 < G, rest
≏ 187; but the omission of 208.603-5 *quos de regibus ... Britannici sermonis*,
which it shares with 187, may also have occurred in 63, which has lost the end.
Indeed, the passage may have occupied a line in 63. 63 and 187 are close relatives
throughout of S (no. 203), where the passage does not occupy a line.

50 G. Ouy, *Les manuscrits de l'abbaye de Saint-Victor: catalogue établi sur la base du répertoire de
Claude de Grandrue* (1514) (Brepols 1999) 2 pp. 592-3.

217   xii   Berlin Lat. 4° 941
≏ 7, but §§ 111-17 at least partly < Π; close to 129 and 186. They share with 21 and its relatives § 109.4 <*milites uel*> *nobiles*, § 118.5 <*suum uel*> *uitae suae.*

218   xii/xiii   Schaffhausen Min. 74
≏ 2; close to 75.

219   xii²   Leipzig UB. 3518 (Haenel 8)
≏ 7; close to 167.

Crick also lists copies of the *Prophecies* (n. 7), which she divides into 76 'independent copies' and 11 copies 'inserted into other texts'; but most of the 'independent copies' must have come from other texts (not necessarily *De gestis Britonum*), and indeed some have a preamble that says as much. Eckhardt's list (n. 7), though less full and accurate, has the advantage of being numbered, to 79. It will save space in a matter unimportant for my edition if I divide them into categories rather than go through them in order, and I include copies inserted into other texts if Eckhardt includes them. Contamination is often evident, but I indicate what seems to be the fundamental allegiance; 'others' are mostly excerpts. Manuscripts of *De gestis Britonum* I cite either by their symbol or by putting 'no.' in front.

Mentioned above as certain or possible descendants of Π: 4, 12, 24, 26, 39, 49, 57, 60, 62, 65-66, 70, 77-79, Boulogne 180, Bruges 428, Paris B. N. Lat. 14465.

Descendants of Δ: 5 (< no. 113), 7, 8, 10 (or Π), 19, 25, 29, 31 (or Π), 32, 37 (≏ 46; < H?), 42 (< no. 113), 46 (≏ 37; < H?), 54 (or Π), 63 (≏ O), 71, 75 (≏ H, no. 215), Cambridge Fitzw. Mus. 379 (≏ O), Cambridge Trin. R 7 23, San Marino Huntington HM 1345 (< H?).

Non-Continental relatives of G: 6, 9 (or ≏ Y?), 22, 28, 35, 38, 43 (2nd Var.), 52, 55, 56 (2nd Var., < no. 108?), 67, 74 (≏ 67), 76, Cambridge Trin. O 1 17. Five of these, written in England from about 1200 and still in British libraries, begin with § 111 *Sedente [itaque] Vortegirno* and continue beyond the prophecies to § 118.3 *collaudat*: 6, 28, 35, 38, 52.

Continental relatives of G: 13 (runs to § 118), 33 (Cleo. C IV, not VI), 59, 64, 68.

Relatives of Y: 30, 36, 40, 45.

Relatives of M: 16, 50, 53.

Not seen: 2-3, 14-15, 17-18, 20, 23, 44, 48, 69, 72-3.

Not a manuscript of the *Prophecies*: 1, Paris B. N. Lat. 2321.

Others: 11, 27 (n. 47), 34 (< Π?), 41, 51, 58, Oxford Bodl. Rawl. D 893 f. 28v.

? Notes: 48, 61.

The most surprising of these manuscripts is 19 (Florence Naz. II I 75, s. xiv^2, Italian), which at § 113.76-7 has the original reading of C, *Succe[dent duo]*, and on a leaf partly missing omits a long passage from a point after § 116.230 *filium proprium quia*, which ends a line, to a point before § 116.284 *]xabitur homo leonem*, the first passage that survives on the next line; C has a break in composition after *filium proprium quia in ore pecudum lasciuient*, for which there is room before *]xabitur homo leonem*.

The apparatus of this edition

My apparatus does not provide a full collation of all the manuscripts that I use. Instead, I have aimed at reconstructing wherever possible Δ and Φ throughout, Π in §§ 110-17, and Σ in §§ 118-208. Except where there are more than two variants, I seldom report single manuscripts, and I also ignore most rejected readings shared by no more than two manuscripts against the agreement of the rest, whether or not they belong to the same cluster.

The apparatus is sometimes positive for the sake of clarity, sometimes negative for the sake of economy. A negative apparatus does not key the variant to a lemma but relies on users to pick out in the text a word that looks similar or has the same function in the sentence.

Except where the lemma forbids or it seemed desirable to keep the closest variants together or put the more primitive first, I cite Δ before Φ throughout with their descendants in the order OCHSE Q(W)YGM. In §§ 1-3 and 5 I put H in its usual place as a descendant of Δ, in the prophecies M after Δ and Π last, in §§ 114-37 H after Y, in §§ 118-208 Σ between Δ and Φ with its descendants in the order UAKND. I insert a space between unrelated manuscripts.

I ignore rubrics except up to § 6 and in §§ 109-11. My collations include variants of spelling, but in the apparatus I ignore them except in some names, because including them would bloat it and serve no purpose known to me; but in the next section I explain the spellings adopted in my text.

Spelling

Fine examples of scribal whim occur in M at § 142.607-8, in G at § 15.273, and in Q at § 119.47-8: *subcubuit succubuerunt* (adjacent words), *a litore auertit dum littora, nefandus populus quem nephandus ille inuitauit*. What editors of classical texts write as *sollemnitas* assumes in the manuscripts of *De gestis Britonum* at least six forms: *soll-/sol-* and *-emn-/-enn-/-empn-*. In §§ 74-5 Geoffrey can hardly have vacillated, as the manuscripts do, between *Fulgenius* and *Sulgenius*. Patterns of agreement in the manuscripts often cut across the usual relationships; individual scribes are often inconsistent; and different scribes in the same manuscript may each be consistent in a different way. The spelling of *Brit(t)annia* and *Brit(t)ones* in C and O, for instance, depends mainly on which scribe is at work. On the other hand, the manuscripts are sometimes unanimous, or nearly so, for one spelling in one passage and another in another, and so Geoffrey himself may well have been inconsistent. I have therefore refrained from imposing consistency against unanimity or near unanimity in the manuscripts.

For an editor of *De gestis Britonum* the worst problem concerns names, of which there are over 900, many recurrent. In collating each manuscript I heaved a sigh of relief when Gualguainus finally perished, but Britain and Britons are there from first to last. I write them both with a single *t*, because Geoffrey quotes two classical hexameters that include *Britann-* with the first syllable short (§§ 62.229, 69.368), and he knew enough metre to compose verse not just in *De gestis Britonum* (§ 16, elegiacs) but at length in his *Vita Merlini* (hexameters); there too metre requires a single *t* in both words (*Britann-* 20, 1525, *Briton-* 58, 580, 965, 1529)[51].

Some variations in names go beyond spelling: *Deira* or *Albania*, *Demetia* or *Kambria*, *Neustria* or *Estrusia*, *Claudiocestria* or *Glauernia*, *Vther Pendragon* or *(H)us Pendragon* or *Vspanus Draconteus* (this last probably scribal whimsy, since Geoffrey offers a translation of 'Pendragon' at § 135.398-9), *Gunhƿuar* (or something like it) or *Gunuasius*, *Worloit* or *Clofaut*, *Kaius* or *Cheudo*. Octa has a *fratruelis* Ebissa (§ 101.385) but later a *cognatus* Eosa (§§ 124-41), who looks suspiciously like the same person. A smaller but alarming variation is that the descendants of Δ write *Tingagol*, not *Tintagol*. In a few places some manuscripts have a gap or omission where others have a name; perhaps Geoffrey never filled in the name. The presence of two guests from Salisbury at § 156.336-8 provoked deletion or conjecture, and at § 87.371 Δ omitted perhaps rightly (it would have been easy to supply from Geoffrey's source) the clause in which Φ named Dionotus's stunning daughter.

Smaller variations in names are as common as in ordinary words but more irritating, especially when they may suggest that a different person or place is in question. With few exceptions, therefore, I have plumped for one attested spelling and stuck to it; would anyone have been grateful for fidelity to the manuscripts? One exception concerns modern Leicester, where the aberrant form used in the etymology from 'Leir's city' is probably deliberate; another concerns Gonorilla's husband, almost unanimously transmitted as Maglaunus twice in § 31 but unanimously twice as Maglaurus in § 32, perhaps far enough away from the earlier instances for Geoffrey to have forgotten what exactly he had called him; another concerns what appear to be alternative forms of the nominative or even the accusative, such as Beli/Belinus, Guider/Guiderius, Katigern/Katigernus, Vortimer/Vortimerium, Gillamuri/Gillamurius, Aschil/Aschillus.

51 B. Clarke, *Life of Merlin* (Cardiff 1973). Earlier editions: W. H. Black (London 1830), J. J. Parry (Urbana 1925), Faral (n. 20) III 305-52.

Next, some of the frequent variations in the spelling of ordinary words:

ae/œ/ę/e/oe/œ

As not all the manuscripts reduce the diphthongs to *e*, I adopt a generally classical spelling, which has the merit of avoiding some ambiguities. Though the commonest form of diphthong in the manuscripts is *ę*, I see no more point in reproducing it than in reproducing the superscript stroke that represents *m* or *n*, because it was simply a way of writing *ae*. In classical spelling even etymological links did not always protect *ae* against reduction: *c(a)ementum* provides an example. Some of my diphthongs may therefore be hypercorrect, and these or others may not actually occur in any manuscript; but I begrudged the time that it would have taken to be more discriminating. Apart from such diphthongs (and conjectures, of course), everything else that I print does occur in manuscripts, and usually in the majority of them.

-ci-/-ti-/sci-

Often I could not tell whether the scribe had written a *c* or a *t*. Treating them as interchangeable before *i* followed by another vowel results in anomalies, because a scribe who writes *tociens*, *audatia*, or *paciebatur*, would not have written *toc*, *audates*, or *paci*, except by mistake. Mostly, however, I follow the majority even at the expense of such anomalies.

The manuscripts agree on *ci-* for *scy-* in the word for 'cup' and more disturbingly on *sciendo* for *ciendo* at § 157.393.

-m-/-n-

When a superscript stroke represents one of these, it is impossible to tell which. I usually resolve it as *m* but accept any *n* supported by the majority. Spellings that strike me as barely defensible, such as *menbrum* and *incunbo*, occur in some manuscripts but never, I think, in the majority.

ca/ka

Variation is common in the initial letter of names even where there is not much excuse for *K*, as in *Carnotensis*, but otherwise confined to *carus*.

i/y

Despite the occasional *hyeme* and *sydus*, the manuscripts are fairly consistent in words, less so in names. What originated as a Greek υ tends to be transmitted as *i*, often unanimously.

(h) and f/ph

On *h* I have nothing more detailed to offer than a list of words in which variation occurs, alphabetized as if the *h* were not there and without brackets if the manuscripts are unanimous or nearly so: *(h)abundo ad(h)olescens anc(h)ora arc(h)a c(h)arta cat(h)ena c(h)oruscare ebdomada heremiticus ex(h)ibere (h)onerare (h)ostium perhennis pro(h)*(exclamatory) *t(h)emo t(h)orus humerus humor.*

What originated as Greek φ becomes *f* in *cifus* (sometimes *ciffus*) *falerata sarcofago,* and what originated as Latin *f* becomes *ph* in *phanatici.*

mi(c)hi, ni(c)hil

The former is usually abbreviated but when written out in full always has the *c.* The latter is usually *nichil,* but *nil* is unanimously attested at § 31.209 and well attested at § 119.29, and individual manuscripts have *nl̄* here and there.

Double consonants

The manuscripts regularly give *Affric-, occeanus,* and *attauus,* often *littus, suppremus,* and *dupplicare,* usually *cominus* and *quatuor,* sometimes *imin-* and *opid-.* Variation in *o(p)portunus* was already common in Antiquity. In classical Latin *c p t* after *re-* in verbs were originally doubled only in proparoxytone trisyllabic perfects and their derivatives (*reccidi, reppereram, rettulisset*), but already in later Antiquity the distinction was often ignored, and the scribes of *De gestis Britonum* do not observe it, though *repp-* is less common than *rep-* where *rep-* is strictly appropriate.

gu/gw/w and non-Latin letters

In the *editio princeps* (Paris 1508) one Alanus Aureus, who addresses the editor as his *praeceptor,* remarks on vacillation in the manuscripts between Saxon *w* and British *gu.* These alternative ways of representing a sound that no Latin word begins with occur in names before a vowel. Though the scribes are indeed capricious, some forms are rarer than others: *Gwalia,* for instance, and *Gwintonia.*

Whereas *w* is nothing more than the Latin *u* written twice, sometimes with overlap, I have met the non-Latin letters ð and Þ in names, though only in single manuscripts, and Y has the non-Latin diphthong *Ea-* in *Estrildis.* The manuscripts so consistently give *Peanda,* however, that Geoffrey may have taken it as trisyllabic.

Prefixes

Assimilation prevails, and in some manuscripts it goes further than in classical Latin: *ammirari, sullimare.* The commonest variations occur in *acquiescere/*

adquiescere and *submittere/summittere*. Negative *in-* tends not to be assimilated. Even where the evidence suggests that Δ had one spelling and Φ another, I plump for one and ignore the other.

Numbers

Some scribes clearly had a policy. In Y, for instance, most numbers are given as numerals, whereas in no. 34 most are written out. I go with the majority and when in doubt write them out.

Geoffrey's Latin

Differences between classical and medieval spelling lead me to other differences between classical Latin and Geoffrey's[52]. Interestingly, scribes react to some of these. Often, for instance, Geoffrey uses a redundant *ita* in expressions like *tantum ... ita ut*, and K usually removes it; K also restores some future tenses in the *Prophetiae* to the right conjugation[53]; and indicatives that in classical syntax would have been subjunctives, for instance in *ut* and *quin* clauses and indirect questions, tend to finish up as subjunctives in some manuscripts.

Few of the differences lie in morphology and vocabulary, and I comment on some of these in my notes below on individual passages. He uses *primitus* twice for *primum*, once for *prius*; *diffugere* often for *fugere*, *deferre* once for *ferre*; *leuiter* for 'easily'; *ueteres nostri* for 'our ancestors'; *patria* for 'country' regardless of who was born in it; *deserere* and *indulgere* with no pejorative connotation; and *documenta* for 'teaching' (a sense attested in classical Latin but rare). To such misuses or extensions I am inclined to add his use of *accedere* interchangeably, or so it seems, with *accidere*, and I suspect that by *asportare* he means not 'carry off', though that sense is appropriate enough in some passages, but *apportare*.

Differences in syntax and idiom are more numerous. Readers familiar with classical Latin will be struck by the frequency and equivalence of *is*, *ille*, *ipse*, and *idem*, especially in the accusative and genitive, and the equivalence of any in the dative or possessive genitive with *sibi* or *suus*. Also frequent is *praedictus* or *supradictus*, often tantamount, as Neil Wright has put it in conversation, to a definite article. Locatival *in* is often replaced by *infra*, not a common preposition in classical Latin; with *in* there is no sharp distinction between the accusative

---

52 With the publication of volume 5, which contains indexes and bibliography, Peter Stotz has completed his *Handbuch zur lateinischen Sprache des Mittelalters* (Munich 1996-2004). The index of words provides the quickest method of consultation; the references indicate not the volumes but the internal division into books and sections, and Book VII is the unnumbered book that takes up the whole of volume 3. Many unclassical usages found in medieval works go back to late Antiquity. Faral (n. 20), II 397-8, has a brief discussion of Geoffrey's style.

53 At § 116.247 Wright in his edition of the First Variant prints *dilaniabit*, but all my manuscripts of the *Historia* have *dilaniet* as if the verb were *dilanire*, and so have all but one of his; on this form see Stotz (n. 52) VIII 102.2, on § 112.42 *tremebit* 107.4 and 129.1. At § 84.326 I wonder if *repleamus* after *promouebo* and *erit* was meant as a future indicative.

and the ablative; in expressions of destination towns sometimes have *in* or *ad*, countries not; *sub* is used only with the ablative; and beside over 250 instances of *ex* there is only one of *e*, § 89.12 *e finibus*, which Geoffrey took over from Gildas 15.2 (contrast *ex finibus* at §§ 18.387, 101.391, 198.435, 200.481). The pluperfect, especially in the subjunctive, often functions as an imperfect, the future perfect as a future; the perfect passive is as often *datus fuit* as *datus est*; and a participle in a subordinate clause may go into the future not because it expresses something that lies in the future with respect to the finite verb of the clause but because the clause itself expresses something that lies in the future with respect to the main clause. In temporal clauses *dum* behaves like *cum*, and there is no unanimously transmitted instance of its classical use with the present indicative for expressing the background against which a momentary event happened; nor, with the subjunctive, does it ever mean 'provided that'. Temporal *ut* sometimes has the subjunctive appropriate to *cum* (§§ 61.147-8, 104.466, 133.360, probably § 56.43), and consecutive *ut* is often replaced by *quod*. The classical practice of using *atque* for *ac* before a vowel is not observed. In neither direct nor indirect questions is *num* ever used; in indirect questions *utrum* replaces it, and besides *utrum ... an* disjunction is conveyed by *utrum ... uel* (emended in K to *utrum ... an*) or *an ... an*. For indirect speech the classical accusative-and-infinitive construction is often replaced by a *quod* or *quia* clause, and further elements are added paratactically, usually in the imperfect subjunctive if they refer to the future and in the indicative if they refer to the present or past. In classical Latin a continuative relative is often combined with *tamen*, but Geoffrey allows coordinating adverbs too, as at § 50.311 *Quo itaque uiso*. Analogical extensions are common, for instance when *iubeo* at § 158.428 is construed with the dative (G substitutes the accusative, no. 48 *praecipio*) or when *permittere* is given not the dative and an *ut* clause but the accusative and infinitive appropriate to *sinere*; among other verbs unclassically construed with the infinitive are *asciscere*, *dirigere*, *progredi* (once each). Geoffrey is fond of *affectare* with the infinitive, and common turns of phrase are *ut quid* for 'why' (more precisely 'to what end'), *ac si* for 'as if', and *sin autem* for 'failing that'.

Hyperbaton, a curse of pretentious prose in the Middle Ages as well as Antiquity, is mercifully rare in *De gestis Britonum*, so rare indeed that one is struck by even modest examples like § 14.218 *cum laeta remeauit uictoria*, § 79.158 *quod amisimus nobis reddere expulso uales Maxentio*.

The quality of the transmitted text

Departures from classical Latinity are one of the things that may bring the transmitted text under suspicion. As will emerge from my 'Critical notes' below on individual passages and from some briefer notes in the apparatus, the oldest text that can be reconstructed from the manuscripts is marred in about 60 places by false concord, lack of a verb, substitution of something just written for what ought to have been written (the type of error known as *Perseverationsfehler*), and even sheer nonsense, though one can usually see what must have been meant[54]. For a work as long as *De gestis Britonum*, though, such lapses cannot be called numerous (one every 800 words). On the contrary, they would be venial even if they originated with Geoffrey himself, because authors slip up almost as much in writing out their own compositions as scribes do in copying out other people's[55]. In my note below on § 14.232 I consider the possibility that Geoffrey dictated to a scribe, but the evidence that I assemble there does not amount to much.

The text may be more corrupt, however, than meets the eye. In some passages the oldest extant reading may be the unacceptable one of some manuscripts rather than the acceptable one of others, because scribes faced with difficulties or anomalies were not slow to introduce conjectures[56]. At § 68.336 Y and H, unrelated at that point, both have *ripam* twice, and at § 186.167 several descendants of both Δ and Φ have *du[a]rum*; much the likeliest explanation is that they are the only manuscripts honest enough to have preserved slips present in the source of all the manuscripts (in H the second occurrence of *ripam* is expunged). Together with the possibility of authorial slips, the possibility of scribal conjectures poses a grave problem for stemmatic analysis, at least in the upper reaches of the tradition. As I said above, the problem seems to me gravest over the definition of Δ.

Geoffrey's sources

Geoffrey's main sources are beyond dispute: Gildas's tirade *De excidio Britanniae*, Bede's *Historia ecclesiastica*, and the *Historia Britonum*. He names Gildas and Bede at the outset and again in the course of the work.

Some readings in *De excidio* for which editors report no variants from the few manuscripts help an editor of Geoffrey either by showing that strange readings are sound or by confirming one variant against another[57]. For examples see §§ 89-91, 119, 195. It may also be, however, that readings peculiar to Geoffrey's manuscript of *De excidio* would provide further help of the same kind if the manuscript could be traced[58].

Editions of the *Historia ecclesiastica* rest on manuscripts that date almost from the time of Bede himself, and later manuscripts run to over 150[59]. Even

54 Faral, *Romania* 55 (1929) 506, listed some errors that he considered archetypal.
55 See 'Errori in autografi' (n. 9).
56 'Les leçons les meilleures' said Faral, *Romania* 55 (1929) 497, 'peuvent n'être que des leçons améliorées', and he repeated the point on p. 508. I am not aware of any general work on the extent and character of the textual criticism practised in the Middle Ages; for medieval work on classical texts see B. Munk Olsen, 'Les classiques latins et la critique textuelle médiévale (IXe-XIIe siècles)', *Comptes Rendus de l'Acad. des Inscriptions et Belles-Lettres* 1995 pp. 817-27 (with closing observations from J. Irigoin).
57 The only edition serviceable in this context is Th. Mommsen's, *Mon. Germ. Hist. Auctores antiquissimi* XIII (Berlin 1898) 1-85. For a revised text with introduction, translation, and notes, see M. Winterbottom, *Gildas: The Ruin of Britain and other works* (London and Chichester 1978).
58 N. Wright, 'Geoffrey of Monmouth and Gildas', *Arthurian Literature* 2 (1982) 1-40, at p. 12 n. 35, mentions links with the 12th-century manuscript A (Avranches 162); but the very idiosyncratic text of A, which I saw in June 2005, shows that it was not Geoffrey's manuscript.
59 B. Colgrave & R. A. B. Mynors, *Bede's Ecclesiastical history of the English people* (Oxford 1969)

if Geoffrey had stayed close to Bede's wording, therefore, it would require a disproportionate amount of work to place his manuscript in the tradition; and he does not seem to have reproduced Bede with the same fidelity as Gildas[60].

Unlike the other two works, the *Historia Britonum* survives only in later recensions[61]. Whether or not Geoffrey used more than one, he certainly used one that included the three *mirabilia* from *Hist. Brit.* 67 and 69-70 described in §§ 149-50. At *Hist. Brit.* 67 his manuscript gave as *lx*, not *cccxl* with the Nennian recension, the number of islands, eagles' nests, and rivers, in Loch Lomond; and at *Hist. Brit.* 69 it included *et mare ... ad sissam*, which the manuscripts that have been used as representatives of the 'Gildasian' recension omit by *saut du même au même*. That he used the Gildasian recension has nevertheless been inferred from his ascription to Gildas of material in § 100 taken from the *Historia Britonum*[62], and to judge from the extant manuscripts it was the recension that circulated most widely in the 12th century. When he mentions Gildas at the outset, therefore, he may have both *De excidio* and the *Historia Britonum* in mind. On the other hand, he says in the same breath that Gildas did not mention Arthur, which is true of Gildas but not of the *Historia Britonum*.

In the apparatus I cite any passage from Geoffrey's sources that I believe to affect the constitution of the text. Rather than add an *apparatus fontium*, I give here a brief indication of where Geoffrey used which source.

> § 5 (Britain) Gildas 3, Bede 1.1, *Hist. Brit.* 7-9
> §§ 6-22 (Brutus) *Hist. Brit.* 10-11
> § 46 (Partholoim) *Hist. Brit.* 13
> §§ 54-93 (the Romans) Gildas 9.2-20.1 (in §§ 77, 86, 88-91), Bede 1.2-14, *Hist. Brit.* 19-30[63]

xxxix-lxxvi.

60 N. Wright, 'Geoffrey of Monmouth and Bede', *Arthurian Literature* 6 (1986) 27-59, at p. 53.

61 Mommsen, op. cit. (n. 57) 111-222; F. Lot, *Nennius et l'Historia Brittonum: étude critique suivie d'une édition des diverses versions de ce texte* (Bibl. de l'École des Hautes Études 273, Paris 1934) 143-231. Much of Lot's apparatus is a selection from Mommsen's. When D. N. Dumville edited the Vatican recension (Cambridge 1985), he was planning editions of six others as well as of an Irish version and a reconstructed original. For a list of the recensions, with bibliography, see M. Lapidge & R. Sharpe, *A bibliography of Celtic-Latin literature 400-1200* (Dublin 1985) 42-5.

62 Mommsen (n. 61) 13, 23, 133. He seems not to have noticed that unlike PQ Geoffrey's manuscript included *et mare ... ad sissam*, from which he takes over the phrase *recipitur in modum uoraginis*. D. N. Dumville, '"Nennius" and the *Historia Brittonum*', *Studia Celtica* 10-11 (1975-6) 78-95, at p. 81, speaks of the passage as 'already missing in the common ancestor of every Gildasian subgroup of the *Historia*'; he does not mention Geoffrey. Geoffrey's version of Hengist's Saxon command at § 104.462, which comes from *Hist. Brit.* 46, is closest to the one added as a correction to Mommsen's L, a manuscript that conflates the Gildasian and Nennian recensions (it is the same as Mommsen's X of Gildas); but at *Hist. Brit.* 67 L has *cccxl*.

63 In §§ 87-8 a subsidiary source was the *Passio II Vrsulae*, edited by the Bollandists in *Acta sanctorum Octobris* IX (Brussels 1858), 157-63, and by J. Klinkenberg, 'Studien zur Geschichte der Kölner Märterinnen', *Bonner Jahrbücher* 93 (1892) 130-79, at pp. 154-63, and translated by Pamela Sheingorn & Marcelle Thiébaux (Toronto 1990, 1996). See also W. Levison, 'Das Werden der Ursula-Legende', *Bonner Jahrbücher* 132 (1927) 1-164, at pp. 90-107, 'Die zweite Passio Ursulae und Galfrid von Monmouth'; he did not say which manuscripts he took to have been in England by the 12th century (p. 102), but current shelfmarks, admittedly an unsafe guide, suggest that what first arrived was the shorter version *Fuit in Britanniae finibus* (pp. 95-6).

§§ 94-132 (Vortigern, Hengist and Horsa, Aurelius Ambrosius) Bede
1.16-17, *Hist. Brit.* 31-2, 36-48

§§ 143-78 (Arthur) *Hist. Brit.* 56 (Arthur's battles in Britain), 67 and
69-70 (the *mirabilia* in §§ 149-50)

§§ 179-87 (Arthur's successors) Gildas 27-36

§§ 188-208 (Augustine, Cadwallon, Northumbrian kings, Penda,
Cadwallader) Bede 1.23-5.7 (especially 1.23, 2.2, 2.20, 3.2, 3.24,
5.7), *Hist. Brit.* 64-5, with moralistic embroidery from Gildas 24
(§§ 184-5) and 21 (§ 195)

Further details, for instance of scattered phrases that Geoffrey took from Gildas, can be found in Wright's articles[64].

Title

When I first studied the transmission, I paid no attention to the title beyond looking in the manuscripts for Geoffrey's byname *Artur* or *Arturus*, and it was only when I returned to the work that I was struck by something that I ought to have noticed before: OCSQM agree on a title seldom found outside them and their immediate relatives, *De gestis Britonum*, followed or preceded by *editio* or *liber*[65]. G too has *De gestis* but continues with *regum maioris Britannie*; as I mentioned above, however, other manuscripts belong to the family of G without either descending from G or representing the Second Variant, and *De gestis Britonum* occurs in the oldest of these, no. 162 (s. xii). Among the Continental manuscripts that descend from G in §§ 1-108 but not in §§ 109-end, it occurs in two of the best, nos. 167 and 219. Furthermore, it is the title that Geoffrey used when he referred to the work at the end of his *Vita Merlini* (1525-9)[66]:

Duximus ad metam carmen. Vos ergo, Britanni,
laurea serta date Gaufrido de Monemuta [Monumeta ms.].
Est etenim uester; nam quondam prelia uestra
uestrorumque ducum cecinit scripsitque libellum
quem nunc Gesta uocant Britonum celebrata per orbem.

Similarly, in §§ 110 he refers to it as *historia quam de gestis regum Britannorum inceperam* (CHSEYΦΠ) or *historia quam de gestis Brittonum inceperam* (O). Keeping the familiar title will do no harm, though, as long as no arguments are founded on it.

Articulation

Of the manuscripts that I use, Y and Q have the most conspicuous division into chapters, and I adopt their division at § 14 *At Brutus*, § 17 *Porro flumen* (GM agree),

---

64 Op. cit. (n. 58) and 'Geoffrey of Monmouth and Gildas revisited', *ibid.* 4 (1984) 155-63; 'Geoffrey of Monmouth and Bede', *ibid.* 6 (1986) 27-59.
65 Crick, *Dissemination* (n. 7) 126-9.
66 Clarke (n. 51) 134.

§ 24 *Duxit itaque* (G agrees), § 31 *Mox ut regio* (G agrees), § 46 *Ea tempestate* (G agrees but not Q), § 119 *Rumore itaque* (H agrees). The digression after § 100 requires a division attested only in E at § 101.377 *Data autem puella*; similarly, when I substitute a dash for the incision in YQ at § 185 *Quid ociosa gens*, I provide it with a partner at § 186 *Postquam autem*. I adopt the well attested division at § 203 *Quo igitur*, where none seems required, and at § 133 *Apparente igitur*, where 349 *Haec dum Guintoniae* seems a better place for one. No manuscript is consistent in its presentation of speeches: sometimes these begin with a decorated initial, and sometimes what immediately follows them begins with a decorated initial. I adopt what I hope is a helpful compromise, namely indenting all speeches throughout their length; I leave unindented what immediately follows them, even where a new paragraph might well have begun if there had been no speech.

Some manuscripts of the *Prophetiae* in the separate tradition mark off sections, but there is not enough agreement to suggest that Π had them. In manuscripts of *De gestis Britonum* only § 116.147 *Tres* receives a decorated initial, and that not often outside the family of Δ.

As regards the division into books, some descendants of Φ, especially G up to § 108 and English relatives of G throughout, indicate it more regularly and more explicitly than any descendant of Δ, and I suggested in 1991 that Φ might have been a presentation copy, in which care was more likely to be taken over such things[67]. It seems clear that in Φ §§ 23-108 formed Books 2-6 (with new books at §§ 35, 54, 73, 89), §§ 118-208 four more books (with new ones at §§ 143, 163, 177); but after the prologue it is not clear whether Book 1 started at § 5 (G) or § 6 (M), and the designation 'Book 7' is poorly attested anywhere in §§ 109-111, presumably because §§ 109-10 constitute another prologue and might or might not be included in it (if the uncertainty had been caused by the status of the prophecies, one might have expected more disagreement over the numbering thereafter, which is usually 8-11). C agrees with M up to § 73, the beginning of Book 5, but then at best leaves a line blank; nevertheless, it differs from M only in starting a new book, or so a blank line suggests, at § 198. O gives three books, §§ 5-53, 54-108, 109-208. In marking off books I dispense with the formulae *explicit* and *incipit*, and in the apparatus I ignore rubrics except up to § 6 and in §§ 109-11.

Though I divide the work into books and the English translation most in use numbers chapters afresh in each book[68], I have decided to ignore the books in numbering the chapters. The existing numeration by book and chapter starts Book 1 at the very beginning, which none of my manuscripts does; treats §§ 190-208 as Book 12, which none of my manuscripts does; and in its Books 2-11 sometimes gives chapters different from those attested by my manuscripts. As a numeration closer to what the manuscripts attest would add a third to the two already in print and still include elements of uncertainty, I adopt instead the continuous numeration

67 'Transmission' (n. 5) 112.
68 L. Thorpe, *Geoffrey of Monmouth: the History of the kings of Britain* (London 1966). The division was introduced by Commelinus (Heidelberg 1587), taken over by J. A. Giles (London 1844) and 'San-Marte' ≈ A. Schulz (Halle 1854), and indicated but not taken over by Griscom; it is also used in the *Dictionary of medieval Latin from British sources*. The *editio princeps* (Paris 1508) already has a division into books and chapters, but one far removed from the evidence of the manuscripts.

introduced by Faral and taken over by Wright[69]. Where it does not correspond to the transmitted divisions, I adjust it only if no more than a short passage is affected.

For narrower reference sections or lines are needed, because some chapters run to pages. As I had to number the lines for the sake of keying the apparatus to the text, it seemed unnecessary to introduce sections as well, but a choice still had to be made between numbering the lines of each page and numbering the lines of each chapter or book or indeed of the whole work. The former would have left ambiguities in the longest chapters, and I chose to number the lines of each book, with prefatory material included.

Punctuation

I make no attempt to reproduce scribal punctuation, because the scribes disagree and some of their shared habits would mislead or annoy a modern reader[70].

The main problem concerns participial phrases. Commonly, for instance, the scribes punctuate after a participial phrase but not before it, with results like § 11.148 *Brutus ergo opem subuectare affectans, internis anxietatibus cruciatur;* and in sentences like § 32.282 *Potitus itaque uictoria Cunedagius monarchiam totius insulae adeptus est* they take the subject not with the main verb but with the participle. In fact, there is often no satisfactory way of dealing with participial phrases if punctuation is felt to be needed round them. They may well include an element that belongs with the rest of the sentence, as at § 2.7-10 *Talia michi ... cogitanti optulit Walterus ... librum*, where *michi* goes with *optulit*, or § 104.468 *Audito (uero) ocius signo abstraxerunt Saxones cultros suos*, where if the text is sound *ocius* must go not with *audito* but with *abstraxerunt* (K actually puts it before *abstraxerunt*) as in Hengist's instructions just before (cf. also § 13.194 *Quo audito enses ocius euaginant*). Conversely, a connecting particle outside a participial phrase may belong more closely with it than with the rest of the sentence, as at § 18.342 *Nuncii ergo classem petentes obuiauerunt Corineo*, where a reason has just been given why they should make for the ships (they were sent) but none yet why they should bump into Corineus. Nevertheless, as editorial practice routinely ignores such complications in subordinate clauses, it is hard to see why they should cause scruples in participial phrases, and so I tend to use commas except where they would sever a grammatical link or a likely semantic link. I also have a strong aversion, rooted in delivery rather than syntax and therefore shared by medieval scribes, to punctuating after words not comfortably followed by a pause, such as conjunctions and relative pronouns; I therefore avoid strictly correct syntactical punctuation like *Qui, ut triumphum habuit, dedit Pictis locum mansionis in Albania* or *Et, ut citius aditum repperiam, faciam me monachum religiosissimum*.

Ambiguities of articulation I leave to be accepted or resolved by the reader, as at § 6.48-9 *Aeneas post Troianum bellum excidium urbis cum Ascanio filio*

---

69 In his single-manuscript edition (n. 23), pp. 172-4, Wright gives a concordance.
70 For a comprehensive account of practices through the ages see M. B. Parkes, *Pause and effect* (Aldershot 1992).

diffugiens Italiam nauigio adiuit, where the participial phrase may begin with either *post* or *excidium.*

In general, the scribes use more punctuation than I do, because they had delivery in view rather than syntactical clarity. Where the syntax is debatable, however, I have used their punctuation as a guide.

Editions

Ponticus Virunius published the first edition (Reggio Emilia, March 27th 1508)[71], but it offers only a much abbreviated version of Books 1-6 as far as § 93 and brief references to §§ 98 and 155-6. The editor's name appears in no. 109, but he used a different manuscript, *argento ornatum sed litteris caducum,* put at his disposal for three days at Ferrara by Battista Fregoso; it divided the work into eleven books and can be seen to have been a descendant of Δ. As the descendants of Δ seldom number books or even divide them clearly, it may not be an accident that two of the few manuscripts now preserved in Italy descend from Δ but have clear numeration, introduced into the older from no. 76 or a relative: no. 71 (s. xii) and its copy no. 181 (s. xiv). At the time of the edition, though, no. 71 had long been at S. Croce, Florence; and no. 181 has been identified in the catalogue of the Visconti-Sforza library drawn up in 1426. Perhaps, then, Fregoso's manuscript was another copy of no. 71[72]. The edition was twice reprinted (Augsburg 1534, London 1585).

Later in 1508, the first complete edition appeared (Paris, July 15th), prepared by Ivo Cavellatus and dedicated to Herveus Kaerquiffinennus. It was reprinted with a few corrections (Paris 1517)[73]. Cavellatus says that he used four manuscripts available in Paris: one *situ et pedore squalentem atque horridum* at his own college (*Collegium Corisopitense,* the Collège de Quimper), one at St-Victor *vetustissimis characteribus scriptum,* another there recently commissioned by the abbot[74], and one chained *inter chronica* at the Carmelite library. As far as I know, the abbot's manuscript could be no. 187, a relative of S, and certainly at least one of Cavellatus's four manuscripts did not descend from Φ. Another was a 'nameless dedication' manuscript, in all probability no. 196 (Vat. Pal. Lat. 962, s. xiii), identifiable, but not yet identified, in the St-Victor catalogue of

71 E. Ph. Goldschmidt, *Medieval texts and their first appearance in print* (London 1943) 74-7. I have used the copy in Cambridge University Library, Norton d 170.

72 Two entries in *Baptistae Fulgosi de dictis factisque memorabilibus collectanea a Camillo Gilino latina facta* (Milan 1509) come from Geoffrey: *De Eliduro qui pius dictus est brithannorum rege* in chapter V 5 *De pietate erga fratres* (from § 50), *De Orso et Engisto Saxonibus Anglis* in chapter IX 6 *De perfidia et proditione* (from §§ 94-105).

73 See Brigitte Moreau, *Inventaire chronologique des éditions parisiennes du XVIᵉ siècle:* I *1501-1510* (Paris 1972) 276 no. 75, II *1511-1520* (Paris 1977) 431 no. 1618. A note at the front of no. 216 (Halle Univ. Stolberg-Wernigerode Za 38) refers to an edition of 1519 as well as the edition of 1517, but I have not met one, and none appears in the *Inventaire.* A note in French at the front of no. 82 (B. L. Add. 15732) refers to an edition of 1555 and T. Wright's edition of the *Prophecies* (Paris 1837), but I have met no edition of 1555.

74 The abbot at the time was Nicaise Delorme; see F. Bonnard, *Histoire de l'Abbaye royale et de l'ordre des chanoines réguliers de St-Victor de Paris* (Paris n. d., c. 1905-7) I 445, 467-8, 471, II 3-5.

1514[75]. The edition has eccentric articulation and a thoroughly unreliable text. Confronted with variants, the editor adopted the simple expedient of combining them:

> § 165.93-5 *Praecepit Beduero ... intuentibus fieret. Praecepit intuentibus fieri silentium*
>
> *praecepit Beduero ... intuentibus fieret* ΔΣΦ, *praecepit intuentibus fieri silentium* 'nameless dedication' mss.

> § 180.101-3 *Exinde tertio anno interfectus est a Conano sententia dei percussus et iuxta Vtherpendragonem intra lapidum structuram sepultus fuit ....*
>
> *interfectus est a Conano et* Φ, *sententia dei percussus* ΔΣ

He or his printer Ascensius, whose help he acknowledges, also made arbitrary changes. Already in §§ 1, for instance, several of his readings are unattested in the manuscripts: 1 *animo <oculisque>*, 2 *miratus sum non modinum* (*modicum* 1517) for *in mirum contuli*, 2-3 *in iis commentariis quos ... luculenter conscripserant* for *infra mentionem quam ... luculento tractatu fecerant*, 4 *<Britanniam> inhabitauerant*, 5 *successerant reperirem* for *successerunt reperissem*, 7 *inscripta <mentibus et>*[76]. This rewriting did not escape the scholar who prepared the *editio Commeliniana* of *Rerum Britannicarum scriptores* (Heidelberg 1587), because the Flemish diplomat Paulus Knibbe put at his disposal a decent relative of G, perhaps to be identified with no. 190 (Paris B. N. Nouv. Acq. Lat. 1001, s. xiv): only in this manuscript, recorded at St Martin's Tournai in 1641, have I found together §§ 1.1 *mecum multa* ~, 2.12 *itaque illius* ~, 119.51 *haec omnia accesserunt <mala>* (*haec omnia <mala> accesserunt* ed.), 120.70 *admittente* for *annitente*, 123.116 *occidebat* for *in interitum*, 123 *praeualuissent Saxones* ~[77]. Nevertheless, he had no way of identifying all Cavellatus's changes, let alone seeing through the contamination. Understandably, therefore, he took over some readings, especially phrases missing from his manuscript. The next editor, J. A. Giles (London 1844), avowedly followed the same principle: on his last page he lists six manuscripts that he collated against the *editio Commeliniana* with the aim of making sure that nothing present in any of them was absent from his edition (M and nos. 16, 27, 100, 114, 115). Like Commelinus, he reprinted Ponticus Virunius's epitome after Geoffrey. 'San-Marte' ≏ A. Schulz (Halle 1854) merely reproduced Giles's text of Geoffrey.

---

75 Veronika Gerz-von Büren and G. Ouy, *Le catalogue de la bibliothèque de l'abbaye de Saint-Victor de Paris de Claude de Grandrue 1514* (Paris 1983) 293 B 7 ff. 56-97; Ouy (n. 50) 2 p. 443. Except that there is no f. 96, the foliation has survived alongside the new foliation, ff. 118-58; Crick's '46-97', *Catalogue* (n. 5) 302, is a slip or misprint.

76 Crick, *Dissemination* (n. 7) 230-39, gives a collation of all the manuscripts in §§ 1-2.

77 Relatives of no. 190, for which see no. 21 in the 'Survey of manuscripts' above, have some of these readings, and apart from no. 206, of unknown provenance, they all come from the area of Tournai and Arras. Knibbe also put at Commelinus's disposal a manuscript of the *Gesta regum Anglorum* that editors regard as particularly close to one formerly at St Martin's Tournai, Brussels II 2541 (Phill. 11604); see Stubbs (n. 37) xcix-cii (the fullest account of Knibbe that I have found), Mynors (n. 38) xiv.

In 1929 Faral and Griscom put a stop to this unintelligent and undetectable conflation by constructing new texts from manuscripts and providing a critical apparatus. Brugger for once had not looked closely enough when he described their actual texts as no improvement on the *editio Commeliniana* and its descendants[78]. That said, Griscom's edition and three of the other four produced in the 20th century, all mentioned in my opening paragraphs, represent no more than small corners of the tradition. The remaining edition, Faral's, has a bad reputation for inaccuracy[79]. Nevertheless, by choosing four manuscripts that had different dedications Faral achieved broad coverage, albeit by accident[80]. For all its faults, his edition is the only one that has had any right to be called the standard edition. In presentation too, as Brugger observed, it leaves Griscom's far behind[81].

The *Prophecies* have also been printed separately, first with a commentary attributed to Alanus de Insulis (Frankfurt 1603, 1608, 1649)[82], then by T. Wright with the sequel as far as § 118.20-21 *aper Cornubiae deuorabit* and variants from unnamed manuscripts in London (Paris 1837)[83], then amongst other prophecies by A. Gfroerer (Stuttgart 1840) and San-Marte (Halle 1853), who both reprinted T. Wright's text, and most recently by Gabriella La Placa (Genoa 1990), who reprinted the text of Neil Wright's *Single-manuscript edition* and listed variants from other editions.

Critical notes

Some of my notes in the apparatus give brief reasons for my choice of reading. Where longer reasons were needed, I decided to put them here in the same language as the rest of this Introduction.

1.7: The sequence of tenses calls for *praedicarentur* even if the commemoration is still going on when Geoffrey writes ('Transmission' 78), and *constarent* makes *praedicentur* still more surprising. Elsewhere he usually observes the sequence of tenses, even to the point of using the present subjunctive in subordinate clauses when the main verb is in the historic present. There are exceptions, however: 12.172 *incederet*, 174 *aduenisset*, 14.216 *distribuerent*, 17.317 *esset*, 18.344 *necaret*, 22.503 *uidear*, 34.320 *opprimeretur*, 92.100 *carea(n)t*, 92.114

---

78 Op. cit. (n. 10) 309-10. Brugger's long review, which has not had the effect that it deserved, never loses sight of essentials, and he is just as level-headed on the nature of *De gestis Britonum* and its relationship with Welsh versions as on editorial procedure.

79 A. C. L. Brown, *Speculum* 6 (1931) 306 (the rest of this review strikes me as largely misguided); Hammer, op. cit. (n. 14) 524; Wright, *Single-manuscript edition* (n. 23), p. xlix. When Hammer without giving examples says 'there is hardly a page in his edition that is free from ... readings non-existent in any MS', one wonders if he was including orthographical variants.

80 In 'Transmission' (n. 5) 109 I gave details of this coverage and suggested how his apparatus could be used.

81 Op. cit. (n. 10) 305 n. 73.

82 Marie-Thérèse d'Alverny, 'Alain de Lille: problèmes d'attribution', in H. Roussel & F. Suard (ed.), *Alain de Lille, Gautier de Châtillon, Jakemart Giélée, et leur temps* (Lille 1980), 27-46, at pp. 29-36, inclines to scepticism.

83 F. Michel & T. Wright, *Galfridi de Monemuta Vita Merlini* (Paris 1837) 61-76.

queat, 110.12-24 in the version of O *placuit ut ... imponam*, 156.328 *deberent*. It therefore seems more likely that *praedicarentur* is a harmonizing conjecture after *constarent* than *praedicentur* a scribal slip.

5.41: Gildas 3.2 *culmina minaci proceritate porrecta*, not specifically of temples, provides inadequate support for *erectis* against *erecta*.

14.227: If *in his quae saluti uestrae reor esse habenda* means 'over things that I believe should be possessed for your salvation', it is awkward that in his next breath he singles out one. Is there another interpretation, or should *habenda* be emended, for instance to a word more readily construed with the dative? Whether conjecture or slip after *utilia* above, *utilia* (no. 167 and First Variant) is such a word, but in sense it amounts to much the same as *habenda*, and a word meaning 'relevant to' would be preferable.

14.232: As a *strages* in battle inflicted on inhabitants is usually inflicted by people from outside, *externam* has no point. Phonetic corruption of *hesternam* would have been easy; the only surprise is the wide attestation of *externam*. Anyone on the hunt for evidence that the text was taken down from dictation might use this corruption together with *diffugierunt*, for which see below on § 18.349, and § 157.393 *sciendo*, on which see the apparatus. These readings seem less likely to be transcriptional errors caused by what has been called *dictation interne* (repeating the text to oneself before writing it down).

16.288-90: Geoffrey himself seems to have been responsible for the slip *circundatus ... statuerunt ... dederunt*. As the plural was firmly in his mind when he went on to write *Ipse Brutus*, it is the participle that does not fit. Other instances of false concord between singular and plural occur at § 85.344-5, *Quoscumque ..., ... illum ...*; at § 88.385, on which see below; at § 92.100, where all the manuscripts but K have *careat* as if the subject were *insula*; and at § 159.469-72, where *Beli ... auxilio fratris sui usus* is treated as though it were *Belinus et frater* but nos. 48 and 93 write *cepit ... possedit*. At § 8.103 *abscedant* is venial, because the subject of the speech has been *gens* (cf. § 188.192-3 *gens ... perstarent*); nevertheless, OSE may be right to give *abscedat*, because *eam* has occurred as recently as the end of the previous sentence.

18.349: The manuscripts so solidly attest *diffugierunt* here and in seven other places that Geoffrey must be presumed to have written it unless he dictated the text to a scribe. See above on § 14.232. Even that possibility, however, would not explain why the manuscripts never add an *i* to the pluperfect indicative.

20.449: Besides the usual sense, 'demand', Geoffrey uses *exigere* in the sense *adire*, *petere*, not just here but also at §§ 31.209 (*adiret* no. 71), 31.228, 37.64, 88.381, 130.269, 148.138; add *Vita Merlini* 406. The sense is missing from *DmLBs*.

21.473: Geoffrey seems to have written *ille*, forgetting *hic* above, which it is very hard to interpret as 'here' after *ibi* in the previous sentence followed by a long description of Goemagog; furthermore, he has 21 instances of initial *hic* that refer to a man just named but only three anywhere of the adverb, two in the oracle at § 16.310-11, both initial, and one in a speech at § 165.59. Of the conjectures *illi*, *illic*, *[ille]*, the best is the last, because he normally uses *superuenire* without a dative or an adverb of place.

22.494: In connexion with naming, *ex* usually conveys the origin of the name, as at § 21.488 *nomen ex praecipitatione gigantis adeptus*, § 23.11 *nomen ei ex nomine suo Albania dedit*; commoner for this purpose is *de*. Geoffrey's Latin for 'called by the name of ...', the only sense possible here, is usually the plain ablative: § 25.60-61 *ut flumen nomine puellae uocaretur*, § 32.281-2 *nomine suo, uidelicet Margan, hucusque a pagensibus appellatus est*, § 92.122-3 *quendam fratrem praedicto nomine uocatum*, § 145.60 *alio nomine Lindocolinum nuncupatur*, § 147.112 *nomine Ron uocabatur*. Geoffrey cannot be saying 'from Troia Noua it eventually came by a process of linguistic corruption to be called Trinouantum', which would leave *multis postmodum temporibus appellata* without any sense or construction. The reading of C, *ea* for *ex*, must therefore be taken seriously. Geoffrey's usual continuative pronoun is *hic* or *qui*, and the only part of *is* that frequently occurs with that function is *id*; but *eam* occurs at § 202.518, and he would hardly have written *Haec hoc nomine*.

24.17: Adjudication is easy between the variants *citra* and *circa*, which are unconnected with the others: Geoffrey surely reasoned that Humber could only have given his name to the river if he had drowned in it while retreating, which required him to have crossed it first. The other variants are harder to assess, not least because this is the only passage where Geoffrey puts the river *Humb-* in the nominative (and who else does?). The variants both in the name and in the relative pronoun suggest that his wording was problematical. At the very least he may have botched the concord; cf. § 99.333 *saxosum locum quod* (for *quem*), where the gender of *saxum* may have been in his mind (though for neuter *locum* see *TLL* 1575.72-1576.1), and § 119.54 *ignem ... quod*, where *adiunctus* suggests miswriting or misreading of *qui*.

31.189-207: Leir sheds retainers in four stages before Cordeilla supplies the wherewithal for more. The original number is not given except perhaps in his nostalgia for the days when he had round him 'so many hundred thousand soldiers', but most manuscripts reduce it first to 40 (line 190), then to 30 by the loss of 20 (lines 194-5), then to five by the loss of 'the rest' (line 199), then to one by the loss of 200 (line 207). Some manuscripts react to the absurdity of this: Q raises 40 to 50 (G to 60: why?), EY reduce 30 to 20, C² reduces 20 to ten and HKM omit it, and Y reduces 200 to 20 (still absurd) and K² to 'the rest'. As I cannot devise a sequence of numbers that plausibly accounts for the readings of the majority, I adopt 'the rest' for each of the three explicit losses. Whether

Cordeilla then supplies the wherewithal for 60 or 40 (lines 239-40), or any other number above one, is a matter not of arithmetical but of narratological coherence.

31.244: As *ex ornamentis* makes no sense, it must be either emended to *exornatus* or written as *exornamentis* and taken to be *b* in *a b et c*. Geoffrey uses *ornare, ornate, ornamentum, exornare*. Unlikely, I think is *et ornamentis*, which would give *a et b et c*.

36.32: Geoffrey often uses *qua quo quibus* locativally without a preposition, as at § 139.538-9 *carceris quo ... uitam ducebant*. The usage is easier to account for when the preposition not expressed has already been expressed with the antecedent, as at § 170.306-7 *in ualle qua uobis insidiantur*.

40.110: As Geoffrey mostly uses *prouenire* with the sense and syntax of *euenire*, one might indeed have expected *peruenerat*; but *prouenire* occurs with *in* at § 116.268 *ne herbae in messes proueniant*, and his four instances of *peruenire* are accompanied by *ad*.

43.179-81: The tenses in *Belinus itaque ... expectauit* do nothing to make *praeterita nocte* intelligible, a task left to *Sequenti deinde die instante*.

46.246: The usual construction is a gerundive or *ad* with the gerund, and *ad inhabitandum* occurs in similar expressions at §§ 14.223, 15.263, 70.381, 120.68. Either Geoffrey muddled the two constructions or *inhabitandam* is a corruption brought about by the gender of *portiunculam*. See also below on § 166.194.

54.12-15: The manuscripts treat the second *ut* as the beginning of a new sentence, in which it has to be read as *sicut* and the subjunctive as jussive. That cannot be right, because *ne nos ... offendamus* plainly goes with *Prius tamen mandandum est eis ....* The transmitted punctuation must therefore be abandoned and the clause taken with the previous sentence, but Caesar can hardly propose demanding tribute from the Britons 'so that other nations too may do obeisance to the senate', because he represents the Britons as the only unconquered nation. A connective must therefore be missing unless *etiam* has that function despite § 98.255-6 *etiam ceteros*, § 162.519 *etiam ceteri*, § 205.571 *etiam ceterorum sanctorum*. I have not found a close parallel in a subordinate clause, but there are some with the infinitive, for instance § 37.47-8 *testatur se totam insulam a mari usque ad mare uastaturum, ipsum etiam fratrem interfecturum*, and there is one in an *ut* clause with *quoque*, § 61.151-2 *ut ... adduceret, adductus quoque praesto esset*. Perhaps, though, *et* has just fallen out before the clause, where no. 15 inserts it, or after *gentes*. Neil Wright suggests an alternative: that *faciant* should be *faciunt*, so that *ut* would mean *sicut*. Elsewhere, however, Geoffrey uses *subiectionem facere* of the initial submission, not the resultant state: 55.22, 63.250, 67.325-6, 153.222, 189.196. Contrast 35.14 *subiectionem teneas*, 69.348-9 *subiectionem ... tenere*. One might therefore have expected *fecerunt*.

60.114: Passive forms of *reuertere* in the sense *redire*, among them *reuerti*, occur some 40 times in the work, but active forms are otherwise confined to the gerund (§§ 40.96, 193.300) and the future participle (§ 91.58). The reading of GK, which must be a conjecture, is therefore a well founded one.

61.171-2: To the question 'Should these services have been repaid?' the answer is all too obviously 'yes'. Unless *-ne* is doing duty for *nonne* (used at §§ 90.44, 95.192), as it may be at § 159.475 but is certainly not at §§ 24.32, 31.221, 62.238, or 90.37, a sharper question is needed, and <*ita*> would give one: 'Is that how these services should have been repaid?'. In the similar question at § 24.32, *Haeccine rependis michi, Locrine, ob tot uulnera quae in obsequio patris tui perpessus sum dum proelia cum ignotis committeret gentibus, ut filia mea postposita tete conubio cuiusdam barbarae summitteres?*, the construction of *rependere* is different.

62.207: Geoffrey has no other instance of *in auxilio* but nine of *in auxilium*: seven with the dative, one with the genitive (§ 43.201), and one with no dependent case. Here, in the presence of *occurrens*, the genitive avoids a syntactical ambiguity; but no such defence offers itself for *in auxilio*. It can hardly be relevant that Geoffrey sometimes uses an unclassical case with *in* of location or destination.

62.242: In classical practice, words that usually come second may come later if preceded by words that closely cohere. As nothing can break up a prepositional phrase, there are dozens of instances like § 31.174 *Post obitum autem eius*; but hardly more surprising are § 141.593 *Praestantius est enim* (OK: *p. enim est* cett.), § 200.485 *Non est enim*, or § 39.89 *Si quis autem* (*si quis* is often written anyway as one word), which in turn lead naturally enough to § 99.307 *Si placet ergo*, § 147.103 *Si aliquis igitur*, § 84.322 *Ne pigeat igitur*, § 170.317 *Vt his itaque*, § 31.167 *Non dico tamen*, § 84.308-9 *Non sufficiebat enim* (*enim* om. G). None of these examples comes near to justifying *Insipientia obducitur itaque* here, let alone at § 159.462 the transmitted punctuation *Qui uiolentiam intulit irrationabilem ergo causam praetendit*.

77.113: Stotz (n. 52) VII 213.6 documents the spelling *ade[m]ptus*, the more surprising because one might have expected an impulse to distinguish the word from *adeptus*, a participle that Geoffrey often uses (from *adipiscor*, 'obtain'). Two other considerations lead me to doubt whether the spelling should be attributed to Geoffrey himself: scribes do not always remember to add superscript strokes, and the manuscripts offer very little support in other compounds of *emere*. Unless I nodded in collating, I find § 64.276 *redemptum*, § 86.359 *interempto*, and 26 instances of *perem(p)tus* (mostly -mp-), against only two passages where the manuscripts disagree, and in these only one manuscript omits the *m*: § 34.324 *intereptorum* C, § 96.226 *pereptoque* Y. The manuscripts of Gildas 10.2 do not help, because he wrote *adimerentur*.

81.228: The plain ablative *copia* must be construed with *subiugare*. The addition of *cum* enables it to be construed with *redire*, as it is with *superuenit* at § 149.161-2.

86.348: The reading of M, *subiugandam*, gives a regular construction (cf. § 165.43), and omitting *ad* would give another, though in classical Latin it is mostly poetic. If Geoffrey wrote *ad ... subiugare*, he must have conflated the two.

88.385: There is no plausible subject for the singular *dissipauit*. I have not found *dissipauerunt* in any manuscript but after *insurrexerunt* should prefer it to *dissipant* if the corruption were easier to explain. Singular for plural at § 136.404-5 in ΔK seems at first sight to have been caused by *conduxerat*, but Geoffrey goes on in the singular, which presumably refers to Octa. For other problems of number see above on § 16.288-90.

89.11-15: At Gildas 15.2 the legion *subiectos ciues tam atroci dilacerationi ex imminenti captiuitate liberauit*, and Gildas continues in 15.3 as follows: *Quos* (with the variant *Ad haec*) *iussit construere inter duo maria trans insulam murum ut esset arcendis hostibus turba* (with the variant *a turba*) *instructus terrori ciuibusque tutamini*. By replacing *ciues* with *plebem* Geoffrey has made the reference of *quos* less clear, and *ad* has no discernible function. Did he find *ad quos* in his copy of Gildas? Winterbottom renders Gildas's *turba instructus* as 'properly manned'; after *arcendis* the variant *a turba* adds syntactical ambiguity to the opacity of the phrase.

90.22: When the Romans are telling the Britons to look after themselves, *soli*, 'on their own', is surely more to the point than that they should concentrate on 'warfare exclusively', *solis ... armis* (unless, as Neil Wright suggests, Geoffrey meant 'unaided arms'). Gildas 18.1 has *sola* and *defenderet*, which pick up *patriae* above, and no other part of *solus* has been reported from any manuscript; but perhaps Geoffrey found *solis* in his copy.

91.62: Geoffrey took *condebitorum* from Gildas 19.1. No more than Mommsen there do I understand it, though Gildas plainly used it at 1.15, where *creditor* follows.

91.78: Though *igitur* sometimes begins a sentence in classical Latin, this is the only place where Geoffrey puts it first. He is following Gildas 20.1. At § 90.19, however, he has just turned Gildas's *Igitur Romani* at 18.1 into *Romani ergo*.

92.115: Geoffrey nowhere uses *alibi*, and *alias* here must have that sense, as it may also on its one other occurrence, § 186.168.

95.213: Geoffrey nowhere else uses *domare*, and it seems inappropriate. With *donare* he uses two constructions, both classical: accusative of gift and dative of recipient ('give something to'), accusative of recipient and ablative of gift ('present someone with'). In no passage, however, is only one of the two elements expressed. For *domare nitebatur* Y has *honorabat*, but closer to the other readings is *honorare nitebatur*, which occurs in no. 87; the verb has just been used, but Geoffrey would not have minded. The original reading of C, *domore*, is probably a sign of trouble, and no. 46, a respectable descendant of Δ at this point, has *donore*.

103.438: Elsewhere Geoffrey uses *associare* with a dative, usually *sibi*. The reading of E is therefore very plausible, but it must be a conjecture.

108.562: If *et* is right, *quasi ilico* will mean 'almost at once', much as *quasi* means 'roughly' at § 16.302 *quasi tertia hora noctis*, § 164.17-18 *quasi media hora noctis*, § 177.19 *quasi octoginta milia*; but the qualification 'almost' seems fussy, and omission of *et*, as in the Second Variant, would give *quasi* its common meaning 'as if', 'on the ground that', which suits the context.

110.16: Though *tot ditiores* could easily have been skipped after *tot doctiores*, wealth is irrelevant, and the phrase seems likely to have originated as a slip for *tot doctiores*; Vat. Reg. Lat. 807, a descendant of Π, has just *tot dictiores*. A manuscript of the First Variant that has §§ 109-10 as a later addition, no. 70, implausibly substitutes *tot discretiores*. More to the point would be *tot disertiores*, but Geoffrey does not use *disertus* elsewhere. Nothing worth having would be added to the sense by *tot eruditiores*.

112.54: It is easier to see how *secabuntur* might have arisen from *truncabuntur* than the reverse: *trū-* might have been omitted after *-trū* and *-cabuntur* then expanded to a suitable word. Attestation, however, favours *secabuntur*.

114.92: Geoffrey seven times has *collaterales*, nowhere else *translaterales*. The agreement of H[1] with the separate text is one of several puzzles in the relationship between the separate text and the manuscripts of the full text.

127.208: The superfluous *et* may betray the loss of a verb, for instance *aduenit* after *igitur* or *nactus/adeptus est* after *iacebant*. There is no other occurrence in the work of *circumspicere*, which does not need an object. Giles accepted *et* and put only a comma after *solutus est*, but with one exception, § 132.338 *Vrbem postremo ingressus*, Geoffrey always puts *postremo* first in its sentence.

130.260: The confusion in the manuscripts seems most likely to have been caused by the miswriting of *ignaua* as *ignauia*, though the conjecture of K[2] is ingenious.

130.296: Geoffrey so often uses *at ille* that it is hard to see why he should suddenly have preferred *ast ille*, which could easily have been caused by *asp-* in the previous word, *asportauerat*. At § 193.313, where *ast ille* has stronger support than here, the previous word is *concupiscebat*.

136.429: Geoffrey several times uses *monitus* in the singular, but in the plural he uses *monitio* (§ 56.74) and *monitum* (§§ 91.52, 132.345). The variants here are unlike *moeniis/moenibus* at § 5.39, *generis/generibus* at § 31.245, and *miliorum/ milium* at § 116.145, because in the nominative there is no alternative to *moenia, generi, milia*.

139.544: The phrase *accendere afficiunt* looks like a hybrid of *afficiunt* and *accendere affectant*. The conjecture in no. 34, *ac caede* for *accendere* (also found in Commelinus's edition of 1587), has the two advantages of restoring the usual construction and killing the inhabitants rather than incinerating them, but Geoffrey nowhere else distributes verbs and objects in that way.

141.592: What does *sequenti uita perfuncturus* mean? If something like 'to live out my allotted span', it adds nothing of substance to *sanus et incolumis*. The compound *perfungi* occurs only here in the work, *fungi* only at § 94.164-5 *uice episcopi functus*. One might have expected a reference to subjection, as at § 55.21-3, § 149.172-3.

143.4: It is hard to see how *arguebat* can be appropriate. In classical Latin its commonest sense is 'convict', usually in the context of demolishing an assertion; at § 7.82, its only other occurrence in the work, it means *accusabat* or something of the kind. For *urgere* see §§ 19.398, 31.217; as it is often spelled *urguere*, one might think of writing *urguebat* here, but in the other two passages most of the manuscripts have no -*u*-.

143.39: If Geoffrey wrote *simultatem*, he misused the word, because it means not 'resemblance' or 'imitation' but 'feud'.

143.40: The manuscripts give *Ex tunc* or *Extunc*. In the sense *ex illo tempore*, documented in *TLL* 'ex' 1126.31-48 and *DmLBs* 'extunc' §§ a-b, it does not fit the context, and as a mere equivalent of *tunc*, a sense reported by *DmLBs* § c from later texts, Geoffrey seems unlikely to have used it just this once when he uses *tunc* over 50 times in either first or second position. The phrase *ex uoto* occurs at § 60.126.

143.42-3: With *incidere* Geoffrey elsewhere uses *in*, and the same phrase recurs at § 193.300. Haplography is to blame when some manuscripts omit *in* at § 100.366.

149.151: Though reported by *DmLBs* from other medieval authors, transitive *dimicare* is not used by Geoffrey elswehere.

150.185-6: From *quod cum* to *uoraginis* the sentence can be construed in various ways, but none makes sense. The sense requires that the subject of both *fluctuat* and *recipitur* should be *mare*, and *ipsum* is a pronoun; *quod* therefore has no function beyond a loosely subordinating one until it becomes the subject of *repletur*. The subject of *eructat* and *tegit et aspergit* can be either *quod* or its antecedent *stagnum*. The sentence would be easier to construe with *recipit*, of which *quod* would be the subject as of *repletur*; but Geoffrey took over *recipitur in modum uoraginis* from *Hist. Brit.* 69.

157.380-81: It is not in Geoffrey's manner to have written *uario* once as the noun ('vair') and once as the adjective; and what would the varieties be? The excellent conjectures found in no. 178 (Faral's P) and other manuscripts not only provide the best explanation for the variants but also restore symmetry to the description. Which participle is right matters less.

157.396: After *ponderosorum lapidum iactu*, what could *saxis* mean? Several instances of *scacci* coupled with *aleae* are given by Du Cange. It seems to have been conjectured independently more than once, because nothing connects the Second Variant (I cite no. 108 as an early representative), no. 15 (a descendant of Δ through H), no. 39 (a relative of Y), and no. 118 (a descendant of Σ).

159.462-3: See the discussion of § 62.242 for my objection to the punctuation adopted here in all the manuscripts but O. Perhaps the transmitted text conflates two versions, *Nichil enim quod ui et uiolentia acquiritur iuste ab ullo possidetur* and *Nichil enim iuste ab ullo possidetur qui uiolentiam intulit*.

160.483: Unless *redoluit* is corrupt, Geoffrey must have meant it as 'devised' (thought up by *dolus*?), a long way from the only meaning attested elsewhere, 'smack of'. If it is corrupt (*edocuit* Y), I had not thought of anything better than *reuoluit* when I met it in no. 69; at §§ 1.1 and 168.236 the verb means 'ponder', at § 16.296 apparently 'unfold'.

160.499-500: As long as *qui* is taken not with *nos* but closely with *ut exalteris* as qualifying the 'you' implicit in the preceding imperatives, there is nothing amiss with *diffugiam*.

162.526: As Geoffrey's adjective from *Gallia* is *Gallicus* only in the metrical oracle at § 16.305 and elsewhere *Gallicanus*, not even if something like *prouinciarum* had fallen out after *autem* would *Gallicarum* be the right form here. Surely it is a slip caused by the -*ca*- of *ducatibus*, and a slip not for *Galliae* (no. 48) but for *Galliarum*.

162.531: For the absurd *exceptus* the obvious remedy is not a present participle like *uidens* (G) or *habens* (no. 100) but a deponent past participle like *expertus* (O[2]) or *compertus* ('Transmission' 100). Neither of these verbs, however, has the same construction elsewhere in the work as it would have here if right.

165.80: At first sight, the *meditatio* is Arthur's intention to stop the giant picking up his club, and the giant rumbles it; but Geoffrey would hardly call Arthur's intention *mala*. It therefore seems likelier that the *mala meditatio* belongs to the giant, 'no stranger to mischief' (cf. § 90.33 *usus belli ignara*, § 178.61 *belli usus ignaros*), and that *malae* was deliberately omitted from Φ through failure to see this.

166.148, 173: Elsewhere Geoffrey uses *subducere* in the sense 'raise', possible here only if *equis* is a dative of destination. It seems likelier that he treated it as equivalent to *subdere*, for which see § 155.274 *subdentes equis calcaria*.

166.194: The usual construction is a gerundive or *ad* with the gerund. Either Geoffrey muddled the two or *ad* has dropped out; corruption of *seruandos* is less likely. See also above on § 46.246.

167.218-19: As Geoffrey does not use the historic infinitive, a finite verb is probably missing; a corrector of E adds *poterant* after *praeualere*, but perhaps Geoffrey at first ended the sentence with *ualuerunt* and then, noticing that he had just used *praeualere*, cancelled *ualuerunt* but neglected to provide a replacement. The reading of KΦ introduces a form of the perfect attested only at § 153.222 *uenere* (why there?) and in K at § 167.230 just below, *requieuere*.

169.267: In classical Latin *profari* never means 'address', and one expects the usual verb, *affatur*. In the only other passage where *profari* occurs, § 165.53, *profata* (*affata* C) could but need not be taken as transitive, with *eum* understood from the preceding clause.

173.393: Elsewhere in the work, *et* after *nam* either precedes a pronoun and means *etiam* (§§ 133.359, 137.488, 190.234) or prepares for a second *et* and means 'both' (§§ 91.73). As neither function is possible here, either it is superfluous or something has dropped out.

177.1: The variants here, doubtless caused by the common practice of leaving the initial letter of a book or chapter to be filled in by a rubricator, raise delicate and tantalizing problems. The manuscripts transmit *ne ... quidem* only at § 198.434 (*nec ... quidem* G) and *nec ... quidem* only at § 55.21, where there may be a connective element in *nec*. On the legitimacy of *nec ... quidem* in classical Latin see Roberta Caldini Montanari, *Tradizione medievale ed edizione critica del 'Somnium Scipionis'* (Florence 2002) 540-42. If *ne* or *nec* is read here, *hoc* must refer forward to *quae proelia ... commiserit*. At §§ 92.125 and 208.604, however, Geoffrey construes *tacere* not with a direct object but with *de*, which may therefore seem preferable here; *hoc* would then refer back to the affair between Modred and the queen, about which Geoffrey would be declining to give details, but it would do so across a division between books. Less important uncertainties caused by space left for a rubricator arise over *cum/dum* and *at/et/ut*.

177.30-31: Unless several words have fallen out after *irruens*, the only correction of *conantur* that accords with Geoffrey's habits is *conabatur*, but corruption to *conantur* seems unlikely. The present tense does not fit the rest of the sentence. Written in abbreviated form, *conaretur*, which I adopt, would have been easier than *conabatur* to misread as *conantur*; but the subjunctive has to be excused as the result of attraction to *intenderet*, because with consecutive *quod* he uses the indicative, at any rate for events in the past (contrast § 3.19 *censeatur*).

177.32: Here and at § 193.307 *in sequent-* is preferable to *insequent-*, because Geoffrey uses *insequi* of pursuit or following an example, never of temporal succession. At § 206.577 I see no way of determining whether he meant *inscriptis* or *in scriptis*, because he has no other use of *concordare* and draws no obvious distinction between *scribere* and *inscribere*.

178.44: Presumably *fugae* is a dative of destination, much as at § 148.147 *deditioni compulit*. The verb *euehi* occurs only once more in the work, just below at § 178.82 with *in insulam*.

194.343: The readings best attested, *nominemur* and *uestri*, attach the relative clause *quae patriam quam uidetis omnibus uicinis aduersatam uiriliter tuetur* to *gens regni uestri* when the argument of the whole speech demands that it should refer to the Britons of Brittany. As there is no other antecedent in the neighbourhood, correction is necessary: read either *nominemini* with the variant *nostri* or *qui ... tuemur* with the antecedent implicit in *nominemur*. The reading of Φ, *nominentur*, must be wrong in any event. This is one of several places where a difficult choice has to be made between forms of *nos/noster* and *uos/ uester*; when scribes abbreviate the adjectives, it is often hard anyway to tell which they intend. At the beginning of the speech, *nostrorum* is less well attested but makes a sharper point.

202.517: An abbreviation of *tantum* is much likelier than *eodem* to have been misread as *tandem*. Whatever the syntax of the ablative (instrumental?), there are comparable instances: § 7.84-5 *Erat autem frater patre et matre Graecus*, § 81.203-5 *Erat autem patre Britannus ..., matre uero et natione Romanus*. With *eodem* the notional participle of *esse* can be understood. If the text of the next clause is sound, taking *mater eius* as the subject of *fuerat* is preferable to punctuating heavily after *diuersa* and extracting *mater* from *matre* to serve as its subject, with an unconvincing asyndeton justifiably emended away by no. 48. In any event, *edita* must go with *ex nobili genere Gewisseorum*, as at § 99.317-18 *ex utrorumque genere edito*, § 152.209-10 *uxorem ... ex nobili genere Romanorum editam*, § 206.581-2 *gens antiquo genere illorum edita*.

207.594-7: The syntax can be rescued with a comma after *Britonum*, so that the ablative absolute is paired with the participles; but as Geoffrey does not write in that way, it seems likelier that he just lost control of the sentence.

A translator must attempt to reconcile two sometimes irreconcilable goals, namely to furnish the reader with an accurate guide to an original text, while at the same time presenting that text in a readable, modern form. The present translation is intended to be consulted primarily in conjunction with Geoffrey's Latin on the facing page. To this end, Geoffrey's original sentences have been retained as far as possible, with the aim of enabling the reader to move smoothly from text to translation and vice versa, even at the cost of occasional longer sentences (particularly in Geoffrey's purple passages). Within this framework, however, the translator has striven at all times to avoid anything slavishly literal or stilted and to present Geoffrey's often fast paced, if sometimes repetitive, narrative in a readily accessible and, it is hoped, enjoyable form.

Geoffrey's work has previously been translated into English four times.[84] For the sake of freshness and independence, the present translation was initially made without reference to the previous versions, which were consulted only occasionally after its completion for comparison.

Personal and place names have been treated here in the following ways. The vast majority of Geoffrey's personal names retain their Latin form, the only exception being very familiar characters such as Vortigern, Merlin and Arthur; lesser Arthurian figures like Kaius and Gualguainus – lesser in Geoffrey's narrative, that is – have not been anglicised and so appear here in Latin form (alongside Brutus, Cordeilla, Cassibellaunus and the rest). This has the added benefit of preserving such names which differ from their conventional Arthurian equivalents (for example, Ganhumara for Guinevere and Caliburnus for Excalibur). Also, in § 26.71 and § 34.306 respectively, two early kings appear as Malim and Clotenis, although it is far from clear whether these are the nominative forms intended by Geoffrey. Conversely, to aid the reader, most places appear under their modern names, in so far as these can be identified; otherwise, the Latin form is retained.[85] For instance, of three cities founded by Ebraucus (§ 27.92-4) Aldclud and Mons Agned appear here as Dumbarton and Edinburgh respectively, whereas Mons Dolorosus has not been modernised, because its identification with Stirling is much later than the twelfth century and so what place Geoffrey intended remains unclear. Cases where Geoffrey contrasts original 'British' and later place names have been similarly treated in the translation (e.g. Trinovantum and London; Dorobernia and Canterbury).

That Geoffrey's text itself contains a few inconsistencies is not perhaps surprising, given the nature of his fanciful pseudohistory. Thus Arthur's steward Kaius appears on one occasion under the name Cheudo (§ 176.470). Likewise, Geoffrey's classicising terminology can result in anachronisms, most frequently in

---

84 A. Thompson (London 1718), revised by J. A. Giles, who published it first separately (London 1842; copy at Selwyn College Cambridge) and then in *Six Old English chronicles* (London 1848) 87-292; S. Evans (London 1904), revised by C. W. Dunn (London 1963); L. Thorpe (n. 68). There are several reprints.

85 An essential aid is J. S. P. Tatlock, *The legendary history of Britain* (Berkeley 1950) 7-115.

the case of France and Gaul, terms which he alternates at will. As regards Geoffrey's vocabulary, there are fewer problems of consistency; the most persistent concerns *milites*, which has been rendered as 'soldiers', 'knights' or simply 'men' as deemed most appropriate to the context.

Indeed, Geoffrey's Latin itself is generally straightforward and problems raised by vocabulary or grammar and syntax are the exception rather than the rule. Two words in particular call for comment. When he makes Leir lament the 'progress of fate' (§ 31.214 *seria fatorum*, neuter plural), Geoffrey appears to have confused the words *seria* and *series* (cf. Lucan, *De bello ciuili* 1.70: *fatorum series*); so at any rate the phrase has been translated here. Later, in Merlin's prophecies, the term *submarini luces* (§ 116.215, masculine) is especially mysterious; here it has been rendered 'pikes beneath the sea, (compare *lucius*).

* * *

We have incurred several debts. With a generous grant from the Vinaver Fund, microfilms were purchased in the 1980s, and later when further manuscripts came to notice, for the Geoffrey of Monmouth Research Project, associated at that time with the Department of Anglo-Saxon Norse and Celtic at Cambridge. Richard Barber undertook the task, and David Dumville served as keeper of the collection, which remains at the Department. For Orderic's quotation from the *Prophetiae* Marjorie Chibnall lent us a reproduction of the autograph. Julia Crick, the author of two books on the tradition, has supplied information, and we have also benefited from the advice of Michael Lapidge, Giovanni Orlandi, Paul Russell, and Oliver Padel. Our warm thanks go to them all.

SYMBOLS AND ABBREVIATIONS

Manuscripts cited:

Ω = the common source of Δ Φ Σ

    Δ = the common source of

	O	Oxford Bodl. Rawl. C 152, s. xii
	C	Cambridge U. L. Dd 6 12, s. xii
	H	Paris B. N. Lat. 6040, s. xii (except in §§ 114-37)
	S	Salisbury Cath. 121, s. xii
	E	Cambridge C. C. C. 281, s. xii

    Φ = the common source of

	Q	Paris B. N. Lat. 13710, s. xv
	W	the First Variant in Neil Wright's edition (n. 15)
	Y	Cambridge Caius 406/627, s. xii
	H	Paris B. N. Lat. 6040, s. xii (in §§ 114-37)
	G	Paris Ste-Geneviève 2113, s. xii
	M	British Library Royal 13 D II, s. xii/xiii

    Π = the common source in §§ 110-17 of

	ζ	Cambridge U. L. Gg 6 42, s. xiii[1]
	λ	Lincoln Cath. 214, s. xii
	β	Bruges 428, s. xiii
	ϱ	Paris B. N. Lat. 14465, s. xii

   and in §§ 111-17 of

	θ	London Lambeth 503, s. xiv

   Also cited in this section:

	Ord.	Ordericus Vitalis (n. 6)

   Σ = the common source in §§ 118-208 of

	U	Ushaw College 6, s. xii
	A	Alençon 12, s. xii
	K	Cambridge U. L. Mm 5 29, s. xii
	N	Oxford All Souls 35, s. xiii[1]
	D	Oxford Bodl. Douce 115, s. xiv

See also 'The apparatus of this edition' above, p. li. Manuscripts cited for conjectures are given the number assigned to them in Crick's catalogue (n. 5) and above in 'Survey of the tradition', pp. xxxi-li. For most variants in names see the Index.

Editions cited

1508	Ivo Cavellatus (Paris)
1587	H. Commelinus (Heidelberg)
1844	J. A. Giles (London)
Faral	E. Faral, *La légende arthurienne* (Paris 1929) III 63-303

Other works cited

DmLBs	*Dictionary of medieval Latin from British sources* (Oxford 1975-)
'Errori'	M. D. Reeve, 'Errori in autografi' (n. 9)
Tatlock	J. S. P. Tatlock, *The legendary history of Britain* (Berkeley 1950)
TLL	*Thesaurus linguae latinae* (Berlin 1900-)
'Transm.'	M. D. Reeve, 'The transmission of the *Historia regum Britanniae*' (n. 5)

Introd. without page number refers to 'Critical notes', pp. lxiv-lxxiv

THE BOOK OF GEOFFREY OF MONMOUTH
CONCERNING THE DEEDS OF THE BRITONS

GALFRIDI ARTVRI MONEMVTENSIS
DE GESTIS BRITONVM EDITIO

Hic et in §§ 1-108 citantur Δ (unde pendent OCHSE), Φ (unde pendent QYGM)

Galfridi monemutensis de gestis britonum secundum caratonum editio *O:*
Incipit editio galfridi arturi monemutensis de gestis britonum *CS:*
Incipit praefatio in libro brittonum *E:*
Galfridi arturi monemutensis de gestis britonum liber incipit *Q:*
Gaufridi arturi monemutensis de gestis britonum prologus incipit *M:*
Incipit prologus gaufridi monemutensis in librum de gestis regum maioris britanniae que nunc
anglia dicitur ad rotbertum comitem gloecestrie *G:*
deest titulus in HY

PROLOGUE

1   While my mind was often pondering many things in many ways, my thoughts turned to the history of the kings of Britain, and I was surprised that, among the references to them in the fine works of Gildas and Bede, I had found nothing concerning the kings who lived here before Christ's Incarnation, and nothing about Arthur and the many others who succeeded after it, even though their deeds were worthy of eternal praise and are proclaimed by many people as if they had been entertainingly and memorably written

2   down. I frequently thought the matter over in this way until Walter archdeacon of Oxford, a man skilled in the rhetorical arts and in foreign histories, brought me a very old book in the British tongue, which set out in excellent style a continuous narrative of all their deeds from the first king of the Britons, Brutus, down to Cadualadrus, son of Caduallo. Though I have never gathered showy words from the gardens of others, I was persuaded by his request to translate the book into Latin in a rustic style, reliant on my own reed pipe; had I larded my pages with bombastic terms, I would tire my readers with the need to linger over understanding my words rather

3   than following my narrative. Therefore, earl Robert of Gloucester, look favourably on my little work; let it be corrected by your instruction and advice so that it does not seem to have arisen from Geoffrey of Monmouth's slight stream but, duly seasoned with the genius of your wit, is called the product of the illustrious king Henry's son, whom philosophy has nurtured in the liberal arts, and whose natural valour has made him a commander of knights in battle; hence the island of Britain now congratulates herself on gaining in you a Henry reborn for our time.[1]

---

1 You too, count Waleran of Meulan, twin pillar of our kingdom, lend your assistance to my book, so that, promoted by the concerted efforts of you both, it may shine forth more brightly for its readers. You can trace your ancestry back to the renowned emperor Charlemagne; wisdom clasped you to her maternal bosom, imbued you with her subtle knowledge and then sent you to gain military fame in the camp of kings, where you surpassed your comrades in boldness, and you learned, like your father before you, to support your vassals. Since you are a trusty supporter of such men, extend your protection to me, your poet, and to my book, written for your delight, so that I may rest beneath the shade of your spreading branches and my muse can play her melody on my rustic pipe, safe from envious critics.

PROLOGVS

1 Cum mecum multa et de multis saepius animo reuoluens in hystoriam
regum Britanniae inciderem, in mirum contuli quod infra mentionem
quam de eis Gildas et Beda luculento tractatu fecerant nichil de regibus
qui ante incarnationem Christi inhabitauerant, nichil etiam de Arturo
ceterisque compluribus qui post incarnationem successerunt repperissem,   5
cum et gesta eorum digna aeternitate laudis constarent et a multis populis
2 quasi inscripta iocunde et memoriter praedicentur. Talia michi et de talibus
multociens cogitanti optulit Walterus Oxenefordensis archidiaconus, uir
in oratoria arte atque in exoticis hystoriis eruditus, quendam Britannici
sermonis librum uetustissimum qui a Bruto primo rege Britonum usque   10
ad Cadualadrum filium Caduallonis actus omnium continue et ex ordine
perpulcris orationibus proponebat. Rogatu itaque illius ductus, tametsi
infra alienos ortulos falerata uerba non collegerim, agresti tamen stilo
propriisque calamis contentus codicem illum in Latinum sermonem
transferre curaui; nam si ampullosis dictionibus paginam illinissem, taedium   15
legentibus ingererem, dum magis in exponendis uerbis quam in historia
3 intelligenda ipsos commorari oporteret. Opusculo igitur meo, Roberte dux
Claudiocestriae, faueas, ut sic te doctore te monitore corrigatur quod non
ex Galfridi Monemutensis fonticulo censeatur exortum sed sale mineruae
tuae conditum illius dicatur editio quem Henricus illustris rex Anglorum   20
generauit, quem philosophia liberalibus artibus erudiuit, quem innata
probitas in militia militibus praefecit; unde Britannia tibi nunc temporibus
nostris ac si alterum Henricum adepta interno congratulatur affectu.

1 Dum *G*
7 praedicarentur *HE (cf. Introd.)*
8-9 [uir ... eruditus] *O*
17-18 Stephane rex Angliae *15*
19 exortum *Φ:* extortum *Δ (cf. 'Transm.' 78)*
20-21 quem ... generauit *Ω:* cuius ... auunculus extitit *15*
22 Britannia <insula> *H (cf. 'Transm.' 78)*
23 gratulatur *Φ*
23 *post* affectu *add. H § 4* Tu quoque, Galeranne consul Mellenti *(*Roberte consul Claudiocestriae
15), altera regni nostri columna, operam adhibeas tuam ut utriusque moderatione communicata
editio in medium producta pulcrius elucescat. Te etenim, ex illius celeberrimi regis Karoli
stirpe *(*illo celeberrimo rege Henrico *15)* progenitum, mater phylosophia in gremio suo excepit
scientiarumque suarum subtilitatem edocuit ac deinde ut in militaribus clareres exercitiis ad castra
regum direxit, ubi commilitones tuos audacter supergressus et terror hostium existere et protectio
tuorum esse paternis auspiciis addidicisti. Fidelis itaque protectio tuorum existens, me tuum uatem
codicemque ad oblectamentum tui editum sub tutela tua recipias, ut sub tegmine tam patulae arboris
recubans calamum musae meae coram inuidis atque improbis tuto modulamine resonare queam,
Galfridi quidem sed in gratiam unius Galeranni posterius ut uid. insertum (cf. Introd. ix-x)

Explicit praefacio. Liber incipit primus *O*: Descriptio insule *C(?)S*: Explicit praefatio. Incipit liber
E: Incipit liber primus *G*: Britannie insule descriptio *M*

DESCRIPTION OF THE ISLAND

5   Britain, the best of islands, lies in the western ocean between France and Ireland; eight hundred miles long by two hundred miles wide, it supplies all human needs with its boundless productivity. Rich in metals of every kind, it has broad pastures and hills suitable for successful agriculture, in whose rich soil various crops can be harvested in their season. It has all kinds of wild beasts in its forests, and in its glades grow not only grasses suitable for rotating the pasture of animals, but flowers of various colours which attract bees to fly to them and gather honey. It has green meadows pleasantly situated beneath lofty mountains, where clear streams flow in silver rivulets and softly murmur, offering the assurance of gentle sleep to those who lie by their banks. Moreover, it is watered by lakes and streams, full of fish, and apart from the straits to the south, which allow one to sail to France, it stretches out, like three arms, three noble rivers, the Thames, the Severn and the Humber, on which foreign goods can be brought in by boat from every land. It was once graced with twenty-eight cities, some of which lie deserted in lonely spots, their walls tumbled down, while others are still thriving and contain holy churches with towers rising to a fine height, in which devout communities of men and women serve God according to the Christian tradition. It is finally inhabited by five peoples, the Normans, the Britons, the Saxons, the Picts and the Scots; of these the Britons once occupied it from shore to shore before the others, until their pride brought divine retribution down upon them and they gave way to the Picts and the Saxons. It remains now to relate how they landed and from where, as will soon be explained.

BOOK ONE

6   After the Trojan war Aeneas fled the devastated city with his son Ascanius and sailed to Italy. He was received with honour by King Latinus, but this attracted the envy of Turnus, King of the Rutulians, who attacked him. Aeneas emerged victorious from their struggle, killed Turnus and was rewarded with the kingdom of Italy and the hand of Lavinia, Latinus' daughter. After Aeneas had breathed his last, Ascanius succeeded him, built Alba by the Tiber and had a son named Silvius. He, indulging a secret passion, married a niece of Lavinia and made her pregnant. When his father Ascanius found out, he ordered his magicians to discover what the sex of the girl's child would be. Once they were certain, the magicians said that the girl was carrying a boy who

DESCRIPTIO INSVLAE

5 Britannia, insularum optima, in occidentali occeano inter Galliam et
Hiberniam sita, octingenta milia in longum, ducenta uero in latum continens, 25
quicquid mortalium usui congruit indeficienti fertilitate ministrat. Omni
etenim genere metalli fecunda, campos late pansos habet, colles quoque
praepollenti culturae aptos, in quibus frugum diuersitates ubertate glebae
temporibus suis proueniunt. Habet et nemora uniuersis ferarum generibus
repleta, quorum in saltibus et alternandis animalium pastibus gramina 30
conueniunt et aduolantibus apibus flores diuersorum colorum mella
distribuunt. Habet etiam prata sub aeriis montibus amoeno situ uirentia, in
quibus fontes lucidi, per nitidos riuos leni murmure manantes, pignus suauis
soporis in ripis accubantibus irritant. Porro lacubus atque piscosis fluuiis
irrigua est et absque meridianae plagae freto, quo ad Gallias nauigatur, tria 35
nobilia flumina, Tamensis uidelicet et Sabrinae nec non et Humbri, uelut
tria brachia extendit, quibus transmarina commercia ex uniuersis nationibus
eidem nauigio feruntur. Bis denis etiam bisque quaternis ciuitatibus olim
decorata erat, quarum quaedam dirutis moeniis in desertis locis squalescunt,
quaedam uero adhuc integrae templa sanctorum cum turribus perpulcra 40
proceritate erecta continent, in quibus religiosi coetus uirorum ac mulierum
obsequium Deo iuxta Christianam traditionem praestant. Postremo quinque
inhabitatur populis, Normannis uidelicet atque Britannis, Saxonibus,
Pictis, et Scotis; ex quibus Britones olim ante ceteros a mari usque ad mare
insederunt donec ultione diuina propter ipsorum superbiam superueniente 45
Pictis et Saxonibus cesserunt. Qualiter uero et unde applicuerunt restat
nunc perarare ut in subsequentibus explicabitur.

LIBER I

6 Aeneas post Troianum bellum excidium urbis cum Ascanio filio diffugiens
Italiam nauigio adiuit. Ibi cum a Latino rege honorifice receptus esset, inuidit
Turnus rex Rutulorum et cum illo congressus est. Dimicantibus ergo illis, 50
praeualuit Aeneas peremptoque Turno regnum Italiae et Lauiniam filiam
Latini adeptus est. Denique, suprema die ipsius superueniente, Ascanius,
regia potestate sublimatus, condidit Albam super Tyberim genuitque filium
cui nomen erat Siluius. Hic, furtiuae ueneri indulgens, nupsit cuidam nepti
Lauiniae eamque fecit praegnantem. Cumque id Ascanio patri compertum 55
esset, praecepit magis suis explorare quem sexum puella concepisset.
Certitudine ergo rei comperta, dixerunt magi ipsam grauidam esse puero qui

39 moeniis *OCH QYM (cf. TLL 1326.14-18):* moenibus *SE G auctorem ut uid. corrigentes*
41 erectis *H (cf. Introd.)*
43 *post* populis *deficit C usque ad § 18.364* timorem non
47 subsequentibus *HSE QY:* sequentibus *O GM*

Narratio istorie *S:* Incipit liber primus *M*

7

would kill his father and mother, wander many lands in exile and in the end receive the highest honour. Their prophecy was not made in vain. When the day of his birth came, the woman had the child, and died while giving birth; the boy was entrusted to the midwife and given the name Brutus. Fifteen years later, when the young Brutus was out hunting with his father, he inadvertently shot and killed him with an arrow; for, while the beaters were driving stags towards them, Brutus aimed an arrow at them, but struck his father in the chest.

7 After Silvius' death, Brutus' grandparents were angry that he had committed such a misdeed and exiled him from Italy. He therefore went in exile to Greece, where he discovered the descendants of Helenus, Priam's son, held in slavery under the power of the Greek king Pandrasus; after the fall of Troy Achilles' son Pyrrhus had taken away Helenus and many others in chains and ordered that they be held in captivity in revenge for his father's death. Once Brutus learned of their descent from his ancient countrymen, he lived among them. He began to manifest so much soldierly prowess and virtue that their kings and chiefs loved him above all the youths in that country; to wise men he displayed his wisdom, to warriors his aggression and, whenever he acquired gold, silver or ornaments, he used to present everything to his men. As Brutus' fame spread through every land, Trojans began to flock to him, asking that he be their leader and free them from their bondage to the Greeks; it would be a simple matter, they claimed, since their population in that land had now grown to seven thousand, not counting women and children. Moreover, there was in Greece a most noble youth named Assaracus, who favoured the Trojan cause. Since his mother had been Trojan, he placed great reliance on their help in repelling Greek raids. For he was in dispute with his brother over three castles that their father had granted to Assaracus on his deathbed, which his brother was trying to take from him because his mother had been a concubine. The brother by contrast was Greek on both sides and had induced the king and the other Greeks to support his faction. Considering the Trojans' numbers and his ready access to Assaracus' three castles, Brutus felt confident enough to agree to their request.

8 Having become their leader, Brutus summoned the Trojans from all directions and put Assaracus' castles in a state of defence. Accompanied by Assaracus, he took possession of the woods and hills with all the multitude of men and women who were with them. Then he sent the king the following letter:

> 'Brutus, leader of the survivors from Troy, sends greetings to Pandrasus, king of the Greeks. It was unjust that people descended from the famous stock of Dardanus should be treated in your kingdom otherwise than their serene nobility demanded, and so they have retired to the heart of the forest; in order to maintain their freedom, they preferred to eke out their lives eating meat and grass like wild beasts, rather than to enjoy every delicacy, while still enduring the yoke of slavery to you. If your highness' power is offended by this, you should not criticise but pardon them, since every captive will always wish to recover his former liberty. Taking pity on them, therefore,

patrem et matrem interficeret, pluribus quoque terris in exilium peragratis ad summum tandem culmen honoris perueniret. Nec fefellit eos uaticinium suum. Nam ut dies partus accessit, edidit mulier puerum et in natiuitate eius 60 mortua est; traditur autem ille obstetrici et uocatur Brutus. Postremo, cum ter quini anni emensi essent, comitabatur iuuenis patrem in uenando ipsumque inopino ictu sagittae interfecit; nam dum famuli ceruos in occursum eorum ducerent, Brutus, telum in ipsos dirigere affectans, genitorem sub pectore

7 percussit. Quo mortuo, expulsus est ab Italia, indignantibus parentibus 65 ipsum tantum facinus fecisse. Exulatus ergo adiuit partes Graeciae et inuenit progeniem Heleni filii Priami, quae sub potestate Pandrasi regis Graecorum in seruitutem tenebatur; Pirrus etenim filius Achillis post euersionem Troiae praedictum Helenum compluresque alios secum in uinclis abduxerat et ut necem patris sui in ipsos uindicaret in captionem teneri praeceperat. Agnita 70 igitur ueterum conciuium prosapia, moratus est Brutus apud eos. In tantum autem militia et probitate uigere coepit ita ut a regibus et principibus prae omni iuuentute patriae amaretur; erat enim inter sapientes sapiens, inter bellicosos bellicosus, et quicquid auri uel argenti siue ornamentorum adquirebat totum militibus erogabat. Diuulgata itaque per uniuersas 75 nationes ipsius fama, Troiani coeperunt ad eum confluere, orantes ut ipso duce a seruitute Graecorum liberarentur, quod leuiter fieri asserebant, cum in tantum iam infra patriam multiplicati essent ita ut septem milia, exceptis paruulis et mulieribus, computarentur. Praeterea erat quidam nobilissimus iuuenis in Graecia nomine Assaracus qui partibus eorum fauebat. Ex 80 Troiana namque matre natus erat fiduciamque in illis habebat maximam ut auxilio eorum inquietudini Graecorum resistere quiuisset. Arguebat enim eum frater suus propter tria castella quae sibi moriens pater donauerat et ea auferre conabatur quia ex concubina natus fuerat. Erat autem frater patre et matre Graecus asciueratque regem ceterosque Graecos parti suae fauere. 85 Inspiciens ergo Brutus et uirorum multitudinem et Assaraci castella quae sibi patebant, securius petitioni illorum adquieuit.

8 Erectus igitur in ducem, conuocat undique Troianos et oppida Assaraci munit. Ipse autem et Assaracus cum tota multitudine uirorum et mulierum quae eis adhaerebat nemora et colles occupant. Deinde litteras suas regi in 90 haec uerba direxit:

'Pandraso regi Graecorum Brutus dux reliquiarum Troiae salutem. Quia indignum fuerat gentem praeclaro genere Dardani ortam aliter in regno tuo tractari quam serenitas nobilitatis eius expeteret, sese infra abdita nemorum recepit; praeferebat namque ferino ritu, carnibus uidelicet et 95 herbis, uitam cum libertate sustentare quam uniuersis deliciis refocillata diutius sub iugo seruitutis tuae permanere. Quod si celsitudinem potentiae tuae offendit, non est ei imputandum sed uenia adhibenda, cum cuiusque captiui communis sit intentio uelle ad pristinam dignitatem redire. Misericordia igitur super eam motus, amissam libertatem largiri 100

63 dum *Δ:* cum *Φ*

do not refuse to restore their lost freedom or forbid them to stay in the forest glades where they are seeking refuge from bondage. Otherwise, grant them permission to depart and join foreign nations'.

9   When Pandrasus read the contents of this letter, he was filled with wonder that people whom he had held in slavery had been so bold as to send him such a message. He called a meeting of his nobles and decided to collect an army and pursue them. As Pandrasus was marching past the castle of Sparatinum towards the wastes that he thought they had occupied, Brutus emerged with three thousand men and suddenly fell on the unsuspecting king. For on hearing of Pandrasus' approach, Brutus had entered Sparatinum the previous night so as to take the unarmed and disordered enemy by surprise. Thus the attack was launched and the Trojans charged in, making a bold effort to cut down the enemy. The Greeks were immediately thunderstruck, fled in all directions and, led by their king, rushed to cross the river Akalon, which flowed near by; but as they crossed, they were at the mercy of its swirling waters. Brutus pursued the fugitives, cutting down some in the water and some on the river-bank, and rejoicing to see them die in either fashion as he dashed from place to place. When Pandrasus' brother Antigonus observed this, his grief knew no bounds, and, calling his fleeing comrades back to the ranks, he swiftly turned about to attack the rampaging Trojans; he preferred to die fighting rather than to drown in muddy water, fleeing like a coward. Advancing in close order, he encouraged his companions to fight bravely and dealt deadly blows with all his strength. But it had little or no effect; for the Trojans had the protection of their weapons, whilst the Greeks were unarmed. Thus the Trojans fought all the more boldly, inflicting dreadful slaughter on their opponents and not relaxing their efforts until almost all the Greeks had been killed and Antigonus and his comrade Anacletus captured.

10   Having won this victory, Brutus provided Sparatinum with a garrison of six hundred knights and returned to the depths of the forest, where the Trojans were awaiting his protection. Pandrasus, deeply troubled by his own flight and the capture of his brother, spent the night rallying his scattered men and, in the morning, advanced with them to lay siege to the castle; for he thought that Brutus was inside with Antigonus and the other prisoners he had taken. As he approached the walls, he examined the castle's layout, divided his army into companies and placed them at various points around it. He told some to prevent the defenders from sallying out and others to divert the rivers, whilst a third group was to break through the walls with relentless blows of the ram and with other siege engines. Executing his orders, they strained every sinew to subject the besieged to the cruellest of assaults. With the onset of night,

digneris et saltus nemorum quos ut seruitutem diffugeret occupauit eam habitare permittas. Sin autem, concede ut ad aliarum terrarum nationes cum licentia tua abscedant'.

9 Pandrasus ergo, agnita litterarum sententia, ultra modum admiratus est ipsos quos in seruitutem tenuerat tanta audacia habundasse ut ei talia 105 mandata dirigerent. Conuocato itaque procerum suorum consilio, exercitum colligere decreuit ut ipsos persequeretur. Dum autem deserta quibus eos adesse auctumauerat per oppidum Sparatinum peteret, egressus est Brutus cum tribus milibus uirorum ipsumque nichil huiusmodi praemeditatum ex inprouiso inuasit. Audito namque aduentu ipsius, sese in praedicto oppido 110 praeterita proxima nocte inmiserat ut in ipsos inermes et sine ordine ituros inopinam irruptionem faceret. Impetu itaque facto, inuadunt acriter Troiani et stragem ingerere nituntur. Porro Graeci confestim stupefacti in omnes partes dilabuntur et rege suo praecedente fluuium Akalon, qui prope fluebat, transire festinant; at in transeundo infra uoraginem fluctus periclitantur. 115 Quos diffugientes Brutus infestat, infestatos uero partim in undis partim super ripam prosternit, et nunc hac nunc illac discurrens duplicem necem ipsis ingestam esse laetatur. Quod ut Antigonus frater Pandrasi intuitus est, ultra modum doluit reuocauitque uagantes socios in turmam et celeri impetu in saeuientes Troas reuersus est; malebat namque resistendo interire 120 quam ignauam fugam faciens luteis gurgitibus submergi. Densa igitur acie incedens, socios uiriliter resistere hortatur letiferaque tela totis uiribus contorquet. Sed parum uel minime profecit; nam Troes armis muniti erant, ceteri uero inermes. Vnde audatiores insistentes caedem miserandam inferebant nec eos hoc modo infestare quieuerunt donec cunctis fere 125 interfectis Antigonum et Anacletum eiusdem socium retinuerunt.

10 Brutus uero, potitus uictoria, oppidum sexcentis militibus muniuit petiuitque nemorum abdita ubi Troiana plebs praesidium illius expectabat. At Pandrasus, ob fugam suam fratrisque captionem anxiatus, nocte illa populum dilapsum resociare uacauit et cum postera lux redisset obsidere 130 oppidum cum resociato populo progressus est; arbitrabatur enim Brutum inmisisse se infra ipsum cum Antigono ceterisque captiuis quos ceperat. Vt igitur moenibus accessit, explorato castelli situ distribuit exercitum suum per turmas et per diuersas partes in circuitu locauit. Indixit etiam ut alii egressum inclusis abnegarent, alii cursus fluminum auerterent, alii crebris 135 arietibus ceterisque machinationibus murorum compagem dissoluerent. Qui praecepta eius effectibus exequentes omni nisu contendebant quibus modis obsessos crudelius infestarent. Superueniente autem nocte, audatiores

103 licentia 3, *113²:* diligentia Ω *(cf. 'Transm.' 97-8)*
103 abscedat *OSE (cf. Introd. ad § 16.288-90)*
108 per Δ: *om. QM:* ante deserta *Y:* et *G*
111 [proxima] *G:* [praeterita] *34²*
125 inquietare Φ
130 rediisset *HS'E QY*
137 [eius] Φ

11

they selected the bolder soldiers to guard against any stealthy attack which the enemy might launch on their camp and tents, while the other soldiers were resting, tired by their exertions.

11   The besieged, stationed on the ramparts, strove with all their might to repel the enemy's engines with counter engines and made concerted efforts to defend themselves by hurling down weapons and torches of pitch. When the enemy used a 'tortoise' to undermine the wall, they forced them back with Greek fire and by pouring boiling water. At last, exhausted by lack of food and unremitting toil, they sent a messenger to Brutus, asking him to hurry to relieve them; they feared they might be so weakened that they would have to abandon the fortress. Brutus wanted to help, but was deeply troubled because he had insufficient soldiers to face the enemy in open battle. Finally he opted for a cunning stratagem, planning to approach the enemy camp at night, slip past the guards and slaughter them as they slept. Realising that this could not be accomplished without the aid and consent of one of the Greeks, he summoned Antigonus' companion Anacletus and, drawing his sword, said to him:

> 'Noble youth, the end of your life and Antigonus' is at hand, unless you do as I tell you and follow my instructions precisely. Tonight I intend to infiltrate the Greek camp and take them unawares, but I fear that their guards will detect the ruse and frustrate my plan. Therefore I need to attack them first and would like to use you to trick them into giving me easier access to the others. To complete this cunning mission, go in the second hour of the night to the siege-lines and lull their suspicions with lies, saying that you have smuggled Antigonus out of my prison to a wooded valley and hidden him there in the bushes, since he could go no further because of the fetters with which you will pretend he has been shackled. Then take them on the pretext of freeing him to the entrance of the wood, where I will be waiting with an armed force to kill them'.

12   Anacletus, eyeing the sword poised at his throat as Brutus spoke, was instantly terror-stricken and swore an oath that he would do exactly as Brutus said as long as he and Antigonus were permitted to live. Having given his word, with the coming of the second hour of the night he set off, as ordered, towards the siege-lines. When at last he neared the camp, up ran the guards from all the hiding-places they were patrolling; they asked what he had come for and whether he meant to betray the army. Feigning great joy, he replied:

> 'I am not here to betray my people, but have escaped from the Trojan prison and have fled to beg you to accompany me to your countryman Antigonus,

eligebant qui dum ceteri labore fessi quietem caperent soporis castra et
tentoria ab hostium furtiua incursione tuerentur. 140

11 At obsessi, in edito murorum astantes, totis uiribus nituntur ut ipsorum
machinationes contrariis machinationibus repellant et nunc tela nunc
sulphureas taedas eicientes sese unanimiter defendere intendunt. Cum
autem parata testudine murus suffoderetur, Graeco igne atque calidarum
aquarum aspergine hostes retrocedere cogebant. Cibi tandem penuria et 145
cotidiano labore afflicti, legatum ad Brutum miserunt, postulantes ut eis
in auxilium festinaret; timebant enim ne in debilitatem redacti oppidum
deserere cogerentur. Brutus ergo, opem subuectare affectans, internis
anxietatibus cruciatur quia tot milites non habebat quot sibi ad campestre
proelium committendum sufficerent. Callido deinde usus consilio, proponit 150
castra hostium noctu adire ipsosque soporatos, deceptis eorundem uigilibus,
interficere. Quoniam autem id fieri non posse callebat absque alicuius Graeci
assensu et auxilio, Anacletum socium Antigoni ad se uocauit illumque
euaginato gladio in hunc modum affatus est:

'Egregie iuuenis, finis uitae tuae Antigonique adest nisi ea quae tibi 155
praecipiam executurus uoluntati meae fideliter adquieueris. Affecto
enim in hac sequenti nocte castra Graecorum adire ut ipsos inopina caede
afficiam, sed timeo ne eorum uigiles, comperto dolo, inceptum meum
impediant. Quia ergo uerti arma in illos prius oporteret, desiderarem
eos per te decipere ut tutiorem aditum aggrediendi ceteros haberem. 160
Tu uero, callide negotium huiusmodi agens, in secunda noctis hora
uade ad obsidionem, et quemque fallacibus uerbis demulcendo dices te
Antigonum a carceribus meis abduxisse usque ad conuallem nemorum
et in eadem illum inter frutices delituisse nec longius abire posse propter
compedes quibus eum impeditum simulaueris. Deinde duces eos ad 165
exitum nemoris quasi ipsum liberaturos, ubi cum armata manu adero
paratus illos perimere'.

12 Anacletus igitur, uiso gladio qui inter haec uerba morti suae imminebat,
continuo perterritus iureiurando promisit sese praeceptum illud executurum
si sibi et Antigono diuturnior uita concederetur. Confirmato denique foedere, 170
in secunda noctis hora, quae iam instabat, uersus obsidionem iussum iter
arripuit. Cum tandem prope castra incederet, occurrunt undique uigiles qui
abdita locorum explorabant; quaerunt quoque aduentus ipsius causam et
utrum ad prodendum exercitum aduenisset. Quibus ille, ingentem laeticiam
simulans, in haec uerba respondit: 175

'Non equidem proditor meae gentis uenio, sed carcerem Troianorum
euadens ad uos orans diffugio ut mecum ad uestrum Antigonum ueniatis,

---

141 stantes Φ
147 [in] auxilium *OE¹*
152 posse *E QY²·* posse esse *OHS Y¹GM*
158 [meum] *S* Φ
169 illud *OSE:* illum *H: om.* Φ

whom I freed from Brutus' chains. Since his fetters were slowing him down, I have just told him to hide in the bushes at the entrance to the wood until I could find someone and bring them to free him'.

They were unsure whether he was speaking the truth, until one arrived who recognised and greeted him, telling his comrades who he was. They hesitated no longer, but swiftly summoned the rest of the guards and followed him directly to the wood where he said Antigonus was hidden. As they made their way through the bushes, Brutus and his armed band revealed themselves, attacked and quickly cut down the terrified guards. Then he advanced to the siege-lines and divided his men into three companies, with orders to separate and infiltrate the camp carefully and silently, and not to kill anyone within until Brutus and his band had reached the king's tent and given them the signal of a trumpet-blast.

13   When they had received their instructions, they swiftly entered the camp and, stealthily occupying their positions, awaited the agreed signal; Brutus was not long in giving it, just as soon as he stood before Pandrasus' tent, the goal he burned to reach. On hearing the trumpet, they quickly drew their swords and entered the quarters of the sleeping men, dealing deadly wounds and showing no mercy as they traversed the camp. The survivors awoke to the groans of the dying and, seeing the Trojans butchering them, were as surprised as sheep who suddenly fall prey to wolves; there was no help at hand, as they had no chance either to snatch up their weapons or take to flight. Armed or unarmed, they ran about in confusion where the fancy took them, only to be cut down as soon as the Trojans fell upon them. Whoever got away more dead than alive, rushing to escape too eagerly, was dashed into the rocks or bushes and choked out his unhappy life together with his blood. Whoever escaped with just his shield or some other protection tumbled into the same rocks and, running in fear for his life, fell in the darkness; those who fell broke their arms or legs. Those who did not suffer either fate, not knowing where to run, drowned in streams that flowed near by. Almost all met some disaster and scarcely any got away unharmed. The garrison too, when they heard of their comrades' arrival, sallied out to increase the carnage they were inflicting.

14   Brutus, on reaching the king's tent, as I described, had him bound and placed under guard. He thought it would be easier to attain his ends by keeping him alive than by executing him. His own troops, however, did not cease killing; they completely destroyed the part of the camp assigned to them. After they had spent the night in this manner and the light of dawn revealed what a crushing defeat the Greeks had suffered, Brutus, brimming with joy, allowed those who had had a part in the slaughter to take their pick of the spoils of the dead;

quem ex uinculis Bruti eripui. Illum quidem, pondere compedum detentum, paulo ante in exitu nemoris inter frutices delitere iussi donec aliquos inuenirem quos ad liberandum eum conducerem'. 180

Dubitantibus autem illis utrum uerum diceret, superuenit unus qui eum agnouerat et salutato ipso indicauit sociis quis esset. At illi, nichil haesitantes, ceteros qui aberant ocius conuocauerunt et secuti sunt eum usque ad siluam qua Antigonum delitere praedixerat. Illis denique inter frutices progredientibus, emergit se Brutus cum armatis cateruis et facto 185 impetu ipsos ocius perterritos dirissima caede affecit. Deinde profectus est ad obsidionem et diuisit socios suos per tres turmas praecepitque ut singulae singulas partes castrorum sapienter et sine tumultu adirent nec intromissae caedem alicui ingererent donec ipse cum sua cohorte tentorio regis potitus lituum suum in signum ipsis sonaret. 190

13   Porro, ut ipsos quicquid acturi erant edocuit, confestim mittunt se leniter infra castra et iussas partes adepti promissum signum expectant; quod Brutus eis dare non distulit postquam stetit ante tentorium Pandrasi, quod super omnia adire aestuabat. Quo audito, enses ocius euaginant, cubilia sopitorum ingrediuntur, letiferos ictus ingeminant, et nullam pietatem habentes castra 195 in hunc modum deambulant. Ad gemitus ergo morientium euigilant ceteri uisisque laniatoribus uelut oues ex inprouiso a lupis occupatae stupefacti fiunt; nichil enim praesidii expectabant, cum neque arma capiendi neque fugam faciendi congruum spacium haberent. Discurrunt etiam sine armis inter armatos quo impetus eos ducebat, sed irruentibus ceteris continuo 200 dilacerantur. Qui semiuiuus euadebat, auiditate fugae festinans, scopulis uel fruticibus allidebatur et infelicem animam cum sanguine emittebat. Qui solo clipeo uel quolibet alio tegmine munitus inter eosdem scopulos incidebat, timore mortis celer, sub obscura nocte cadebat; cadenti quoque uel brachia uel crura frangebantur. Cui neutrum horum contingebat, inscius 205 quo fugam faceret, in prope fluentibus fluuiis submergebatur. Vix aliquis illaesus abibat quin aliquo infortunio periclitaretur. Oppidani quoque agnito commilitonum aduentu egressi cladem quae dabatur dupplicabant.

14   At Brutus, tentorium regis ut praedictum est nactus, ipsum uincire et conseruare uacauit; deliberabat enim se magis uita illius quam morte 210 adepturum quod affectauerat. Turma autem quae cum eo erat non cessabat stragem facere; quae partem quam sortita fuerat usque ad internitionem deleuerat. Vt igitur noctem in hunc modum consumpserunt et sub luce aurorae tanta ruina patuit populi, Brutus, maximo gaudio fluctuans, sociis peractae caedis spolia peremptorum iuxta libitum suum tractare permittit; 215

180 deliberandum *E Y*
190 sonaret ipsis *Φ*
194 [adire] *Φ*
196 ergo *OHS:* autem *E:* uero *Φ*
206 fluuiis fluentibus *Φ ut uid. (QYM)*
210 ipsius *S YG*

then he entered the castle with the king, to wait while they distributed their loot. When this had been accomplished, he again fortified the castle, ordered that the corpses be buried and gathered his troops to return to the forest, happy and victorious. Since all were overjoyed at their success, their renowned leader summoned the elders and asked them what they thought he should demand from Pandrasus; since he was in their power, he would agree to any request to secure his release from captivity. They made various proposals for various reasons, some saying that he should ask for part of the kingdom to live in, others for permission to depart and what would be necessary for the journey. For a long time they were undecided until one of them, named Mempricius, rose, asked for silence and addressed the others as follows:

'Why, fathers, do you hesitate over measures which I consider vital for your safety? If you desire lasting peace for yourselves and your descendants, there is only one request you can make, permission to depart. If you wish to grant Pandrasus his life in return for a part of Greece where you can live among the Greeks, you will never enjoy uninterrupted peace as long as the brothers, sons and grandsons of those you slaughtered yesterday dwell among you or near you. They will never forget their fathers' deaths and will hate you forever; they will burn to take revenge on the slightest pretext. Nor do you, with your inferior numbers, have the strength to resist an attack by all their countrymen. If hostilities break out between you, their numbers will increase every day, just as yours will diminish. Therefore I propose that you ask Pandrasus for his eldest daughter, named Innogin, to marry our leader, and also gold, silver, ships, corn and everything necessary for our journey; if he is amenable, let us set sail for foreign lands with his permission'.

15　When he had finished making these and other proposals, the whole assembly agreed, saying that Pandrasus should be brought forward and condemned to a frightful death if he did not submit to this request. He was immediately produced, and placed on a throne higher than the rest. On being informed of the tortures he faced if he did not do their bidding, he replied:

'Since the gods have turned against me and delivered myself and my brother Antigonus into your hands, I must agree to your requests, or otherwise we shall lose our lives, which you can give or take away at will, if I refuse you. I consider nothing to be better or sweeter than life, so you should not be surprised if I am prepared to secure it at the cost of material goods. Though I am reluctant to agree to your terms, yet I derive some consolation from marrying my daughter to a young man of such prowess, whose descent from the race of Priam and Anchises is proclaimed both by his inherent nobility and by the reputation

deinde cum rege oppidum ingreditur, expectaturus dum gazas distribuerent. Quibus impertitis, muniuit iterum castellum et cadauera dari sepulturae praecepit, resociatisque cateruis ad nemora cum laeta remeauit uictoria. Quae ut tantam laeticiam animis cunctorum infudit, inclitus dux maiores natu conuocauit quaesiuitque ab illis quid a Pandraso petendum laudarent; 220 nam cum in potestate eorum positus esset, per omnia peticioni ipsorum adquiesceret si liber abire sineretur. Mox illi, diuersis affectibus diuersa cupientes, pars partem regni ad inhabitandum petere hortatur, pars uero licentiam abeundi et ea quae itineri suo utilia forent. Cumque diu in ambiguo extitissent, surrexit unus ex illis, Mempricius nomine, rogatoque 225 silentio audientibus ceteris ait:

'Vt quid haesitatis, patres, in his quae saluti uestrae reor esse habenda? Vnum petendum est, licentia uidelicet eundi, si uobis posterisque uestris aeternam pacem habere desideraueritis. Nam si eo pacto uitam concesseritis Pandraso ut per eum partem Graeciae adepti inter Danaos 230 manere uelitis, nunquam diuturna pace fruemini dum fratres et filii et nepotes eorum quibus hesternam intulistis stragem uobis uel inmixti uel uicini fuerint. Semper enim necis parentum suorum memores, aeterno uos habebunt odio; quibusque etiam nugis incitati, uindictam sumere nitentur. Nec uobis, pauciorem turbam habentibus, ea uis est ut tot ciuium 235 inquietationi resistere queatis. Quod si decertatio inter uos accesserit, numerus eorum cotidie augebitur, uester uero minuetur. Laudo igitur ut petatis ab illo filiam suam primogenitam, quam Innogin uocant, ad opus ducis nostri, et cum ea aurum et argentum, naues et frumentum et quodcunque itineri nostro necessarium erit; et si id impetrare poterimus, 240 licentia sua alias nationes petamus'.

15 Vt his et consimilibus finem dicendi fecit, acquieuit ei tota multitudo atque suasit ut Pandrasus in medium adduceretur et nisi huic peticioni faueret saeuissima morte dampnaretur. Nec mora, adductus est et in cathedra celsior ceteris positus. Edoctus quoque quibus tormentis affligendus erat 245 nisi faceret quae iubebatur, in hunc modum respondit:

'Quoniam aduersi dii me meumque fratrem Antigonum in manus uestras tradiderunt, parendum est peticioni uestrae, ne uitam, quae nobis arbitrio uestro et adimi et concedi potest, si repulsam passi fueritis amittamus. Nichil enim uita praestantius, nichil iocundius censeo, nec 250 est mirandum si illam exteris rebus redimere uelim. Quamquam tamen inuitus praeceptis uestris oboediam, solatium habere uideor quia filiam meam tantae probitatis adolescenti daturus sum, quem ex genere Priami et Anchisae creatum et nobilitas quae in ipso pullulat et fama nobis

216 expecturus *OH:* expectans *SE*
216 gaza *Φ ut uid. (sic Q:* gazam *G)*
221 ipsorum *Δ M:* eorum *QYG*
227 *de* habenda *cf. Introd.*
229 desideratis *Φ*
232 hesternam (est- *G) Y²G:* extremam *M:* externam *cett. (cf. Introd.)*
247 Antigonum *Y, auctorem ut uid. corrigens (cf. 'Errori' 40-41):* Anacletum *cett.*

we know so well. Who else, when the exiles from Troy were enslaved by so many mighty chiefs, could have freed them from their bonds? Who could have stood up to the king of the Greeks with them, challenging his great army with so small a force and, after battle was joined, leading off their king in chains? Because this fine young man has resisted me so stoutly, I give him my daughter Innogin. I also give you gold and silver, ships, corn, wine and oil and whatever you say is necessary for your journey. Should you change your minds and decide to stay among the Greeks, I grant you a third of my kingdom to live in; otherwise, I shall fulfil my promises and, as a further guarantee, I shall remain as your hostage until everything is complete'.

This agreement reached, envoys were despatched to collect ships from all the shores of Greece. When the ships had been assembled, they numbered three hundred and twenty-four and were loaded with all kinds of grain; Brutus married the king's daughter; gold and silver was presented to each man according to his rank. When all this had been done, the king was freed from prison and favourable winds carried the Trojans out of his reach. Innogin stood at the high stern, frequently swooning into Brutus' arms; weeping and sobbing, she lamented at leaving behind her parents and country, and kept her gaze fixed on the coastline until it faded from view. Brutus soothed her with endearments, giving her sweet embraces and sweet kisses, and did not cease until she had fallen asleep, worn out by her
16   tears. Meanwhile following winds carried them along for two days and a single night until they landed at an island called Leogetia, which had long before been laid waste by raiding pirates and was now uninhabited. Brutus sent three hundred armed men into the interior to find out what lived there; having met no one, they killed wild beasts of various kinds that they found in the glades and woods. They came to an abandoned city in which they discovered a temple to Diana. In it was a statue of the goddess which answered questions posed to it. Loaded with the prey they had found, the scouts returned to the ships and described to their comrades the lie of the land and the abandoned city. They suggested that their leader should visit the temple, offer sacrifices and ask the local goddess what land could offer them a safe and sure haven; when all agreed, Brutus took the augur Gerio and twelve elders and visited the temple with everything necessary for a sacrifice. When they arrived, they bound garlands round their foreheads and, at the temple's entrance, set up according to hallowed practice three altars to three gods, Jupiter, Mercury and Diana; to each they made a special offering. Brutus himself, standing before Diana's altar and holding in his right hand a sacrificial goblet filled with wine and the blood of a white hind, raised his eyes to her statue and broke the silence as follows:

'Mighty goddess of the forest, terror of woodland boars,
    you who can travel through celestial orbits

cognita declarat. Quis etenim alter exules Troiae, in seruitutem tot et   255
tantorum principum positos, eorumdem uinculis eriperet? quis cum illis
regi Graecorum resisteret aut cum tam paucis tantam armatorum copiam
proelio prouocaret initoque congressu regem eorum uinctum duceret?
Quia ergo tantus iuuenis tanta probitate michi resistere potuit, do ei
filiam meam Innogin; do etiam aurum et argentum, naues, frumentum   260
uinum et oleum, et quicquid itineri eius necessarium esse dixeritis. Et si a
proposito uestro diuertentes cum Graecis commanere uolueritis, tertiam
regni mei partem uobis ad inhabitandum concedo; sin autem, promissa
mea effectu prosequar, et ut securiores sitis uobis quasi obses manebo
dum omnia perficiam'.   265

Conuentione itaque facta, diriguntur legati per uniuersa Graeciae litora
colligere naues. Quae ut collectae fuerunt, trecentae uiginti quatuor numero
praesentantur, omni genere farris onerantur; filia Bruto maritatur; quisque
prout dignitas expetebat auro et argento donatur. Peractis cunctis, rex liber
a carcere, Troes ab eius potestate secundis uentis abscedunt. At Innogin, in   270
excelsa puppi stans, saepius inter brachia Bruti in extasi collabitur; fusis
quoque cum singultu lacrimis, parentes ac patriam deserere conqueritur, nec
oculos a litore auertit dum litora oculis patuerunt. Quam Brutus blandiciis
mitigans nunc dulces amplexus, nunc dulcia basia innectit, nec coeptis suis
16 desistit donec fletu fatigata sopori summittitur. Inter haec et alia duobus   275
diebus et una nocte prospero uentorum flatu cucurrerunt applicueruntque
in quandam insulam uocatam Leogetia, quae antiquitus ab incursione
piratarum uastata a nemine inhabitabatur. In illam ergo misit Brutus trecentos
armatos ad explorandum quid inhabitaret; qui neminem reperientes feras
diuersi generis infra saltus ac nemora inuentas caede afficiunt. Venerunt ad   280
quandam ciuitatem desertam in qua templum Dianae reppererunt. In eodem
imago deae responsa dabat si forte ab aliquo peteretur. Onerati tandem
reperta uenatione, reuertuntur ad naues suas patriaeque situm et ciuitatem
consociis praedicant. Suggerunt duci templum adire atque litatis donis a
numine loci inquirere quae patria eis sedem certae mansionis praeberet;   285
communicatoque omnium assensu, assumpsit Brutus secum Gerionem
augurem et duodecim maiores natu petiuitque templum cum omnibus quae
ad sacrificium necessaria erant. Quo ubi uentum est, circundati timpora
uittis ante aditum ueterrimo ritu tribus diis, Ioui uidelicet et Mercurio nec
non et Dianae, tres focos statuerunt; singulis singula libamina dederunt.   290
Ipse Brutus ante aram deae, uas sacrificii plenum uino et sanguine candidae
ceruae dextra tenens, erecto uultu ad effigiem numinis silentium in haec
uerba dissoluit:

'Diua potens nemorum, terror siluestribus apris,
  cui licet amfractus ire per aethereos   295

264 et *E Φ: om. OHS*
274 dulces ... dulcia *suspectum*
276 cucurrerunt *54², 15:* concurrerunt *HSE QYG:* concurrunt *O M*
288 circundati *1844:* circundatus *Ω (cf. Introd.)*
289 aditum *an pro* adytum *(1587) ?*

and through the halls of death, unfold your earthly powers
  and say in which lands you wish us to dwell.
Prophesy a sure home where I can worship you forever,
  and where I can dedicate to you temples and choirs of virgins'.

After repeating this nine times and four times circling the altar, he poured the wine he held into its flames, lay down on the skin of the hind, which he had spread before the altar, and, closing his eyes, fell asleep at last. It was around the third hour of the night, when our repose is sweetest. Then the goddess seemed to stand before him and address him as follows:

'Brutus, to the west, beyond the kingdoms of Gaul,
  lies an island of the ocean, surrounded by the sea;
an island of the ocean, where giants once lived,
  but now it is deserted and waiting for your people.
Sail to it; it will be your home for ever.
  It will furnish your children with a new Troy.
From your descendants will arise kings, who
  will be masters of the whole world'.

17 Awakened by this vision, the Trojan leader did not know whether he had experienced a dream, or the goddess had, with her own voice, foretold the land to which he would sail. At length he called his companions and recounted what had happened to him as he slept. They were filled with joy, urging him to return to the ships and, as soon as the wind was favourable, to sail with all speed towards the west and seek the land promised by the goddess. They returned at once to their comrades and put to sea. They ploughed the waves for thirty days until they came to Africa, still unsure where to direct the ships' prows. Next they came to the altars of the Philistines and the lake of Salinae and sailed between Russicada and the mountains of Azara. There they were attacked by pirates and put in great danger; but the Trojans beat them off and took possession of their rich spoils.

Next they passed the river Malva and landed in Mauritania. Lack of food and water forced them to leave the ships, draw up their forces and ravage the land from end to end. With the ships restocked, they sailed to the Pillars of Hercules and saw there the sea monsters called the Sirens, which swam around their ships and almost sank them; but they somehow escaped and came to the Tyrrhenian sea. There on the shore they found four generations descended from the Trojan exiles who had accompanied Antenor when he fled. Their leader was called Corineus, a just man and a good advisor, of great character and boldness; if he met a giant, Corineus could overcome him at once, as if he were fighting a child. When the Trojans realised their common ancestry, they took Corineus and his people with them. Later they were called Cornish after their chief and in every battle proved more helpful to Brutus than the rest. Next they came to Aquitaine and

infernasque domos, terrestria iura reuolue
et dic quas terras nos habitare uelis.
Dic certam sedem qua te uenerabor in aeuum,
qua tibi uirgineis templa dicabo choris'.

Haec ubi nouies dixit, circuiuit aram quater fuditque uinum quod tenebat 300
in foco atque procubuit super pellem ceruae, quam ante aram extenderat,
inuitatoque sompno tandem obdormiuit. Erat tunc quasi tercia hora noctis,
qua dulciore sopore mortales premuntur. Tunc uisum est illi deam astare
ante ipsum et sese in hunc modum affari:

'Brute, sub occasu solis trans Gallica regna   305
insula in occeano est undique clausa mari;
insula in occeano est habitata gigantibus olim,
nunc deserta quidem, gentibus apta tuis.
Hanc pete; namque tibi sedes erit illa perhennis.
Hic fiet natis altera Troia tuis.   310
Hic de prole tua reges nascentur, et ipsis
tocius terrae subditus orbis erit'.

17 Tali uisione expergefactus dux in dubio mansit an sompnus fuerat quem
uidit an dea uiua uoce praedixerat patriam quam aditurus erat. Vocatis
tandem sociis, indicauit per ordinem quod sibi dormienti contigerat. At illi, 315
maximo gaudio fluctuantes, hortantur ut ad naues repedent et dum uentus
secundus esset citissimis uelis uersus occasum eant ad inquirendum quod
diua spoponderat. Nec mora, remeant ad socios altumque ingrediuntur.
Sulcantes aequora, cursu triginta dierum uenerunt ad Affricam, nescii
adhuc quorsum proras uerterent. Deinde uenerunt ad aras Philistinorum et 320
ad lacum Salinarum et nauigauerunt inter Russicadam et montes Azarae. Ibi
ab incursione piratarum maximum passi sunt periculum; uictoriam tamen
adepti, spoliis eorum et rapinis ditati sunt.

Porro, flumen Maluae transeuntes, applicuerunt in Mauritaniam. Deinde,
penuria cibi et potus coacti, egressi sunt ex nauibus et dispositis turmis 325
uastauerunt patriam a fine usque ad finem. Refertis uero nauibus, petierunt
columpnas Herculis, ubi apparuerunt eis monstra maris uocata Sirenes, quae
ambiendo naues fere ipsas obruerunt; utcumque tamen elapsi, uenerunt
ad Tyrrenum aequor. Ibi iuxta littora inuenerunt quatuor generationes de
exulibus Troiae ortas quae Antenoris fugam comitatae erant. Erat eorum 330
dux Corineus dictus, uir modestus, consilii optimus, magnae uirtutis et
audaciae; qui si cum aliquo gigante congressum faceret, ilico obruebat
eum ac si cum puero contenderet. Agnita itaque ueteris originis prosapia,
associauerunt illum sibi nec non et populum cui praesidebat. Hic, de nomine
ducis postmodum Cornubiensis uocatus, Bruto in omni decertatione prae 335
ceteris auxilium praestabat. Deinde uenerunt ad Aequitaniam et hostium

302 inuitatoque *Φ*: inuitato *Δ*
335 postmodum *E Φ*: postmodo *OHS*

entered the estuary of the Loire, where they dropped anchor. They stayed there for seven days, scouting out the lie of the land.

18   At that time Aquitaine was ruled by Goffarius Pictus, king of the land; when he heard reports of a foreign people landing in his country with a large fleet, he sent envoys to find out whether they brought peace or war. As they headed for the ships, the envoys met Corineus, who had gone out at the head of two hundred men to hunt in the woods. They approached, asking who had given him the right to enter the king's glades and kill his beasts; for it had long been unlawful for anyone to bring them down without royal permission. When Corineus answered that no one should need permission to hunt, one of them, named Imbertus, rushed forward, drew his bow and fired an arrow at him. Corineus ducked, fell on Imbertus and brained him with the very bow Imbertus had in his hands. The others, having only escaped his hands with difficulty, fled and reported the killing of their comrade to the king. Filled with sorrow, the leader of the Poitevins assembled a great army to avenge the murder of his messenger. Hearing that Goffarius was coming, Brutus fortified his ships and, ordering the women and children to remain on board, set off to meet the opposing army with a force made up of all the able-bodied men. When at last battle was joined, there was fierce fighting on both sides; after they had spent most of the day amid such carnage, Corineus was ashamed that the Aquitanians were resisting so valiantly and cheating the Trojans of victory. Summoning his courage, he shifted his troops to the right wing, closed them up and made a swift charge against the enemy; the dense formation of his men allowed him to get among the enemy, where he cut them down without respite until he had broken their ranks and put them all to flight. Having lost his sword, he chanced on an axe, with which he sliced down the middle anyone he met. Corineus' boldness and courage amazed Brutus and his comrades, and even the enemy. Brandishing his axe among the fleeing cohorts, he shouted these menacing words:

'Cowards, sluggards, where are you fleeing to? Come back, come back and face Corineus. For shame! Do you in your thousands flee from one man? Yet take solace for your flight from the fact that you flee before me, who have so often forced Tyrrhenian giants to run and sent them down to hell three or four at a time.'

In response to these taunts, an earl named Suhardus turned to attack him with three hundred knights. Corineus parried Suhardus' blow with his shield, then, remembering the axe in his hand, raised it

Ligeris ingressi anchoras fixerunt. Morati sunt ibi septem diebus situmque regni explorauerunt.

18   Regnabat tunc in Aequitania Goffarius Pictus, eiusdem patriae rex; cui ut fama indicauit externam gentem cum magna classe in fines regni 340 sui applicuisse, misit legatos ad inquirendum utrum pacem uel guerram aduectasset. Nuncii ergo classem petentes obuiauerunt Corineo, egresso iam cum ducentis uiris ut infra nemora uenationem adquireret. Mox allocuti eum quaerunt cuius licentia saltus regis ingressus feras necaret; statutum enim ab antiquo fuerat neminem sine principis iussu eas debere prosternere. 345 Quibus cum Corineus respondisset licentiam huius rei nequaquam debere haberi, irruit unus ex illis, Imbertus nomine, et curuato arcu sagittam in ipsum direxit. Vitauit eam Corineus cucurritque ocius in Imbertum et arcu quem tenebat caput ei in frusta contriuit. Diffugierunt ergo ceteri, uix ex manibus eius elapsi, atque Goffario necem socii nuntiauerunt. Contristatus 350 ilico dux Pictauensium collegit exercitum grandem ut in ipsos mortem nuntii sui uindicaret. At Brutus, diuulgato eius aduentu, naues munit, mulieres et paruulos infra ipsas iubet manere, ipse cum tota multitudine cui uigor florebat obuius exercitui progreditur. Inito tandem certamine, dira pugna utrobique committitur; et cum multum diei in agendo caedem 355 consumpsissent, puduit Corineum Aequitanos tam audacter resistere nec Troianos cum triumpho insistere. Vnde resumpta audatia seuocauit suos in dexteram partem proelii et facto agmine celerem impetum in hostes fecit; et ut infra eorundem turmas sese densa acie intromisit, non cessauit hostes prosternere donec penetrata cohorte cunctos in fugam coegit. Fortuna 360 ei amisso gladio bipennem amministrauerat, cum qua quemcumque attingebat a summo usque ad imum disiungebat. Miratur Brutus, mirantur socii, mirantur etiam hostes audaciam uiri et uirtutem. Qui bipennem inter fugientes cohortes librans timorem non minimum cum his uerbis inferebat: 365

'Quo fugitis timidi, quo fugitis segnes? Reuertimini, o reuertimini et congressum cum Corineo facite. Proh pudor! Tot milia me solum diffugitis? At tamen habetote solatium fugae uestrae quod ego uos insequor, qui tociens soleo Tyrrenos gigantes in fugam propellere, qui ternos atque quaternos ad Tartara detrudere'. 370

Ad haec uerba illius reuertitur quidam consul, uocabulo Suhardus, cum trecentis militibus et impetum fecit in eum. Cuius ictum Corineus praetenso clipeo excipiens non oblitus est bipennis quam tenebat sed erecta illa

349 conscidit *QG²M:* concidit *YG¹*
349 *de* Diffugierunt *cf. Introd.*
350 atque *O Φ: om. HS:* et *E*
361 ei am. gl. bip. amm. *Φ:* am. gl. ei bip. amm. *HSE:* ei bip. am. amm. gl. *O*
364 *ante* minimum *redit* C
369-70 qui ternos *Δ:* et ternos *Φ*
371 nomine *Φ*
373 est oblitus *Φ*

and struck down through his helmet, cutting him completely in two. Next he swiftly rushed on the others, wielding his axe to slaughter them horribly, and, as he ran back and forth, he neither shrank from receiving blows nor ceased cutting down the enemy. He hacked off one man's arm and hand, sliced another's shoulders from his body, beheaded another with one stroke and cut another man's legs out from under him. All kept charging at him alone and he alone met every attacker. At this spectacle Brutus could not contain his love for the man and ran to his aid with a single company. Then shouts arose from the contending armies, blows were redoubled and there was terrible slaughter on both sides. Soon the Trojans were victorious and put Goffarius and his Poitevins to flight. Having escaped only with difficulty, the king visited various parts of Gaul to obtain help from his relatives and friends. At that time there were twelve kings in Gaul, who exercised equal authority over the whole country; they received Goffarius warmly and promised to unite to drive off the foreigners who had landed in Aquitaine.

19   Brutus meanwhile, cheered by his victory, awarded the spoils of the dead to his comrades, reordered their ranks and marched through the country with the aim of ravaging it completely and loading all its wealth on his ships. He lit fires to burn down all the cities, carrying off their hidden treasures, and laid waste the fields, slaughtering townsfolk and country-dwellers alike in an effort to wipe out those unhappy people to the last man. When he had ravaged almost all Aquitaine in this way, he came to the future site of the city of Tours, which, according to Homer, Brutus himself later built on that spot. Having discovered this suitable place of refuge, he laid out a camp there, to which he could retire if it became necessary. He was apprehensive about the arrival of Goffarius, who was near by with the kings and princes of Gaul and a huge armed force preparing to fight. Once his camp was finished, for two days Brutus waited there for Goffarius, trusting in his own resourcefulness and the boldness of the young men he commanded.

20   Hearing of the Trojans' presence, Goffarius marched day and night until he was close enough to see Brutus' camp. After casting a scornful gaze at it and smiling for a short time, he burst out:

'Oh cruel destiny! These dishonoured exiles have even made a camp in my kingdom. To arms, men, to arms, close your ranks and advance. We shall soon capture these effeminates as if they were sheep, and make them slaves in our country'.

The men he had brought with him all donned their armour, formed twelve columns and advanced on the enemy. Opposite them, Brutus also formed up his troops and advanced valiantly, but carefully instructed them what to do,

percussit eum in summitatem galeae percussumque a summo usque ad imum
in ambas partes dissecuit. Sed et confestim irruens in ceteros bipennem 375
rotat, stragem acerrimam facit, et nunc hac nunc illac discurrens nec ictus
recipere diffugit nec hostes prosternere quiescit. Huic brachium cum manu
amputat, illi scapulas a corpore separat, alii caput uno ictu truncat, alteri
crura a summo dissecat. Omnes in illum solum et ipse solus in omnes
irruebat. Quod Brutus aspiciens, motus amore uiri, cucurrit cum una turma 380
ut ei auxilium subuectaret. Tunc oritur clamor inter diuersas gentes, tunc
crebri ictus inferuntur, tunc in utraque parte fit caedes dirissima. Nec mora,
uictoria potiuntur Troes et regem Goffarium cum Pictauensibus suis in fugam
propellunt. Qui uix euadens partes Galliarum adiuit ut a cognatis et notis
succursum haberet. Erant tunc temporis duodecim reges in Gallia, quorum 385
regimine tota patria pari dignitate regebatur; qui benigne suscipientes eum
promittunt sese unanimiter expulsuros ex finibus Aequitaniae externam
gentem quae aduenerat.

19   At Brutus, ob praedictam uictoriam laetus, peremptorum spoliis socios
ditat, ditatos autem iterum in turmas resociat, resociatos per patriam ducit, 390
affectans eam penitus desolare et naues suas uniuersis diuiciis replere.
Accumulato igitur igne, ciuitates undique incendit, absconditas quoque opes
ab eisdem extrahit, agros etiam depopulat, stragem miserandam ciuibus
atque plebanis infert, uolens infelicem gentem usque ad unum delere. Ac
dum tali clade totius fere Aequitaniae partes affecisset, uenit ad locum ubi 395
nunc est ciuitas Turonorum, quam ut Omerus testatur ipse postmodum
construxit. Vt igitur loca conuenientia refugio inspexit, metatus est ibi
castra sua ut si opus accidisset sese infra ipsa reciperet. Vrgebatur namque
timore propter aduentum Goffarii, qui cum regibus et principibus Galliae
et maxima armatorum copia prope eundem locum aduenerat ut cum illo 400
bellum committeret. Peractis deinde castris, expectauit ibi biduo Goffarium,
confidens in prudentia sua atque audatia iuuentutis cui praesidebat.

20   Goffarius ergo, audita ibidem praesentia Troianorum, nec noctu nec
die cessauit incedere donec castra Bruti prope aspexit. Toruo igitur lumine
intuens, paulisper subridens in haec uerba erupit: 405

'Proh fatum triste! Castra etiam sua in regno meo fecerunt ignobiles
exules. Armate uos, uiri, armate et per densatas turmas incedite. Nulla
mora erit quin semimares istos uelut oues capiemus atque captos per
regna nostra mancipabimus'.

Armauerunt itaque se omnes quos secum adduxerat et per duodena agmina 410
statuti uersus hostes suos incedunt. Contra quos Brutus etiam dispositis
cateruis non muliebriter graditur sed turmas suas quid acturae essent

374 summitate *E QY*
376 stragemque *E Y*
382 durissima *H G, sed cf. § 21.473*
392 [opes] *Φ ut uid. (QY: post* eisdem *M: recte G)*
393 depopulat *Δ QYM (sic §§ 42.163, 146.80, codd. praeter G):* depopulatur *C²(?) G*
394 Ac *OCHS QYG:* At *E M (cf. §§ 155.262, 281, 158.434, 166.124)*
407 densas *SE Q*

telling them when to attack and when to defend. When the armies met, success at first went to the Trojans, who inflicted heavy losses on their opponents. Almost two thousand of the latter fell; and in their amazement the rest were all but routed. However, superior numbers usually secure victory. The Gauls enjoyed a thirty-to-one superiority, and, although driven back at first, eventually rallied and attacked the Trojans from all sides, cutting them down and forcing them into their camp. Once victorious, they besieged them there, intending to remain until the besieged either allowed chains to be placed on their necks or, worn down by protracted hunger, were dying a miserable death. That night Corineus laid a plan before Brutus: he would go out that night by a side-road and hide in a nearby wood until dawn; at daybreak Brutus was to come out to face the enemy, whilst he and his cohort would attack from the rear and slaughter them. Brutus was delighted with Corineus' plan; so with three thousand men he cunningly sallied out, as he had said, and found a hiding-place in the wood. When day dawned, Brutus drew up his forces, opened the gates and came out to fight. The Gauls ran up at once and formed to attack him. Many thousands fell on both sides as they exchanged blows, giving quarter to none. Among the Trojans was Brutus' nephew, named Turnus, the strongest and boldest of them, except for Corineus. Armed only with his sword, he accounted for six hundred men, but all too soon he was killed by the onrushing Gauls. The city of Tours, where he was buried, took its name from him. When both armies were bitterly engaged, Corineus unexpectedly arrived and swiftly took the enemy in the rear. At this Brutus' men fought all the more boldly, striving to cut down the enemy. The Gauls were astonished by the mere shouts of Corineus' men at their backs and, overestimating their numbers, hurried to abandon the field of battle. The Trojans pursued, hacking and killing, and did not cease until they had secured victory. Brutus was most satisfied with this triumph, but anxious because his numbers were diminishing every day, whilst those of the Gauls grew continually. At last, doubting the wisdom of a protracted struggle, he decided to board ship while the majority of his companions were unharmed and his victory still unsullied, and to sail for the island vouchsafed to him by divine prophecy. With his comrades' agreement, he returned to his fleet, loaded it with all the riches he had acquired and then went on board. Favourable winds brought him to the promised isle, where he came ashore at Totnes.

21   The island was at that time called Albion; it had no inhabitants save for a few giants. The choice position of this pleasant land, its numerous rivers, good for fishing,

sapienter docens qualiter debeant et inuadere et resistere edicit. Vt ergo congressum inceperunt, praeualuerunt in initio Troes et caedem acerrimam ex hostibus faciunt. Ceciderunt namque ex eis fere duo milia hominum; 415 unde ceteri stupefacti fere in fugam uersi fuerunt. Sed ubi maior numerus hominum habundat, euenire solet triumphum accedere. Galli igitur, quoniam tricies plures erant ceteris, quamquam primo oppressi fuerant, tandem tamen resociati impetum fecerunt undique in Troas et illata strage ipsos castra ingredi coegerunt. Victoriam itaque adepti, obsederunt eos 420 infra castra, meditantes se nequaquam prius illinc abscedere antequam ipsi inclusi uel colla uincienda catenis traderent uel longa fame afflicti saeuissima morte tormentarentur. Sequenti interea nocte Corineus iniuit consilium cum Bruto: se uelle scilicet per quaedam diuorcia in eadem nocte egredi et infra nemus quod prope fuerat usque ad diem delitere; et dum 425 Brutus cum diluculo egressus cum hostibus dimicaret, ipse cum cohorte sua a dorso superueniret et facto impetu stragem ingereret. Placuit itaque Bruto sententia Corinei; qui ut praedixerat callide egressus est cum tribus milibus occultaque nemorum petiuit. Adueniente autem postera die, statuit Brutus suos per turmas et apertis castris pugnaturus egreditur. Occurrunt 430 igitur confestim Galli et facto agmine cum ipso congrediuntur. Concidunt ilico in utraque parte multa milia uirorum dum mutua uulnera dantur, quia nullus aduersario suo parcebat. Erat ibi quidam Tros nomine Turnus, Bruti nepos, quo forcior siue audatior nullus excepto Corineo aderat. Hic solus solo gladio suo sexcentos uiros peremit, sed ab irruentibus Gallis cicius 435 quam debuisset interfectus est. De nomine ipsius praedicta ciuitas Turonis uocabulum nacta est, quia ibidem sepultus fuit. Cum igitur utraeque turmae acrius pugnarent, superuenit ex inprouiso Corineus et a tergo hostes celeriter inuasit. Audatiores proinde insurgentes ceteri ex altera parte incumbunt stragemque facere contendunt. Itaque Galli solo clamore Corineiensium, 440 qui a tergo inuaserant, stupefacti sunt et arbitrantes plures aduenisse quam aduenerant campum deserere festinant. Quos Troes usque ferientes insequuntur, insequendo uero prosternunt, nec prosternere cessauerunt donec uictoriam habuerunt. Brutus itaque, licet tantus triumphus illi maximum intulisset gaudium, dolore tamen angebatur quia numerus suorum 445 cotidie minuebatur, Gallorum autem semper multiplicabatur. In dubio tandem existens utrum diutius eos oppugnaret, praeelegit naues suas salua adhuc maiori parte sociorum nec non et reuerentia uictoriae adire atque insulam quam ei diuinus praedixerat monitus exigere. Nec plura, petiuit suorum assensu classem suam et repleuit eam ex uniuersis diuiciis quas 450 acquisiuerat et ipsam ingressus est. Prosperis quoque uentis promissam insulam exigens, in Totonesio littore applicuit.

21   Erat tunc nomen insulae Albion; quae a nemine, exceptis paucis gigantibus, inhabitabatur. Amoeno tamen situ locorum et copia piscosorum

---

433 [suo] *Φ, sed cf. §§ 123.130, 141.577*
449 *de exigere cf. Introd.*
449 Nec mora *G ut solet noster*

and its woods led Brutus and his companions to want to settle there. After exploring its various territories and driving off to mountain caves any giants they came upon, they portioned out the land, at their leader's invitation, and began to till the fields and build homes so that, in a short time, the country appeared to have been occupied for many years. Brutus named the island Britain after himself and called his followers Britons. He wanted to be remembered for ever for giving them his name. For this reason the language of his people, previously known as Trojan or 'crooked Greek', was henceforth called British. Corineus followed his leader's example by similarly calling the area of the kingdom allotted to him Corineia and his people Corineians, after himself. He could have had his pick of the provinces before any other settler, but preferred the region now called Cornwall, either after Britain's horn or through a corruption of the name Corineia. He loved to fight giants, and there were more of them to be found there than in any of the districts divided amongst his companions. One of these Cornish giants was a monster called Goemagog, twelve cubits tall and so strong that he could loosen and uproot an oak tree as if it were a twig of hazel. One day when Brutus was holding a feast for the gods at the port where he had landed, Goemagog arrived with twenty giants and inflicted terrible carnage on the Britons. Eventually. as more Britons flocked to their aid, they beat the giants and killed them all except Goemagog. Brutus had ordered that his life be spared because he wanted to see him wrestle with Corineus, who was always most eager to fight giants. Overjoyed, Corineus hitched up his tunic, threw his weapons aside and challenged the giant to wrestle. The bout began, both Corineus and the giant closing to encircle each other with their arms, whilst their panting breath disturbed the air. Goemagog swiftly gripped Corineus with all his strength and broke three of his ribs, two on the right side and one on the left. This goaded Corineus to fury and, summoning all his might, he lifted the giant on his shoulders and ran to the nearby shore as fast as his burden would allow. Coming to the edge of a high cliff, he hurled over the fearful monster he bore on his shoulders, casting him into the sea. As he fell down the rocky crag, the giant was torn into a thousand pieces and stained the sea red with his blood. The place took its name from the giant's plunge and is still called Goemagog's Leap.

22 Once the kingdom had been divided up, Brutus desired to build a city. To achieve his aim, he toured the whole extent of the country to find a suitable

fluminum nemoribusque praeelecta, affectum habitandi Bruto sociisque 455
inferebat. Peragratis ergo quibusque prouinciis, repertos gigantes ad
cauernas montium fugant, patriam donante duce sorciuntur, agros incipiunt
colere, domos aedificare, ita ut in breui tempore terram ab aeuo inhabitatam
censeres. Denique Brutus de nomine suo insulam Britanniam appellat
sociosque suos Britones. Volebat enim ex diriuatione nominis memoriam 460
habere perpetuam. Vnde postmodum loquela gentis, quae prius Troiana
siue curuum Graecum nuncupabatur, dicta fuit Britannica. At Corineus
portionem regni quae sorti suae cesserat ab appellatione etiam sui nominis
Corineiam uocat, populum quoque suum Corineiensem, exemplum ducis
insecutus. Qui cum prae omnibus qui aduenerant electionem prouinciarum 465
posset habere, maluit regionem illam quae nunc uel a cornu Britanniae uel per
corruptionem praedicti nominis Cornubia appellatur. Delectabat enim eum
contra gigantes dimicare, quorum copia plus ibidem habundabat quam in ulla
prouinciarum quae consociis suis distributae fuerant. Erat ibi inter ceteros
detestabilis quidam nomine Goemagog, staturae duodecim cubitorum, 470
qui tantae uirtutis existens quercum semel excussam uelut uirgulam corili
euellebat. Hic quadam die, dum Brutus in portu quo applicuerat festiuum
diem deis celebraret, superuenit cum uiginti gigantibus atque dirissima caede
Britones affecit. At Britones, undique tandem confluentes, praeualuerunt
in eos et omnes praeter Goemagog interfecerunt. Hunc Brutus uiuum 475
reseruari praeceperat, uolens uidere luctationem ipsius et Corinei, qui cum
talibus congredi ultra modum aestuabat. Itaque Corineus, maximo gaudio
fluctuans, succinxit se et abiectis armis ipsum ad luctandum prouocat. Inito
deinde certamine, instat Corineus, instat gigas, et alter alterum uinculis
brachiorum adnectens crebris afflatibus aera uexant. Nec mora, Goemagog, 480
Corineum maximis uiribus astringens, fregit ei tres costas, duas in dextro
latere, unam uero in sinistro. Vnde Corineus compulsus in iram reuocauit
uires suas et imposuit illum humeris suis et quantum uelocitas pro pondere
sinebat ad proxima littora cucurrit. Deinde, summitatem excelsae rupis
nactus, excussit se et praedictum letabile monstrum, quod super humeros 485
suos ferebat, infra mare proiecit. At ille, per abrupta saxorum cadens, in
mille frusta dilaceratus est et fluctus sanguine maculauit. Locus autem
ille, nomen ex praecipitatione gigantis adeptus, Saltus Goemagog usque in
praesentem diem uocatur.

22   Diuiso tandem regno, affectauit Brutus ciuitatem aedificare. Affectum 490
itaque suum exequens, circuiuit tocius patriae situm ut congruum locum

458 in *C Y* (*cf. § 80.191*): *om. cett.*
462 [fuit] *Φ*
463 [etiam] *H G*
464 quoque *OCSE:* -que *H Φ*
472 Brutus dum *Φ*
473 superuenit *54:* ille *add. Ω, unde* illi *H,* illic *15* (*cf. Introd.*)
479 instat ... instat *C¹H:* hinc stat ... instat *C²OSE:* hinc stat ... hinc stat *Φ*
482 in iram compulsus *Φ*
485 letale *S, et deest* letabile *apud DmLBs, sed cf. TLL*
487 mille *Δ:* multa *Φ*
490 Viso *QG*

site. When he came to the river Thames, he walked its banks and found the very spot for his plans. There he founded a city which he called New Troy. It retained this name for a long time until it was eventually corrupted to Trinovantum. When Lud, the brother of Cassibellaunus, who fought against Julius Caesar, came to the throne, he surrounded the city with fine walls and wonderfully built towers; and he commanded that it be named Kaerlud or Lud's city. Afterwards this was the cause of a mighty argument between him and his brother Nennius, who was indignant that Lud wished to suppress the name of Troy in the realm. Since their argument has been discussed at length by the historian Gildas, I have chosen to omit it, lest my poor style should appear to spoil what a great author has described so well.

After Brutus had built his city, he furnished it with dwellers to inhabit it lawfully and established a code under which they could live in peace. At that time the priest Eli was ruling in Judea and the Ark of the Covenant had been captured by the Philistines. The sons of Hector were ruling at Troy after the descendants of Antenor were exiled. In Italy there ruled the third of the Latins, Silvius Aeneas, the son of Aeneas and the uncle of Brutus.

BOOK TWO

23 By his union to Innogin, Brutus had three fine sons, named Locrinus, Albanactus and Kamber. When their father passed away, twenty-four years after his landing, they buried him in the city he had founded and divided up the kingdom of Britain among them, each living in his own region. Locrinus, the first-born, received the central part of the island, afterwards called Loegria after him; Kamber received the region across the river Severn, now known as Wales, which for a long time was named Kambria after him, and for this reason the inhabitants still call themselves Cymry in British; Albanactus, the youngest, received the region known today as Scotland, which he named Albania after himself. For a considerable time they ruled in peace together until Humber the king of the Huns landed in Scotland, killed Albanactus in battle and forced his people to flee to Locrinus.

24 On hearing of this, Locrinus joined his brother Kamber, assembled all the country's forces and marched to meet Humber to the south of the river which now bears his name. In the ensuing battle he put to flight Humber, who fled

inueniret. Perueniens ergo ad Tamensem fluuium, deambulauit littora locumque nactus est proposito suo perspicuum. Condidit itaque ciuitatem ibidem eamque Troiam Nouam uocauit. Ea, hoc nomine multis postmodum temporibus appellata, tandem per corruptionem uocabuli Trinouantum 495 dicta fuit. At postquam Lud frater Cassibellauni, qui cum Iulio Caesare dimicauit, regni gubernaculum adeptus est, cinxit eam nobilissimis muris nec non et turribus mira arte fabricatis; de nomine quoque suo iussit eam dici Kaerlud, id est ciuitas Lud. Vnde postea maxima contentio orta est inter ipsum et Nennium fratrem suum, qui grauiter ferebat illum uelle nomen 500 Troiae in patria sua delere. Quam contentionem quia Gildas hystoricus satis prolixe tractauit, eam praeterire praeelegi, ne id quod tantus scriba tanto stilo perarauit uidear uiliori dictamine maculare.

Postquam igitur praedictus dux praedictam urbem condidit, dedicauit eam ciuibus iure uicturis deditque legem qua pacifice tractarentur. 505 Regnabat tunc in Iudaea Heli sacerdos et archa testamenti capta erat a Philisteis. Regnabant etiam in Troia filii Hectoris, expulsis posteris Antenoris. Regnabat in Italia Siluius Aeneas, Aeneae filius, auunculus Bruti, Latinorum tercius.

LIBER II

23 Cognouerat autem Brutus Innogin uxorem suam et ex ea genuit tres inclitos filios, quibus erant nomina Locrinus, Albanactus, Kamber. Hii, postquam pater in .xx.iiii. anno aduentus sui ab hoc saeculo migrauit, sepelierunt eum infra urbem quam condiderat et diuiserunt regnum Britanniae inter se et secesserunt unusquisque in loco suo. Locrinus, qui primogenitus fuerat, 5 possedit mediam partem insulae, quae postea de nomine suo appellata est Loegria; Kamber autem partem illam quae est ultra Sabrinum flumen, quae nunc Gualia uocatur, quae de nomine ipsius postmodum Kambria multo tempore dicta fuit, unde adhuc gens patriae lingua Britannica sese Kambro appellat; at Albanactus iunior possedit patriam quae lingua nostra 10 his temporibus appellatur Scotia et nomen ei ex nomine suo Albania dedit. Illis deinde concordi pace diu regnantibus, applicuit Humber rex Hunorum in Albaniam et commisso proelio cum Albanacto interfecit eum et gentem patriae ad Locrinum diffugere coegit.

24 Locrinus igitur, audito rumore, associauit sibi Kambrum fratrem 15 suum et collegit totam iuuentutem patriae et iuit obuiam regi Hunorum citra fluuium qui nunc uocatur Humber. Inito ergo congressu, compulit

494 Ea *C:* Ex *cett. mei:* quae *88 (cf. Introd.)*
501 historiographus *Φ*
17 circa *HS QG, sed cf. Introd.*
17 flumen *QY*
17 qui *E G:* quod *OCHS QYM*
17 Humbrum *Φ (cf. Introd.)*

to the river, drowned in its waters and gave it its name. Having gained victory, Locrinus divided the enemy plunder among his comrades, keeping nothing for himself except the gold and silver he found in their ships. He also kept for himself three girls of striking beauty, one of them a king's daughter from Germany, who had been captured along with the other two women when Humber raided their country. Named Estrildis, she was so beautiful that it was difficult to find her like; neither Indian ivory, new fallen snow nor any lily could surpass her white skin. Overcome with love for her, Locrinus wished to share her bed and become her lawful husband. When Corineus discovered this, he was exceedingly angry, as Locrinus had promised to marry his daughter.

He went to the king and, hefting his axe in his right hand, said:

> 'Locrinus, is this how you repay me for all the wounds I suffered in your father's service while he fought unknown peoples—to spurn my daughter and marry some barbarian? You will pay for it, while there is yet strength in this right hand of mine, which has deprived so many giants of life's joys on Tyrrhenian shores'.

Shouting this again and again, he was raising his axe as if to strike the king, when their friends separated them. They calmed Corineus and forced Locrinus to fulfil his promise.

So Locrinus married Corineus' daughter, called Guendoloena, but he did not forget his love for Estrildis, making instead an underground chamber in Trinovantum, where he had her shut up, though on his instructions she was well treated by his household servants. He wanted to make love to her, if only in secret; for in his fear of Corineus he did not dare take her openly, but, as I said, he hid her and visited her for seven whole years, with the knowledge only of his very closest associates. Whenever he wanted to visit her, he pretended that he wished to make a private offering to his gods; and so he easily induced everybody to believe it was true. During this time, Estrildis became pregnant and gave birth to a most beautiful daughter, whom she named Habren. Guendoloena became pregnant too and had a son, who was called Maddan. He was entrusted to his grandfather Corineus and learned his ways.

25   When Corineus eventually died, Locrinus repudiated Guendoloena and made Estrildis queen. Guendoloena, enraged, went to Cornwall, gathered all the forces of the region and began to harry Locrinus. Their armies met in battle by the river Stour, where Locrinus was struck by an arrow and departed from the joys of this life. After his death,

Humbrum in fugam; qui usque ad fluuium diffugiens submersus est infra fluctus et nomen suum flumini reliquit. Locrinus ergo, potitus uictoria, spolia hostium sociis largitur, nichil sibi ipsi retinens praeter aurum et 20 argentum quod infra naues inuenit. Retinuit quoque sibi tres puellas mirae pulcritudinis, quarum prima filia fuerat cuiusdam regis Germaniae quam praedictus Humber cum duabus rapuerat dum patriam uastaret. Erat nomen illius Estrildis, et erat tantae pulcritudinis quod non leuiter reperiebatur quae ei conferri poterat; candorem carnis eius nec Indicum ebur nec nix recenter 25 cadens nec lilia ulla uincebant. Amore itaque illius Locrinus captus uoluit cubilia eius inire ipsamque sibi maritali taeda copulare. Quod cum Corineo compertum esset, indignatus est ultra modum, quoniam Locrinus pactus fuerat sese filiam ipsius ducturum.

   Adiuit ergo regem et bipennem in dextera manu librans illum hoc modo 30 allocutus est:

   'Haeccine rependis michi, Locrine, ob tot uulnera quae in obsequio
   patris tui perpessus sum dum proelia cum ignotis committeret gentibus,
   ut filia mea postposita tete conubio cuiusdam barbarae summitteres?
   Non impune feres dum uigor huic inerit dexterae, quae tot gigantibus per 35
   Tyrrena littora gaudia uitae eripuit'.

Hoc iterum iterumque proclamans, librabat bipennem quasi percussurus eum, cum amici utrorumque sese interposuerunt. Sedato uero Corineo, Locrinum quod pepigerat exequi coegerunt.

   Duxit itaque Locrinus filiam Corinei, Guendoloenam nomine, nec tamen 40 Estrildidis amoris oblitus est sed facto infra urbem Trinouantum subterraneo inclusit eam in ipso familiaribusque suis honorifice seruandam tradidit. Volebat saltem furtiuam uenerem cum illa agere; timore namque Corinei anxiatus, non audebat eam patenter habere sed ut praedictum est occuluit illam frequentauitque septem annis integris, nemine comperiente exceptis 45 illis qui eiusdem familiaritati proximiores fuerant. Nempe quotienscumque adibat illam fingebat se uelle occultum sacrificium diis suis facere; unde quosque falsa credulitate mouebat id ipsum aestimare. Interea grauida facta est Estrildis ediditque filiam mirae pulcritudinis, quam uocauit Habren. Grauida etiam facta est Guendoloena genuitque puerum, cui impositum est 50 nomen Maddan. Hic, Corineo auo suo traditus, documenta ipsius discebat.
25   Subsequente tandem tempore defuncto Corineo deseruit Locrinus Guendoloenam et Estrildidem in reginam erexit. Itaque Guendoloena, ultra modum indignans, adiuit Cornubiam collectaque iuuentute totius regni illius coepit inquietationem Locrino ingerere. Conserto tandem 55 utrorumque exercitu, commiserunt proelium iuxta fluuium Sturam, ubi Locrinus ictu sagittae percussus gaudia uitae amisit. Perempto igitur illo,

25 Indicum (-tum *C*, -cium *E*) *OCSE M:* inclitum *H QYG(?)*
30 Adiit *Φ*
41 Estrildidis *OCS:* Astrildidis *Q:* Eastrildis *Y:* Astrildis *GM*
49 Astarildis *C QM:* Eastrildis *Y:* Astrildis *G*
53 Estrildidem *OE:* Astarildidem *C QM:* Astrildam *H G:* Estrildem *S:* Estrildam *Y*

Guedoloena took the throne, inheriting all the fury of her father. For she ordered Estrildis and her daughter Habren to be thrown into the river now called the Severn, and issued instructions throughout Britain that the river should be named after the girl; she wanted Habren to enjoy immortality since her own husband had been the girl's father. Hence the river is called Habren in British even today, although in the other tongue this has been corrupted to Severn.

26   Guendoloena reigned for fifteen years after the death of Locrinus, who had himself ruled for ten; when she saw that her son Maddan was grown up, she had him crowned king, being herself content with the region of Cornwall for the rest of her days. At that time the prophet Samuel was ruling in Judea, Silvius Aeneas was still alive and Homer was a famous writer and poet. Maddan took a wife, had two sons, Mempricius and Malim, and ruled the kingdom well and in peace for forty years. After his death, a dispute over the kingdom arose between his two sons, since each of the brothers longed to rule the whole island. Eager to realise his ambition, Mempricius held talks with Malim as if he wished to settle matters, but, fired by the torch of betrayal, struck his brother down among the negotiators. Once crowned king of the whole island, Mempricius ruled his subjects with such despotism that he killed almost all the nobility. He also loathed his own family, eliminating by force or treachery anyone he feared might succeed him. He abandoned his wife, by whom he had fathered a fine young man named Ebraucus, and gave himself over to the pleasures of sodomy, rejecting natural desire in favour of unnatural vice. Eventually, in the twentieth year of his reign, he left his hunting-companions to enter a valley, where he was surrounded by a pack of ravening wolves and wretchedly devoured. At that time Saul was ruling in Judea, and Euristeus in Sparta.

27   After Mempricius' death, his son Ebraucus, a man of great size and wonderful courage, succeeded to the throne and ruled for thirty-nine years. He was the first after Brutus to take a fleet to Gaul and subject the land to war, killing its people and oppressing its cities, before returning victorious, laden with huge quantities of gold and silver. Then he built a city north of the Humber, which he called Kaerebrauc, or the city of Ebraucus, after himself. At that time King David was ruling in Judea, Silvius Latinus was king in Italy, and Gad, Nathan and Asaph were prophesying in Israel. Ebraucus also built the city of Dumbarton towards Scotland, the town of Mount Agned, now called Edinburgh, and Mons Dolorosus.

By his twenty wives Ebraucus fathered twenty sons and thirty daughters and ruled the kingdom of Britain with great energy for sixty years. His sons were named Brutus Greenshield, Margadud, Sisillius,

cepit Guendoloena regni gubernaculum, paterna insania furens. Iubet enim Estrildidem et filiam eius Habren praecipitari in fluuium qui nunc Sabrina dicitur fecitque edictum per totam Britanniam ut flumen nomine puellae 60 uocaretur; uolebat etenim honorem aeternitatis illi impendere quia maritus suus eam generauerat. Vnde contigit quod usque in hunc diem appellatum est flumen Britannica lingua Habren, quod per corruptionem nominis alia lingua Sabrina uocatur.

26   Regnauit deinde Guendoloena .xv. annis post interfectionem Locrini, 65 qui decem annis regnauerat; et cum uidisset Maddan filium suum aetate adultum, sceptro regni insigniuit illum, contenta regione Cornubiae dum reliquum uitae deduceret. Tunc Samuel propheta regnabat in Iudaea et Siluius Aeneas uiuebat adhuc et Omerus clarus rethor et poeta habebatur. Insignitus igitur Maddan uxore ex illa genuit duos filios, Mempricium et 70 Malim, regnumque cum pace et diligentia quadraginta annis tractauit. Quo defuncto, discordia orta est inter praedictos fratres propter regnum, quia uterque totam insulam possidere aestuabat. Mempricius ergo, affectum suum perficere desiderans, colloquium iniuit cum Mali quasi concordiam facturus, sed taeda proditionis inflammatus ipsum inter prolocutores 75 interfecit. Deinde, regimen tocius insulae nactus, tantam tyrannidem exercuit in populum quod fere quemque nobilissimum perimebat. Sed et totam progeniem suam exosus quemcumque sibi in regno posse succedere timebat uel ui uel proditione opprimebat. Relicta etiam propria uxore sua, ex qua inclitum iuuenem Ebraucum progenuerat, sese sodomitanae uoluptati 80 dedit, non naturalem uenerem naturali libidini praeferens. Vigesimo tandem regni sui anno, dum uenationem faceret, secessit a sociis suis in quandam conuallem, ubi a multitudine rabiosorum luporum circundatus miserrime deuoratus est. Tunc Saul regnabat in Iudaea et Euristeus in Lacedaemonia.

27   Defuncto itaque Mempricio, Ebraucus filius suus, uir magnae staturae et 85 mirae fortitudinis, regimen Britanniae suscepit et triginta nouem annis tenuit. Hic primus post Brutum classem in partes Galliarum duxit et illato proelio affecit prouincias caede uirorum atque urbium oppressione infinitaque auri et argenti copia ditatus cum uictoria reuersus est. Deinde trans Humbrum condidit ciuitatem, quam de nomine suo uocauit Kaerebrauc, id est ciuitas 90 Ebrauci. Et tunc Dauid rex regnabat in Iudaea et Siluius Latinus in Italia et Gad Nathan et Asaph prophetabant in Israel. Condidit etiam Ebraucus urbem Aldclud uersus Albaniam et oppidum Montis Agned, quod nunc Castellum Puellarum dicitur, et Montem Dolorosum.

      Genuit etiam .xx. filios ex uiginti coniugibus quas habebat nec non 95 et .xxx. filias regnumque Britanniae .lx. annis fortissime tractauit. Erant autem nomina filiorum eius Brutus Viride Scutum, Margadud, Sisillius,

---

59 Estrildidem *OE:* Astarildidem *CS QM:* Astrildam *H:* Astrildidem *G:* Estrildam *Y*
66 cum *YGM:* tunc cum *OCSE:* cum tunc *H:* tunc *Q*
69 adhuc uiuebat *Φ*
80 genuerat *Φ*
81 non *(in- E) hic OE G:* ante naturali *CHS QYM: fort.* naturali ueneri non naturalem libidinem
86 .lx. *Φ*

Regin, Morvid, Bladud, Iagon, Bodloan, Kincar, Spaden, Gaul, Dardan, Eldad, Ivor, Cangu, Hector, Kerin, Rud, Assarach and Buel; the names of his daughters were Gloigin, Innogin, Oudas, Guenlian, Gaurdid, Angarad, Guenlodee, Tangustel, Gorgon, Medlan, Methahel, Ourar, Mailure, Kambreda, Ragan, Gael, Ecub, Nest, Chein, Stadud, Gladus, Ebrein, Blangan, Aballac, Angaes, Galaes (in her day the most beautiful woman in Britain or Gaul), Edra, Anor, Stadiald and Egron. Ebraucus sent all his daughters to Italy to Silvius Alba, who had succeeded Silvius Latinus. There they wedded Trojan nobles, whom the Latin and Sabine women refused to marry. His sons, led by their brother Assaracus, took ship to Germany, where with Silvius Alba's help they subdued the inhabitants and conquered the kingdom.

28   Brutus Greenshield stayed behind with his father, succeeded him and ruled for twelve years. He in turn was succeeded by his own son Leil, a lover of peace and justice, who, while his reign prospered, built in the north of Britain a city named Carlisle after him. At that time Solomon began to build the Lord's temple in Jerusalem, where the queen of Sheba came to hear his wisdom, and in Italy Silvius Alba was succeeded by his son Silvius Epitus. Leil lived on for twenty-five years after ascending the throne, but in the end proved a weak ruler. Because of his neglect civil war suddenly

29   erupted in the kingdom. After Leil, his son Rud Hudibras reigned for thirty-nine years. He suppressed civil strife, pacified his subjects and built Kaerkein, or Canterbury. He also built Kaergueint, or Winchester, and the town of Mons Paladur, now known as Shaftesbury. While the city-wall was being constructed there, an eagle spoke; and if I thought that its prophecies were true, I would not hesitate to set them down here with the rest. At that time Capys, son of Epitus, was reigning and Haggai, Amos, Jehu, Joel and Azariah prophesied.

30   Rud Hudibras was succeeded by his son Bladud, who ruled the kingdom for twenty years. Bladud built the city of Kaerbadum, which is now called Bath, where he made warm baths, suitable for the use of mankind. These he put under the protection of Minerva, placing in her temple undying flames which would never turn to ash, but became lumps of stone whenever they began to fail. At that time Elijah prayed that there should be no rain upon the earth and it did not rain for three years and six months. Bladud was a very clever man, who taught magic throughout the kingdom of Britain. He did not cease to work wonders until he tried to fly high through the air on wings he had made; he fell over the temple of Apollo in Trinovantum and was completely dashed to pieces.

31   After Bladud met his fate, his son Leir became king and for sixty years ruled the country well. He built a city by the river Soar, named after him Kaerleir in British, and Leicester in English. He had no male offspring, only three daughters, called Gonorilla, Regau and Cordeilla. Their father loved them with wonderful affection, especially Cordeilla, the youngest. When

Regin, Moruid, Bladud, Iagon, Bodloan, Kincar, Spaden, Gaul, Dardan,
Eldad, Iuor, Cangu, Hector, Kerin, Rud, Assarach, Buel; nomina autem
filiarum Gloigin, Innogin, Oudas, Guenlian, Gaurdid, Angarad, Guenlodee, 100
Tangustel, Gorgon, Medlan, Methahel, Ourar, Mailure, Kambreda, Ragan,
Gael, Ecub, Nest, Chein, Stadud, Gladus, Ebrein, Blangan, Aballac,
Angaes, Galaes (omnium pulcherrima quae tunc in Britannia siue in Gallia
fuerant), Edra, Anor, Stadiald, Egron. Has omnes direxit pater in Italiam ad
Siluium Albam, qui post Siluium Latinum regnabat. Fuerunt ibi maritatae 105
nobilioribus Troianis, quorum cubilia et Latinae et Sabinae diffugiebant. At
filii duce Assaraco fratre duxerunt classem in Germaniam et auxilio Siluii
Albae usi subiugato populo adepti sunt regnum.

28   Brutus autem cognomento Viride Scutum cum patre remansit regnique
gubernaculo post illum potitus .xii. annis regnauit. Huic successit Leil filius 110
suus, pacis amator et aequitatis, qui ut prosperitate regni usus est urbem in
aquilonari parte Britanniae aedificauit, de nomine suo Kaerleil uocatam.
Tunc Salomon coepit aedificare templum Domino in Ierusalem et regina
Saba uenit audire sapientiam eius, et tunc Siluius Epitus patri Albae in
regnum successit. Vixit deinde Leil post sumptum regnum .xxv. annis sed 115
regnum in fine tepide rexit. Quocirca segnicia eius insistente ciuilis discordia
29   subito in regno orta est. Post hunc regnauit filius suus Rud Hudibras .xxxix.
annis. Ipse, populum ex ciuili discidio in concordiam reducens, condidit
Kaerkein, id est Cantuariam. Condidit etiam Kaergueint, id est Guintoniam,
atque oppidum Montis Paladur, quod nunc Seftonia dicitur. Ibi tunc aquila 120
locuta est dum murus aedificaretur; cuius sermones si ueros esse arbitrarer
sicut cetera memoriae dare non diffugerem. Tunc Capis filius Epiti regnabat
et Aggeus Amos Ieu Iohel Azarias prophetabant.
30   Successit ei deinde Bladud filius tractauitque regnum uiginti annis. Hic
aedificauit urbem Kaerbadum, quae nunc Bado nuncupatur, fecitque in illa 125
calida balnea ad usus mortalium apta, quibus praefecit numen Mineruae,
in cuius aede inextinguibiles posuit ignes, qui nunquam deficiebant in
fauillas sed ex quo tabescere incipiebant in saxeos globos uertebantur.
Tunc Helias orauit ne plueret super terram et non pluit annos tres et menses
sex. Hic admodum ingeniosus homo fuit docuitque nigromantiam per 130
regnum Britanniae nec praestigia facere quieuit donec paratis sibi alis ire
per summitatem aeris temptauit ceciditque super templum Apollinis infra
urbem Trinouantum, in multa frusta contritus.
31   Dato igitur fatis Bladud, erigitur Leir filius eiusdem in regem, qui
.lx. annis patriam uiriliter rexit. Aedificauit autem super flumen Soram 135
ciuitatem, quae Britannice de nomine eius Kaerleir, Saxonice uero
Lerecestre nuncupatur. Cui negata masculini sexus prole natae sunt
tantummodo tres filiae, uocatae Gonorilla, Regau, Cordeilla. Pater eas miro
amore sed magis iuniorem, uidelicet Cordeillam, diligebat. Cumque in

112 aquilonali *QM (cf. uu. ll. §§ 116.280, 120.74)*
116 insi[stente] *Q: om. YM*
118 deducens *Φ*
124 filius *CS QYG:* filius suus *O:* filius eius *E M*

Leir began to grow old, he decided to share his kingdom with them and give them husbands worthy of themselves and their realm. In order to find out which of them deserved the largest share of the kingdom, he approached them, one after the other, to ask which loved him most. Gonorilla, whom he asked first, declared before the powers of heaven that he was dearer to her than the soul in her body. Leir replied:

'Dearest daughter, since you value my old age more than your own life, I shall marry you to the man of your choice and give you a third of the kingdom of Britain'.

Next his second daughter, Regau, wishing to win her father's goodwill just as her sister had, swore that she could say nothing except that she loved him above all living creatures. Her gullible father swore that she would be married with the same honour that he had promised the eldest, with a third of the kingdom. But Cordeilla understood that he had succumbed to the flattery of her sisters and proceeded to answer differently, in order to test him:

'Father, is there any daughter who would presume to love her father more than a father? As far as I am concerned, no one would dare to say that, unless she were trying to conceal the truth with playful words. Certainly I have always loved you as a father, and will not be diverted from that course now. If you persist in trying to get more out of me, hear the true love I bear you and put an end to your questions: you are worth what you have, and that much I love you'.

Her father thought that she had spoken wholeheartedly. Filled with anger, he was swift to make the following reply:

'Since you despise your old father so much that you do not honour me even with the same love as your sisters, I in turn will dishonour you: you shall never have a share in my kingdom with your sisters. I do not refuse, however, since you are my daughter, to marry you to some foreign husband at least, should chance bring one. But I am adamant that I shall never contrive to marry you as honourably as your sisters, seeing that you love me less than they do, despite the fact that I used to love you more'.

With the approval of the kingdom's nobles he immediately married the elder daughters to two dukes, of Cornwall and Scotland, with no more than half the island while he lived, but granting them possession of the entire kingdom of Britain after his death. Afterwards Aganippus, the king of the French, happened to hear reports of Cordeilla's beauty. He instantly sent messengers to the king, requesting that she be sent to him to be joined in solemn matrimony. Her father, his earlier anger unabated, replied that he would gladly send her, but without land or money, since he had divided his kingdom along with all its gold and silver

senectutem uergere coepisset, cogitauit regnum suum ipsis diuidere easque 140
talibus maritis copulare qui easdem cum regno haberent; sed ut sciret quae
illarum parte regni potiore dignior esset, adiuit singulas ut interrogaret quae
ipsum magis diligeret. Interrogante igitur illo, Gonorilla prius numina caeli
testata est ipsum sibi maiori dilectioni esse quam animam quae in corpore
suo degebat. Cui pater: 145

'Quoniam senectutem meam uitae tuae praeposuisti, te, carissima
filia, maritabo iuueni quemcumque elegeris cum tercia parte regni
Britanniae'.

Deinde Regau, quae secunda erat, exemplo sororis suae beniuolentiam
patris allicere uolens, iureiurando respondit se nullatenus aliter exprimere 150
nisi quod illum super omnes creaturas diligeret. Credulus ergo pater iurauit
quod eadem dignitate quam primogenitae promiserat ipsam cum alia parte
regni maritaret. At Cordeilla iunior, cum intellexisset eum praedictarum
adulationibus acquieuisse, temptare illum cupiens aliter respondere
perrexit: 155

'Est uspiam, pater mi, filia quae patrem suum plus quam patrem
praesumat diligere? Non reor equidem ullam esse quae hoc fateri audeat
nisi iocosis uerbis ueritatem celare nitatur. Nempe ego dilexi te semper
ut patrem et adhuc a proposito meo non diuertor. Et si ex me magis
extorquere insistis, audi certitudinem amoris quem aduersum te habeo 160
et interrogationibus tuis finem impone. Etenim quantum habes tantum
uales tantumque te diligo'.

Porro pater, ratus eam ex habundantia cordis dixisse, uehementer indignans
quod responsurus erat hoc modo manifestare non distulit:

'Quia in tantum senectutem patris tui spreuisti ut uel eo amore quo me 165
sorores tuae dedignata es diligere, et ego dedignabor te, nec umquam
partem in regno meo cum sororibus habebis. Non dico tamen, cum
filia mea sis, quin te alicui externo si illum fortuna optulerit utcumque
maritem. Illud autem affirmo, quod numquam eo honore quo sorores tuas
maritare laborabo, quippe cum te plus quam ceteras hucusque dilexerim, 170
tu uero me minus quam ceterae diligas'.

Nec mora, consilio procerum regni dedit praedictas puellas duas duobus
ducibus, Cornubiae uidelicet et Albaniae, cum medietate tantum insulae
dum ipse uiueret; post obitum autem eius totam monarchiam Britanniae
concessit habendam. Contigit deinde quod Aganippus rex Francorum, 175
audita fama pulcritudinis Cordeillae, continuo nuntios suos ad regem
direxit, rogans ut ipsa sibi coniugali taeda copulanda traderetur. At pater, in
praenominata ira adhuc perseuerans, respondit se illam libenter daturum,
sed sine terra et pecunia; regnum namque suum cum omni auro et argento

---

151-2 iurauit quod *addidi codd. 88 et 116 secutus, ubi* iurat quod: *infra* maritare spopondit *W*,
maritare promisit *37 (cf. 'Transm.' 98)*
167 sororibus <tuis> *Φ*

between the girl's sisters, Gonorilla and Regau. This was reported to Aganippus; he, burning with love for the girl, sent again to king Leir. He said that, since he ruled a third of France, he had plenty of gold, silver and other possessions; he wanted no more than the girl, to beget heirs by her. So a treaty was struck and Cordeilla sent to France, where she married Aganippus.

Much later, when Leir began to grow weary with age, the dukes to whom he had given Britain and his daughters rose up against him. They deprived him of the kingdom and his royal authority, which up to then he had exercised well and with glory. Agreement was reached that he should stay with one of his sons-in-law, Maglaunus duke of Scotland, with a company of forty knights so that his guest would not lack majesty. Leir remained with his son-in-law for two years, until Gonorilla became angry with his many knights, who insulted her servants because the rations provided were not more lavish. Addressing her husband, she said that her father should content himself with a retinue of thirty knights, dispensing with the remainder. This angered Leir, who left Maglaunus and visited Henuinus duke of Cornwall, to whom he had married his other daugher, Regau. The duke received him with honour, but before a year was out trouble arose between his household and the king's. Irritated at this, Regau told her father to dismiss all his companions, except five to serve him. Leir, now very anxious, returned once more to his eldest daughter, expecting her to show pity and receive him and his retinue. But Gonorilla's anger had not at all diminished, and she swore by the powers of heaven that she was quite unable to receive him unless he would be content with a single knight and dismiss the rest; she rebuked him, an old man without possessions, for wanting to go about with so large a retinue. As she would in no way agree to his request, Leir complied, keeping a single knight and dismissing the rest. Yet when he recalled his former pomp, he could not bear the wretchedness to which he had been reduced. He began to think that he should seek out his youngest daughter across the sea; but he was unsure whether she would want to help him, since, as we know, he had married her off so dishonourably. But he crossed to France, unwilling to endure his wretchedness any longer. During the crossing he realised that he ranked third among the princes who were aboard ship and exclaimed with tearful sobs:

'O the implacable progress of fate, marching onwards down a familiar path! Why did it ever want to raise me to fickle good fortune, the recollection of whose loss outweighs the crushing presence of the ensuing unhappiness? The memory of the time when I used to overthrow city-walls and lay waste enemy lands, at the head of so many

Gonorillae et Regau puellae sororibus distribuerat. Cumque id Aganippo 180
nunciatum fuisset, amore uirginis inflammatus remisit iterum ad Leirem
regem, dicens se satis auri et argenti aliarumque possessionum habere, quia
tertiam partem Galliae possidebat; se uero tantummodo puellam captare, ut
heredes ex illa haberet. Denique, confirmato foedere, mittitur Cordeilla ad
Galliam et Aganippo maritatur. 185

Post multum uero temporis, ut Leir torpere coepit senio, insurrexerunt
in illum praedicti duces quibus Britanniam cum filiabus diuiserat;
abstulerunt autem ei regnum regiamque potestatem, quam usque ad illud
tempus uiriliter et gloriose tenuerat. Concordia tamen habita, retinuit eum
alter generorum Maglaunus, dux Albaniae, cum quadraginta militibus, ne 190
secum inglorius maneret. Elapso deinde biennio, moram eo apud generum
faciente, indignata est Gonorilla filia sua ob multitudinem militum eius, qui
conuicia ministris inferebant quia sibi profusior epimonia non praebebatur.
Proinde maritum suum affata iussit patrem obsequio triginta militum
contentum esse, relictis ceteris quos habuerat. Vnde ille iratus relicto 195
Maglauno petiuit Henuinum ducem Cornubiae, cui alteram natam Regau
maritauerat; et cum a duce honorifice receptus fuisset, non praeteriit annus
quin inter utrorumque familias discordia orta fuerat. Quam ob rem Regau in
indignationem uersa praecepit patri cunctos socios deserere praeter quinque
qui ei obsequium praestarent. Porro pater, ultra modum anxius, reuersus est 200
iterum ad primogenitam, existimans se posse commouere illam in pietatem
ut cum familia sua retineretur. At illa nequaquam a coepta indignatione
reuersa est sed per numina caeli iurauit quod nullatenus secum commaneret
nisi postpositis ceteris solo milite contentus fuisset; increpabat etiam eum
senem et in nulla re abundantem uelle cum tanta familia incedere. Cumque 205
illa assensum uoluntati eius nullo modo praebuisset, paruit ipse et relictis
ceteris cum solo milite remansit. At cum in memoria pristinae dignitatis
reductus fuisset, detestando miseriam in quam redactus erat, cogitare coepit
quod iuniorem filiam trans occeanum exigeret, sed dubitabat ipsam nil
uelle sibi facere, quoniam eam tam ingloriose ut praedictum est dedisset. 210
Indignans tamen miseriam suam diutius ferre, transfretauit ad Gallias;
sed transfretando cum se tercium infra nauim inter principes qui aderant
aspexisset, in haec uerba cum fletu et singultu prorupit:

'O inreuocabilia seria fatorum, quae solito cursu fixum iter tenditis, cur
unquam me ad instabilem felicitatem promouere uoluistis, cum maior 215
poena sit ipsam amissam recolere quam sequentis infelicitatis praesentia
urgeri? Magis etenim aggrauat me illius temporis memoria quo tot

191 ingloriosus *CSE (§ 31.210 ingloriose, 82.262 inglorium)*
193 epimenia *Gildas 23.5 non solus*
195 ceteris *H M:* ceteris uiginti *OSE QYG:* ? *C¹:* ceteris .x. *C² (cf. Introd.)*
202 a coepta *H²S Φ:* accepta *OCH¹:* arepta *E*
207 ceteris *54²:* ducentis *Δ QG:* .cc. *M:* .xx. *Y (cf. Introd.)*
212 cum transfretando *Φ*
214 seria *quid sunt ?*

hundreds of thousands of knights, oppresses me more than this disastrous humiliation, which makes those who so recently grovelled at my feet abandon me in my weakness. O angry fortune! Will the day ever come when I shall be able to repay those time-servers who have thus shunned me in my poverty? O daughter Cordeilla, how true was the reply you made to me when I asked how much you loved me! You said: 'you are worth what you have, and that much I love you'. While I had something I could give, I was respected by those who were friendly not to me but to my gifts. For a time they loved me, but really my gifts; when my gifts were gone, so were they. But how will I have the effrontery to entreat you, dearest daughter, after I planned, because of my anger at what you said, a worse marriage for you than for your sisters, sisters who, after the kindnesses I have done them, can endure seeing me as a penniless outcast?'.

With this and similar complaints he eventually landed and came to Karitia, where his daughter was. He waited outside the city, sending her a messenger to report that he had fallen into such misery, and asking her to take pity on him as he had nothing to eat or wear. Moved by this news, Cordeilla wept bitterly and inquired how many knights he had with him. The messenger replied that he had none, except for a single squire waiting outside with him. Then Cordeilla took as much gold and silver as was necessary and gave it to him, with instructions that he should take her father to another city, where he was to pretend that Leir was ill, and bathe, dress and care for him. She further commanded that Leir should have a retinue of sixty well-dressed and equipped knights and only then should he announce his arrival to king Aganippus and his daughter. The messenger returned, took Leir to another city and hid him there until he had done all Cordeilla had ordered.

As soon as Leir had been furnished with the apparel and household of a king, he informed Aganippus and his daughter that he had been driven from the kingdom of Britain by his sons-in-law and had come to them so that with their help he could recover his realm. They in turn came to meet him with their earls and nobles, greeted him with respect and gave him jurisdiction over all France until they could restore him to his former glory.

Meanwhile Aganippus sent messengers throughout France to collect all the armed soldiers there, with whose aid he could attempt to return the kingdom of Britain to his father-in-law, Leir. When this was done, Leir took his daughter and the assembled army to Britain. He fought with his sons-in-law and beat them. Three years later he died, having restored all to their rightful positions.

centenis milibus militum stipatus et moenia urbium diruere et prouincias
hostium uastare solebam quam calamitas miseriae meae, quae ipsos qui
iam sub pedibus meis iacebant debilitatem meam deserere coegit. O irata   220
fortuna! Venietne dies umquam qua ipsis uicem reddere potero qui sic
tempora mea secuti paupertatem meam diffugierunt? O Cordeilla filia,
quam uera sunt dicta illa quae michi respondisti quando quaesiui a te quem
amorem aduersum me haberes! Dixisti enim "quantum habes tantum
uales tantumque te diligo". Dum igitur habui quod potui dare, uisus fui   225
ualere eis qui non michi sed donis meis amici fuerant. Interim dilexerunt
me sed magis munera mea; nam abeuntibus muneribus et ipsi abierunt.
Sed qua fronte, karissima filia, te audebo exigere, qui ob praedicta uerba
iratus putaui te maritare deterius quam sorores tuas, quae post beneficia
quae eis impendi me exulem et pauperem esse patiuntur?'.   230

Vt tandem haec et similia dicendo applicuit, uenit Karitiam, ubi filia sua
erat. Expectans autem extra urbem, misit ei nuncium suum qui indicaret
ipsum in tantam miseriam collapsum; et quia non habebat quid comederet
uel indueret, misericordiam illius petebat. Quo indicato, commota est
Cordeilla et fleuit amare quaesiuitque quot milites secum habuisset. Qui 235
respondit ipsum neminem habere, excepto quodam armigero qui foris cum
eo expectabat. Tunc illa cepit quantum opus erat auri et argenti deditque
nuncio, praecipiens ut patrem ad aliam ciuitatem duceret ibique ipsum
infirmum fingeret et balnearet, indueret, foueret. Iussit etiam ut sexaginta
milites bene indutos et paratos retineret et tunc demum mandaret regi 240
Aganippo et filiae suae sese aduenisse. Nuncius ilico reuersus duxit Leirem
regem ad aliam ciuitatem absconditque eum ibi donec omnia quae Cordeilla
iusserat perfecisset.

Mox, ut regio apparatu exornatus et familia insignitus fuit, mandauit
Aganippo et filiae sese a generis suis expulsum fuisse ex regno Britanniae 245
et ad ipsos uenisse ut auxilio eorum patriam suam recuperare ualuisset. At
illi, cum consulibus et proceribus obuiam uenientes, honorifice susceperunt
illum dederuntque ei potestatem totius Galliae donec eum in pristinam
dignitatem restaurassent.

Interea misit Aganippus legatos per uniuersam Galliam ad colligendum 250
in ea omnem armatum militem ut auxilio suo regnum Britanniae Leiri
socero reddere laboraret. Quo facto, duxit secum Leir filiam et collectam
multitudinem in Britanniam pugnauitque cum generis et triumpho potitus
est. Deinde, cum quosque potestati suae reddidisset, in tercio anno mortuus

222 secuti *OCE:* sicuti *HS Φ (de loco uix sano cf. 'Transm.' 90)*
225 dare potui *Φ*
226 fuerunt *SE M*
231 <his> similia *YG*
239 .xl. *H Φ*
244 exornatus *scripsi:* ex ornamentis *Ω (cf. Introd.):* et ornamentis *197²*
245 generibus *CHSE QY¹M*
251 Leiri *CSE QYM:* Leir *OH:* Leiro *G*
252 socero <suo> *OHE Y*
252 filiam <suam> *OE Φ*

The French king Aganippus also died. Leir's daughter Cordeilla therefore took over the kingdom and buried her father in an underground chamber which he had commanded be built under the river Soar in Leicester. The chamber had been constructed in honour of Janus, the god with two faces. During Janus' festival, all the builders of the city used to inaugurate in the chamber all the projects on which they were going to work in the coming year.

32   After Cordeilla had ruled the kingdom peacefully for five years, Marganus and Cunedagius (the two sons of her sisters, married to Maglaurus and Henuinus) began to attack her. Both were youths of great worth, the former Maglaurus' son, the latter Henuinus'. After their fathers' deaths, they succeded as dukes and resented a woman having power over Britain. They therefore assembled their armies and rose up against the queen, unwilling that hostilities should cease until they had devastated all her provinces and joined battle with her; finally they captured and imprisoned her, where, overwhelmed by grief at the loss of her kingdom, she killed herself. The youths then divided the island, the part extending from the Humber to Caithness going to Marganus, and the part to the west of the river to Cunedagius. After two years passed, certain people who took pleasure in disrupting the kingdom approached Marganus; to twist his mind, they asserted that it was a foul disgrace that he, the elder, was not master of the whole island. Induced by this and many other ploys, Marganus led his army through Cunedagius' provinces and started fire after fire. Now that strife had arisen, Cunedagius met him with his whole army; after battle was joined, Cunedagius inflicted no little slaughter and put Marganus to flight. He pursued him from region to region, eventually catching him in a district of Wales which ever since Marganus' death has been called Margam by its inhabitants. The victorious Cunedagius took control of the whole island and for thirty-three years ruled it in splendour. At that time lived the prophets Isaiah and Hosea; and Rome was founded on April 21st by the twins Romulus and Remus.

33   When Cunedagius finally died, he was succeeded by his son Rivallo, a peaceful and fortunate youth, who ruled the kingdom well. While he was king, it rained blood for three days and people died from a plague of flies. He was succeeded by his son Gurgustius; next came Sisillius, next Iago, Gurgustius' nephew, then Kinmarcus, Sisillius' son, and finally Gorbodugo. He had two sons, called Ferreux and Porrex. When their father grew old, they quarreled about which of them should succeed to the throne. Porrex felt the greater desire and tried to kill his brother Ferreux by setting an ambush, but the latter discovered the plot and escaped his brother by crossing to France. Aided by the French king Suhardus, he returned to fight his brother. In the battle Ferreux and all the troops with him were killed.

est. Mortuus est etiam Aganippus rex Francorum. Cordeilla ergo filia, regni 255
gubernaculum adepta, sepeliuit patrem in quodam subterraneo quod sub
Sora fluuio infra Legecestriam fieri praeceperat. Erat autem subterraneum
illud conditum in honore bifrontis Iani. Ibi omnes operarii urbis, adueniente
sollempnitate dei, opera quae per annum acturi erant incipiebant.

32   Cum igitur Cordeilla regnum per quinquennium pacifice tractasset, 260
coeperunt eam inquietare duo filii sororum suarum, Marganus et
Cunedagius, quae Maglauro et Henuino ducibus coniugatae fuerant. Ambo
iuuenes praeclarae probitatis famam habebant; quorum alterum, uidelicet
Marganum, Maglaurus generauerat, Cunedagium uero Henuinus. Hi itaque,
cum post obitum patrum in ducatus eisdem successissent, indignati sunt 265
Britanniam femineae potestati subditam esse. Collectis ergo exercitibus,
in reginam insurrexerunt nec saeuiciae suae desistere uoluerunt donec
quibusque prouinciis uastatis proelia cum ipsa commiserunt; eam quoque
ad ultimum captam in carcerem posuerunt, ubi ob amissionem regni dolore
obducta sese interfecit. Exin partiti sunt iuuenes insulam, cuius pars illa quae 270
trans Humbrum extenditur uersus Katanesiam Margano cessit, alia uero,
quae in altera parte fluuii ad occasum solis uergit, Cunedagio summittitur.
Emenso deinde biennio, accesserunt quibus turbatio regni placebat ad
Marganum animumque illius subducentes aiebant turpe et dedecus esse
ipsum, cum primogenitus esset, totius insulae non dominari. Cumque his 275
et pluribus aliis modis incitatus fuisset, duxit exercitum per prouincias
Cunedagii ignemque accumulare incepit. Orta igitur discordia, obuiauit ei
Cunedagius cum omni multitudine sua factoque congressu caedem intulit
non minimam et Marganum in fugam propulit. Deinde secutus est eum
fugientem a prouincia in prouinciam. Tandem intercepit eum in pago 280
Kambriae qui post interfectionem nomine suo, uidelicet Margan, hucusque
a pagensibus appellatus est. Potitus itaque uictoria Cunedagius monarchiam
totius insulae adeptus est eamque .xxxiii. annis gloriose tractauit. Tunc
Ysaias et Osea prophetabant et Roma condita est .xi. kl Mai a geminis
fratribus Remo et Romulo.   285

33   Postremo defuncto Cunedagio successit ei Riuallo filius ipsius, iuuenis
pacificus atque fortunatus, qui regnum cum diligentia gubernauit. In
tempore eius tribus diebus cecidit pluuia sanguinea et muscarum affluentia
homines moriebantur. Post hunc successit Gurgustius filius eius, cui
Sisillius, cui Iago Gurgustii nepos, cui Kinmarcus Sisillii filius, post hunc 290
Gorbodugo. Huic nati fuerunt duo filii, quorum unus Ferreux, alter Porrex
nuncupabatur. Cum autem pater in senium uergisset, orta est contentio
inter eos quis eorum in regno succederet. At Porrex, maiori cupiditate
subductus, paratis insidiis Ferreucem fratrem interficere parat. Quod cum
illi compertum fuisset, uitato fratre transfretauit in Gallias sed usus auxilio 295
Suhardi regis Francorum reuersus est et cum fratre dimicauit. Pugnantibus
autem illis, interfectus est Ferreux et tota multitudo quae eum comitabatur.

255 [filia] *Φ*
287 [pacificus] *Φ*

Their mother, named Iudon, was greatly angered by the news of the death of one of her sons and came to hate the other, whom she had loved less. She burned with such fury over Ferreux's death that she desired to take revenge on his brother. Waiting until he was asleep, she and her serving women attacked and tore him to pieces. For a long time after that, civil strife troubled the people and the kingdom was ruled by five kings, who inflicted defeats one upon the other.

34   After some time had passed, a young man named Dunuallo Molmutius was singled out by his prowess. The son of king Cloten of Cornwall, he was more handsome and bold than all the kings of Britiain. On becoming ruler of his region after his father's death, he rebelled against Pinner, king of Loegria, and killed him in battle. Then Rudaucus king of Wales and Staterius king of Scotland met together and made an alliance. They led their armies into Dunuallo's provinces, bent on destroying buildings along with their inhabitants. Dunuallo himself faced them with thirty thousand men, and battle was joined. When Dunuallo had spent much of the day fighting without success, he separated six hundred of his boldest men and ordered them all to take up the equipment of the enemy dead and put it on; he too, removing his own armour, did the same. Then he led them among the attacking enemy formations, advancing as if they were part of them. Reaching the place where Rudaucus and Staterius stood, he ordered his fellow-soldiers to attack them. The two kings and many others with them were killed in this assault. Dunuallo Molmutius, apprehensive of being killed by his own men, returned with his companions and took off his armour. Putting on again the equipment he had removed, he urged his men to attack the enemy, leading a desperate assault himself. The enemy was soon scattered in flight and he had won a victory. Finally, ravaging the countries of the two dead kings, he destroyed cities and towns and made the inhabitants his subjects; when he had gained complete control over the whole island, he made himself a crown of gold and restored the country to its former position. He established among the Britons the laws called Molmutine, which are still renowned even today among the English. Amongst other enactments recorded much later by St Gildas, he ordained that the temples of the gods and the cities should be treated with such respect that any fugitive or criminal who fled to them should be allowed to depart with a full pardon from his enemies. He further ordained that the roads leading to the temples and cities and also farmers' ploughlands should enjoy the same privilege. In Dunuallo's time the knives of thieves were idle, the savagery of robbers was allayed and no one anywhere

Porro mater eorum, cui nomen erat Iudon, cum de nece filii certitudinem
habuisset, ultra modum commota in odium alterius uersa est. Diligebat
namque illum magis altero. Vnde tanta ira ob mortem ipsius ignescebat ut 300
ipsum in fratrem uindicare affectaret. Nacta ergo tempus quo ille sopitus
fuerat, aggreditur eum cum ancillis suis et in plurimas sectiones dilacerauit.
Exin ciuilis discordia multo tempore populum afflixit et regnum quinque
regibus summissum est, qui sese mutuis cladibus infestabant.

34   Succedente tandem tempore, suscitauit probitas quendam iuuenem qui 305
Dunuallo Molmutius uocabatur. Erat ipse filius Clotenis regis Cornubiae,
pulcritudine et audacia omnes reges Britanniae excellens. Qui ut regimen
patriae post obitum patris suscepit, insurrexit in Pinnerem regem Loegriae
et facto congressu interfecit eum. Deinde conuenerunt Rudaucus rex
Kambriae atque Staterius rex Albaniae confirmatoque inter se foedere 310
duxerunt exercitus suos in prouincias Dunuallonis, aedificia et colonos
depopulaturi. Quibus obuiauit ipse Dunuallo cum .xxx. milibus uirorum
proeliumque commisit. Cumque multum diei dum pugnarent praeterisset
nec sibi uictoria prouenisset, seuocauit sexcentos audacissimos iuuenes et
cunctis arma defunctorum hostium sumere praecepit et indui; ipse etiam, 315
proiectis illis quibus armatus erat, fecit similiter. Deinde duxit illos inter
concurrentes hostium cateruas, incedendo quasi ex ipsis essent. Nactus
quoque locum quo Rudaucus et Staterius erant, commilitonibus indixit ut
in ipsos irruerent. Facto igitur impetu, perimuntur praedicti duo reges et
plures alii cum illis. At Dunuallo Molmutius, timens ne a suis opprimeretur, 320
reuertitur cum sociis et sese exarmauit. Resumptis deinde armis quae
proiecerat, hortatur consocios in hostes irruere ipsosque acriter inuasit.
Nec mora, potitus est uictoria, fugatis ac dispersis hostibus. Denique per
patrias supradictorum interemptorum uagando subuertit urbes et oppida
populumque potestati suae summittit; et cum totam insulam omnino 325
subiugasset, fecit sibi diadema ex auro insulamque in pristinum statum
reduxit. Hic leges quae Molmutinae dicebantur inter Britones statuit,
quae usque ad hoc tempus inter Anglos celebrantur. Statuit siquidem inter
cetera quae multo tempore post beatus Gildas scripsit ut templa deorum
et ciuitates talem dignitatem haberent ut quicumque fugitiuus siue reus 330
ad ea confugeret cum uenia coram inimico suo abiret. Statuit etiam ut
uiae quae ad praedicta templa et ad ciuitates ducebant nec non et aratra
colonorum eadem lege confirmarentur. In diebus itaque eius latronum
mucrones cessabant, raptorum saeuiciae obturabantur, nec erat usquam qui

---

306 ipse *Δ*: enim *Φ (cf. § 73.8)*
312 depopulaturi *C*: -aturos *E Φ*: -antes *HS: ? O*
312 [ipse] *Φ*
316 similiter fecit *Φ*
316-17 [inter] *Φ, unde* concurrentes <in> *GM*
319 duo praedicti *YG*
322 socios *SE Φ*
332 [ad] ciuitates *O Q*

wished to do violence to another. At last, having devoted to such deeds the forty years since he assumed the crown, Dunuallo died and was buried in the city of Trinovantum, near the temple of Harmony, which he himself had built to bolster his laws.

BOOK THREE

35   Dunuallo's two sons, Beli and Brennius, both wished to succeed him as king and fell prey to great disagreement. They argued to determine which of them should wear the crown. After many altercations, their mutual friends intervened and reconciled them. They decided terms to divide the kingdom between them, with Loegria, Wales and Cornwall along with the crown going to Belinus, since he was the elder and Trojan custom demanded that the chief inheritance should fall to him. Brennius, since he was younger, obtained Northumbria from the Humber to Caithness, subject to his brother. Having cemented this agreement with a treaty, they ruled the country peacefully and with justice for five years. Yet because strife always tries to interrupt success, certain spinners of lies emerged who went to Brennius, saying:

> 'Why does sloth so overmaster you that you are subject to Belinus, when the same father, the same mother, and the same nobility make you his equal? Moreover, you have proved youself in many battles, since you have so often been able to repulse Cheulfus, duke of the Flemings, when he landed in our region, and drive him from your kingdom. Break this treaty which so dishonours you, and marry the daughter of Elsingius, king of the Norsemen, with whose help you can recover the dignity you have lost'.

After they had twisted the youth's mind with these and other arguments, he consented, sailed to Norway and married the king's daughter as those flatterers had told him.

36   When his brother was informed, he was angry that Brennius had acted without his permission and against his will. He marched on Northumbria, took the cities of its neighbours and garrisoned them with his troops. On hearing reports of what his brother was doing, Brennius, taking with him a great number of Norsemen, built a fleet and returned to Britain. As he ploughed the waves, confident and with a following wind, he was met by Guichtlacus king of the Danes, who had followed him; Guichtlacus burned with love for the girl Brennius had married and, overcome by grief, had assembled a fleet and army and made a hasty voyage to shadow him. A naval battle ensued, in which Guichtlacus had the good fortune to capture the ship on which the girl was and drag it off among his followers with grappling hooks. As the battle swayed to and fro upon the ocean,

uiolentiam alicui ingereret. Denique, cum inter talia .xl. annos post sumptum 335
diadema expleuisset, defunctus est et in urbe Trinouantum prope templum
Concordiae sepultus, quod ipse ad confirmationem legum construxerat.

LIBER III

35 Exin duo filii eius, Beli uidelicet et Brennius, in regnum succedere uolentes
maxima contriti sunt discordia. Contendebant enim quis eorum diademate
regni insigniretur. Cum itaque plures decertationes inter se commiscuissent,
interfuerunt amici utrorumque, qui ipsos in concordiam reduxerunt.
Censuerunt quoque regnum inter eos ea conditione diuidendum esse ut 5
Belinus diadema insulae cum Loegria atque Kambria nec non et Cornubia
possideret; erat enim primogenitus, petebatque Troiana consuetudo ut
dignitas hereditatis ei proueniret. At Brennius, quoniam iunior fuerat, fratri
subditus Northamhimbriam ab Humbro usque ad Katanesiam adeptus est.
Confirmato igitur super his pactionibus foedere, tractauerunt patriam per 10
quinquennium cum pace et iusticia. Sed quia discordia sese prosperis rebus
semper miscere conatur, affuerunt quidam fabricatores mendacii qui ad
Brennium accesserunt dicentes:

'Vt quid ignauia te tantum occupauit ut Belino subiectionem teneas, cum
idem pater et mater eademque nobilitas te ei parificet? Adde quod in 15
pluribus debellationibus expertus es, qui tociens Cheulfo duci Morianorum
in prouinciam nostram applicanti resistere potuisti ipsumque ex regno
tuo fugare. Rumpe foedus quod tibi dedecori est et duc filiam Elsingii
regis Norguegensium, ut ipsius auxilio amissam dignitatem recipias'.

Postquam igitur his et pluribus aliis animum iuuenis corruperunt, adquieuit 20
ipse adiuitque Norguegiam duxitque filiam regis ut a praedictis adulatoribus
edoctus fuerat.

36 Interea, cum id fratri nunciatum esset, indignatus est quia sic sine licentia
sua et contra ipsum egisset. Petiuit itaque Northamhimbriam cepitque
comprouincialium ciuitates et eas custodibus suis muniuit. Porro Brennius, 25
audito rumore qui actum fratris notificauerat, adducit secum magnam
copiam Norguegensium paratoque nauigio redit in Britanniam. Cumque
aequora securius et prospero uento sulcaret, obuiauit ei Guichtlacus rex
Dacorum, qui ipsum insecutus fuerat; aestuauerat namque amore puellae
quam Brennius duxerat, unde ultra modum dolens classem parauerat et 30
exercitum ipsumque citissimis uelis sequebatur. Nauali igitur aggressu facto,
cepit forte nauem qua praedicta puella fuerat illatisque uncis illam inter
consocios attraxit. Illis autem hinc et inde infra profundum congredientibus,

2 Contenderant Φ
8-9 At Brennius ... subditus Northanhimbriam ... adeptus est Δ: Brennius uero ... subderetur
Northanhimbriamque ... optineret Φ
27 rediit OSE
32 <in> qua E G, sed cf. Introd.

contrary winds suddenly arose, creating a storm which scattered the ships and drove them to different shores. The king of Denmark was driven on by the force of adverse winds and, after sailing for five days, landed with the girl in Northumbria, full of apprehension, as he did not know to what country these unexpected events had brought him. When the locals heard of it, they arrested them and took them to Belinus, who was at the coast, awaiting his brother's return. With Guichtlacus' ship there were three others, one of which belonged to Brennius' fleet. After their identity was made known to the king, Belinus was overjoyed that these events had occurred at the time when he was planning to revenge himself on his brother.

37   A few days later, Brennius landed in Scotland with his fleet reunited. After he discovered that his wife and the others had been captured and that his brother had deprived him of the kingdom of Northumbria in his absence, he sent messengers to Belinus demanding the return of his kingdom and wife; otherwise he undertook to lay waste the whole island from sea to sea and also to kill his brother if an opportunity for battle presented itself. Hearing this, Belinus flatly denied his request and, collecting every knight in the island, came to Scotland to fight him. Once he knew he had been rebuffed and that his brother was marching against him, Brennius set off to meet him, to join battle in the forest called Calaterium. When they arrived at the field of battle, they divided their companions into companies and advanced to begin the fight. The battle lasted most of the day, because the warriors on both sides fought skilfully. Much blood was spilt by both armies, while they wielded their spears with all their might to deal deadly wounds. As the cohorts clashed, the wounded fell like corn before the reapers. At last the Britons got the upper hand and the mangled ranks of the Norsemen fled to their ships; Belinus pursued them as they ran, cutting them down without mercy. Fifteen thousand men fell in the battle, and of the survivors scarcely a thousand got away unwounded. Brennius, having boarded just a single ship by a stroke of luck, made for the French coast; the remainder of his followers sought refuge wherever they could.

38   Having won this battle, Belinus summoned all the nobles of the kingdom to York, to advise him what to do about the Danish king, who had sent him a message from prison that he would submit himself and his kingdom and pay tribute every year if he were allowed to go free with his lover. He said that he would seal the agreement with a solemn oath and hostages. When the assembled nobles were informed of this, they unanimously agreed that Belinus should grant Guichtlacus' request on the above terms. He too agreed, and Guichtlacus was released from prison and returned to Denmark with his lover.

ruunt ex inprouiso aduersi uenti factoque turbine naues dissipant, dissipatas
uero in diuersa littora compellunt. Rex igitur Daciae inimica ui uentorum   35
compulsus, peracto quinque dierum cursu, cum timore applicuit cum puella
in Northamhimbriam, nescius quam patriam inopinabilis euentus optulisset.
Cumque id a pagensibus compertum esset, ceperunt illos duxeruntque ad
Belinum, qui super maritima aduentum fratris expectabat. Erant ibi cum
naue Guichtlaci tres aliae naues, quarum una fuerat ex Brennii nauigio.   40
Postquam autem quid essent regi indicauerunt, gaudens admodum gauisus
est id sibi contigisse dum sese in fratrem uindicare captaret.

37   Emensis deinde aliquot diebus, ecce Brennius resociatis nauibus in
Albaniam applicuit. Exin, cum ei captio coniugis ceterorumque notificata
fuisset et quod frater sibi regnum Northamhimbriae dum aberat surripuisset,   45
misit nuncios suos ad eum mandauitque ut regnum et sponsa redderentur;
sin autem, testatur se totam insulam a mari usque ad mare uastaturum,
ipsum etiam fratrem interfecturum si copia congrediendi sibi praestaretur.
Quod cum Belinus sciuisset, negauit plane quod petebat collectoque omni
milite insulae uenit Albaniam, contra illum pugnaturus. At Brennius,   50
ut se sciuit repulsam passum fuisse germanumque hoc modo contra se
uenire, iuit in obuiam illi in nemore quod uocatur Calaterium ut cum eo
congrederetur. Vt igitur eundem nacti sunt campum, diuiserunt uterque
socios suos in turmas cominusque accedentes proeliari coeperunt. Multum
diei in bellando consumpserunt, quia in utraque parte probissimi uiri dextras   55
commiscebant. Multum cruoris hinc et inde fuderunt, quia tela ipsorum
uiribus uibrata letifera uulnera ingerebant. Concidebant inter corruentes
cohortes uulnerati quemadmodum segetes cum a falcatoribus aggrediuntur.
Denique, praeualentibus Britonibus, diffugiunt Norguegenses laceratis
agminibus ad naues; et cum fugam facerent, insequitur illos Belinus,   60
caedem sine pietate faciens. Ceciderunt in illo proelio .xv. milia hominum,
nec ex residuis mille superfuerunt qui illaesi abscederent. At Brennius, uix
unam nauim nactus ut fortuna conduxerat, Gallicana littora petiuit; ceteri
uero qui cum illo aduenerant quo casus ducebat latebras exigebant.

38   Cum igitur Belino uictoria cessisset, conuocauit omnes regni proceres   65
infra Eboracum, consilio ipsorum tractaturus quid de rege Dacorum
faceret; mandauerat namque sibi ex carcere quod sese regnumque Daciae
sibi submitteret, tributum quoque singulis annis donaret, si cum amica sua
liber sineretur abire. Mandauit etiam quod pactum suum foedere iuramenti
et obsidibus confirmaret. Conuocatis ergo proceribus cum id indicatum   70
fuisset, assensum praebuerunt cuncti ut Belinus peticioni Guichtlaci cum
praedicta conditione acquiesceret. Acquieuit igitur ipse, et Guichtlacus ex
carcere solutus cum amica sua in Daciam reuersus est.

41 qui *Φ, sed cf. § 16.279*
55 dexteras *CS Φ*
69 Mandauerat *CSE*

39   Now that nobody in the kingdom of Britain could prevent him, Belinus took control of the whole island from shore to shore. He reinforced the laws which his father had passed and ordered that justice should be observed throughout the land. Above all, he proclaimed that the cities and the roads leading to them should continue to enjoy the peace established by Dunuallo; but disputes had arisen about the roads because nobody knew their prescribed boundaries. Therefore the king, wishing to eliminate all uncertainty from his laws, summoned all the workmen from the whole island. He ordered them to make a road of cement and stone which would traverse the length of the island from the Cornish sea to the shore at Caithness and lead directly to the cities on the way. He commanded that another road be built across the width of the island from the city of St David's on the coast of Demetia to Southampton, to lead to the cities there, as well as two more roads diagonally across the island, leading to the remaining cities. He inaugurated them with all honour and dignity, proclaiming that it would be his own responsibility to take retribution for any act of violence committed upon them. If anyone wishes to discover all his edicts concerning the roads, they should read the Molmutine laws, which the historian Gildas translated from British into Latin, and King Alfred from Latin into English.

40   Whilst Belinus ruled Britain in peace and tranquility, his brother Brennius, who, as we have seen, had been driven to the shores of France, was tortured by inner doubts; he was mortified at having been exiled from his country with no chance of regaining his former position. In this quandary, he visited the leaders of France with a retinue of only twelve knights. He revealed his misfortune to each of them, but was unable to obtain help from any, until he came at last to Seginus, duke of the Allobroges, who received him with honour. Brennius stayed with him and grew so close to the duke that he became his favourite at court. He showed such ability in all matters, of both peace and war, that the duke loved him like a son. Moreover, he was handsome, of tall and slender build and well versed in hunting and hawking. The duke, since he loved him so much, decided that Brennius should marry his only daughter. Further, he granted him after his own death the kingdom of the Allobroges, to rule with his daughter should he have no male heir; if on the other hand the duke were to have a son, he promised his aid in making Brennius king of Britain. This was the intention not only of the duke but also of all his loyal followers, so dear

39   Porro Belinus, cum neminem sibi infra regnum Britanniae resistere
animaduertisset, totiusque insulae a mari usque ad mare potitus, leges   75
quas pater inuenerat confirmauit, stabilem quoque iusticiam per regnum
fieri praecepit. Maxime autem indixit ut ciuitates et uiae quae ad ciuitates
ducebant eandem pacem quam Dunuallo statuerat haberent; sed de uiis
orta fuerat discordia, quia nesciebatur quibus terminis definitae essent.
Rex igitur, omne ambiguum legi suae auferre uolens, conuocauit omnes   80
operarios totius insulae iussitque uiam ex caemento et lapidibus fabricari
quae insulam in longitudinem a Cornubico mari usque ad Katanesium litus
secaret et ad ciuitates quae infra erant recto limite duceret. Iussit etiam aliam
fieri in latitudinem regni quae a Meneuia urbe, quae super Demeticum mare
sita est, usque ad Portum Hamonis extensa ad urbes infra positas ducatum   85
ostenderet, alias quoque duas ab obliquo insulae quae ad ceteras ciuitates
ducatum praestarent. Deinde sanciuit eas omni honore omnique dignitate
iurisque sui esse praecepit quod de illata super eas uiolentia uindicta
sumeretur. Siquis autem scire uoluerit omnia quae de ipsis statuerit, legat
Molmutinas leges, quas Gildas hystoricus de Britannico in Latinum, rex   90
uero Aluredus de Latino in Anglicum sermonem transtulit.

40   Belino autem regnum cum pace et tranquillitate regente, frater suus
Brennius, in Gallicano litore ut praedictum est appulsus, internis anxietatibus
cruciatur; ferebat enim grauiter sese expulsum ex patria esse nec copiam
reuertendi habere ut amissa dignitate frueretur. Nescius ergo quid faceret,   95
principes Galliae adiuit, .xii. solummodo militibus comitatus. Cumque
infortunium suum singulis ostendisset neque auxilium ab ullo impetrare
quiuisset, uenit tandem ad Seginum ducem Allobrogum et ab eo honorifice
susceptus est. Morans autem apud ipsum, accessit in tantam familiaritatem
ducis ita ut non esset alter in curia qui sibi praeferretur. In omnibus namque   100
negociis tum in pace tum in bello probitatem suam monstrabat ita ut dux
illum amore patris diligeret. Erat etiam pulcher aspectu, procera et gracilia
membra habens, in uenatu uero ut decebat et in aucupatu edoctus. Cum
igitur in tantam amiciciam ducis incidisset, statuit dux de eo ut unicam
quam habebat filiam sibi maritali lege copularet. Et si masculino deinceps   105
sexu careret, concedebat ei regnum Allobrogum post obitum suum cum
filia possidendum; si autem filius ei superueniret, promittebat auxilium
ut in regem Britanniae promoueretur. Et non solum id a duce sed etiam
ab omnibus sibi subditis heroibus appetebatur, quia in tantam eorum

75 animaduerteret *Φ*
75 totius insulae *QYM:* tota insula *G*
82 longitudine *Φ*
82 Cornubio *E Y*
88 uindicta *G: om. Δ QYM:* supplicium *W (cf. 'Transm.' 101)*
97 ostenderet *Φ*
99 Morans autem *C Φ:* Morante autem *OSE:* Morante autem eo *H (cf. §§ 61.174, 157.359-60)*
104 [dux] *C¹HE*
107 filia <sua> *O Q*
108 regnum *Φ*

had Brennius become to them. Soon the girl married Brennius, the leaders of the country became his vassals and a throne was given to him. Within a year the duke's last hour had come and he breathed his last. Brennius, already popular with the local chiefs, hastened to win their loyalty by presenting them with the duke's treasure, hoarded since the days of his ancestors. Above all, he won over the Allobroges by holding feasts, turning no one away from his door.

41 Once he had won devotion from all, Brennius pondered how he could take revenge on his brother. When he informed his subjects of this, they all agreed to accompany him to any kingdom he wished. He immediately formed a great army and made a treaty with the French, allowing him to march through their provinces towards Britain without molestation. He built a fleet on the coastline of the Normans, set sail and landed in Britain after a successful voyage. As news of his arrival spread, his brother Belinus summoned all the young men of the kingdom and marched to do battle against him. But when the armies, drawn up opposite each other, were just about to engage, their mother, who was still living, hurried between the ranks. Named Tonwenna, she was eager to see her long-lost son. With trembling steps she arrived beside her son and threw her arms around him, kissing him again and again as she had longed to. She even bared her bosom and, sobbing, said to him:

'Do not forget, my son, do not forget these breasts which gave you suck nor your mother's womb, in which the Creator gave you life and brought you forth into the world while your birth-pangs wracked my body. Remember the pain I endured for you and grant my plea; forgive your brother and swallow your anger. Indeed, you need bear no anger against him, as he has never done you harm. You claim to have been exiled from your country by him, but if you examine the circumstances more carefully, you will find nothing to call unjust. His banishment of you did not lead to disgrace, but made you overcome it and climb higher. Under him, you shared a kingdom. After losing it, you became his equal by winning the kingdom of the Allobroges. What has he done other than to transform you from a poor subruler into a mighty monarch? Moreover, it was not he who caused the dispute between you, but you yourself by wanting to attack him, assisted by the king of Norway'.

amiciciam prouenerat. Nec mora, maritatur puella Brennio principesque 110
patriae subduntur soliumque regni donatur. Nec annus quo haec facta
sunt integre emensus fuerat cum suprema dies ducis adueniens ipsum
ex hac uita rapuit. Tunc Brennius principes patriae, quos prius amicicia
illexerat, obnoxios sibi facere non diffugit largiendo eis thesaurum ducis,
qui a tempore attauorum suorum reseruatus fuerat. Et quod Allobroges 115
pro maximo habebant, profusus erat in dandis cibis, nulli ianuam suam
prohibens.

41   Attractis ergo quibusque in dilectionem suam, deliberauit apud se
qualiter sese in Belinum fratrem suum uindicaret. Quod cum populo
sibi subdito indicasset, assensum fecerunt cuncti ut cum illo irent ad 120
quodcumque regnum ipsos conducere affectasset. Nec mora, collecto grandi
exercitu foedus cum Gallis iniuit ut per prouincias eorum Britanniam cum
tranquillitate adire sineretur. Exin, parato in litore Estrusensium nauigio,
mare ingressus est secundisque uelis in insulam applicuit. Diuulgato igitur
aduentu ipsius, Belinus frater, ascita totius regni iuuentute, obuiam perrexit, 125
proelium cum illo commissurus. Sed cum hinc et inde statutae cohortes fere
commisceri incepissent, accelerauit mater amborum, quae adhuc uiuebat,
per dispositas turmas incedens. Erat nomen eius Tonwenna aestuabatque
filium uidere quem multo tempore non aspexerat. Vt igitur tremulis gradibus
locum quo ipse stabat nacta fuit, brachia collo eius iniecit, desiderata basia 130
ingeminans. Nudatis quoque uberibus, illum in hunc modum affata est,
sermonem impediente singultu:

'Memento, fili, memento uberum istorum quae suxisti matrisque tuae
uteri, quo te opifex rerum in hominem ex non homine creauit, unde te in
mundum produxit angustiis mea uiscera cruciantibus. Anxietatum igitur 135
quas pro te passa sum reminiscens, peticioni meae acquiesce fratrique
tuo ueniam concede atque inceptam iram compesce. Nullam enim
aduersus eum habere debes, qui tibi nullam contumeliam intulerit. Nam
quod causaris te a natione tua per eum expulsum fuisse, si euentum rei
diligentius intueri institeris, nullatenus reperies quod iniusticiam uocabis. 140
Non enim fugauit te ut deterius tibi contingeret sed coegit deteriora
postponere ut ad potiora sublimareris. Subditus namque illi partem regni
possidebas. Quam ut amisisti, par sibi factus es Allobrogum regnum
adeptus. Quid igitur fecit nisi quod te ex paupere regulo in sublimem
regem promouit? Adde quod discidium inter uos ortum non per ipsum 145
sed per te inceptum fuit, qui auxilio regis Norguegiae fretus in ipsum
exurgere aestuaueras'.

110 peruenerat *Y, sed cf. Introd.*
113 rapuit *scripsi (corripuit 1508: eripuit 1587: fort.* surripuit*): migrauit Ω (cf. 'Transm.' 98)*
123 extrusensium *Δ ut uid. supra scripto* neustriensium *uel inuicem (*neustriensium *C¹:* ex
neustriensium trusensium *OSE¹,* trusensium del. *E²:* extrusensium *C²:* ex neustriensium *H):*
neustriensium *Φ (cf. §§ 155.301, 171.359, 176.468)*
139 a *CHS YG:* uidelicet a *OE QM*
144 te *post* regulo *Φ*
146 coeptum *Φ*

Touched by her tearful words, Brennius calmly assented, readily removing his helmet and accompanying her to his brother. Belinus, seeing his brother approaching with a peaceful expression, threw down his weapons and rushed to hug and kiss him. They immediately became friends, disarmed their troops and went to the city of Trinovantum. There they considered what to do and made ready to take their combined forces to France to conquer all its provinces.

42   A year later they crossed to France and began to ravage it. When the French heard of this, all their princes assembled and marched to fight them. Belinus and Brennius won a victory and the French fled with their ranks depleted. The triumphant Britons and Allobroges mercilessly pursued the fleeing French until they captured their kings and forced them to surrender. They sacked the fortified cities and within a year had conquered the whole country. After compelling all the provinces to submit, they directed their army against Rome and laid waste cities and towns throughout Italy.

43   At Rome, government rested in the hands of two consuls, Gabius and Porsenna; they, recognising that no nation could resist the fury of Belinus and Brennius, with the senate's approval approached them, asking for peace and friendship. They also brought many gifts of gold and silver and the promise of yearly tribute if they and their possessions were left in peace. The kings granted their request, took hostages and led their troops against Germany. Once they had begun their assault on that people, the Romans thought better of this agreement, recovered their spirits and marched to help the Germans. On discovering this, the kings were extremely angry and discussed how to attack both their enemies. For the numbers of the approaching Italians were intimidating. It was decided that Belinus and the Britons should remain in Germany to fight the enemy there, whilst Brennius and his army should go to Rome to punish the Romans for breaking their word. The Italians discovered this and separated from the Germans, making for Rome to intercept Brennius. When Belinus was informed of this, he mustered his army and hurried that night to occupy a valley through which his enemies must pass, hiding there to await their arrival. The next day the Italians' march brought them to the spot. When they saw hostile weapons glittering in the valley, they were instantly amazed, thinking that it was Brennius and the Senones from Gaul. As soon as he saw the enemy, Belinus charged and engaged them fiercely. The Romans, unarmed and disordered because they had been taken by surprise, immediately left the field in flight; Belinus pursued without pity, cutting them down ceaselessly until night brought an end to the massacre.

Super his igitur quae ipsa cum fletu expresserat motus, sedato animo oboediuit et ultro deposita galea cum illa ad fratrem perrexit. Belinus ergo, ut illum cum uultu pacis ad se uenire calluit, abiectis armis in amplexus 150 eiusdem cum osculo cucurrit. Nec mora, amici facti sunt adinuicem et cohortibus exarmatis urbem Trinouantum uenerunt. Ibi consilio coepto quid facerent parauerunt exercitum communem in Galliarum partes ducere cunctasque prouincias potestati suae submittere.

42   Emenso deinde anno, transfretauerunt ad Gallias patriamque uastare 155 coeperunt. Quod cum per nationes diuulgatum esset, conuenerunt omnes reguli Francorum obuiamque uenientes contra eos dimicauerunt. At Belino et Brennio uictoria proueniente Franci uulneratis cateruis diffugierunt. Mox Britones et Allobroges, ut triumpho potiti sunt, fugientes Gallos insequi non cessauerunt donec captis regibus ipsos deditioni coegerunt. Munitis etiam 160 urbibus euersis, totum regnum infra unum annum submiserunt. Postremo, cum uniuersas prouincias deditioni compulissent, petierunt Romam cum tota multitudine sua urbesque et colonos per Italiam depopulant.

43   Erant tunc Romae duo consules, Gabius et Porsenna, quorum regimini patria commissa fuerat; qui cum uidissent nullam gentem saeuitiae Belini 165 atque Brennii resistere ualere, assensu senatorum uenerunt ad illos, concordiam et amiciciam petentes. Optulerunt etiam plurima donaria auri et argenti singulisque annis tributum ut sua cum pace possidere sinerentur. Sumptis igitur obsidibus, ueniam donauerunt reges cohortesque suas in Germaniam duxerunt. Cumque populum infestare institissent, piguit 170 Romanos praedicti foederis et reuocata audatia Germanis in auxilium processerunt. Quod cum regibus compertum esset, ultra modum id grauiter ferentes, consilium inierunt quomodo utrumque populum oppugnarent. Tanta namque multitudo Italorum superuenerat ita ut illis terrori essent. Consilio igitur habito, remansit Belinus cum Britonibus in Germania, 175 proelia hostibus illaturus, Brennius uero cum exercitibus suis Romam adiuit ut ruptum foedus in Romanos uindicaret. Id autem Itali scientes deseruerunt Germanos et Romam reuerti captantes iter Brennii praecedere festinauerunt. Belinus itaque, ut id sibi nunciatum fuerat, reuocato exercitu praeterita nocte accelerauit quandamque uallem nactus qua hostes praeterituri erant infra 180 illam delituit et aduentum illorum expectauit. Sequenti deinde die instante, uenerunt Itali ad eundem locum, coeptum iter facientes. Et cum uallem armis hostium fulgere prospexissent, confestim stupefacti arbitrati sunt Brennium Senonesque Gallos adesse. Belinus ergo, compertis hostibus, subito impetu irruptionem fecit in illos atque acriter inuasit. Nec mora, Romani ex inprouiso 185 occupati, quia inermes et sine ordine incesserant, cum fuga campum deseruerunt; quos Belinus sine pietate sequens trucidare non cessauit donec superueniente nocte inceptam stragem nequiuit perficere. Cum uictoria

156 fuisset Φ
169 igitur *OCHS:* ergo *E:* itaque Φ
179 *de* praeterita nocte *cf. Introd.*
184 compertis *ut § 143.39*

Then he marched in triumph to Brennius, who had been besieging Rome for three days. Once they had joined forces, they attacked the city from all sides, trying to pierce its walls; and, to increase its suffering, they set up gallows before the gates, informing the besieged that, unless they surrendered, they would hang the hostages they had been given. But the Romans, despite their attachment to their sons and nephews, remained unshaken and continued to defend themselves. Sometimes they destroyed the enemy engines with the same or counter-engines, sometimes they used weapons of all kinds to drive the foe back from their walls. At this, the brothers, blazing with remorseless anger, ordered that twenty-four of the noblest hostages be hung before their parents' eyes. This and a message from the consuls Gabius and Porsenna saying that they would arrive to relieve them the next day made the Romans more determined, and they decided to come out of the city to fight. As they were carefully drawing up their forces, the two consuls arrived on the battlefield, having reunited their scattered men. They advanced in deep columns and attacked the unsuspecting Allobroges and Britons. The citizens came out to join them and at first inflicted not inconsiderable casualties. The brothers were concerned at the sudden slaughter of their men, but began to encourage them and reorder their ranks. By making frequent charges they began to force the enemy back. After thousands of troops had fallen on both sides, victory finally went to the brothers. After the death of Gabius and the capture of Porsenna they took the city and gave to their soldiers the riches its inhabitants had hoarded.

44   Once the brothers had triumphed, Brennius stayed in Italy, where he subjected the people to unparalleled oppression; the histories of Rome record his subsequent career and death, so I have omitted them to avoid making this work too long and also losing the thread by repeating what has been dealt with by others. Belinus returned to Britain and ruled the country in peace for the rest of his days. He repaired the existing cities where they were dilapidated and built many new ones. Amongst others he built one on the river Usk near the mouth of the Severn, which became the metropolitan city of Demetia and for a long time was known as Kaerusk; after the Romans came, it was called instead Caerleon, taking its name from the Roman legions which used to winter there. In the city of Trinovantum Belinus made a wonderful gate beside the Thames, which the inhabitants now call Billingsgate after him. Above it he built a huge tower and at its foot a port where ships could land. Throughout his kingdom he reestablished his father's laws, always maintaining justice. During his reign the people enjoyed riches surpassing any period before or after. When death finally carried him off from this world, his body was burned and his ashes placed in a golden vessel, skilfully positioned on the top of his tower in Trinovantum.

deinde Brennium petiuit, qui iam die tercio instante Romam obsidebat. Vt
igitur communem exercitum fecerunt, inuadentes undique urbem moenia 190
prosternere insistunt et ut maiorem cladem ingererent erexerunt furcas ante
portas ciuitatis obsessisque mandauerunt quod obsides quos dederant in
patibulo suspenderent nisi sese deditioni summitterent. Verum Romani,
in proposito suo perseuerantes, despecta natorum et nepotum pietate, sese
defendere intendunt; nam quandoque machinationes eorum contrariis uel 195
consimilibus machinationibus conterebant, quandoque uero omnimodis telis
ipsos a moenibus repellebant. Cumque id conspexissent fratres, confestim
proterua ignescentes ira .xxiiii. nobilissimos obsidum in conspectu
parentum suspendi praeceperunt. Itaque Romani, proteruiores insistentes
et freti legatione Gabii et Porsennae consulum, qui ipsis mandauerant quod 200
in auxilium eorum sequenti die uenirent, urbem egredi statuerunt et cum
hostibus proelia committere. Et dum turmas suas sapienter distribuerent,
ecce praedicti consules, resociatis sociis qui dispersi fuerant, proeliaturi
aduenerunt. Densis autem agminibus incedentes, ex inprouiso inuaserunt
Allobroges et Britones. Egressis quoque ciuibus consociati, stragem primo 205
non minimam fecerunt. Porro fratres, cum cladem commilitonum tam subito
illatam inspexissent, admodum anxiati socios coeperunt hortari atque in
turmas resociare. Crebras etiam irruptiones facientes, hostes retro cedere
coegerunt. Postremo, peremptis in utraque parte ad milia pugnantibus,
uictoria fratribus prouenit. Interfecto etiam Gabio et capto Porsenna, urbem 210
ceperunt et absconditas conciuium opes commilitonibus dederunt.

44 Habita ergo uictoria, remansit Brennius in Italia, populum inaudita
tyrannide afficiens; cuius ceteros actus et exitum quia Romanae hystoriae
declarant nequaquam tractare curaui, cum et nimiam prolixitatem huic
operi ingessissem et id quod alii tractauerunt perarans a proposito meo 215
diuertissem. Belinus uero in Britanniam reuersus est et cum tranquillitate
reliquis uitae suae diebus patriam tractauit. Renouauit etiam aedificatas
urbes ubicumque collapsae fuerant et multas nouas aedificauit. Inter
ceteras composuit unam super Oscam flumen prope Sabrinum mare,
quae multis temporibus Kaerusc appellata metropolis Demetiae fuerat; 220
postquam autem Romani uenerunt, praefato nomine deleto uocata est Vrbs
Legionum, uocabulum trahens a Romanis legionibus quae ibidem hiemare
solebant. Fecit etiam in urbe Trinouantum ianuam mirae fabricae super
ripam Tamensis, quam de nomine suo ciues temporibus istis Belinesgata
uocant. Desuper uero aedificauit turrim mirae magnitudinis portumque 225
subtus ad pedem applicantibus nauibus idoneum. Leges patris ubique per
regnum renouauit, constanti iusticiae indulgens. In diebus igitur eius tanta
copia diuiciarum populum refecit quantam nec retro aetas habuisse testetur
nec subsequens consecuta fuisse. Postremo, cum supprema dies ipsum
ex hac uita rapuisset, combustum est corpus eius et puluis in aureo cado 230
reconditus, quem in urbe Trinouantum in summitate praedictae turris mira
arte locauerunt.

205-6 non minimam primo Φ

45   He was succeeded by his son Gurguint Barbtruc, a wise and moderate man, who, as a lover of peace and justice, was guided in all things by his father's example. When his neighbours rose against him, he summoned his courage like his father before him and fought stern battles before reducing his foes to a proper state of subjection. Amongst other things it happened that the king of the Danes refused to Gurguint the tribute he used to pay when Belinus was king, and withheld the submission he owed him; Gurguint angrily sailed to Denmark with a fleet and subjected its people to terrible defeats, killing their king and returning the country to its former position of servitude.

46   At the time he won this victory, as he was sailing homewards through the Orkneys, Gurguint came upon thirty ships filled with men and women; when he asked the reason for their coming, their leader, named Partholoim, came and bowed low before him, asking for his pardon and for peace. He said that he had been expelled from Spain and was roving those waters to find a new home. He asked for a part of Britain to live in and so bring an end to his tiresome voyage; it had been a year and a half since he and his companions had been driven from their country to sail the ocean. After learning the wishes of these people, who had come from Spain and were called Basques, Gurguint sent them with guides to Ireland, an island at that time devoid of inhabitants, which he granted to them. They increased and multiplied there and have occupied the island ever since, up to the present day. Gurguint Barbtruc ended his days peacefully and was buried in Caerleon, in which, after his father's death, he had constructed fine buildings and walls.

47   After him Guithelinus inherited the crown of the kingdom, which throughout his life he ruled with kindness and moderation. He had a noble wife, called Marcia, skilled in all the arts. Among the many novelties devised by this intelligent woman was the law which the British called Marcian. This and much else was translated by King Alfred, who named it Merchenelage in English. On his death, Guithelinus' crown passed to his wife Marcia and his son, called Sisillius. The latter was then seven years old, too young for the government of the country to be entrusted to him. His able and intelligent mother therefore came to rule the whole island; and after her demise, Sisillius reigned as king. After him ruled his son Kimarus, who was succeeded by his brother Danius. When Danius died, he was followed by Morvidus, his son by his concubine Tangustela. Morvidus would have enjoyed a fine reputation were it not for his excessive cruelty: once roused, he would ruthlessly kill anybody if he could lay his hands on a weapon. He was handsome, a generous giver of gifts and so strong that no one in the kingdom could overcome him.

45   Exin successit ei Gurguint Barbtruc filius eiusdem, uir modestus et
prudens, qui per omnia paternos actus imitans pacem et iusticiam amabat. Et
cum uicini aduersus eum rebellabant, audaciam exemplo genitoris reuocans 235
proelia dira committebat et hostes ad debitam subiectionem reducebat. Inter
plura alia contigit quod rex Dacorum, qui diebus patris tributum eidem
reddebat, huic reddere diffugeret et ei debitam subiectionem denegaret;
quod ipse grauiter ferens duxit nauigium in Daciam afflictoque dirissimis
proeliis populo interfecit regem patriamque pristino iugo subposuit.   240

46   Ea tempestate, cum post istam uictoriam domum per insulas Orcadum
rediret, inuenit .xxx. naues uiris et mulieribus plenas; et cum causam
aduentus eorum inquisiuisset, accessit ad ipsum dux illorum, Partholoim
nomine, et adorato eo ueniam et pacem rogauit. Dicebat autem se ex partibus
Hispaniarum expulsum fuisse et maria illa circuire ut locum mansionis   245
haberet. Petebat etiam ab illo portiunculam Britanniae ad inhabitandam ne
odiosum iter maris diutius pererraret; annus enim et dimidius iam emensus
fuerat ex quo a patria sua pulsus per occeanum cum sociis nauigauerat.
Vt igitur Gurguint Barbtruc et ipsos ex Hispania uenisse et Basclenses
uocatos esse et petitionem eorum edoctus fuit, misit homines cum eis   250
ad insulam Hiberniae, quae tunc uasta omni incola carebat, eamque illis
concessit. Deinde creuerunt illic et multiplicati sunt insulamque usque in
hodiernum diem tenuerunt. Gurguint uero Barbtruc, cum dies uitae suae
cum pace explesset, sepultus fuit in Vrbe Legionum, quam post obitum
patris aedificiis et muris decorare studuerat.   255

47   Post illum autem Guithelinus diadema regni suscepit, quod omni tempore
uitae suae benigne et modeste tractauit. Erat ei nobilis mulier Marcia nomine,
omnibus artibus erudita. Haec inter multa et inaudita quae proprio ingenio
reppererat inuenit legem quam Britones Marcianam appellauerunt. Hanc
etiam rex Aluredus inter cetera transtulit et Saxonica lingua Merchenelage 260
uocauit. At ut Guithelinus obiuit, remansit gubernaculum regni praedictae
reginae et filio ipsius, qui Sisillius uocabatur. Erat tunc Sisillius .vii.
annorum nec aetas ipsius expetebat ut regnum moderationi illius cessisset.
Qua de causa mater, quia consilio et sensu pollebat, imperium totius
insulae optinuit; et cum ab hac luce migrasset, Sisillius sumpto diademate 265
gubernaculo potitus est. Post illum Kimarus filius suus regimen optinuit,
cui successit Danius eiusdem frater. Quo defuncto, insignitus est Moruidus,
quem ex Tangustela concubina genuerat. Hic nimia probitate famosissimus
esset nisi plus nimiae crudelitati indulsisset; nemini namque parcebat iratus
quin eum interficeret si copiam telorum repperiret. Erat namque pulcher 270
aspectu et in dandis muneribus profusus, nec erat alter tantae fortitudinis in
regno qui congressum eius sustentare quiuisset.

233 Exin *OCSE:* Exinde *H:* Post haec *Φ*
243 inquiuisset *Q:* inquisisset *YM*
246 ad inhabitandum *S (cf. Introd.)*
251 tum *CH*
253 hodiernam *QGM*

48   During his reign the king of the Flemings landed in Northumbria and began to ravage it. Morvidus collected all his able-bodied subjects and marched to fight him. In the ensuing battle he achieved more by himself than almost the entire army which he commanded. After he had won, no one escaped his clutches alive. He ordered the men to be brought to him one after another so that he could indulge his savagery by dispatching each one; and when he paused for a while exhausted, he ordered that they be flayed and then burned alive. In the midst of these and similar acts of cruelty he suffered a misfortune which put an end to his wickedness. A beast of incredible ferocity came from the region of the Irish sea and began to devour without respite those living near the coast. When reports of this reached Morvidus' ears, he came in person and fought against it single-handed. But when he had used up all his missiles on it without effect, the monster rushed up and swallowed him in its open jaws like a little fish.

49   Morvidus had five sons, the eldest of whom, Gorbonianus, ascended the throne. No man of that time was fairer than him, a greater promoter of justice or a more diligent ruler of his people. He never failed to show above all the honour due to the gods and then justice and equity to his people. In every city of Britain he repaired the gods' temples and built many new ones. Throughout his reign the island enjoyed an abundance of riches beyond that of any of its neighbours. He also encouraged farmers to till their fields and protected them from the injustices of their masters. He gave the young warriors so much gold and silver that they had no need to squabble. Amid these many deeds of his inherent goodness he met his end, and his corpse was buried in the city of Trinovantum.

50   After Gorbonianus his brother Arthgallo was crowned king, though all his actions were the opposite of his brother's: at every opportunity he strove to remove nobles and promote the low-born, to strip everybody of their wealth and to amass huge riches. The nobles of the kingdom could bear it no longer, rose up and deprived him of the throne. In his place they crowned his brother Elidurus, who was later called 'the dutiful' because he took pity on his brother. For, after Elidurus had reigned for five years, he happened, while hunting in the forest of Calaterium, to meet his deposed brother. He had been wandering through all the neighbouring realms seeking help to recover his lost crown, but without success; when he could bear the onset of poverty no longer, he returned to Britain with no more than ten knights. So he came to be passing through the forest in search of his former friends when his brother unexpectedly saw him. Elidurus at once ran to embrace him, showering him with kisses. For a long time he wept over his brother's misfortune, then took him to the city of Dumbarton and hid him in his bedroom. Next he pretended to be ill and sent messengers throughout the kingdom

48   Temporibus ipsius applicuit quidam rex Morianorum cum magna manu in Northamhimbriam et patriam uastare incepit. Cui Moruidus, collecta totius potestatis suae iuuentute, obuiam perrexit et cum illo proeliatus est. 275 Plus ipse solus in proeliando proficiebat quam maxima pars exercitus cui principabatur. Et ut uictoria potitus est, non euasit ullus uiuus quin ipsum interficeret. Iubebat enim unum post alium ante se adduci ut quemque perimendo crudelitatem suam saciaret; et cum fatigatus paulisper cessasset, praecipiebat ipsos uiuos excoriari et excoriatos comburi. Inter haec et alia 280 saeuiciae suae gesta contigit ei infortunium quoddam quod nequitiam suam deleuit. Aduenerat namque ex partibus Hibernici maris inauditae feritatis belua, quae incolas iuxta maritima sine intermissione deuorabat. Cumque fama aures eius attigisset, accessit ipse ad illam et solus cum ea congressus est. At cum omnia tela sua in illa in uanum consumpsisset, accelerauit 285 monstrum illud et apertis faucibus ipsum uelut pisciculum deuorauit.

49   Generauerat ipse quinque filios, quorum primogenitus, Gorbonianus nomine, solium regni suscepit. Nullus ea tempestate iustior erat aut amantior aequi nec qui populum maiori diligentia tractaret. Mos eius continuus erat debitum honorem diis primum impendere et rectam plebi iusticiam. Per 290 cunctas regni Britanniae ciuitates templa deorum renouabat et plura noua aedificabat. Omnibus diebus eius tanta diuitiarum copia insula affluebat quantam nullae collaterales prouinciae habebant. Quippe colonos ad agri culturam inanimabat, ipsos ab iniuriis dominorum defendens. Bellatores quoque iuuenes auro et argento ditabat ita ut nulli opus esset iniuriam alteri 295 facere. Inter haec et plurima innatae bonitatis ipsius gesta debita naturae soluens ab hac luce migrauit et in urbe Trinouantum sepultus est.

50   Post illum Arthgallo frater regio diademate insignitur, qui in omnibus suis actibus germano diuersus extitit; nobiles namque ubique laborabat deponere et ignobiles exaltare, diuitibus quibusque sua auferre, infinitos 300 thesauros accumulans. Quod heroes regni diutius ferre recusantes insurrexerunt in illum et a solio regio deposuerunt. Exin erexerunt Elidurum fratrem suum, qui postea propter misericordiam quam in fratrem fecit Pius uocatus fuit. Nam cum regnum emenso quinquennio possedisset, forte in Calaterio nemore uenans obuiauit fratri suo, qui depositus fuerat. Ipse 305 uero, peragratis quibusque prouincialibus regnis, auxilium quaesiuerat ut amissum honorem recuperare quiuisset, nec usquam inuenerat; et cum superuenientem paupertatem diutius ferre non potuisset, reuersus est in Britanniam, .x. solummodo militibus sociatus. Petens igitur illos quos dudum habuerat amicos, praedictum nemus praeteribat cum Elidurus frater 310 eius ipsum non speratum aspexit. Quo itaque uiso, cucurrit Elidurus et amplexatus est illum, infinita oscula ingeminans. Et ut diu miseriam ipsius defleuit, duxit illum secum in ciuitatem Aldclud et in thalamo suo occuluit. Exin finxit se infirmum ibi nuntiosque suos per totum regnum direxit

274 coepit Φ
284 ea Δ: sola Φ
294 animabat H Y (cf. § 66.299)
314 Post haec Φ

to tell his chief subjects to come to see him. When they had all arrived in the city where he lay ill, he instructed that they should enter his room quietly, one after another; he said that, if they came in all together, their talking would make his head ache. They all readily obeyed his command and entered his dwelling one after another. As they did so, Elidurus ordered his servants, who were ready at hand, to seize them and cut off their heads unless they submitted once more to Arthgallo. He did this to each of them, reconciling them all to Arthgallo through fear. Having ratified this arrangement, Elidurus took Arthgallo to York, removed the crown from his own head and placed it on his brother's. So he won the name 'the dutiful' because of his love for his brother. Arthgallo ruled for ten years and mended his ways; he now began to remove the low-born and promote the nobles, to let each person enjoy their possessions, and to be fair and just. Finally he fell ill and died, and was buried in the city of Leicester.

51   Elidurus was then crowned for a second time and restored to his old position; he showed all the good qualities of his elder brother Gorbonianus, but his other brothers, Iugenius and Peredurus, assembled troops from all quarters to attack him. They won, capturing Elidurus and placing him under armed guard in the tower at Trinovantum. They then divided the kingdom: the portion to the west of the river Humber went to Iugenius, the remainder and all of Scotland to Peredurus. When Iugenius died seven years later, Peredurus gained control over the whole country. After being crowned, he ruled with such kindness and moderation that people thought he surpassed his brothers and forgot about Elidurus. Death, however, spares no one and brought Peredurus' life to a sudden end. Elidurus was immediately freed from prison and ascended the throne for a third time; he lived out his days in goodness and justice until he finally passed away, a paragon of virtue for his successors.

52   After Elidurus had died, Gorbonianus' son Regin inherited the crown and was guided by the same good sense and wisdom as his uncle; he avoided despotism, treated his subjects with justice and mercy, and never deviated from the right path. He was succeeded by Arthgallo's son Marganus, who was also chastened by the example of his parents and ruled the British people in peace. He was succeeded by his brother Enniaunus, who treated the people quite differently and was deposed in the sixth year of his reign; he had neglected justice and preferred tyranny, which led to his downfall. He was replaced by his relative Iduallo, Iugenius' son,

qui principibus sibi subditis suggessissent ut ad se uisitandum uenirent. 315
Cumque cuncti in urbe qua iacebat conuenissent, praecepit ut unusquisque
thalamum suum singulatim et sine tumultu ingrederetur; asserebat enim
sermonem plurium capiti suo nociturum si cateruatim superuenissent.
Credulus ergo quisque iussioni eius paruit unusque post alterum domum
ingressus est. Singulos itaque ingredientes praecipiebat Elidurus ministris 320
qui ad hoc parati fuerant capere ipsisque capita amputare nisi se iterum
Arthgalloni fratri suo summisissent. Sic faciebat separatim de cunctis, et
omnes Arthgalloni mediante timore pacificauit. Confirmato denique foedere,
duxit Elidurus Arthgallonem Eboracum cepitque diadema de capite suo et
fratris capiti imposuit. Vnde sortitus est hoc nomen Pius, quia praedictam 325
pietatem in fratrem habuerat. Regnauit igitur Arthgallo decem annis et sese
ab incepta nequitia correxit; uice etenim uersa coepit ignobiles deponere
et generosos exaltare, quod suum erat unicuique permittere, rectamque
iusticiam exercere. Denique, superueniente languore, defunctus est et in
urbe Kaerleir sepultus.   330

51   Erigitur Elidurus iterum in regem et pristinae dignitati restituitur; sed
dum Gorbonianum primogenitum fratrem in omni bonitate insequeretur,
duo residui fratres eius, Iugenius et Peredurus, collectis undique armatis
cum illo proeliari aggrediuntur. Potiti uero uictoria, ceperunt illum et infra
turrim urbis Trinouantum incluserunt, imponentes custodes. Exin partiti 335
sunt regnum in duo; cuius pars quae ab Humbro flumine uersus occidentem
uergit in sortem cecidit Iugenii, altera uero cum tota Albania Pereduro.
Emensis deinde .vii. annis, obiuit Iugenius et totum regnum cessit Pereduro.
Insignitus itaque illud benigne postmodum et modeste gubernauit ita ut
antecessores fratres excellere diceretur nec de Eliduro mentio fieret. Sed 340
cum nemini mors parcere nesciat, ipsa repentino cursu ueniens ipsum
uitae surripuit. Eripitur continuo Elidurus carceri et tercio in solium regni
sublimatur; et cum omne tempus suum in bonitate et iusticia expleuisset, ab
hac luce migrans exemplum pietatis successoribus suis deseruit.

52   Defuncto itaque Eliduro, suscepit Regin Gorboniani filius diadema 345
regni et auunculum in sensu et prudentia imitatus est; postposita namque
tyrannide iusticiam atque misericordiam in populum exercebat nec unquam
a tramite rectitudinis deuiauit. Post illum regnauit Marganus Arthgallonis
filius, qui etiam exemplo parentum serenatus gentem Britonum cum
tranquillitate tractauit. Huic successit Enniaunus frater suus, qui longe ab 350
illo distans in tractando populum sexto anno regni sui a regia sede depositus
est; postposita namque iusticia, tyrannidem praeelegerat, quae illum a solio
regni deposuit. In loco eius positus fuit cognatus suus Iduallo Iugenii filius,

319 unus quisque *O YG*
321 erant *Φ*
332 insequeretur *C²HSE (cf. §§ 21.464-5, 72.410, 125.163, 147.101):* insequitur *C¹O:* sequeretur *Φ*
333 [collectis undique armatis] *Φ*
335 Postea *Φ*
341 sciat *E, fort. auctorem corrigens*

who was persuaded by Enniaunus' fate to respect what was lawful and right. After him there succeeded Peredurus' son Runo, then Elidurus' son Gerontius, then his son Catellus, then Coillus, then Porrex and finally Cherin. He had three sons, Fulgenius, Eldadus and Andragius, who ruled one after the other. They were succeeded by Andragius's son Urianus, next came Eliud, then Cledaucus, then Clotenus, then Gurgintius, then Merianus, then Bledudo, then Cap, then Oenus, then Sisillius and finally Bledgabred. He surpassed all previous singers in melody and in playing all musical instruments to such an extent that he was called the performers' god. He was succeeded by his brother Arthmail, next came Eldol, then Redion, then Rederchius, then Samuil Penissel, then Pir, then Capoir. Capoir was succeeded by his son Cligueillus, who showed moderation and wisdom in all he did and above all treated his subjects fairly and justly.

53   He was succeeded by his son Heli, who ruled for sixty years. Heli had three sons, Lud, Cassibellaunus and Nennius. Lud, as eldest, succeeded after his father's death. He was a great builder of cities, who repaired the walls of Trinovantum and surrounded it with numerous towers. He commanded its citizens to build homes and houses there, so that no foreign city could boast finer palaces. A warrior and a generous feast-giver, he possessed many cities, but always preferred Trinovantum and used to spend the greater part of the year there. Later it was renamed Kaerlud, a name afterwards corrupted to Kaerlundein; as time passed and languages changed, it was called Lundene and then Lundres when foreigners landed and conquered the country. When Lud died, his body was buried there beside the gate which is still named after him, Porhlud in British and Ludgate in English. He had two sons, Androgeus and Tenuantius; but because they were too young to rule, his brother Cassibellaunus was crowned in their place. As soon as Cassibellaunus occupied the throne, he began to show such generosity and goodness that his fame spread through far-off kingdoms; for this reason the island's crown passed to him, not his nephews. Out of affection, however, Cassibellaunus did not want them to be deprived of power and gave them a considerable share; to Androgeus he granted the city of Trinovantum and the duchy of Kent, and to Tenuantius the duchy of Cornwall. He, as crowned monarch, ranked above them and the chiefs of the whole island.

qui euentu Enniauni correctus ius atque rectitudinem colebat. Huic successit Runo Pereduri filius, cui Gerontius Eliduri filius, post illum Catellus filius 355 suus, post Catellum Coillus, post Coillum Porrex, post Porrecem Cherin. Huic nati fuerunt tres filii, Fulgenius uidelicet atque Eldadus nec non et Andragius, qui omnes alter post alterum regnauerunt. Exin successit Vrianus Andragii filius, cui Eliud, cui Cledaucus, cui Clotenus, cui Gurgintius, cui Merianus, cui Bledudo, cui Cap, cui Oenus, cui Sisillius, cui Bledgabred. 360 Hic omnes cantores quos retro aetas habuerat et in modulis et in omnibus musicis instrumentis excedebat ita ut deus ioculatorum diceretur. Post illum regnauit Arthmail frater suus, post Arthmail Eldol, cui successit Redion, cui Rederchius, cui Samuil Penissel, cui Pir, cui Capoir. Deinde successit Cligueillus Capoirri filius, uir in omnibus actibus modestus et prudens et 365 qui super omnia rectam iusticiam inter populos exercebat.

53   Post illum successit Heli filius eius regnumque .lx. annis tractauit. Hic tres generauit filios, Lud, Cassibellaunum, Nennium. Quorum primogenitus, uidelicet Lud, regnum post obitum patris suscepit. Exin, gloriosus aedificator urbium existens, renouauit muros urbis Trinouantum 370 et innumerabilibus turribus eam circumcinxit. Praecepit etiam ciuibus ut domos et aedificia sua in eadem construerent ita ut non esset in longe positis regnis ciuitas quae pulcriora palacia contineret. Fuit ipse bellicosus homo et in dandis epulis profusus, et cum plures ciuitates possideret hanc prae omnibus amabat et in illa maiori tempore totius anni commanebat. Vnde 375 nominata fuit postmodum Kaerlud et deinde per corruptionem nominis Kaerlundein; succedente quoque tempore, per commutationem linguarum dicta fuit Lundene et postea Lundres, applicantibus alienigenis qui patriam sibi submittebant. Defuncto tandem illo, corpus eius reconditum fuit in praedicta ciuitate iuxta portam illam quae adhuc de nomine suo Porhlud 380 Britannice, Saxonice uero Ludesgata nuncupatur. Nati fuerant ei duo filii, Androgeus et Tenuantius; qui cum propter aetatem regnum tractare nequiuissent, Cassibellaunus frater suus loco illorum sublimatur. Mox, ut diademate insignitus fuit, coepit ita largitate atque probitate uigere ut fama illius per remota regna diuulgaretur; unde contigit ut totius regni monarchia 385 sibi et non nepotibus cederet. Cassibellaunus tamen, pietati indulgens, noluit iuuenes expertes esse regni sed eis magnam partem distribuit; urbem etenim Trinouantum cum ducatu Cantiae largitus est Androgeo, ducatum uero Cornubiae Tenuantio. Ipse autem diademate praelatus illis et totius insulae principibus imperabat.   390

362 excedebat *Φ* (*cf. § 173.407*): *om. Δ*: exsuperauerat *O²*: *melius* superabat *15 ut §§ 78.138, 137.456, 152.211 (cf. 'Transm.' 90)*
367 .xl. *E Φ*

BOOK FOUR

54 Meanwhile, as we read in the histories of Rome, it happened that after his conquest of Gaul Julius Caesar had arrived on the coast of Flanders; and when, as he surveyed the ocean, he spied the island of Britain from there, he asked those standing beside him about the country and its inhabitants. On learning the name of the kingdom and its people, he exclaimed:

'By Hercules, we Romans and the Britons share a common ancestry, being both descended from the Trojans. After the sack of Troy our first ancestor was Aeneas, theirs Brutus, whose father was Silvius, son of Aeneas's son Ascanius. But, unless I am mistaken, they are no longer our equals and have no idea of soldiering, since they live at the edge of the world amid the ocean. We shall easily force them to pay tribute to us and obey Roman authority forever. However, as they have not yet been approached or affected by the Roman people, we must first instruct them to pay taxes and like other nations submit to the senate, lest we offend the ancient dignity of our ancestor Priam by shedding the blood of our cousins'.

55 He sent a letter to this effect to Cassibellaunus, who angrily returned the following response:

'Cassibellaunus king of the Britons sends greetings to Gaius Julius Caesar. The greed of the Roman people, Caesar, is remarkable. In their thirst for gold and silver, they cannot bring themselves, though we live at the world's edge amid the perils of the ocean, to forgo seeking the wealth which we have so far enjoyed in peace. If that were not enough, they also demand we submit and become their slaves forever. Your request disgraces you, Caesar, since Briton and Roman share the same blood-line from Aeneas, a shining chain of common ancestry which ought to bind us in lasting friendship. Friendship, not slavery, is what you should have asked us for, since we are more accustomed to give that than to bear the yoke of servitude. We are so used to freedom that we have no idea what it is to serve a master; if the gods themselves tried to take it from us, we would strive with every sinew to retain our liberty. Let it therefore be clear to you, Caesar, that, whatever your intentions, we will fight for our freedom and our country if you attempt to carry out your threat of landing in the island of Britain'.

56 After reading this letter, Gaius Julius Caesar prepared his fleet and awaited favourable winds in order to put his message to Cassibellaunus into effect. When the wind changed, he hoisted his sails and landed with his army at the mouth of the river Thames. Just as Caesar's ships made land, Cassibellaunus set off with his whole army to the town of Dorobellum, where he consulted his nobles as to how he could best drive away the enemy.

LIBER IIII

54 Interea contigit, ut in Romanis repperitur hystoriis, Iulium Caesarem
subiugata Gallia ad litus Rutenorum uenisse; et cum illinc Britanniam
insulam aspexisset, quaesiuit a circumstantibus quae patria et quae gens
inhabitasset dum ad occeanum intueretur. Cumque nomen regni didicisset
et populi, dixit: 5

'Hercle ex eadem prosapia nos Romani et Britones orti sumus, quia ex
Troiana gente processimus. Nobis Aeneas post destructionem Troiae
primus pater fuit, illis autem Brutus, quem Siluius Ascanii filii Aeneae
filius progenuit. Sed nisi fallor ualde degenerati sunt a nobis nec quid sit
milicia nouerunt, cum infra occeanum extra orbem commaneant. Leuiter 10
cogendi erunt tributum nobis dare et continuum obsequium Romanae
dignitati praestare. Prius tamen mandandum est eis ut inaccessi a Romano
populo et intacti uectigal reddant, ut ceterae etiam gentes subiectionem
senatui faciant, ne nos ipsorum cognatorum nostrorum sanguinem
fundentes antiquam nobilitatem patris nostri Priami offendamus'. 15

55 Quod cum litteris suis Cassibellauno regi mandauisset, indignatus est
Cassibellaunus et ei epistulam suam in haec uerba direxit:

'Cassibellaunus rex Britonum Gaio Iulio Caesari. Miranda est, Caesar,
Romani populi cupiditas, qui quicquid est auri uel argenti sitiens nequit
nos infra pericula occeani extra orbem positos pati quin census nostros 20
appetere praesumat, quos hactenus quiete possedimus. Nec hoc quidem
sufficit nisi postposita libertate subiectionem ei faciamus, perpetuam
seruitutem subituri. Opprobrium itaque tibi petiuisti, Caesar, cum
communis nobilitatis uena Britonibus et Romanis ab Aenea defluat et
eiusdem cognationis una et eadem catena praefulgeat, qua in firmam 25
amicitiam coniungi deberent. Illa a nobis petenda esset, non seruitus, quia
eam potius largiri didicimus quam seruitutis iugum deferre. Libertatem
namque in tantum consueuimus habere quod prorsus ignoramus quid sit
seruituti oboedire; quam si ipsi dii conarentur nobis eripere, elaboraremus
utique omni nisu resistere ut eam retineremus. Liqueat igitur dispositioni 30
tuae, Caesar, nos pro illa et pro regno nostro pugnaturos si ut comminatus
es infra insulam Britanniae superuenire inceperis'.

56 His itaque uisis, Gaius Iulius Caesar nauigium suum parat prosperosque
uentos expectat ut quod Cassibellauno mandauerat effectibus prosequeretur.
Optato igitur uento instante, erexit uela sua et in hostium Tamensis 35
fluminis cum exercitu suo applicuit. Iamque rates tellurem appulerant, ecce
Cassibellaunus cum tota fortitudine sua occurrit et ad Dorobellum oppidum
ueniens ibi consilium cum proceribus regni iniuit qualiter hostes longius

3 *fort.* patria <esset>
13-14 ut ceterae etiam *pro* 'et sicut ceterae' *ut uid.:* <et> ut *15 et ita fere W:* faciunt *pro* faciant
Wright (cf. Introd.)
23 petisti *YG*
27 deferre *pro* ferre *(DmLBs § 3)*

With him was Bellinus, the general of his forces, on whose advice the governance of the whole kingdom depended; also present were his two nephews, Androgeus duke of Trinovantum and Tenuantius duke of Cornwall, and three sub-rulers, Cridious of Scotland, Gueithaet of Venedotia and Britahel of Demetia. When they had inspired the others to fight, they advised an immediate attack on Caesar's camp to drive him out before he had taken any city or town; they said that it would be harder to drive him away after he had occupied the country's strongpoints, since it would then be clear to him where he and his soldiers could retreat. Everybody agreed and made for the coast where Caesar had erected his camp and tents. When the opposing forces were drawn up, they fought there, matching spear for spear and blow for blow. Men immediately fell on both sides, pierced by enemy weapons. The earth was as wet with the blood of the dying as if a south wind was raining down the sea water it had soaked up. As the two forces clashed, fate brought Nennius and Androgeus, with the men of Kent and the citizens of Trinovantum whom they commanded, up against the troops of the emperor. When they met, the dense formation of the Britons almost scattered the emperor's cohort. While they traded blows in the melee, Nennius got the chance of attacking Caesar. As he rushed at him, Nennius congratulated himself on being able to exchange even a single blow with so famous a man. Caesar saw him coming, held up his shield and with his drawn sword struck him as hard as he could on the helmet. Raising his sword again, he tried to deal a fatal wound with a second blow. Nennius spotted it and blocked with his shield, in which Caesar's sword, glancing off the helmet, stuck so fast that, as they were forced to break off their duel by onrushing troops, the emperor could not pull it out. Having got Caesar's sword in this way, Nennius cast aside the one he was holding, freed the other and hastened to attack the enemy. Once he struck anybody with it, he either cut off his head or left him too badly wounded to hope for recovery. As he rampaged in this way, the tribune Labienus finally faced him, but fell to his first thrust. After most of the day had passed, victory went with God's help to the Britons, who attacked in formation and charged boldly, whilst Caesar and the shattered Romans retreated to their camp and ships. That night Caesar gathered his men and embarked, happy to use the sea as his camp. His companions were against renewing the fighting, advice which Caesar took and turned back to Gaul.

57   Cheered by this triumph, Cassibellaunus gave thanks to God, summoned his victorious comrades and gave each of them generous gifts according to their services. He was grieved, however, that his brother Nennius lay between life and death, seriously injured; for the wound Caesar had inflicted in their duel had proved incurable. A fortnight after the battle Nennius breathed his last and was buried in the city of Trinovantum by the northern gate.

arceret. Aderat secum Bellinus, princeps miliciae suae, cuius consilio totum regnum tractabatur; aderant etiam duo nepotes sui, Androgeus uidelicet 40 dux Trinouantum et Tenuantius dux Cornubiae, tres quoque reges subditi sibi, Cridious Albaniae et Gueithaet Venedociae atque Britahel Demetiae. Qui ut ceteros in affectum pugnandi induxissent, consilium dederunt ut recenter castra Caesaris adirent et antequam ciuitatem aliquam siue oppidum cepisset ipsum expellere insisterent; nam si sese infra munitiones 45 patriae immisisset, dicebant eum difficilius expellendum, cum sciret ubi se et commilitones suos reciperet. Assensum igitur praebentes cuncti petierunt littora quibus Iulius castra et tentoria sua erexerat. Ibi, dispositis in utraque parte cateruis, dextras cum hostibus commiscuerunt, pila pilis et ictus ictibus obicientes. Nec mora, hinc et inde corruunt uulnerati, telis 50 infra uitalia receptis. Manat tellus cruore morientium ac si repentinus auster absortum mare reuomuisset. Concurrentibus ergo aduersis cateruis, obtulit casus Nennium et Androgeum cum Cantuaritis et ciuibus urbis Trinouantum, quibus praesidebant, agmini quo imperator aderat. Vt ergo conuenerunt, paene dissipata fuit imperatoria cohors, Britonibus densa 55 acie inuadentibus. Et cum mixtim ictus ingeminarent, dedit casus aditum Nennio congressum cum Iulio faciendi. Irruens ergo in illum Nennius ultra modum laetatur se posse uel solum ictum tanto uiro ingerere. Quem Caesar ut impetum in se facientem aspexit, praetenso clipeo excepit et quantum uires permiserunt cum nudato ense ipsum super cassidem percussit. Erecto 60 iterum gladio, uoluit exequi primum ictum ut letiferum uulnus imprimeret. Quod cum Nennius calluisset, interposuit clipeum suum, in quo mucro Iulii a casside maximis labens uiribus inhaesit ita ut, cum irruentibus turmis diutius congredi nequirent, ipsum imperator extrahere non potuisset. Nennius ergo, gladium Caesaris praedicto modo adeptus, abiecit suum quem 65 tenuerat et abstracto altero in hostes irruere festinat. Quemcumque cum ipso percutiebat, uel ei caput amputabat uel ipsum sauciatum praeteribat ita ut nulla spes uiuendi in eo maneret. Illi tandem in hunc modum saeuienti obuiauit Labienus tribunus, sed in primo congressu ab eo peremptus est. Denique, plurima parte diei emensa, irruentibus Britonibus strictis turmis 70 et audaces impetus facientibus uictoria fauente Deo prouenit, et Caesar sese infra castra et naues laceratis Romanis recepit. Deinde nocte illa resociatis ceteris naues suas intrauit et Neptunum pro castris habere laetatur. Cumque sibi dissuasissent socii proelia diutius ingerere, acquiescens monitionibus eorum reuersus est in Galliam. 75

57 Cassibellaunus ergo, ob receptum triumphum laetus, grates Deo soluens socios uictoriae suae conuocauit et quemque iuxta meritum probitatis maximis muneribus donauit. Angebatur tamen ex alia parte dolore, quia frater suus Nennius, letaliter uulneratus, in dubio uitae iacebat; uulnerauerat enim illum Iulius in supradicto congressu et plagam inmedicabilem 80 intulerat. Vnde infra quindecim dies post proelium irrepente morte ab hac luce migrauit et in urbe Trinouantum iuxta aquilonarem portam sepultus

61 iterum *CHSE: om. O:* igitur *Φ*

They gave him a royal funeral and placed beside him in his coffin the sword which Caesar had fixed in his shield in their duel. It was called 'Yellow Death', because nobody wounded by it ever escaped with his life.

58   Once Caesar had been forced to retreat and driven back to the Gallic coast, the Gauls attempted to rebel and throw off his yoke; they thought that he had been so weakened that they needed to fear him no longer. All had heard the same report, that the sea was alive with Cassibellaunus' ships following up his flight. Emboldened by this, they plotted to expel Caesar from their country. When he learned of it, Caesar did not want to risk war against so fierce a race, but opened his coffers and approached all the nobles individually to reward them and win back their friendship. To the people he promised liberty, to the dispossessed their former property and to slaves freedom. Formerly he had taken everything from them and roared like a savage lion, now he bleated meekly like a harmless sheep, happy to return it all; he did not cease his flattery until all were won over and he had regained his lost power. In the meantime not a day passed when he did not brood over his retreat and the Britons' victory.

59   So, after two years had gone by, Caesar prepared to cross the sea again and take his revenge on Cassibellaunus. On receiving the news, Cassibellaunus fortified all his cities, repaired broken walls and placed armed garrisons in every port. Moreover, in the bed of the Thames, where Caesar would sail to Trinovantum, he planted beneath the waterline stakes of iron and lead, as thick as a man's thigh, to hole Caesar's ships from below. He also gathered all the island's forces and stationed himself near the coast, awaiting the arrival of the enemy.

60   When Caesar had made all necessary preparations, he set sail with a great host of soldiers, eager to fulfil his desire of slaughtering the people that had defeated him. And he certainly would have done, had he landed with his fleet intact, but he failed to do so. For as he sailed up the Thames towards Trinovantum, his ships struck the stakes and were suddenly wrecked; thousands of his troops were drowned as the river-water entered and sunk the holed ships. Seeing this, Caesar changed tack with all his might and hurried to reach land. The survivors of the disaster escaped with difficulty and got to the bank with him. Cassibellaunus was on the bank, watching the plight of the drowned with glee, but saddened by the escape of the remainder. Then he gave his comrades the signal to attack the Romans. Despite the dangers they had faced on the river, as soon as they were on dry land, the Romans resisted the British assault. Making boldness their defence, they inflicted heavy casualties, but suffered worse themselves. Because of their losses in the river, their numbers were inferior, whereas the Britons outnumbered them thirty to one, and were being strengthened at every moment by the arrival of fresh troops.

est. Exequias autem regias facientes, posuerunt cum illo gladium Caesaris in sarcofago, quem infra clipeum suum pugnans retinuerat. Erat nomen gladii Crocea Mors, quia nullus euadebat uiuus qui cum illo uulnerabatur. 85

58 Terga igitur uertente Iulio et in Gallicano litore appulso, rebellionem moliuntur Galli, dominium Iulii abicientes; arbitrabantur namque ipsum ita debilitatum ut nullatenus eis amplius timori esset. Fama etiam apud omnes una et eadem erat totum mare iam nauibus Cassibellauni feruere, fugam ipsius insecuturi. Vnde audaciores insistentes cogitabant quomodo Caesarem 90 a finibus suis expellerent. Quod Iulius callens noluit anceps bellum cum feroci populo committere sed apertis thesauris quosque nobiliores adire ut singulos munificatos in concordiam reduceret. Plebi libertatem pollicetur, exheredatis amissas possessiones, seruis etiam libertatem. Qui prius leonina feritate fulminans ipsis omnia abstulerat nunc mitis agnus humili uoce 95 balans omnia posse reddere laetatur; nec ab his blandiciis quieuit donec pacificatis cunctis amissam potestatem recuperauit. Nullus interim dies praeteribat quin fugam suam Britonumque uictoriam recoleret.

59 Emenso itaque biennio, parat iterum occeanum transfretare et sese in Cassibellaunum uindicare. Quod cum Cassibellaunus comperisset, urbes 100 ubique muniuit, diruta moenia renouauit, armatos milites in singulis portibus statuit. Praeterea alueo Tamensis fluminis, quo ad urbem Trinouantum Caesar nauigaturus erat, palis ferreis atque plumbatis et ad modum humani femoris grossis subtus amnem infixit ut naues Iulii superuenturae illiderentur. Collecta etiam tota iuuentute insulae, mansionem iuxta maritima fecit, 105 aduentum hostium expectans.

60 Iulius autem, cum omnia quae sibi necessaria essent parauisset, cum innumerabili multitudine militum mare ingressus est, optatam stragem populo qui eum deuicerat inferre affectans. Quam procul dubio ingessisset si illaesa classe tellure potiri quiuisset, quod ad effectum ducere nequiuit. 110 Nam dum per Tamensem praedictam ciuitatem peteret, naues eius, praefatis palis infixae, subitum passae sunt periculum; unde ad milia submergebantur milites dum ipsas foratas ingrediens fluuius absorberet. Cumque id Caesari compertum esset, uelis maxima ui retortis ad terram reuertere festinauit. Ipsi quoque qui in tanto periculo superfuerant uix elapsi cum illo tellurem 115 scandunt. Hoc igitur Cassibellaunus ex ripa qua aderat aspiciens gaudet propter periculum submersorum sed tristatur ob salutem ceterorum. Dato uero commilitonibus suis signo, impetum in Romanos facit. At Romani, quamquam periculum in fluuio perpessi fuissent, ut terra potiti sunt uiriliter Britonum irruptioni restiterunt. Audatiam quoque pro muro habentes, 120 stragem non minimam fecerunt, sed tamen maiorem paciuntur quam inferebant. Periclitati namque in fluuio, pauciores incedebant, Britones uero, omni hora affluentia suorum augmentati, tricies maiorem numerum

87 ita *Δ:* esse *Φ*
94 exhereditatis *H¹SE QY (cf. § 61.172, 79.150)*
110 quiuisset *Δ:* potuisset *Φ (cf. 'Transm.' 103)*
110 [quod ... nequiuit] *CHSE*
114 reuerti *G (cf. Introd.)*

Their victory was assured by the weakness of the Romans. Caesar saw that he was beaten, fled with a few companions to his ships and reached the safety of open water as he had hoped. The winds were favourable, so he set sail for the coast of Flanders. He landed at a tower which he had built in a place called Odnea, before embarking on his present invasion. For he feared that he could place no reliance on the loyalty of the Gauls, who were likely to attack him again just as they had before when they first heard that he had fled from the Britons. For this reason he had built the tower as a stronghold from which to resist any rebellion should the Gauls, as we have said, rise up against him.

61   Cassibellaunus, overjoyed at having triumphed for a second time, issued an edict that all the British nobles should gather with their wives in the city of Trinovantum to hold fitting ceremonies for their native gods, who had granted them victory over so mighty an emperor. They came without delay and slaughtered animals in various sacrifices. At these were offered forty thousand cows, a hundred thousand sheep, innumerable birds of different species and also a collection of thirty thousand woodland beasts of every kind. After they had completed their offerings to the gods, they refreshed themselves with the left-over food, as was the custom at sacrifices. Then they spent the rest of the night and the following day in various sports. In these games, it happened that two noble youths, one the nephew of the king, the other of duke Androgeus, contested in a wrestling-match and could not agree who had won. The king's nephew was called Hirelglas, and Androgeus' Cuelinus. After an exchange of insults, Cuelinus snatched up a sword and cut off the head of the king's nephew. Hirelglas' death threw the court into uproar, and the news swiftly reached Cassibellaunus. Agitated by his friend's fate, Cassibellaunus commanded Androgeus to bring Cuelinus before him at court, where he should be prepared to accept the verdict of the nobles, so that Hirelglas would not go unavenged if his death had been unjust. Distrustful of the king's intentions, Androgeus replied that he had a court of his own, in which any complaint against his household should be decided; if the king wanted a verdict on Cuelinus, ancient custom demanded that it be handed down in the city of Trinovantum. His plans frustrated, Cassibellaunus threatened to put Androgeus' territories to fire and the sword if he did not agree to his demands. Androgeus angrily refused to obey, and Cassibellaunus equally angrily hastened to lay waste his lands. Every day Androgeus approached the king through relatives and friends, requesting him to cease his rage. Since he was unable to soften the king's fury, Androgeus reviewed various ways of resisting him.

habebant. Vnde debilitatis ceteris potiti sunt triumpho. Caesar igitur, cum sese deuictum inspexisset, cum paucis ad naues diffugit et tutamen maris 125 ex uoto nactus est. Tempestiuis etiam uentis instantibus, erexit uela sua et Morianorum litus petiuit. Ingressus est deinde quandam turrim quam in loco qui Odnea uocatur construxerat antequam Britanniam hac uice adiuisset. Timebat namque Gallorum fidem et instabilitatem, ne in sese secundo irruerent sicut supradictum est ipsos fecisse quando primo Britonibus 130 terga testatus est ostendisse. Ob hanc ergo causam turrim in refugium sibi aedificauerat ut rebelli populo resistere ualuisset si in illum ut praedictum est insurrexisset.

61 Cassibellaunus autem, secundo triumphum adeptus, maximo gaudio fluctuans edictum fecit ut omnes proceres Britanniae in urbe Trinouantum 135 cum uxoribus suis conuenirent debitasque sollempnitates patriis deis celebrarent, qui uictoriam sibi de tanto imperatore concesserant. Cumque omnes postposita mora aduenissent, diuersa sacrificia facientes occisioni pecudum indulserunt. Litauerunt ibi .xl. milia uaccarum et centum milia ouium diuersorumque generum uolatilia quae leuiter sub numero non 140 cadebant, praeterea .xxx. milia siluestrium ferarum cuiusque generis collectarum. Mox, cum diis suos honores perfecissent, refecerunt se residuis epulis ut in sacrificiis fieri solebat. Exin quod noctis et diei restabat diuersos ludos componentes praeterierunt. Ludentibus ergo ipsis, contigit inclitos iuuenes, quorum unus nepos erat regis, alter uero Androgei ducis, 145 pariter in palaestra contendere et ob dubiam uictoriam litigare. Erat nomen nepotis regis Hirelglas, alterius uero Cuelinus. Qui ut mutua conuicia adinuicem intulissent, arripuit Cuelinus gladium nepotique regis caput amputauit. Quo interfecto, perturbata est curia, et rumor ad Cassibellaunum uolauit. Commotus igitur super casu amici sui Cassibellaunus Androgeo 150 praecepit ut Cuelinum in curia coram praesentia sua adduceret, adductus quoque praesto esset sententiam quam proceres dictarent subire, ne Hirelglas inultus permaneret si iniuste interfectus fuisset. Cumque animum regis dubitasset Androgeus, respondit sese suam curiam habere et in illa diffiniri debere quicquid aliquis in homines suos clamaret; si igitur 155 rectitudinem de Cuelino decreuisset appetere, ipsam in urbe Trinouantum ex ueterum traditione recepisset. Cassibellaunus itaque, cum affectui suo satisfactionem nequiuisset ingerere, comminatus est Androgeo, testans se ferro et flamma prouinciam suam populaturum nisi peticioni suae acquiesceret. Indignatus ergo Androgeus distulit peticioni eius parere. 160 Indignatus autem Cassibellaunus accelerauit prouincias ipsius uastare. At Androgeus cotidie per cognatos et notos regem adibat petebatque ut irae coeptae desisteret. Et cum furorem eius nullatenus mitigare quiuisset, diuersas meditationes iniuit qualiter ipsi resistere ualuisset. Denique, ab

143 diei et noctis *Φ*
158 nequisset *OHE QYG*
163 desisteret coeptae irae *Φ*

Having exhausted all hope, he finally decided to seek Caesar's aid and sent him the following letter:

'Gaius Julius Caesar, Androgeus duke of Trinovantum, who used to wish you dead, now wishes you well. I regret opposing you when you fought against my king. Had I refrained from my acts of daring, you would have beaten Cassibellaunus, whose victory has made him so proud that he is trying to drive me, the author of his success, from my lands. Are these my just desserts? I ensured his inheritance, now he is attempting to disinherit me. I returned his kingdom to him for a second time, now he wants to turn me out. I presented all this to him by fighting against you. The powers of heaven bear witness that I have not deserved his anger, unless I may be judged to have done so by refusing to hand over to him my nephew, whom he unjustly wishes to condemn to death. To understand this more clearly, consider the facts of the case. Rejoicing over our triumph, we happened to hold ceremonies for our native gods; at them, after the completion of the due sacrifices, our young men held contests against each other. Among them, our two nephews, following the others' example, had a wrestling-match. My nephew won, whereupon the other was consumed by unmerited anger and hastened to strike him down. My nephew avoided the blow and seized the sword in his fist, to snatch it away. In the struggle the king's nephew fell upon the blade and was stabbed to death. After being informed of it, the king ordered me to deliver up the boy to be punished for murder. When I refused, he brought his whole army to subject my lands to terrible devastation. Therefore I throw myself upon your mercy and request your aid so that I, through you, may regain my proper position and you, through me, may conquer Britain. Have no qualms on my account, for I have no thought of betrayal. It is part of life for enemies to become friends and for defeat to be followed by victory'.

62   Having read this letter, Caesar's advisors suggested that he should not go to Britain merely on the duke's invitation, but that he should receive suitable hostages to make his landing more secure. Androgeus immediately sent him his son Scaeva and thirty noble young men of his own family. Caesar, reassured by having them as hostages, reassembled his troops and landed with a following wind at Richborough. Meanwhile Cassibellaunus had embarked on a siege at Trinovantum and was laying waste neighbouring towns; but when he heard of Caesar's intervention, he abandoned the siege and hurried to meet the emperor. As he entered a valley near Canterbury, he spied the Roman army pitching its camp and tents; they had been brought there by Androgeus to make a surprise attack on the city. Seeing the Britons coming, the Romans swiftly armed themselves, and drew up their soldiers in ranks. Their British opponents donned their armour and marshalled their forces. Androgeus concealed himself with five thousand armed warriors

omni alia spe decidens, auxilium Caesaris petere decreuit litterasque suas   165
ei in hanc direxit sententiam:

'Gaio Iulio Caesari Androgeus dux Trinouantum post optatam mortem
optandam salutem. Paenitet me aduersum te egisse dum proelia cum rege
meo committeres. Si enim me a talibus ausis abstinuissem, deuicisses
Cassibellaunum, cui post triumphum suum tanta irrepsit superbia ut me,   170
per quem triumphauit, a finibus meis exterminare insistat. Haeccine ergo
merita rependenda essent? Ego illum hereditaui, ipse me exheredare
conatur. Ego eum in regno secundo restitui, ipse me destituere affectat.
Me etenim contra te pugnante omnia ista largitus sum. Numina caelorum
testor me non promeruisse iram ipsius, nisi promereri dicar quia diffugio   175
nepotem meum tradere, quem iniusta nece dampnare adoptat. Quod ut
manifestius discretioni tuae liqueat, causam rei aduerte. Contigerat nos
ob laeticiam triumphi nostri sollempnitates patriis deis celebrasse; in
quibus, cum quae agenda essent peregissemus sacrificia, iuuentus nostra
ludos mutuos componebat. Inter ceteros inierunt duo nepotes nostri   180
palaestram, exemplo aliorum conducti. Cumque meus triumphasset,
succensus est alter iniusta ira festinauitque eum percutere. At ille, uitato
ictu, cepit eum per pugnum quo gladium tenebat, uolens eum eripere.
Interea cecidit nepos regis super mucronem confossusque morti subiacuit.
Id itaque cum regi nuntiatum esset, praecepit michi liberare puerum   185
meum ut pro homicidio supplicio plecteretur. Cui cum contradixissem,
uenit cum omni multitudine sua in prouincias meas, grauissimam inferens
inquietudinem. Vnde misericordiam tuam implorans auxilium a te peto
ut ego per te dignitati meae restituar et tu per me Britannia potiaris. De
hoc autem nichil in me haesitaueris, quia omnis abest proditio. Ea enim   190
conditione mouentur mortales ut post inimicicias amici fiant et post
fugam ad triumphum accedant'.

62 His igitur inspectis, consilium habuit Iulius a familiaribus suis ne uerbis
solummodo ducis inuitatus Britanniam adiret nisi tales dirigerentur obsides
quibus securius applicare quiuisset. Nec mora, misit ei Androgeus Scaeuam   195
filium suum et .xxx. nobiles iuuenes ex cognatione sua propinquos.
Datis igitur obsidibus, securus factus est Caesar reuocatisque cateruis
cum instante uento in Rutupi Portu applicuit. Interea obsidere incipiebat
Cassibellaunus urbem Trinouantum et uillas prouinciales uastabat; sed
cum aduentum Iulii comperisset, deseruit obsidionem et imperatori obuiare   200
festinauit. Vt igitur uallem prope Doroberniam intrauit, aspexit in eadem
Romanorum exercitum castra et tentoria ponentem; adduxerat enim eos
Androgeus ibidem ut illic occultum impetum urbi ingererent. Nec mora,
aduertentes Romani Britones superuenire armauerunt sese ocius militesque
suos per cateruas statuerunt. Ex alia uero parte armis induuntur Britones et   205
sese per turmas consociant. At Androgeus cum quinque milibus armatorum

171 meis *Δ YM:* suis uel meis *Q:* suis *G*
172 *fort.* merita <ita> *(cf. Introd.)*
172 exhereditare *OHE QG (cf. § 58.94, 79.150)*
185 liberare *Δ:* tradere *Φ*
199 uastare *Φ*

in a nearby wood, to aid Caesar by making an unexpected attack on Cassibellaunus and his unsuspecting comrades. When the two armies met, they immediately hurled their deadly weapons and exchanged mortal blows. The opposing formations met and much blood was shed. On both sides the wounded fell as thick as leaves from the trees in autumn. As they charged, Androgeus emerged from the wood and, coming up from behind, attacked Cassibellaunus' company, on which the outcome of the war depended. Already weakened by the Romans attacking in front, and now taken from behind by their fellow-countrymen, they could not stand for long; with his companions scattered, the king abandoned the field in flight. Near by stood a hill with a rocky summit thickly covered with hazel trees. The defeated king and his men fled to it. Reaching the top, Cassibellaunus put up a brave defence and slaughtered the pursuing enemy. Both the Romans and Androgeus' troops had followed him, cutting down his fleeing men. They climbed the hill, launching several assaults, but without success. The rocks on the hill and its steep summit protected the Britons, allowing them to charge down and slaughter the enemy. Darkness began to fall, and Caesar blockaded the hill all night, to prevent any escape. He had decided to starve the king out since he could not defeat him by force. How admirable were the Britons of that age, who twice put to flight the conqueror of the whole world! Even after being routed, they faced a man the whole world could not resist, and were ready to lay down their lives for the liberty of their country. It was in praise of them that the poet Lucan described how Caesar 'in terror turned his back upon the Britons he had attacked'. By the end of the second day Cassibellaunus had run out of supplies and feared that hunger would force him to surrender and become Caesar's prisoner. So he sent a message to Androgeus, asking him to reconcile him to Caesar, lest his capture should dishonour the race to which they both belonged. He also said that, although he had harried Androgeus, that was no reason for the latter to desire his death. On receipt of the message, Androgeus said:

> 'No one can love a prince who is gentle as a lamb in war, and in peace as fierce as a lion. Gods of heaven and earth, the lord who used to command me is now begging me. Does the king whom Caesar once sued for peace now want to be reconciled to Caesar and become his vassal? He should have realised that the man whose assistance he needed to drive the mighty emperor from our kingdom could also bring him back again. I should not have been treated unjustly, I who could render him that service then, and can now render him another. Only a fool wrongs and insults those who have ensured his triumph.

in prope sito nemore delituit ut in auxilio Caesaris occurrens furtiuam et inprouisam irruptionem Cassibellauno consociisque suis faceret. Vt itaque hinc et inde conuenerunt, non distulerunt mortalia tela emittere nec letiferos ictus ingeminare. Concurrunt aduersae cateruae et multum cruoris diffundunt. 210 Concidunt in utraque parte uulnerati quemadmodum folia arborum in auctumno. Illis igitur irruentibus, egreditur Androgeus ex nemore et aciem Cassibellauni, ex qua totum bellum pendebat, a tergo inuadit. Mox illa, in una parte irruptione Romanorum paulo ante uastata, in alia uero conciuibus suis modo oppressa, nequiuit stationem facere; unde dissipatis sociis arrepta 215 fuga campum deseruit. Astabat prope quidam mons in cacumine saxosus densum coriletum habens. Ad illum confugit Cassibellaunus cum suis postquam in debiliorem partem ceciderat. Summitatem quoque eius nactus, sese uiriliter defendebat et insequentes hostes nece afficiebat. Insecuti namque fuerant ipsum Romani et Androgei cateruae, fugientes turmas eius 220 lacerantes. Montem quoque ascendentes, crebros impetus faciebant nec praeualebant. Saxa etenim montis eiusdemque cacuminis arduitas Britonibus defensio erat ita ut a summo occurrentes hostibus stragem darent. Obsedit igitur Caesar montem illum tota nocte quae iam superueniebat, omnes exitus praecludens. Affectabat namque regem fame cogere, quem armis nequiuerat. 225 O ammirabile tunc genus Britonum, qui ipsum bis in fugam propulerunt qui totum orbem sibi submiserat! Cui totus mundus nequiuit resistere, illi etiam fugati resistunt, parati mortem pro patria et libertate subire. Hinc ad laudem illorum cecinit Lucanus de Caesare 'territa quaesitis ostendit terga Britannis'. Emenso iam die secundo, cum non haberet Cassibellaunus quid comederet, 230 timuit ne fame caperetur, carcerem Caesaris subiturus. Mandauit itaque Androgeo ut sese cum Iulio pacificaret, ne dignitas gentis ex qua natus fuerat capto ipso deleretur. Mandauit etiam ei se non promeruisse ut mortem ipsius optaret, quamuis inquietudinem sibi intulisset. Cumque haec retulissent nuncii, ait Androgeus: 235

'Non est diligendus princeps qui in bello est mitis ut agnus, in pace ferus ut leo. Dii caeli et terrae, orat me nunc dominus meus, qui prius imperabat. Pacificarine Caesari et subiectionem facere desiderat cuius pacem prius desiderauerat Caesar? Proinde aduertere debuerat illum per quem tantum imperatorem ex regno suo pepulit posse ipsum iterum 240 restituere. Non eram igitur iniuste tractandus, qui tunc illud obsequium, nunc istud inferre poteram. Insipientia obducitur qui commilitones quibus triumphat iniuriis uel contumeliis infestat. Non enim est ullius ducis

207 [delituit] *OCHS (cf. 'Transm.' 90)*
207 auxilium *Y (cf. Introd.)*
207 Caesari *Φ (cf. Introd.)*
222 eiusque *Φ*
229 *Bellum Ciuile 2.572*
231 Caesaris carcerem *Φ*
231 namque *Φ*
234 hoc *C Y*
239 aduertere *E M:* uertere *OCS QYG:* uereri *H (cf. 'Transm.' 98)*
240 iterum ipsum *O YM*
242 obducitur <itaque> *Δ (cf. Introd.)*

Victory is not the property of the leader, but of the men who have shed their blood for him in battle. Yet I will reconcile him if I can, since by begging me for mercy he has redressed the wrong he did me'.

63   Androgeus then hurried to Caesar and, embracing his knees, addressed him as follows:

'Your revenge on Cassibellaunus is complete. Take pity on him. Do you wish for more than that he should submit and pay tribute in the name of Rome?'.

When Caesar made no reply, Androgeus repeated:

'I agreed no more, Caesar, than to work to make Britain subject to you and Cassibellaunus your vassal. Well, with my help Cassibellaunus has now been beaten and Britain overcome. What more do I owe you? The Creator of the world would never want me to allow even the imprisonment of my lord now that he begs me for mercy and is righting the wrong he did me. To kill Cassibellaunus is no easy task while I am still alive, and I shall not hesitate to help him if you do not do as I say'.

Out of fear of Androgeus, Caesar relented and made peace with Cassibellaunus in return for the payment of yearly tribute; the king promised a sum of three thousand pounds of silver. Caesar and Cassibellaunus then swore friendship and exchanged gifts. Caesar spent the winter in Britain and returned to Gaul in spring. Some time later he gathered troops from all nations and marched on Rome against Pompey.

64   Seven years later Cassibellaunus died and was buried at York. He was succeeded by Androgeus' brother Tenuantius duke of Cornwall; Androgeus himself had set off for Rome with Caesar. Once crowned, Tenuantius ruled well. He was a warrior and promoted justice. After him, the throne passed to his son Kimbelinus, a tireless soldier, who had been brought up by Augustus Caesar and knighted by him. Kimbelinus was so fond of the Romans that he freely paid them the tribute which he could have withheld. In his reign was born Our Lord Jesus Christ, whose precious blood redeemed the human race, bound beforehand in the chains of idolatry.

65   After he had ruled Britain for ten years, Kimbelinus had two sons, the elder named Guider, the other Arviragus. When the king's life ended, the crown passed to Guider. Because Guider refused to pay the tribute demanded by the Romans, Claudius, newly created emperor, made a landing. Claudius had with him his general,

uictoria sed illorum qui pro eo sanguinem suum pugnando diffundunt. Tamen pacificabo illum si potero, quia iniuria quam michi intulit satis 245 uindicata est in illo cum misericordiam meam imploret'.

63 Post haec festinauit Androgeus ad Iulium amplexusque ipsius genua eum in hunc allocutus est sermonem:

'Ecce satis uindicasti te in Cassibellaunum. Misericordiam de illo habe. Quid amplius agendum est quam ut subiectionem faciens uectigal 250 Romanae dignitati reddat?'.

Cumque nichil respondisset Caesar, ait iterum Androgeus:

'Hoc solum pactus sum tibi, Caesar, ut summisso Cassibellauno Britanniam tibi subdere laborarem. Ecce uictus est Cassibellaunus et Britannia tibi auxilio meo subdita. Quid ultra tibi debeo? Nolit creator 255 omnium ut dominum meum misericordiam meam orantem rectumque michi de illata iniuria offerentem patiar umquam uel in uinculis uinciri. Non leue est interficere Cassibellaunum me uiuente, cui auxilium meum reddere non erubescam nisi consilio meo parueris'.

Timore igitur Androgei mitigatus Iulius cepit a Cassibellauno concordiam 260 cum uectigali singulis annis reddendo; erat autem uectigal quod spopondit tria milia librarum argenti. Exin amici facti adinuicem Iulius et Cassibellaunus mutua donaria alter alteri dederunt. Deinde hiemauit Caesar in Britannia et redeunte uere in Gallias transfretauit. Succedente postmodum tempore, collectis undique ex omni genere militibus Romam 265 contra Pompeium perrexit.

64 Cumque postmodum septem anni praeterissent, defunctus est Cassibellaunus et in Eboraco sepultus. Cui successit Tenuantius dux Cornubiae, frater Androgei; nam Androgeus Romam cum Caesare profectus fuerat. Diademate igitur insignitus Tenuantius regnum in diligentia 270 optinuit. Erat ipse bellicosus uir et qui uigorem iusticiae colebat. Post illum promotus est ad culmen regale Kimbelinus filius suus, miles strenuus, quem Augustus Caesar nutriuerat et armis decorauerat. Hic in tantam amiciciam Romanorum inciderat ut cum posset tributum eorum detinere gratis impendebat. In diebus illis natus est dominus noster Iesus Christus, 275 cuius precioso sanguine redemptum est humanum genus, quod anteacto tempore daemonum catena obligabatur.

65 Kimbelinus igitur, cum Britanniam decem annis gubernasset, genuit duos filios, quorum primogenito nomen erat Guider, alteri Aruiragus. Exin, expletis uitae suae diebus, cessit gubernaculum regni Guiderio. Cum igitur 280 tributum quod appetebant Romanis denegaret, superuenit Claudius, qui in imperium subrogatus fuerat. Aderat secum princeps miliciae suae, uocabulo

245 eum *E Φ*
253 <solummodo> submisso *Φ*
263 mutuaque *Φ*
279 Deinde *Φ*

Laelius Hamo, who advised him on military affairs. After he came ashore
at Portchester, Claudius blockaded its gates with a wall, trapping the
inhabitants inside. He wanted to starve them into submission or leave them
to die without mercy.

66   As news of Claudius' landing spread, Guider collected all the armed
soldiers in the kingdom and marched towards the Roman army. Once battle
was joined, he launched a bitter assault on the enemy, killing more of them
with his own sword than most of his men. Claudius was already retiring to
his ships and the Romans were almost broken, when Hamo craftily shed
his own equipment, put on British armour and began to attack his own men
as if he were a Briton. Then he began to urge the British to follow him,
promising them a swift victory; Hamo knew the language and customs of
the British because he had been brought up among their hostages in Rome.
Little by little he got closer and closer to the king until he struck him down,
all unsuspecting. Then he melted back into the enemy ranks, returning to
his men in undeserved triumph. But when Arviragus saw that his brother
had been killed, he immediately took off his own equipment and donned
the king's, urging the Britons on all sides to stand firm, as if he were Guider
himself; unaware of the king's death, they stood and fought as he urged,
and slaughtered the enemy. Eventually the Romans broke and shamefully
abandoned the field in two bodies; Claudius with one sought the safety
of his ships, whilst Hamo, cut off from the ships, made for the woods.
Arviragus, thinking that Claudius was fleeing with Hamo, hurried after him
and chased him on and on until he caught up with the fugitives by the coast,
at the place now called Southampton after Hamo. It was a safe harbour, at
which some merchant ships were moored. Hamo was trying to board them
when Arviragus arrived unexpectedly and swiftly slew him. From that day
to this the port has been known as Southampton.

67   Meanwhile Claudius had reassembled his troops and was besieging
the city now named Portchester, which at that time was called Kaerperis.
He broke down its walls without delay, overcame its inhabitants and
marched after Arviragus, who was now at Winchester. There he besieged
the city, trying to capture it with various engines. Seeing himself besieged,
Arviragus mustered his troops, opened the gates and came out to fight. As he
prepared to attack, Claudius sent him envoys suggesting that they came to
terms. Intimidated by the king's boldness and the bravery of the Britons, he
preferred to overcome them by wise judgement rather than to hazard a battle.
He therefore offered Arviragus a truce and the promise of his daughter's hand
if he were prepared merely to recognise Rome's authority over the kingdom
of Britain. Hostilities were suspended and Arviragus' elders persuaded him
to comply with Claudius' promises; they said that it was no

Laelius Hamo, cuius consilio proelia quae gerenda erant tractabantur. Hic itaque, ut in ciuitate Portcestria applicuit, coepit portas eius muro praecludere exitumque ciuibus abnegare. Cupiebat namque ipsos fame 285 affectos uel deditioni compellere uel sine clementia interire.

66   Diuulgato igitur Claudii Caesaris aduentu, collegit Guiderius omnem armatum regni militem et Romanum exercitum petiuit. Commisso deinde proelio, acerrime coepit hostes infestare, plus solus cum gladio suo quam maior pars exercitus sui perimens. Iam Claudius naues petebat, iam Romani 290 paene dissipabantur, cum uersutus Hamo, proiectis illis quibus indutus fuerat, arma Britannica cepit et quasi Britannus contra suos pugnabat. Deinde hortabatur Britones ad insequendum, festinatum triumphum promittens; didicerat enim linguam eorum et mores, quia inter Britannicos obsides Romae nutritus fuerat. Exin accessit ipse paulatim iuxta regem adituque 295 inuento ipsum nichil tale timentem mucrone suffocauit. Elapsus deinde inter hostium cuneos, sese cum nefanda uictoria inter suos recepit. At Aruiragus eiusdem frater, ut ipsum peremptum inspexit, confestim deposuit arma sua armisque regis indutus hinc et inde Britones ad perstandum inanimabat quasi ipse Guiderius fuisset; qui nescientes casum regis monitu eius 300 resistebant, pugnabant, stragemque non minimam inferebant. Ad ultimum dilabuntur Romani in duas partes, campum turpiter deserentes; Caesar namque in una parte tutamina nauium petebat, Hamo autem nemora, quia non habebat spacium naues adeundi. Aruiragus igitur, arbitrans Claudium cum eo diffugere, festinauit sequi eum nec cessauit de loco in locum fugare 305 donec occupauit illos super ripam maris quae nunc de nomine eiusdem Hamonis Hamtonia nuncupatur. Erat ibi portus applicantibus congruus nauesque mercatorum appulsae. Quas igitur cum ingredi affectasset Hamo, superuenit ex inprouiso Aruiragus ipsumque subito interfecit. Portus autem ille ab illo tempore usque in hodiernum diem Portus Hamonis appellatur.   310

67   Interea Claudius resociatis sociis oppugnabat praedictam ciuitatem, quae tunc Kaerperis, nunc autem Portcestria uocatur. Nec mora, moenibus eius dirutis ciuibusque subactis insecutus est Aruiragum, iam in Guintoniam ingressum. Exinde obsedit ciuitatem diuersisque machinationibus illam opprimere nitebatur. Aruiragus uero, ut sese obsessum inspexit, consociauit 315 cateruas suas apertisque portis ad proeliandum egressus est. Cumque irruptionem facere affectasset, direxit Claudius nuntios ad ipsum, mandans ut concordiam inirent. Quippe timebat regis audatiam Britonumque fortitudinem praeferebatque ipsos sensu et sapientia subiugare quam dubium certamen inire. Mandabat igitur ei concordiam daturumque promittebat 320 sese filiam suam si tantummodo regnum Britanniae sub Romana potestate recognouisset. Postpositis ergo debellationibus, suaserunt maiores natu Aruirago promissionibus Claudii acquiescere; dicebant autem non esse ei

289 inuadere *Φ*
299 animabat *M*
312-13 moenia eius diruit *Φ*
314 Exin *S:* Postmodum *Φ*

disgrace for him to be a subject of the Romans, since they were masters of the whole world. Mollified by this and other considerations, he accepted their advice and submitted to Caesar. Claudius then sent to Rome for his daughter and with Arviragus' help conquered the Orkneys and adjacent islands.

68   That spring the envoys returned with the girl and presented her to her father. She was named Gewissa, and was so beautiful that those who saw her were amazed. After they were married, the king was inflamed with such passion that he valued her above all things. Wishing to secure the fame of the place where he first married her, he suggested to Claudius that they build there a city to perpetuate the memory of so happy a union. Claudius agreed and ordered the construction of the city, named Kaerglou, or Gloucester, after him, which to this day stands beside the Severn between Wales and Loegria. Others claim that it took its name from Claudius' son duke Gloius, who was born there and became duke of Wales after Arviragus' death. Once the city had been built and peace established throughout the land, Claudius returned to Rome, leaving Arviragus in control of the neighbouring islands. At that time the apostle Peter, after founding the church of Antioch, came to Rome, became its bishop and sent the evangelist Mark to Egypt to preach the text of his gospel.

69   After Claudius' departure, Arviragus began to show judgement and ability and to rebuild cities and towns, displaying such justice towards his people that foreign kings feared him. His pride made him contemptuous of Roman authority and, unwilling to remain subject to the senate, he took everything into his own hands. When Claudius got to hear of it, he sent Vespasian to quieten Arviragus or bring him back under Roman control. Vespasian attempted to land at Richborough, but Arviragus met him and prevented him from entering the port. The king had brought sufficient forces to intimidate the Romans and dissuade them from landing in fear of an attack. Vespasian retreated from the port and sailed on to land at Totnes. Disembarking there, he set off for Kaerpenhuelgoit, or Exeter, to besiege it. After the siege had gone on for seven days, Arviragus arrived with his army and attacked. Both armies suffered major casualties that day, but neither could get the upper hand. The following morning their leaders were reconciled by the efforts of queen Gewissa and sent their troops into winter quarters. The following spring Vespasian returned to Rome, leaving Arviragus in Britain. As he grew older, he began to respect the senate and to rule

dedecori subditum fuisse Romanis, cum totius orbis imperio potirentur. His uero et pluribus aliis mitigatus, paruit consiliis suorum et subiectionem 325 Caesari fecit. Mox Claudius misit propter filiam suam Romam et auxilio Aruiragi usus Orcadas et prouinciales insulas potestati suae submisit.

68 Emensa deinde hieme, redierunt legati cum filia eamque patri tradiderunt. Erat autem nomen puellae Gewissa, eratque ei tanta pulcritudo ut aspicientes in ammirationem duceret. Et ut maritali lege copulata fuit, tanto feruore 330 amoris succendit regem ita ut ipsam solam cunctis rebus praeferret. Vnde locum quo ei primo nupserat celebrem esse uolens suggessit Claudio ut aedificarent in illo ciuitatem quae memoriam tantarum nuptiarum in futura tempora praeberet. Paruit ergo Claudius praecepitque fieri urbem, quae de nomine eius Kaerglou, id est Gloucestria, nuncupata usque in hodiernum 335 diem in confinio Kambriae et Loegriae super ripam Sabrinae sita est. Quidam uero dicunt ipsam traxisse nomen a Gloio duce, quem Claudius in illa generauerat, cui post Aruiragum gubernaculum Kambrici ducatus cessit. Aedificata igitur urbe ac pacificata insula, rediit Claudius Romam regimenque prouincialium insularum Aruirago permisit. Eodem tempore 340 Petrus apostolus Antiochenam ecclesiam fundauit Romamque deinde ueniens tenuit ibidem episcopatum misitque Marcum euangelistam in Aegyptum praedicare euangelium quod scripserat.

69 At Aruiragus, ut Claudius recessit, coepit sensum et probitatem habere coepitque ciuitates et oppida reaedificare populumque regni tanta iusticia 345 coercere ita ut longe positis regibus timori esset. Hinc autem subsequente superbia despexit Romanam potestatem nec senatui subiectionem uoluit tenere diutius sed sibimet omnia uendicauit. Quo audito, missus est Vespasianus a Claudio ut Aruiragum uel pacificaret uel Romanae subiectioni restitueret. Cum igitur in Rutupi Portu applicare incepisset Vespasianus, 350 obuiauit ei Aruiragus prohibuitque ne portum ingrederetur. Tantam namque multitudinem armatorum conduxerat ita ut Romanis terrori esset nec ob eius irruptionem terram adire auderent. Retraxit itaque se Vespasianus a portu illo retortisque uelis in Totonesio littore applicuit. Nactus deinde tellurem Kaerpenhuelgoit, quae Exonia uocatur, obsessurus eandem adiuit. Cumque 355 eam septem diebus obsedisset, superuenit Aruiragus cum exercitu suo proeliumque commisit. Die illa ualde laceratus fuit utrorumque exercitus, sed neuter potitus est uictoria. Mane autem facto, mediante Gewissa regina concordes effecti sunt duces commilitonesque suos in hiberna legauerunt. Hieme uero emensa, rediuit Vespasianus Romam et Aruiragus in Britannia 360 remansit. Deinde in senectutem uergens coepit senatum diligere regnumque

325 uero *Ω: an* ergo ?
326 misit *post* Romam *Φ*
329 ei *Y: om. cett., unde* tanta pulcritudine *M*, tantae pulcritudinis *34 (cf. § 24.24),* tanta pulcritudo <eius> *G*
336 Kambriae *Δ:* Demeciae *Φ*
338 Demetici *Φ*
355 quae <nunc> *M*
359 hiberna *M¹:* -nia *OCS QG:* -niam *HE YM²*

in peace and harmony, enforcing the old laws, passing new ones and rewarding all upright men with generous gifts. His fame spread throughout Europe and the Romans so respected and feared him that no king was more talked about at Rome; Juvenal in his satires tells how a blind man said to Nero, while discussing a newly caught turbot: 'you will capture a king or Arviragus shall fall from his British chariot'. No one was fiercer in war than he, no one more mild in peace, no one more witty, no one more generous in the giving of gifts. Having lived out his days, he was buried at Gloucester in a temple he had dedicated in Claudius' honour.

70   Arviragus was succeeded by his son Marius, a man of great wisdom and knowledge. During his reign, a Pictish king named Rodric arrived from Scythia with a large fleet, landed in the northern part of Britain, called Scotland, and began to ravage the region. Marius gathered his people to march against him, won several engagements and killed Rodric. To mark his victory, in the province later named Westmorland after him, Marius set up a stone; upon it is an inscription which preserves his memory to the present day. With Rodric dead, Marius allowed the defeated people who had accompanied him to live in the part of Scotland called Caithness; it was deserted, having been uninhabited and uncultivated for many years. Since the Picts had no wives, they asked the Britons for their daughters and relatives, but they refused to marry their daughters to such people. On suffering this rebuff, the Picts sailed to Ireland and in that country took wives, whose offspring increased their numbers. But enough of the Picts, since it is not my intention to write either their history or that of the Scots, who are descended from them and the Irish. After Marius had secured peace throughout the island, he showed himself to be a friend to the Romans, paying the tribute which they demanded from him. Inspired by his father, he ruled the kingdom with justice and peace, law and all honour.

71   When Marius' life came to an end, the crown passed to his son, named Coillus. Since he had been brought up from infancy in Rome, Coillus understood the ways of the Romans and had become very well disposed towards them. He too used to pay their tribute, being unwilling to offend them; he realised that they ruled the whole world and that their might could conquer any region or province. He therefore paid what they demanded and was able to enjoy his possessions in peace. None of Britain's kings showed greater respect for her nobles, allowing them to live in peace and awarding them frequent gifts.

72   Coillus had only one son, called Lucius. When he had been crowned after his father's death, Lucius continued all his good deeds so successfully that everybody thought of him as Coillus himself. Wishing to put his end above

suum cum pace et tranquillitate tractare, leges etiam ueteris traditionis confirmare, nouas uero inuenire, maxima donaria cuique probo impertiens. Fama igitur per totam Europam diuulgata, diligebant eum Romani et timebant ita ut prae omnibus regibus sermo de eo apud Romam fieret; unde 365 Iuuenalis caecum quendam Neroni dixisse in libro suo commemorat cum de capto rumbo loqueretur inquiens 'regem aliquem capies aut de themone Britanno decidet Aruiragus'. Nullus in bello ferocior illo fuit, nullus in pace mitior, nullus iocosior, nullus in dandis muneribus profusior. At ut dies uitae suae expleuit sepultus est Claudiocestriae in quodam templo quod in 370 honorem Claudii dicauerat.

70   Successit ei in regnum filius suus Marius, uir mirae prudentiae et sapientiae. Regnante postmodum illo, quidam rex Pictorum uocabulo Rodric, de Scithia cum magna classe ueniens, applicuit in aquilonarem partem Britanniae, quae Albania appellatur, coepitque prouinciam illam 375 uastare. Collecto igitur populo suo, petiuit illum Marius illatisque proeliis ipsum interfecit et uictoria potitus est. Deinde erexit lapidem in signum triumphi sui in prouincia, quae postea de nomine suo Wistmaria dicta fuit; in quo inscriptus titulus memoriam eius usque in hodiernum diem testatur. Perempto uero Rodric, dedit deuicto populo qui cum eo uenerat partem 380 Albaniae ad inhabitandum quae Katanesia nuncupatur; erat autem deserta, nullo habitatore multis diebus inculta. Cumque uxores non habentes filias et cognatas Britonum ab illis petiuissent, dedignati sunt Britones huiusmodi populo natas suas maritare. At illi, ut passi fuerunt repulsam, transfretauerunt in Hiberniam duxeruntque ex patria illa mulieres, ex 385 quibus creata sobole multitudinem suam auxerunt. Sed haec hactenus, cum non proposuerim tractare historiam eorum siue Scotorum qui ex illis et Hibernensibus originem duxerunt. At Marius, cum totam insulam summa pace composuisset, coepit amorem cum Romano populo habere, tributa soluens quae exigebantur ab illo. Exemplo etiam patris incitatus, iusticiam 390 et pacem, leges et omnia honesta per regnum suum exercebat.

71   Cum autem cursum uitae suae expleuisset, filius suus, uocabulo Coillus, regni gubernaculum suscepit. Hic ab infantia Romae nutritus fuerat moresque Romanorum edoctus in maximam ipsorum amiciciam inciderat. Sed et ipse tributum eis reddebat, aduersari diffugiens; quippe uidebat totum mundum 395 subditum illis eorumque potestatem quosque pagos, quamque prouinciam superare. Soluens igitur quod exigebatur, in pace quod possidebat optinuit. Nullus in regibus maiorem reuerentiam nobilibus regni praestabat, quia ipsos aut in pace manere permittebat aut assiduis donariis munerabat.

72   Natus est ei unicus filius, cui nomen erat Lucius. Qui cum defuncto patre 400 regni diademate insignitus fuisset, omnes actus bonitatis illius imitabatur ita ut ipse Coillus a cunctis censeretur. Exitum quoque suum praeferre

365-8 *4.126-7*
372 regnum <suum> *Φ*
395 reddebat eis *Φ*
400 [ei] *OCHS*

his beginning, he sent a letter to pope Eleutherius, asking to receive instruction in the Christian religion from him; for his spirit had been illuminated by the miracles that were being worked in various lands by the soldiers of Christ. Lucius' eager desire for the true faith meant that his pious prayer was answered, since on learning of his devotion the holy pontiff sent him two religious instructors, Faganus and Duvianus, who preached the Word of God made flesh, anointed him in holy baptism and brought him to Christ. The people of his country immediately flocked from all quarters to follow their king's example, and were cleansed from the same font and restored to the kingdom of heaven. When the blessed teachers had eradicated paganism from nearly the whole island, they rededicated to the One God and his saints the temples which had been built to honour many gods, and they filled them with various communities of men in clerical orders. At that time there were in Britain twenty-eight priests and three high priests, who were responsible for the remaining spiritual advisors and temple-servants. Following the command of the pope, they converted them from idolatry and set up bishops in place of priests, and archbishops in place of high priests. The high priests had been based in three of the noblest cities, London, York and Caerleon, whose site beside the river Usk in Glamorgan is marked by ancient walls and buildings. Once paganism had been suppressed, twenty-eight bishops were placed under the authority of these three archbishoprics. The dioceses were divided as follows: Deira and Scotland, which are separated from Loegria by the river Humber, were subject to the metropolitan of York; Loegria and Cornwall to the metropolitan of London; and Kambria, or Wales, which is separated from the two former dioceses by the Severn, was under Caerleon.

When at last everything had been reorganised, the priests returned to Rome to obtain from his holiness the pope confirmation of all they had achieved. With it they came back to Britain, accompanied by many others, whose teaching, shortly after they arrived, strengthened the British people's faith in Christ. Their names and acts can be found in the book which Gildas wrote about the victory of Aurelius Ambrosius. I saw no need to repeat in my inferior style what he had narrated in so distinguished a work.

BOOK FIVE

73   Meanwhile the glorious king Lucius, rejoicing that the worship of the true faith was esteemed in his kingdom, turned to better use the holdings and lands formerly owned by the pagan temples by permitting that they should remain in the possession of the churches of the faithful. And to afford the churches the greater honour that was their due, he increased their lands and holdings

uolens principio, epistulas suas Eleutherio papae direxit, petens ut ab eo
Christianitatem reciperet; serenauerant enim mentem eius miracula quae
tyrones Christi per diuersas nationes faciebant. Vnde in amorem uerae fidei 405
anhelans piae peticionis effectum consecutus est, siquidem beatus pontifex,
comperta eius deuotione, duos religiosos doctores, Faganum et Duuianum,
misit ad illum, qui uerbi Dei incarnationem praedicantes abluerunt ipsum
baptismate sacro et ad Christum conuerterunt. Nec mora, concurrentes
undique nationum populi exemplum regis insecuntur eodemque lauacro 410
mundati caelesti regno restituuntur. Beati igitur doctores, cum per totam
fere insulam paganismum deleuissent, templa quae in honore plurimorum
deorum fundata fuerant uni Deo eiusque sanctis dedicauerunt diuersisque
coetibus ordinatorum repleuerunt. Fuerant tunc in Britannia .xx. et .viii.
flamines nec non et tres archiflamines, quorum potestati ceteri iudices 415
morum atque phanatici submittebantur. Hos etiam ex praecepto apostolici
idolatriae eripuerunt et ubi erant flamines episcopos, ubi archiflamines
archiepiscopos posuerunt. Sedes autem archiflaminum in tribus nobilioribus
ciuitatibus fuerant, Lundoniis uidelicet atque Eboraci et in Vrbe Legionum,
quam super Oscam fluuium in Glamorgantia ueteres muri et aedificia sitam 420
fuisse testantur. His igitur tribus euacuata supersticione .xxviii. episcopi
subduntur. Diuisis quoque parrochiis, subiacuit metropolitano Eboracensi
Deira et Albania, quas magnum flumen Humbri a Loegria secernit;
Lundoniensi uero metropolitano submissa est Loegria et Cornubia; has duas
prouincias seiungit Sabrina a Kambria, id est Gualia, quae Vrbi Legionum 425
subiacuit.

Denique, restauratis omnibus, redierunt antistites Romam et cuncta
quae fecerant a beatissimo papa confirmari impetrauerunt. Confirmatione
igitur facta, reuersi sunt in Britanniam, compluribus aliis comitati, quorum
doctrina gens Britonum in fide Christi ex quo uenerunt in breui corroborata 430
fuit. Eorum nomina et actus in libro reperiuntur quem Gildas de uictoria
Aurelii Ambrosii inscripsit. Quod autem ipse tam lucido tractatu perarauerat
nullatenus opus fuit ut inferiori stilo renouaretur.

LIBER V

73 Interea gloriosus ille rex Lucius, cum infra regnum suum cultum uerae
fidei magnificatum esse uidisset, maximo gaudio fluctuans possessiones et
territoria quae prius templa idolorum possederant in meliorem usum uertens
ipsa ecclesiis fidelium permanere concessit. Et quia maiorem honorem
ipsis impendere debuerat, augmentauit illas amplioribus agris et mansis 5

---

420 quae *OS QYM*
429 cum pluribus *OHE YM*
430 [gens] *Δ*
430 in fide Christi *O Φ:* fides *(*fideles *H)* in Christo *CHSE*
430 [ex quo uenerunt] *CHSE*
432 parauerat *CHE*

and granted them every freedom. While engaged in realising these and other goals, he departed this life in the city of Gloucester and received honourable burial in the chief metropolitan church in the year of Our Lord 156. Since he had no child to succeed him, his death caused strife among the Britons and weakened the authority of Rome.

74   On the receipt of this news, the Roman senate chose one of their number, Severus, and two legions to restore the island to Roman control. After Severus had landed, he fought with the Britons, conquering some, and continually subjecting those he could not overcome to such terrible assaults that he drove them through Deira and into Scotland. Led by Fulgenius, the Britons fought back with all their might, often inflicting considerable slaughter both on their fellow-countrymen and on the Romans. To help them they brought in all the island-dwellers they could find and so won many victories. Annoyed by their raids, the emperor ordered a rampart to be built between Deira and Scotland to prevent their attacks penetrating any further. The rampart was constructed from coast to coast at public expense and for a long time afterwards held back enemy incursions. Fulgenius, unable to resist Severus any longer, sailed to Scythia, hoping to be restored to power with the help of the Picts; he gathered all the forces of that region, returned to Britain with a great fleet and besieged York. When the neighbouring provinces learned of this, most of the Britons deserted Severus and went over to Fulgenius. Severus however did not give up on this account, but summoned the Romans and those Britons who remained faithful to him, marched to the siege and attacked Fulgenius; in a bitterly fought battle Severus and many of his men were killed, whilst Fulgenius was mortally wounded. Severus was buried at York, which his legions had captured. He left two sons, Bassianus and Geta, the latter by a Roman mother, the former by a British. On the death of his father the Romans made Geta king, preferring him because he was fully Roman; the Britons rejected the Roman candidate, choosing Bassianus because he was related to them on his mother's side. When the brothers fought, Geta was killed and Bassianus crowned king.

75   At that time there was in Britain a young man of common birth named Carausius, who, after proving his worth in many battles, set out for Rome and asked the senate's permission to employ ships to protect Britain's coastline against barbarian attack; he promised, if

omnique libertate sublimauit. Inter haec et ceteros propositi sui actus in urbe Claudiocestriae ab hac uita migrauit et in ecclesia primae sedis honorifice sepultus est anno ab incarnatione Domini .clvi. Caruerat ipse sobole quae sibi succederet, unde defuncto illo et discidium inter Britones ortum fuit et Romana potestas infirmata. 10

74   Cumque id Romae nuntiatum fuisset, legauerunt senatus Seuerum senatorem duasque legiones cum illo ut patriam Romanae potestati restituerent. Qui ut appulsus fuit, proelium commisit cum Britonibus partemque sibi submisit, partem uero illam quam subiugare nequibat diris debellationibus infestare laborauit ita ut eam trans Deiram in Albaniam 15 fugaret. At illa duce Fulgenio omni nisu resistebat saepiusque stragem maximam et conciuibus et Romanis inferebat. Conducebat autem in auxilium sibi quoscumque insulanos populos inueniebat et sic multociens cum uictoria redibat. Irruptionem igitur eius grauiter ferens imperator iussit construi uallum inter Deiram et Albaniam ut impetum eius propius accedere 20 prohiberet. Communicato igitur sumptu, fecerunt illud a mari usque ad mare, quod multo tempore post hostium accessus detinuit. At Fulgenius, cum diutius Seuero resistere nequiuisset, transfretauit in Scithiam ut Pictorum auxilio dignitati restitueretur; cumque ibi omnem iuuentutem patriae collegisset, reuersus est maximo nauigio in Britanniam atque Eboracum 25 obsedit. Quod cum per ceteras nationes diuulgatum esset, maxima pars Britonum Seuerum deseruit et ad Fulgenium abiuit. Nec ob id ab inceptis suis destitutus est Seuerus sed conuocatis Romanis ceterisque Britonibus qui sibi adhaerebant obsidionem petiuit et cum Fulgenio dimicauit; sed cum pugnam acrius confecisset, interfectus est cum multis suorum et Fulgenius 30 letaliter uulneratus est. Exin sepultus est Eboraci, quam legiones eius optinuerunt. Reliquit ipse duos filios, Bassianum et Getam, quorum Geta Romana matre genitus erat, Bassianus uero Britannica. Defuncto igitur patre, sublimauerunt Romani Getam in regem, fauentes illi quia ex utraque parte Romanus fuerat; quod abnegantes Britanni Bassianum elegerunt quia 35 materno sanguine ipsis coniunctus erat. Proinde commiserunt pugnam fratres, unde Geta interficitur et Bassianus regno potitur.

75   Eo tempore fuerat in Britannia iuuenis quidam nomine Carausius, ex infima gente creatus, qui cum probitatem suam in multis debellationibus examinasset profectus est Romam petiuitque licentiam a senatu ut 40 maritima Britanniae ab incursione barbarica nauigiis tueretur; quod si

8 ipse *Δ (cf. § 78.140):* namque *Φ (cf. § 81.224), male*
8 qui *Φ*
12-13 patria suae ... restitueretur *Φ*
13 Qui *Δ:* Mox *Φ*
15 Deiram *Δ:* Scotiam *Φ*
26 fuisset *Φ*
29 adhaeserunt *Φ*
30 [est] *QG*
31 *fort.* uulneratus [est]
35 [parte] *QYG*
36-7 fratres pugnam *Φ*

permission was granted, to take so much booty that he could be of more service to the state than if they had made him Britain's king. Having deceived the senate with such promises, he got what he wanted and returned to Britain with official documents. He immediately assembled a fleet, gathered huge numbers of local youths and, setting sail and marauding round all the shoreline, threw the inhabitants into uproar. He landed on the nearby islands, ravaging crops, destroying cities and towns and stripping the natives of all they owned. His actions caused all those who were eager for plunder to flock to him so that he quickly possessed an army that no neighbouring chief could match. Puffed up by this, he told the Britons that, if they made him king, he would kill or expel the Romans and free the whole island from the barbarians. When they agreed, he immediately attacked and killed Bassianus and took the throne. Bassianus had been betrayed by the Picts who had been brought to Britain by duke Fulgenius, his maternal uncle; they were induced by Carausius' promises and bribes to desert Bassianus as soon as the battle began and turn on their comrades, so that they, not knowing friend from foe, quickly fled in surprise, leaving Carausius the winner. After his victory he gave the Picts a home in Scotland, where they have remained ever since, mixed with the British.

76   When Carausius' usurpation became known in Rome, the senate dispatched Allectus and three legions to kill the pretender and restore the kingdom of Britain to Roman authority. As soon as Allectus landed, he fought with Carausius, killed him and took the throne. Then he subjected the Britons to great oppression for deserting the Roman state to join Carausius. In retaliation, they crowned as king Asclepiodotus, duke of Cornwall, turning unanimously on Allectus and challenging him to battle. At that time Allectus was in London, conducting a ceremony for his native gods. When he heard that Asclepiodotus was coming, he broke off the sacrifice, led out his whole army against him and opened a fierce battle. Asclepiodotus got the upper hand, scattering his troops in flight and killing Allectus and thousands of his men in the pursuit. After his victory, Allectus' colleague, Livius Gallus, gathered the Roman survivors in the city, closed the gates and manned the towers and other fortifications, in the hope of holding Asclepiodotus off and escaping imminent death. Seeing this, Asclepiodotus swiftly blockaded the city and informed all Britain's leaders that he had killed Allectus and thousands of his men and held Gallus and the remaining Romans under siege in London; he therefore humbly begged them all

sibi committeretur, promittebat se tot et tanta adepturum quibus rem
publicam magis augmentaret quam si sibi regnum Britanniae traderetur.
Cumque senatum promissis suis illusisset, impetrauit quod poposcerat et
cum sigillatis cartis in Britanniam rediuit. Mox, collectis nauibus, asciuit   45
sibi magnam uirtutem iuuentutis patriae et ingressus est mare et circuiuit
omnia littora regni et maximum tumultum per populum faciebat. Interea,
in comprouincialibus insulis appulsus, agros populando, ciuitates et oppida
diruendo, incolis omnia sua eripiebat. Sic igitur ipso agente, confluebant
ad illum quicumque in aliena anhelabant, ita ut in breui tantum haberet   50
exercitum quanto nullus uicinus princeps resistere quiuisset. Ob hoc itaque
tumidum habens animum, dixit Britonibus ut sese sibi facerent regem et
ipse interfectis atque exterminatis Romanis totam insulam a barbara gente
liberaret. Quod cum impetrauisset, dimicauit confestim cum Bassiano et
interfecit eum et gubernaculum regni suscepit. Prodiderant enim Bassianum   55
Picti quos dux Fulgenius, matris suae frater, in Britanniam conduxerat;
nam dum sibi auxiliari debuissent, promissis et donariis Carausii corrupti
in ipso proelio diuerterunt se a Bassiano et in commilitones suos irruerunt,
unde stupefacti ceteri, cum ignorarent quis socius esset, quis hostis, ocius
dilabuntur, et uictoria cessit Carausio. Qui ut triumphum habuit, dedit Pictis   60
locum mansionis in Albania, ubi cum Britonibus mixti per subsequens
aeuum permanserunt.

76   Cum igitur inuasio Carausii Romae nunciata fuisset, legauit senatus
Allectum cum tribus legionibus ut tyrannum interficeret regnumque
Britanniae Romanae potestati restitueret. Nec mora, postquam appulsus   65
fuit, proeliatus est cum Carausio ipsoque interfecto solium regni suscepit.
Deinde maximam intulit cladem Britonibus quia relicta re publica societati
Carausii adhaeserant. Britones uero, id grauiter tolerantes, erexerunt
in regem Asclepiodotum ducem Cornubiae communique assensu facto
persecuti sunt Allectum et ad proelium prouocauerunt. Erat ipse tunc   70
Lundoniis festumque patriis diis celebrabat. At cum aduentum Asclepiodoti
comperisset, relicto sacrificio egressus est cum tota fortitudine sua contra
ipsum et acerrimam pugnam ingessit. Praeualuit autem Asclepiodotus
dissipauitque turmas suas atque in fugam coegit et usque insequendo multa
milia et regem Allectum peremit. Cum itaque sibi cessisset uictoria, Liuius   75
Gallus, Allecti collega, residuos Romanos conuocauit in urbe clausisque
ianuis turres ac ceteras munitiones muniuit cogitabatque sic Asclepiodoto
resistere uel imminentem necem uitare. At Asclepiodotus, cum ita factum
esse uidisset, obsedit ocius ciuitatem mandauitque omnibus ducibus
Britanniae quod Allectum cum multis milibus interfecerat obsidebatque   80
Gallum et reliquias Romanorum infra Lundonias, unde quosque supplici

---

48 <et> ciuitates *Φ*
48 oppida *Δ:* urbes *Φ*
53 ipse <eis> *QYM*
54 impetrasset *GM*
68 uero *O Q:* ergo *CHSE GM: om. Y*

to hurry to his assistance. The Roman race, he said, could easily be eliminated from Britain, if the Britons combined their efforts to attack them, trapped as they were. In response to his edict, there arrived the Demeti and Venedoti, the Deiri and Albani, and all the Britons; and when all were assembled under the eyes of their leader, he ordered them to construct great numbers of siege-engines to batter down the city walls. They obeyed, each man boldly and bravely assaulting the city with all his might. They soon forced their way in by demolishing the walls and began to slaughter their foes. The Romans realised that they were being cut down without respite and persuaded Gallus to surrender and beg Asclepiodotus for mercy, so that they might be allowed to depart with their lives. Almost all of them had been killed except one single legion that was still resisting as best it could. Gallus agreed and surrendered himself and his men. Asclepiodotus was about to show them mercy, when the Venedoti came in a body and in a single day beheaded every one beside a stream in the city, called after the Roman commander Nantgallun in British, and Galabroc in English.

77 Having overcome the Romans, Asclepiodotus took the crown and placed it on his own head with the approval of the people. He then ruled the country in full justice and peace for ten years, repressing the fury of robbers and the blades of thieves. His reign witnessed the persecution of the emperor Diocletian, in which Christianity nearly perished in Britain, even though it had flourished there unsullied since the days of king Lucius. There had arrived Maximianus Herculius, the tyrannical emperor's military governor, by whose command all the churches were demolished, all the sacred writings that could be found were burned in the public squares and all the chosen priests along with their faithful congregations were executed, so that they strove all together to hasten in a single body to the welcoming kingdom of heaven as if to their allotted home. God magnified his mercy among us, who in a generous gift at this time of persecution, lest the people of Britain be enveloped in a thick mist of the blackest night, provided holy martyrs as the brightest of lamps to enlighten them; their graves and places of martyrdom would even now inspire the minds of onlookers with the great warmth of divine love, had our people not been deprived of them by the lamentable partition with the barbarians. Among the men and women who stood firm in Christ's army were the martyrs Alban of Verolamium, and Julius and Aaron, citizens of Caerleon. Alban, burning with the virtue of love, first concealed in his home his confessor Amphibalus, who was being pursued by persecutors and was about to be caught, and then faced impending death by exchanging clothes with him, thus imitating Christ, who laid down his life for his flock; the other two, after enduring frightful bodily torture, swiftly ascended to Jerusalem's splendid gates with the trophy of martyrdom.

78 Meanwhile Coel duke of Kaercolum, or Colchester, rebelled against king Asclepiodotus, killed him in battle and took

rogatu poscebat ut sibi in auxilium festinarent; leuiter enim exterminandum erat Romanorum genus ex Britannia si communi uirtute illos, inclusos ut aiebat, inuaderent. Ad edictum itaque ipsius uenerunt Demeti et Venedoti, Deiri et Albani, et quicumque ex genere Britonum fuerant; cumque omnes 85 ante conspectum ducis conuenissent, iussit machinationes innumeras fieri et moenia ciuitatis prosternere. Paruit ilico quisque fortis et audax et urbem acerrime inuaserunt. Nec mora, diruerunt muros atque sibi introitum fecerunt stragemque Romanis dabant. At Romani, cum sese interfici sine intermissione uidissent, suaserunt Gallo ut sese et ipsos deditioni traderet et 90 misericordiam Asclepiodoti rogaret ut uiui abscedere sinerentur. Interfecti etenim omnes fere fuerant praeter unam solam legionem quae adhuc utcumque resistebat. Assensum ergo praebens Gallus tradidit se atque suos Asclepiodoto. Cumque ipse misericordiam de illo habere captaret, uenerunt Venedoti et facto agmine decollauerunt omnes una die super torrentem infra 95 urbem, qui postea de nomine ducis Britannice Nantgallun, Saxonice uero Galabroc nuncupatus fuit.

77   Triumphatis itaque Romanis, cepit Asclepiodotus regni diadema et capiti suo annuente populo imposuit. Exin tractauit patrias recta iusticia et pace decem annis raptorumque saeuitiam atque latronum mucrones 100 coercuit. In diebus eius orta est Dioclitiani imperatoris persecutio, qua fere deleta fuit Christianitas in insula, quae a tempore Lucii regis integra et intemerata permanserat. Superuenerat Maximianus Herculius, princeps miliciae praedicti tyranni, cuius imperio omnes subuersae sunt ecclesiae et cunctae sacrae scripturae quae inueniri poterant in mediis foris exustae 105 atque electi sacerdotes cum fidelibus sibi subditis trucidati ita ut agmine denso certatim ad amoena caelorum regna quasi ad propriam sedem festinarent. Magnificauit igitur misericordiam suam nobis Deus, qui gratuito munere persecutionis tempore, ne penitus crassa atrae noctis caligine populus Britonum offuscaretur, clarissimas lampades sanctorum 110 martirum ei accendit; quorum nunc sepulturae et passionum loca non minimum diuinae caritatis ardorem intuentium mentibus incuterent si non lugubri barbarorum diuortio ciuibus adempta fuissent. Inter ceteros utriusque sexus summa magnanimitate in acie Christi perstantes passus est Albanus Verolamius, Iulius quoque et Aaron Vrbis Legionum ciues. 115 Quorum Albanus, caritatis gratia feruens, confessorem suum Amphibalum, a persecutoribus insectatum et iamiamque comprehendendum, primum in domo sua occuluit et deinde mutatis uestibus sese discrimini mortis optulit, imitans in hoc Christum animam suam pro ouibus ponentem; ceteri autem duo, inaudita membrorum discerptione lacerati, ad egregias Ierusalem 120 portas absque cunctamine cum martyrii trophaeo conuolauerunt.

78   Interea insurrexit in regem Asclepiodotum Coel dux Kaercolun, id est Colecestriae, et conserto proelio peremit illum regnique diademate

83-4 [ut aiebat] *Φ*
89 stragem *O Q*
93 tradiditque *QGM*
113 adempta *M²*: adepta *cett. (cf. Introd.)*

his crown. When the senate heard this news, they rejoiced over the death of a king who had weakened Roman power in every way he could. Recalling the injury they had suffered through the loss of the kingdom, they dispatched the senator Constantius, a wise and brave man, who had conquered Spain for them and who was second to none in his efforts to strengthen the state. When the British king Coel heard he was coming, he was afraid to fight a man whom, it was rumoured, no king could defeat. After Constantius landed, Coel therefore sent envoys to him asking for peace and promising his submission, on condition that he be allowed to retain the crown and pay the Roman authorities nothing more than the customary tribute. On receiving this message, Constantius agreed, and they sealed the pact by an exchange of hostages. After a month went by, Coel fell gravely ill and died eight days later; on his death, Constantius was crowned king and married Coel's daughter, Helena. She was more beautiful than any girl in the country and was considered to have no equal in playing musical instruments and in the liberal arts. Lacking any other offspring to inherit the throne, her father had taken pains to educate her in such a way that she could rule the country more easily when he died. After making her his partner in marriage, Constantius had a son by her whom he called Constantine. Then, when eleven years had passed, Constantius died at York and passed on the crown to his son. After acceding to the throne, Constantine began a few years later to show great ability, displaying the fierceness of a lion and maintaining justice among his subjects. He curbed the greed of robbers, trampled the cruelty of tyrants and strove to reestablish peace everywhere.

79   At that time there was a despot at Rome called Maxentius, who was trying to dispossess all the nobles and most upright citizens and oppressing the state with terrible tyranny. The victims of his savagery fled in exile to Britain, where Constantine received them with due honour. Eventually, when many such people had flocked to him, they stirred up in his heart hatred for the despot, with such repeated taunts as:

'How long will you permit our calamitous exile, Constantine? Why do you hesitate to restore us to our native soil? You are the only one of our countrymen who can return to us our lost possessions by driving out Maxentius. What prince can match the king of Britain in the bravery and strength of his soldiers or in the abundance of his gold and silver? Restore our property, we beg you, return our wives and children by taking your army to Rome with us'.

sese insigniuit. Cumque id senatui nunciatum fuisset, gauisi sunt propter mortem regis, qui per omnia Romanam potestatem turbauerat. Recolentes 125 quoque dampnum quod de amisso regno habuerant, legauerunt Constantium senatorem, qui Hispaniam ipsis subdiderat, uirum sapientem, audacem, et qui prae ceteris rem publicam augere laborauerat. Porro Coel rex Britonum, cum aduentum ipsius comperisset, timuit ei proelia ingerere quia fama ipsius asserebat nullum regem ipsi resistere posse. Vt igitur infra insulam 130 Constantius applicuit, direxit Coel legatos suos ad illum petiuitque pacem et subiectionem promisit, eo tamen pacto ut regnum Britanniae possideret nichilque aliud praeter solitum tributum Romanae dignitati solueret. Hoc igitur nunciato, acquieuit ei Constantius, pacemque receptis obsidibus confirmauerunt. Emenso deinde mense, grauissima infirmitas occupauit 135 Coel ipsumque infra octo dies morte affecit; quo defuncto, insigniuit se Constantius regni diademate duxitque filiam Coel, cui nomen erat Helena. Pulcritudo eius prouinciales puellas superabat, nec uspiam reperiebatur altera quae in musicis instrumentis siue in liberalibus artibus doctior illa censeretur. Caruerat pater alia sobole quae solio regni potiretur, unde eam 140 ita docere laborauerat ut regimen patriae post obitum suum facilius tractare quiuisset. Cum igitur illam in societatem thori recepisset Constantius, generauit ex ea filium uocauitque eum Constantinum. Exin, cum undecim anni praeterissent, ipse apud Eboracum morti subiacuit regnumque filio donauit. Qui ut solio honoris potitus est, coepit infra paucos annos 145 probitatem maximam habere, leoninam feritatem ostendere, iusticiam inter populos tenere. Latronum rapacitatem hebetabat, tyrannorum saeuitiam conculcabat, pacem ubique renouare studebat.

79   Ea tempestate erat quidam tyrannus Romae, uocabulo Maxentius, qui quosque nobiles, quosque probissimos ciues exhereditare nitebatur 150 pessimaque tyrannide rem publicam opprimebat. Incumbente igitur ipsius saeuicia, diffugiebant exterminati ad Constantinum in Britanniam et ab ipso honorifice excipiebantur. Denique, cum multi tales ad illum confluxissent, incitauerunt eum in odium aduersus praedictum tyrannum et talia ei saepissime obiciebant: 155

'Quousque calamitatem et exilium nostrum patieris, Constantine? Vt quid moraris nos in natale solum restituere? Tu solus es ex generatione nostra qui quod amisimus nobis reddere expulso uales Maxentio. Quis etenim princeps regi Britanniae conferri queat siue in fortitudine robustorum militum siue in copia auri et argenti? Obsecramus te, redde 160 nobis possessiones nostras, redde coniuges et liberos nostros Romam cum exercitu nobiscum petendo'.

131 [Coel] *Φ*
132 [tamen] *Φ*
149 [Romae] *OCSE*
150 exheredare *YG²M (cf. §§ 58.94, 61.172)*
150 conabatur *Φ*
153 eum *YG*

80   Roused by these and other reproaches, Constantine marched on Rome, conquering it and subsequently gaining control over the whole world. He had taken with him Helena's three uncles, Loelinus, Trahern and Marius, whom he made senators. Meanwhile Octavius, duke of the Gewissei, had rebelled against the authority of the Roman proconsuls, to whom government of the island had been entrusted, killed them and occupied the throne of the kingdom. When this was reported to Constantine, he sent Helena's uncle Trahern with three legions to restore the island to Roman power. Trahern came ashore near the city which in British is called Kaerperis, attacked it and took it in two days. When news of this spread among all his peoples, king Octavius assembled all the armed forces of the whole island and came to meet him not far from Winchester, on the plain whose British name is Maisurian. Battle commenced and Octavius was victorious. Trahern and his mangled troops made for their ships, on which he embarked, travelled by sea to Scotland and proceeded to lay waste those regions. When this was again reported to Octavius, he reassembled his men in pursuit. He attacked in the province called Westmorland, but retreated without success. Trahern, seeing that victory was in his grasp, followed Octavius and, harrying him, deprived him of his cities and crown. Octavius, aggrieved at the loss of his kingdom, sailed to Norway to enlist the aid of its king, Gumbertus. In the meantime, he had issued instructions to his retinue to spare no effort in engineering Trahern's death, a command which a count of a free town, who loved Octavius more than the rest, was quick to put into effect. One day, when Trahern was returning from the city of London, the count hid with a hundred knights in a wooded valley where he would pass; as Trahern did so, the count launched an unexpected attack and killed him among his men. On receiving the news, Octavius returned to Britain, scattered the Romans and recovered the throne of the kingdom. He then in a short time acquired such a reputation and so much gold and silver that he feared no man. From that time until the days of Gratianus and Valentinianus, Octavius ruled the kingdom of Britian unopposed.

81   Finally exhausted by old age and wishing to make arrangements for his subjects, he asked his advisors which of his family they wanted to become king after his demise. He had no son to pass on the crown to, only a daughter. Some suggested that he should give the daughter in marriage to a Roman noble, along with the crown so that they could be surer of peace; others prefered that his nephew Conanus Meriadocus be crowned as king, and the daughter married to the ruler of some other kingdom with a dowry of gold and silver. While they were discussing these proposals, Caradocus duke of Cornwall arrived and advised that they should summon the senator Maximianus, give him the king's daughter and crown, and so enjoy lasting peace. Maximianus had a British father, since he was the son of Constantine's uncle, Loelinus, mentioned above, whilst his mother and his nation were Roman, so that he was of royal blood on both sides. Hence Caradocus could promise an enduring

80 His igitur et aliis incitatus Constantinus adiuit Romam subiugauitque
illam sibi et postmodum monarchiam totius mundi optinuit. Conduxerat
secum tres auunculos Helenae, Loelinum uidelicet et Trahern nec non 165
et Marium, ipsosque in senatorium ordinem promouit. Interea insurrexit
Octauius dux Gewisseorum in proconsules Romanae dignitatis, quibus
regimen insulae permissum fuerat, et solio regni ipsis interfectis potitus
est. Cumque id Constantino nuntiatum fuisset, direxit Trahern auunculum
Helenae cum tribus legionibus ut insulam Romanae dignitati restitueret. 170
Appulsus itaque Trahern in littore iuxta urbem quae Britannice Kaerperis
nuncupatur impetum fecit in ipsam atque infra duos dies cepit. Quo per
uniuersas nationes diuulgato, rex Octauius omnem armatam manum totius
insulae collegit uenitque sibi in obuiam haut longe a Guintonia in campo
qui Britannice Maisurian appellatur coepitque proeliari et uictoria potitus 175
est. Trahern itaque naues laceratis militibus adiuit ingressusque eas petiuit
Albaniam aequoreo itinere et prouincias uastare uacauit. Cumque id regi
Octauio iterum nuntiatum fuisset, resociatis turmis secutus est eum et in
prouintia quae Westmarialanda uocata fuit dimicauit sed sine uictoria diffugit.
At Trahern, ut sibi uictoriam cedere perspexit, insecutus est Octauium 180
nec eum quietem habere permisit donec illi urbes cum diademate eripuit.
Octauius igitur, propter amissum regnum anxius, nauigio Norguegiam
petiuit ut auxilium a rege Gumberto acquireret. Interea familiaribus suis
edictum fecerat ut omni nisu elaborarent neci Trahern imminere. Comes
ergo oppidi municipii, qui ipsum prae ceteris diligebat, praeceptis illius 185
parere non distulit. Nam dum Trahern ex urbe Lundoniarum quadam die
recederet, delituit cum centum militibus in quadam conualle nemoris qua
ille transiturus erat atque in ipsum praetereuntem inopinum fecit impetum
ac inter commilitones interfecit. Quod cum nunciatum esset Octauio,
reuersus est in Britanniam et dissipatis Romanis solium regni recuperauit. 190
Exin tantam probitatem tantamque copiam auri et argenti in breui tempore
nactus fuit ita ut neminem timeret. Regnum autem Britanniae ab illo
tempore usque in diebus Gratiani et Valentiniani feliciter optinuit.

81 Denique senio confectus, disponere populo uolens, quaesiuit a
consiliariis suis quem post ipsius fata in regem de progenie sua erigere 195
affectassent. Vnicam tantum filiam habens, filio caruerat cui regimen
patriae permitteret. Fuerunt itaque qui laudabant ut filiam suam alicui
nobilium Romanorum cum regno maritaret ut firmiori pace fruerentur;
alii uero censebant Conanum Meriadocum nepotem suum in solium regni
iniciandum, filiam uero alicui alterius regni principi cum auro et argento 200
copulandam. Dum haec inter ipsos gererentur, accessit Caradocus dux
Cornubiae consiliumque dedit ut Maximianum senatorem inuitarent
filiamque ei cum regno donarent et sic perpetua pace fruerentur. Erat autem
patre Britannus, quia Loelinus auunculus Constantini, de quo superius
mentionem feceram, ipsum genuerat; matre uero et natione Romanus ex 205
utroque sanguine regalem ferebat procreationem. Iccirco igitur stabilitatem

180 prospexit *SE* Y

peace, since he knew that Maximianus' claim to Britain rested both on imperial descent and British birth. When the duke of Cornwall presented his plan, the king's nephew Conanus, who was very eager to succeed him, was furious and disrupted the whole court on account of it. Caradocus, unwilling to relinquish his project, sent his son Mauricus to Rome to inform Maximianus. This Mauricus was handsome, able and bold, a man who in the face of opposition could uphold his judgement by recourse to arms. Coming into Maximianus' presence, he was fittingly received by him and honoured above his companions. At that time there was great enmity between the two emperors, Gratianus and his brother Valentinianus, and Maximianus, who had been refused the third share in the empire he desired. Perceiving that Maximianus had been slighted by the emperors, Mauricus addressed the following words to him:

'Maximianus, why be frightened of Gratianus, when there is an easy way for you to take the empire from him? Come with me to the island of Britain, and you will have its crown. King Octavius is worn out by age and weakness, and desires nothing better than to find someone worthy of receiving his kingdom and his daughter. Lacking a male heir, he asked his nobles to whom he should give his daughter and the crown. In obedience to his request, those mighty men decided that the kingdom and the girl should be given to you, and they have sent me to inform you. If you come with me and carry this out, you, with all Britain's gold and silver and all her warlike knights, will be able to return to Rome, drive out the emperors and take the city, just as your kinsman Constantine did and many other kings of ours who became emperors'.

82 Maximianus was persuaded by this speech and made for Britain. On the way he conquered the cities of the French, thus amassing gold and silver and attracting knights from all quarters. He then set sail on the ocean and, after a successful voyage, landed at Southampton. The king was greatly alarmed by this news, as he thought that an enemy army had landed. He therefore summoned his nephew Conanus, instructing him to assemble all the island's armed soldiers and advance to meet the foe. Conanus swiftly gathered all the kingdom's young men and came to Southampton, where Maximianus had pitched his tents. When Maximianus learned of the arrival of this host, he was deeply troubled, not knowing what to do; he had no hope of making peace and, since he commanded the smaller army, placed no confidence in either his men's numbers or their bravery. So he summoned his elders and Mauricus, commanding them to say what should be done in this situation. Mauricus replied:

pacis promittebat quia sciebat illum et ex genere imperatorum et ex origine Britonum ius in Britanniam habere. Cum itaque tale consilium dedisset dux Cornubiensium, indignatus est Conanus nepos regis, qui omni nisu in regnum anhelabat, totamque curiam propter talia turbauit. At Caradocus, coeptis suis desistere nolens, misit Mauricum filium suum Romam ut ea Maximiano indicaret. Erat ipse Mauricus pulchrae staturae magnaeque probitatis atque audaciae et qui ea quae iudicabat armis si contradictio fieret et duellio probabat. Qui ut praesentiam Maximiani adiuit, receptus est ab illo ut decebat et super commilitones honoratus. Erat tunc maxima inquietudo inter ipsum Maximianum et duos imperatores, Gratianum fratremque suum Valentinianum, quia passus fuerat repulsam de tercia parte imperii quam petebat. Vt igitur Mauricus uidit Maximianum ab imperatoribus oppressum, eum in haec uerba affatur:

'Vt quid Gratianum times, Maximiane, cum tibi pateat uia qua ei imperium eripere poteris? Veni mecum in Britanniam insulam, et diadema regni possidebis. Octauius enim rex, senio et languore grauatus, nichil aliud desiderat nisi ut aliquem talem inueniat cui regnum suum cum filia donet. Masculina namque prole caret consiliumque a proceribus suis petiuit cui unicam filiam suam cum regno copularet. Et ut affectui eius parerent heroes decreuerunt ut tibi concederetur regnum et puella direxeruntque me ad te ut id tibi notificarem. Si igitur mecum ueniens inceptum istud perpetraueris, copia auri et argenti Britanniae, multitudine etiam bellicosorum militum ibidem manentium Romam ualebis redire expulsisque imperatoribus eam subiugare. Sic enim egit cognatus tuus Constantinus pluresque reges nostri qui imperium ascenderunt'.

82   Acquiescens igitur uerbis eius Maximianus petiuit Britanniam, petendo subiugabat Francorum urbes, subiugando aurum et argentum coaceruabat, milites undique sibi associabat. Exin, occeanum mare ingressus, in Portum Hamonis secundis uelis applicuit. Cumque id regi nunciatum esset, expauit stupore uehementi, existimans hostilem exercitum superuenisse. Vocato igitur Conano nepote suo, iussit eum colligere omnem armatum militem insulae atque in obuiam hostibus procedere. Collegit ilico Conanus cunctam iuuentutem regni uenitque ad Portum Hamonis, ubi tentoria sua Maximianus erexerat. Qui ut aduentum tantae multitudinis comperit, maximis angustiis cruciabatur, quia ignorabat quid faceret; paucioribus namque cateruis comitatus, dubitabat et uirorum multitudinem et audatiam, quia de pace nullam spem habebat. Conuocatis igitur maioribus natu et Maurico, dicere praecepit quid contra talem euentum agendum fieret. Cui Mauricus:

214 duello *O QG*
228 <cum> copia *54 (cf. Introd.)*
234 sibi undique *QY*
234 Postmodum *Φ*
235 fuisset *O Y*
243 [et] *M*

'We must not fight against so many warlike knights, nor have we come with the aim of conquering Britain in battle. We should seek peace and permission to remain until we know the king's intentions. Let us claim to have been sent by the emperors, bringing their instructions to Octavius, and lull these people with crafty words'.

This pleased everybody. Mauricus went to meet Conanus with twelve grey-haired nobles, wiser than the rest and carrying olive branches in their right hands. Once the British saw these reverend old men bearing the peace-sign of the olive, they rose as a mark of respect and made way for them to reach the duke more easily. As soon as they stood before Conanus, they greeted him in the name of the emperors and senate, saying that Maximianus had been sent to king Octavius with instructions for him from Gratianus and Valentinianus. Conanus replied:

'Why then does such a host accompany him? They resemble not so much ambassadors, but rather invaders who are planning to inflict harm on us'.

Mauricus retorted:

'It was not fitting for such an individual to travel in private without the protection of soldiers, especially when many kings hate him because of the power of the Romans and the deeds of his forebears. Were he to travel with a small retinue, he might be killed by the enemies of the republic. He comes in peace, seeking peace, as his actions amply demonstrate. Since we have landed, we have so conducted ourselves as to harm no one. We bear our costs like peaceful men, buying what we need and having taken nothing from anyone by force'.

Conanus hesitated between declaring himself for peace or war. Then Caradocus duke of Cornwall and the other nobles came and persuaded him that after this request he should not initiate hostilities. Conanus would have preferred to fight, but laid down his weapons and granted them peace. He took Maximianus to London to see the king, and told him the whole story.

83   Then Caradocus duke of Cornwall with his son Mauricus, after commanding the attendants to withdraw, said to the king:

There! Something which those who are truly loyal to your service have for a long time desired can be counted, with God's grace, among your accomplishments. You commanded your nobles to advise you what you should do about your daughter and your kingdom, since your age is now against your ruling your people for much longer. Some judged that the crown should be given to your nephew Conanus, and that your daughter should make some other suitable match, since they feared the extinction of our citizens if a foreign prince were brought in. Others were for presenting the kingdom to your daughter and to some nobleman who speaks our own tongue, who could succeed after your

'Non est nobis cum tot bellicosis militibus pugnandum, nec ea de   245
causa uenimus ut Britanniam proelio subiugaremus. Pax roganda est et
hospitandi licentia donec animum regis sciamus. Dicamus nos missos
esse ab imperatoribus eorundemque mandata Octauio deferre et callidis
uerbis populum istum mulceamus'.

Cumque id omnibus placuisset, assumpsit secum duodecim canutos proceres 250
sapientiores ceteris et ramos oliuae in dextris ferentes uenitque Conano in
obuiam. Videntes ergo Britones uiros reuerendae aetatis et oliuam in signum
pacis gestantes assurgunt eis honori et uiam patefaciunt ut ducem liberius
adeant. Mox illi, in praesentia Conani Meriadoci stantes, salutauerunt eum
ex parte imperatorum et senatus dixeruntque Maximianum missum ad   255
regem Octauium ut mandata Gratiani et Valentiniani eidem portaret. Ad
haec Conanus:

'Vt quid ergo eum tanta sequitur multitudo? Non haec facies legatorum
esse solet, immo superuenientium hostium qui iniuriam inferre
meditantur'.   260

Tunc Mauricus:

'Non decebat tantum uirum inglorium sine commilitonibus incedere,
praesertim cum propter Romanam potentiam et propter actus auorum
suorum pluribus regibus odiosus habeatur. Nam si raro comitatu incederet,
fortasse ab inimicis rei publicae perimeretur. Pace uenit pacemque petit,   265
quod ex actu suo credi debeat. Ex quo namque applicuimus, sic nosmet
ipsos habuimus ut nemini iniuriam intulimus. Expensam nostram ut gens
pacis ferimus, quia necessaria ementes nichil ui cuipiam surripuimus'.

Cumque haesitasset Conanus an pacem an proelium committeret, accessit
Caradocus dux Cornubiae, accesserunt ceteri proceres, et dissuaserunt 270
Conano post hanc peticionem bellum ingerere. Qui licet dimicare maluisset,
depositis armis concessit eis pacem duxitque Maximianum Lundonias ad
regem et rem ex ordine manifestauit.

83   Tunc Caradocus dux Cornubiae, assumpto secum Maurico filio suo,
iussit astantes semoueri regemque in haec uerba adiuit: 275

'Ecce, quod longo tempore desiderabant qui fidelitati tuae ueriori
affectu oboedientiam seruant disponente Deo successibus tuis accessit.
Praeceperas namque proceribus tuis consilium dare quid de filia tua, quid
de regno tuo tibi agendum foret, cum tua aetas in tantum his diebus repugnet
ut populum tuum diutius gubernes. Alii itaque censebant diadema Conano   280
nepoti tuo tradendum filiamque tuam alicubi digne maritandam, timentes
ciuium exterminationem si alterius linguae princeps superueniret. Alii
concedebant regnum filiae et alicui nostrae loquelae nobili, qui tibi post

---

248 eorumque *H*
251 ferentes *54 (cf.§ 158.413): om. cett. (cf. 'Transm.' 98)*
264 habebatur *C*
266 debebat *C¹*: debet *O*
267 intulerimus *E M*

death. However, the majority argued that someone related to the emperors should be sent to marry your daughter and to receive the crown, promising that firm and lasting peace would be the result, since they would be under the protection of Roman authority. See now, God has deigned to send you this young man, of Roman blood and descended from the British royal family; in my opinion you should marry your daughter to him with all speed. Even if you were to refuse, how could your claim to the throne of Britain compare with his? He is Constantine's kinsman and the nephew of our king Coel, the hereditary claim of whose daughter Helena to this kingdom we cannot deny'.

When he had heard Caradocus out, Octavius agreed with him and with the consent of all gave Maximianus the throne of Britain and his daughter. Conanus Meriadocus was unbelievably angry at this and retired to Scotland, where he began to assemble an army to attack Maximianus. Having gathered a host, he crossed the river Humber, ravaging all the provinces on either bank. When this news reached Maximianus, he collected all his forces. Hastening to attack, he fought Conanus and returned victorious. Conanus however did not give up, but reunited his army and threatened those provinces with destruction. Maximianus therefore returned and in the ensuing battles emerged sometimes victorious, sometimes defeated. Eventually, after inflicting serious losses on each other, they were persuaded by their friends to make peace.

84   Five years passed, and the huge amounts of gold and silver which daily flowed into Maximianus' coffers went to his head. He readied a great fleet and assembled all Britain's armed soldiers. Not content with the kingdom of Britain, he desired to conquer France. After crossing over, he went first to the kingdom of Armorica, which is now called Brittany, and began to subdue its French inhabitants. Led by Imbaltus, they came to attack him, but after most of them had been killed, they fled, their leader Imbaltus and fifteen thousand armed men, drawn from the whole kingdom, being among the dead. Maximianus was overjoyed to have inflicted such losses, knowing as he did that the country could easily be conquered after the death of so many men. He summoned Conanus from the ranks and said with a brief smile:

'See, we have overcome one of the mightiest kingdoms of France, and can hope to take the rest. Let us make haste to capture the cities and towns before news of the threat spreads further in France and rouses all her population to arms. If we can gain this kingdom, all France will doubtless fall into our hands. Have no regrets that you

obitum succederet. Maior autem pars laudabat ut ex genere imperatorum
mandaretur aliquis cui nata cum diademate donaretur; promittebant enim   285
firmam et stabilem pacem inde prouenturam, cum Romana potestas
ipsos protegeret. Ecce ergo tibi dignatus est subuectare Deus iuuenem
istum, et ex genere Romanorum et ex regali prosapia Britonum creatum,
cui filiam tuam meo consilio maritare non differes. Quamquam autem
id abnegares, quid iuris tibi contra illum in regnum Britanniae fieret?   290
Constantini etenim consanguineus est et nepos Coel nostri regis, cuius
filiam Helenam nequimus abnegare hereditario iure regnum istud
possidere'.

Cumque haec retulisset Caradocus, adquieuit ei Octauius communique
assensu illato regnum Britanniae cum filia sua illi donauit. Quod uidens   295
Conanus Meriadocus indignatus est ultra quam credi potest secessitque
in Albaniam et exercitum colligere uacauit ut Maximianum inquietaret.
Multitudine ergo consociata, praeteriuit Humbri flumen, quasque
prouincias ultra et citra depopulans. Quod cum Maximiano nuntiaretur,
collecta tota fortitudine sua festinauit in obuiam et cum illo proeliatus est   300
et cum uictoria rediuit. Nec tamen deficiebat Conanus sed resociatis iterum
cateruis destructioni prouinciarum imminebat. Redibat ergo Maximianus et
commissis proeliis quandoque cum triumpho, quandoque superatus abibat.
Denique, cum alter alteri dampnum maximum intulisset, concordiam
annitentibus amicis fecerunt.   305

84   Emenso deinde quinquennio, superbiuit se Maximianus propter
infinitam copiam auri et argenti quae illi cotidie affluebat parauitque
nauigium maximum omnemque armatum militem Britanniae collegit; non
sufficiebat enim ei regnum Britanniae quin affectaret Gallias subiugare.
Vt igitur transfretauit, adiuit primitus Armoricum regnum, quod nunc   310
Britannia dicitur, et populum Francorum qui inerat debellare incepit. At
Franci duce Imbalto obuiam uenientes pugnam fecerunt contra illum, sed
in maiori parte periclitati fugam inierunt; ceciderat namque dux Imbaltus
et quindecim milia armatorum, qui ex omni regno illo conuenerant. Vt
igitur tantam cladem ingessit Maximianus maximo fluctuauit gaudio quia   315
interitu tot uirorum sciebat patriam leuiter deinde subdendam. Vocauit ergo
Conanum ad se extra turmas et paulisper subridens ait:

'Ecce, unum ex potioribus Galliae regnis subiugauimus: ecce, spem ad
cetera habere possumus. Festinemus urbes et oppida capere antequam
rumor huius periculi, in ulteriorem Galliam euolans, uniuersos populos ad   320
arma prouocet. Nam si istud regnum habere poterimus, non haesito quin
totam Galliam potestati nostrae subdemus. Ne pigeat igitur te regnum

291 regis nostri *E YM*
295 assensu *M ut § 144.50:* sensu *cett.*
296 exprimi *Φ*
311 coepit *O*
322 subdamus *GM*
322 ergo *Φ*

surrendered the crown of Britain to me, despite the fact that you hoped for it; for whatever you lost there, I shall restore to you in this country. I shall make you the ruler of this kingdom; we shall drive out its inhabitants, and it will be another Britain, occupied by our people. It is a country rich in crops with rivers full of fish, beautiful woods and pleasant glades, more welcoming, to my mind, than any other'.

To this, Conanus thankfully bowed his head and promised that he would be faithful in his service as long as he lived.

85   Next they gathered their troops, marched to Rennes and captured it that very day. For when they heard of the savagery of the British and the fate of the dead, its citizens hastened to flee, abandoning their wives and children. The inhabitants of the other cities and towns followed their example, allowing the British easy access. Wherever they gained entry, the Britons killed all males and spared only the women. Finally, when they had left all the provinces completely desolate, they placed British knights as garrisons in the cities, towns and castles in their various locations. News of Maximianus' cruelty spread through the remaining regions of France and all its dukes and princes were gripped by such panic that they could rely on nothing other than their prayers. From every village they fled to the cities and towns, anywhere that offered a safe haven. When he saw how much he was feared, Maximianus became bolder and hastened to increase his army by lavish donations. He attracted to him all those he knew lusted after the possessions of others, readily enriching them with gold, silver and other presents.

86   Finally Maximianus assembled a host sufficient in his opinion to conquer all France. Yet for a short time he halted his cruel progress until he had pacified the captured kingdom and filled it with a British population. He issued an edict to the effect that a hundred thousand common people should be gathered to be sent to him, as well as thirty thousand knights to protect them from hostile attack in the country they were to inhabit. Once all this was organised, he spread them throughout all the regions of Armorica, making it a second Britain, which he presented to Conanus Meriadocus. Maximianus himself and his fellow-soldiers marched further into France and, after a series of major engagements, conquered not only it but also all of Germany, being victorious in every battle. Setting up the throne of his empire at Trier, he unleashed such frenzy on the two emperors, Gratianus and Valentinianus, that he killed the former and drove the latter from Rome.

87   Meanwhile the French and Aquitanians were harrying Conanus and the Armorican Britons, making frequent assaults and attacking them at every opportunity. Conanus in

Britanniae insulae cessisse michi, licet spem possidendi eam habuisses, quia quicquid in illa amisisti tibi in hac patria restaurabo. Promouebo etenim te in regem regni huius, et erit haec altera Britannia, et eam ex 325 genere nostro expulsis indigenis repleamus. Patria namque fertilis est segetibus et flumina piscosa sunt, nemora perpulchra, et saltus ubique amoeni, nec est uspiam meo iudicio gratior tellus'.

Ad haec inclinato capite grates egit Conanus promisitque se fidelem in obsequio suo mansurum dum uiueret. 330

85   Exin, conuocatis cateruis, ierunt Redonim ipsamque eodem die ceperunt. Audita namque saeuitia Britonum peremptorumque casu, diffugerant ciues cum festinatione, mulieribus relictis atque infantibus. Exemplo istorum fecerunt ceteri per urbes et oppida, ita ut facilis aditus Britonibus pateret. Qui ubicumque intrabant interficiebant quicquid erat masculini sexus, solis 335 mulieribus parcentes. Postremo, cum uniuersas prouincias penitus ab omni incola deleuissent, muniuerunt ciuitates et oppida militibus Britanniae et promunctoria in diuersis locis statuta. Saeuitia ergo Maximiani per ceteras Galliarum prouintias diuulgata, timor nimius quosque duces, quosque principes inuadebat, ita ut nullam aliam spem nisi in uotis soluendis 340 haberent. Diffugiebant itaque ab omni pago ad ciuitates et oppida et ad quaecumque loca tutum praestabant refugium. Maximianus ergo, sese timori esse comperiens, maiorem audatiam resumit exercitumque suum profusis donariis augere festinat. Quoscumque enim aliena captare callebat associabat sibi et nunc auro, nunc argento ceterisque muneribus illum ditare 345 non diffugiebat.

86   Exin tantam multitudinem collegit quantam existimabat sibi sufficere ad omnem Galliam subiugare. Distulit tamen saeuitiam suam paulisper ulterius ingerere donec sedato regno quod ceperat ipsum Britannico populo repleuisset. Fecit itaque edictum suum ut centum milia plebanorum in 350 Britannia insula colligerentur qui ad eum uenirent, praeterea triginta milia militum qui ipsos infra patriam qua mansuri erant ab hostili irruptione tuerentur. Cumque omnia perpetrasset, distribuit eos per uniuersas Armorici regni nationes fecitque alteram Britanniam et eam Conano Meriadoco donauit. Ipse uero cum ceteris commilitonibus suis ulteriorem Galliam 355 adiuit grauissimisque proeliis illatis subiugauit eam nec non et totam Germaniam, in omni proelio uictoria potitus. Thronum autem imperii sui apud Treueros statuens, ita debachatus est in duos imperatores, Gratianum et Valentinianum, quod uno interempto alterum ex Roma fugauit.

87   Interea inquietabant Conanum Armoricosque Britones Galli atque 360 Aequitani crebrisque irruptionibus saepissime infestabant. Quibus ipse

323 spem *post* eam *Φ*
331 Exinde *H:* Post haec *Φ*
332 casu *1508:* casum *Ω*
337 uacuassent *54 auctorem corrigens (cf. § 200.490)*
337 munierunt *HSE Y*
345 illos *M:* om. *96 (cf. Introd. ad § 16.288-90)*
347 <posse> sufficere *YGM*
348 subiugandam *M (cf. Introd.)*

turn was fighting back, matching slaughter with slaughter, and bravely defending the country entrusted to him. When finally he was victorious, he wanted to present his fellow soldiers with wives, by whom they might father heirs to occupy the country for ever. To avoid intermarriage with the French, he ordered that women should come from the island of Britain to be their brides. For this purpose he sent messengers there to Dionotus king of Cornwall, who had succeeded his brother Caradocus as ruler, instructing him to arrange this. Dionotus was a powerful nobleman to whom Maximianus had entrusted the government of the island while he himself was engaged in the schemes outlined above. He also had a very beautiful daughter, called Ursula, whom Conanus had desired more than any other thing.

88   After an interview with Conanus' messenger, Dionotus willingly obeyed his instructions. In various provinces he gathered eleven thousand noblemen's daughters, as well as sixty thousand girls of common birth, and ordered them all to assemble in the city of London. He also commanded that ships be brought from various shores to carry them to their husbands. Many amid such a throng were pleased by the plan, but more objected, having greater affection for their parents and country; probably there were also some who preferred virginity to marriage, being willing to die anywhere on earth rather than to seek wealth in such a way. Indeed different things would have pleased different women, had they only been able to bring their plans to fruition. Once the fleet was ready, the women embarked on the ships and sailed down the river Thames towards the sea. When they set sail for Armorica, the fleet was struck by adverse winds, which swiftly scattered it utterly. The ships were imperilled on the sea and mostly sank. The few women who escaped the danger were driven to foreign islands, where they were butchered or enslaved by an unknown people; they had chanced upon the evil army of Wanius and Melga, who had been ordered by Gratianus to subject the nations who lived by the ocean and the Germans to terrible slaughter. Wanius was king of the Huns, and Melga of the Picts. Gratianus had made them his allies and sent them to Germany to attack Maximianus' supporters. While ravaging the shore-line, they came upon the girls who had been driven there and, when they saw how beautiful they were, they wanted sex with them. When the girls refused, the villains fell on them and most of the Britons were quickly killed. Then Wanius and Melga, the wicked leaders of the Huns and Picts, who had sided with Gratianus and Valentinianus,

resistens et mutuam cladem reddebat et commissam patriam uiriliter
defendebat. Cumque sibi cessisset uictoria, uoluit commilitonibus suis
coniuges dare ut ex eis nascerentur heredes qui terram illam perpetuo
possiderent. Et ut nullam commixtionem cum Gallis facerent, decreuit ut 365
ex Britannia insula mulieres uenirent quae ipsis maritarentur. Direxit ergo
nuntios suos in Britanniam insulam ad Dionotum regem Cornubiae, qui
fratri suo Caradoco in regnum successerat, ut curam huius rei susciperet.
Erat ipse nobilis et praepotens et cui Maximianus principatum insulae
commendauerat dum ipse praedictis negociis intenderet. Habebat etiam 370
filiam mirae pulcritudinis, cui nomen erat Vrsula, quam Conanus super
omnia adoptauerat.

88   Dionotus igitur, uiso Conani nuntio, uolens mandatis suis parere collegit
per diuersas prouintias filias nobilium numero undecim milia, de ceteris
ex infima gente creatis sexaginta milia, et omnes infra urbem Lundoniae 375
conuenire praecepit. Naues quoque ex diuersis litoribus iussit adduci
quibus ad praedictos coniuges transfretarent. Quod licet multis in tanto
coetu placuisset, displicebat tamen pluribus, quae maiori affectu et parentes
et patriam diligebant; nec deerant forsitan aliquae quae castitatem nuptiis
praeferentes maluissent in qualibet natione uitam amittere quam hoc modo 380
diuitias exigere. Quippe diuersas diuersa iuuarent si quod adoptabant ad
effectum ducere quiuissent. Parato autem nauigio, ingrediuntur mulieres
naues et per Tamensem fluuium maria petunt. Postremo, cum uela uersus
Armoricanos diuertissent, insurrexerunt contrarii uenti in classem et in
breui totam societatem dissipauerunt. Periclitabantur ergo naues infra maria 385
in maiori parte submersae. Quae uero tantum periculum euaserunt appulsae
sunt in barbaras insulas et ab ignota gente siue trucidatae siue mancipatae.
Inciderant siquidem in nefandum exercitum Wanii et Melgae, qui iussu
Gratiani nationes maritimorum et Germaniae dira clade opprimebant.
Erat enim Wanius rex Hunorum, Melga uero Pictorum. Ipsos asciuerat 390
sibi Gratianus miseratque in Germaniam ut eos qui Maximiano fauerent
inquietarent. Per maritima ergo saeuientes, obuiauerunt praedictis puellis in
partes illas appulsis. Inspicientes ergo earum pulcritudinem, lasciuire cum
eis uoluerunt. Quod cum abnegauissent puellae, irruerunt in eas ambrones
maximamque partem sine mora trucidauerunt. Tunc nefandi Pictorum et 395
Hunorum duces Wanius et Melga, qui parti Gratiani et Valentiniani fauebant,

---

366 qui *OCH*
371 [cui nomen erat Vrsula] *Δ, fort. recte (cf. 'Transm.' 103, Introd. p. lii)*
376 [ex] *C:* de *O*
379 dirigebant *OCS*
381 quod adoptabant *Δ:* optatum suum *Φ*
385 dissipauerunt *scripsi:* dissipauit *Ω:* dissipant *C²H (cf. Introd.)*
390 enim *Δ:* autem *Φ*
394 Quod *Δ:* Sed *Φ*
394 abnegassent *OH Y*
395 mora *Δ:* pietate *Φ*
395 Tunc *Δ:* Deinde *Φ*

learned that the island of Britian had been stripped of all its armed soldiers; they hurriedly sailed there and, in league with the neighbouring islanders, landed in Scotland. Forming an army, they attacked the leaderless and defenceless kingdom and slaughtered its unthinking population. For, as has been stated, Maximianus had taken with him all the young warriors he could find and left behind helpless and feckless farmers. When the two invaders realised that these could offer no resistance, they created havoc, ceaselessly laying waste cities and provinces like sheepfolds. When Maximianus learned of the disaster, he sent Gratianus Municeps and two legions to help. On their arrrival, they engaged the enemy, whom they subjected to terrible slaughter and drove to Ireland. Meanwhile Maximianus had been murdered in Rome by Gratianus's friends, and the Britons whom he had brought with him were killed or scattered. Those who could escape returned to their fellow-citizens in Armorica, which was now known as a second Britain.

BOOK SIX

89   When Gratianus Municeps heard of Maximianus' murder, he seized the crown and made himself king. So tyrannically did he treat the people that a crowd of commoners attacked and killed him. When this news spread through neighbouring kingdoms, his two foes returned from Ireland. Bringing with them Irish, Norwegians and Danes, they put the land to fire and the sword from sea to sea. On account of this attack and unbearable oppression, envoys were sent to Rome with letters, requesting with tearful entreaties an armed force to avenge them and pledging their submission for ever, if the foe could be warded off. They were soon sent a legion which, suppressing the memory of their previous offences, embarked across the ocean to the island and engaged their enemies. They cut them down in great numbers, drove them all out of the country and freed the oppressed population from their terrible depredations. They ordered the people to build a wall from coast to coast between Scotland and Deira, which, when garrisoned by the crowd, would overawe such enemies as needed to be kept away and would protect the Britons. For Scotland had been completely devastated by barbarian occupation, and provided a useful base for any enemies who arrived there. The Britons set to work and built the wall, using both private and public funds.

90   The Romans then proclaimed to the British that it was out of the question for them to be troubled further by such demanding expeditions or for Rome's standards and her mighty army to be worn down by land and sea

cum didicissent insulam Britanniae ab omni armato milite uacuatam, iter
festinatum uersus illam direxerunt associatisque sibi collateralibus insulis
in Albaniam applicuerunt. Agmine igitur facto, inuaserunt regnum, quod
rectore et defensore carebat, uulgus irrationabile caedentes. Abduxerat   400
enim secum Maximianus ut praedictum est omnes bellicosos iuuenes
qui repperiri potuerunt inermesque colonos atque inconsultos reliquerat.
Quos cum praedicti duces compererunt minime resistere posse, stragem
non minimam facientes urbes et prouintias ut ouium caulas uastare non
cessabant. Cum igitur tanta calamitas Maximiano nuntiata fuisset, misit   405
Gratianum Municipem cum duabus legionibus ut auxilium subuectaret.
Qui ut in insulam uenerunt, proeliati sunt cum praefatis hostibus et
acerrima nece affectos ipsos in Hiberniam fugauerunt. Interea interfectus
fuit Maximianus Romae ab amicis Gratiani et Britones quos secum duxerat
interfecti et dissipati. Qui euadere potuerunt uenerunt ad conciues suos   410
Armoricam, quae iam altera Britannia uocabatur.

LIBER VI

89 Gratianus Municeps, cum de nece Maximiani audiuisset, cepit diadema regni
et sese in regem promouit. Exin tantam tyrannidem in populum exercuit ita
ut cateruis factis irruerunt in illum plebani et interfecerunt. Quod cum per
cetera regna diuulgatum fuisset, reuersi sunt praedicti hostes ex Hibernia
et secum Scotos, Norguegenses, Dacos conducentes regnum a mari usque   5
ad mare ferro et flamma affecerunt. Ob hanc infestationem ac dirissimam
oppressionem legati Romam cum epistulis mittuntur, militarem manum ad
se uindicandam lacrimosis postulationibus poscentes et subiectionem sui
in perpetuum uouentes si hostis longius arceretur. Quibus mox committitur
legio praeteriti mali immemor, quae ratibus trans occeanum in patriam uecta   10
cominus cum hostibus congressa est. Magnam denique ex his multitudinem
sternens, omnes e finibus depulit atque oppressam plebem a tam atroci
dilaceratione liberauit. Ad quos iussit construere murum inter Albaniam et
Deiram a mari usque ad mare ut esset arcendis hostibus a turba instructus
terrori, ciuibus uero tutamini. Erat autem Albania penitus frequentatione   15
barbarorum uastata, et quicumque hostes superueniebant oportunum infra
illam habebant receptaculum. Collecto igitur priuato et publico sumptu,
incumbunt indigenae operi et murum perficiunt.

90   Romani ergo, patriae denuntiantes nequaquam se tam laboriosis
expeditionibus posse frequentius uexari et ob imbelles et erraticos   20
latrunculos Romana stegmata, tantum talemque exercitum, terra ac mari

---

403 duces *Δ (sequitur lac. in C):* Guanius et Melga *Φ (cf. § 91.59)*
3 eum *HE YG*
6 durissimam *C Φ cum Gildae cod. X*
8 uindicandam *male ex Gilda sumptum (cf. N. Wright apud 'Transm.' 102), cui debetur etiam
anacoluthon § 90.19-25*
13 Ad quos *uix sanum (cf. Introd.)*

on account of weak, wandering bands of robbers; rather, the Britons should get used to defending themselves and, by fighting bravely, protect with all their strength their country, possessions, wives, children and, above all, their freedom and lives. To deliver this message, they ordered all the men of military age to assemble in London, as they were preparing to return to Rome. When they had all arrived, the task of delivering a speech to them was entrusted to Guithelinus, metropolitan bishop of London, who said:

'At the behest of the chiefs here present I must address you, yet I am forced to burst into tears rather than floods of rhetoric, filled as I am with pity for the leaderless weakness which has afflicted you since Maximianus stripped our country of all its armed soldiers and youths. You who were left behind are commoners ignorant of war and concerned with other matters, such as tilling the fields and various enterprises of trade. When foes arrived from foreign countries, they forced you to abandon your folds like wandering sheep without a shepherd, until the might of Rome restored you to your possessions. Will you always rely on the help of others? Will you not take up shields, swords and spears against robbers who would be no braver than you, were it not for your slothful laziness? The Romans have grown tired of the unremitting travel they must endure to fight your enemies for you. They prefer to forgo all the tribute you pay them rather than to continue being exhausted like this on land and sea. Before your soldiers left, you were the common people; did you think that made you less than men? Surely generations change so that a farmer can father a soldier and vice versa, and a soldier can be born to a trader, just as a trader to a soldier? But though the one can produce the other, I do not think that either lose their humanity. Since you are men, conduct yourselves like men, beg Christ to make you brave, and defend your freedom'.

When he finished speaking, the crowd cheered so much that one would have thought them suddenly filled with boldness.

91   The Romans then delivered strict instructions to the fearful populace and left them plans for military equipment. They told them to build a chain of forts looking out to sea on the southern coast where their ships were moored, and from where a barbarian incursion was feared. However, it is easier to turn a kite into a hawk than to make a countryman suddenly wise; to give him sound advice is just like casting pearls before swine. As soon as the Romans bade farewell and departed, apparently with no intention of returning,

fatigari, sed ut pocius solis consuescendo armis ac uiriliter dimicando terram, substantiam, coniuges, liberos, et quod his maius est libertatem uitamque totis uiribus defenderent – ut igitur hanc ammonitionem facerent, iusserunt conuenire omnes bellicosos uiros insulae infra Lundoniam; 25 nam Romam repedare moliebantur. Cum autem conuenissent cuncti, commissus fuit sermo Guithelino Lundoniensi metropolitano, qui ipsos in haec uerba adiuit:

'Cum uos iussu astantium principum alloqui deberem, magis in fletum prorumpere cogor quam in excelsum sermonem. Miseret enim me 30 orphanitatis et debilitatis quae uobis accessit postquam Maximianus regnum istud omni milite omnique iuuentute spoliauit. Vos autem reliquiae eratis, plebs usus belli ignara, quae ceteris negociis, ut in terris colendis diuersisque commercii machinationibus, intendebat. Cum igitur superuenerunt ab alienis nationibus inimici, uelut oues sine pastore 35 errantes uos ouilia uestra deserere coegerunt donec Romana potestas uos possessionibus uestris restituit. Eritne ergo spes uestra semper in alieno tutamine, et non instruetis manus uestras peltis, ensibus, hastis in latrones nequaquam uobis fortiores si segnitia et torpor abesset? Iam taedet Romanos tam assidui itineris quo uexantur ut pro uobis cum hostibus 40 congrediantur. Prius omne tributum quod soluitis amittere praeeligunt quam hoc modo diutius terra et ponto fatigari. Quid si tempore militum uestrorum fueratis uulgus? Putabatis iccirco humanitatem a uobis diffugisse? Nonne homines transuerso ordine nascuntur ita ut ex rustico generetur miles et ex milite rusticus? Miles etiam de mangone uenit 45 et mango de milite. Hac ergo consuetudine quamuis unus ab altero procedat, non existimo eos esse quod est hominis amittere. Cum igitur sitis homines, habetote uos ut homines et inuocate Christum ut audatiam adhibeat et libertatem uestram defendite'.

Cumque finem dicendi fecisset, tanto murmure infremuit populus ut ipsos 50 subita audatia repletos diceres.

91   Post haec Romani fortia monita formidoloso populo tradunt, exemplaria instruendorum armorum relinquunt. In littore quoque occeani quo naues illorum habebantur ad meridianam plagam, quia exinde barbari timebantur, turres per interualla ad prospectum maris collocari praecipiunt. Sed 55 facilius est accipitrem ex miluo fieri quam ex rustico subitum eruditum, et qui profundam doctrinam ei diffundit idem facit ac si margaritam inter porcos spargeret. Nam ut 'uale' dicto Romani tanquam ultra non reuersuri

22 soli *1587:* sola *et infra* defenderet *Gildas (cf. Introd.)*
23 his *Δ QG:* id *M: om. Y*
27 est *Φ*
36 <et> ouilia *OH*
39 nisi ... adesset *Φ*
47 eos *OHS Φ:* nos *C: om. E*
54 eorum *E YM*
57 eis *Φ*
57 margaritas *OE Y*

their old enemies disembarked again from the ships which had carried them to Ireland and, accompanied by foul crowds of Scots, Picts, Norsemen, Danes and other allies, occupied all Scotland as far as the wall. News of the Romans' departure and refusal to return boosted the enemy's confidence, and they prepared to destroy the island. Against them, the farmers, stationed high on their walls, unenthusiastic for battle and too unwieldy to run, were unmanned by their trembling hearts and fretted day and night on their foolish perches. At the same time the enemy ceaselessly used hooked weapons to drag the wretched herd off the walls and dash them to the ground. Their unexpected deaths were a blessing in disguise, since the swift demise of those who were carried off in this way spared them the dreadful suffering that would engulf their brothers and sons. Alas for the divine retribution upon their previous sins! Alas for the absence of so many warlike knights through Maximianus' madness! Had they been faced with this disaster, they could have driven off any invading peoples, as they had demonstrated before they left, by conquering far-off lands and maintaining peace in Britain. So it goes when defence of a realm is left to farmers. In short, the cities and the lofty wall were abandoned. Again the people fled, more desperately scattered than ever, again the enemy pursued, eager for ever crueller slaughter; the wretched people were torn apart by their enemies like lambs by wolves. Their sad remnants again sent a letter to Agitius, the representative of Roman power, beginning:

'To Agitius, three times consul, the groans of the Britons'.

Further on they lamented:

'The sea turns us back to the barbarians, the barbarians to the sea. One way or another we die, either drowned or massacred'.

Their envoys got no help for them, but returned sadly to announce their rejection to their fellow-citizens.

92   An assembly was held and Guithelinus archbishop of London crossed to Brittany, then called Armorica or Letavia, to seek the aid of their fellow-countrymen. At that time Brittany was ruled by Aldroenus, fourth to succeed Conanus, to whom Maximianus had presented the crown, as has been related. On seeing so reverend a figure, Aldroenus received him honourably and asked the reason for his journey. Guithelinus replied:

abscesserunt, emergunt iterum praedicti hostes ex nauibus quibus in Hiberniam uecti fuerant cum taetris cuneis Scotorum et Pictorum et cum 60 Norguegensibus, Dacis, et ceteris quos conduxerant, et omnem Albaniam muro tenus capessunt. Cognita etiam condebitorum reuersione et reditus denegatione, confidentiores solito destructioni insulae imminent. Ad haec in edito murorum statuuntur rustici segnes ad pugnam, inhabiles ad fugam, trementibus praecordiis inepti, qui diebus ac noctibus stupido sedili 65 marcebant. Interea non cessant uncinata hostium tela, quibus miserrimum uulgus de muris trahebatur et solo allidebatur. Hoc scilicet eis proficiebat immaturae mortis supplicium, qui tali funere rapiebantur quo fratrum pignorumque suorum miserandas imminentes poenas cito exitu deuitarent. O diuinam ob praeterita scelera ultionem! O tot bellicosorum militum per 70 uesaniam Maximiani absentiam! Qui si in tanta calamitate adessent, non superuenisset populus quem non in fugam propellerent. Quod manifestum fuit dum manebant; nam et longe posita regna adiciebant potestati suae et Britanniam cum tranquillitate possidebant. Sic est cum regnum tutamini rusticorum deseritur. Quid plura? Relictis ciuitatibus muroque celso, 75 iterum ciuibus fugae, iterum dispersiones desperabiliores solito, iterum ab hoste insectationes, iterum crudeliores strages accelerant; et sicut agni a lupis, ita deflenda plebs ab inimicis discerpitur. Igitur rursum miserae reliquiae mittunt epistulas ad Agitium Romanae potestatis uirum, hoc modo loquentes: 80

'Agitio ter consuli gemitus Britonum'.

Et post pauca querentes adiciunt:

'Nos mare ad barbaros, barbari ad mare repellunt. Interea oriuntur duo genera funerum: aut enim submergimur aut iugulamur'.

Nec pro eis quicquam adiutorii habentes tristes redeunt atque conciuibus 85 repulsam suam denuntiant.

92 Inito itaque consilio, transfretauit Guithelinus Lundoniensis archiepiscopus in minorem Britanniam, quae tunc Armorica siue Letauia dicebatur, ut auxilium a confratribus suis postularet. Regnabat tunc in illa Aldroenus quartus a Conano, cui Maximianus regnum illud donauerat, 90 sicut iam praedictum est. Qui uiso tantae reuerentiae uiro excepit illum cum honore causamque aduentus sui inquisiuit. Cui Guithelinus:

---

59 emerguntur *CHSE (cf. § 12.185)*
59 hostes *CHSE:* duces *(hostes Y)* Guanius et Melga *O Φ (cf. § 88.403)*
62 *de* condebitorum *cf. Introd.*
63 imminent *QM (cf. §§ 12.168, 80.184, 83.302, 102.416, 104.477, 115.106, 116.205, 166.137, 173.395):* eminent *cett.*
69 imminentesque *Φ contra Gildam 19.2*
72 propelleret *Φ*
78 *de* Igitur *cf. Introd.*
81 Britones *QYM*

'Your honour is well aware of, and can be moved to tears by, the plight of your fellow-Britons since Maximianus stripped our island of all its knights and settled them in this kingdom you hold—and may you continue to hold it in everlasting peace! We, the few you left behind, have been attacked by our neighbours, who have emptied our island of all the store of riches which filled it, so that all our provinces lack the sustenance of any food, except for the relief brought by the art of hunting. There was no one to stop them, since no one strong or warlike remained among us. The Romans have turned their backs on us and refused all help. With nowhere else to turn, we ask you to take pity on us and we beg for your protection to save from barbarian invasion a kingdom which you will inherit. For who else should wear the crown of Constantine and Maximianus against your wishes, seeing that it adorned the brows of your fathers' fathers? Prepare a fleet and sail. I hereby entrust the kingdom of Britain to your hands'.

Aldroenus replied:

'There was once a time when I would not have refused to take Britain if it were offered; no other country was in my opinion more fertile, while it enjoyed peace and tranquility. But now that it is prey to misfortune, it has been cheapened and become hateful both to me and to other chiefs. Above all, the evil sway of Rome has done it so much harm that no one can enjoy lasting power there without losing their freedom, oppressed beneath the yoke of slavery. Who would not prefer a poorer life in freedom elsewhere to the possession of Britain's riches under the yoke of servitude? This kingdom which I rule is mine by title and without obedience due to higher authority; I choose to prefer it to other countries since I govern it in freedom. Yet since my fathers' fathers had a claim on your island, I entrust to you my brother Constantinus with two thousand knights so that with God's help he can free your country from barbarian attack and assume its crown. Yes, I have a brother of that name who is, amongst his other achievements, an excellent soldier. If you are willing to receive him, I am ready to release him to you with the agreed number of troops; I can say nothing of committing more, since the French threaten to attack us daily'.

Aldroenus had scarcely finished speaking before the archbishop thanked him and, summoning Constantinus, said to him with a smile:

'Christ conquers, reigns and commands. In you, with Christ's help, we have a king for our abandoned country; in you, our defender; in you, our hope and our joy'.

Without further ado, ships were made ready on the shore, and knights chosen from various parts of the kingdom were entrusted to Guithelinus.

'Satis patet nobilitati tuae et te in fletum mouere potest miseria quam
nos combritones tui passi sumus ex quo Maximianus insulam nostram
suis spoliauit militibus istudque regnum quod possides – et utinam cum   95
diuturna pace possideas! – ab ipsis inhabitari praecepit. Insurrexerunt
etenim in nos, pauperculas uestrum reliquias, omnes comprouinciales
insulae et insulam nostram omni copia diuitiarum repletam euacuauerunt
ita ut uniuersae eiusdem nationes tocius cibi baculo, excepto uenatoriae
artis solatio, careant. Nec fuit qui obuiaret, cum nullus potens nullusque   100
bellicosus ex nostris remansit. Nam Romani in taedium nostri uersi sunt
et omnino auxilium suum abnegauerunt. Ab omni igitur alia spe repulsi,
adiuimus misericordiam tuam, te implorantes ut praesidium adhibeas et
debitum tibi regnum a barbarorum irruptione protegas. Quis etenim alius
te inuito diademate Constantini et Maximiani coronari debeat, cum aui   105
tui atque proaui ipso insigniti fuerint? Para ergo nauigium tuum et ueni.
Ecce, regnum Britanniae in manus tuas trado'.

Ad haec Aldroenus:

'Olim tempus erat quo non negarem insulam Britanniae recipere si quis
eam largiretur; non enim existimo alteram patriam fertiliorem fuisse dum   110
pace et tranquillitate frueretur. At nunc, quoniam infortunia accesserunt,
uilior facta est et michi et ceteris principibus odiosa. Super omnia
uero mala potestas Romanorum in tantum nocuit ita ut nemo stabilem
dignitatem infra illam habere queat quin iugo seruitutis oneratus libertatem
amittat. Quis igitur non mallet minus alias cum libertate possidere quam   115
diuitias ipsius sub iugo seruicii habere? Regnum istud, quod nunc
potestati meae subditum est, cum honore et sine obsequio quod altiori
impendam possideo; unde illud ceteris nationibus praeferre praeelegi,
cum ipsum cum libertate gubernem. At tamen, quoniam ius in insulam
aui et attaui mei habuerunt, trado tibi Constantinum fratrem meum et   120
duo milia militum ut si Deus permiserit patriam a barbarica irruptione
liberet et sese diademate illius insigniat. Habeo namque quendam fratrem
praedicto nomine uocatum, qui in militia ceterisque probitatibus uiget.
Illum tibi cum praefato numero committere non diffugiam, si placet ut
recipiatur; nam de ampliori numero commilitonum tacendum censeo,   125
cum inquietudo Gallorum cotidie immineat'.

Vix finem dicendi fecerat, grates egit archiepiscopus uocatoque Constantino
ei in haec uerba arrisit:

'Christus uincit, Christus regnat, Christus imperat. Ecce rex Britanniae
desertae, assit modo Christus; ecce defensio nostra; ecce spes nostra et   130
gaudium'.

Quid plura? Paratis in littore nauibus, eliguntur ex diuersis partibus regni
milites et Guithelino traduntur.

100 careant *54:* careat *cett.*
100 nullusque *Δ:* nullus *Φ*
106 [ergo] *Φ*
109 negarent *OE QG*
115 *de* alias *cf. Introd.*

93   When everything was prepared, they set sail and landed at Totnes. They swiftly joined up with the remaining forces of the island and engaged the enemy, winning a victory thanks to the blessed archbishop. Then the Britons who had been dispersed assembled from all directions to hold a meeting at Silchester, where they made Constantinus king and placed the island's crown upon his head. As a wife they gave him a woman of noble Roman descent, who had been brought up by archbishop Guithelinus. She became pregnant and bore him three sons, named Constans, Aurelius Ambrosius and Uther Pendragon. The king presented the eldest, Constans, to the church of St Amphibalus in Winchester to become a monk; the other two, Aurelius and Uther, he entrusted to Guithelinus to bring up. Ten years passed; then a Pict in the king's service, having taken him aside into a thicket on the pretext of a private conversation, killed him with a dagger.

94   After Constantinus' death the nobles could not agree who should succeed to the throne, some supporting Aurelius Ambrosius, others Uther Pendragon and yet others various men related to them. After much disagreement Vortigern, earl of the Gewissei, eager to win the crown for himself, intervened by visiting the monk Constans and addressing him as follows:

> 'Look, your father has died, your brothers are too young to succeed him and, in my opinion, there is no one else in your family that the people can make king. If you agree to follow my advice and increase my wealth, I shall induce them to be willing to crown you and divest you of your monkish habit, even against the rules of your order'.

Constans was overjoyed to hear this and swore to go along with all his presumed wishes. So Vortigern dressed him in regal robes, took him to London and made him king, though hardly with the people's agreement. Archbishop Guithelinus had recently died and no one else was willing to anoint an ex-monk. This did not, however, hinder the coronation, since Vortigern himself performed the role of bishop and placed the crown on Constans' head with his own hands.

95   Once king, Constans entrusted the entire administration of the realm to Vortigern, putting himself so firmly in his hands as to do nothing except what Vortigern told him. This was the result of his lack of sense; how to be a king had not been part of his monastic instruction. When Vortigern realised this, he began to plot how to take the throne, always his overriding aim. He saw that the moment was at hand when he could easily fulfil his ambition. The whole realm was in his power and Constans, the supposed king, was a mere puppet who lacked the sternness and judgement to instil fear in his people or their neighbours. His two brothers,

93   Cumque omnia parata fuissent, ingressi sunt mare atque in Totonesio portu applicuerunt. Nec mora, collegerunt reliquam iuuentutem insulae et 135 cum hostibus congressi uictoriam per meritum beati uiri adepti sunt. Exin confluxerunt undique Britones prius dispersi et facta infra Silcestriam contione erexerunt Constantinum in regem regnique diadema capiti suo imposuerunt. Dederunt etiam ei coniugem ex nobili genere Romanorum ortam, quam Guithelinus archiepiscopus educauerat. Cumque illam 140 cognouisset, progenuit ex ea tres filios, quorum nomina fuerunt Constans, Aurelius Ambrosius, Vther Pendragon. Constantem uero primogenitum tradidit in ecclesia Amphibali infra Guintoniam ut monachilem ordinem susciperet; ceteros autem duos, Aurelium uidelicet et Vther, Guithelino ad nutriendum commisit. Postremo, cum decem anni praeterissent, uenit 145 quidam Pictus qui in obsequium suum fuerat et quasi secretum colloquium habiturus in uirgulto quodam, semotis cunctis, eum cum cultro interfecit.

94   Defuncto igitur Constantino, fuit dissensio inter proceres quis in regnum sublimaretur. Alii itaque acclamabant Aurelium Ambrosium, alii Vther Pendragon, alii ceteros ex generatione propinquos. Denique, cum nunc sic, 150 nunc aliter contendissent, accessit Vortegirnus consul Gewisseorum, qui omni nisu in regnum anhelabat, et adiuit Constantem monachum illumque in haec uerba allocutus est:

    'Ecce, pater tuus defunctus est et fratres tui propter aetatem sublimari nequeunt, nec alium uideo in progenie tua quem in regem populus 155 promoueret. Si igitur consilio meo adquiescere uolueris possessionemque meam augmentare, conuertam populum in affectum sublimandi te in regnum et ex tali habitu, licet ordo repugnet, te abstrahendi'.

Quod cum audisset Constans, maximo gaudio fluctuauit et quicquid callebat ipsum uelle ei iureiurando promittebat. Cepit itaque eum Vortegirnus 160 duxitque regiis ornamentis indutum Lundonias atque uix annuente populo in regem erexit. Tunc defunctus fuerat Guithelinus archiepiscopus nec affuit alter qui ipsum inungere praesumpsisset, quia ex monacho transferebatur. Nec tamen iccirco postposuit diadema, quod ipse Vortegirnus uice episcopi functus manibus suis capiti suo imposuit. 165

95   Sublimatus igitur Constans totam iusticiam regni commisit Vortegirno et semet ipsum in consilium eiusdem tradidit ita ut nichil absque praecepto ipsius faceret. Quippe debilitas sensus ipsius id faciebat; nam infra claustra aliud quam regnum tractare didicerat. Quod cum calluisset Vortegirnus, coepit apud se deliberare qualiter sublimari potuisset in regem; nam id 170 prius super omnia concupiuerat. Videbat etenim congruum tempus instare quo desiderium suum leuiter ad effectum duci poterat. Totum namque dispositioni eius regnum commissum fuerat, nec Constans, qui rex dicebatur, nisi pro umbra principis astabat. Nullius enim asperitatis, nullius iusticiae fuerat, nec a populo suo nec a uicinis gentibus timebatur. Duo autem pueri 175

158 abstraham Φ
165 functus C: functurus H *(an recte ? cf. § 11.156):* fruens O: fretus SE: *om.* Φ

Uther Pendragon and Aurelius Ambrosius, were babes in their cradles, too young to be crowned. The elder statesmen of the land had unfortunately died and only Vortigern seemed able, wise and experienced; the others were almost all boys or youths who had somehow or other acceded to their fathers' or uncles' titles after the latter had died in the recent wars. Passing all this in review, Vortigern plotted a cunning subterfuge to depose the monk Constans and usurp the throne. He decided to wait until he had brought various nationalities under his power and influence. He therefore began asking to be allowed to guard the king's treasure and walled cities, claiming that it was rumoured that the men of the neighbouring islands were planning an attack. Once his request was granted, he everywhere appointed his own men to keep the cities loyal to him. Then, embarking on his treacherous plot, he went to Constans, saying that he needed to increase the size of his retinue to be sure of repelling the enemy attack. Constans replied:

> 'Have I not placed everything in your hands? Do whatever you wish, provided that it does not compromise your loyalty to me.'

Vortigern answered:

> 'I have been informed that the Picts plan to bring the Danes and Norsemen upon us to inflict the greatest harm. I therefore suggest as the safest plan that you keep some Picts in your court to act as go-betweens for you. If the Picts really do intend to rebel, they will uncover their countrymen's cunning plots so you can foil them more easily'.

Covert betrayal, this was, of an unsuspecting friend. The advice was not given to save Constans, but because Vortigern knew the Picts were a fickle nation, ready for anything; if he made them drunk or enraged, they could easily be stirred to kill the king without a thought, and then he would have the chance to become king as he had so often longed. Sending messengers to Scotland, he summoned a hundred Pictish knights and made them part of the royal household; he showed them special honour, lavishing gifts upon them and loading them with food and drink, so that they treated him as their king. They used to worship him and sing in the street:

> 'It is Vortigern that is worthy of the crown, worthy of the sceptre of Britain, not Constans'.

fratres eiusdem, Vther Pendragon atque Aurelius Ambrosius, in cunis adhuc iacentes inhabiles erant ut in regnum promouerentur. Praeterea infortunium illud acciderat, quod proceres regni qui maiores erant natu defuncti fuerant solusque Vortegirnus astutus et sapiens magnique consilii uidebatur, ceteri autem paene omnes pueri erant ac iuuenes peremptisque in anteactis proeliis 180 eorundem patribus atque auunculis honores utcumque possidebant. Haec igitur omnia comperiens Vortegirnus meditabatur quo ingenio tectius et callidius Constantem monachum deponeret, ut in locum ipsius erumperet. Quod tandem differre praeelegit donec prius diuersas nationes melius potestati et familiaritati suae submisisset. Coepit igitur petere thesauros 185 regis ab ipso in custodiam eiusque ciuitates cum munitionibus, dicens quia rumor asserebat collaterales insulanos superuenire affectasse. Quod cum impetrauisset, posuit ubique familiares suos qui easdem urbes in fidelitate sua seruarent. Deinde, praemeditatam proditionem machinans, adiuit Constantem dixitque illi oportere numerum familiae suae augmentare ut 190 securius superuenturis hostibus resisteret. Cui Constans:

'Nonne omnia dispositioni tuae commisi? Fac ergo quaecumque uolueris, ita tamen ut in fidelitate mea proueniant'.

Ad haec Vortegirnus:

'Dictum est michi Pictos uelle conducere Dacos et Norguegenses super 195 nos ut inquietudinem maximam inferant. Quamobrem laudarem et consilium saluberrimum esse censeo ut quosdam ex Pictis in curia tua retineas qui mediatores inter te et ceteros existant. Nam si uerum est quod rebellare inceperint, explorabunt tibi consociorum suorum machinationes et uersutias, quas leuius uitare poteris'. 200

Ecce occulta incauti amici proditio! Non enim id laudabat ut salus inde proueniret Constanti sed quia sciebat Pictos gentem esse instabilem et ad omne scelus paratam; inebriati ergo siue in iram inducti, commoueri possent facile aduersus regem ita ut absque cunctamine ipsum interficerent, unde si id contigisset haberet aditum promouendi sese in regem ut saepius 205 affectauerat. Directis itaque in Scotiam nuntiis, inuitauit centum Pictos milites ipsosque infra familiam regis recepit, receptos autem honorabat super omnes diuersisque donariis ditabat, cibis etiam et potibus ultra modum saciabat, ita ut pro rege illum haberent. Adorantes igitur illum, per plateas psallebant: 210

'Dignus est Vortegirnus imperio dignusque sceptro Britanniae, Constans uero indignus'.

---

178 natu erant *Φ*
201 incauti *scripsi:* occulti *OCHE QGM: om. S Y:* latentis *54:* inimici *pro* amici *E, 54 (cf. 'Transm.' 99)*

Vortigern in turn strove to honour them more and more, to win them over. When they had become completely devoted to him, he plied them with drink and pretended that he wished to leave Britain to increase his wealth, saying that the little he had was not enough for him to support fifty knights. Then, feigning sorrow, he returned to his rooms and left them drinking in the palace. At this the Picts, who believed his story, were very downcast. They muttered to each other:

'Why do we let this monk live? Why not kill him so that Vortigern can ascend the throne? Who else would succeed? This man who never ceases to enrich us is worthy of royal power, worthy of every honour'.

96   Immediately they burst into Constans' bedroom, attacked and killed him and took his head to Vortigern. On seeing it, he burst into tears as if in sorrow, when he had in fact never felt greater joy. Summoning the citizens of London (where these events took place), he ordered all the traitors to be bound and then beheaded for daring to commit such an outrage. Some suspected that Vortigern was behind this act of treason, which the Picts would never have undertaken without his connivance; others did not hesitate to clear him of suspicion. The matter remained unresolved, but the guardians of the king's two brothers, Aurelius Ambrosius and Uther Pendragon, fled with them to Brittany, fearing that they would be murdered by Vortigern. King Budicius received them there and brought them up with due honour.

97   When Vortigern saw that no rival remained in the country, he placed the crown on his own head, raising himself above his fellow-nobles. As his treachery became known, the peoples of the neighbouring islands whom the Picts had brought to Scotland rose up against him; the Picts were angry that their countrymen had been killed on account of Constans and wanted to take revenge on him. So Vortigern was troubled daily by the losses his army suffered in battle. Equally he was troubled by fear of Aurelius Ambrosius and his brother Uther Pendragon, who, as I said, had fled to Brittany because of him. Every day his ears were filled with reports that they had grown up and built a great fleet and were planning to return and claim their kingdom.

98   Meanwhile there landed in Kent three keels, or warships as we call them, full of armed knights, led by two brothers, Horsus and Hengest.

Ad haec Vortegirnus magis ac magis eos honorare nitebatur ut magis placeret. At cum amorem eorum omnino adeptus fuisset inebriauit illos finxitque se uelle recedere ex Britannia ut ampliores possessiones perquireret; dicebat 215 autem id tantillum quod habebat non posse sibi sufficere ut quinquaginta militibus stipendia donaret. Deinde quasi tristis secessit ad hospitium suum ipsosque potantes in aula deseruit. Quo uiso, ultra quam credi potest contristati sunt Picti, arbitrantes uerum fuisse quod dixerat. Murmurantes uero adinuicem dicebant: 220

'Vt quid monachum istum uiuere permittimus? Vt quid non interficimus eum ut Vortegirnus solio regni potiatur? Quis etenim alius ei in regnum succederet? Dignus namque est imperio et honore, dignus etiam omni dignitate, qui nos ditare non cessat'.

96 Post haec, irrumpentes thalamum, impetum fecerunt in Constantem 225 peremptoque illo caput coram Vortegirno tulerunt. Quod cum inspexisset Vortegirnus, quasi contristatus in fletum erupit, nec unquam prius maiori gaudio fluctuauerat. Vocatis tamen ciuibus Lundoniae (nam id infra eam contigerat), iussit cunctos proditores alligari alligatosque decollari quia tantum scelus facere praesumpserant. Fuerunt ergo qui aestimabant 230 proditionem illam per Vortegirnum fuisse machinatam, Pictos uero nullatenus nisi assensu illius incepisse; fuerunt etiam qui nichil haesitantes ipsum a tali crimine purgabant. Re tandem in dubio relicta, nutritores duorum fratrum Aurelii Ambrosii atque Vther Pendragon diffugierunt cum eis in minorem Britanniam, timentes ne a Vortegirno perimerentur. Ibidem 235 excepit illos rex Budicius et honore quo decebat educauit.

97 At Vortegirnus, cum neminem sibi parem in regno conspexisset, imposuit capiti suo diadema regni et conprincipes suos supergressus est. Proditione tandem eius diuulgata, insurrexerunt in eum comprouintialium populi insularum quos Picti in Albaniam conduxerant; indignati namque 240 Picti commilitones suos qui propter Constantem interfecti fuerant in ipsum uindicare nitebantur. Anxiabatur igitur Vortegirnus cotidie dampnumque exercitus sui in proeliando perpetiebatur. Anxiabatur etiam ex alia parte timore Aurelii Ambrosii fratrisque sui Vther Pendragon, qui ut praedictum est in minorem Britanniam propter ipsum diffugerant. Cotidianus etenim 245 rumor aures eius impleuerat ipsos iam adultos esse maximumque nauigium construxisse atque reditum suum in debitum regnum uelle moliri.

98 Interea applicuerunt tres cuilae, quas longas naues dicimus, in partibus Cantiae plenae armatis militibus, quibus duo fratres Horsus et Hengistus

213 eos honorare 87: eos domare (domore *C¹*) OCHS: eos donare *E M*: donare *QG¹*: eis donare *G*: eos honorabat [nitebatur] *Y (cf. Introd.)*
214 finxit- *C²HS*: stinxit- *C¹*: dixit- *OE Φ*
216 [sibi] *Φ*
220 [uero] *H Φ*
240 insularum populi *Φ*
242 Anxiebatur *OS Y*
243 Anxiebatur *OS*
249 <de> armatis *Φ*

Vortigern was then at Dorobernia, now named Canterbury, a city he was accustomed to visit frequently. When messengers informed him of the landing of warships full of unknown men of large stature, he granted them peace, ordering that they be brought before him. As soon as they arrived, his gaze fell on the two brothers, who, noble and handsome, stood out from their men. After he had cast his eyes over the rest, Vortigern asked their country of origin and their reason for coming to his kingdom. As befitted his greater age and wisdom, Hengest replied for the others:

'Most noble king, our home is the land of Saxony, one of the provinces of Germany. Our purpose in coming is to offer our service to you or some other lord. We have been exiled from our land, but only because the custom of our kingdom demanded it. For it is the practice in our country, whenever it becomes overpopulated, that our leaders come from its various provinces and order all the young men of the entire realm to assemble before them; they then cast lots and choose the best and bravest to support themselves by going to foreign lands, thus relieving their native country of its excessive population. When such overpopulation recently occurred in our own province, the chiefs met, cast lots, chose these young men you see before you and ordered them to obey our ancient custom. They made me, Hengest, and my brother Horsus here their leaders, since we are descended from dukes. So we obeyed the time-honoured decree, set sail and came to your kingdom, guided by Mercury'.

At the name Mercury, the king raised his head and asked their religion. Hengest replied:

'We worship our native gods, Saturn, Jupiter and the others who rule this world, and especially Mercury, whom in our tongue we call Woden. To him our ancestors dedicated the fourth day of the week, which up to the present takes from his name that of Wednesday. After him we worship Frea, the most powerful of the goddesses, to whom they dedicated the sixth day, which we call Friday after her'.

Vortigern replied:

'Your faith, or rather faithlessness, makes me truly sorry. Your coming, however, brings me joy, since God or some other has brought you at an opportune time for my needs.

ducatum praestabant. Fuerat tunc Vortegirnus Doroberniae, quae nunc 250
Cantuaria dicitur, ut consuetudo eum conduxerat ciuitatem illam saepissime
uisitare. Cui cum retulissent nuntii ignotos uiros magnaeque staturae
homines in magnis nauibus applicuisse, dedit pacem ipsosque ad se conduci
praecepit. Mox, ut conducti fuerunt, uertit oculos suos in duos germanos;
nam ipsi prae ceteris et nobilitate et decore praeminebant. Cumque etiam 255
ceteros aspectu peragrasset, quaesiuit quae patria produxerat illos et quae
causa eos in regnum suum direxerat. Cui Hengistus respondere pro aliis
incepit (nam ipsum et maturior aetas et sapientia praeponebat):

> 'Rex ceterorum nobilissime, Saxonia tellus edidit nos, una ex regionibus
> Germaniae. Causa autem aduentus nostri est ut tibi siue alteri principi 260
> obsequium nostrum offeramus. Fueramus etenim expulsi a patria nostra
> nec ob aliud nisi quia consuetudo regni expetebat. Consuetudo namque
> in patria nostra est ut cum habundantia hominum in eadem superuenerit
> conueniunt ex diuersis prouinciis principes et tocius regni iuuenes coram
> se uenire praecipiunt; deinde, proiecta sorte, potiores atque fortiores 265
> eligunt qui extera regna petituri uictum sibi perquirant et patria ex qua
> orti sunt a superflua multitudine liberetur. Superfluente igitur nouiter in
> regno nostro hominum copia, conuenerunt principes nostri sortemque
> proitientes elegerunt iuuentutem istam quam in praesentia tua cernis
> praeceperuntque ut consuetudini ab antiquo statutae parerent. Nos 270
> quoque duos germanos, quorum ego Hengistus, iste Horsus nuncupamur,
> praefecerunt ei duces; nam ex ducum progenie progeniti fueramus.
> Oboedientes ergo decretis ab aeuo sancitis, ingressi sumus maria
> regnumque tuum duce Mercurio petiuimus'.

Ad nomen itaque Mercurii erecto uultu rex inquirit cuiusmodi religionem 275
haberent. Cui Hengistus:

> 'Deos patrios Saturnum, Iouem atque ceteros qui mundum istum
> gubernant colimus, maxime autem Mercurium, quem Woden lingua nostra
> appellamus. Huic ueteres nostri dicauerunt quartam feriam septimanae,
> quae usque in hodiernum diem nomen Wodenesdei de nomine ipsius 280
> sortita est. Post illum colimus deam inter ceteras potentissimam uocabulo
> Fream, cui etiam dicauerunt sextam feriam, quam ex nomine eius Fridei
> uocamus'.

Ad haec Vortegirnus:

> 'De credulitate uestra, quae pocius incredulitas dici potest, uehementer 285
> doleo. De aduentu autem uestro gaudeo, quia in congruo tempore

257 [eos] Φ
259 Saxonica Φ
260 autem Δ: haec Φ
261 offeremus Δ
271 nuncupatur *QGM*
277 [istum] Φ
279 dedicauerunt *OH*
282 dedicauerunt *O*
282 ex Δ: de Φ

My enemies press me on all sides, and, should you share the burden of my battles with me, I shall maintain you with honour in my kingdom and enrich you with various gifts and lands'.

The barbarians instantly agreed, signed a treaty and stayed in his court. Soon after, the Picts emerged from Scotland with a huge army and began to ravage the north of the island. Hearing the news, Vortigern assembled his troops and set off across the Humber to meet them. Battle was joined, the Britons and their foes face to face in a bitter engagement. But the Britons did not have to fight hard, as the Saxons among their ranks fought so bravely that they quickly routed the enemy, accustomed though they were to winning.

99   Vortigern, victorious thanks to the Saxons' efforts, increased his gifts to them and gave their leader Hengest extensive lands in the region of Lindsey to support himself and his fellow-warriors. Realising he had won the king's friendship, Hengest, who was an experienced and clever man, said to him:

'My lord, your enemies harass you on all sides and few of your subjects love you. They all threaten you, saying that they will bring Aurelius Ambrosius from Brittany to crown him in your place. Let us, with your permission, send to our country and invite from it knights to increase our fighting-strength. Also I would ask one favour of your merciful wisdom, if I did not fear rejection'.

Vortigern replied:

'Send your envoys to Germany, then; invite whomever you wish; and ask me what you want, without fear of rejection'.

Bowing his head in thanks, Hengest said:

'You have given me generous holdings and lands, but not the honour due to a duke, even though I number dukes among my ancestors. You should also have given me a city or towns to increase my standing amongst the nobles of your kingdom. I should have received the title of earl or prince, since I count both in my family tree'.

Vortigern answered:

'I am forbidden to grant such favours because you are foreigners and pagans, and I am not yet well enough acquainted with your character and customs to treat you like my fellow-countrymen; even if I did, I would not give something of which my nobles would disapprove'.

uos necessitati meae siue deus siue alius optulit. Opprimunt etenim me inimici mei undique, et si laborem proeliorum meorum mecum communicaueritis retinebo uos honorifice infra regnum meum et diuersis muneribus et agris ditabo'. 290

Paruerunt ilico barbari et foedere confirmato in curia ipsius remanserunt. Nec mora, emergentes ex Albania Picti exercitum ualde grandem fecerunt coeperuntque aquilonares partes insulae deuastare. Cumque id Vortegirno nunciatum fuisset, collegit milites suos atque trans Humbrum in obuiam perrexit. Deinde, ut cominus conuenerunt, hinc et illinc et ciues et hostes 295 acerrimam pugnam commiserunt. Nec multum oportuit ciues pugnare; nam Saxones qui aderant tam uiriliter proeliabantur ita ut hostes, qui prius solebant uincere, sine mora in fugam propellerent.

99 Vortegirnus ergo, per illos uictoria potitus, donaria sua ampliauit eis atque duci eorum Hengisto dedit agros plurimos in Lindiseia regione quibus 300 sese et commilitones suos sustentaret. Hengistus ergo, cum esset uir doctus atque astutus, comperta amicicia quam rex aduersus illum gerebat, ipsum in hunc sermonem adiuit:

'Domine, undique inquietant te inimici tui, et pauci sunt ex conciuibus tuis qui te diligunt. Omnes minantur tibi dicuntque se conducturos 305 Aurelium Ambrosium ex Armorico tractu ut te deposito ipsum in regem promoueant. Si placet ergo, mittamus in patriam nostram et inuitemus milites ex ea, ut numerus noster ad certandum augeatur. Sed unum discretionem clementiae tuae implorarem nisi repulsam pati timerem'.

Ad haec Vortegirnus: 310

'Mitte ergo legatos tuos ad Germaniam et inuita quos uolueris, et pete a me quod desideras et nullam repulsam patieris'.

Inclinato igitur capite, grates agit Hengistus et ait:

'Ditauisti me largis mansionibus et agris nec tamen eo honore quo ducem decuerat, cum duces me progenuerint. Quippe inter cetera danda esset 315 michi ciuitas siue oppida ut dignior inter proceres regni tui censerer. Dignitas namque consulis siue principis adhibenda esset ex utrorumque genere edito'.

Cui Vortegirnus:

'Prohibitus sum huiusmodi donaria uobis largiri, quia alienigenae estis 320 et pagani nec adhuc mores uestros et consuetudines agnosco ut uos conciuibus meis parificem; nec si uos ut proprios ciues existimassem inciperem donare quod proceres regni dissuaderent'.

287 optulerit *OHSE*
308 unam *OH²*
309 discretione *QY²*: discretioni *Y¹GM*
313 autem *QGM: om. Y*
314 ditasti *Φ*
316 oppidum *M*
321 consuetudinem *YM*

Hengest replied:

> 'Grant me, your servant, just as much of the land you have already given me as can be encompassed by a single string, so that I can build there a stronghold to retreat to if need be; I am, have been, and will be, true to you and will carry out my plan in good faith'.

Persuaded by these words, the king granted his request and told him to send messengers to Germany to summon knights to bring swift help. Having sent the envoys without delay, Hengest took a bull's hide and cut it into a single string. Then with great care he selected a rocky spot, encircled it with the string and began work on a castle within the space marked out. Once completed, the fortress took its name from the string with which it had been measured out; for it was later called in British Kaercarrei, and in English Thanccastre, or Castrum Corrigiae in Latin.

100   Meanwhile the envoys had returned from Germany, bringing with them eighteen ships full of chosen knights. They also brought Hengest's daughter Ronwein, a girl of unsurpassed beauty. After their arrival Hengest invited king Vortigern to his home to view the new construction and the newly arrived knights. The king immediately arrived in private, praised the swiftly completed work and engaged the knights who had been summoned. After he had been refreshed by a royal banquet, the girl came out of her chamber, carrying a golden goblet full of wine. Going up to the king, she curtseyed and said:

> 'Lauerd king, wasseil'.

At the sight of the girl's face he was amazed by her beauty and inflamed with desire. He asked his interpreter what the girl had said and what he should reply. He answered:

> 'She called you lord king and honoured you with a word of greeting. You should reply "drincheil"'.

Then Vortigern, giving the reply 'drincheil', told the girl to drink, took the goblet from her hand with a kiss and drank. From that day forward it has been the custom in Britain that at feasts a drinker says to his neighbour 'wasseil' and the one who receives the drink after him replies 'drincheil'. Vortigern became drunk on various kinds of liquor and, as Satan entered into his heart, asked her father for the girl he loved. Satan, I repeat, had entered into his heart, for despite being a Christian he wanted to sleep with a pagan woman.

Cui Hengistus

> 'Concede' inquit 'mihi, seruo tuo, quantum una corrigia possit ambiri   325
> infra terram quam dedisti, ut ibidem promontorium aedificem quo me si
> opus fuerit recipiam; fidelis etenim tibi sum et fui et ero, et in fidelitate
> tua quae agere desidero faciam'.

Motus itaque rex uerbis ipsius eiusdem petitioni acquieuit praecepitque
legatos suos in Germaniam mittere ut milites ex ea inuitati festinatum   330
auxilium subuectarent. Nec mora, missa in Germaniam legatione cepit
Hengistus corium tauri atque ipsum in unam corrigiam redegit. Exin
saxosum locum quod maxima cautela elegerat circuiuit cum corrigia et
infra spacium metatum castellum aedificare incepit. Quod ut aedificatum
fuit, traxit nomen ex corrigia, quia cum ea metatum fuerat; dictum namque   335
fuit postmodum Britannice Kaercarrei, Saxonice uero Thanccastre, quod
Latino sermone Castrum Corrigiae appellamus.

100   Interea uero reuersi sunt nuncii ex Germania conduxeruntque decem
et octo naues electis militibus plenas. Conduxerunt etiam filiam Hengisti
uocabulo Ronwein, cuius pulcritudo nulli secunda uidebatur. Postquam   340
autem uenerunt, inuitauit Hengistus Vortegirnum regem in domum suam
ut et nouum aedificium et nouos milites qui applicuerant uideret. Venit
ilico rex priuatim et laudauit tam subitum opus et milites inuitatos retinuit.
Vt ergo regiis epulis refectus fuit, egressa est puella de thalamo, aureum
ciphum plenum uino ferens. Accedens deinde propius regi, flexis genibus   345
dixit:

> 'Lauerd king, wasseil'.

At ille, uisa facie puellae, ammiratus est tantum eius decorem et incaluit.
Denique interrogauit interpretem suum quid dixerat puella et quid ei
respondere debebat. Cui interpres dixit: 350

> 'Vocauit te dominum regem et uocabulo salutationis honorauit. Quod
> autem respondere debes est "drincheil"'.

Respondens deinde Vortegirnus 'drincheil', iussit puellam potare cepitque
ciphum de manu ipsius et osculatus est eam et potauit. Ab illo die usque
in hodiernum mansit consuetudo illa in Britannia quia in conuiuiis qui   355
potat ad alium dicit 'wasseil', qui uero post illum recipit potum respondet
'drincheil'. Vortegirnus autem, diuerso genere potus inebriatus, intrante
Sathana in corde suo, amauit puellam et postulauit eam a patre suo. Intrauerat,
inquam, Sathanas in corde suo quia cum Christianus esset cum pagana coire

331 subuectarent *scripsi ('Transm.' 99):* inuitarent Ω
331 Germania *E QYM*
333 quem *G (cf. Introd. ad § 24.17)*
334 coepit *M*
342 ut [et] *QY*
344 uero *CSE QG*
344 [est] *Δ*
350 debebat *OHS QY:* debeat *C GM:* deberet *E*

Hengest in his wisdom immediately recognised the king's lack of judgement and asked his brother Horsus and the other elders present what they should do about his request. All agreed that the girl should be given to the king and that they should ask for the province of Kent in return. Without delay the king received the girl and Kent was given to Hengest, without the knowledge of count Gorangonus, its ruler. The king married the pagan girl that very night, and she pleased him greatly; but he swiftly incurred the enmity of his nobles and sons on her account. For he already had three sons, Vortimer, Katigern and Paschent.

101   At that time St Germanus bishop of Auxerre came with Lupus of Troyes to preach the word of God to the Britons. For their faith had fallen into decline, both because of the pagans whom the king had brought among them and through the heresy of Pelagius, which had already been poisoning it for a long time. Their belief in the true faith was restored by the preaching of these blessed men, who became famous for their many, daily miracles. Gildas in his book described in a clear style the many miracles that God revealed through them.

Once Ronwein had been given to the king, as has been related, Hengest said to him:

> 'I am your father-in-law and should be your adviser. Do not ignore my advice, because you will overcome all your enemies thanks to my people. Let us summon also my son Octa and his cousin Ebissa; for they are warlike men. Give them the regions in the north of Britain beside the wall which separates Deira from Scotland. They will stop the barbarians' attacks there and you will remain in peace to the south of the Humber'.

Vortigern acceded, instructing them to summon as many as they thought necessary to help him. Envoys were immediately dispatched and Octa, Ebissa and Cherdich arrived with three hundred ships full of armed men, all of whom Vortigern welcomed warmly and rewarded with generous gifts; for with their help he continually beat his enemies and was victorious in every battle. Little by little Hengest invited more ships, increasing his numbers day by day. When the Britons saw this, they feared that they would be betrayed and told the king to expel the Saxons from the kingdom. Pagans ought not to communicate or mix with Christians, as it was forbidden by Christian law; moreover so many of them had arrived that his subjects feared them; no one knew who was pagan and who Christian, since the pagans had married their daughters and relatives. With such objections they urged the king to expel them lest they get the upper hand over his subjects by some act of treachery. Yet Vortigern was reluctant to accept this advice because for the sake of his wife he loved the pagans more than any other people. At this, the Britons quickly abandoned Vortigern and in their anger unanimously made his son Vortimer king. He, being in complete agreement with them, began to drive out the barbarians,

desiderabat. Hengistus ilico, ut erat prudens, comperta leuitate animi regis, 360
consuluit fratrem suum Horsum ceterosque maiores natu qui secum aderant
quid de petitione regis facerent; sed omnibus unum consilium fuit ut puella
regi daretur et ut peterent pro ea prouinciam Cantiae ab illo. Nec mora, data
fuit puella Vortegirno et prouincia Cantiae Hengisto, nesciente Gorangono
comite, qui in eadem regnabat. Nupsit itaque rex eadem nocte paganae, 365
quae ultra modum placuit ei; unde in inimicitiam procerum et filiorum
suorum citissime incidit. Generauerat namque filios primitus, quibus erant
nomina Vortimer, Katigern, Paschent.

101   In tempore illo uenit sanctus Germanus Altissiodorensis episcopus et
Lupus Trecacensis ut uerbum Dei Britonibus praedicarent. Corrupta namque 370
fuerat Christianitas eorum tum propter paganos quos rex in societatem
eorum posuerat, tum propter Pelagianam haeresim, cuius uenenum ipsos
multis diebus affecerat. Beatorum igitur uirorum praedicatione restituta est
inter eos uerae fidei religio, quia multis miraculis cotidie praeclarebant.
Multa per eos miracula ostendebat Deus, quae Gildas in tractatu suo 375
luculento dictamine perarauit.

Data autem puella regi ut praedictum est, dixit Hengistus ad eum:

'Ego sum pater tuus et consiliator tibi esse debeo. Noli praeterire consilium
meum, quia omnes inimicos tuos uirtute gentis meae superabis. Inuitemus
adhuc filium meum Octam cum fratruele suo Ebissa; bellatores enim uiri 380
sunt. Da eis regiones quae sunt in aquilonaribus partibus Britanniae iuxta
murum inter Deiram et Scotiam. Detinebunt namque ibidem impetum
barbarorum ita ut in pace citra Humbrum remanebis'.

Paruit Vortegirnus praecepitque illis inuitare quoscumque scirent ad
auxilium sibi ualere. Missis ilico legatis, uenerunt Octa et Ebissa et 385
Cherdich cum trecentis nauibus armata manu repletis, quos omnes suscepit
Vortegirnus benigne maximisque muneribus donauit; uincebat namque
inimicos suos per eos et in omni proelio uictor existebat. Hengistus etiam
inuitabat paulatim naues et cotidie numerum suum augebat. Quod cum
uidissent Britones, timentes proditionem eorum dixerunt regi ut ipsos 390
ex finibus regni sui expelleret. Non enim debebant pagani Christianis
communicare nec intromitti, quia Christiana lex prohibebat; insuper
tanta multitudo aduenerat ita ut ciuibus terrori essent; iam nesciebatur
quis paganus esset, quis Christianus, quia pagani filias et consanguineas
eorum sibi associauerant. Talia obicientes, dissuadebant regi retinere illos, 395
ne in proditione aliqua ciues supergrederentur. At Vortegirnus diffugiebat
consilio eorum acquiescere, quia super omnes gentes propter coniugem
suam ipsos diligebat. Quod cum uidissent Britones, deseruerunt ilico
Vortegirnum et unanimiter irati Vortimer filium suum in regem erexerunt.
Qui acquiescens eis per omnia incepit expellere barbaros atque oppugnare 400

362 faceret *O M*
362 fuit *Δ Y: om. QG:* placuit *M*
363 daretur regi *Φ*
365 rex <in> *Φ*
366 [in] *CH QY*

131

fighting them and launching sharp attacks. Four battles he fought against them, all of which he won: the first was by the river Derwent; in the second at the ford of Episford Horsus opposed Katigern, another of Vortigern's sons, and both died in the fighting, inflicting mortal wounds on each other; the third was by the sea-shore, where the enemy boarded their ships like cowards and sought refuge on the isle of Thanet; but Vortimer besieged them there, attacking every day with his ships. When they could endure the British assaults no longer, the Saxons sent king Vortigern (who had been with them in all the battles) to his son Vortimer, asking permission to depart and to sail in safety to Germany. While this proposal was still being discussed, they boarded their warships and returned to Germany, leaving behind their women and children.

102   After this victory, Vortimer began to restore to his subjects the possessions of which they had been deprived, to treat them with affection and respect and, prompted by St Germanus, to rebuild churches. But his good deeds stirred up the envy of the Devil, who entered the heart of his step-mother Ronwein and moved her to plot his murder. After collecting potions of all kinds, she administered poison to Vortimer by means of one of his household, whom she had bribed with countless gifts. When the famous warrior had drunk it, he suddenly fell ill beyond hope of recovery. Without delay he ordered all his knights to his side and, telling them of his impending death, gave them all the gold and silver amassed by himself and his ancestors. They wept and wailed, but he comforted them, reminding them that he, like all men, was doomed to die. He begged the bold and warlike youths who had been with him in his battles to fight for their country in order to protect it from enemy invasion. His own great courage inspired him to order that a lofty pyramid be built in the port where the Saxons used to land, at the summit of which his body was to be entombed after his death so that the barbarians would see his place of burial and sail straight back to Germany; he said that none of them would dare to approach any nearer once they had merely glimpsed his tomb. The boldness of that man, who even after death wished to terrorise those who had feared him while he lived! Yet after he died, the Britons did differently and buried his body at Trinovantum.

103   After Vortimer's death, Vortigern became king once more and was persuaded by the entreaties of his wife to send messengers to Hengest in Germany telling him to return to Britain, but in private with a few retainers, fearing that otherwise trouble would arise between the barbarians and the British. On hearing of Vortimer's demise, Hengest assembled three hundred thousand armed men, prepared a fleet and returned to Britain. Learning of their arrival in such numbers, Vortigern and his nobles were angered and decided to fight them and drive them from their shores. Hengest was informed of this by his daughter's agents

et diris irruptionibus afficere. Quatuor bella gessit cum eis et in omnibus superauit: primum super flumen Derwend; secundum super uadum Episford, ubi conuenerunt Horsus et Katigernus, alter filius Vortegirni, congressuque facto ceciderunt ambo, alter alterum letaliter aggressus; tercium bellum super ripam maris, quo naues muliebriter ingressi diffugierunt hostes et 405 insulam Thaneth pro refugio adiuerunt; at Vortimerius obsedit illos ibidem et nauali proelio cotidie infestabat. Cumque impetum Britonum diutius tolerare nequirent, miserunt Vortegirnum regem, qui in omnibus bellis cum ipsis aderat, ad filium suum Vortimerium, petentes licentiam abscedendi petendique Germaniam cum salute. Cumque inde colloquium haberent, 410 interim ingressi sunt ciulas suas relictisque mulieribus et filiis Germaniam redierunt.

102   Victoria deinde potitus Vortimerius coepit reddere possessiones ereptas ciuibus ipsosque diligere atque honorare et ecclesias iubente sancto Germano renouare. Sed bonitati eius inuidit ilico Diabolus, qui in corde Ronwein 415 nouercae suae ingressus incitauit eam ut neci ipsius immineret. Quae ergo, ascitis uniuersis ueneficiis, dedit illi per quendam familiarem suum uenenum potare, quem innumerabilibus donariis corruperat. Quod cum hausisset inclitus bellator ille, subita infirmitate grauatus est ita ut nullam spem uiuendi haberet. Nec mora, iussit omnes milites suos uenire ad se et 420 indicata morte quae superueniebat distribuit eis aurum atque argentum suum et quicquid attaui congesserant. Flentes quoque et eiulantes consolabatur, docens uiam uniuersae carnis esse quam initurus erat. Audaces autem et bellicosos iuuenes qui ei in debellationibus suis astare solebant hortabatur ut pro patria pugnantes eam ab hostili irruptione tueri niterentur. Audatia 425 autem maxima docente, iussit piramidem fieri sibi aeriam locarique in portu quo Saxones applicare solebant, corpus uero suum, postquam defunctum foret, sepeliri desuper, ut uiso busto barbari retortis uelis in Germaniam redirent; dicebat enim neminem illorum audere propius accedere si etiam bustum ipsius aspicerent. O maximam uiri audaciam, qui eis quibus uiuus 430 terrori fuerat post obitum etiam ut timeretur optabat! Sed defuncto illo aliud egerunt Britones, quia in urbe Trinouantum corpus illius sepelierunt.

103   Post obitum autem ipsius restitutus est Vortegirnus in regnum, qui precibus coniugis suae commotus misit nuncios suos ad Hengistum in Germaniam mandauitque sibi ut iterum in Britanniam rediret, at tamen 435 priuatim et cum paucis, quia timebat ne si aliter superuenisset discordia inter barbaros et ciues oriretur. Hengistus ergo, audito obitu Vortimerii, trecenta milia armatorum associauit paratoque nauigio in Britanniam reuersus est. Sed cum tantae multitudinis aduentus Vortegirno et principibus regni nunciatus esset, indignati sunt ualde initoque consilio constituerunt 440 proeliari cum eis atque ipsos ex littoribus expellere. Quod cum filia sua

---

414 atque *OSE Φ*: et *H: om. C*
417 [ergo] *Φ*
423 iturus *YG*
438 associauit <sibi> *E (cf. Introd.)*

and immediately considered what would be his best response. Of the many possible plans, he chose a plot to betray the British under a show of peace. He sent messengers to the king with orders to say that his intention in bringing so many men had not been that they should remain with him or do any harm to the country. Rather, in the belief that Vortimer was still alive, he had hoped to use them to repel him, should he attack. Now he was sure that Vortimer was dead, Hengest placed himself and his people in Vortigern's hands, to retain as many as he wanted in his kingdom, and he undertook that those he rejected would return to Germany without delay; and if it was agreeable to the king, he asked Vortigern to name a time and place for them to meet and arrange everything as he wished. This message pleased the king inordinately, as he was unwilling for Hengest to leave. He commanded that Britons and Saxons should meet in the village of Ambrius to finalise matters there on the next May Day.

104   Both parties agreed, but Hengest, resorting to unheard-of treachery, ordered that each of his companions should have a long knife hidden in his boot and, while the unsuspecting Britons were negotiating, on his signal, 'nimet oure saxas', each should be ready to grab the Briton beside him boldly, draw the knife and slit his throat. Soon May Day came and they all met together in the prescribed place to begin peace-talks. When he saw that the moment was ripe for treachery, Hengest shouted, 'nimet oure saxas', and immediately seized Vortigern and held him by his robe. On hearing the signal, the Saxons drew their daggers, grabbed the chiefs beside them and killed around four hundred and sixty barons and earls, who had expected nothing of the sort. Their bodies were later interred and given Christian burial by Eldadus not far from Kaercaradoc, now called Salisbury, in a cemetery beside the monastery which abbot Ambrius founded long ago. All the Britons had come unarmed and with no thought except making peace; so those who had come to betray them found it all the easier to kill their unarmed foes. Yet the pagans did not escape lightly, since many were killed by their intended victims. The Britons, snatching up rocks from the ground and clubs, tried to defend themselves by striking down their betrayers.

Hengisto per internuntios indicauisset, confestim cogitauit quid potius contra id agendum esset. Diuersis igitur machinationibus peragratis, unum ex omnibus elegit, ut gentem regni sub specie pacis adoriretur prodere. Misit itaque legatos suos ad regem iussitque nuntiare quod non conduxerat tantam 445 multitudinem uirorum ut uel secum in regno remanerent uel uiolentiam aliquam cum eis patriae ingereret. Erat namque causa cur eam conduxisset quia existimabat Vortimerium adhuc uiuere, cui per eos affectabat resistere si illum expugnare incepisset. Quoniam autem non haesitabat ipsum defunctum esse, committebat sese et populum suum dispositioni Vortegirni, 450 ut quot optaret ex tanto numero in regnum suum retinuisset, et quot refutandos censeret concedebat ut in Germaniam sine dilatione rediissent; et si id Vortegirno placuisset, tunc petebat ipse ut diem et locum nominasset Vortegirnus quo pariter conuenirent et omnia ex uoluntate sua disposuisset. Talia itaque ut regi nunciata fuerunt, placuerunt ei uehementer, quia inuitus 455 sineret Hengistum abire. Postremo iussit et ciues et Saxones kalendis Maii, quae iam instare incipiebant, in pago Ambrii conuenire ut ibidem praedicta statuerentur.

104   Quod cum in utraque parte concessum esset, Hengistus, noua proditione usus, praecepit commilitonibus suis ut unusquisque longum cultrum infra 460 caligas absconditum haberent et cum colloquium securius tractarent Britones ipse daret eis hoc signum, 'nimet oure saxas', unde quisque paratus astantem Britonem audacter occuparet atque abstractis cultris ocius ipsum iugularet. Nec mora, statuta die instante conuenerunt omnes infra nominatam prouinciam et de pace habenda colloquium inceperunt. 465 Vt igitur horam proditioni suae idoneam inspexisset Hengistus, uociferatus est 'nimet oure saxas' et ilico Vortegirnum accepit et per pallium detinuit. Audito uero ocius signo, abstraxerunt Saxones cultros suos et astantes principes inuaserunt ipsosque nichil tale praemeditatos iugulauerunt circiter quadringentos sexaginta inter barones et consules. Quorum corpora 470 beatus Eldadus postmodum sepeliuit atque Christiano more humauit haud longe a Kaercaradoc, quae nunc Salesberia dicitur, in cimiterio quodam iuxta coenobium Ambrii abbatis, qui olim fundator ipsius extiterat. Omnes enim sine armis aduenerant nec aliud nisi de pace tractanda existimabant; unde ceteri, qui propter proditionem accesserant, leuius ipsos inermes 475 interficere potuerunt. Non impune tamen hoc egerunt pagani, quia multi eorum perempti fuerunt dum neci ceterorum imminerent. Eripiebant enim Britones ex tellure lapides et fustes atque sese defendere uolentes proditores illidebant.

442 indicasset *OS Φ*
451 quot optaret *GM:* quod optaret *Δ QY*
455 itaque *54 ('Transm.' 99):* namque *Ω*
457 in pago *Δ:* iuxta coenobium *Φ (cf. 'Transm.' 104)*
459 statutum *Φ*
465 prouinciam *Δ:* urbem *Φ*
468 [uero] *Φ, fort. recte*
470-73 [Quorum ... extiterat] *Φ (cf. 'Transm.' 104)*
474 [nisi] *OC*

105   Among these men was Eldol earl of Gloucester, who, seeing that they were betrayed, found a staff to wield and defended himself. Whoever he struck with it had a limb broken by the blow and was dispatched straight to hell. He inspired great fear, breaking heads, arms, shoulders and very often legs; he did not leave the place until he had broken his staff and killed seventy men. Overwhelmed by their numbers, he escaped and made for his own city. Many men died on both sides, but victory went to the Saxons. For the unsuspecting Britons had come unarmed and so could put up little resistance. Once their wicked plot had succeeded, the Saxons were reluctant to kill Vortigern, but bound him and threatened him with death unless he surrendered his cities and castles in return for his life. He straightaway gave them what they wanted, in order to escape unharmed. When he had sworn an oath, they freed him and went first to London, which they took. Next they took York, Lincoln and Winchester and laid waste to all regions. Everywhere they attacked the people like wolves attacking shepherdless sheep. In the face of such slaughter, Vortigern retreated into Wales, unsure what to do against the terrible barbarians.

106   Finally he summoned and consulted his magicians, commanding them to tell him what to do. They said that he should build a very strong tower as a refuge, since he had lost his other fortresses. He visited many places in order to build it in a good spot and came at last to mount Snowdon, where he gathered stonemasons from various regions and ordered them to build the tower. They met and began to lay foundations. But whenever they completed a day's work, it would be swallowed up by the ground the next day, so that they had no idea where it had gone. When Vortigern was informed of this, he again consulted his magicians in order to find out what was causing it. They told him to seek out a young man who had no father and, when found, to kill him and pour his blood over the cement and stones; this, they claimed, would make the foundations sound. Envoys were immediately despatched throughout all regions to find such a person. When they arrived at the city later called Kaermerdin, they discovered youths playing in front of the gate; they approached the players, but, tired by their journey, sat in a circle around them, looking for what they sought. After most of the day had passed, a quarrel suddenly broke out between two youths, whose names were Merlin and Dinabutius. As they argued, Dinabutius said to Merlin:

> 'You fool, why do you quarrel with me? You will never enjoy the same degree of nobility as I do. I am of royal descent on both sides of my family, whereas your identity is unknown since you have no father'.

105   Aderat ibi consul Claudiocestriae, uocabulo Eldol, qui uisa proditione 480
sustulit palum quem forte inuenerat et defensioni uacauit. Quemcumque
attingebat cum illo, confringens ei membrum quod percutiebat dirigebat
confestim ad Tartara. Alii caput, alii brachia, alii scapulas, compluribus
etiam crura elidens, terrorem non minimum inferebat; nec prius ex loco
illo abscessit donec septuaginta uiros consumpto palo interfecit. Nam cum 485
tantae multitudini resistere nequiuisset, diuertit sese ab illis atque ciuitatem
suam petiuit. Multi hinc et inde ceciderunt, sed uictoriam habuerunt
Saxones. Britones namque, nichil tale praemeditati, inermes aduenerant,
unde minime resistere potuerunt. Vt igitur nefandum inceptum peregerunt
Saxones, noluerunt interficere Vortegirnum sed mortem comminantes 490
ligauerunt eum petieruntque ciuitates suas atque munitiones pro uita.
Quibus ilico quicquid affectauerant concessit ut uiuus abscedere sineretur.
Cumque id iureiurando confirmatum fuisset, soluerunt eum a uinculis atque
urbem Lundoniae primitus adeuntes ceperunt. Ceperunt deinde Eboracum
et Lindocolinum nec non et Guintoniam, quasque prouincias deuastantes. 495
Inuadebant undique ciues quemadmodum lupi oues quas pastores
deseruerunt. Cum ergo tantam cladem inspexisset Vortegirnus, secessit in
partibus Kambriae, inscius quid contra nefandam gentem ageret.

106   Vocatis denique magis suis, consuluit illos iussitque dicere quid faceret.
Qui dixerunt ut aedificaret sibi turrim fortissimam quae sibi tutamen foret, 500
cum ceteras munitiones amisisset. Peragratis ergo quibusque locis ut eam
in congruo loco statueret, uenit tandem ad montem Erir, ubi coadunatis
ex diuersis patriis caementariis iussit turrim construere. Conuenientes
itaque lapidarii coeperunt eam fundare. Sed quicquid una die operabantur,
absorbebat tellus illud in altera, ita ut nescirent quorsum opus suum 505
euanesceret. Cumque id Vortegirno nunciatum fuisset, consuluit iterum
magos suos ut causam rei indicarent. Qui dixerunt ut iuuenem sine patre
quaereret quaesitumque interficeret ut sanguine ipsius caementum et lapides
aspergerentur; id enim prodesse asserebant ut fundamentum constaret.
Nec mora, mittuntur legati per uniuersas prouincias ut talem hominem 510
inuenirent. At cum in urbem quae postea Kaermerdin uocata fuit uenissent,
conspexerunt iuuenes ante portam ludentes et ad ludum accesserunt, fatigati
autem itinere sederunt in circo, exploraturi quod quaerebant. Denique, cum
multum diei praeterisset, subita lis orta est inter duos iuuenes, quorum erant
nomina Merlinus atque Dinabutius. Certantibus uero ipsis, dixit Dinabutius 515
ad Merlinum:

        'Quid mecum contendis, fatue? Numquam nobis eadem erit nobilitas.
        Ego enim ex origine regum editus sum ex utraque parte generationis
        meae, de te autem nescitur quis sis, cum patrem non habeas'.

---

482 [cum illo] *Φ*
484-5 illo loco *OH, sed cf. § 196.412*
485 [cum] *E: post* multitudini *Φ*
501 quibus *O:* quibusdam *H*
503 diuersa patria *Φ*

At this the envoys looked up and, gazing at Merlin, asked the bystanders who he was. They said that no one knew who his father had been, but his mother was the daughter of the King of Demetia, who was living in the city as a nun at the church of St Peter.

107   The envoys hurried to the governor of the city and ordered him in the king's name to send the boy and his mother to Vortigern. When he learned the purpose of their mission, the governor immediately sent Merlin and his mother to Vortigern to do with them as he wished. When they had been brought before him, the king received the mother graciously, since he knew her to be of noble lineage. Then he began to ask her who had been the youth's father. She said:

'Upon your soul and mine, my lord king, I knew no man who begot this child of me. One thing, however, I do know, that when my companions and I were in our cells, someone resembling a handsome young man used to appear to me very often, holding me tight in his arms and kissing me. After remaining with me for a while, he would suddenly disappear from my sight. Often he would talk to me without appearing, while I sat alone. He visited me in this way for a long time and often made love to me in the form of a man, leaving me with a child in my womb. In your wisdom, you should know, my lord, that in no other way have I known a man who could have been this youth's father'.

The king, amazed, ordered Maugantius to be summoned to inform him if what the woman had said was possible. Maugantius was brought and, after hearing the full story, said to Vortigern:

'I have discovered in the books of our philosophers and in very many histories that many people have been born in this way. As Apuleius records in *De deo Socratis*, between the moon and the earth there live spirits whom we call incubi. They are part human, part angel, and take on human form at will and sleep with women. Perhaps it was one of them who appeared to this woman and fathered this youth'.

108   When Merlin had heard all this, he approached the king and said:

'Why have my mother and I been brought before you?'.

Vortigern answered:

'My magicians have told me to find someone without a father so that my tower could be sprinkled with his blood and so stand firm'.

Then Merlin said:

Ad uerbum istud erexerunt legati uultus suos atque intuentes in Merlinum 520
interrogauerunt circumstantes quis esset. Quibus illi dixerunt quia nesciebatur
quis pater eum progenuerat, mater uero filia fuerat regis Demetiae, quae in
ecclesia sancti Petri in eadem urbe inter monachas degebat.

107 Festinantes itaque nuncii uenerunt ad praefectum urbis praeceperuntque
ei ex parte regis ut Merlinus cum matre sua ad regem mitteretur. Praefectus 525
ilico, cum causam legationis eorum cognouisset, misit Merlinum et
matrem suam ad Vortegirnum ut de eis libitum suum perficeret. Et cum
in praesentiam ipsius adducti fuissent, excepit rex diligenter matrem, quia
eam sciebat nobilibus natalibus ortam. Deinde inquirere coepit ab illa ex
quo uiro iuuenem conceperat. Cui illa dixit: 530

'Vivit anima tua et uiuit anima mea, domine mi rex, quia neminem
agnoui qui illum in me generauerit. Vnum autem scio, quod cum essem
inter consocias meas in thalamis nostris apparebat michi quidam in
specie pulcherrimi iuuenis et saepissime amplectens me strictis brachiis
deosculabatur. Et cum aliquantulum mecum moram fecisset, subito 535
euanescebat ita ut nichil ex eo uiderem. Multociens quoque alloquebatur
dum secreto sederem nec usquam comparebat. Cumque me diu in hunc
modum frequentasset, coiuit mecum in specie hominis saepius atque
grauidam in aluo deseruit. Sciat prudentia tua, domine mi, quod aliter
uirum non agnoui qui iuuenem istum genuerit'. 540

Ammirans itaque rex iussit Maugantium ad se uocari ut sibi manifestaret si
id quod dixerat mulier fieri potuisset. Adductus autem Maugantius, auditis
omnibus ex ordine, dixit ad Vortegirnum:

'In libris philosophorum nostrorum et in plurimis historiis repperi multos
homines huiusmodi procreationem habuisse. Nam ut Apulegius de deo 545
Socratis perhibet, inter lunam et terram habitant spiritus quos incubos
daemones appellamus. Hii partim habent naturam hominum, partim
uero angelorum, et cum uolunt assumunt sibi humanas figuras et cum
mulieribus coeunt. Forsitan unus ex eis huic mulieri apparuit et iuuenem
istum in ipsa generauit'. 550

108 Cumque omnia auscultasset Merlinus, accessit ad regem et ait:

'Vt quid ego et mater mea in praesentia tua adducti sumus?'.

Cui Vortegirnus:

'Magi mei dederunt michi consilium ut hominem sine patre perquirerem
ut opus meum sanguine ipsius irroraretur et staret'. 555

Tunc ait Merlinus:

---

522 fuerat filia *Φ*
530 [iuuenem] *Φ*
531 mea ... tua *H G:* tua *Q*
544 pluribus *E YM*
555 irrogaretur *Q:* irrigaretur *YGM*

'Order your magicians here before me, and I shall prove that they have lied'.

Amazed at what he said, the king ordered the magicians to come and sit before Merlin. To them Merlin said:

'Without knowing what is hindering the foundation of the tower that is being built, you have advised that the cement be sprinkled with my blood, whereupon it would almost instantly stand firm. But tell me what is hidden beneath the foundations. There is something beneath which prevents the tower standing firm'.

The magicians were cowed into silence. Then Merlin, who was also called Ambrosius, said:

'My lord king, call your workmen and set them digging; you will find a pool beneath the tower which prevents it from standing'.

This was done and a pool discovered beneath the tower, undermining it. Ambrosius Merlin went again to the magicians, saying:

'Tell me what is beneath the pool, you lying flatterers'.

They made not a word of reply. Merlin said:

'Have the pool drained through channels and at the bottom you will see two hollow rocks with two dragons asleep in them'.

Because he had been right about the pool, the king believed him and had it drained, full of wonder at Merlin. All the bystanders too were filled with wonder at his wisdom, thinking he was inspired.

'Iube magos tuos uenire coram me, et conuincam illos mendacium adinuenisse'.

Ammirans continuo rex super uerbis illius iussit uenire magos et coram Merlino sedere. Quibus ait Merlinus: 560

'Nescientes quid fundamentum inceptae turris impediat, laudauistis ut sanguis meus diffunderetur in caementum et quasi ilico opus constaret. Sed dicite michi quid sub fundamento latet. Nam aliquid sub illo est quod ipsum stare non permittit'.

Expauescentes autem magi conticuerunt. Tunc ait Merlinus, qui et 565 Ambrosius dicebatur:

'Domine mi rex, uoca operarios tuos et iube fodere terram, et inuenies stagnum sub ea quod turrim stare non permittit'.

Quod cum factum fuisset, repertum est stagnum sub terra, quod eam instabilem fecerat. Accessit iterum Ambrosius Merlinus ad magos et ait: 570

'Dicite michi, mendaces adulatores, quid sub stagno est'.

Nec unum uerbum respondentes obmutuerunt.

'Praecipe hauriri stagnum per riuulos, et uidebis in fundo duos concauos lapides et in illis duos dracones dormientes'.

Credidit rex uerbis eius quia uerum dixerat de stagno et iussit illud hauriri, 575 et Merlinum super omnia ammirabatur. Ammirabantur etiam cuncti qui astabant tantam in eo sapientiam, existimantes numen esse in illo.

---

562 [et] *54, 108 (cf. Introd.)*
573 <Tunc ait Merlinus ad regem> praecipe *E, similia multi*

PREFACE TO THE PROPHECIES OF MERLIN

109 Before I had reached this point in my history, news of Merlin spread and I was being pressed to publish his prophecies by all my contemporaries, and particularly by Alexander bishop of Lincoln, a man of the greatest piety and wisdom. No one among the clergy or the people enjoyed the service of so many nobles, whom he bound to him with his gentle goodness and kind generosity. Wishing to please him, I translated the prophecies and sent them to him with the following letter:

110 'Alexander bishop of Lincoln, my love for your noble person compelled me to translate from British into Latin the prophecies of Merlin, before completing the history which I had begun concerning the deeds of the kings of the British. It had been my intention to finish the history first and only then set out this work so that the twin task should not make me less attentive to either. All the same, because I was sure that the discernment of your subtle mind would grant me pardon, I have put my rustic pipe to my lips and, to its humble tune, have translated the tongue which is unknown to you. I am surprised that you deigned to entrust this task to my poor pen when your staff of office can command so many men of greater learning to soothe the ears of your intellect with the sweetness of a more sublime song. And to say nothing of all the scholars in the whole of Britain, I readily admit that you alone could sing it best of all with your bold lyre, if your lofty office did not call you to other business.

PROLOGVS IN PROPHETIAS MERLINI

109 Nondum autem ad hunc locum historiae perueneram cum de Merlino
diuulgato rumore compellebant me undique contemporanei mei prophetias
ipsius edere, maxime autem Alexander Lincolniensis episcopus, uir summae
religionis et prudentiae. Non erat alter in clero siue in populo cui tot nobiles
famularentur, quos mansueta pietas ipsius et benigna largitas in obsequium   5
suum alliciebat. Cui cum satisfacere praeelegissem, prophetias transtuli et
eidem cum huiusmodi litteris direxi:

110 'Coegit me, Alexander Lincolniensis praesul, nobilitatis tuae dilectio
prophetias Merlini de Britannico in Latinum transferre antequam historiam
perarassem quam de gestis regum Britannorum inceperam. Proposueram   10
enim illam prius perficere istudque opus subsequenter explicare, ne dum
uterque labor incumberet sensus meus ad singula minor fieret. At tamen,
quoniam securus eram ueniae quam discretio subtilis ingenii tui donaret,
agrestem calamum meum labellis apposui et plebeia modulatione
ignotum tibi interpretatus sum sermonem. Admodum autem ammiror   15
quia id pauperi stilo dignatus eras committere, cum tot doctiores uirga
potestatis tuae coherceat, qui sublimioris carminis delectamento aures
mineruae tuae mulcerent. Et ut omnes philosophos totius Britanniae
insulae praeteream, tu solus es, quod non erubesco fateri, qui prae cunctis
audaci lira caneres, nisi te culmen honoris ad cetera negocia uocaret.   20

---

*In §§ 109-10 citantur O, CHSE, Y, Φ (unde pendent QGM); accedit in § 110 Π (unde pendent
ζλβρ)*

Incipit prologus in librum septimum qui continet prophetia Ambrosii Merlini G: Incipit prologus
in prophetias Merlini M: *tit. nullus huiusmodi in cett.*

3 [ipsius] Y
3 maxime uero O
3 Lincolniensis praesul Y
3-6 summae ... alliciebat CHSE Y Φ: prudens et eruditus O
6-10 Cui cum ... inceperam CHSE Y Φ (et Π inde a Coegit): Quibus satisfacere uolens eius
prophetias antequam historiam quam de gestis Brittonum inceperam perarassem de Brittannico
in Latinum transtuli O

Ante § 110 Prologus S: Incipit prologus ad Alexandrum Lincolniensem episcopum G: Epistula magistri
Galfr. Monomutensis directa Alexandro Lincolniensi episcopo ζ: Editio Gaufridi Monemutensis de
edictis Merlini Ambrosii β: Incipit editio Gaufridi Monemutensis de dictis Merlini ρ: *tit. nullus in λ*

10 britannicorum H ζ: britonum E
11 enim illam CHSE Y Φ Π: namque historiam O
12 minor fieret H G² Y Π: minus fieret CSE QG¹M: minus sufficeret O (cf. 'Transm.' 79-80)
12-24 At tamen ... concentum CHSE Y Φ Π: Quoniam igitur sic illis placuit ut huic uaticinio
fistulam meam imponam, siquid uitiose minusue ordinate sonuerit uenia donanda est, quia libens
pareo et pudibundus Brito non doctus canere quod in Brittannico Merlinus dulciter et metrice
cecinit utcumque potui licet immodulate tamen Latine persono O
14 plebeio CS Φ
14 modulamine Φ
16 tot doctiores <tot ditiores> HS Φ λ, sed cf. Introd.
19 quod CSE Y Φ ζλ: quem H
19 ceteris Φ
20 audaciori (-dic- Y) Y Π

Since it is your wish, therefore, that the reed of Geoffrey of Monmouth pipes this prophecy, please favour his playing and with the rod of your muses restore to harmony anything irregular or faulty.'

THE PROPHECIES

111   As Vortigern, King of the Britons, sat on the bank of the drained pool, the two dragons emerged, one white, one red. As they neared each other, they fought a terrible battle, breathing fire. The white dragon began to get the upper hand and drove the red to the edge of the pool. But it was irked at being driven back and attacked the white, forcing it back in turn. As the dragons fought in this way, the king commanded Ambrosius Merlin to tell him the meaning of their battle. He burst into tears and was inspired to prophesy thus:

112   'Alas for the red dragon, its end is near. Its caves will be taken by the white dragon, which symbolises the Saxons whom you have summoned. The red represents the people of Britain, whom the white will oppress. Its mountains will be levelled with the valleys, and the rivers in the valleys will flow with blood. Religious observance will be destroyed and churches stand in ruins. At last the oppressed will rise up and resist the foreigners' fury. The boar of Cornwall will lend his aid and trample the foreigners' necks beneath his feet. The islands of the ocean will fall under his sway and he will occupy the glades of France. The house of Rome will tremble before his rage, and his end shall be unknown. He will be celebrated in the mouth of the nations and his deeds will feed those who tell them. His six successors will wield the sceptre, but after them the German worm will rise. It will be raised up by a wolf from the sea, who will be accompanied by the forests of Africa. Religion will be destroyed again and archbishoprics will be displaced. London's honour will adorn Canterbury and the seventh pastor of York will dwell in the kingdom of Armorica. St David's will wear the pallium of Caerleon, and the preacher of Ireland will fall silent because of a baby growing in the womb.

Quoniam ergo placuit ut Galfridus Monemutensis fistulam suam in hoc uaticinio sonaret, modulationibus suis fauere non diffugias et siquid inordinate siue uitiose protulerit ferula camenarum tuarum in rectum aduertas concentum'.

PROPHETIAE

111 Sedente itaque Vortegirno rege Britonum super ripam exhausti stagni, 25 egressi sunt duo dracones, quorum unus erat albus et alius rubeus. Cumque alter alteri appropinquasset, commiserunt diram pugnam et ignem anhelitu procreabant. Praeualebat autem albus draco rubeumque usque ad extremitatem lacus fugabat. At ille, cum se expulsum doluisset, impetum fecit in album ipsumque retro ire coegit. Ipsis ergo in hunc 30 modum pugnantibus, praecepit rex Ambrosio Merlino dicere quid proelium draconum portendebat. Mox ille, in fletum erumpens, spiritum hausit prophetiae et ait:

112 'Vae rubeo draconi; nam exterminatio eius festinat. Cauernas ipsius occupabit albus draco, qui Saxones quos inuitasti significat. Rubeus 35 uero gentem designat Britanniae, quae ab albo opprimetur. Montes itaque eius ut ualles aequabuntur, et flumina uallium sanguine manabunt. Cultus religionis delebitur, et ruina ecclesiarum patebit. Praeualebit tandem oppressa et saeuiciae exterorum resistet. Aper etenim Cornubiae succursum praestabit et colla eorum sub pedibus suis conculcabit. 40 Insulae occeani potestati ipsius subdentur, et Gallicanos saltus possidebit. Tremebit Romulea domus saeuiciam ipsius, et exitus eius dubius erit. In ore populorum celebrabitur, et actus eius cibus erit narrantibus. Sex posteri eius sequentur sceptrum, sed post ipsos exsurget Germanicus uermis. Sublimabit illum aequoreus lupus, quem Affricana nemora comitabuntur. 45 Delebitur iterum religio, et transmutacio primarum sedium fiet. Dignitas Lundoniae adornabit Doroberniam, et pastor Eboracensis septimus in Armorico regno frequentabitur. Meneuia pallio Vrbis Legionum induetur, et praedicator Hiberniae propter infantem in utero crescentem

---

23 uitiose *CHSE Φ λβρ:* ociose *Y:* incuriose *ζ*
24 auertas *H M*

In §§ 111-17 citantur Δ (unde pendent OCSE, H usque ad § 114.104 fauorem), *M, hic illic W, Y (cui accedit H inde a § 114.104* Tonantis), *G, Π (qui saltem 110-116.194 ante cetera editum separatim tradit; ad ζλβρ accedit θ)*

Prophetiae Merlini Britonis *O:* Hic incipit prophetia Ambrosii Merlini *S:* Explicit prologus. Incipiunt prophetiae *M:* Incipit liber .vii. qui continet prophetias Merlini Ambrosii *G:* Incipit liber Ambrosii Merlini *β: tit. nullus in θ cett.*

28 anhelitu <suo> *Π*
39 enim *Π*
43 Sed *pro* Sex *O G*
45 [Sublimabit ... comitabuntur] *λβρθ*
46 erit *WYG*

A rain of blood will fall and men will suffer a terrible famine. At this the red dragon will lament, but will recover its strength once the travail is over. Then the misfortune of the white will be hastened and the buildings in its gardens be destroyed. Seven sceptre-bearers will be killed, and one of them become a saint. Mothers' bellies will be cut open and infants aborted. People will suffer greatly in order that the natives be restored. He who achieves this will don a man of bronze and for many years guard the gates of London upon a bronze steed. Then the red dragon will return to its old ways and strive to tear at itself. Upon it will come the retribution of the Thunderer, for every field will disappoint its cultivators. Pestilence will smite the people and empty every region. The survivors will leave their native soil and plant in foreign fields. A blessed king will prepare a fleet and be numbered among the saints in the palace of the twelfth. There will be grievous desolation in the kingdom and the threshing-floors for harvest will revert to scrubby glades. The white dragon will rise again and summon Germany's daughter. Our gardens will be filled again with foreign seed and the red dragon will languish at the pool's edge. Then the German worm will be crowned, and the prince of bronze buried. A limit has been set for the white dragon beyond which it will not be able to fly; for a hundred and fifty years it will endure harassment and submission, but for three hundred it will be in occupation. Then the north wind will rise against it and blow away the flowers the western breeze has nurtured. There will be gilding in the temples, nor will sword-blades cease to be busy. The German dragon will be hard put to keep possession of its caves, since retribution will be visited on its treason. Then it will prosper for a short time, but Normandy's tithe will injure it. A people will come clad in wood and tunics of iron to take vengeance on its wickedness. They will restore the former inhabitants to their dwellings, and the ruin of the foreigners will be plain to see. The seed of the white dragon will disappear from our gardens and the remnants of its generation will be decimated. They will bear the yoke of unending slavery and wound their mother with hoes and ploughs. Two dragons will succeed, one of which will be suffocated by the arrow of envy, while the other will return beneath the shadow of a name. They will be succeeded by the lion of justice, whose roar will set trembling the towers of France and the island dragons. In his time gold will be extracted from the lily and the nettle, and silver shall drip from the hooves of lowing cattle. Men with curled hair will wear fleeces of varied hue, and their outer apparel will betray their inner selves. The paws of barking dogs will be cut off. Wild beasts will enjoy peace. Men will suffer punishment. The shape for trading will be cut; the half will be circular. The greed of kites will be ended, and the teeth of wolves blunted. The lion's cubs will become fishes of the sea, and his eagle will nest on mount Aravius. Venedotia will run red with a mother's blood, and the house

113

obmutescet. Pluet sanguineus imber, et dira fames mortales afficiet. His superuenientibus, dolebit rubeus sed emenso labore uigebit. Tunc infortunium albi festinabit et aedificia ortulorum eius diruentur. Septem sceptrigeri perimentur, et unus eorum sanctificabitur. Ventres matrum secabuntur, et infantes abortiui erunt. Erit ingens supplicium hominum ut indigenae restituantur. Qui faciet haec aeneum uirum induet et per multa tempora super aeneum equum portas Lundoniae seruabit. Exin in proprios mores reuertetur rubeus draco et in se ipsum saeuire laborabit. Superueniet itaque ultio Tonantis, quia omnis ager colonos decipiet. Arripiet mortalitas populum cunctasque nationes euacuabit. Residui natale solum deserent et exteras culturas seminabunt. Rex benedictus parabit nauigium et in aula duodecimi inter beatos annumerabitur. Erit miseranda regni desolatio, et areae messium in fruticosos saltus redibunt. Exurget iterum albus draco et filiam Germaniae inuitabit. Replebuntur iterum ortuli nostri alieno semine, et in extremitate stagni languebit rubeus. Exin coronabitur Germanicus uermis et aeneus princeps humabitur.
113 Terminus illi positus est quem transuolare nequibit; centum namque quinquaginta annis in inquietudine et subiectione manebit, ter centum uero insidebit. Tunc exurget in illum aquilo et flores quos zephirus procreauit eripiet. Erit deauratio in templis, nec acumen gladiorum cessabit. Vix obtinebit cauernas suas Germanicus draco, quia ultio prodicionis eius superueniet. Vigebit tandem paulisper, sed decimatio Neustriae nocebit. Populus namque in ligno et ferreis tunicis superueniet, qui uindictam de nequitia ipsius sumet. Restaurabit pristinis incolis mansiones, et ruina alienigenarum patebit. Germen albi draconis ex ortulis nostris abradetur, et reliquiae generationis eius decimabuntur. Iugum perpetuae seruitutis ferent matremque suam ligonibus et aratris uulnerabunt. Succedent duo dracones, quorum alter inuidiae spiculo suffocabitur, alter uero sub umbra nominis redibit. Succedet leo iusticiae, ad cuius rugitum Gallicanae turres et insulani dracones tremebunt. In diebus eius aurum ex lilio et urtica extorquebitur et argentum ex ungulis mugientium manabit. Calamistrati uaria uellera uestibunt, et exterior habitus interiora signabit. Pedes latrantum truncabuntur. Pacem habebunt ferae. Humanitas supplicium dolebit. Findetur forma commercii; dimidium rotundum erit. Peribit miluorum rapacitas, et dentes luporum hebetabuntur. Catuli leonis in aequoreos pisces transformabuntur, et aquila eius super montem Arauium nidificabit. Venedocia rubebit materno sanguine, et domus

51 rubeus <draco> *λβϱθ*
52-3 Octo sceptrigeri <illius> ... glorificabitur *Π*
54 obtruncabuntur *G:* truncabuntur *54 (cf. Introd.)*
57 et *Ω:* nam *Π*
62 fruticosos *M*^{2} *G λβ:* fructicosos *CHSE M*^{1} *ζϱθ*: fructuosos *O Y*
65 humiliabitur *O M*
67 [in] *OC*^{1}*SE*^{2}
67 ter centum *W M Π:* trecentum *Δ Y:* trecentis *G*
70 draco *Δ M WG Π:* uermis *Y*
72 - 108 Populus ... orietur *citat Ord.*
74 albi draconis *Ω:* ipsius *Π, Ord.*
82 latrantium *M WG βθ, Ord.*
85 montes *M θ, Ord.*
86 Araunium *Ord.*

of Corineus kill six brothers. The island will be soaked in nightly tears, and so all men will be provoked to all things. Their progeny will try to fly beyond the heavens, but the favour of new men will be raised up. The possessor will be harmed by the goodness of the wicked until he dresses himself as his father. Girt thus with the teeth of the boar, he will rise above the mountain peaks and the shadow of the helmeted man. Scotland will be angered and, summoning its neighbours, will spend its time in bloodshed. Upon its jaws will be placed a bridle, made in the bay of Brittany. The eagle of the broken treaty will gild the bridle and rejoice in a third nesting. The cubs of the ruler will awake, leave the forests and hunt within city walls. They will do great execution among those who oppose them and cut out the tongues of bulls. They will load with chains the necks of those who roar and renew the times of their grandfathers. Then the thumb will be rolled in oil from the first to the fourth, from the fourth to the third and from the third to the second. The sixth will overthrow the city walls of Ireland and turn its forests into a plain. He will reduce various shares to one and be crowned with the lion's head. His beginning will be weakened by uncertain desires, but his end will ascend to the heavens. For he shall rebuild the homes of the saints throughout his lands and appoint shepherds where they are needed. He will dress two cities in two pallia and give virginal gifts to virgins. For this he will earn the favour of the Thunderer and be numbered among the blessed. From him will emerge a lynx, which will pierce through everything and threaten to destroy its own people. Because of it Normandy will lose both islands and be stripped of its former honour. Then the natives will return to the island; for strife will break out among the foreigners. An old man in white on a snow-white horse will divert the river Periron and with a white rod measure out a mill on its bank. Cadualadrus will summon Conanus and make Scotland his ally. Then the foreigners will be slaughtered, the rivers flow with blood, and the hills of Brittany burst forth and be crowned with Brutus' diadem. Wales will be filled with rejoicing and the Cornish oaks will flourish. The island will be called by Brutus' name and the foreign term will disappear. From Conanus will come forth a warlike boar, who will sharpen his tusks on the forests of France. He will break all the tallest trees, but give protection to the smaller. The Arabs and Africans will tremble before him; for his charge will carry him all the way to further Spain. He will be succeeded

114

115

Corinei sex fratres interficiet. Nocturnis lacrimis madebit insula, unde
omnes ad omnia prouocabuntur. Nitentur posteri transuolare superna,
sed fauor nouorum sublimabitur. Nocebit possidenti ex impiis pietas
donec sese genitore induerit. Apri igitur dentibus accinctus, cacumina
montium et umbram galeati transcendet. Indignabitur Albania et
conuocatis collateralibus sanguinem effundere uacabit. Dabitur maxillis
eius frenum, quod in Armorico sinu fabricabitur. Deaurabit illud aquila
rupti foederis et tercia nidificatione gaudebit. Euigilabunt regentis catuli
et postpositis nemoribus infra moenia ciuitatum uenabuntur. Stragem
non minimam ex obstantibus facient et linguas taurorum abscident. Colla
rugientium onerabunt catenis et auita tempora renouabunt. Exin de primo
in quartum, de quarto in tercium, de tercio in secundum rotabitur pollex
in oleo. Sextus Hiberniae moenia subuertet et nemora in planiciem
mutabit. Diuersas portiones in unum reducet et capite leonis coronabitur.
Principium eius uago affectui succumbet, sed finis ipsius ad superos
conuolabit. Renouabit namque beatorum sedes per patrias et pastores
in congruis locis locabit. Duas urbes duobus palliis induet et uirginea
munera uirginibus donabit. Promerebitur inde fauorem Tonantis et inter
beatos collocabitur. Egredietur ex eo linx penetrans omnia, quae ruinae
propriae gentis imminebit. Per illam enim utramque insulam amittet
Neustria et pristina dignitate spoliabitur. Deinde reuertentur ciues in
insulam; nam discidium alienigenarum orietur. Niueus quoque senex in
niueo equo fluuium Perironis diuertet et cum candida uirga molendinum
super ipsum metabitur. Cadualadrus Conanum uocabit et Albaniam
in societatem accipiet. Tunc erit strages alienigenarum, tunc flumina
sanguine manabunt, tunc erumpent Armorici montes et diademate Bruti
coronabuntur. Replebitur Kambria laeticia, et robora Cornubiae uirescent.
Nomine Bruti uocabitur insula, et nuncupatio extraneorum peribit. Ex
Conano procedet aper bellicosus, qui infra Gallicana nemora acumen
dentium suorum exercebit. Truncabit namque quaeque maiora robora,
minoribus uero tutelam praestabit. Tremebunt illum Arabes et Affricani;
nam impetum cursus sui in ulteriorem Hispaniam protendet. Succedet

114 / 115 / 90 / 95 / 100 / 105 / 110 / 115

88 *post* prouocabuntur *add. YG* Vae tibi Neustria, quia cerebrum leonis in te *(*in te cerebrum leonis *Y)* effundetur dilaceratisque *(*et dissipatis *Y)* membris a patrio *(*natiuo *Y)* solo eliminabitur
90 genitorem *Ord.*
90 acumina *Ord.*
92 translateralibus H^1 Π, *Ord.* (*cf. Introd.*)
94 regentis O^1CS^1 *YG* $\zeta\lambda\varrho$, *Ord.*: rugientis $O^2HS^2E^1$ *M* θ: rugientes $E^2\beta$: rugientis *uel* -tes *W*
97 Exinde de *Ord.*
98 rorabitur *Ord.*
100 [et] *Ord.*
101 subiacebit *YG*
103 [duobus] *Ord.*
105 coronabitur *Ord.*
105 linx Ω Π: lues *Ord.*
105 qua *Ord.*
105 ruina $\zeta\varrho\beta\theta$, *Ord.*
110 uocabit Conanum *YHG*
111 tunc flumina Δ *WYHG* Π: et flumina *M*
116 exacuet *M* ζ
118 Succedet <uero> *M* ζ

by the goat of the Camp of Venus, with golden horns and a silver beard, who will breathe forth from his nostrils a cloud which will cover the whole surface of the island. There will be peace in his time and the rich soil will increase its crops. Women will move like snakes and their every step will be filled with pride. The Camp of Venus will be renewed, and Cupid's arrows will not cease to wound. The spring of Anna will turn to blood, and two kings will fight over the lioness of Stafford. All the soil will be rank, and mankind will not cease to fornicate. Three generations will witness all this until the kings buried in the city of London are revealed. Hunger and plague will return and the natives will lament for their empty cities. The boar of trade will arrive and call the scattered flocks back to their lost pasture. His breast shall be food for the needy and his tongue drink for the thirsty. Out of his mouth will issue rivers to moisten the parched throats of men. Then a tree will grow above the tower of London, whose three branches will shade the surface of the whole island with their spreading leaves. The north wind will come as its enemy and its cruel blast will rip off the third branch. The remaining two will take its place until one chokes the other with its abundant foliage. Then it will replace the first two and feed birds from foreign lands. It will prove harmful to native birds; for they will not be able to fly freely in fear of its shadow. It will be succeeded by the ass of wickedness, swift against makers of gold, but slow against predatory wolves. In its time oak trees will burn in the forests and acorns will grow on the branches of lindens. The Severn estuary will flow through seven channels and the river Usk will boil for seven months. The heat will kill its fish and snakes will take their place. The springs of Bath will run cold and their healing waters will bring death. London will grieve for the demise of twenty thousand, and the Thames will turn to blood. The wearers of cowls will be challenged to marry, and their complaint will be heard in the mountains of the Alps.

116   Three springs will appear in the city of Winchester, and their streams will cut the island in three. Whoever drinks from the first will live a longer life, free from disease. Whoever drinks from the second will die of a thirst that cannot be quenched, and a ghastly pallor will appear on his face. Whoever drinks from the third will die a sudden death, and no one will be able to bury his body. To escape this menace, they will try to hide it under various things. Whatever is placed upon it will assume a different form. If earth is put over the spring, it will become stones, stones become water, wood become ashes and ash become water. In response, a girl will be sent forth from the city of the hoary forest to bring curing medicine. After she has tried all her arts, she will dry up the deadly springs with her breath alone. Then, after

hircus Venerii Castri, aurea habens cornua et argenteam barbam, qui ex naribus suis tantam efflabit nebulam quanta tota superficies insulae 120 obumbrabitur. Pax erit in tempore suo et ubertate glebae multiplicabuntur segetes. Mulieres incessu serpentes fient, et omnis gressus earum superbia replebitur. Renouabuntur castra Veneris, nec cessabunt sagittae Cupidinis uulnerare. Fons Annae uertetur in sanguinem, et duo reges duellum propter leaenam de Vado Baculi committent. Omnis humus luxuriabit, et 125 humanitas fornicari non desinet. Omnia haec tria saecula uidebunt donec sepulti reges in urbe Lundoniarum propalabuntur. Redibit iterum fames, redibit mortalitas, et desolationem urbium dolebunt ciues. Superueniet aper commercii, qui dispersos greges ad amissam pascuam reuocabit. Pectus eius cibus erit egentibus, et lingua eius sedabit sicientes. Ex ore 130 ipsius procedent flumina, quae arentes hominum fauces rigabunt. Exin super turrim Lundoniarum procreabitur arbor, quae tribus solummodo ramis contenta superficiem tocius insulae latitudine foliorum obumbrabit. Huic aduersarius Boreas superueniet atque iniquo flatu suo tercium illi ramum eripiet. Duo uero residui locum extirpati occupabunt donec alter 135 alterum foliorum multitudine adnichilabit. Deinde uero locum duorum optinebit ipse et uolucres exterarum regionum sustentabit. Patriis uolatilibus nociuus habebitur; nam timore umbrae eius liberos uolatus amittent. Succedet asinus nequitiae, in fabricatores auri uelox sed in luporum rapacitatem piger. In diebus illis ardebunt quercus per nemora 140 et in ramis tiliarum nascentur glandes. Sabrinum mare per septem hostia discurret, et fluuius Oscae per septem menses feruebit. Pisces illius calore morientur, et ex eis procreabuntur serpentes. Frigebunt Badonis balnea, et salubres aquae eorum mortem generabunt. Lundonia necem uiginti miliorum lugebit, et Tamensis in sanguinem mutabitur. Cucullati ad 145 nuptias prouocabuntur, et clamor eorum in montibus Alpium audietur.

116   Tres fontes in urbe Guintonia erumpent, quorum riuuli insulam in tres portiones secabunt. Qui bibet de uno diuturniori uita fruetur nec superuenienti languore grauabitur. Qui bibet de altero indeficienti fame peribit, et in facie ipsius pallor et horror sedebit. Qui bibet de tercio subita 150 morte periclitabitur, nec corpus ipsius subire poterit sepulchrum. Tantam ingluuiem uitare uolentes, diuersis tegumentis eam occultare nitentur. Quaecunque ergo moles superposita fuerit formam alterius corporis recipiet. Terra namque in lapides, lapides in limpham, lignum in cineres, cinis in aquam, si superiecta fuerint, uertentur. Ad haec ex urbe canuti 155 nemoris eliminabitur puella ut medelae curam adhibeat. Quae ut omnes artes inierit, solo anhelitu suo fontes nociuos siccabit. Exin, ut sese

---

127 Lundoniae *M:* Lundonia ζ
128 desolationem *CSE YH Π:* -tium *O:* -tione *M G*
129 amissa pascua *OE WG* ζβρθ
138 habebitur *Δ WYHG Π:* erit *M*
140 rapacitatem luporum *Π*
144 illorum λβρθ
145 milium *M H:* .m. *Y:* milia β
149 superueniente *C²S Π*
149 indeficiente *S¹E Π*
150 bibit *OC*
151 poterit subire *M* ζ

refreshing herself with healing water, she will bear in her right hand the forest of Colidon and in her left the battlements of London's walls. Wherever she goes, she will leave tracks of sulphur, which will burn with a double flame. Their smoke will rouse the Flemings and provide food for the creatures of the deep. She will be drenched with pitiful tears and fill the island with a terrible cry. She will be killed by a stag with ten branches, four of which will wear golden crowns, while the remaining six will become the horns of buffalos and stir up Britain's three islands with their dreadful sound. The forest of Dean will awaken and shout in a human voice: "come, Wales, stand with Cornwall at your side, and say to Winchester, 'the earth will swallow you up; move the seat of your shepherd to the place where ships land, and let the remaining limbs follow the head; the day is at hand when your citizens will perish because of their sins of betrayal; the whiteness of wool and the many colours it has been dyed have done you harm; woe to the treacherous people on whose account a famous city will fall'". The ships will rejoice at this great increment and two will become one. The city will be rebuilt by a hedgehog laden with fragrant apples, to which the birds will flock from various forests. It will add a huge palace, fortified with six hundred towers. London will be filled with envy and will increase its walls threefold. The Thames will form a moat around the city, and the fame of this feat will penetrate beyond the Alps. The hedgehog will hide his apples there and construct pathways beneath the earth. At that time stones will speak and the sea where one sails to France will become a narrow strait. Men will call from shore to shore and the island's surface will grow larger. The secrets of the deep will be revealed, and France will tremble in fear. Afterwards a heron will emerge from the forest of Calaterium and will circle the island for two years. At night it will summon the birds of the air with its cry and assemble all their species. They will fall upon men's crops and eat all the grains of corn. The people will be afflicted by hunger and after that by a deadly plague. When this calamity is over, the accursed bird will visit the valley of Galahes and raise it into a lofty mountain. At the summit the heron will plant an oak and nest in its branches. In the nest it will lay three eggs, from which will hatch a fox, a wolf and a bear. The fox will devour its mother and wear the head of an ass. In this unnatural form it will frighten its brothers and drive them off to Normandy. They will stir up a tusked boar against it and sail back with a fleet to fight the fox. In the battle the fox will feign death and

salubri liquore refecerit, gestabit in dextera sua nemus Colidonis, in sinistra uero murorum Lundoniae propugnacula. Quacumque incedet passus sulphureos faciet, qui dupplici flamma fumabunt. Fumus ille 160 excitabit Rutenos et cibum submarinis conficiet. Lacrimis miserandis manabit ipsa et clamore horrido replebit insulam. Interficiet eam ceruus decem ramorum, quorum quatuor aurea diademata gestabunt, sex uero residui in cornua bubalorum uertentur, quae nefando sonitu tres insulas Britanniae commouebunt. Excitabitur Daneum nemus et in humanam 165 uocem erumpens clamabit "accede, Kambria, et iunge lateri tuo Cornubiam, et dic Guintoniae 'absorbebit te tellus; transfer sedem pastoris ubi naues applicant, et cetera membra caput sequantur; festinat namque dies qua ciues ob scelera periurii peribunt; candor lanarum nocuit atque tincturae ipsarum diuersitas; uae periurae genti, quia urbs 170 inclita propter eam ruet'". Gaudebunt naues augmentatione tanta, et unum ex duobus fiet. Reaedificabit eam hericius oneratus pomis, ad quorum odorem diuersorum nemorum conuolabunt uolucres. Adiciet palacium ingens et sexcentis turribus illud uallabit. Inuidebit ergo Lundonia et muros suos tripliciter augebit. Circuibit eam undique 175 Tamensis fluuius, et rumor operis transcendet Alpes. Occultabit infra illam hericius poma sua et subterraneas uias machinabitur. In tempore illo loquentur lapides et mare quo ad Galliam nauigatur infra breue spacium contrahetur. In utraque ripa audietur homo ab homine, et solidum insulae dilatabitur. Reuelabuntur occulta submarinorum, et Gallia prae 180 timore tremebit. Post haec ex Calaterio nemore procedet ardea, quae insulam per biennium circumuolabit. Nocturno clamore conuocabit uolatilia et omne genus uolucrum associabit sibi. In culturas mortalium irruent et omnia grana messium deuorabunt. Sequetur fames populum atque dira mortalitas famem. At cum calamitas tanta cessauerit, adibit 185 detestabilis ales uallem Galahes atque eam in excelsum montem leuabit. In cacumine quoque ipsius plantabit quercum atque infra ramos nidificabit. Tria oua procreabuntur in nido, ex quibus uulpes et lupus et ursus egredientur. Deuorabit uulpes matrem et asininum caput gestabit. Monstro igitur assumpto, terrebit fratres suos ipsosque in Neustriam 190 fugabit. At ipsi excitabunt aprum dentosum in illa et nauigio reuecti cum uulpe congredientur. Quae cum certamen inierit, finget se defunctam et

160 ille *Ω:* exortus *Π*
161 excaecabit *W*
162 ipsa *Ω:* puella *Π*
165 Excitabunt *G β*
168 [caput] *M Y*
170 [ipsarum] *Π*
174 illud uallabit *Δ θ:* ipsum uallabit *M ζλβϱ:* uallabit illud *WYHG: sequitur in Π* In una quaque statuetur decurio qui leges subditis dabit, *errore ut uid. in Ω omissum ('Transm.' 95-6, Introd. ix)*
178 illo *Δ WYHG:* suo *M Π*
184 genera *C² WY β*
188 Quatuor *ζλβϱ¹*
188 uulpis *M G Π*
189 uulpis *λβϱθ*
191 illam *M ζθ*

move the boar to pity. It will approach the fox's body and, standing over it, will breathe into its eyes and face. But the fox, mindful of its old cunning, will bite the boar's left foot and tear it from its body. Then, leaping up, it will bite off its right ear and tail and hide in the mountain-caves. The tricked boar will demand that the wolf and bear restore its lost limbs. Plotting together, they will promise it two feet and ears and a tail to replace the boar's members. The boar will consent and await their restitution. Meanwhile the fox will come down from the mountains, transform itself into the wolf and, after cunningly approaching as if to talk with the boar, will eat all that remains of him. Next it will disguise itself as the dismembered boar and await its brothers. When they arrive, it will swiftly bite them also to death and be crowned with a lion's head. In its time will be born a snake which will threaten men with death. It will coil itself around London and devour all who pass by. A mountain-ox will put on the head of the wolf and polish its teeth in the Severn's forge. It will ally itself to the flocks of Scotland and Wales, which will drink the Thames dry. An ass will summon a shaggy-bearded goat and borrow its form. The mountain-ox will be angry, summon the wolf, and gore them like a horned bull. After this savage deed, it will eat their flesh and bones, but will be burned on the height of Urian. The sparks from its funeral pyre will become swans, which will swim on dry land as if on a river. They will eat fish upon fish and devour man upon man. In old age they will become pikes beneath the sea and set traps there. They will sink ships and amass much silver. The Thames will flood again, summoning the rivers and bursting its banks. It will hide neighbouring cities and overthrow mountains in its path. It will have as its ally the spring of Galahes, full of wicked treachery. From it will arise strife, which will provoke the Venedoti to fight. The trees of the forests will gather to do battle with the stones of the Gewissei. A crow will swoop with kites to devour the corpses of the slain. An owl will build its nest on the walls of Gloucester and an ass will be born in it. The snake of Malvern will foster the ass and inspire it to many acts of trickery. It will assume the crown, mount on high and terrify the inhabitants of the land with its braying. In its time the mountains of Pacau will be shaken and the regions

aprum in pietatem mouebit. Mox adibit ipse cadauer et dum superstabit
anhelabit in oculos eius et faciem. At ipsa, non oblita praeteriti doli,
mordebit sinistrum pedem ipsius totumque ex corpore euellet. Saltu   195
quoque facto, eripiet ei dexteram aurem et caudam et infra cauernas
montium delitebit. Aper ergo illusus requiret lupum et ursum ut ei amissa
membra restituant. Qui ut causam inierint, promittent ei duos pedes et
aures et caudam et ex eis porcina membra component. Acquiescet ipse
promissamque restaurationem expectabit. Interim descendet uulpes de   200
montibus et sese in lupum mutabit et quasi colloquium habitura cum apro
adibit illum callide et ipsum totum deuorabit. Exin transuertet sese in
aprum et quasi sine membris expectabit germanos. Sed et ipsos postquam
aduenerint subito dente interficiet atque capite leonis coronabitur. In
diebus eius nascetur serpens, quae neci mortalium imminebit. Longitudine   205
sua circuibit Lundoniam et quosque praetereuntes deuorabit. Bos
montanus caput lupi assumet dentesque suos in fabrica Sabrinae dealbabit.
Associabit sibi greges Albanorum et Kambriae, qui Tamensem potando
siccabunt. Vocabit asinus hircum prolixae barbae et formam ipsius
mutuabit. Indignabitur igitur montanus uocatoque lupo cornutus taurus   210
in ipsos fiet. Vt autem saeuitiae indulserit, deuorabit carnes eorum et ossa
sed in cacumine Vriani cremabitur. Fauillae rogi mutabuntur in cignos,
qui in sicco quasi in flumine natabunt. Deuorabunt pisces in piscibus et
homines in hominibus deglutient. Superueniente uero senectute,
efficientur submarini luces atque submarinas insidias machinabuntur.   215
Submergent naualia et argentum non minimum congregabunt. Fluctuabit
iterum Tamensis conuocatisque fluminibus ultra metas aluei procedet.
Vrbes uicinas occultabit oppositosque montes subuertet. Adhibebit sibi
fontem Galahes dolo et nequitia repleti. Orientur ex eo seditiones,
prouocantes Venedotos ad proelia. Conuenient nemorum robora et cum   220
saxis Gewisseorum congredientur. Aduolabit coruus cum miluis et
corpora peremptorum deuorabit. Super muros Claudiocestriae nidificabit
bubo, et in nido suo procreabitur asinus. Educabit illum serpens
Maluerniae et in plures dolos commouebit. Sumpto diademate,
transcendet excelsa et horrido racanatu populum patriae terrebit. In   225
diebus eius titubabunt montes Pacau et prouinciae nemoribus suis

193 pietate *M G*
193 [et] *Δ WYH*
post 194 faciem *deficit* λ
200 uulpis *M G* ζ*[β]*ϱθ
201 mactabit *OCS* ζ¹
202 callide et *15:* callide *Δ M YH* ζ*:* et callide *G [β]*ϱθ
202 ipsumque *M Y*
204 subita *O M*
205 qui *E M WYH* ζϱθ
210 cornutus *WG* βϱθ*:* cornu *Δ YH* ζ*:* cornua *M*
211 figet *M YH, non male si abesset* taurus
215 luces *pro 'lucii' ut uid. (cf. TLL 'lucius'):* duces *G*
218 opsitos- *C ,* obsitos- *SE* ζ
219 galahes *O M HG: lac. C: om. SE¹:* galaes *E²* ζ*:* galabes *β:* galathes ϱ*:* galeas θ
219 repleti *OCS M WY* ζϱ*:* repletus *G* βθ*:* repletos *H:* repletum *E*
225 recanatu *HG* θ*:* rachatu ζ*:* rachanatu βϱ
226 Pacau *M HG:* Pacaii *Y* ϱ*: lac. OC: om. SE:* Pacuuii ζ*:* Pachaii βθ

stripped of their forests. For a fire-breathing worm will come and the heat it emits will burn the trees. From it will emerge seven lions, disfigured with the heads of goats. By the stench of their nostrils they will corrupt women and turn wives into whores. Fathers will not recognise their own sons, because they will rut like animals. An evil giant will arrive and terrify everybody with his flashing eyes. The dragon of Worcester will rise up and try to drive him out. When they fight, the dragon will be beaten, overwhelmed by the victor's wickedness. For he will mount the dragon and, casting off his clothes, will ride naked upon it. The dragon will carry the naked giant into the heavens and strike him with its thrashing tail. Recovering his strength, the giant will smash its jaws with his sword. Finally the dragon will die of poison, entangled beneath its own tail. After it will come the boar of Totnes, which will crush the people with its terrible despotism. Gloucester will send forth a lion, which will make several assaults on the raging boar. The lion will trample it beneath his feet and frighten it with his gaping maw. At length the lion will quarrel with the kingdom and mount over the backs of the nobles. A bull will intervene in the quarrel and strike the lion with his right foot. It will drive the lion through the by-ways of the kingdom, but will break its horns on the walls of Exeter. The fox of Caerdubalum will avenge the lion and with its teeth devour the bull whole. The serpent of Lincoln will encircle the fox and with dreadful hissing signal its presence to several dragons. Then the dragons will fight and tear one another to pieces. The winged dragon will overcome the wingless, and fasten its claws into its poisonous cheeks. Two others will join the battle and each will kill the other. The dead will be succeeded by a fifth person. He will crush the rest by various stratagems. He will climb on the back of one dragon with his sword and sever its head from its body. Stripping off his clothes, he will mount another and grasp its tail with both his right and left hands. Once naked, he will master it, though, when clothed, he achieved nothing. He will torture the rest from behind and drive them around the kingdom. A roaring lion will arrive, terrifying in his dreadful ferocity. He will reduce fifteen shares to one and take the people for himself. A giant will shine with brilliant whiteness and beget a white people. Luxury will corrupt princes and their subjects will become beasts. A lion sated with human blood will rise up against them. A wielder of the scythe will replace him in the corn, but, while he toils with his mind, he will be overcome by the lion. Both will be calmed by the chariot-driver of York, who will expel his master and mount the chariot he leads. Drawing his sword, he will threaten the east and fill the tracks of his wheels with blood. Then he will become a fish in the sea, and be called back by a hissing serpent, with which he will mate. Their offspring will be three flashing bulls, who will eat up their pastures and become trees. The eldest will bear a scourge of vipers and will turn his back on the second. The latter will try to seize his whip, but will be chastised by the third.

spoliabuntur. Superueniet namque uermis ignei anhelitus, qui emisso
uapore comburet arbores. Egredientur ex eo septem leones capitibus
hircorum turpati. Fetore narium mulieres corrumpent et proprias
communes facient. Nesciet pater filium proprium, quia more pecudum   230
lasciuient. Superueniet uero gigas nequiciae, qui oculorum acumine
terrebit uniuersos. Exurget in illum draco Wigorniae et eum exterminare
conabitur. Facto autem congressu, superabitur draco et nequitia uictoris
opprimetur. Ascendet namque draconem et exuta ueste insidebit nudus.
Feret illum ad sublimia draco erectaque cauda uerberabit nudatum.   235
Resumpto iterum uigore, gigas fauces illius cum gladio confringet.
Implicabitur tandem sub cauda sua draco et uenenatus interibit. Succedet
post illum Totonesius aper et dira tirannide opprimet populum. Eliminabit
Claudiocestria leonem, qui diuersis proeliis inquietabit saeuientem.
Conculcabit eum sub pedibus suis apertisque faucibus terrebit. Cum   240
regno tandem litigabit leo et terga nobilium transcendet. Superueniet
taurus litigio et leonem dextro pede percutiet. Expellet illum per regni
diuersatoria sed cornua sua in muros Exoniae confringet. Vindicabit
leonem uulpes Caerdubali et totum suis dentibus consumet. Circumcinget
eam Lindocolinus coluber praesentiamque suam draconibus multis   245
horribili sibilo testabitur. Congredientur deinde dracones et alter alterum
dilaniet. Opprimet alatus carentem alis et ungues in genas uenenatas
configet. Ad certamen conuenient alii, et alius alium interficiet. Succedet
quintus interfectis. Residuos diuersis machinationibus confringet.
Transcendet dorsum unius cum gladio et caput a corpore separabit. Exuta   250
ueste, ascendet alium et dexteram caudae laeuamque iniciet. Superabit
eum nudus, cum nichil indutus proficeret. Ceteros tormentabit a dorso et
in rotunditatem regni compellet. Superueniet leo rugiens immani feritate
timendus. Ter quinque portiones in unum reducet et solus possidebit
populum. Splendebit gigas colore niueo et candidum populum germinabit.   255
Deliciae principes eneruabunt, et subditi in beluas mutabuntur. Orietur in
illis leo humano cruore turgidus. Supponetur ei in segete falcifer, qui
dum laborabit mente opprimetur ab illo. Sedabit illos Eboracensis auriga
expulsoque domino in currum quem ducit ascendet. Abstracto gladio,
minabitur orienti et rotarum suarum uestigia replebit sanguine. Fiet   260
deinde piscis in aequore, qui sibilo serpentis reuocatus coibit cum illo.
Nascentur inde tres tauri fulgurantes, qui consumptis pascuis conuertentur
in arbores. Gestabit primus flagellum uipereum et a postgenito dorsum
suum diuertet. Nitetur ipse flagellum ei eripere sed ab ultimo corripietur.

231 uero *CSE M WH* ζ: ergo *O* βϱθ: igitur *G: om. Y*
235 electaque *OCS¹*
post 237 interibit deficit β
243 diuersoria *E G* ζθ
244 uulpis *G* ζθ
244 dentibus suis *C* ζ
249 residuosque *Y* θ
250 unius *CSE M G* ζϱθ: illius *O:* tertius *H:* uiuus *Y*
255 et ϱ: ad *OCS Y* ζ: et ad *E G* θ: at *M:* ac *W, sed deest in Prophetiis*
257 falcifer *WYHG* θ: falufer *Δ* ζ²: saltifer *M* ϱ: salufer *E* ζ¹
263 a postgenito *CSE M* ζθ: postgenito *O YH:* aprogenito *G* ϱ

They will all turn their faces away from each other until they cast forth the goblet of poison. They will be succeeded by a farmer of Scotland, behind whom will loom a snake. The farmer will devote himself to ploughing the land so that the regions are white with corn. The snake will toil to spread its poison and to prevent the plants coming to harvest. The people will die in this fatal disaster and the walls of cities will stand empty. A remedy will be found in the city of Claudius, which will send the daughter of the whip-bearer. She will carry a platter of medicine, and the island will quickly be restored. Then two will bear the sceptre in succession, served by a horned dragon. Another will come in iron and ride the flying serpent. Exposing his body, he will sit on its back and grasp its tail in his right hand. His cry will rouse the seas, which will inspire fear for a second time. The second will ally himself with a lion, but they will quarrel and fight. Both will suffer setbacks at the other's hand, but the savage beast will prevail. Someone will intervene with timbrel and lute, and soothe the lion's rage. So the nations of the kingdom will be at peace and bring the lion to the platter. Taking his seat, he will apply himself to the provisions, but stretch out his palms to Scotland. The northern provinces will be saddened by this and the entrances of the temples unlocked. A wolf bearing a standard will lead out his companies and curl his tail around Cornwall. He will be opposed by a knight in a chariot, who will turn the Cornish into a boar. The boar will lay regions waste, but hide his head in the depths of the Severn. A man will embrace a lion in wine, and the glint of gold will blind the eyes of those who behold it. Silver will gleam all around and trouble various wine-presses.

117 When the wine has been served, mortals befuddled with drink will neglect the heavens and gaze at the ground. The planets will look away from men and alter their customary paths. Because of their wrath crops will wither and rain not fall from the sky. Roots will change place with branches, and people will marvel at the strange sight. The brightness of the sun will be outshone by Mercury's amber, to the horror of observers. Arcadian Stilbon will change his shield, and Mars' helmet will summon Venus. Mars' helmet will cast a shadow, and Mercury's rage will know no bounds. Steely Orion will unsheathe his sword, and a watery sun will trouble the clouds. Jupiter will turn from his permitted course, and Venus abandon her established paths. The spite of Saturn's star will rain down and slaughter mortals with a curved scythe. The twelvefold band that is home to the stars will weep to see its travellers run amok in this way. The Twins will forgo their usual embraces and call Aquarius to the spring. The scales of Libra will hang awry until Aries supports them with his curved horns. Lightning bolts will flash from Scorpio's tail and Cancer will quarrel with the sun. Virgo will mount on Sagittarius' back and defile her virginal flowers. The moon's chariot will disrupt the zodiac and the Pleiades burst into tears. Janus will not perform his duties, but will close his door and hide in the precinct of Ariadne. In the flash of its beam, the seas will rise and the dust of the long-dead will be reborn. The winds will contend with a terrible blast and the stars will hear them howl'.

Auertent mutuo a sese facies donec uenenatum cifum proiecerint.   265
Succedet eis colonus Albaniae, cui a dorso imminebit serpens. Vacabit
ipse tellurem subuertere ut patriae segetibus candeant. Laborabit serpens
uenenum diffundere ne herbae in messes proueniant. Letali clade deficiet
populus, et moenia urbium desolabuntur. Dabitur in remedium Vrbs
Claudii, quae alumpnam flagellantis interponet. Stateram namque   270
medicinae gestabit et in breui renouabitur insula. Deinde duo subsequentur
sceptrum, quibus cornutus draco ministrabit. Adueniet alter in ferro et
uolantem equitabit serpentem. Nudato corpore, insidebit dorso et
dexteram caudae iniciet. Clamore ipsius excitabuntur maria et timorem
secundo inicient. Secundus itaque sociabitur leoni, sed exorta lite   275
congressum facient. Mutuis cladibus succumbent mutuo, sed feritas
beluae praeualebit. Superueniet quidam in timpano et cythara et
demulcebit leonis saeuiciam. Pacificabuntur ergo nationes regni et
leonem ad stateram prouocabunt. Locata sede, ad pensas studebit sed
palmas in Albaniam extendet. Tristabuntur ergo aquilonares prouinciae   280
et hostia templorum reserabunt. Signifer lupus conducet turmas et
Cornubiam cauda sua circumcinget. Resistet ei miles in curru, qui
populum illum in aprum mutabit. Vastabit igitur aper prouincias sed in
profundo Sabrinae occultabit caput. Amplexabitur homo leonem in uino,
et fulgor auri oculos intuentium excaecabit. Candebit argentum in circuitu   285
et diuersa torcularia uexabit. Imposito uino, inebriabuntur mortales
postpositoque caelo in terram respicient. Ab eis uultus auertent sydera et
solitum cursum confundent. Arebunt segetes his indignantibus, et humor
conuexi negabitur. Radices et rami uices mutabunt, nouitasque rei erit in
miraculum. Splendor solis electro Mercurii languebit, et erit horror   290
inspicientibus. Mutabit clipeum Stilbon Archadiae, uocabit Venerem
galea Martis. Galea Martis umbram conficiet, transibit terminos furor
Mercurii. Nudabit ensem Orion ferreus, uexabit nubes Phoebus aequoreus.
Exibit Iupiter licitas semitas, et Venus deseret statutas lineas. Saturni
sideris liuido corruet et falce recurua mortales perimet. Bissenus numerus   295
domorum siderum deflebit hospites ita transcurrere. Obmittent Gemini
complexus solitos et Vrnam in fontes prouocabunt. Pensa Librae oblique
pendebunt donec Aries recurua cornua sua supponat. Cauda Scorpionis
procreabit fulgura, et Cancer cum sole litigabit. Ascendet Virgo dorsum
Sagittarii et flores uirgineos obfuscabit. Currus lunae turbabit zodiacum,   300
et in fletum prorumpent Pleiades. Officia Iani nulla redibunt, sed clausa
ianua in crepidinibus Adriannae delitebit. In ictu radii exurgent aequora,
et puluis ueterum renouabitur. Confligent uenti diro sufflamine et sonitum
inter sidera conficient'.

117

---

265 cisum *OCE:* cibum *θ*
267 paterae *OSE*
275 iniciet *G ζθ*
280 aquilones *(-nis O) Δ ζ:* aquilonales *ϱ*
281 reserabuntur *C G*
282 causa *C¹SE*
285 fulgur *Δ M H ϱ*
301 officia *54:* officio *Ω ζϱθ*
301 iam *E H*
302 delitebunt *Δ*

BOOK EIGHT

118 Merlin foretold these things and more, and his riddling words reduced the
bystanders to amazement. Vortigern was the most amazed of all and praised
the insight of the youth's prophecies. No man of his time had spoken so
wonderfully in his presence. Wishing to know how his life would end, he
asked Merlin to tell him what he knew. Merlin answered:

> 'Beware the fire of Constantinus' sons, if you can. Even now they are
> preparing their ships, leaving the shores of Armorica and setting their
> sails for the crossing. They will land on this island, attack the Saxons and
> conquer that wicked race; but first they will besiege your tower and burn
> you in it. Your betrayal of their father and the summoning of the Saxons
> to Britain have recoiled upon you. You invited them to protect you, but
> they became your scourge. You face two deaths, and it is not easy to tell
> which you will escape first. On the one hand the Saxons are laying your
> kingdom waste, eager to kill you, on the other the two brothers Aurelius
> and Uther are landing to try to avenge their father's death upon you. Take
> refuge if you can. Tomorrow they will come ashore at Totnes. The faces of
> the Saxons will be red with blood, and Hengest will be killed and Aurelius
> Ambrosius crowned. He will pacify the people and rebuild the churches,
> but will die by poison. His brother Uther Pendragon will succeed him, but
> his days will also be cut short by poison. Your offspring will have a share
> in this treason, before the boar of Cornwall devours them'.

As soon as the next day dawned, Aurelius Ambrosius and his brother
landed, accompanied by ten thousand knights.

119   As news of his landing spread, the Britons assembled from all the places
to which the recent disasters had scattered them and were strengthened and
encouraged by the sight of their fellow-countrymen. Summoning the clergy,
they anointed Aurelius king and duly did homage to him. They wanted to
attack the Saxons, but the king disagreed; he preferred to pursue Vortigern
first. He was so aggrieved by the betrayal of his father that he felt that
nothing would be achieved unless he first took revenge on Vortigern. With
this end in view, he directed his army to Wales and made his way to the
castle of Genoriu; Vortigern had fled there, seeking safe refuge. The castle
was in the region of Hergign on a hill named Doartius above the river Wye.
When he arrived there, Aurelius, remembering how his father and brother
had been betrayed, said to Eldol duke of Gloucester:

LIBER VIII

118 Cum igitur haec et alia prophetasset Merlinus, ambiguitate uerborum suorum astantes in ammirationem commouit. Vortegirnus uero prae ceteris ammirans et sensum iuuenis et uaticinia collaudat. Neminem enim praesens aetas produxerat qui ora sua in hunc modum coram ipso soluisset. Scire igitur uolens exitum uitae suae, rogauit iuuenem sibi indicare quod sciebat. 5 Ad haec Merlinus:

'Ignem filiorum Constantini diffuge, si diffugere ualueris. Iam naues parant, iam Armoricanum litus deserunt, iam uela per aequora pandunt. Petent Britanniam insulam, inuadent Saxonicam gentem, subiugabunt nefandum populum; sed te prius infra turrim inclusum comburent. Malo 10 tuo patrem eorum prodidisti et Saxones infra insulam inuitasti. Inuitasti ipsos tibi in praesidium, sed superuenerunt in tuum supplicium. Imminent tibi duo funera, nec est promptum quod prius uitabis. Hinc enim regnum tuum deuastant Saxones et leto tuo incumbunt, hinc autem applicant duo fratres, Aurelius et Vther, qui mortem patris sui in te uindicare nitentur. 15 Quaere tibi diffugium si poteris. Cras Totonesium litus tenebunt. Rubebunt sanguine Saxonum facies, et interfecto Hengisto Aurelius Ambrosius coronabitur. Pacificabit nationes, restaurabit ecclesias, sed ueneno deficiet. Succedet ei germanus suus Vther Pendragon, cuius dies anticipabuntur ueneno. Aderunt tantae proditioni posteri tui, quos aper 20 Cornubiae deuorabit'.

Nec mora, cum crastina dies illuxit, applicuit Aurelius Ambrosius cum germano suo, decem milibus militum comitatus.

119   Rumore itaque aduentus ipsius diuulgato, conuenerunt undique Britones, qui in tanta clade dispersi fuerant, et societate conciuium suorum 25 roborati hilariores solito efficiuntur. Conuocato autem clero, inunxerunt Aurelium in regem et sese sibi more suo submiserunt. Cumque impetum in Saxones fieri cohortarentur, dissuasit rex; nam prius Vortegirnum persequi affectauerat. Adeo enim propter proditionem patri illatam doluerat quod nil agere uideretur nisi ipsum prius uindicaret. Affectum itaque suum exequi 30 desiderans, conuertit exercitum suum in Kambriam oppidumque Genoriu petiuit; diffugerat enim eo Vortegirnus ut tutum refugium haberet. Erat autem oppidum illud in natione Hergign super fluuium Guaiae in monte qui Doartius nuncupatur. Vt igitur ad illud peruenit Ambrosius, proditionis patri ac fratri illatae reminiscens Eldol ducem Claudiocestriae affatur: 35

In §§ 118-208 citantur Δ (unde pendent OCSE, H inde a § 137.506 Commansit), Σ (unde pendent UAKND), Φ (unde pendent QYGM, H usque ad § 137.505 adesse)

Expliciunt prophetie Merlini. Sequitur liber .viii. unde supra M: *tit. nullus in UA: in cett. nihil notabile*

1 Dum *QM*
10 prius te *Φ*
22-3 [cum germano ... comitatus] *Σ Φ*
27 more solito *E K*
34 Cloartius *OC A(?) Φ, sed cf. Tatlock 72-3*

'Consider, noble duke, whether the towers and walls of this city can protect Vortigern and prevent me from thrusting my sharp sword into his vitals with my own hand. He deserves to die, and I think you know the reason. That most wicked of men ought to perish through exquisite torture. First he betrayed my father Constantinus, who had saved him and our country from the invading Picts; then he betrayed my brother Constans, having made him king in order to do so; finally, after his cunning had won him the crown, he infiltrated pagans among our countrymen to drive out those who had remained faithful to me. But God ensured that he fell blindly into the trap he had set for his own subjects. Once the Saxons discovered his wickedness, they drove him from the kingdom, an act that ought to be applauded by all. I think, however, that we ought to be sorry that a wicked people, called in by that wicked king, has driven out our noble countrymen, laid waste our fertile land, destroyed our holy churches and wiped out the Christian faith almost from shore to shore. So now, Britons, show your courage and first avenge yourselves on the author of all these disasters. Then let us turn our weapons upon the enemies who threaten us, and free our country from their greedy hands'.

They immediately tried various devices to break down the walls. When all else failed, they resorted to fire. Once set, it took hold and consumed the tower and Vortigern with it.

120   When this news reached Hengest and the Saxons, he was filled with terror, since he feared Aurelius' prowess. Such was his strength and boldness that, when he had been in France. no one had dared to face him. If they had, Aurelius would have toppled them from their horses or splintered their lances. Furthermore he was a generous giver, attentive to divine offices, moderate in all things and averse in particular to falsehood; he was a fine warrior on foot, better on horseback and a skilled commander of armies. Fame had incessantly winged the news of his virtues to the island while he still resided in Brittany. In fear of him, therefore, the Saxons retreated behind the Humber. There they fortified cities and towns; the region had always provided them with a refuge. They were further protected by the proximity of Scotland, a continual deadly threat to the British. It was an inhospitable place, devoid of Britons, but readily accessible to foreigners. Its very position had made it suitable for Picts, Scots, Danes, Norsemen and the others who landed to lay the island waste; reassured by the nearness of that country, the Saxons retreated towards it, to retire there, if necessary, as if to a welcoming base. When Aurelius learned of this, he was encouraged to hope for victory. He swiftly

'Respice, dux nobilis, huius urbis turres et moenia utrum poterint
Vortegirnum protegere quin gladii mei mucronem ipse infra uiscera ipsius
recondam. Promeruit enim necem, nec tibi ignotum esse existimo ipsum
eam promeruisse. O hominem omnium sceleratissimum, o ineffabilibus
tormentis perdendum! Primo prodidit patrem meum Constantinum, qui   40
ipsum et patriam a Pictorum irruptione liberauerat; deinde Constantem
fratrem meum, quem ut proderet in regem promouit; denique, cum
ipsemet uersutia sua insignitus fuisset, intromisit cum conciuibus paganos
ut ipsos qui fidelitati meae adhaerebant exterminaret. Sed permittente
Deo in laqueum quem fidelibus suis parauerat incautus cecidit. Nam ut   45
nequitiam ipsius compererunt Saxones, eiecerunt illum ex regno, quod
neminem pigere debeat. Illud uero dolendum censeo, quod nefandus
populus quem nefandus ille inuitauit nobiles ciues exterminauit, fertilem
patriam deuastauit, sacras ecclesias destruxit, et Christianitatem fere a
mari usque ad mare deleuit. Nunc igitur, ciues, uiriliter agite et uindicate   50
uos in istum prius, per quem haec omnia accesserunt. Deinde uertamus
arma in hostes imminentes et patriam ab eorum ingluuie liberemus'.

Nec mora, diuersis machinationibus incumbunt, moenia diruere nituntur.
Postremo, cum cetera defecissent, ignem adhibuerunt. Qui cum alimentum
reperisset, non quieuit adiunctus donec turrim et Vortegirnum exarsit.   55

120   Quod cum Hengisto Saxonibusque suis relatum esset, inuasit eum timor,
quia probitatem Aurelii timebat. Tanta namque uirtus et audatia uiro inerat
quod dum Galliarum partes frequentaret non erat alter qui cum illo congredi
auderet. Nam si congressum fecisset, uel hostem ab equo prosterneret uel
hastam in frusta confringeret. Praeterea largus erat in dandis, sedulus in   60
diuinis obsequiis, modestus in cunctis, et super omnia mendatium uitans,
fortis pede, fortior equo, et ad regendum exercitum doctus. Tales probitates
ipsius, dum adhuc in Armoricana Britannia moraretur, fama assiduis
uolatibus in insulam detulerat. Timuerunt igitur eum Saxones et sese trans
Humbrum receperunt. In partibus illis munierunt ciuitates et oppida; nam   65
patria illa semper refugio eis patuerat. Vicinitas etenim Scotiae tutelam
adhibebat, quae in omne dampnum ciuium imminere consueuerat. Natio
namque ad inhabitandum horribilis, euacuata ciuibus, tutum receptaculum
alienigenis praestauerat. Siquidem Pictis, Scotis, Dacis, Norguegensibus,
ceterisque qui ad uastandam insulam applicuerant, situ locorum annitente   70
patuerat; securi igitur affinitatis patriae, uersus illam diffugerant, ut si opus
fuisset sese infra eam quasi in propria castra recepissent. Cumque id Aurelio
indicatum fuisset, audatior effectus spem uictoriae recepit. Ocius ergo

36 urbis *(ante* huius *K)* turres et *Δ Σ:* urbes et *Q:* loci urbes et *YH:* urbis *GM*
46 comperuerunt *OC*
47 debeat *OCS UND QGM:* debebat *AK YH:* deberet *E*
53 <a> diuersis *U:* admensis *N*
54 Qui *69, 86, 113, 167:* Quod *Ω (cf. Introd. ad § 24.17)*
55 adquieuit *Φ, sed cf. § 184.137, ubi Gildam 24.1 propius sequitur*
63 Armorica *Φ*
66-7 adhibebat tutelam *Σ Φ*

gathered the Britons to increase his army and force-marched to the North. As he passed through the countryside, he was distressed by the devastation, and especially by churches razed to the ground; he promised to repair them if he was victorious.

121   When Hengest heard that Aurelius was coming, he recovered his nerve and encouraged each of his chosen companions, telling them to fight bravely and not to fear Aurelius' onset. He said that Aurelius had few Breton soldiers, who did not number more than ten thousand; the Britons of the island Hengest discounted, since he had overcome them in battle so often. For that reason he promised his soldiers victory, assured by their superiority in numbers; some two hundred thousand of them were under arms. With this encouragement, he went to meet Aurelius on the plain called Maisbeli, where he was sure to pass. Hengest planned a sudden, concealed assault to catch the Britons unawares. But he did not deceive Aurelius, who, undaunted, made all the more haste to reach the plain. Once Aurelius saw the enemy, he drew up his forces. He ordered three thousand of the Bretons to remain mounted, the rest he distributed along the British line. He placed the Demetae on the hills and the Venedoti in nearby woods. His aim was for them to cut off any Saxons fleeing in those directions.

122   Meanwhile Eldol duke of Gloucester approached the king, saying:

'I would gladly exchange my whole life for the day on which God permits me to fight Hengest. One of us would certainly die, once we had crossed swords. I remember the day when we met to discuss peace. While the talks progressed, he betrayed us all and killed with knives everybody except me, because I found a staff and thus escaped. On that day there perished four hundred and eighty barons and earls, who had all come unarmed. In this extremity, God provided me with a staff, to defend myself and escape'.

Such were Eldol's words, but Aurelius urged his comrades to let all their hopes rest on the Son of God, then to attack the enemy boldly and fight all together for their country.

123   Opposite them Hengest marshalled his forces, arranging them for battle and visiting each formation to inspire the same fighting spirit in each one. When at last both armies were ready, the lines met, exchanging blows and spilling much blood. On both sides Britons and Saxons were wounded and fell. Aurelius encouraged the Christians, Hengest the pagans. While the battle raged, Eldol strove continually to get a chance to attack Hengest, but without success. For, when Hengest saw that his men were losing, and that God meant the British to win, he immediately retreated towards the town of Kaerconan, today called Conisbrough.

conuocatis ciuibus, exercitum suum augmentauit atque uersus aquilonares
prouincias iter arripuit. Et cum nationes praeteriret, inspiciens eas desolatas   75
condolebat, maxime autem propter ecclesias usque ad solum destructas;
quibus restaurationem promittebat si triumpho potiretur.

121   At Hengistus, cum aduentum ipsius comperisset, reuocata audatia
commilitones suos elegit atque unumquemque inanimans hortabatur eos
uiriliter resistere nec congressum Aurelii Ambrosii abhorrere. Dicebat   80
autem ipsum paucos ex Armoricanis Britonibus habere, cum numerus
eorum ultra decem milia non procederet; insulanos uero Britones pro
nichilo reputabat, cum tociens eos in proeliis deuicisset. Proinde promittebat
suis uictoriam et ob ampliorem numerum securitatem; aderant enim
circiter ducenta milia armatorum. Et cum omnes hoc modo inanimasset,   85
iuit obuiam Aurelio in campo qui dicebatur Maisbeli, quo ipse Aurelius
transiturus erat. Affectabat namque et subitum et furtiuum impetum facere
Britonesque non praemeditatos occupare. Quod tamen non latuit Aurelium,
nec iccirco distulit campum adire sed festinantius ingressus est. Vt igitur
hostes prospexit, disposuit turmas suas. Tria milia ex Armoricanis iussit   90
equis adesse, ceteros cum insulanis mixtim in acies constituit. Demetas in
collibus, Venedotos in prope sitis nemoribus locauit. Erat autem causa ut si
Saxones ad ea diffugerent adessent qui obuiarent.

122   Interea accessit Eldol dux Claudiocestriae ad regem et ait:

'Sola dies pro omnibus diebus uitae meae michi sufficeret si congredi   95
cum Hengisto Deus concederet. Nempe succumberet alter nostrum dum
gladiis insisteremus. Reminiscor namque diei qua conuenimus quasi
pacem habituri. Cumque de concordia ageretur, prodidit omnes qui
aderant et cum cultris interfecit praeter me solum, qui reperto palo euasi.
Succubuerunt eadem die .cccclxxx. barones ac consules, qui omnes   100
inermes aduenerant. In tanto periculo subuectauit Deus palum, quo
defensus euasi'.

Talia referebat Eldol, sed Aurelius socios hortabatur totam spem suam
in filium Dei ponere, hostes deinde suos audacter inuadere, pro patria
unanimiter pugnare.   105

123   At Hengistus econtra turmas suas componebat, componendo proeliari
docebat, docendo singulas perambulabat ut omnibus unam audatiam
pugnandi ingereret. Dispositis tandem in utraque parte cuneis, congrediuntur
acies, mutuos ictus ingeminant, cruorem non minimum diffundunt. Hinc
Britones hinc Saxones uulnerati moriuntur. Hortatur Aurelius Christianos,   110
monet Hengistus paganos. Et dum talem decertationem facerent, nitebatur
semper Eldol habere aditum congrediendi cum Hengisto; sed non habuit.
Nam Hengistus, ut uidit suos succumbere, Britones uero nutu Dei praeualere,
confestim diffugit petiuitque oppidum Kaerconan, quod nunc Cunengeburg

74 aquilonales (-lis *C¹*) *OCS AK*
75 prouincias *Δ Σ:* partes *Φ*
80 [Ambrosii] *Σ Φ*
101 subuectauit <mihi> *Φ*

Aurelius pursued, killing or enslaving all those he found in Hengest's wake. Seeing Aurelius at his back, Hengest decided not to enter the town, but reformed his men to renew the battle. He realised that the town could not hold Aurelius off and that sword and spear were his only chance. When Aurelius came up, he too reordered his troops and launched a bitter attack. The Saxons fought back and men fell mortally wounded. On both sides blood flowed and the groans of the dying sharpened the anger of the living. In the end the Saxons would have prevailed, but for the intervention of the Breton cavalry. Aurelius had drawn them up separately, as in the first engagement. In the face of their intervention the Saxons wavered and, falling back a little, rallied only with difficulty. Then the Britons advanced more fiercely and attacked their foe together. Aurelius ceaselessly urged on his comrades, wounding attackers, pursuing fugitives, all to comfort his men. Eldol likewise charged hither and thither, inflicting deadly wounds on his enemies. And all the time he burned for the opportunity of meeting Hengest.

124   As the various formations swayed back and forth, the pair encountered each other by chance and began to exchange blows. As the swords of those unmatched champions clashed, their blows scattered sparks like lightning from thunderclaps. For a long time it was unclear whose strength was greater; sometimes Hengest yielded to Eldol, sometimes Eldol to Hengest. In the midst of this struggle, Gorlois duke of Cornwall arrived with his troops, attacking the enemy battalions. When Eldol caught sight of him, he took heart and, seizing Hengest with all his might by the nasal of his helmet, dragged him into the ranks of his fellow-Britons. Overjoyed, he shouted out:

> 'God has granted my desire. Men, cut down these villains, cut them down. Victory is assured. Hengest's defeat means your triumph'.

Meanwhile the Britons pressed home their onslaught on the pagans, attacking them over and over and, if forced to retreat, steeling their spirits to fight again; thus they continued until victory was theirs. The Saxons fled as best they could. Some made for their cities, some the wooded hills and some their ships. Most with Hengest's son Octa went to York, whilst his relative Eosa retreated to Dumbarton, both of which cities they garrisoned with great numbers of armed men.

appellatur. Insequitur eum Aurelius et quoscumque in itinere repperiebat 115
uel in interitum uel in seruitutem compellebat. Cum ergo uidisset Hengistus
quia insequeretur eum Aurelius, noluit introire in oppidum sed conuocato
in turmas populo iterum proeliari disposuit. Quippe sciebat quod oppidum
nequaquam Aurelio resisteret et quod omne tutamen suum in gladio et hasta
consisteret. Denique, cum superuenisset Aurelius, composuit et ipse socios 120
suos in turmas et acerrimam pugnam ingessit. Porro Saxones unanimiter
resistunt et inuicem letaliter uulnerantur. Diffunditur sanguis utrobique,
clamor morientium uiuos in iram ducebat. Postremo praeualuissent Saxones
nisi equestris turma Armoricanorum Britonum superuenisset. Constituerat
namque eam Aurelius sicut in primo proelio fecerat. Superueniente 125
ergo illa, cesserunt ei Saxones et aliquantulum dilapsi uix iterum sese
consociauerunt. Acriores deinde incumbunt Britones et hostes unanimiter
infestant. Non cessabat Aurelius socios monere, obuiantes uulnerare,
fugientes insequi, atque suos hoc modo consolari. Similiter Eldol, nunc
hac nunc illac discurrens, infestis uulneribus aduersarios suos afficiebat. 130
Quicquid autem ageret, aestuabat semper habere copiam congrediendi cum
Hengisto.

124   Cum itaque diuersas irruptiones diuersae turmae facerent, conuenerunt
forte pariter et mutuos ictus ingeminare coeperunt. O uiros prae ceteris
pugnaces! Qui dum mutuos enses alter in alterum immitterent, prosiliebant 135
ex ictibus ignes ac si tonitrua choruscationes procrearent. Diu dubium fuit
cui praestantior uigor inerat; quandoque enim praeualebat Eldol et cedebat
Hengistus, cedebat Eldol et praeualebat Hengistus. Dum itaque in hunc
modum decertarent, superuenit Gorlois dux Cornubiae cum phalange cui
praeerat turmas diuersorum infestans. Quem cum aspexisset Eldol, securior 140
effectus cepit Hengistum per nasale cassidis atque totis uiribus utens ipsum
infra conciues extraxit. Maximo igitur gaudio fluctuans, excelsa uoce
dicebat:

'Desiderium meum adimpleuit Deus. Prosternite, uiri, obstantes
ambrones, prosternite. Vobis est in manu uictoria. Vicistis enim deuicto 145
Hengisto'.

Inter haec Britones non cessant paganos expugnare, saepius ac saepius
inuadere, et cum retro cedebant iterum reuocata audatia resistere; nec in
hunc modum quieuerunt donec potiti sunt uictoria. Diffugierunt itaque
Saxones quo impetus quemque ducebat. Alii urbes, alii montana nemorosa, 150
alii naues petebant. At Octa filius Hengisti cum maiori multitudine
Eboracum adiuit, Eosa uero cognatus suus urbem Aldclud, atque eas
innumeris armatis munierunt.

117 [in] oppidum *Φ*
133 Dum *SE QHM*
138 <quandoque uero> cedebat *66:* <quandoque> cedebat *76, 178 (cf. 'Transm.' 100)*
138 [itaque] *Σ Φ*
144 impleuit *Φ, sed cf. § 160.494*
152 Aldclud atque eas *Δ:* Aldclud adiuit atque eam *U: lac. A: om. ND QYH:* secum *K G (et mox*
muniuit *K):* Alclud et sic se *M*

125   After this victory, Aurelius captured the city called, as I said, Cunengeburg and remained there for three days. During this time he ordered that the dead be buried and the wounded tended and that the weary should rest and enjoy various refreshments. Then he assembled the leaders to decide what to do with Hengest. Among those present was Eldadus bishop of Gloucester, Eldol's brother and a man of great wisdom and piety. When he saw Hengest standing before the king, he told the others to be silent and said:

> 'Even if everybody were eager for his release, I would still cut him to pieces. I would be following the example of the prophet Samuel, who, when he had Agag king of the Amalekites in his power, cut him in pieces, saying: "Just as you have made women childless, so today shall I make your mother childless among women". Do the same to him, this second Agag'.

So Eldol took a sword, led Hengest outside the city and cut off his head, dispatching him to hell. But Aurelius, showing his usual moderation, ordered him to be buried and a mound raised over his body as was the custom of the pagans.

126   Aurelius next led his army to York to defeat Hengest's son Octa. After Aurelius commenced a siege, Octa despaired of resisting and holding the city against such a host. After taking counsel, he came out with the nobler men who were accompanying him, with chains on his hands and gravel in his hair, and presented himself before the king with the following words:

> 'My gods are beaten and I am certain that your God is King, since he forces so many noble men to come to you in this manner. Receive us and our chains and, unless you take pity on us, keep us as prisoners, ready to face any punishment'.

Full of pity, Aurelius ordered his men to decide what to do with them. Various opinions were aired, until bishop Eldadus rose and pronounced the following judgement:

> 'When the Gibeonites came of their own free will to the sons of Israel, they received the mercy they asked for. Shall we Christians prove worse than Jews by refusing it? Let them have the mercy they request. The island of Britain is large and in many places uninhabited. Let us allow them by treaty to occupy at least the empty places, and be our servants forever'.

Aurelius agreed with Eldadus' pronouncement and granted them mercy. Eosa and the others who had fled followed Octa's example and received the same answer. The king gave them the region adjacent to Scotland and ratified his treaty with them.

125   Vt itaque triumphauit Aurelius, cepit Vrbem Conani, quam supra
memoraueram, et ibidem tribus diebus moratus est. Interea iussit peremptos 155
sepeliri, uulneratos curari, fatigatos requiescere, et eosdem diuersis
leuaminibus reficere. Post haec, conuocatis ducibus, decernere praecepit
quid de Hengisto ageretur. Aderat Eldadus Claudiocestrensis episcopus,
frater Eldol, uir summae prudentiae et religionis. Hic, cum Hengistum
coram rege stantem aspiceret, iussit ceteros tacere et in hunc modum 160
locutus est:

'Etsi omnes istum liberare niterentur, ego eum in frusta conciderem.
Insequerer namque prophetam Samuelem, qui cum Agag regem Amalech
in potestatem tenuisset concidit illum in frusta, dicens "sicut fecisti matres
sine liberis, sic faciam hodie matrem tuam sine liberis inter mulieres". 165
Sic igitur facite de isto, qui alter Agag existit'.

Accepit itaque Eldol gladium et duxit eum extra urbem et amputato capite
ad Tartara direxit. At Aurelius, ut erat in cunctis rebus modestus, iussit
sepeliri eum et cumulum terrae super corpus pagano more apponi.

126   Deinde duxit Aurelius exercitum suum ad Eboracum ut Octam filium 170
Hengisti expugnaret. Cumque ciuitatem obsideret, dubitauit Octa resistere
et urbem contra tantam multitudinem defendere. Communicato itaque
consilio, egressus est cum nobilioribus qui secum aderant, gestans catenam
in manu et sablonem in capite, et sese regi in haec uerba praesentauit:

'Victi sunt dii mei deumque tuum regnare non haesito, qui tot nobiles ad 175
te uenire hoc modo compellit. Accipe ergo nos et catenam istam, et nisi
misericordiam adhibueris habe nos ligatos et ad quodlibet supplicium
uoluntarie paratos'.

Motus igitur Aurelius pietate iussit adiudicari quid in illos agendum foret.
Cum autem diuersi diuersa proferrent, surrexit Eldadus episcopus et 180
sententiam hoc sermone disseruit:

'Gabaonitae uoluntarie uenerunt ad filios Israel petentes misericoridam
et impetrauerunt. Erimus ergo Christiani peiores Iudaeis, abnegantes
misericordiam? Misericordiam petunt, misericordiam habeant. Ampla
est insula Britanniae et in pluribus locis deserta. Foederatos itaque illos 185
sinamus saltem deserta inhabitare, et nobis in sempiternum seruiant'.

Acquieuit itaque rex Eldadi sententiae et misericordiam de eis habuit.
Exemplo etiam Octae uenit Eosa ceterique qui diffugerant et misericordiam
impetrauerunt. Dedit ergo eis rex nationem iuxta Scotiam et foedus cum eis
confirmauit.   190

154 At *O UAKN:* Et *C Q*
154 ita *YHM*
160 aspexit *Φ*
171 possideret *Σ Φ*
189 [rex] *Σ Φ*

127   Having defeated his foes, Aurelius summoned the earls and chiefs of the kingdom to York and commanded them to rebuild the churches destroyed by the Saxons. He himself began work on restoring the metropolitan see in that city and the remaining bishoprics of its diocese. A fortnight later, after setting up various teams of workmen in various places, he went to London, which had not been spared barbarian attack. Moved by the damage it had suffered, he recalled the surviving citizens from all directions and began repair-work. There he made provision for his kingdom, revived the long-forgotten laws and restored to grandchildren their grandparents' lost possessions. Such holdings as had no heir after so much slaughter he presented to his own followers. His sole concerns were the restitution of his kingdom, the reorganisation of the churches, the renewal of peace and law, and the enforcement of justice. Next he went to Winchester to repair it too. After putting that in motion, he was advised by bishop Eldadus to visit the monastery near Kaercaradoc, now Salisbury, in which were buried the earls and chiefs betrayed by Hengest. It was a community of three hundred monks on the hill of Ambrius, by whom, it is said, it had been founded. Looking round at the place where the dead rested, Aurelius was moved to tears of pity. He pondered for a long time, wondering how to make the place a monument. For he considered that the turf that covered so many nobles who had died for their country's sake deserved to be remembered.

128   So Aurelius summoned carpenters and stonemasons from all districts and instructed them to employ their skills to build a new structure to stand forever as a memorial to such heroes. When, however, lack of confidence in their skills led them all to refuse, Tremorinus archbishop of Caerleon came to the king and said:

> 'If there exists anywhere someone to carry out your orders, then it is Vortigern's prophet Merlin. I do not think there is anyone in your kingdom more distinguished in foretelling the future or in feats of engineering. Command him to come and employ his skills to build the monument you desire'.

After asking many questions about Merlin, Aurelius sent various messengers to various regions of the country to find and fetch him. Scouring the regions, they found him in the province of the Gewissei at the spring of Galahes, his favourite haunt. They told him their mission and took him to the king. Aurelius received him gladly and, wishing to hear marvels, commanded him to prophesy. Merlin replied:

127   Triumphatis itaque hostibus, conuocauit consules ac principes regni
infra Eboracum praecepitque eis restaurare ecclesias quas gens Saxonum
destruxerat. Ipse uero metropolitanam sedem illius urbis atque ceteros
episcopatus prouinciae reaedificare incepit. Emensis deinde quindecim
diebus, cum operarios diuersos in diuersis locis statuisset, adiuit urbem   195
Lundoniae, cui hostilis irruptio non pepercerat. Condolens igitur ipsius
excidium, reuocat undique ciues residuos et eam restituere aggreditur.
Ibidem disponit regno suo legesque sopitas renouat, amissas auorum
possessiones nepotibus distribuit. Quae autem in tanta calamitate heredes
amiserant largitae sunt commilitonibus suis. Tota intentio ipsius uersabatur   200
circa regni restitutionem, ecclesiarum reformationem, pacis ac legis
renouationem, iusticiae compositionem. Exin petiuit Guintoniam ut eam
sicut ceteras restitueret. Cumque in restaurationem eius quae ponenda erant
posuisset, monitu Eldadi episcopi iuit ad monasterium prope Kaercaradoc,
quod nunc Salesberia dicitur, ubi consules ac principes iacebant quos   205
nefandus Hengistus prodiderat. Erat ibi coenobium .ccc. fratrum in monte
Ambrii, qui ut fertur fundator eiusdem olim extiterat. Vt igitur locum
quo defuncti iacebant circumspexit, motus pietate in lacrimas solutus est.
Postremo, in diuersas meditationes inductus, deliberauit apud se qualiter
locum faceret memorabilem. Dignam namque memoria censebat caespitem   210
quae tot nobiles pro patria defunctos protegebat.

128   Conuocatis itaque undique artificibus lignorum et lapidum, praecepit
ingeniis uti nouamque structuram adinuenire quae in memoriam tantorum
uirorum in aeuum constaret. Cumque omnes ingeniis suis diffidentes
repulsam intulissent, accessit Tremorinus Vrbis Legionum archiepiscopus   215
ad regem et ait:

'Si uspiam est qui praeceptum tuum aggredi ualuerit, Merlinus uates
Vortegirni aggredietur. Quippe non existimo alterum esse in regno tuo
cui sit clarius ingenium siue in futuris dicendis siue in operationibus
machinandis. Iube eum uenire atque ingenio suo uti ut opus quod affectas   220
constet'.

Cum itaque de eo multa interrogasset Aurelius, misit diuersos nuntios per
diuersas nationes patriae ut inuentum illum adducerent. Qui peragratis
prouinciis inuenerunt eum in natione Gewisseorum ad fontem Galahes,
quem fuerat solitus frequentare. Indicato autem quid uellent, duxerunt illum   225
ad regem. Excepit illum rex cum gaudio iussitque futura dicere, cupiens
miranda audire. Cui Merlinus:

192 praecepit *AD QHG*
202 Exinde *C N H*
203 restauratione *O QHM*
208 <et> motus *Δ UAKN (cf. Introd.)*
217 [tuum] *Φ*
218 aestimo *N YHM*
224 fontes *S AK H*

'Such mysteries should only be revealed in times of dire necessity. If I prophesied for entertainment or without purpose, the spirit that instructs me would fall silent and abandon me when I needed it'.

Faced with complete refusal, the king refrained from bothering him about the future, but spoke instead of his projected plan. Merlin answered:

'If you wish to mark their graves with a lasting monument, send for the Giants' Ring, which is on Mount Killaraus in Ireland. There is there a ring of stones which no man of this era could erect save by skill and art combined. The stones are huge, beyond the strength of any man. If you set them up in the same pattern around the burial-place, they will stand forever'.

129 Merlin's words made Aurelius laugh, and he asked how it could be that such huge stones should be brought from so far, as if Britain did not have stones for the job. Merlin replied:

'Do not waste your laughter, king, for my words are not in vain. The stones are magic and can effect various cures. They were brought long ago from the farthest shores of Africa by giants, who erected them in Ireland while they lived there. Their purpose was to set up baths among them whenever they were ill. They used to wash the stones and pour the water into the baths to cure illnesses. They also used to mix in herbal compounds to heal wounds. There is not a stone among them that does not have some medicinal power'.

When they heard this, the Britons decided to send for the stones and to fight the Irish people if they refused to surrender them. For the mission was chosen Uther Pendragon, the king's brother, with fifteen thousand armed men. Merlin too was chosen to supply them with brains and advice. As soon as ships were ready, they set sail and were carried to Ireland by favourable winds.

130 At that time Ireland was ruled by Gillomanius, a very able young man. When he heard that the Britons had landed in Ireland, he collected a great host and set off to meet them. On learning the purpose of their mission, he smiled to his companions, saying:

'I am not surprised that a cowardly race has been able to lay Britain waste, since its people are dull and stupid. Who has ever heard of such foolishness? Are Ireland's stones so much better than Britain's that they challenge us to fight for them? To arms, men, defend your country, for they shall not take so much as the smallest pebble from the ring as long as I live'.

'Non sunt reuelanda huiusmodi misteria nisi cum summa necessitas incubuerit. Nam si ea in derisionem siue uanitatem proferrem, taceret spiritus qui me docet et cum opus superueniret recederet'. 230

Denique, cum omnibus repulsam intulisset, noluit rex infestare eum de futuris sed de operatione praemeditata allocutus est. Cui Merlinus:

'Si perpetuo opere sepulturam uirorum decorare uolueris, mitte pro chorea gigantum quae est in Killarao monte Hiberniae. Est etenim ibi structura lapidum quam nemo huius aetatis construeret nisi ingenium 235 artem subuectaret. Grandes sunt lapides, nec est aliquis cuius uirtuti cedant. Qui si eo modo quo ibidem positi sunt circa plateam locabuntur, stabunt in aeternum'.

129 Ad uerba ipsius solutus est Aurelius in risum, dicens qualiter id fieri posset ut tanti lapides ex tam longinquo regno adueherentur ac si Britannia 240 lapidibus careret qui ad operationem sufficerent. Ad haec Merlinus:

'Ne moueas, rex, uanum risum, quia haec absque uanitate profero. Mistici sunt lapides et ad diuersa medicamenta salubres. Gigantes olim asportauerunt eos ex ultimis finibus Affricae et posuerunt in Hibernia dum eam inhabitarent. Erat autem causa ut balnea infra ipsos conficerent 245 cum infirmitate grauarentur. Lauabant namque lapides et infra balnea diffundebant, unde aegroti curabantur. Miscebant etiam cum herbarum confectionibus, unde uulnerati sanabantur. Non est ibi lapis qui medicamento careat'.

Cumque hoc audissent Britones, censuerunt pro lapidibus mittere 250 populumque Hiberniae proelio infestare si ipsos detinere niterentur. Postremo eligitur Vther Pendragon frater regis et quindecim milia armatorum ut huic negotio pareant. Eligitur et ipse Merlinus, ut ipsius ingenio et consilio agenda tractentur. Paratis deinde nauibus, mare ingrediuntur, prosperis uentis Hiberniam adeunt. 255

130 Ea tempestate regnabat in Hibernia Gillomanius, iuuenis mirae probitatis. Hic, cum audiuisset quia in Hibernia applicuissent Britones, collegit exercitum grandem et eis obuiam perrexit. Cumque didicisset causam aduentus eorum, astantibus arrisit et ait:

'Non miror si ignaua gens insulam Britonum deuastare potuit, cum 260 Britones bruti sint et stulti. Quis etenim huiusmodi stulticiam audiuit? Numquid meliora sunt saxa Hiberniae quam Britanniae, ut regnum nostrum pro ipsis ad proeliandum prouocetur? Armate uos, uiri, et defendite patriam uestram, quia dum michi uita inerit non auferent etiam nobis minimum lapillum choreae'. 265

231 [rex] Σ Φ
257 audisset *E AKN YGM*
259 irrisit Σ Φ
260 ignaua *OC²SE D Y²HGM:* ignaui *C¹A:* ignaua + *lac. U:* ignaui + *lac. K¹ Q:* ignauis *N:* ignauia *Y¹:* ignauissima Saxonum *K²*
263 [ad proeliandum] Φ
264-5 nobis etiam *K*

When Uther saw that they were prepared to fight, he hurried his army to the attack. They won an easy victory, slaughtering and killing the Irish and putting Gillomanius to flight. The victorious British then marched to mount Killaraus and came to the ring of stones, full of satisfaction and wonder. As they stood there, Merlin approached them, saying:

'Employ your might, men, to take down the stones and we shall see whether brains yield to brawn or vice versa'.

At his command they all at once tried contrivances of all kinds in their efforts to take down the ring. To this end some employed ropes, others pulleys, others ladders, but without being rewarded by any success. Merlin laughed at their failure, then prepared contrivances of his own. As soon as everything was ready, he took down the stones with incredible ease and had them carried to the ships and loaded, and so they joyfully embarked to return to Britain. The winds were favourable and they soon landed and set off for the burial-ground with the stones. When Aurelius had been informed, he sent messengers throughout Britain with instructions to summon the clergy and people to come to mount Ambrius and dedicate the cemetery with rejoicing and honour. At his command there gathered bishops, abbots and their attendants from all classes. When they had all assembled, on the appointed day Aurelius placed the crown upon his head in royal observance of the feast of Whitsun and spent the following three days in unbroken celebrations. At these he distributed unclaimed titles to his followers to reward their efforts in his service. Two of the metropolitan sees, York and Caerleon, had no incumbents; wishing to remedy this, with the common assent of the people Aurelius bestowed York on Samson, a distinguished candidate noted for his great piety, and Caerleon on Dubricius, whom divine providence had singled out for that honour. Having settled his kingdom in this way, Aurelius ordered Merlin to set up around the burial-place the stones which he had brought from Ireland. Merlin obeyed and erected them round the cemetery exactly as they had stood on mount Killaraus in Ireland, so proving the superiority of brains over brawn.

131   At the same time Vortigern's son Pascentius, who had fled to Germany, stirred up all the armed soldiers of that kingdom against Aurelius Ambrosius in an effort to avenge his father. He promised them huge rewards of gold and silver if they helped him to conquer Britain. Having tempted all the young men with such promises, he readied

Vther igitur, ut uidit ipsos ad proeliandum paratos, festinato agmine in eos irruit. Nec mora, praeualuerunt Britones Hiberniensibusque laceratis ac interfectis Gillomanium in fugam propulerunt. Potiti autem uictoria, exegerunt Killaraum montem lapidumque structuram adepti gauisi sunt et ammirati. Circumstantibus itaque cunctis accessit Merlinus et ait: 270

'Vtimini uiribus uestris, iuuenes, ut in deponendo lapides istos appareat utrum ingenium uirtuti an uirtus ingenio cedat'.

Ad imperium igitur eius indulserunt unanimiter multimodis machinationibus et aggressi sunt choream deponere. Alii funes, alii restes, alii scalas parauerunt ut quod affectabant perficerent, nec ullatenus perficere ualuerunt.   275
Deficientibus itaque cunctis, solutus est Merlinus in risum suasque machinationes confecit. Denique, cum quaeque necessaria apposuisset, leuius quam credi potest lapides deposuit, depositos autem fecit deferri ad naues et introponi, et sic cum gaudio in Britanniam reuerti coeperunt. Nec mora, prosperantibus uentis applicant sepulturasque uirorum cum   280
lapidibus petunt. Quod cum indicatum fuisset Aurelio, diuersos nuntios per diuersas partes Britanniae direxit iussitque clerum ac populum submonere, submonitos uero in monte Ambrii conuenire ut cum gaudio et honore praedictam sepulturam repararent. Ad edictum ergo illius uenerunt pontifices et abbates et ex unoquoque ordine qui ei subditi fuerant. Et cum omnes   285
conuenissent, instante die quae praedestinata fuerat imposuit Aurelius diadema capiti suo festumque Pentecostes regaliter celebrauit tribusque sequentibus diebus continuae celebrationi uacauit. Interea honores qui possessoribus carebant domesticis suis largitur ut eis laborem obsequii sui remuneraret. Euacuatae erant duae metropolitanae sedes, Eboraci uidelicet   290
atque Vrbis Legionum, a pastoribus suis; quibus communi populorum consilio consulere uolens, concessit Eboracum Samsoni, illustri uiro summaque religione famoso, Vrbem uero Legionis Dubricio, quem diuina prouidentia in eodem loco profuturum elegerat. Cumque haec et cetera in regno suo statuisset, praecepit Merlino lapides circa sepulturas erigere quos   295
ex Hibernia asportauerat. At ille, praeceptis eius oboediens, eodem modo quo in Killarao monte Hiberniae positi fuerant erexit illos circa sepulturam ingeniumque uirtuti praeualere comprobauit.

131   Eodem tempore Pascentius filius Vortegirni, qui in Germaniam diffugerat, commouebat omnem armatum militem illius regni in Aurelium   300
Ambrosium patremque suum uindicare uolebat. Promittebat autem infinitam copiam auri et argenti si auxilio eorum Britanniam sibi subdidisset. Denique, cum promissis suis uniuersam iuuentutem corrupisset, parauit

271 appareat *Δ: om. Σ* (cedat <sciatis> *N*): sciatis *Φ (cf. 'Transm.' 91)*
280 Nec mora *Δ:* nec *U Q:* et *AKD YHG:* ac *N:* nec non *M*
281 petunt *Δ Σ G:* applicant *Q:* adeunt *YHM*
289 laborem *post* sui *Φ*
293 Legionum *E A QG*
294 *fort.* praefuturum
296 Ast *OCS (cf. Introd.)*

a great fleet, landed in the north of the island and began to lay it waste. At this news, the king assembled his army, marched out and challenged the enemy raiders to battle. They came to fight without hesitation and attacked the Britons, but by God's will they were beaten and put to flight.

132   Having been forced to flee, Pascentius did not dare to return to Germany, but set sail instead for Gillomanius in Ireland, where he was well received. When he described his misfortune, Gillomanius took pity on him and promised him help, complaining of the injury Aurelius' brother Uther had done him in his quest for the Giants' Ring. At length they agreed a pact, prepared and boarded ships and landed at St David's. This news led Uther Pendragon to assemble his forces to march into Wales and oppose them; his brother Aurelius lay ill in Winchester and could not go himself. Discovering this, Gillomanius, Pascentius and their Saxon confederates were greatly heartened, thinking that the king's illness would make it easy to conquer Britain. As the people muttered over this, Eopa, one of the Saxons, went to Pascentius saying:

> 'What reward will you give to the man who can kill Aurelius Ambrosius for you?'.

Pascentius replied:

> 'If only I could find someone with that intention! He would have a thousand pounds of silver and my friendship for life. Should it come about that I win the crown, I would make him a centurion, confirmed by my oath'.

Eopa answered:

> 'I can speak British and I know the ways of men, being a skilled doctor. If you guarantee me what you have promised, I shall pretend to be a Christian, British and a doctor, to gain access to the king and administer a deadly potion. To make access easier, I shall pose as a most pious monk, well versed in all dogma'.

At this promise, Pascentius agreed terms with him, confirming his reward with an oath. Eopa shaved off his beard and tonsured his hair, put on a monk's habit and hurried to Winchester, laden with his jars of medicine. Entering the city, he offered his services to the king's attendants and found favour in their eyes; they desired nothing better than a doctor. He was admitted and

maximum nauigium applicuitque in aquilonaribus insulae partibus ac eas
uastare incepit. Cumque id regi nunciatum fuisset, collegit exercitum suum 305
obuiamque perrexit atque saeuientes hostes ad proelium prouocauit. Qui
ultro ad bellum uenientes commiserunt pugnam cum ciuibus, sed uolente
Deo deuicti fuerunt et in fugam compulsi.

132   Pascentius ergo, in fugam propulsus, non ausus est redire in Germaniam
sed retortis uelis adiuit Gillomanium in Hiberniam et ab illo receptus est. 310
Et cum infortunium suum notificasset, miseratus Gillomanius pactus
est ei auxilium, conquerens de iniuria quam Vther frater Aurelii sibi
intulerat dum choream gigantum perquireret. Confirmato tandem inter
ipsos foedere, parauerunt sibi naues et ingressi sunt eas et in Meneuiam
urbem applicuerunt. Quo diuulgato, Vther Pendragon, excita armatorum 315
copia, iuit in Kambriam ut cum eis pugnaret; frater etenim suus Aurelius in
Guintonia urbe morbo grauatus iacebat nec poterat ipsemet adire. Cumque
id Pascentio et Gillomanio Saxonibusque qui aderant compertum fuisset,
gauisi sunt ualde, quia existimabant propter infirmitatem eius regnum
Britanniae leuiter subdendum. Et dum murmuratio inde per populos fieret, 320
accessit unus ex Saxonibus, uocabulo Eopa, ad Pascentium et ait:

'Quibus donariis ditabis hominem qui Aurelium Ambrosium tibi
interficiet?'.

Cui Pascentius:

'O si quempiam repperirem cui hoc in animo staret! Darem ei mille libras 325
argenti familiaritatemque meam dum uiuerem. Et si fortuna permiserit
ut diademate regni potiar, faciam illum centurionem atque iuramento
confirmabo'.

Ad haec Eopa:

'Didici linguam Britannicam moresque hominum scio, in medicina 330
arte peritus. Si ergo ea quae promittis executus michi fueris, fingam me
Christianum et Britannum et quasi medicus praesentiam regis nactus ei
potionem qua obibit conficiam. Et ut citius aditum reperiam, faciam me
monachum religiosissimum et omni dogmate eruditum'.

Cumque hoc promisisset, pepigit Pascentius foedus cum illo et ea quae 335
spoponderat iuramento confirmauit. Rasit igitur Eopa barbam suam
capiteque tonso monachalem cepit habitum et uasis medicamentorum
suorum oneratus iter uersus Guintoniam arripuit. Vrbem postremo ingressus,
obtulit obsequium suum clientibus regis et gratiam in oculis eorum inuenit;
nichil enim desiderabilius expectabant quam medicum. Exceptus itaque et 340

306 perrexit *Δ Σ YM: om. QH:* ei iuit *G*
317 ipse *Φ*
319 aestimabant *Σ Φ*
320 [Britanniae] *Σ Φ*
325 illi *C AK*
335 petiit *Δ Σ*

presented to the king, whom he promised to restore to health if he took his potions. Eopa was immediately commanded to mix a draught, which he stealthily poisoned before handing it to the king. When Aurelius had received and drunk it, the wicked villain straight away told him to cover himself with his blanket and go to sleep, so that the cursed poison would be all the more effective. The king immediately followed the traitor's instructions and went to sleep, expecting to be cured. The poison quickly spread through the arteries and veins of his body and his sleep became death, which spares no one. Meanwhile the wicked traitor, who had escaped in the crowd, had disappeared from court. While this was happening at Winchester, there appeared a comet of great size and brightness, with a single tail. Attached to the tail was a fiery mass stretching out like a dragon, from whose mouth issued two rays, one of which seemed to extend beyond the skies of France, the other towards the Irish sea and to end in seven smaller rays.

133 All who saw the comet were filled with fear and awe by its appearance. As he marched towards the enemy army in Wales, the king's brother Uther was also not a little apprehensive and consulted all his wise men to find out what it meant. Among the rest he ordered that Merlin be summoned; he was accompanying the army to advise on matters of strategy. Brought before the duke, he was commanded to explain the comet's meaning. Immediately overwhelmed by tears, he summoned his spirit, exclaiming:

'Oh irreparable loss, oh the bereavement of the British people, oh the passing of a most noble king! Aurelius Ambrosius, the renowned king of the Britons, is dead, and with him, without God's help, we shall all die too. Make haste, noble duke Uther, make haste and attack the enemy without delay. Victory shall be yours and you shall be king of all Britain. It is you that are represented by the comet and the fiery dragon beneath it. The ray that extends over France foretells that you will have a most powerful son, whose might shall possess all the kingdoms beneath it; the other ray indicates a daughter, whose sons and grandsons will rule Britain in turn'.

134 Uther, uncertain whether what Merlin had said was true, continued his advance on the enemy; and by midday he was nearing St David's.

in praesentia regis ductus, promisit se redditurum ei sanitatem si potionibus suis frueretur. Nec mora, potionem conficere iussus submiscuit uenenum et regi porrexit. Quod cum cepisset Aurelius et hausisset, iussus est confestim a nefando ambrone sub coopertorio suo delitere atque obdormire, ut magis potio detestanda profecisset. Paruit ilico rex monitis proditoris illius et 345 quasi sanitatem recepturus obdormiuit. Nec mora, illabente ueneno per poros corporis et uenas consecuta est mors soporem, quae nemini parcere sueuit. Interea nefandus proditor ille, inter unum et alium elapsus, in curia nusquam comparuit. Haec dum Guintoniae gererentur, apparuit stella mirae magnitudinis et claritatis uno radio contenta. Ad radium uero erat globus 350 igneus in similitudinem draconis extensus, et ex ore eius procedebant duo radii, quorum unus longitudinem suam ultra Gallicana climata uidebatur extendere, alter uero, uersus Hibernicum mare uergens, in septem minores radios terminabatur.

133   Apparente itaque praefato sydere, perculsi sunt omnes metu et 355 ammiratione qui istud inspiciebant. Vther etiam frater regis, hostilem exercitum in partibus Kambriae petens, non minimo timore perculsus quosque sapientes adibat ut quid portenderet stella notificarent. Inter ceteros iussit uocari Merlinum; nam et ipse in exercitu uenerat ut consilio ipsius res proeliorum tractarentur. Qui ut in praesentia ducis astitisset, iussus est 360 significationem syderis enucleare. Mox ille, in fletum erumpens, reuocato spiritu exclamauit et ait:

'O dampnum inrecuperabile, o orbatum populum Britanniae, o nobilissimi regis migrationem! Defunctus est inclitus rex Britonum Aurelius Ambrosius, cuius obitu obibimus omnes nisi Deus auxilium 365 subuectauerit. Festina ergo, dux nobilissime Vther, festina et conflictum facere cum hostibus ne differas. Victoria tibi in manu erit, et rex eris tocius Britanniae. Te etenim sidus istud significat et igneus draco sub sidere. Radius autem qui uersus Gallicanam plagam porrigitur portendit tibi filium futurum et potentissimum, cuius potestas omnia regna quae 370 protegit habebit; alter uero radius significat filiam, cuius filii et nepotes regnum Britanniae succedenter habebunt'.

134 At Vther, in dubio tamen extans an uerum protulisset Merlinus, in hostes ut coeperat progreditur; aduenerat namque prope Meneuiam, ita ut iter

---

342 iussit *O K*
349 Haec dum *OC A Φ:* et dum *S¹ U:* et dum haec *S² KND:* et haec dum *E*
349 agerentur *Φ*
355 percussi *C UA QG*
357 partibus Kambriae *Δ Σ:* Kambria *Φ*
357 percussus *A QG*
358 protenderet *OCS UND QH*
359 uocare *Φ*
360 tractarent *Φ*
366 subuectaret *Σ:* subuectet *Φ*
367 [facere] *Φ*
371 proteget *UAND Φ, sed cf. § 116.259*
373 *fort.* tandem *(cf. § 20.447, § 96.233)*

When Gillomanius, Pascentius and the Saxons heard he was approaching, they came out to meet and fight him. As they came in sight of one another, both sides drew up their lines and closed to engage. As is usual in battle, soldiers fell on both sides. When evening drew near, Uther prevailed and won, whereas Gillomanius and Pascentius were killed. The barbarians rushed to their ships in flight, but were slaughtered by the pursuing Britons as they ran. Having won a victory thanks to Christ, the duke hurried as quickly as he could after such a struggle to Winchester; messages had arrived that the king was dead and had already been buried by his bishops near the monastery of Ambrius in the Giants' Ring, which he had had erected in his lifetime. On hearing of his demise, the bishops, abbots and clergy of the whole region had gathered at Winchester and conducted a funeral befitting so great a monarch. Before his death Aurelius had instructed that he be buried in the cemetery he himself had built, so they took his body there and gave it a royal burial.

135   His brother Uther summoned the clergy and people of the kingdom and took the crown, becoming king of the island with the consent of all. Remembering Merlin's interpretation of the comet, he ordered that two dragons be cast in gold, to resemble the dragon he had seen in the comet's tail. After these had been fashioned with great skill, he presented one to the cathedral in Winchester, and kept the other to take into battle. From that time he was known as Uther Pendragon, which means 'dragon's head' in British. He had received the name because Merlin had used the dragon to prophesy his succession as king.

136   Meanwhile Hengest's son Octa and his relative Eosa, released from their undertaking to Aurelius Ambrosius, attempted to harry the king and extend their boundaries. They had allied themselves with the Saxons brought in by Pascentius and sent envoys to Germany for more. Octa, at the head of a huge host, invaded the northern districts, and did not cease ravaging them until he had destroyed the cities and castles all the way from Scotland to York. He began a siege there, until finally Uther arrived with all the forces of the kingdom to attack him. The Saxons fought bravely, resisting the British assaults and driving them back. Victorious, they pursued the British all day until they fled to mount Damen.

medietatis diei restaret. Cumque aduentus eius Gillomanio, Pascentio, 375
Saxonibusque qui aderant, relatus fuisset, egressi sunt ei obuiam ut cum ipso
congrederentur. Porro, ut sese adinuicem conspexerunt, statuerunt agmina
sua in utraque parte cominusque accedentes pugnauerunt. Pugnantes autem
interficiuntur hinc et inde milites ut in tali euentu fieri solet. Denique, cum
multum diei praeterisset, praeualuit Vther interfectisque Gillomanio et 380
Pascentio triumpho potitus est. Fugientes itaque barbari festinauerunt ad
naues suas, sed in fugiendo a persequentibus ciuibus trucidabantur. Cessit
prorsus uictoria duci fauente Christo, qui post tantum laborem quam citius
potuit progressus est Guintoniam; praeuenerant namque nuntii qui casum
regis indicauerant ipsumque iam ab episcopis patriae sepultum fore prope 385
coenobium Ambrii infra choream gigantum, quam uiuens fieri praeceperat.
Audito etenim ipsius obitu, conuenerant in urbe Guintoniae pontifices et
abbates atque totus clerus eiusdem prouintiae et ut tantum regem decebat
funus ipsius procurauerunt. Et quia uiuens adhuc praeceperat ut in cimiterio
quod ipse parauerat sepeliretur, tulerunt corpus eius ibidem atque cum 390
regiis exequiis humauerunt.

135   At Vther frater eius, conuocato regni clero et populo, cepit diadema
insulae annuentibusque cunctis sublimatus est in regem. Reminiscens autem
expositionis quam Merlinus de supradicto sidere fecerat, iussit fabricari
duos dracones ex auro ad similitudinem draconis quem ad radium stellae 395
inspexerat. Qui ut mira arte fabricati fuerunt, optulit unum in ecclesia primae
sedis Guintoniae, alterum uero sibi ad ferendum in proelia retinuit. Ab illo
itaque tempore uocatus fuit Vther Pendragon, quod Britannica lingua caput
draconis sonamus. Iccirco hanc appellationem receperat quia Merlinus eum
per draconem in regem prophetauerat.   400

136   Interea Octa filius Hengisti atque Eosa cognatus suus, cum soluti
essent a foedere quod Aurelio Ambrosio pepigerant, moliti sunt inferre
inquietudinem regi atque nationes suas dilatare. Associabant namque sibi
Saxones quos Pascentius conduxerat nuntiosque suos propter ceteros in
Germaniam dirigebat. Maxima itaque multitudine stipatus, aquilonares 405
prouintias inuasit nec saeuitiae suae indulgere quieuit donec urbes et
promontoria ab Albania usque ad Eboracum destruxit. Postremo, cum
urbem obsidere incepisset, superuenit Vther Pendragon cum tota fortitudine
regni et cum illo proeliatus est. Restiterunt uiriliter Saxones irruptionesque
Britonum tolerantes ipsos in fugam propulerunt. Victoria autem potiti, 410
insecuti sunt eos cedentes usque ad montem Damen dum sol diem stare

375 <et> Pascentio *AK GM*
388 [decebat] *Φ, unde* tanti regis *GM*
390 corpus [eius] *G:* eum *YHM*
392 [et] *S UAN*
393 admittentibusque *Q:* annitentibusque *HGM*
405 dirigebant *ND YHGM (cf. Introd. ad § 88.385)*
406 [suae] *Φ*
407 [ad] *E QHGM*
409 irruptiones *Q:* et irruptiones *YHGM*

It was a high mountain, crowned with hazel trees and flanked with craggy rocks, which provided lairs for wild beasts. The Britons occupied it, spending the night among the crags and trees. When the pole star began to fade, Uther ordered that his earls and chiefs be summoned to advise him how to attack the enemy. They all swiftly assembled before the king and, when they were commanded to give their opinions, allowed the first words to Gorlois duke of Cornwall. He was an older man of considerable experience. He said:

> 'As long as it is still night, there is no need for empty evasion or discussion. Boldness and bravery are needed if you wish to go on living as free men. The pagan host is large and eager to fight, and we are outnumbered. If we wait until daylight, it will not be to our advantage to attack them. While the darkness lasts, then, let us close ranks and move down to make an unexpected assault on their camp. If we all rush boldly at them while they are careless and unconcerned about an attack, we shall certainly overcome them'.

His plan pleased everybody, including the king, and they followed his advice. Armed and in formation, they approached the enemy camp and prepared to launch a concerted attack. But as they got nearer, the sentries heard them coming and woke their sleeping comrades with trumpet blasts. Confused and dazed, some of them hurriedly grabbed their weapons, others, overwhelmed by fear, ran blindly. The Britons, advancing with closed ranks, got quickly to the camp, burst in and fell upon the enemy with drawn swords. In their surprise the Saxons could not fight back, whilst the Britons had boldness and planning on their side. The Britons' aim was to fight bitterly and, as they strove to cut them down, they killed the pagans in their thousands. Eventually Octa and Eosa were captured and the rest of the Saxons completely scattered.

137   After this victory Uther went to the city of Dumbarton, made provision for the region and completely pacified it. He visited all the Scottish tribes and made that unruly people forget their savagery. He displayed greater justice throughout their homelands than any of his predecessors. In his days wrongdoers trembled, since they were punished without mercy. When the northern provinces were at last at peace, Uther went to London, ordering Octa and Eosa to be imprisoned there. As Easter was approaching, he ordered his nobles to

permittebat. Erat autem mons ille arduus, in cacumine coriletum habens, in medio uero saxa praerupta, latebris ferarum habilia. Occupauerunt eum Britones totaque nocte infra saxa et corileta commanserunt. At cum Arctos temonem uertere coepit, praecepit Vther consules suos atque principes 415 ad se uocari ut consilio eorum tractaret qualiter in hostes irruptionem facerent. Conuenerunt ocius cuncti in praesentia regis iussique dicere quid consiliarentur Gorloi duci Cornubiae prius sententiam suam proferre praeceperunt. Erat enim ipse consilii magni atque aetatis maturae.

'Non opus est' inquit 'ambagibus uanis aut sermonibus dum adhuc 420 noctem restare conspicimus. Vtendum nobis est audatia et fortitudine si uita et libertate frui diutius uolueritis. Magna est paganorum multitudo et pugnandi auida, nos uero rariores existimus. Si autem diem superuenire expectauerimus, non censeo nobis utile ut cum eis congrediamur. Eia ergo, dum tenebrae durant, densatis turmis descendamus ipsosque infra 425 castra sua subito impetu inuadamus. Nam dum nichil haesitauerint nec nos hoc modo uenturos existimauerint, si unanimiter irruentes usi fuerimus audatia, triumpho sine dubio potiemur'.

Placuit regi omnibusque sententia illius, monitisque suis paruerunt. Statuti namque per turmas et armati, castra hostium petunt et unanimi affectu in 430 ipsos irruere proponunt. At dum prope incederent, compererunt uigiles aduentum eorum, qui soporatos socios sonitu lituorum euigilauerunt. Turbati itaque hostes et stupefacti partim armare sese festinant, partim formidine praeoccupati quo impetus ducebat discurrebant. At Britones, densatis incedentes turmis, ocius adeunt castra et inuadunt repertoque aditu 435 nudatis ensibus in hostes concurrunt. Qui ita ex inprouiso occupati non utiliter reddiderunt proelium, cum ceteri audatiam cum praemeditatione recepissent. Porro Britones acriter irruere intendunt, trucidare conantur, et paganos ad milia interficiunt. Denique capti sunt Octa et Eosa et Saxones penitus dissipati. 440

137 Post illam uero uictoriam petiuit urbem Aldclud prouinciaeque illi disposuit pacemque ubique renouauit. Circuiuit etiam omnes Scotorum nationes rebellemque populum a feritate sua deposuit. Tantam namque iusticiam exercebat per patrias quantam alter antecessorum suorum non fecerat. Tremebant ergo in diebus eius quicumque peruerse agebant, 445 cum sine misericordia plecterentur. Denique, pacificatis aquilonaribus prouinciis, iuit Lundoniam iussitque ibidem Octam atque Eosam in carcere seruari. Festo etiam paschali superueniente, praecepit proceribus regni in

417 citius *ND* Φ
417 iussit- *E K¹N Y¹HG*
419 [ipse] Φ
421 est nobis *C KN Q, sed cf. §§ 166.167-8, 194.328*
422 uoluerimus *SE M:* uolueris *N YH*
429 monitibusque *OS UA² (cf. Introd.)*
441 prouinciae *C:* et prouinciae *O*

assemble in the same city so that he could mark the day with due honour by wearing the crown. All obeyed and, as the day neared, came together from their various cities. The king observed the feast as he had intended, making merry with his nobles. All were pleased that the king was glad to receive them. As befitted a joyous banquet, many nobles attended with their wives and daughters. Among them was the duke of Cornwall, Gorlois, with his wife Igerna, the most beautiful woman in Britain. As soon as the king saw her among the rest, he suddenly burned with love for her and had eyes only for her, neglecting the others. To her alone he constantly presented dishes, to her alone he directed goblets of gold with friendly messages. He kept on smiling and joking with her. Her husband noticed and angrily stormed out of court without permission. No one could call him back, since he feared to lose the thing he valued above all else. Uther angrily commanded him to return to court, intending to punish him for the slight he had inflicted. When Gorlois refused, Uther was enraged and swore to ravage his province if he did not comply immediately. When neither's fury abated, the king gathered a large army, marched to Cornwall and set about burning its cities and towns. Gorlois did not dare to oppose him, since his forces were outnumbered; so he decided to fortify his strongholds until he could get help from Ireland. Fearing less for himself than for his wife, he placed her in the fort of Tintagel, a safe place of refuge on the coast. He himself entered the castle of Dimilioc, so that both of them should not be endangered together in case of a setback. When this was reported to the king, he marched on the castle where Gorlois was and besieged it, cutting off all access. After a long week had passed, he recalled his passion for Igerna and summoned Ulfin of Ridcaradoc, a knight of his household, expressing his desire as follows:

'I am aflame with love for Igerna and cannot go on living if I do not have her. Tell me how I can fulfil my desire before my inner turmoil kills me'.

Ulfin answered:

eandem urbem conuenire ut sumpto diademate tantum diem cum honore
celebraret. Paruerunt ergo cuncti et diuersi ex diuersis ciuitatibus uenientes 450
instante festiuitate conuenerunt. Celebrauit itaque rex sollempnitatem ut
proposuerat et gaudio cum proceribus suis indulsit. Laeticiam agebant
cuncti, quia ipsos rex laeto animo receperat. Aduenerant namque tot
nobiles cum coniugibus et filiabus suis, laeto conuiuio digni. Aderat inter
ceteros Gorlois dux Cornubiae cum Igerna coniuge sua, cuius pulcritudo 455
mulieres tocius Britanniae superabat. Cumque inter alias inspexisset eam
rex, subito incaluit amore illius ita ut postpositis ceteris totam intentionem
suam circa eam uerteret. Haec sola erat cui fercula incessanter dirigebat,
cui aurea pocula familiaribus internuntiis mittebat. Arridebat ei multociens
et iocosa uerba interserebat. Quod cum comperisset maritus, confestim 460
iratus ex curia sine licentia recessit. Non affuit qui eum reuocare quiuisset,
cum id solum amittere timeret quod super omnia diligebat. Iratus itaque
Vther praecepit ei redire in curiam suam ut de illata iniuria rectitudinem ab
eo sumeret. Cui cum parere diffugisset Gorlois, admodum indignatus est
iurauitque iureiurando se uastaturum nationem ipsius nisi ad satisfactionem 465
festinasset. Nec mora, manente praedicta ira inter eos collegit rex exercitum
magnum petiuitque prouinciam Cornubiae atque ignem in urbes et oppida
accumulauit. At Gorlois non ausus est congredi cum eo, quia eius minor
erat armatorum copia; unde praeelegit munire oppida sua donec auxilium
ab Hibernia impetrasset. Et cum magis pro uxore sua quam pro semet 470
ipso anxiaretur, posuit eam in oppido Tintagol in littore maris, quod
pro tuciori refugio habebat; ipse uero ingressus est castellum Dimilioc,
ne si infortunium superuenisset ambo insimul periclitarentur. Cumque
id regi nuntiatum fuisset, iuit ad oppidum quo inerat Gorlois et obsedit
illud omnemque aditum ipsius praeclusit. Emensa tandem ebdomada, 475
reminiscens amoris Igernae, uocauit Vlfin de Ridcaradoc, familiarem sibi
commilitonem, indicauitque in haec uerba quod affectauerat:

'Vror amore Igernae nec periculum corporis mei euadere existimo nisi ea
potitus fuero. Tu igitur adhibe consilium quo uoluntatem meam expleam,
aut aliter internis anxietatibus interibo'. 480

Ad haec Vlfin:

449 eandem urbe *(-bem N) N YHGM*
451 sollempnitatem rex *Φ*
453 [rex] *Φ*
456 totius *Δ Σ:* omnes *Φ*
459 Assidebat *Δ*
466 manente *post* eos *Φ*
466 [rex] *N Φ*
467 prouincias *Φ*
471 Tingagol *Δ ubique*
474 quo inerat *S Σ Φ:* quod inerat *OC:* in quo erat *E*

'What advice can there be, seeing that no power on earth can get us to her in the stronghold of Tintagel? It stands completely surrounded by the sea and can be reached only by a narrow cliff. Three armed knights could hold it against you, even though you had the whole kingdom of Britain at your back. Yet were Merlin prepared to help, I think he could tell you how to achieve your aim'.

The king was persuaded, and ordered that Merlin be called, since he too was present at the siege. Merlin was swiftly summoned and, when he stood before the king, was commanded to advise him how to fulfil his desire for Igerna. When he saw how troubled the king was on her account, Merlin was moved by Uther's great passion and said:

'For your wish to be granted, you must resort to strange arts, unheard of in your time. With my herbs I can give you the exact appearance of Gorlois. If you agree, I will make you his double, and Ulfin that of his retainer Jordanus of Tintagel. I shall accompany you in another disguise, and you will be able to get into the castle safely and gain access to Igerna'.

The king agreed with a ready spirit. He entrusted the siege to his retinue and himself to Merlin's herbs, being transformed into Gorlois. Ulfin became Jordanus and Merlin Britahel, so that their true identities were concealed. Then they set off on the path to Tintagel, where they arrived at dusk. The gatekeeper was immediately informed that the duke was approaching, and the gates were opened and the men admitted; what else could have happened, since it was thought that Gorlois himself was really there? The king spent the night with Igerna and cured himself through the love-making he had longed for. Igerna was deceived by his false appearance and also by the lies he wove so well; for he said that he had stolen out of his castle to look after the thing he most loved and his refuge. So she trustingly denied nothing that he asked. That very night she conceived the renowned Arthur, whose prowess afterwards secured his fame.

138   Meanwhile the king's absence was noticed at the siege and his army made a foolish attempt to break down the walls and force the besieged duke to fight. Gorlois equally foolishly came out with his comrades, expecting to hold off so many armed men with a handful. As both sides engaged, Gorlois was among the first to be killed and his companions were scattered. The besieged castle was taken and the riches it contained divided up unfairly; with greedy fingers each man snatched what chance or bravery offered.

'Et quis tibi consiliari ualuerit, cum nulla uis accedere queat qua eam infra oppidum Tintagol adeamus? Etenim situm est in mari et undique circumclausum ab ipso, nec est alter introitus nisi quem angusta rupes praebeat. Ipsum tres armati milites prohibere queunt, licet cum toto   485 regno Britanniae astitisses. At tamen, si Merlinus uates operam insisteret dare, arbitror te posse consilio ipsius desiderio tuo potiri'.

Credulus itaque rex iussit uocari Merlinum; nam et ipse ad obsidionem uenerat. Vocatus confestim Merlinus, cum in praesentia regis astitisset, iussus est consilium dare quo rex desiderium suum in Igerna expleret. Qui 490 comperta anxietate quam rex patiebatur pro ea commotus est super tanto amore ipsius et ait:

'Vt uoto tuo potiaris, utendum est tibi nouis artibus et tempore tuo inauditis. Scio medicaminibus meis dare tibi figuram Gorlois ita ut per omnia ipse uidearis. Si itaque parueris, faciam te prorsus similare eum,   495 Vlfin uero Iordanum de Tintagol, familiarem suum. Alia autem specie sumpta, adero tercius, poterisque tuto adire oppidum ad Igernam atque aditum habere'.

Paruit itaque rex diligentemque animum adhibuit. Postremo, commissa familiaribus suis obsidione, commisit se medicaminibus Merlini et in 500 speciem Gorlois transmutatus est. Mutatur etiam Vlfin in Iordanum, Merlinus in Britahelem, ita ut nemini quod fuerant comparerent. Deinde aggressi sunt uiam uersus Tintagol et cum crepusculo ad oppidum uenerunt. Indicato ocius ianitori quod consul adueniret, apertae sunt ianuae et intromissi sunt uiri; quid enim aliud accessisset, cum prorsus ipse Gorlois reputaretur adesse? 505 Commansit itaque rex ea nocte cum Igerna et sese desiderata uenere refecit. Deceperat namque illam falsa specie quam assumpserat, deceperat etiam ficticiis sermonibus quos ornate componebat; dicebat enim se egressum esse furtim ab obsesso oppido ut sibi tam dilectae rei atque oppido suo disponeret. Vnde ipsa credula nichil quod poscebatur abnegauit. Concepit 510 quoque eadem nocte celeberrimum uirum illum Arturum, qui postmodum ut celebris foret mira probitate promeruit.

138 Interea, cum compertum esset per obsidionem regem non adesse, exercitus, inconsulte agens, muros diruere conatur et obsessum comitem ad proelium prouocare. Qui etiam inconsulte faciens egressus est cum 515 commilitonibus suis, arbitrans parua manu tot armatis se posse resistere. Pugnantes ergo hinc et inde inter primos peremptus est Gorlois et socii sui dissipati. Captum est quoque oppidum quod obsederant et opes intropositae non aequa sorte diuisae; nam ut cuique amministrabat fortuna et fortitudo

486 astitisset *OCE*[1]
494 dare tibi *C ND*[2] *YG:* tibi dare *OSE:* dare *UAKD*[1] *QHM*
501 Vlfinus *Δ*
507 etiam *Δ Σ Y:* namque *Q:* et *G:* eam *M (*namque ... deceperat *om.)*
511 [uirum] *Σ Φ*
512 esset *Φ*
517 interfectus *Σ Φ*

When the savage deed was done, messengers came to Igerna to report the duke's death and the result of the siege. When they saw the king sitting beside her in the duke's guise, they were abashed and amazed that the man they had left for dead at the siege was alive and had arrived before them; they had no idea of the effect of Merlin's herbs. The king laughed at their stories and embraced the duchess, saying:

'I have certainly not been killed, but am alive, as you see. However, I am grieved by the destruction of my fort and the slaughter of my comrades. It is to be feared that the king will come to cut us off in this castle. Therefore I shall set out first to meet him and make peace, so that no worse fate overtakes us'.

Leaving, he returned to his troops and shed the appearance of Gorlois, to become Uther Pendragon again. When he had learned the whole story, he regretted Gorlois' death, but rejoiced that Igerna was now free from the bond of marriage; so he returned to the castle of Tintagel, took it and Igerna and fulfilled his desire. They remained together thereafter, united by no little passion, and had a son and daughter. Their son was called Arthur, their daughter Anna.

139   After the days and years had passed, the king fell prey to a sickness that troubled him for a long time. Meanwhile the custodians of the prison in which Octa and Eosa, as I mentioned above, were eking out a miserable existence, escaped with them to Germany, spreading fear throughout Britain. Rumors circulated that they had roused the Germans and built a huge fleet to return and destroy the island. And so they did. They returned with a huge fleet and countless companions and, having landed in Scotland, threatened the cities and their inhabitants with fire. The army of Britain was entrusted to Loth of Lothian to keep the enemy at bay. He was the earl of Carlisle, a good soldier, wise and experienced. Impressed by his talents, the king had given him his daughter Anna's hand and stewardship of the realm while he was ill. Loth advanced against the enemy, but was often repulsed and forced to seek refuge in the cities. More often, however, he routed and scattered the enemy, driving them sometimes to the woods and sometimes to their ships. In these see-saw battles it was unclear who was winning. The Britons' downfall was their pride, which led them to scorn the earl's orders; and so they were too weak to beat off the enemy threat.

140   When the king learned that the island had been almost laid waste, more angry than was good for his illness, he ordered all the nobles to meet so that he could rebuke them for their pride and weakness. Seeing them gathered before him, he taunted them with harsh words and swore to lead them against

capaci ungue rapiebat. Peracta tandem huius ausi saeuitia, uenerunt nuntii 520
ad Igernam qui et necem ducis et obsidionis euentum indicarent. Sed cum
regem in specie consulis iuxta eam residere inspexissent, erubescentes
ammirabantur ipsum, quem in obsidione interfectum deseruerant, ita
incolumem praeuenisse; nesciebant enim quae medicamenta Merlinus
confecerat. Ad tales ergo rumores arridebat rex atque cum his uerbis 525
comitissam amplexabatur:

'Non equidem interfectus sum sed ut ipsa uides uiuo. Doleo tamen oppidi
mei destructionem sociorumque meorum caedem. Vnde nobis timendum
est ne superueniat rex et nos in oppido isto intercipiat. Ibo igitur prius in
obuiam et me pacificabo cum ipso, ne nobis deterius contingat'. 530

Egressus itaque petiuit exercitum suum et exuta specie Gorlois in Vther
Pendragon rediuit. Cumque omnem euentum didicisset, ob caedem Gorlois
doluit sed ob Igernam a maritali copula solutam gauisus est. Reuersus itaque
ad oppidum Tintagol, cepit illud cepitque Igernam et uoto suo potitus est.
Commanserunt deinde pariter non minimo amore ligati progenueruntque 535
filium et filiam. Fuit autem nomen filii Arturus, filiae uero Anna.

139   Cumque dies et tempora praeterissent, occupauit infirmitas regem
eumque multis diebus uexauit. Interim uero custodes carceris quo Octa
atque Eosa, quos supra memoraui, taediosam uitam ducebant diffugierunt
cum eis in Germaniam terroremque per regnum intulerant. Asserebat 540
namque rumor ipsos iam commouisse Germaniam classemque maximam
parauisse in exitium insulae redituros. Quod et factum est. Redierunt enim
cum maxima classe sociisque innumerabilibus et partes Albaniae ingressi
ciuitates atque ciues igne accendere afficiunt. Committitur itaque exercitus
Britanniae Loth de Lodonesia ut hostes longius arceret. Erat autem ille 545
consul Leil, miles strenuissimus, sapientia et aetate maturus. Probitate ergo
ipsius acclamante, dederat ei rex Annam filiam suam regnique sui curam
dum infirmitati subiaceret. Hic, cum in hostes progressus esset, multociens
repulsus est ab eis ita ut sese infra ciuitates reciperet, saepius uero fugabat
illos atque dissipabat et nunc ad nemora, nunc ad naues diffugere cogebat. 550
Fuit inter eos dubia proeliorum decertatio ita ut nesciretur cui uictoria
proueniret. Superbia enim ciuibus nocebat, quia dedignabantur praeceptis
consulis oboedire; unde debiliores insistentes nequibant imminentes hostes
triumphare.

140   Vastata itaque fere insula, cum id regi nuntiaretur, ultra quam infirmitas 555
expetebat iratus est iussitque cunctos proceres conuenire, ut ipsos de superbia
et debilitate sua corriperet. Et cum omnes in praesentia sua inspexisset,
conuitia cum castigantibus uerbis intulit iurauitque quod ipsemet eos in

520 saeuitia *Δ Σ:* audatia *Φ*
527 [ipsa] *Σ Φ*
532 rediit *OC*
542 redituros *E A²:* redituri *cett.*
544 ac caede *pro* accendere *34 (cf. Introd.)*
547 illius *E AK M*

the enemy in person. He had a litter made for himself as he was too ill to travel in any other way. He ordered them to be ready to attack the enemy as soon as an opportunity presented itself. Soon the litter was ready, they were all prepared and the opportunity arose.

141   When the king had been lifted in, they marched to St Albans, where the Saxons were harrying all the people. After Octa and Eosa had been told that the Britons had arrived carrying their king in a litter, they refused to fight a man who had to be carried there; they said that it was beneath their dignity to fight someone who was half-dead already. They retired into the city, leaving the gates open as if they had nothing to fear. Hearing this, the king ordered that the city be besieged and its walls attacked from all directions. Obeying his orders, his people laid siege to the city and assaulted its walls. The Britons slaughtered the Saxons and, once the walls were almost demolished, would have broken in if the enemy had not begun to fight back at last. Now that the Britons were victorious, the Saxons repented their former arrogance and began to defend themselves. They manned the walls and drove back the Britons with weapons of every kind. As the battle raged on all sides, night fell, a sign for each man to lay down his weapons and rest. Many wanted to sleep, but the majority plotted their enemy's destruction. The Saxons realised that they had been undone by their pride and that the Britons had almost triumphed, and therefore decided to come out at dawn to challenge their foes to fight on the plain. And so they did. As the sun came up, the Saxons drew up their lines to execute their plan. When the Britons saw them, the soldiers fell in and attacked first, meeting them head on. The Saxons countered the British assault and each side slaughtered the other. When the day was almost done, the British king was victorious and the Saxons fled, leaving Octa and Eosa dead. The king was so overjoyed that, whereas before he could not lift himself up without assistance, now he rose easily and sat on his litter as though suddenly cured. Laughing out loud, he pronounced in happy tones:

'The villains called me a king half-dead, because I lay sick on a litter. And so I was. Yet I prefer conquering them when half-dead to being beaten when hale and hearty, and having to endure a long life thereafter. It is better to die with honour than to live in shame'.

142 Although the Saxons had been beaten, as I described, they did not cease their wicked ways, but attacked the northern regions, constantly harrying the inhabitants. King Uther wanted to pursue them as he had intended, but his chiefs dissuaded him,

hostes conduceret. Praecepit itaque fieri sibi feretrum quo asportaretur, cum gressum alterius modi abnegaret infirmitas. Praecepit etiam cunctos paratos 560 esse ut cum oportunitas accederet in inimicos progrederentur. Nec mora, paratum est feretrum, parati sunt omnes, diesque oportunus instabat.

141   Introposito itaque rege, Verolamium perrexerunt, ubi praedicti Saxones uniuersum populum affligebant. Cumque edocti essent Octa atque Eosa aduentum Britonum regemque feretro aduectum, dedignati sunt cum eo 565 proeliari, quia in uehiculo aduenerat; aiebant enim ipsum semimortuum esse nec tantos uiros cum huiusmodi homine pugnare decere. Receperunt itaque sese infra urbem et ualuas quasi nichil timerent deseruerunt apertas. At Vther, cum id sibi relatum fuisset, iussit ocius obsidere ciuitatem atque moenia undique inuadere. Paruerunt ergo ciues et urbem obsederunt et 570 moenia inuaserunt. Stragem autem Saxonibus dantes, fere dirutis muris ingressi sunt nisi Saxones ad ultimum resistere incepissent. Praeualentibus namque ciuibus, piguerat eos inceptae superbiae, unde se defendere institerunt. Scandentes itaque muros, omnimodis telis Britones repellebant. Denique, cum utrimque decertarent, superuenit nox, quae singulos ab armis 575 ad quietem inuitauit. Quietem desiderabant multi, plures uero consilium quo aduersarios suos perderent. At Saxones, cum inspexissent superbiam suam sibi nocuisse, Britones autem fere triumphasse, proposuerunt cum diluculo egredi inimicosque suos ad campestre proelium prouocare. Quod factum est. Nam ut diem protulit Titan, egressi sunt dispositis cateruis ut 580 propositum suum exequerentur. Quod uidentes Britones diuiserunt milites suos per turmas atque in obuiam uenientes prius inuadere coeperunt. Resistunt ilico Saxones, inuadunt Britones, et mutuam necem utrobique conficiunt. Postremo, cum multum diei praeterisset, cessit uictoria regi Britonum interfectisque Octa atque Eosa terga dederunt Saxones. Cepit 585 inde tanta laeticia regem ita ut cum prius sine iuuamine alterius sese erigere nequiret leui conamine erectus resedit in feretro ac si subitam sanitatem recepisset. Solutus etiam in risum, hilari uoce in hunc sermonem prorumpebat:

    'Vocabant me ambrones regem semimortuum, quia infirmitate grauatus 590 in feretro iacebam. Sic equidem eram. Malo tamen semimortuus ipsos superare quam sanus et incolumis superari sequenti uita perfuncturus. Praestantius enim est mori cum honore quam cum pudore uiuere'.

142 Deuicti autem ut dictum est Saxones non iccirco a malicia sua destiterunt sed aquilonares prouincias ingressi populos incessanter infestabant. Quos 595 Vther rex, ut proposuerat, affectabat insequi, sed dissuaserunt principes,

564 et *E Φ*
565 <in> feretro *Σ Φ*
565 aduectum *H N YG:* aduentum *OCS UAKD QM:* aduectatum *E*
592 *de* sequenti uita perfuncturus *cf. Introd.*
593 enim est *C QGM (cf. § 62.243):* est enim *OHSE Σ (cf. § 200.485):* est *Y*
594 Defuncti *Δ*
594 autem *OHSE UAND Φ:* itaque *C K*
594 ut dictum est *post* Saxones *C: om. Σ Φ*

as his illness had worsened after his victory. This made his enemies bolder and they tried all means to conquer the kingdom. Resorting to their customary treachery, they plotted to kill the king by deceit. They decided to poison him as it was the only practicable method. And so they did. While he lay ill at St Albans, they sent men dressed as beggars to spy on the court. When the spies had become thoroughly familiar with it, they discovered, among other things, one detail upon which they seized to betray Uther. Near the palace there was a spring of sparkling water, which the king used to drink since he could not bear other liquids because of his illness. The wicked traitors went to the spring and completely poisoned it, so that all the flowing water was affected. As soon as the king drank from it, he quickly died. A hundred more men fell victim after him until the treacherous deed was discovered and the spring buried under a mound of earth. After news of the king's death had spread, the bishops and clergy of the kingdom came to escort his body to the monastery of Ambrius, where they gave it a royal burial beside Aurelius Ambrosius in the Giants' Ring.

BOOK NINE

143 On Uther Pendragon's death, British nobles from various regions assembled in Silchester and urged Dubricius archbishop of Caerleon to crown Uther's son Arthur as his successor. They were motivated by necessity because the Saxons, when they learned of Uther's death, had invited in their countrymen from Germany and, led by Colgrimus, were aiming to expel the Britons. They had already occupied all the island from the Humber to the sea at Caithness. Moved by his country's plight, Dubricius and his bishops placed the crown of the kingdom on Arthur's head. He was a youth of fifteen, of great promise and generosity, whose innate goodness ensured that he was loved by almost everybody. As newly-crowned king, he displayed his customary open-handedness. Such a crowd of knights flocked to him that he ran out of gifts. Yet a man who combines an upright character with natural generosity may be out of pocket for a short time, but will never be the victim of lasting poverty. Arthur, who was both upright and generous, decided on war against the Saxons, to use their wealth to reward his household retainers. Right was on his side as he should have been ruler of the entire island by lawful inheritance. He gathered his younger subjects and set off for York. At this news, Colgrimus gathered the Saxons, Scots and Picts to meet him with a great host by the river Duglas, where they fought

quia eum grauior infirmitas post uictoriam occupauerat. Vnde audatiores insistentes hostes omnibus modis regnum subdere nituntur. Proditioni etiam solitae indulgentes, machinantur qualiter regem dolo interficiant. Et cum alter aditus defecisset, statuerunt illum ueneno perdere. Quod factum 600 est. Nam cum in urbe Verolamii iaceret, direxerunt in paupere cultu legatos qui statum curiae addiscerent. Qui cum totum didicissent, inter cetera compererunt unum quod proditioni ipsius praeelegerunt. Erat namque prope aulam fons nitidissimae aquae, quam solitus fuerat potare cum ceteros liquores propter infirmitatem abhorreret. Fontem itaque aggressi 605 sunt nefandi proditores ipsumque undique affecerunt ueneno, ita ut manans aqua tota corrumperetur. Vt igitur potauit ex ea rex, festinae morti succubuit. Succubuerunt etiam centeni homines post illum, donec comperta fraude cumulum terrae superapposuerunt. Cum autem obitus regis diuulgatus fuisset, aduenerunt pontifices cum clero regni tuleruntque corpus eius ad 610 coenobium Ambrii et infra choream gigantum iuxta Aurelium Ambrosium regio more humauerunt.

LIBER VIIII

143 Defuncto igitur Vther Pendragon, conuenerunt ex diuersis prouinciis proceres Britonum in ciuitatem Silcestriae, Dubricio Vrbis Legionum archiepiscopo suggerentes ut Arturum filium eius in regem consecraret. Vrgebat enim eos necessitas, quia audito praedicti regis obitu Saxones conciues suos ex Germania inuitauerant et duce Colgrimo ipsos exterminare 5 nitebantur. Subiugauerant etiam sibi totam partem insulae quae a flumine Humbri usque ad Katanesium mare extenditur. Dubricius ergo, calamitatem patriae dolens, associatis sibi episcopis Arturum regni diademate insigniuit. Erat autem Arturus quindecim annorum iuuenis inauditae uirtutis atque largitatis, in quo tantam gratiam innata bonitas praestiterat ut a cunctis fere 10 populis amaretur. Insignibus itaque regiis iniciatus, solitum morem seruans largitati indulsit. Confluebat ad eum tanta multitudo militum ut ei quod dispensaret deficeret. Sed cui naturalis inest largitio cum probitate, licet ad tempus indigeat, nullatenus tamen continua paupertas ei nocebit. Arturus ergo, quia in illo probitas largitionem comitabatur, statuit Saxones inquietare, 15 ut eorum opibus quae ei famulabatur ditaret familiam. Commonebat etiam id rectitudo, cum tocius insulae monarchiam debuerat hereditario iure optinere. Collecta deinde sibi subdita iuuentute, Eboracum petiuit. Cumque id Colgrimo compertum esset, collegit Saxones, Scotos, et Pictos, uenitque ei obuius cum multitudine maxima iuxta flumen Duglas, ubi facto 20

602 totum *1508 (cf. § 196.399-400)*: totum esse Ω
605 itaque *5 ('Transm.' 99)*: namque Ω
1 Huspendragon *(Vs- S) OS U (cf. § 180.102)*
4 Vrgebat *34 (possis Vrguebat)*: Arguebat Ω *(cf. Introd.)*: Angebat *1587*
13 Sed *5, 21, 46, 56, 104, 111, 113² (cf. 'Transm.' 100)*: Sic Ω
20 obuiam *YM*

a battle damaging to both sides. Arthur, however, was the victor, pursuing the retreating Colgrimus and, when he entered York, subjecting him to a siege. When Colgrimus' brother Baldulfus learned that he had fled, he marched on the siege-lines with six thousand men to free his brother from blockade. While Colgrimus was fighting the battle, Baldulfus had been on the coast, awaiting the arrival of duke Chelricus, who was coming to their assistance from Germany. When Baldulfus was ten miles from the city, he resolved to march all night to deliver a surprise attack. Arthur discovered this, and that very night sent Cador duke of Cornwall with six hundred cavalry and three thousand infantry to intercept him. Cador, reaching the road on which the enemy were passing, launched an unexpected attack and broke up and slaughtered the Saxons, whom he forced to flee. Concerned because he had failed to bring aid to his brother, Baldulfus pondered how he could get to talk with him. He thought that, if he could meet him, they could together devise a plan of escape. Seeing no other way, he shaved off his hair and beard and assumed the dress of a player with a harp. Then, walking into the camp, he posed as a performer, playing music on his harp. Having attracted no suspicion, he went up to the city walls little by little, maintaining his disguise. At last he was noticed by those within, pulled up inside the walls by ropes and taken to his brother. On seeing the brother he had longed for, Baldulfus indulged his emotions, kissing and embracing him as if he was back from the dead. After protracted discussion they despaired of escaping, when suddenly the envoys returned from Germany, bringing to Scotland six hundred ships laden with brave knights, led by Chelricus. At this news, Arthur's advisors persuaded him to break off the siege, as the intervention of such a host of enemies would make the outcome of the battle uncertain.

144   Arthur deferred to the views of his retainers and retired to London. There he gathered all the clergy and nobles of the realm to ask what was the best and safest course to adopt against the enemy invasion. By unanimous agreement messengers were sent to Armorica to inform king Hoelus of Britain's peril. Hoelus was the son of Arthur's sister and of Budicius, king of the Armorican Britons. Hearing of the troubles inflicted on his uncle, Hoelus ordered his fleet prepared, gathered fifteen thousand armed men, sailed with the first favourable winds and landed at Southampton. Arthur received him with due honour and they shared many embraces.

congressu utrorumque exercitus in maiori parte periclitatus fuit. Victoria
tamen potitus Arturus Colgrimum fugientem insecutus est ingressumque
infra Eboracum obsedit. Audita itaque fratris sui fuga, Baldulfus cum sex
milibus uirorum obsidionem petiuit ut ipsum inclusum liberaret. Erat autem
tunc ipse quando frater pugnauerat expectans aduentum Chelrici ducis   25
iuxta maritima, qui eis ex Germania in auxilium uenturus erat. Cum itaque
esset spatio decem miliariorum ab urbe, statuit nocturnum iter arripere
ut furtiuam irruptionem faceret. Quod edoctus Arturus iusserat Cadorem
ducem Cornubiae cum sexcentis militibus et tribus milibus peditum eadem
nocte illi obuiare. Qui uiam qua hostes praeteribant nactus, inopinum   30
impetum fecit dilaceratisque ac interfectis Saxonibus fugam facere coegit.
Qui ultra modum anxius, quoniam fratri suo auxilium subuectare nequiret,
deliberauit apud se qualiter colloquio ipsius frueretur. Existimabat enim
aditum salutis utrorumque consilio machinari posse si illius praesentiam
adire quiuisset. Cum igitur alterius modi aditum non haberet, rasit capillos   35
suos et barbam cultumque ioculatoris cum cythara cepit. Deinde, infra castra
deambulans, modulis quos in lira componebat sese cytharistam exibebat.
Cumque nulli suspectus esset, accessit ad moenia urbis paulatim, coeptam
simultatem faciens. Postremo, cum ab inclusis compertus esset, tractus est
funiculis infra muros et ad fratrem conductus. Ex uoto tunc uiso germano,   40
osculis et amplexibus desideratis sese refecit ac si ex morte resuscitatus
esset. Denique, cum post multimodas deliberationes in desperationem
egrediendi incidissent, remeabant iam legati ex Germania, qui duce Chelrico
sexcentas naues milite forti oneratas in Albaniam conduxerant. Quo audito,
dissuaserunt consiliarii sui Arturo obsidionem diutius tenere, ne si tanta   45
multitudo hostium superuenisset dubium certamen commisissent.

144   Paruit igitur Arturus domesticorum suorum consilio recepitque sese
infra urbem Lundoniarum. Ibi conuocato clero et primatibus tocius
potestatis suae, quaerit consilium quid optimum quidue saluberrimum
contra paganorum irruptionem faceret. Communi tandem assensu   50
illato, mittuntur Armoricam nuntii ad regem Hoelum qui ei calamitatem
Britanniae notificarent. Erat autem Hoelus filius sororis Arturi, ex Budicio
rege Armoricanorum Britonum generatus. Vnde audita inquietatione quae
auunculo ingerebatur iussit nauigium suum parari collectisque quindecim
milibus armatorum proximo uentorum flatu in portu Hamonis applicuit.   55
Excepit illum Arturus quo honore decebat, mutuos amplexus saepissime
innectens.

31 <Baldulfum> in fugam coegerunt *W, sed subauditur ut uid.*
39 simulationem *Y (cf. Introd.)*
39 [ab] *Σ Φ*
40 uoto *addidi:* et *pro* Ex *1508 (cf. Introd.)*
41-2 [ac si ... esset] *Σ Φ*
42 [in] *Φ, sed cf. Introd.*
44 conduxerant *E KD:* conduxerat *cett.: an* qui *post* Chelrico *transponendum ?*
55 in portu *Δ Σ:* portum *Φ*

145   After a few days had passed, they went to the city of Kaerluidcoit, which was under siege by the pagans whom I mentioned before. That city, also known as Lincoln, lay on a hill between two rivers in the province of Lindsey. Arriving there with their combined armies, Arthur and Hoelus attacked the Saxons and inflicted unparalleled losses on them. Six thousand Saxons died that day, either drowned in the rivers or mortally wounded. The rest abandoned the siege in confusion and took to flight. Arthur pursued them relentlessly until they reached the forest of Colidon. As fugitives arrived from all directions, the Saxons tried to make a stand there. Once battle was joined, they defended themselves valiantly and slaughtered the Britons. Moreover the trees permitted them to avoid the Britons' weapons. Noting this, Arthur ordered the trees surrounding that part of the forest to be cut down and their trunks to be placed as a barricade around it; he intended to keep the Saxons trapped there until they starved to death. Then he commanded his troops to surround the forest and remained in position for three days. When the Saxons ran out of food, to avoid starvation they asked to be allowed to leave, on condition that they returned to Germany with only their ships, leaving behind all their gold and silver. They promised to pay him tribute from Germany and to leave behind hostages as surety. After taking advice, Arthur agreed to their terms. He kept their wealth and the hostages to guarantee the tribute, giving them in return no more than
146 permission to leave. As they ploughed the waves on their return voyage, the Saxons repudiated the agreement they had made, set sail round the shores of Britain and made for the coast at Totnes. Having made land, they ravaged the country as far as the Severn estuary, dealing the inhabitants deadly blows. Hurrying to the region of Bath, they subjected the city to a siege. This news caused the king to wonder at their wickedness and to order that the hostages be sentenced to hang without delay. He abandoned the expedition he had launched against the Scots and Picts and hurried to lift the siege, though he was extremely troubled at leaving behind his nephew Hoelus, who was ill in the city of Dumbarton. When he eventually reached the region of Somerset and saw the siege-lines from close quarters, Arthur said:

> 'Since the wicked Saxons, true to their evil repute, refuse to keep faith with me, I shall preserve my faith in my God by attempting to take revenge on them today for the blood of my fellow-countrymen. To arms, men, to arms, and bravely attack these traitors, whom we are sure to defeat with Christ's aid'.

147 At his words, holy Dubricius, archbishop of Caerleon, climbed to a hilltop and cried loudly:

145   Emensis postmodum paucis diebus, urbem Kaerluidcoit petunt, a paganis quos supra memoraui obsessam. Haec autem, in Lindiseiensi prouintia inter duo flumina super montem locata, alio nomine Lindocolinum nuncupatur. Vt 60 igitur cum omni multitudine sua eo uenerunt, proeliati sunt cum Saxonibus, inauditam caedem inferentes. Ceciderunt namque ex illis ea die sex milia, qui partim fluminibus submersi, partim telis percussi uitam amiserunt. Vnde ceteri stupefacti, relicta obsidione, fugam fecerunt. Quos Arturus insequi non cessauit donec in nemore Colidonis uenerunt. Ibi undique ex 65 fuga confluentes, conati sunt Arturo resistere. Conserto itaque proelio, stragem Britonibus faciunt, sese uiriliter defendentes. Vsi etenim arborum auxilio, tela Britonum uitabant. Quod Arturus intuens iussit arbores circa illam partem nemoris incidi et truncos ita in circuitu locari ut egressus eis abnegaretur; uolebat namque ipsos inclusos tam diu obsidere donec fame 70 interirent. Quo facto, iussit turmas suas ambire nemus mansitque tribus diebus ibidem. Cum igitur Saxones quo uescerentur indigerent, ne subita fame perirent petierunt eo pacto egressum ut relicto omni auro et argento cum solis nauibus Germaniam redire sinerentur. Promiserunt quoque se daturos ei tributum ex Germania obsidesque inde mansuros. Tunc Arturus, 75 quaesito consilio, peticioni eorum acquieuit. Retinuit namque ipsorum opes

146 reddendique uectigalis obsides solumque abscessum largitus est. Cumque illi in redeundo domum aequora sulcarent, piguit peractae pactionis retortisque uelis ambierunt Britanniam et Totonesium litus adiuerunt. Nacti deinde tellurem, patriam usque ad Sabrinum mare depopulant, colonos letiferis 80 uulneribus afficientes. Inde arrepto itinere uersus pagum Badonis, urbem obsident. Idque cum regi nunciatum esset, ammirans ultra modum ipsorum facinus, iudicium fieri iussit de illorum obsidibus breui mora suspendendis. Praetermissa etiam inquietatione qua Scotos et Pictos opprimere inceperat, obsidionem dispergere festinauit, maximis uero angustiis cruciatus quoniam 85 Hoelum nepotem suum grauatum morbo in ciuitatem Aldclud deserebat. Postremo, Sumersetensem prouintiam ingressus, uisa cominus obsidione in haec uerba locutus est:

> 'Quoniam impiissimi atque inuisi nominis Saxones fidem michi dedignati sunt tenere, ego fidem Deo meo conseruans sanguinem conciuium 90 meorum in ipsos hodie uindicare conabor. Armate uos, uiri, armate, et proditores istos uiriliter inuadite, quos procul dubio auxiliante Christo triumphabimus'.

147 Haec eo dicente, sanctus Dubricius Vrbis Legionum archiepiscopus, ascenso cuiusdam montis cacumine, in hunc modum celsa uoce exclamauit: 95

---

58 Mensis *Δ*
61 sunt *add. D, 167² (cf. § 88.407):* inferebant *pro* inferentes *48*
79 ambierunt *OHS UAK:* abierunt *CE D:* ad *N:* redierunt *Φ*
85 [uero] *K¹*
85 <est> cruciatus *Φ:* cruciabatur *48*
86 ciuitate *YM*

'Men, distinguished as you are by your Christian faith, do not forget your love for your land and fellow-countrymen, whose expulsion by the treacherous pagans will be a reproach against you forever if you fail to protect them. Fight for your country, ready to die for it if you must. Such a death means victory and the salvation of your souls. Whoever lays down his life for his fellow-Christians, dedicates himself as a living sacrifice to God and patently follows Christ, who deigned to die for his brothers. If any of you falls in this battle, let his death, provided he does not shrink from it, be the repentance and cleansing of all his sins'.

Heartened by the saint's blessing, every man immediately began to arm himself in order to obey his instructions. Arthur himself donned a hauberk worthy of a mighty king, placed on his head a golden helmet engraved with the image of a dragon and shouldered his shield called Pridwen, on which was depicted Mary, the Holy Mother of God, to keep her memory always before his eyes. He also buckled on Caliburnus, an excellent blade forged on the isle of Avallon, and graced his hand with his spear, called Ron. It was a long and broad-bladed spear, ready for the fray. Then he drew up his soldiers and rushed boldly at the Saxons, who were formed in wedges as was their custom. The Saxons fought back valiantly all day, cutting down the Britons without respite. As the sun began to set, the Saxons occupied a nearby hill, to use it as a camp; the bare hillside seemed sufficient, so confident were they in their numbers. But when the next day dawned, Arthur climbed to the summit with his army, though he lost many of them in the ascent; the Saxons, charging down from the crest, found it easier to inflict wounds, since they were faster as they ran down than the Britons who were climbing up. However, the Britons made a mighty effort to reach the top and the fighting quickly became hand to hand. The Saxons stood firm, striving to put up the best resistance they could. Much of the day passed like this, until Arthur was angered that their prowess was denying him victory. Unsheathing his sword Caliburnus, he called out the name of St Mary and swiftly hurled himself upon the dense ranks of the enemy. As he called on God, he killed any man he touched with a single blow and pressed forward until with Caliburnus alone he had laid low four hundred and seventy men. At this sight, the Britons closed ranks and followed him, spreading slaughter. Colgrimus, his brother Baldulfus and many thousands of others fell at once.

'Viri Christiana professione insigniti, maneat in uobis conciuium uestrorum pietas et patriae, qui proditione paganorum exterminati uobis sempiternum erunt opprobrium nisi ipsos defendere institeritis. Pugnate pro patria uestra et mortem si superuenerit ultro pro eadem patimini. Ipsa enim uictoria est et animae remedium. Quicumque etenim pro confratribus suis mortem inierit uiuam hostiam se praestat Deo Christumque insequi non ambigitur, qui pro fratribus suis animam suam dignatus est ponere. Si aliquis igitur uestrum in hoc bello mortem subierit, sit ei mors illa omnium delictorum suorum paenitentia et ablutio, dum eam hoc modo recipere non diffugerit'. 100

105

Nec mora, beati uiri benedictione hilarati festinauit quisque armari se et praeceptis eius parere. Ipse uero Arturus, lorica tanto rege digna indutus, auream galeam simulacro draconis insculptam capiti adaptat, humeris quoque suis clipeum uocabulo Pridwen, in quo imago sanctae Mariae Dei genitricis inpicta ipsum in memoriam ipsius saepissime reuocabat. 110 Accinctus etiam Caliburno gladio optimo et in insula Auallonis fabricato, lancea dextram suam decorat, quae nomine Ron uocabatur. Haec erat ardua lataque lancea, cladibus apta. Deinde, dispositis cateruis, Saxones suo more in cuneos dispositos audacter inuasit. Ipsi tota die uiriliter resistebant, Britones usque prosternentes. Vergente tandem ad occasum sole, proximum 115 occupant montem, pro castro eum habituri; multitudine etenim sociorum confisis solus mons sufficere uidebatur. At ut posterus sol diem reduxit, ascendit Arturus cum exercitu suo cacumen sed in ascendendo multos suorum amisit; Saxones namque, ex summitate occurrentes, facilius ingerebant uulnera, dum ipsos cicior cursus in descensu ageret quam eos in 120 ascensu. Britones tamen, cacumen maxima ui adepti, dextris hostium dextras suas confestim conferunt. Quibus Saxones pectora praetendentes omni nisu resistere nituntur. Cumque multum diei in hunc modum praeterisset, indignatus est Arturus ipsis ita successisse nec sibi uictoriam aduenire. Abstracto ergo Caliburno gladio, nomen sanctae Mariae proclamat et sese 125 cito impetu infra densas hostium acies immisit. Quemcumque attingebat Deum inuocando solo ictu perimebat, nec requieuit impetum suum facere donec quadringentos septuaginta uiros solo Caliburno gladio peremit. Quod uidentes Britones densatis turmis illum sequuntur, stragem undique facientes. Ceciderunt ilico Colgrimus et Baldulfus eius frater et multa milia 130

---

98 erit *E Σ*
98 insisteritis *OC M*
100 Quicumque enim *CE Y*
100 fratribus *O AD QYM*
104 absolutio *OS Σ YM*
106 armare *K M (cf. § 136.433), sed cf. § 20.421*
110 ipsum *CHS UAKD QM²*: ipsam *OE N YGMᵗ, non male, sed cf. § 31.207-8*
112 dexteram *OSE K*
115 insequentes *Φ*
117 confisis (-sisis *Q*) *CHSE UAD Q*: confisus *O*: confisi *K N YM*: confusus *G*
123 praeterisset *O KND ut §§ 34.313, 106.514, 134.380, 141.584*: praeterissent *CSE UA Φ ut §§ 61.144, 157.398, 202.515*

Chelricus witnessed his comrades' peril and immediately turned to flee with the rest.

148   Having gained this victory, the king ordered Cador duke of Cornwall to pursue the Saxons, while he himself hurried to Scotland. He had heard reports that the Scots and Picts were besieging Hoelus in the city of Dumbarton, where, as I said before, he lay ill. Arthur therefore hastened to assist, and to prevent the barbarians from capturing him. The duke of Cornwall with his ten thousand men was reluctant to pursue the fleeing Saxons without first making a forced march to their ships to prevent them embarking. As soon as Cador reached the ships, he left his best soldiers to guard them and stop the pagans from boarding if they retreated that way. Then he pursued swiftly, cutting the fugitives down without mercy, as Arthur had told him. Though the inborn fury of the Saxons had once blazed like lightning, now they fled with fear in their hearts, rushing to deep forests or to hills and caves to preserve their lives. Having failed to find refuge, the tattered remnants came at last to the island of Thanet. The duke of Cornwall pursued them there, slaughtering all the way, and did not cease until he had killed Chelricus and forced the rest to surrender and give him hostages.

149   Once hostilities were over, Cador set out for Dumbarton, now freed by Arthur from barbarian attack. Then he took his army to Moray, where Arthur was blockading the Scots and Picts, who had fled there after fighting three battles against the king and his nephew. After reaching Loch Lomond, they occupied its islands in their search for refuge. The loch, which contains sixty islands, is fed by sixty rivers, but only one flows out of it into the sea. On the islands sixty crags can be seen, each topped by the nest of an eagle, eagles which every year used to gather to mark with loud and conserted cries any marvel about to occur in the kingdom. The enemy had fled to these islands, hoping to be protected by the loch. Their hopes, however, were dashed. Arthur collected a fleet to patrol the rivers and, by blockading them for a fortnight, starved them until they died in their thousands. As they were suffering in this way, Gillamurius, king of Ireland, came to their assistance, arriving by ship with a great host of barbarians. Arthur lifted the blockade and turned his troops on the Irish, whom he mercilessly cut down and forced to sail home. Once victorious, he redirected his attention to the Scots and Picts and began wiping them out with utter ruthlessness. No one he came upon was spared, until all the bishops and subordinate clergymen of that wretched country came to the king barefoot, carrying holy relics and church treasures, to beg him for mercy

aliorum. At Chelricus, uiso sociorum periculo, continuo in fugam cum ceteris uersus est.

148 Rex igitur, potitus uictoria, Cadorem ducem Cornubiae iussit persequi illos dum ipse Albaniam petere festinaret. Nuntiatum namque illi fuerat Scotos atque Pictos obsedisse Hoelum in urbe Aldclud, qua ipsum supra 135 dixi infirmitate grauatum. Quocirca properabat ei in auxilium, ne a barbaris occuparetur. Dux itaque Cornubiae, decem milibus comitatus, fugientes Saxones nondum insequi uoluit, immo naues eorum festinanter exigere ut ipsis ingressum prohiberet. Mox, ut ipsis potitus est, muniuit eas militibus optimis qui introitum abnegarent paganis si ad easdem confugerent. 140 Deinde festinat hostes sequi, sectatos sine pietate trucidare, praeceptum Arturi facturus. Qui modo genuina feritate fulminabant nunc timido corde fugientes aliquando occulta nemorum, aliquando montes et cauernas montium petebant ut spacium uiuendi haberent. Postremo, cum nichil eis tutamini accessisset, insulam Thaneth lacero agmine ingrediuntur. Insequitur 145 eos ibidem dux Cornubiae, solitam caedem inferens, nec requieuit donec perempto Chelrico cunctos deditioni compulit, receptis obsidibus.

149 Pace itaque firmata, profectus est Aldclud, quam Arturus iam a barbarica oppressione liberauerat. Deinde duxit exercitum suum Mureif, ubi obsidebantur Scoti et Picti, qui tercio contra regem nepotemque suum 150 dimicati ipsos usque ad eandem prouinciam diffugerant. Ingressi autem stagnum Lumonoi, occupauerunt insulas quae infra erant, securum refugium quaerentes. Hoc autem stagnum, sexaginta insulas continens, sexaginta flumina recipit, nec ex eo nisi unum solum ad mare decurrit. In insulis uero sexaginta rupes manifestum est esse, totidem aquilarum nidos sustentantes, 155 quae singulis annis conuenientes prodigium quod in regno uenturum esset celso clamore communiter edito notificabant. Ad has itaque insulas confugerant praedicti hostes, ut praesidio stagni fruerentur. Sed parum illis profuit. Nam Arturus, collecto nauigio, flumina circuiuit ipsosque per quindecim dies obsidendo tanta afflixit fame ut ad milia morerentur. Dumque 160 illos in hunc modum opprimeret, Gillamurius rex Hiberniae cum maxima barbarorum copia classe superuenit ut ipsis oppressis auxilium subuectaret. Praetermissa itaque obsidione, coepit Arturus arma uertere in Hibernenses, quos sine pietate laceratos coegit domum refretare. Potitus ilico uictoria, uacauit iterum delere gentem Scotorum atque Pictorum, incommutabili 165 saeuitiae indulgens. Cumque nulli prout reperiebatur parceret, conuenerunt omnes episcopi miserandae patriae cum omni clero sibi subdito, reliquias sanctorum et ecclesiastica sacra nudis ferentes pedibus, misericordiam regis

140 [ad] *OC U QY*
151 dimic<antes et ab eo super>ati *48,* dimicantes *108, 93 (cf. Introd.)*
153 .xl. insulas *CHSE contra Hist. Brit. 67*
154 <nec> solum *OC¹HS UN QG:* <et> solum *D*
163 igitur *Σ G*
164 refrenare *Φ*
164 ilico *Δ Σ:* igitur *Φ*

for the sake of their flock. As soon as they stood before him, they knelt and implored him to take pity on their shattered people; he had inflicted damage enough, and there was no need to kill the few survivors down to the last man; if he let them keep a small portion of their country, they would willingly bear the yoke of slavery for ever. Such was their plea to the king, who, moved to tears of pity, agreed to the holy men's request and granted them pardon.

150   After this, Hoelus visited the site of the loch, amazed at the presence of the sixty rivers, islands, crags and eagles' nests. As he stood in awe, Arthur approached him, saying that there was another, still more wonderful loch in the same region. Quite near, it was twenty feet wide, twenty feet long and five feet deep; square in shape, either by the hand of man or naturally, it supported in its four corners four species of fish, none of which ever strayed into the space of the other three. He added that there was another lake in Wales near the Severn, called Linligwan by the locals, which sucks in the incoming tide and absorbs all the waves without ever flooding its banks. Yet when the tide turns, it vomits back a mountain of water, which only then covers and soaks its banks. If the inhabitants of the whole district stood facing it, once the water spattered their clothes they would have little chance of escape without being drowned in the lake. But if you turn your back, the flood is not dangerous even to people standing beside the water.

151   Having granted pardon to the Scots, the king returned to York to celebrate Christmas there. When he entered the city, he was saddened to see that its holy churches were abandoned. Because archbishop Samson and other men of the Christian faith had been driven out, divine services were no longer held in the half-burnt churches; such had been the extent of the pagans' fury. Arthur gathered the clergy and people, and appointed his chaplain Piramus to the archiepiscopal see. He rebuilt the churches that had been razed and filled them with throngs of religious men and women. Moreover he restored their family titles to the nobles who had been dispossessed by the Saxon incursion.

152   Attending the king were three brothers of regal descent, Loth, Urianus and Auguselus, who had been princes in the region before the Saxons took control. Wishing to return their ancestral rights

pro salute populi sui imploraturi. Mox, ut praesentiam ipsius habuerunt, flexis genibus deprecati sunt ut pietatem super contrita gente haberet; satis 170 etenim periculi intulerat, nec erat opus perpaucos qui remanserant usque ad unum delere; sineret illos portiunculam habere patriae, perpetuae seruitutis iugum ultro gestaturos. Cumque regem in hunc modum rogauissent, commouit eum pietas in lacrimas sanctorumque uirorum peticioni acquiescens ueniam donauit. 175

150 His itaque gestis, explorat Hoelus situm praedicti stagni ammiraturque tot flumina, tot insulas, tot rupes, tot nidos aquilarum eodem numero adesse. Cumque id in mirum contulisset, accessit Arturus dixitque illi aliud stagnum magis esse mirandum in eadem prouincia. Erat quippe haut longe illinc, latitudinem habens uiginti pedum eademque mensura longitudinem cum 180 quinque pedum altitudine; in quadrum uero siue hominum arte siue natura constitutum, quatuor genera piscium infra quatuor angulos procreabat, nec in aliqua partium pisces alterius partis reperiebantur. Adiecit etiam aliud stagnum in partibus Gualiarum prope Sabrinam esse quod pagenses Linligwan appellant, quod cum in ipsum mare fluctuat recipitur in modum 185 uoraginis sorbendoque fluctus nullatenus repletur ut riparum marginem operiat. At dum mare decrescit, eructat ad instar montis absortas aquas, quibus demum ripas tegit et aspergit. Interim, si gens totius regionis illius facie uersa prope astaret, recepta infra uestes undarum aspergine uel uix uel numquam elabi ualeret quin a stagno uoraretur. Tergo autem uerso, non est 190 irroratio timenda etiam si in ripis astaret.

151 Data igitur uenia Scotorum populo, petiuit rex Eboracum, instantis natalis Domini festum celebraturus. Cumque urbem ingressus fuisset, uisa sacrarum ecclesiarum desolatione condoluit. Expulso namque beato Samsone archiepiscopo ceterisque sanctae religionis uiris, templa semiusta 195 ab officio Dei cessabant; tanta etenim paganorum insania praeualuerat. Exin, conuocato clero et populo, Piramum capellanum suum metropolitanae sedi destinat. Ecclesias usque ad solum destructas renouat atque religiosis coetibus uirorum ac mulierum exornat. Proceres autem inquietatione Saxonum expulsos patriis honoribus restituit. 200

152 Erant ibi tres fratres regali prosapia orti, Loth uidelicet atque Vrianus nec non et Auguselus, qui antequam Saxones praeualuissent principatum illarum partium habuerant. Hos igitur ut ceteros paterno iure donare

170 contritam gentem *CE G*
172 patriae habere *Φ*
177 eodem numero *Δ:* numero *ND Φ:* numquam *U:* nusquam *A:* ibidem *K*
185 *de* quod *cf. Introd.*
188 totius patriae *Φ contra Hist. Brit. 69*
192 [igitur] *Σ Φ*
193 ingressus fuisset *A:* om. *Δ U Q (*uenisset ad *ante* urbem *E,* ad urbem praeuenisset *D):* ingrederetur *K:* intraret *N:* intrasset *YM:* transisset *G*
196 praeualuerant *CHS*
198 destinauit *(*fest- *N) E Σ Φ*
199 inquietudine *Φ*

to them too, Arthur restored to Auguselus royal power over the Scots and made his brother Urianus king of Moray. Loth, who in the reign of Aurelius Ambrosius had married the king's sister and fathered Gawain and Modred, recovered the earldom of Lothian and its associated provinces. Then, when he had reestablished the old institutions of the whole region, Arthur took as his wife Ganhumara, a woman of noble Roman ancestry brought up at the court of duke Cador, who was the most beautiful woman in the island.

153 That summer Arthur prepared his fleet to go to Ireland, which he desired to conquer. As he landed, he was opposed by king Gillamuri with great numbers of his subjects, ready to fight. Battle was joined, but quickly Gillamuri's bare and defenceless warriors were horribly butchered and fled wherever they could find refuge. Gillamuri too was swiftly captured and forced to surrender. The other chiefs of Ireland were stunned and surrendered like their king. Having subdued the whole country, Arthur took his fleet to Iceland, where he defeated the natives and conquered their land. As the news spread through the islands that no one could stop Arthur, kings Doldauius of Gotland and Gunuasius of the Orkneys came unbidden to submit and promised to pay tribute. That spring Arthur returned to Britain, restored lasting peace throughout the land and remained there for twelve years.

154 Then Arthur began to increase his household by inviting all the best men from far-off kingdoms and conducted his court with such charm that he was envied by distant nations. All the noblest were stirred to count themselves as worthless if they were not dressed or armed in the manner of Arthur's knights. As his reputation for generosity and excellence spread to the farthest corners of the world, kings of nations overseas became very frightened that he would attack and deprive them of their subjects. Overcome by nagging doubts, they began to put their cities and fortifications in order and built castles in appropriate spots as places of last resort should Arthur attack them. When Arthur learned of this, he exulted at being universally feared and decided to conquer all Europe. He readied his fleets and headed first for Norway to make his brother-in-law Loth its king. Loth was the nephew of Sichelmus king of Norway, who had recently died and left his kingdom to Loth. But the Norsemen had refused to accept him and had made a certain Riculfus king, thinking they could defeat Arthur by fortifying their cities. Loth's son Gawain was then a boy of twelve, who had been placed by his uncle in the service of pope Sulpicius, who had knighted him. When Arthur landed, as I said, in

uolens, reddidit Auguselo regiam potestatem Scotorum fratremque suum Vrianum sceptro Murefensium insigniuit. Loth autem, qui tempore Aurelii 205 Ambrosii sororem ipsius duxerat, ex qua Gualguainum et Modredum genuerat, ad consulatum Lodonesiae ceterarumque comprouinciarum quae ei pertinebant reduxit. Denique, cum tocius patriae statum in pristinam dignitatem reduxisset, duxit uxorem nomine Ganhumaram ex nobili genere Romanorum editam, quae in thalamo Cadoris ducis educata tocius insulae 210 mulieres pulcritudine superabat.

153   Adueniente deinde sequenti aestate, parauit classem suam adiuitque Hiberniae insulam, quam sibi subdere desiderabat. Applicanti autem sibi praedictus rex Gillamuri cum innumerabili gente obuius uenit, contra illum dimicaturus. Cumque proelium incepisset, confestim gens eius nuda et 215 inermis misere lacerata confugit quo ei locus refugii patebat. Nec mora, captus est etiam Gillamuri et deditioni coactus. Vnde ceteri principes patriae stupefacti exemplo regis deditionem fecerunt. Subiugatis itaque tocius Hiberniae partibus, classem suam direxit in Islandiam eamque debellato populo subiugauit. Exin, diuulgato per ceteras insulas rumore quod ei 220 nulla prouintia resistere poterat, Doldauius rex Godlandiae et Gunuasius rex Orcadum ultro uenere promissoque uectigali subiectionem fecerunt. Emensa deinde hyeme, reuersus est in Britanniam statumque regni in firmam pacem renouans moram duodecim annis ibidem fecit.

154   Tunc, inuitatis probissimis quibusque ex longe positis regnis, coepit 225 familiam suam augmentare tantamque faceciam in domo sua habere ita ut aemulationem longe manentibus populis ingereret. Vnde nobilissimus quisque incitatus nichili pendebat se nisi sese siue in induendo siue in arma ferendo ad modum militum Arturi haberet. Denique, fama largitatis atque probitatis illius per extremos mundi cardines diuulgata, reges transmarinorum 230 regnorum nimius inuadebat timor ne inquietatione eius oppressi nationes sibi subditas amitterent. Mordacibus ergo curis anxiati, urbes atque urbium turres renouabant, oppida in congruis locis aedificabant, ut si impetus Arturum in illos duceret refugium si opus esset haberent. Cumque id Arturo notificatum esset, extollens se quia cunctis timori erat, totam Europam 235 sibi subdere affectat. Paratis deinde nauigiis, Norguegiam prius adiuit ut illius diademate Loth sororium suum insigniret. Erat autem Loth nepos Sichelmi regis Norguegensium, qui ea tempestate defunctus regnum suum eidem destinauerat. At Norguegenses, indignati illum recipere, erexerant iam quendam Riculfum in regiam potestatem munitisque urbibus Arturo 240 se posse resistere existimabant. Erat tunc Gualguainus filius praedicti Loth duodecim annorum iuuenis, obsequio Sulpicii papae ab auunculo traditus, a quo arma recepit. Vt igitur Arturus sicut dicere inceperam in

209 [nomine] *Σ Φ*
216 mire lacerata *Φ*
216 refrigerii *YM*
217 [et] *QYG*
222 uenerunt *1587* (uenereunt *1508*) (*cf. Introd. ad § 167.218-19*)

Norway, king Riculfus opposed him with all the kingdom's men, and battle was joined. Much blood was spilt on both sides, but at last the Britons gained the upper hand and charged forward, killing Riculfus and many of his men. Once victorious, they assaulted the cities with fire at the ready, and scattered the country-dwellers with unabated fury until they had subjected 155 the. whole of Norway and Denmark to Arthur's control. After accepting their surrender and making Loth king of Norway, Arthur sailed to Gaul, marshalled his forces and began to ravage the entire country. At that time Gaul was a Roman province under the tribune Frollo, who ruled it in the name of emperor Leo. When he heard of Arthur's arrival, Frollo collected all the armed soldiers under his jurisdiction in order to fight him. Yet Frollo was unable to stand against him. For with Arthur were all the youths from the islands he had conquered. Hence it was claimed that his army was too large to be defeated by any man. The best of the Gallic knights too were in Arthur's service, won over by his generosity. Realising that he was certain to be defeated, Frollo left the battlefield and fled with a handful of followers to Paris. There he reassembled the scattered men, fortified the city and set about facing Arthur again. But while he was trying to recruit neighbouring peoples to reinforce his army, Arthur arrived unexpectedly and trapped him in the city. A month passed until Frollo, concerned that his people were starving, challenged Arthur to single combat, the victor to deprive the vanquished of his kingdom. Frollo was tall, bold and strong, qualities upon which he staked his hopes of salvation. On receiving the challenge, Arthur was delighted with Frollo's proposal and replied that he was prepared to accept his terms. Both parties having agreed, the pair met on an island outside the city, while their men awaited the outcome. Both were well armed and mounted on the swiftest of horses, so that it was not easy to predict the winner. They faced each other with lances held high, then clapped their spurs to their steeds and struck mighty blows. Arthur directed his lance with greater skill and hit Frollo full in the chest, avoiding his lance and dashing him to the ground with all his strength. Drawing his sword, Arthur charged to strike him, but Frollo leapt to his feet and braced his spear to drive it into the breast of Arthur's horse, killing it and bringing them both down. When they saw that their king had fallen, the Britons feared that he was dead and were only prevented with difficulty from breaking the agreement and rushing in a body upon the Gauls. But even as they were about to abandon the terms of the truce, Arthur sprang up and, with his shield held before him,

Norguegensi littore applicuit, obuiauit ei rex Riculfus cum uniuerso patriae populo proeliumque commisit. Et cum multum cruoris in utraque parte 245 diffusum esset, praeualuerunt tandem Britones factoque impetu Riculfum cum multis peremerunt. Victoria igitur potiti, ciuitates accumulata flamma inuaserunt dispersisque pagensibus saeuitiae indulgere non cessauerunt donec totam Norguegiam nec non et Daciam dominio Arturi summiserunt.

155 Quibus subactis, cum Loth in regem Norguegiae promouisset, nauigauit 250 Arturus ad Gallias factisque turmis patriam undique uastare incepit. Erat tunc Gallia prouincia Romae, Frolloni tribuno commissa, qui eam sub Leone imperatore regebat. Qui cum aduentum Arturi comperisset, collegit omnem armatum militem qui potestati suae parebat et cum Arturo proeliatus est. Sed minime resistere quiuit. Nam Arturum iuuentus omnium 255 insularum quas subiugauerat comitabatur. Vnde tantum perhibebatur habere exercitum quantus erat difficilis ab ullo posse superari. Famulabatur quoque ei melior pars Gallicanae militiae, quam sua largitate sibi obnoxiam fecerat. Frollo igitur, cum sese in deteriorem proelii partem incidere uidisset, relicto confestim campo Parisius cum paucis diffugit. Ibi resociato 260 dilapso populo, muniuit urbem iterumque affectauit cum Arturo dimicare. At dum exercitum suum uicinorum auxilio roborare intenderet, uenit ex inprouiso Arturus ipsumque infra ciuitatem obsedit. Emenso deinde mense, cum Frollo gentem suam fame perire doluisset, mandauit Arturo ut ipsi soli duellum inissent et cui uictoria proueniret alterius regnum optineret. Erat 265 enim ipse magnae staturae et audatiae et fortitudinis, quibus ultra modum confisus ista mandauerat, ut hoc modo aditum salutis haberet. Quod cum Arturo nunciatum fuisset, placuit ei uehementer affectus Frollonis renuntiauitque sese paratum fore praedictam conuentionem tenere. Dato igitur in amba parte foedere, conueniunt uterque in insulam quae erat extra 270 ciuitatem, populo expectante quod de eis futurum erat. Ambo erant decenter armati, super equos etiam mirae uelocitatis residentes, nec erat promptum dinoscere cui triumphus proueniret. Vt itaque erectis lanceis in aduersis partibus steterunt, confestim subdentes equis calcaria sese maximis ictibus percusserunt. At Arturus gestando cautius lanceam Frollonem in summitate 275 pectoris infixit eiusque telo uitato quantum uigor sinebat illum in terram prostrauit. Euaginato quoque ense, festinabat eum ferire, cum Frollo uelocius erectus praetensa lancea occurrit illatoque infra pectus equi Arturi letifero uulnere utrumque concidere coegit. Britones, ut regem prostratum uiderunt, timentes eum peremptum esse uix potuerunt retineri quin foedere 280 rupto in Gallos unanimiter irruerent. Ac dum metam pacis iam egredi meditarentur, erectus est ocius Arturus praetensoque clipeo imminentem

266 magnae staturae *OHSE Σ Y:* mirae magnitudinis *C:* staturae staturae *Q:* staturae *GM (*magnae *post* fortitudinis *G)*
266 atque fortitudinis *OHSE*
268 esset *C K*
272 etiam *Δ Σ QY:* et *G: om. M*
275 gestans *Φ*
281 At *K Φ (cf. §§ 19.394, 155.262, 158.434, 166.124)*

ran at the oncoming Frollo. They exchanged blows at close quarters, each eager to dispatch the other. Then Frollo, getting past Arthur's guard, struck him a blow on the forehead which could have proved fatal had his helmet not deflected the blade. When Arthur saw his hauberk and shield red with his own flowing blood, his anger knew no bounds and, raising Caliburnus with all his strength, he brought it down through Frollo's helmet and cut his head in two. Frollo fell mortally wounded, drumming the earth with his heels, and breathed his last. As the news spread through the army, the citizens rushed to open their gates and surrender the city to Arthur. After winning this victory, Arthur divided his force, giving part to duke Hoelus with instructions to march to attack Guitardus, duke of Poitou. With the rest Arthur devoted himself to subduing the remaining rebellious provinces. Hoelus marched into Aquitaine, attacked its cities and, after defeating Guitardus in several battles, forced him to surrender. Gascony too he put to fire and the sword, and received the submission of its chiefs. After nine years had passed, in which he secured the surrender of all the Gallic provinces, Arthur returned to Paris and held court there, summoning clergy and laymen to confirm the rule of peace and law in the kingdom. He presented Estrusia, now called Normandy, to his butler Beduerus, the province of Anjou to his steward Kaius, and many other regions to noble men of his retinue. Then, having secured peace for his cities and their people, he returned to Britain at the beginning of spring.

156   Now that the feast of Whitsun was imminent, Arthur, delighted at his great triumph, decided to hold court immediately, wearing the royal crown upon his head, and summoned the kings and dukes subject to him to the same ceremony, to mark it solemnly and to establish lasting peace among his nobles. He put his plan to his advisors, who suggested that the celebrations be held at Caerleon. The superior wealth of Caerleon, admirably positioned on the river Usk not far from the mouth of the Severn in Glamorgan, made it the most suitable of all cities for such a ceremony. On one side there flowed a noble river, on which could be brought by boat the kings and princes visiting from overseas. On the other, it was surrounded by meadows and woods, and so fine were its royal palaces that the gold that decked their roofs reminded one of Rome. Site of the third metropolitan see of Britain, it boasted two churches, one of which, in honour of the martyr Julius, was distinguished by a convent of devout nuns, and the other, dedicated to his companion Aaron, housed a group of canons.

sibi Frollonem cito cursu petiuit. Instantes ergo cominus, mutuos ictus ingeminant, alter neci alterius insistens. Denique Frollo, inuento aditu, percussit Arturum in frontem, et nisi collisione cassidis mucronem 285 hebetasset mortiferum uulnus forsitan induxisset. Manante igitur sanguine, cum Arturus loricam et clipeum rubere uidisset, ardentiori ira succensus est atque erecto totis uiribus Caliburno impressit eum per galeam infra caput Frollonis, quod in duas partes dissecuit. Quo uulnere cecidit Frollo, tellurem calcaneis pulsans, et spiritum in auras emisit. Cumque id per exercitum 290 diuulgatum fuisset, concurrerunt ciues apertisque ualuis ciuitatem Arturo tradiderunt. Qui deinde, uictoria potitus, diuisit exercitum suum in duo et unam partem Hoelo duci commisit praecepitque illi ut ad expugnandum Guitardum Pictauensium ducem iret. Ipse uero cum reliqua parte ceteras prouintias sibi rebelles subiugare uacauit. Mox Hoelus, Aequitaniam 295 ingressus, urbes patriae inuasit Guitardumque pluribus proeliis anxiatum deditioni coegit. Guasconiam quoque ferro et flamma depopulans principes eiusdem subiugauit. Emensis interim nouem annis, cum totius Galliae partes potestati suae submisisset, uenit iterum Arturus Parisius tenuitque ibidem curiam, ubi conuocato clero et populo statum regni pace et lege 300 confirmauit. Tunc largitus est Beduero pincernae suo Estrusiam, quae nunc Normannia dicitur, Kaioque dapifero Andegauensium prouinciam, plures quoque alias prouincias nobilibus uiris qui in obsequio eius fuerant. Deinde, pacificatis quibusque ciuitatibus et populis, incipiente uere in Britanniam reuersus est. 305

156   Cum igitur sollempnitas Pentecostes aduenire inciperet, post tantum triumphum maxima laeticia fluctuans Arturus affectauit curiam ilico tenere regnique diadema capiti suo imponere, reges etiam et duces sibi subditos ad ipsam festiuitatem conuocare, ut et illam uenerabiliter celebraret et inter proceres suos firmissimam pacem renouaret. Indicato autem familiaribus 310 suis quod affectauerat, consilium cepit ut in Vrbe Legionum suum exequeretur propositum. In Glamorgantia etenim super Oscam fluuium non longe a Sabrino mari amoeno situ locata, prae ceteris ciuitatibus diuitiarum copiis abundans tantae sollempnitati apta erat. Ex una namque parte praedictum nobile flumen iuxta eam fluebat, per quod transmarini reges 315 et principes qui uenturi erant nauigio aduehi poterant. Ex alia uero parte pratis atque nemoribus uallata, regalibus praepollebat palaciis ita ut aureis tectorum fastigiis Romam imitaretur. Duabus autem eminebat ecclesiis, quarum una, in honore Iulii martiris erecta, uirgineo dicatarum choro perpulchre ornabatur, alia quidem, in beati Aaron eiusdem socii nomine 320 fundata, canonicorum conuentu subnixa, terciam metropolitanam sedem

288 in caput *Φ*
293 [ad] *QM*
295 [rebelles] *Φ*
301 Neustriam *AKN M*
319 <monialium deo> dicatarum *N*: <deo> dicatarum <puellarum> *GM (cf. tamen § 157.366)*

It also possessed a college of two hundred scholars, skilled in astronomy and other sciences, who attentively studied the paths of the stars and accurately predicted to the king the portentous events that were to come. Since it was renowned for so many refinements, Caerleon was chosen for the celebrations. Next, envoys were sent to various lands, and guests were invited to visit the court from Gaul and from the neighbouring islands out at sea. Among those attending were Auguselus, king of Albania, now called Scotland; Urianus, king of Moray; Caduallo Lauihr, king of the Venedoti, now known as the North Welsh; Stater, king of the Demetae, or South Welsh; Cador, king of Cornwall; and the three archbishops of the metropolitan sees, London, York and Caerleon. Archbishop Dubricius of Caerleon, primate of Britain and papal legate, was a man of such piety that his prayers could cure any invalid. Also present were earls of noble cities: Morvid, earl of Gloucester; Mauron of Worcester; Arthgal of Kaergueir, now named Warwick; Iugein of Leicester; Cursalem of Chester; Kinmarc of Canterbury; Gualauc of Salisbury; Urbgennius of Bath; Jonathal of Dorchester; and Boso of Ridochen, or Oxford. In addition to these earls, men of no lesser rank were also present: Donaut Mappapo, Cheneus Mapcoil, Peredur Maberidur, Grifud Mapnogoid, Regin Mapclaut, Eddelein Mapcledauc, Kincar Mabbangan, Kinmarc, Gorbonian Masgoit, Clofaut, Run Mapneton, Kinbelin Maptrunat, Cathleus Mapcatel, Kinlith Mapneton and many others too numerous to name; from neighbouring islands came Gillamurius king of Ireland, Maluasius king of Iceland, Doldauius king of Gotland, Gunuasius king of the Orkneys, Loth king of Norway and Aschillus king of the Danes; and from the continent Holdinus duke of the Flemings, Leodegar earl of Boulogne, the butler Beduerus duke of Normandy, Borellus of Le Mans, the steward Kaius duke of Anjou, Guitardus of Poitou, the twelve peers of France, led by Gerinus of Chartres, and Hoelus duke of the Armorican Britons with the nobles subject to him. They travelled with such ostentation of trappings, mules and horses as defies description. In addition to them there was no prince worth his salt this side of Spain who did not answer such a call. Nor was it surprising; Arthur's world-famous openhandedness had made them all love him.

157   When they had all arrived at Caerleon, on the day of the festival the archbishops were led to the palace to place the royal diadem upon the king's head. Undertaking this duty because the court was being held in his diocese, Dubricius

Britanniae habebat. Praeterea gymnasium ducentorum philosophorum habebat, qui astronomia atque ceteris artibus eruditi cursus stellarum diligenter obseruabant et prodigia eo tempore uentura regi Arturo ueris argumentis praedicebant. Tot igitur deliciarum copiis praeclara, festiuitati 325 edictae disponitur. Missis deinde in diuersa regna legatis, inuitantur tam ex Galliis quam ex collateralibus insulis occeani qui ad curiam uenire deberent. Venerunt ergo Auguselus rex Albaniae, quae nunc Scotia dicitur; Vrianus rex Murefensium; Caduallo Lauihr rex Venedotorum, qui nunc Norgualenses dicuntur; Stater rex Demetarum, id est Suthgualensium; 330 Cador rex Cornubiae; trium etiam metropolitanarum sedium archipraesules, Lundoniensis uidelicet atque Eboracensis nec non et ex Vrbe Legionum Dubricius. Hic Britanniae primus et apostolicae sedis legatus tanta religione clarebat ut quemque languore grauatum orationibus suis sanaret. Venerunt nobilium ciuitatum consules: Moruid consul Claudiocestriae; Mauron 335 Wigornensis; Arthgal Cargueirensis, quae nunc Warwic appellatur; Iugein ex Legecestria; Cursalem ex Kaicestria; Kinmarc dux Doroberniae; Gualauc Salesberiensis; Vrbgennius ex Badone; Ionathal Dorecestrensis; Boso Ridochensis, id est Oxenefordiae. Praeter praedictos consules uenerunt non minoris dignitatis heroes: Donaut Mappapo, Cheneus Mapcoil, Peredur 340 Maberidur, Grifud Mapnogoid, Regin Mapclaut, Eddelein Mapcledauc, Kincar Mabbangan, Kinmarc, Gorbonian Masgoit, Clofaut, Run Mapneton, Kinbelin Maptrunat, Cathleus Mapcatel, Kinlith Mapneton, plures quoque alii, quorum nomina longum est enumerare; ex collateralibus etiam insulis Gillamuri rex Hiberniae, Maluasius rex Islandiae, Doldauius rex 345 Godlandiae, Gunuasius rex Orcadum, Loth rex Norguegiae, Aschillus rex Dacorum; ex transmarinis quoque partibus Holdinus dux Rutenorum, Leodegarius consul Boloniae, Beduerus pincerna dux Normanniae, Borellus Cenomanensis, Kaius dapifer dux Andegauensium, Guitardus Pictauensis, duodecim quoque pares Galliarum quos Gerinus Carnotensis conducebat, 350 Hoelus dux Armoricanorum Britonum cum proceribus sibi subditis. Qui tanto apparatu ornamentorum, mularum et equorum incedebant quantum difficile est describere. Praeter hos non remansit princeps alicuius precii citra Hispaniam quin ad istud edictum ueniret. Nec mirum; largitas namque Arturi, per totum mundum diuulgata, cunctos in amorem ipsius allexerat. 355

157   Omnibus denique in urbe congregatis, sollempnitate instante archipraesules ad palacium ducuntur ut regem diademate regali coronent. Dubricius ergo, quoniam in sua diocesi curia tenebatur, paratus ad

322-3 [Praeterea ... habebat] *Φ (cf. 'Transm.' 88)*
332 [et] *Σ Φ*
334 quemque *H² Σ Φ*: quem *OCS*: quemquam *H¹*: quemlibet *E*
336 Wigornensis <Anaraut Salesberiensis> *OCH²SE Σ QY, sed u. infra et § 172.381*
336 [Arthgal Cargueirensis] *H¹ M*
337-8 Gualauc Salesberiensis *om. Y: fort. supra pro* Anaraut Salesberiensis *legendum*
339 [praedictos] *Φ*
354 Nec mora *UAN*
355 illexerat *Σ Φ*

performed the act. After the coronation, the king was duly escorted to the metropolitan cathedral. He was flanked to right and left by two archbishops; four kings, of Scotland, Cornwall, Demetia and Venedotia, walked before him, bearing four golden swords, as was their right; a choir of clergy of all stations sang before him. From the other direction the archbishops and prelates led the queen, wearing her own regalia, to the convent church of the nuns; as was the custom, the queens of the four kings already mentioned bore four white doves before her; all the women attending followed her with great joy. After the parade there was such music and singing in both churches that the knights who were taking part were too captivated to decide which to enter first. They rushed in crowds from one to the other and would not have felt bored even if the ceremony had lasted all day. When at last the religious services in each church were over, the king and queen removed their crowns and put on lighter robes, and the king went with the men to dine at his palace, the queen to another with the women; for the Britons used to observe the old Trojan custom that men and women should celebrate feastdays separately. After they had all been seated according to their rank, Kaius the steward, dressed in ermine, and with him a thousand nobles similarly attired, served them courses. Opposite, a thousand men dressed in vair followed Beduerus the butler, similarly attired, offering various drinks of every sort in goblets. In the queen's palace numerous attendants in various liveries were also doing service and performing their roles; if I were to describe it all in detail, my history would become too wordy. So noble was Britain then that it surpassed other kingdoms in its stores of wealth, the ostentation of its dress and the sophistication of its inhabitants. All its doughty knights wore clothes and armour of a single colour. Its elegant ladies, similarly dressed, spurned the love of any man who had not proved himself three times in battle. So the ladies were chaste and better women, whilst the knights conducted themselves more virtuously for the sake of their love.

When at last they had had their fill at the banquets, they separated to visit the fields outside the city and indulge in varied sports. The knights exercised on horseback, feigning battle. The ladies, watching from the battlements,

celebrandum obsequium huius rei curam suscepit. Rege tandem insignito, ad templum metropolitanae sedis ordinate conducitur. A dextro enim et 360 a laeuo latere duo archipontifices ipsum tenebant; quatuor autem reges, Albaniae uidelicet atque Cornubiae, Demetiae et Venedotiae, quorum ius id fuerat, quatuor aureos gladios ferentes ante illum praeibant; conuentus quoque multimodorum ordinatorum miris modulationibus praecinebat. Ex alia autem parte reginam, suis insignibus laureatam, archipraesules atque 365 pontifices ad templum dicatarum puellarum conducebant; quatuor quoque praedictorum regum reginae quatuor albas columbas more praeferebant; mulieres omnes quae aderant illam cum maximo gaudio sequebantur. Postremo, peracta processione, tot organa, tot cantus in utrisque fiunt templis ita ut prae nimia dulcedine milites qui aderant nescirent quod templorum 370 prius peterent. Cateruatim ergo nunc ad hoc, nunc ad illud ruebant, nec si totus dies celebrationi daretur taedium aliquod ipsis generaret. Diuinis tandem obsequiis in utroque celebratis, rex et regina diademata sua deponunt assumptisque leuioribus ornamentis ipse ad suum palatium cum uiris, ipsa ad aliud cum mulieribus epulatum incedunt; antiquam namque consuetudinem 375 Troiae seruantes Britones consueuerant mares cum maribus, mulieres cum mulieribus festiuos dies separatim celebrare. Collocatis postmodum cunctis ut dignitas singulorum expetebat, Kaius dapifer, herminio ornatus, mille uero nobilibus comitatus, qui omnes herminio induti fercula cum ipso ministrabant. Ex alia uero parte Beduerum pincernam uario indutum totidem 380 amicti uario secuntur, qui in ciphis diuersorum generum multimoda pocula cum ipso distribuebant. In palatio quoque reginae innumerabiles ministri, diuersis ornamentis induti, obsequium suum praestabant, morem suum exercentes; quem si omnino describere pergerem, nimiam prolixitatem historiae generarem. Ad tantum etenim statum dignitatis Britannia tunc 385 reducta erat quod copia diuitiarum, luxu ornamentorum, facetia incolarum cetera regna excellebat. Quicumque uero famosus probitate miles in eadem erat unius coloris uestibus atque armis utebatur. Facetae etiam mulieres, consimilia indumenta habentes, nullius amorem habere dignabantur nisi tercio in milicia probatus esset. Efficiebantur ergo castae et meliores et 390 milites pro amore illarum probiores.

Refecti tandem epulis, diuersi diuersos ludos composituri campos extra ciuitatem adeunt. Mox milites, simulacrum proelii ciendo, equestrem ludum componunt. Mulieres in edito murorum aspicientes

360 ornate *O Φ*
367 columbae *C U Q*
368 omnes *Δ Σ*: autem *Φ*
372 daretur *K: om. OCHS UAND Q: male* uacaret *E YM,* esset *G,* indulgeret *O²* (cf. *Introd.*)
378-80 Kaius ... ministrabant *negligenter compositum*
380 indutum *add. N, 8, 113, 123,* amictum *178, 88: prius* uario *om. C YG,* alterum *OH M* (cf. *Introd.*)
386 coma *CHSE*
390 <mulieres> et meliores *C:* et mulieres *A¹ G:* mulieres *Faral*
393 ciendo *69* (cf. *Verg. Aen. 5.585, 674):* sciendo *Ω*

playfully fanned the flames in the knights' hearts into furious passion. Then they peacefully passed the remainder of the day in various games, some contending with boxing gloves, some with spears, some in tossing heavy stones, some at chess, and others with dice. Arthur rewarded all those who had been victorious with liberal gifts. After they had devoted the first three days to these pursuits, on the fourth all those who were serving the king in expectation of some title were summoned and each was rewarded with a city or castle, with archbishoprics, bishoprics, abbeys or some other honour.

158   The saintly Dubricius relinquished his position as archbishop, being eager to live as a hermit. His place was taken by the king's uncle David, whose life was a model of goodness for all his pupils. Archbishop Samson of Dol was replaced by Teliaus, a distinguished priest of Llandaff, with the full support of Hoelus king of the Armorican Britons, who was impressed by his conduct and good character. Maugannius became bishop of Silchester and Duvianus of Winchester. The episcopal mitre of Dumbarton was awarded to Eledenius. While these honours were being distributed, twelve men of mature age with reverend expressions suddenly entered at a measured pace, carrying in their right hands olive branches as a token of their mission, and after greeting the king, presented him with the following letter from the hand of Lucius Hiberius:

> 'Lucius, procurator of the republic, wishes Arthur, king of Britain, his just deserts. I am filled with amazement at the boldness of your despotism. I repeat, I am amazed and, when I recall the slight that you have inflicted on Rome, I am angered that you do not acknowledge it in your pride, and are slow to realise what it means to have offended with your unjust actions the senate, to which the whole world owes allegiance, as you well know. The senate ordered you to pay Britain's tribute, because it had been paid for many years to Julius Caesar and other representatives of Roman power, but you dared to withhold it and disregard the command of that august body. You have taken from them Gaul, the province of the Allobroges and all the islands of the ocean, whose kings were tributory to my forebears, when Roman power prevailed in those parts. The senate has decreed that redress must be sought for the insults you have heaped upon it; therefore I set the middle of August next year as the time by which you are ordered to appear in Rome, to satisfy your masters and accept the sentence they will justly hand down. Otherwise I shall enter your territory in person and take steps to recover with the sword whatever you in your frenzy have stolen from the republic'.

in furiales amores flammas more ioci irritant. Alii cum caestibus, alii 395
cum hasta, alii ponderosorum lapidum iactu, alii cum scaccis, alii cum
aleis ceterorumque iocorum diuersitate contendentes, quod diei restabat
postposita lite praetereunt. Quicumque ergo uictoriam ludi sui adeptus
erat ab Arturo largis muneribus ditabatur. Consumptis autem primis in
hunc modum diebus tribus, instante quarta uocantur cuncti qui ei propter 400
honores obsequium praestabant et singuli singulis possessionibus,
ciuitatibus uidelicet atque castellis, archiepiscopatibus, episcopatibus,
abbatiis, ceterisque honoribus donantur.

158   Beatus igitur Dubricius, in heremiticam uitam anhelans, sese ab
archiepiscopali sede deposuit. In cuius loco sacratur Dauid auunculus regis, 405
cuius uita exemplum tocius bonitatis erat his quos doctrina imbuebat. In
loco uero sancti Samsonis Dalensis archipraesulis destinatur Teliaus illustris
presbiter Landauiae, annitente Hoelo rege Armoricanorum Britonum, cui
uita et boni mores uirum commendauerant. Episcopatus quoque Silcestriae
Maugannio et Guintoniae Duuiano decernitur. Decernitur quoque 410
pontificalis infula Aldclud Eledenio. Dum haec inter eos distribueret, ecce
duodecim uiri maturae aetatis, reuerendi uultus, ramos oliuae in signum
legationis dextris ferentes, moderatis passibus ingrediuntur et salutato rege
litteras ei ex parte Lucii Hiberii in haec uerba optulerunt:

'Lucius rei publicae procurator Arturo regi Britanniae quod meruit. 415
Ammirans uehementer ammiror super tuae tyrannidis proteruia. Ammiror,
inquam, et iniuriam quam Romae intulisti recolligens indignor quod extra
te egressus eam cognoscere diffugias nec animaduertere festines quid sit
iniustis actibus senatum offendisse, cui totum orbem famulatum debere
non ignoras. Etenim tributum Britanniae, quod tibi senatus reddere 420
praeceperat quia Gaius Iulius ceterique Romanae dignitatis uiri illud
multis temporibus habuerunt, neglecto tanti ordinis imperio detinere
praesumpsisti. Eripuisti quoque illi Galliam, eripuisti Allobrogum
prouintiam, eripuisti omnes occeani insulas, quarum reges, dum Romana
potestas in illis partibus praeualuit, uectigal ueteribus meis reddiderunt. 425
Quia ergo de tantis iniuriarum tuarum cumulis senatus rectitudinem
petere decreuit, mediantem Augustum proximi anni terminum praefigens
Romam tibi uenire iubeo, ut dominis tuis satisfaciens sententiae quam
eorum dictauerit iusticia acquiescas. Sin autem, ego ipse partes tuas
adibo et quicquid uesania tua rei publicae eripuit eidem mediantibus 430
gladiis restituere conabor'.

395 amoris *AD G*
395 cestibus *K G:* celtibus *cett., absurde*
396 scaccis *108, 15, 39, 118:* saxis *Ω (cf. Introd.)*
400 tribus diebus *H NK*
406 imbuerat *HSE K*
413 <in> dextris *Φ*
420 [reddere] *Φ*
423 [illi] *Φ*
429 dictauerit *OH UAK:* dictauit *CSE ND Φ*

After the letter had been read out before the king and his earls, Arthur retired with them to the giants' tower above his gateway, to determine how they ought to reply to such demands. As they began to climb the steps, Cador duke of Cornwall, in happy mood, smiled and said to the king:

'I had feared that the ease which the Britons have enjoyed in this long period of peace would make them slack and completely forgetful of the reputation for fighting which marks them out from other nations. When military expeditions cease and their place is taken by dice, love-affairs and other pleasures, then it is certain that the prowess, honour, boldness and renown of former days is tainted by slackness. For nearly five years we have pursued such pleasures without being tried in war. To ensure that sloth does not sap our strength, God has therefore set the Romans on this course to allow us to recover our old virtue'.

159 As Cador voiced these and similar opinions to the others, they came at last to their seats, where all of them gathered to hear Arthur deliver the following speech:

'You, my companions in success and adversity, whose worth has thus far been proven to me in council and on the battlefield, now consider together and make wise provision for our response to such demands. Wise and careful forethought ensures that what must be done can be the more easily endured. We shall therefore endure Lucius' provocation more easily if we plan together in advance how we can counter it. In my opinion we need not fear it greatly, because Lucius has no justification for demanding the tribute he wishes to have from Britain. He claims that he ought to receive it on the grounds that it was paid to Julius Caesar and his successors, who landed with an army after being called in because of dissent on our ancestors' part, and who by force of arms subjected our country to their power, when it was weakened by internal strife. Because they obtained it by these means, the tribute they exacted from us was unjust. What is obtained by force of arms is never the rightful possession of the aggressor. Therefore Lucius has no valid reason to claim the right to receive tribute from us. Indeed, since he has presumed to make unjust demands on us, let us by the same token ask him for tribute from Rome, and let the stronger party obtain what they desire. If Lucius judges that he ought to receive tribute from Britain because Julius Caesar and other Roman emperors once

Quae ut in praesentia regum et consulum recitatae fuerunt, secessit Arturus cum eis in giganteam turrim quae in introitu erat, tractaturus quae contra talia mandata disponi deberent. Ac dum gradus ascendere incepissent, Cador dux Cornubiae, ut erat laeti animi, in hunc sermonem cum risu 435 coram rege solutus est:

'Hucusque in timore fueram ne Britones longa pace quietos ocium quod ducunt ignauos faceret famamque militiae, qua ceteris gentibus clariores censentur, in eis omnino deleret. Quippe ubi usus armorum uidetur abesse, aleae autem et mulierum inflammationes ceteraque oblectamenta 440 adesse, dubitandum non est ne id quod erat uirtutis, quod honoris, quod audatiae, quod famae, ignauia commaculet. Fere namque transacti sunt quinque anni ex quo praedictis deliciis dediti exercitio martis caruimus. Deus igitur, ne nos debilitaret segnitia, Romanos in hunc affectum induxit ut in pristinum statum nostram probitatem reducerent'. 445

159 Haec et his similia illo cum ceteris dicente, uenerunt tandem ad sedilia, ubi collocatis singulis Arturus illos in hunc modum affatus est:

'Consocii' inquit 'prosperitatis et aduersitatis, quorum probitates hactenus et in dandis consiliis et in militiis agendis expertus sum, adhibete nunc unanimiter sensus uestros et sapienter praeuidete quae super talibus 450 mandatis nobis agenda esse noueritis. Quicquid enim a sapiente diligenter praeuidetur, cum ad actum accedit, facilius toleratur. Facilius ergo inquietationem Lucii tolerare poterimus si communi studio praemeditati fuerimus quibus modis eam debilitare institerimus. Quam non multum nobis timendam esse existimo, cum irrationabili causa exigat tributum 455 quod ex Britannia habere desiderat. Dicit enim ipsum sibi dari debere quia Iulio Caesari ceterisque successoribus suis redditum fuerit, qui discidio ueterum nostrorum inuitati cum armata manu applicuerunt atque patriam domesticis motibus uacillantem suae potestati ui et uiolentia summiserunt. Quia igitur eam hoc modo adepti fuerunt, uectigal ex illa 460 iniuste ceperunt. Nichil enim quod ui et uiolentia acquiritur iuste ab ullo possidetur qui uiolentiam intulit. Irrationabilem ergo causam praetendit qua nos iure sibi tributarios esse arbitratur. Quoniam autem id quod iniustum est a nobis praesumpsit exigere, consimili ratione petamus ab illo tributum Romae, et qui fortior superuenerit ferat quod habere exoptauit. 465 Nam si quia Iulius Caesar ceterique Romani reges Britanniam olim

433 [erat] *OCHS UAND*
434 deberet *Φ*
434 At *E AKD QY*
438 qua *CE AND YM:* quae *OHS U Q:* qui *K:* quam *G*
440 autem *OCSE Σ: om. H:* uero *Φ*
444 ut nos *O AK²:* ut ne nos *N*
444 debilitaret *N:* deliberaret *Δ UAKD:* liberaret *Φ*
445 [in] *OC¹HS Y: post* statum *E*
460 ex ea *Φ*
462 *ante* Qui *interpungunt codd. praeter O, uix recte, unde* ergo *om. Y (cf. Introd.)*
463 sibi iure *A QY*

conquered us, I likewise judge that Rome owes tribute to me, because my predecessors once captured her. That most serene British king Beli, aided by his brother Brennius, duke of the Allobroges, once hung twenty of the noblest Romans in the middle of the forum, captured the city and occupied it for a considerable time. Helena's son Constantine and Maximianus, close relatives of mine who were crowned king of Britain one after the other, have both sat upon the throne as emperor of Rome. Should we then demand tribute from the Romans? As for Gaul and the neighbouring islands of the ocean, no reply is called for, since Lucius failed to defend them when we replaced his jurisdiction with our own'.

160 After Arthur had voiced these and similar opinions, Hoelus, king of the Armorican Britons, was bidden to make the first reply and said:

'Even if each of us could look into his heart and ponder each detail in every way, I do not think that we could offer a better plan than that which your discernment and painstaking wisdom has just unfolded. Your arguments, soaked in Cicero's honey, have made ample provision for us, and we ought to offer unceasing praise for your feeling as a man of resolve, for steeling your wise mind and for revealing an excellent plan. If you wish to march on Rome on the terms you have proposed, I have no doubt that we shall be successful, since we would be protecting our freedom and demanding justly from our enemies what they are trying unjustly to demand from us. Whoever attempts to steal another's property, deserves to lose his own to the man he has wronged. Since the Romans are attempting to deprive us of our possessions, we will surely deprive them of theirs, if we get the chance to fight them. That is a battle every Briton ought to long for, nor should we forget the prophecies of the Sibyl, whose truthful verses proclaim that for a third time one born of British blood will rule the Roman state. Her prophecies have come true for two men already, since it is clear, as you said, that the noble princes Beli and Constantine have worn the crown of Rome. You now stand before us as the third to whom that high title has been vouchsafed. Make haste, then, to accept what God so freely offers, conquer what begs for conquest, and do honour to us all; for the sake of your honour, I am ready both to endure wounds and to sacrifice my life. So that you can attain your goal, I shall accompany your person with ten thousand armed men'.

subiugauerunt uectigal nunc debere sibi ex illa reddi decernit, similiter
ego censeo quod Roma michi tributum dare debet, quia antecessores mei
eam antiquitus optinuerunt. Beli etenim, serenissimus ille rex Britonum,
auxilio fratris sui usus, Brennii uidelicet ducis Allobrogum, suspensis 470
in medio foro uiginti nobilioribus Romanis urbem ceperunt captamque
multis temporibus possederunt. Constantinus etiam Helenae filius nec non
Maximianus, uterque michi cognatione propinquus, alter post alterum
diademate Britanniae insignitus, thronum Romani imperii adeptus est.
Censetisne ergo uectigal ex Romanis petendum? De Gallia autem siue de 475
collateralibus insulis occeani non est respondendum, cum illas defendere
diffugeret quando easdem potestati eorum subtrahebamus'.

160 Haec et his similia eo dicente, Hoelus rex Armoricanorum Britonum,
ceteros praecedere iussus, in haec uerba respondit:

'Licet unusquisque nostrum, totus in se reuersus, omnia et de omnibus 480
animo retractare ualeret, non existimo eum praestantius consilium
posse inuenire quam istud quod modo discretio sollertis prouidentiae
tuae reuoluit. Prouide etenim prouidit nobis tua deliberatio Tulliano
liquore lita, unde constantis uiri affectum, sapientis animi effectum,
optimi consilii profectum laudare indesinenter debemus. Nam si iuxta 485
praedictam rationem Romam adire uolueris, non dubito quin triumpho
potiamur dum libertatem nostram tueamur, dum iuste ab inimicis nostris
exigamus quod a nobis iniuste petere inceperunt. Quicumque enim sua
alteri eripere conatur merito quae sua sunt per eum quem impetit amittit.
Quia ergo Romani nobis nostra demere affectant, sua illis procul dubio 490
auferemus si licentia nobis congrediendi praestabitur. En congressus
cunctis Britonibus desiderandus, en uaticinia Sibillae, quae ueris
uersibus testantur ex Britannico genere tercio nasciturum qui Romanum
optinebit imperium. De duobus autem adimpleta sunt ipsius oracula, cum
manifestum sit praeclaros ut dixisti principes Beli atque Constantinum 495
imperii Romani gessisse insignia. Nunc uero te tercium habemus cui
tantum culmen honoris promittitur. Festina ergo recipere quod Deus
non differt largiri, festina subiugare quod ultro uult subiugari, festina
nos omnes exaltare; qui ut exalteris, nec uulnera recipere nec uitam
amittere diffugiam. Vt autem hoc perficias, decem milibus armatorum 500
praesentiam tuam comitabor'.

471 .xxiiii. *YM ex § 43.198*
471-2 cepit ... possedit *48, 93, sed cf. Introd. ad § 16.288-90*
472 nec non <et> *Y ut solet noster*
475 siue [de] *Φ*
476 [occeani] *E Σ Φ*
476-7 diffugeret defendere *Φ*
479 ceterosque *QYM*
483 reuoluit *69:* redoluit *Ω (cf. Introd.)*
493 uersibus *addidi (pro* ueris *48):* argumentis *add. 93 ex § 156.324-5,* auguriis *1508*
494 [ipsius] *H¹ Φ*
497 [tantum] *Φ*
500 *de* diffugiam *cf. Introd.*

161 When Hoelus had finished speaking, Auguselus king of Scotland expressed his view as follows:

> 'As soon as I realised that my lord's desires were as he said, my heart felt greater joy than I can tell here and now. I count as nothing all the campaigns we have waged against so many mighty kings as long as the Romans and Germans remain unpunished and the harm they have inflicted on our countrymen in the past goes unavenged. Now that we have permission to fight them, I am overjoyed and long for the day of battle, thirsting for their blood as if I had been denied water for three days. When I see that dawn, how sweet will be the wounds I give and receive when we exchange blows! Death itself will be sweet, as long as I die avenging our forefathers, preserving our freedom and securing the fame of our king. Let us attack these effeminates and never relent until we have won a welcome victory and deprived the vanquished of their titles. I shall provide two thousand armed knights for our army, and foot soldiers besides'.

162 After the others had also said what was necessary in the circumstances, each of them pledged their full required contingents, so that from the island of Britain alone there were reckoned sixty thousand troops of all arms, in addition to those promised by the duke of Armorica. The kings of the neighbouring islands, who did not employ cavalry, promised their full complement of infantry, a total of one hundred and twenty thousand men from the six lands of Ireland, Iceland, Gotland, the Orkneys, Norway and Denmark. Eighty thousand troops were contributed by the French dukedoms of Flanders, Ponthieu, Normandy, Maine, Anjou and Poitou; and twelve hundred from the twelve earldoms of Gerinus of Chartres and his peers. In total there were a hundred and eighty-three thousand, two hundred knights, in addition to countless numbers of infantry.

King Arthur, now that he was sure of their unanimous support, commanded that they return home quickly to gather their promised contingents and hasten on the first day of August to the habour of Barfleur, from which town they would advance with him to the territory of the Burgundians against the Romans. To the emperors he sent a message by their own envoys to the effect that he would never pay them tribute, nor

161 Auguselus etiam rex Albaniae, ut Hoelus finem dicendi fecerat, quod super
hac re affectabat in hunc modum manifestare perrexit:

'Ex quo dominum meum ea quae dixit affectare conieci, tanta laeticia
animo illapsa est quantam nequeo in praesentiarum exprimere. Nichil   505
enim in transactis debellationibus quas tot et tantis regibus intulimus
egisse uidemur dum Romani et Germani illaesi permaneant nec in illos
clades quas olim nostratibus ingesserunt uiriliter uindicemus. At nunc,
quoniam nobis licentia congrediendi promittitur, gaudens admodum
gaudeo et desiderio diei quo conueniemus exaestuans sitio cruorem   510
illorum quemadmodum fontem si triduo prohiberer ne biberem. O si illam
lucem uidebo quam dulcia erunt uulnera quae uel recipiam uel inferam
quando dexteras conseremus! Ipsa etiam mors dulcis erit dum eam in
uindicando patres nostros, in tuendo libertatem nostram, in exaltando
regem nostrum perpessus fuero. Aggrediamur igitur semiuiros illos et   515
aggrediendo perstemus ut deuictis ipsis eorum honoribus cum laeta
potiamur uictoria. Exercitum autem nostrum duobus milibus armatorum
militum, exceptis peditibus, augebo'.

162 Postquam etiam ceteri ad hoc quae dicenda erant dixerunt, promiserunt
ei singuli quot in obsequium suum debebant, ita ut praeter eos quos   520
promiserat dux Armoricae ex sola insula Britanniae .lx. milia omnibus
armis armatorum computarentur. At reges ceterarum insularum, quoniam
non duxerant in morem milites habere, pedites quot quisque debebat
promittunt, ita ut ex sex insulis, uidelicet Hiberniae, Islandiae, Godlandiae,
Orcadum, Norguegiae atque Daciae, sexies .xx. milia essent annumerata;   525
ex Galliarum autem ducatibus Rutenorum, Portiuensium, Estrusiensium,
Cenomannorum, Andegauensium, Pictauensium, .lxxx. milia; ex duodecim
autem consulatibus illorum qui cum Gerino Carnotensi aderant duodecies
centum. Quod inter totum fuit centum octoginta milia et tria milia et .cc.
praeter pedites, qui sub numero non leuiter cadebant.   530

Rex igitur Arturus, expertus omnes in obsequium suum unanimiter
paratos, praecepit eis celeriter repatriare et exercitum promissum disponere
et in kalendis Augusti ad portum Barbae fluuii festinare, ut illinc Allobrogum
fines cum ipso adituri Romanis in obuiam uenirent. Imperatoribus autem
per eorundem legatos mandauit se nequaquam eis redditurum tributum nec   535

---

509 permittitur *K Φ*
513 dextras *CHE D*
521 Armoriae *codd. praeter G, uix recte*
523 quos *OH D*
525 .xx. *bis CS U*
526 Galliarum *AND, Aluredus Beuerlac. (cf. Introd. n. 31) p. 65:* Gallicarum *cett. mei (cf. Introd.)*
526 Pontiuorum *34, et cf. Tatlock 90-91*
526 Neustrensium *H AK²*
528 [autem] *CE K*
530 leuiter non *Φ*
531 expertus *O², 93: fort.* compertus: exceptus *Ω (cf. Introd.)*
533 [ad] *Δ, sed cf. §§ 77.107-8, 134.381-2*

was he coming to Rome to face their sentence, but rather to demand from them what their court had decided to demand from him. Then the envoys, kings and nobles speedily went on their way to complete their missions.

BOOK TEN

163 Once he discovered the contents of Arthur's reply, Lucius Hiberius by the senate's command instructed the kings of the East to muster their forces and join him in conquering Britain. There swiftly assembled Epistrophus king of the Greeks, Mustensar king of the Africans, Aliphatima king of Spain, Hirtacius king of the Parthians, Boccus king of the Medes, Sertorius king of Libya, Serses king of the Itureans, Pandrasus king of Egypt, Micipsa king of Babylon, Politetes duke of Bithynia, Theucer duke of Phrygia, Evander of Syria, Echion of Boetia and Ypolitus of Crete, with the dukes and nobles subject to them; and from the ranks of the senators, Lucius Catellus, Marius Lepidus, Gaius Metellus Cocta, Quintus Milvius Catulus and Quintus Carucius; and so many others that they numbered four hundred and sixty thousand, one hundred.

164 Once all necessary preparations had been made, they set off towards Britain on the first day of August. On learning that they were coming and after entrusting the running of the country to his nephew Modred and queen Ganhumara, Arthur went with his army to Southampton, from where he sailed with a following wind. While he was ploughing the waves with his huge fleet, enjoying a safe passage, at about midnight he fell into a deep sleep. In it he dreamed he saw a bear flying through the air and making all the shores tremble with its growls; and also a terrible dragon swooping from the west, whose blazing eyes lit up the land; they met to fight a wondrous duel, in which the bear repeatedly attacked the dragon, but was burned by its fiery breath and cast to the ground. Arthur awoke and told the dream to his retinue. They interpreted the dragon as meaning the king, and the bear as a giant he would fight; their battle meant the impending combat between the king and the giant; and the dragon's victory foretold that of the king. Arthur understood the dream differently, thinking that it concerned himself

ob id ut sententiae eorum adquiesceret Romam aditurum, immo ut ex illis appeteret quod ab illo iudicio suo appetere decreuerant. Digrediuntur ergo legati, digrediuntur reges, digrediuntur proceres, et quod eis praeceptum fuerat perficere non differunt.

LIBER X

163 Lucius igitur Hiberius, agnita sententia huius responsi, iussu senatus orientalibus edixit regibus ut parato exercitu secum ad subiugandum Britanniam uenirent. Conuenerunt ocius Epistrophus rex Graecorum, Mustensar rex Affricanorum, Aliphatima rex Hispaniae, Hirtacius rex Parthorum, Boccus Medorum, Sertorius Libiae, Serses rex Ituraeorum, 5 Pandrasus rex Aegypti, Micipsa rex Babiloniae, Politetes dux Bithiniae, Theucer dux Frigiae, Euander Syriae, Echion Boetiae, Ypolitus Cretae, cum ducibus et proceribus sibi subditis; ex senatorio quoque ordine Lucius Catellus, Marius Lepidus, Gaius Metellus Cocta, Quintus Miluius Catulus, Quintus Carutius; tot etiam alii quod inter totum quadringenta milia et .lx. 10 et .c. computati fuerunt.

164   Dispositis itaque quibusque necessariis, incipientibus kalendis Augusti iter uersus Britanniam arripiunt. Comperto igitur aduentu ipsorum, Arturus, Modredo nepoti suo atque Ganhumarae reginae Britanniam ad conseruandum permittens, cum exercitu suo Portum Hamonis adiuit, ubi 15 tempestiuo uentorum afflatu mare ingressus est. Dum autem innumeris nauibus circumsaeptus prospero cursu et cum gaudio altum secaret, quasi media hora noctis instante grauissimus sompnus eum intercepit. Sopitus etiam per sompnium uidit ursum quendam in aere uolantem, cuius murmure tota littora intremebant; terribilem quoque draconem ab occidenti aduolare, 20 qui splendore oculorum suorum patriam illuminabat; alterum uero alteri occurrentem miram pugnam committere, sed praefatum draconem ursum saepius irruentem ignito anhelitu comburere combustumque in terram prosternere. Expergefactus ergo Arturus astantibus quod sompniauerat indicauit. Qui exponentes dicebant draconem significare eum, ursum uero 25 aliquem gigantem qui cum ipso congrederetur; pugnam autem eorum portendere bellum quod inter ipsos futurum erat; uictoriam uero draconis illam quae ei proueniret. At Arturus aliud coniectabat, existimans ob se

---

537 decreuerunt *SE:* decreuerat *AK G*
1 sententia *Δ (cf. § 9.104): om. Σ Φ, unde alius aliud AKND (etiam* huius responsi *om. U),* responsi <edicto> *mire Φ (antea* agnito *GM) (cf. 'Transm.' 91-2)*
2 subiugandam *A YG*
5 Boccus <rex> *H YM*
10 quod *Σ Φ:* quot *Δ*
15 conseruandam *K² QG*
18 somnis *C G*
19 sompnum *S AND GM*
20 occidente *E Σ Φ*
22 <in> ursum *YM*
26 cum eo *YM*

and the emperor. When the night was over and dawn was breaking, they landed at Barfleur. They immediately pitched their tents and waited there for the arrival of the kings of the islands and the continental dukes.

165   Meanwhile news reached Arthur that a huge giant had come from Spain, abducted Helena, duke Hoelus' niece, from her guards and fled with her to the summit of the mount now known as St Michael's, where the pursuing Breton knights were unable to get at him. Whether they approached by sea or land, he either sank their boats with great boulders or killed some with various weapons, capturing the majority and eating them alive. That night at the second hour Arthur took Kaius the steward and Beduerus the butler and, leaving camp without the others' knowledge, set off for the mount. So mighty a warrior as Arthur was unwilling to lead his army against such a monster, as he could destroy it single-handed and wanted to encourage his troops by doing so. When they neared the mount, they observed a fire burning on it, and another on a smaller hill not far away. As they did not know on which of them the giant could be found, they immediately sent Beduerus to discover the truth. He came upon a small boat and sailed first to the smaller mount, which could be approached only in this manner because it was located in the sea. As he began to climb to the top, he heard above him a woman wailing and he started, uncertain whether the giant was there. Swiftly summoning his courage, he drew his sword, but on reaching the top, found nothing except the fire he had seen. He saw too a freshly made grave, beside which an old woman was weeping and lamenting. As soon as she noticed him, she straightaway said between her sobs:

> 'What mischance brings you here, unfortunate man? You will suffer a death of unspeakable agony. I pity you, I pity you, because tonight the foul monster will devour you, in the flower of your youth. That wicked giant of accursed name, who brought the duke's niece and myself, her nurse, to this mount, where I have just buried her, will soon come and subject you to an unheard-of death. Oh wretched fate! My sweetest charge felt in her most tender heart such terror at his wicked embraces that she breathed her last, though she deserved a longer life. When he could not inflict his foul desires on her - she was my second soul, my second life, my second dear delight -, maddened by vile lust, he raped me, against my will, by God and my old age. Flee, my friend, flee, for should he come, as is his habit, to have sex with me, he will wretchedly tear you to pieces if he finds you like this'.

Beduerus, as touched as a human soul can be, soothed her with friendly words and, promising that help would soon be at hand, returned to Arthur and

et imperatorem talem uisionem contigisse. Rubente tandem post cursum noctis aurora, in portu Barbae fluuii applicuerunt. Mox, tentoria sua figentes,   30
expectauerunt ibidem insulanos reges et comprouincialium prouinciarum duces uenturos.

165   Interea nunciatur Arturo quendam mirae magnitudinis gigantem ex partibus Hispaniarum aduenisse et Helenam neptim ducis Hoeli custodibus eiusdem eripuisse et in cacumine montis qui nunc Michaelis dicitur cum illa   35
diffugisse, milites autem patriae insecutos nichil aduersus eum proficere; nam siue mari siue terra illum inuadebant, aut naues eorum ingentibus saxis obruebat aut diuersorum generum telis interimebat, sed plures capiebat, quos deuorabat semiuiuos. Nocte ergo sequenti in secunda hora, assumpto Kaio dapifero et Beduero pincerna, clam ceteris tentoria egressus uiam   40
uersus montem arripuit. Tanta namque uirtute praeualendo negligebat contra talia monstra exercitum ducere, cum et suos hoc modo inanimaret et solus ad illa destruenda sufficeret. Vt igitur prope montem uenerunt, aspexerunt quendam rogum super eum ardere, alium uero super minorem qui non longe ab altero distabat. Dubitantes ilico super quem eorum habitaret gigas,   45
Beduerum dirigunt ut certitudinem rei exploret. At ille, inuenta quadam nauicula, prius ad minorem nauigauit, quem aliter nequibat adire, quoniam infra mare situs fuerat. Cuius dum cacumen incepisset ascendere, audito desuper femineo ululatu primo inhorruit, quia dubitabat monstrum illud adesse. Reuocata ocius audatia, gladium euaginauit et ascenso culmine   50
nichil aliud repperit praeter rogum quem prospexerat. Inspexit quoque tumulum recenter factum et iuxta eum quandam anum flentem et eiulantem. Quae ut eum aspexit, confestim fletu impediente in hunc modum profata est:

'O infelix homo, quod infortunium te in hunc locum subuectat? O   55
inenarrabiles mortis poenas passure! Miseret me tui, miseret, quia tam detestabile monstrum florem iuuentutis tuae in hac nocte consumet. Aderit namque sceleratissimus ille inuisi nominis gigas qui neptim ducis, quam modo hic intumulaui, et me illius altricem in hunc montem aduexit, qui inaudito mortis genere te absque cunctamine afficiet. Proh   60
tristia fata! Serenissima alumpna, recepto infra tenerrimum pectus timore dum eam nefandus ille amplecteretur, uitam diuturniori luce dignam finiuit. Vt igitur illam, quae erat michi alter spiritus, altera uita, altera dulcedo iocunditatis, foedo coitu suo deturpare nequiuit, detestanda uenere succensus michi inuitae – Deum et senectutem meam testor – uim   65
et uiolentiam ingessit. Fuge, dilecte mi, fuge, ne si more suo mecum coiturus aduenerit te hoc modo repertum miserabili caede dilaniet'.

At ille, quantum humanae naturae possibile est commotus, eam amicis sedauit uerbis et promisso festinati auxilii solamine ad Arturum reuersus

39 semiuiuos deuorabat *E Σ Φ*
40 <in> uiam *C¹HSE UAK¹ Q*
48 erat *Σ Φ*
61 Precepto *tamquam initium capituli O Q, item* Recepto *S U:* quae percepto *E:* namque recepto *G:* re + *lac.* + Praecepto *A: lac. ante* recepto *UKN (cf. 'Transm.' 113)*

225

described everything he had found. Saddened by the girl's fate, the king commanded them to let him attack the giant alone, but to lend assistance and fight bravely if the need arose. Then they strode off to the higher mount and, led by Arthur, began to ascend, after handing their horses over to their squires. The monster was by the fire, his mouth smeared with the blood of half-devoured pigs, some of which he had eaten, some of which, fixed on spits, he was roasting over coals. As soon as he saw the unexpected sight, he rushed to get his club, which two men could scarcely have lifted from the ground. The king unsheathed his sword and, raising his shield, hurried as fast as he could to prevent the giant reaching his club. But he, full of evil cunning, had already grasped it and brought it down so hard on the king's shield that the sound filled all the shores and made his ears ring. Arthur, blazing with fierce anger, raised his sword and struck him on the forehead a blow which, though it was not mortal, made blood stream over his face and into his eyes, blinding him; the giant had parried the sword with his club, so protecting his forehead from a lethal wound. Blinded by the flowing blood, the giant leapt forward and, like a boar rushing on a hunter along his spear, found the king by means of his sword, threw his arms around his waist and forced him to his knees. Summoning his courage, Arthur quickly escaped and swiftly struck the monster with his sword, now from one side, now from the other, never resting until he had mortally wounded him by driving the whole blade into his head where the skull protected his brain. The monster roared and fell with a mighty crash, like an oak tree uprooted by raging winds. Immediately the king laughed, telling Beduerus to cut off his head and give it to one of the squires to take back to the camp as a sight for his men to gaze upon. He said that he had not encountered anyone of such strength since he had killed upon mount Aravius the giant Ritho, who had challenged him to a duel. Ritho had turned the beards of the kings he had slain into a cloak and had dispatched instructions to Arthur to shave off his beard carefully and send it to him, so he could place it above the rest, to reflect Arthur's preeminence over other kings. Otherwise, he challenged Arthur to a duel, to the victor of which would go the cloak together with the beard of the vanquished. Arthur won the duel and took Ritho's beard and the trophy, but had never, as he said, subsequently met Ritho's equal.

est et omnia quae inuenerat indicauit. Arturus igitur, casum ingemiscens 70
puellae, praecepit eis ut sibi soli illum inuadere permitterent sed si necessitas
accideret in auxilium procedentes uiriliter aggrederentur. Direxerunt inde
gressus ad maiorem montem et equos suos armigeris commiserunt et eum
Arturo praecedente ascenderunt. Aderat autem inhumanus ille ad ignem,
illitus ora tabo semesorum porcorum, quos partim deuorauerat, partim 75
uero uerubus infixos subterpositis prunis torrebat. Mox, ut illos nichil tale
praemeditatus aspexit, festinauit clauam suam sumere, quam duo iuuenes
uix a terra erigerent. Euaginauit ergo rex gladium suum et praetenso clipeo
quantum uelocitas sinebat properauit eum praecedere antequam clauam
cepisset. At ille, non ignarus malae meditationis, iam ceperat eam regemque 80
in interpositum clipeum tanto conamine percussit quod sonitu ictus et tota
littora repleuit et aures eiusdem ultra modum hebetauit. Arturus uero, acri
ignescens ira, erecto in frontem ipsius ense uulnus intulit, tametsi non
mortale, unde tamen sanguis in faciem et oculos eius profluens eorundem
excaecauit aciem; interposuerat namque clauam ictui et frontem suam a 85
letali uulnere muniuerat. Excaecatus autem profluente sanguine acrior
insurgit et uelut aper per uenabulum in uenatorem ita irruit per gladium in
regem et complectendo eum per medium coegit illum genua humi flectere.
Arturus itaque, reuocata uirtute, ocius elabitur et celeriter nunc hinc nunc
illinc nefandum gladio diuerberabat, nec requieuit donec letali uulnere 90
illato totum mucronem capiti impressit qua cerebrum testa protegebatur.
Exclamauit uero inuisus ille et uelut quercus uentorum uiribus eradicata
cum maximo sonitu corruit. Rex ilico in risum solutus praecepit Beduero
amputare ei caput et dare uni armigerorum ad deferendum ad castra, ut
spectaculum intuentibus fieret. Dicebat autem se non inuenisse alium 95
tantae uirtutis postquam Rithonem gigantem in Arauio monte interfecit,
qui ipsum ad proeliandum inuitauerat. Hic namque ex barbis regum
quos peremerat fecerat sibi pelles et mandauerat Arturo ut suam barbam
diligenter excoriaret atque excoriatam sibi dirigeret et quemadmodum ipse
ceteris praeerat regibus ita in honore eius eam ceteris barbis superponeret; 100
sin autem, prouocabat eum ad proelium et qui fortior superuenisset pelles
et barbam deuicti tulisset. Inito itaque certamine, triumphauit Arturus et
barbam alterius cepit et spolium, et postea nulli fortiori isto obuiauerat

73 [gressus] Σ Φ, *unde antea* perrexerunt *N*
73 eum *OC UA(?)K¹D QGM:* cum *HS(?)E K²N Y*
76 suterpositis *A:* superpositis *QYG:* suppositis *M*
76 illos ut Φ
79 properabat Σ Φ
80 [malae] Φ *(cf. Introd.)*
81 in *OC² G:* om. *C¹HSE Σ QYM*
81 [et] *O G*
83 tametsi *scripsi (cf. §§ 2.12, 167.207, 177.26):* tantum etsi *CE:* etsi *K:* tamenetsi *cett.*
88 coegit eum *SE ND YG*
89-90 huc ... illuc *OC*
95 alterum *YM*
100 [eam] Σ Φ *(barbis <eam> N)*

Having gained this victory, at the dawn of the third day they returned to their tents with the head, which the soldiers rushed in crowds to see, praising the man who had freed the land from such a pest. Hoelus, however, was saddened by the death of his niece, and ordered a church to be constructed over the place where the girl's body was buried on the mount, which to this very day is called Tumba Helenae because of her grave.

166   After the arrival of all those for whom he was waiting, Arthur marched off to Autun, where he expected to find the emperor. When he arrived at the river Aube, he learned that the emperor was camped not far off with a huge force which was considered unbeatable. Undaunted, Arthur decided to continue, but laid out on the river bank a camp, from which his army could freely advance and to which it could retreat, if need be. To Lucius Hiberius he sent two earls, Boso of Oxford and Gerinus of Chartres, and his nephew Gawain to convey the message that he should either leave the territory of France, or advance the following day in order to determine which of them had the better claim to the country. The young men of the court, rejoicing heartily, began to encourage Gawain to create in the emperor's camp some pretext for them to attack the Romans. The envoys visited Lucius and told him to leave France or come out to fight the next day. When the emperor replied that he ought not to retreat but rather advance to occupy France, his nephew Gaius Quintilianus, who was also present, said that the Britons showed more prowess in boasts and threats than they did in boldness and courage. Gawain, quick to anger, drew the sword at his belt, attacked and beheaded Quintilianus and then returned to the horses with his companions. The Romans pursued, some on foot, some on horseback, to revenge their fellow-citizen on the envoys, who were now fleeing as fast as they could. As soon as one of the Romans was about to catch him, Gerinus of Chartres suddenly turned with his lance lowered, thrust it straight through his armoured body and with all his might dashed him to the ground. Boso of Oxford envied his brave deed and, whirling round his steed, drove his lance into the throat of the first man he met and made him fall mortally wounded from the horse he rode in pursuit. Meanwhile, in his great eagerness to avenge Quintilianus, Marcellus Mutius was now close behind Gawain and trying to grasp him, when the Briton turned quickly and with the sword in his hand sliced through his head and helmet down to the chest. He told Mutius that in hell he should inform Quintilianus, whom he had killed in camp, that this was how the Britons showed their prowess in boasts and threats. Gathering his comrades, Gawain encouraged them to charge together and each to kill his man. They readily agreed, turned and each killed an opponent. The Romans, however, pressed their pursuit, striking at them now with swords, now with lances, but could neither catch nor

ut superius asserebat. Victoriam igitur ut praedictum est adepti, in
secundae noctis diluculo ad tentoria sua cum capite remeauerunt, ad quod 105
ammirandum cateruatim concurrebant, ei ascribentes laudes, qui patriam a
tanta ingluuie liberauerat. At Hoelus, ob casum neptis suae tristis, praecepit
aedificari basilicam super corpus ipsius in monte quo iacebat, qui nomen ex
tumulo puellae nactus Tumba Helenae usque in hodiernum diem uocatur.

166 Congregatis tandem cunctis quos expectauerat Arturus, illinc 110
Augustudunum progreditur, quo imperatorem adesse existimabat. Vt
autem ad Albam fluuium uenit, nuntiatum est ei illum castra sua non longe
posuisse et tanto incedere exercitu quanto ut aiebant resistere nequiret. Nec
iccirco perterritus coeptis suis desistere uoluit sed super ripam fluminis
castra sua metatus est, unde posset exercitum suum libere conducere et si 115
opus accidisset sese infra ea recipere. Duos etiam consules, Bosonem de
Vado Boum et Gerinum Carnotensem, Gualguainum etiam nepotem suum,
Lucio Hiberio direxit ut suggereret ei quatinus recederet a finibus Galliae
aut in postero die ad experiendum ueniret quis eorum maius ius in Galliam
haberet. Iuuentus ergo curiae, maximo gaudio fluctuans, coepit instimulare 120
Gualguainum ut infra castra imperatoris aliquid inciperet quo occasionem
haberent congrediendi cum Romanis. Perrexerunt illi ad Lucium et
praeceperunt ei a Gallia recedere aut in postero die ad pugnandum uenire.
Ac dum responderet eis quod non deberet recedere, immo ad regendum
illam accedere, interfuit Gaius Quintilianus eiusdem nepos, qui dicebat 125
Britones magis iactantia atque minis habundare quam audatia et probitate
ualere. Iratus ilico Gualguainus, euaginato ense quo accinctus erat, irruit in
eum et eiusdem capite amputato ad equos cum sociis digreditur. Insequuntur
itaque Romani partim pede partim equis, ut conciuem suum in legatos omni
nisu diffugientes uindicent. At Gerinus Carnotensis, dum quidam eorum 130
ipsum attingere inciperet, ex inprouiso reuersus direxit lanceam suam
atque ipsum per arma et medium corpus foratum humi quantum potuit
prostrauit. Inuidit ergo Boso de Vado Boum quoniam tantam probitatem
fecisset Carnotensis et retorquens equum suum cui primo obuiauit ingessit
lanceam sibi infra gulam et letaliter uulneratum coegit caballum deserere 135
quo eum insequebatur. Interea Marcellus Mutius, maximo affectu uolens
Quintilianum uindicare, Gualguaino iam imminebat a tergo atque coeperat
retinere, cum ipse continuo reuersus galeam cum capite usque ad pectus
gladio quem tenebat abscidit. Praecepit etiam ei Quintiliano, quem infra
castra trucidauerat, in infernum renuntiare Britones minis et iactantia hoc 140
modo habundare. Sociis deinde resociatis, hortatur ut pari impetu reuersi
quisque suum prosternere laboraret. Acquiescentes igitur ei, reuertuntur et
quisque unum prosternit. At Romani usque insequentes quandoque cum
gladiis quandoque cum lanceis percutiebant eos, sed nec retinere nec

104 Victoriam ... adepti *CHSE Σ*: Victoriam ... adeptus *(et mox* remeauit*) O*: Victoria ... potitus *Φ*
105 secundo *Φ*
121 aliquid *48: om. Ω (cf. 'Transm.' 101)*
124 At *E N M*
143-4 quandoque cum gladiis *post* eos *M: om. G*

kill them. As the pursuers neared a wood, there suddenly emerged from it about six thousand Britons, who had heard of the earls' flight and hidden there to help them. Coming out, they clapped their spurs to their horses and, filling the air with their cries and protecting their chests with their shields, fell on the surprised Romans and routed them. They pressed on together, unhorsing some of the Romans with their lances, and capturing or killing others. When the senator Petreius was informed, he hastened with ten thousand men to aid his comrades. He forced the Britons to retreat to the wood from which they had charged, but not without suffering losses of his own. During the retreat, the Britons continually turned where the path narrowed and cut down their pursuers. As they fell back, Hiderus, son of Nu, rushed to their assistance with five thousand men. The Britons rallied and, turning to face the men from whom they had just been fleeing, strove valiantly to land telling blows. The Romans too fought back, sometimes cutting them down, sometimes being cut down themselves. The Britons simply wanted to fight, not caring about the consequences as long as they could do so. The Romans were more circumspect, being supported by the skilful generalship of Petreius Cocta, who sensibly ordered them to charge at one moment and retire at the next and so to inflict grievous losses. Noticing this, Boso called aside several of his men whom he knew to be the boldest and said:

> 'We have started this battle without Arthur's knowledge, so we must be careful that our efforts are not turned against us. If we fail, we will lose many knights and make our king curse us. Take heart and follow me into the Roman ranks to kill or capture Petreius if we can'.

They spurred their horses and, charging all together into the Roman formations, came to the spot where Petreius was exhorting his comrades. Boso immediately made for him and seized him around the neck, toppling to the ground with him, as he had planned. The Romans rushed to free Petreius from the enemy, and the Britons rushed to help Boso. The fighting grew hot, as amid shouting and confusion one side tried to free their leader, the other to capture him. They traded blows, killed and were killed in return. There it was plain to see who fought best with sword, spear or other weapon. Finally the Britons closed ranks, beat off the Roman assaults and retreated

prosternere praeualebant. Dum autem prope quandam siluam ut dictum est 145
insequerentur, confestim egrediuntur ex illa circiter sex milia Britonum, qui
fugam consulum comperti infra eam delituerant ut eis auxilium subuectarent.
Egressi autem subduxerunt calcaria equis suis et aera clamore replentes
et clipeos pectoribus praetendentes Romanos ex inprouiso inuadunt et
confestim in fugam propellunt. Sed et unanimiter insequentes quosdam 150
eorum ab equis suis cum lanceis seiungunt, quosdam autem retinent,
quosdam interficiunt. Quod cum Petreio senatori nuntiatum est, decem
milibus comitatus subuenire sociis suis festinauit. Coegit Britones ad siluam
ex qua egressi fuerant recurrere, nec sine detrimento suorum. Diffugiendo
etenim Britones reuertebantur in strictis locis atque insequentibus stragem 155
ingerebant maximam. Quibus hoc modo cedentibus, Hiderus filius Nu
cum quinque milibus accelerabat ut eisdem subueniret. Resistunt ergo et
ipsi, et quibus terga paulo ante dederant nunc pectora opponentes ualidos
ictus uiriliter inferre elaborabant. Resistunt etiam Romani et quandoque
eos prosternunt, quandoque uero ab illis prosternuntur. At Britones toto 160
affectu desiderabant militiam, sed nec multum curabant in quem euentum
inciderent dum eam incipiebant. Romani autem sapientius agebant, quos
Petreius Cocta more boni ducis nunc ad inuadendum nunc ad diffugiendum
sapienter edocebat, et ita maximum dampnum ceteris impendebat. Quod
cum Bosoni compertum esset, plures suorum quos audatiores nouerat 165
seiunxit a ceteris et eos hoc modo affatus est:

'Quoniam nesciente Arturo istud proelium incepimus, cauendum nobis
est ne in peiorem partem incepti nostri decidamus. Nam si in illam
deciderimus, et maximum dampnum militum nostrorum incurremus et
regem nostrum ad execrandum nos commouebimus. Resumite audatiam 170
et sequimini me per cateruas Romanorum, ut si fortuna fauerit Petreium
interficiamus siue capiamus'.

Subduxerunt itaque calcaria equis suis et cuneos hostium pari impetu
penetrantes ad locum quo Petreius socios suos commonebat uenerunt.
In quem ocius Boso irruens eundem per collum amplectitur et sicut 175
praemeditatus fuerat cum illo in terram corruit. Concurrunt ergo Romani
ut eum hostibus eripiant, concurrunt autem Britones ut Bosoni auxilientur.
Fit itaque inter eos maxima caedes, fit clamor, fit turbatio, dum hi ducem
suum liberare, illi eundem retinere conarentur. Inuicem ergo uulnerabant et
uulnerabantur, prosternebant et prosternebantur. Illic itaque uideri poterat 180
quis hasta, quis gladio, quis telo praeualeret. Denique Britones, densata
caterua incedentes impetumque Romanorum ferentes, sese infra fortitudinem

146 congrediuntur *QGM*
148 *de* subduxerunt *cf. Introd.*
148 complentes *Φ*
152 quosdam \<autem\> *QGM*
157 et *C KN: om. cett.*
164 docebat *Φ*
165 eorum *Φ*

with Petreius to their main body. Then they immediately charged the Romans, who, now leaderless and seriously weakened, wavered and turned tail. Pressing them from behind, they cut at and slaughtered them, stripping the dead before leaving them to continue the pursuit. Many more they took prisoner to present to the king. Then, after they had inflicted sufficient damage, they returned to camp with their booty and captives and, overjoyed by their victory, told their tale and presented Petreius Cocta and the other prisoners to Arthur. He congratulated them with promises of titles and promotions because they had acted so valiantly in his absence. Wishing to keep the captives in custody, he selected men to escort them the next day to Paris and to turn them over to the city-guards until they received his orders as to what should be done next with them. He also instructed duke Cador, Beduerus the butler and two earls, Borellus and Richerius, to accompany the party with their retainers until they reached a point where Roman interference was no longer to be feared.

167   Arthur's plan, however, came to the ears of the Romans, who on the emperor's orders picked fifteen thousand men to overtake them that night and attack them so as to free the prisoners. In command they placed the senators Vulteius Catellus and Quintus Carutius and kings Evander of Syria and Sertorius of Libya, who marched with their troops that very night and lay in ambush, having selected a suitable place where they judged the Britons must pass. Next morning the Britons set out with the prisoners and were now nearing the spot, not suspecting that the enemy had laid a cunning trap. As they began to pass, the Romans suddenly charged out and broke into their unsuspecting ranks. Yet, although they were surprised and scattered, the British bravely rallied to fight back, stationing some men around the prisoners and forming up others to attack the enemy. Richerius and Beduerus commanded the group guarding the captives, whilst duke Cador of Cornwall and Borellus commanded the rest. The Romans had charged out in disorder and were not maintaining formation; rather they made every effort to cut the Britons down while they were organising and trying to defend themselves. Diminished in numbers, the Britons would have suffered the humiliating loss of their charges, if fate had not brought them speedy relief. When he heard of the ambush, duke Guitardus of Poitou came up with three thousand men, with whose help the Britons at last

proelii sui cum Petreio recipiunt. Sed confestim impetum fecerunt in illos,
iam rectore suo orbatos, iam in maiore parte debilitatos, iam etiam dilapsos
atque terga eisdem ostendentes. Incumbentes igitur ipsos a tergo caedunt, 185
caesos prosternunt, prostratos despoliant, despoliatos praetereunt ut ceteros
insequantur; sed et plures capiunt, quos regi praesentare affectant. Postremo,
postquam satis periculi ipsis ingesserunt, remeauerunt cum spoliis et captiuis
ad castra et indicantes quod sibi contigerat Petreium Coctam et ceteros
captiuos Arturo cum laeticia uictoriae optulerunt. Quibus ille congratulans 190
et honores et honorum augmentationes promisit, quoniam eo absente
tantam probitatem egerant. Captiuos autem in carceribus trudere uolens,
seuocauit quosdam qui eos in crastinum Parisius ducerent et custodibus
oppidi seruandum traderent donec ex illis aliud fieri praecepisset. Iussit
etiam Cadorem ducem Beduerumque pincernam nec non et duos consules, 195
Borellum et Richerium, cum familiis suis ipsos conducere donec uenirent
eo quo minime disturbationem Romanorum timuissent.

167　　At Romani, forte comperientes apparatum istum, imperatore iubente
elegerunt quindecim milia suorum qui nocte illa iter eorum praecederent atque
cum ipsis congressuri suos liberare perstarent. Ipsis quoque praefecerunt 200
Vulteium Catellum et Quintum Carutium senatores, Euandrum etiam regem
Syriae et Sertorium Libiae, qui nocte illa cum praedictis milibus iussum iter
arripuerunt et locum latibulis conuenientem adepti delituerunt quo ipsos
ituros arbitrabantur. Mane autem facto, Britones uiam ineunt cum captiuis
et iam prope locum incedunt, nescii quos dolos uersuti hostes instituerant. 205
Cum uero praeterire incepissent, egressi ex inprouiso Romani ipsos nichil
tale praemeditatos occupauerunt et penetrauerunt. At illi, tametsi ex
inprouiso occupati atque dissipati fuissent, tandem tamen resociati uiriliter
resistunt et quosdam circa captiuos statuunt, quosdam autem per cateruas
distribuunt qui cum hostibus congrediantur. Agmini autem illi quod ad 210
conseruandum captiuos statuerant Richerium et Beduerum praefecerunt,
Cador uero dux Cornubiae atque Borellus ceteris praeponuntur. Sed Romani
omnes sine ordine eruperant nec curabant suos per turmas disponere; immo,
omni nisu perstantes, Britonibus stragem dabant dum turmas disponere,
dum semet ipsos defendere elaborarent. Vnde ultra modum debilitati 215
illos quos conducebant turpiter amisissent nisi fortuna optatum auxilium
eis accelerasset. Guitardus etenim dux Pictauensium, comperto praedicto
dolo, cum tribus milibus aduenerat, cuius auxilio freti tandem coeperunt

184 maiori *OCSE Σ*
191 bonorum *UK, non male, nisi quod bona noster possessiones uocat*
194 seruandos *178: melius* <ad> seruandum *(cf. Introd.)*
196 famulis *OE UAKD YM*
202 <regem> Libiae *HSE N QY:* Libiae <regem> *UAKD GM*
206 penetrare *QYG*
208 et *E Σ Φ*
218 freti auxilio *Σ Φ*
218 coeperunt *93: incipiunt 178²:* poterant *post* praeualere *96²: om. Ω, unde* praeualuere ...
reddidere *K Φ (cf. Introd.)*

recovered and turned the tables on their impudent assailants. Nevertheless, they were deprived of many men in the first attack. They lost Borellus, the noted earl of Le Mans, who charged king Evander of Syria, but was wounded in the throat by his lance and choked on his own blood. They also lost four distinguished noblemen, Hirelglas of Perirun, Mauricius of Cardorcan, Aliduc of Tintagol and Er, son of Hider, all men whose bravery could not easily be equalled. Yet they did not forget their courage nor give in to despair, but tried with all their strength both to guard their prisoners and kill their enemies. At length the Romans could stand up to them no longer, but swiftly abandoned the field and began to make for their camp. The Britons pursued, cutting them down and capturing many, and did not rest until they had killed Vulteius Catellus and king Evander of Syria and completely scattered the rest. Having defeated them, they sent on to Paris the prisoners they were conducting, and, returning to the king with their new captives, promised that ultimate victory was at hand, since with their inferior numbers they had fought off so many attackers.

168   Unsettled by his defeats, Lucius Hiberius was sick at heart and, unable to make up his mind between conflicting strategies, could not decide whether to press on to fight Arthur or retreat to Autun and await help from the emperor Leo. At last he gave in to his fears and entered Langres with his armies, intending to march to Autun that night. When Arthur discovered this, he resolved to cut him off and that same night, leaving the city on his left, occupied a valley called Siesia, through which Lucius would pass. Wishing to deploy for battle, Arthur instructed one legion, led by earl Morvid, to remain at the ready so that, should the need arise, he would know where he might retreat to rally his forces for a second attack on the enemy. He drew up the remainder in seven bodies, assigning to each five thousand, five hundred and fifty-five men of all arms. Each formation was part cavalry, part infantry. Their orders were that, when the infantry advanced, the cavalry should immediately charge from the flank with ranks closed and attempt to scatter the enemy. The bodies of infantry were formed as columns with a right and left wing in the British manner, the first being commanded by king Auguselus of Scotland on the right and duke Cador of Cornwall on the left; the second by two noble earls, Gerinus of Chartres and Boso of Ridichen, or Oxford in

praeualere et uicem praedictae stragis impudentibus grassatoribus reddere. At tamen multos suorum in primo congressu amiserunt. Amiserunt etenim 220 illum inclitum Cenomannorum consulem Borellum, qui dum cum Euandro rege Syriae congrederetur lancea ipsius infra gulam infixus uitam cum sanguine eructauit. Amiserunt quoque quatuor proceres nobiles, Hirelglas de Perirun, Mauricum Cardorcanensem, Aliduc de Tintagol, Er filium Hider, quibus audatiores non facile reperiri poterant. Nec tamen audatiae 225 suae desistentes sibi desperauerunt sed omni nisu instantes et captiuos custodire et inimicos prosternere intendebant. Romani tandem, congressum eorum ferre non ualentes, ocius reliquerunt campum et castra sua petere coeperunt. At Britones usque insequentes stragem inferunt, complures capiunt, nec requieuerunt donec Vulteio Catello et Euandro rege Syriae 230 peremptis ceteros penitus dissipauerunt. Habita igitur uictoria, captiuos quos ducebant miserunt Parisius atque cum illis quos recenter ceperant ad regem suum repedantes spem summae uictoriae promittebant, cum admodum pauci de tot superuenientibus hostibus triumphum habuissent.

168   Lucius autem Hiberius, tales casus moleste ferens, animum suum diuersis 235 cruciatibus uexatum nunc huc nunc illuc reuoluit, haesitando an coepta proelia cum Arturo committat an infra Augustudunum receptus auxilium Leonis imperatoris expectet. Acquiescens tandem formidini, nocte sequenti praedictam ciuitatem aditurus Lengrias cum exercitibus suis ingreditur. Quod ut Arturo compertum est, affectans iter eius praecedere eadem nocte 240 relicta a laeua ciuitate quandam uallem qua Lucius transgressurus erat ingreditur, quae Siesia uocabatur. Commilitones igitur suos per cateruas disponere uolens, legionem unam, cui praefecerat Moruid Claudiocestriae consulem, iussit adesse ut si opus accidisset sciret ubi posset sese recipere et resociatis turmis iterum hostibus proelia ingerere. Ceteros etiam per 245 cateruas septenas distribuens, in unaquaque caterua quinquies mille et quingentos et quinquaginta quinque uiros omnibus armis instructos collocauit. Pars quoque statutarum turmarum disponitur equestris, pars autem altera pedestris. Daturque praeceptum tale inter eos, ut dum pedestris turma ad inuadendum intendat equestris ilico ab obliquo superueniens 250 stricto agmine dissipare hostes nitatur. Erant autem pedestres cateruae Britannico more cum dextro et sinistro cornu in quadrum statutae, quarum uni Auguselus rex Albaniae et Cador dux Cornubiae, unus in dextro cornu et alius in sinistro cornu, praeficiuntur, alii uero duo insignes consules, Gerinus uidelicet Carnotensis et Boso de Ridichen, quae lingua Saxonum 255

221 [dum] *Φ*
232 ceperunt *CE*
237 aut infra *UAKD Φ*
243 Moruid Claudiocestriae (Glauwerniae *S, locum post* consulem *SG) S N GM : lac. OC UA Q: om. HE KD:* hoelem *Y*
246 in *48:* et in *Ω*
250 obliquo *HS²E K² Φ:* aliquo *OCSⁱ Σ*
254 sinistro [cornu] *O A Y*

English; the third by kings Aschil of Denmark and Loth of Norway; and the fourth by Hoelus duke of Armorica and the king's nephew Gawain. Behind the first four formations were drawn up four more, the first led by Kaius the steward and Beduerus the butler; the second by dukes Holdinus of the Flemings and Guitardus of Poitou; the third by Iugenis of Leicester, Ionathal of Dorchester and Cursalem of Chester; and the fourth by Urbgennius of Bath. Behind them, Arthur selected a position for a legion he had decided to command personally, planting there his standard of a golden dragon, so that the wounded and weary could retire to it as if to a fortress, should it prove necessary. The legion which he kept with him numbered six thousand, six hundred and sixty-six men.

169   When they were all in place, Arthur addressed the following speech to his comrades:

'You, my friends, have made Britain the mistress of thirty kingdoms, and I congratulate you on your resolve, which, I see, never falters, but grows ever stronger. Although you have not campaigned for five years and were devoted to the pleasures of rest rather than to military service, you have by no means lost your natural prowess, but have stood firm and put the Romans to flight. In their arrogance they desired to deprive you of your freedom and advanced to attack in superior numbers, yet they could not stand up to your assaults and have retreated in disgrace to this city, from which they will shortly emerge to march to Autun down this valley, where you will be able to take them by surprise and catch them like sheep. Clearly they considered you to be as cowardly as easterners when they planned to exact tribute from your country and make you slaves. Have they not heard of the wars you waged against the Danes, the Norsemen and the leaders of the French, whom you placed in my power and freed from the shameful domination of Rome? Having won that greater victory, we will surely prevail in this lesser affair, as long as we show the same determination to crush these effeminates. What rewards each of you will obtain if, like faithful comrades, you obey my wishes and commands! Once the enemy is defeated, we shall march on Rome, capture it and take it over, so that you shall have gold, silver, palaces, towers, castles, cities and all the spoils of victory'.

Oxeneford nuncupatur, terciae uero turmae Aschil rex Dacorum atque Loth rex Norguegensium, quartae Hoelus dux Armoricorum atque Gualguainus nepos regis. Post has autem .iiii. fuerunt aliae .iiii. a dorso statutae, quarum uni praeponuntur Kaius dapifer et Beduerus pincerna, alii autem praeficiuntur Holdinus dux Rutenorum et Guitardus dux Pictauensium, 260 terciae Iugenis de Legecestria et Ionathal Dorecestrensis atque Cursalem de Kaicestria, quartae uero Vrbgennius de Badone. Ipse quoque post hos elegit sibi et legioni uni quam sibi adesse affectauerat locum quendam, quo aureum draconem infixit quem pro uexillo habebat, ubi uulnerati et fatigati, si necessitas compulisset, quasi ad castrum diffugissent. Aderant autem in 265 legione illa quam secum habebat sex milia et sexcenti sexaginta sex.

169   Dispositis itaque cunctis, commilitones suos in haec uerba profatur:

'Domestici mei, qui Britanniam terdenorum regnorum fecistis dominam, uestrae congratulor probitati, quam nullatenus deficere, immo magis ac magis uigere considero. Quamquam quinque annis inexercitati 270 oblectamentis ocii potius quam usui miliciae dediti sitis, nequaquam tamen ab innata bonitate degenerauistis sed in ipsa perseuerantes Romanos propulistis in fugam. Qui instimulante superbia sua libertatem uobis demere affectauerunt, qui ampliori numero incedentes ingerere proelia coeperunt, qui congressui uestro resistere non ualuerunt, sese 275 turpiter infra ciuitatem istam receperunt, ex qua ad praesens egressuris et per istam uallem Augustudunum petituris obuiam poteritis adesse et nichil tale praemeditatos uelut pecudes occupare. Sane orientalium gentium segnitiam in uobis esse existimabant dum patriam uestram facere tributariam et uosmet ipsos subiugare affectarent. Numquid 280 nouerunt quae bella Dacis atque Norguegensibus Gallorumque ducibus intulistis, quos meae subdidistis potestati et ab eorum pudendo dominio liberauistis? Qui igitur in grauiore decertatione ualuimus in hac leuiori sine dubio praeualebimus si pari affectu semiuiros illos elaborauerimus opprimere. Quantos honores quisque uestrum possidebit si uoluntati meae 285 atque praeceptis meis ut fideles commilitones adquieueritis! Subiugatis etenim ipsis, continuo Romam petemus, petitam capiemus, captam autem possidebimus, et sic aurum, argentum, palatia, turres, oppida, ciuitates, et ceteras uictorum diuicias habebitis'.

257 Armoricanorum *OE Σ Y*
258 [autem] *OG*
259 praeponitur *OE M*
265 castra *Φ*
267 praefatur *UA¹K¹ND Φ*: affatur *93 (cf. Introd.)*
270 [ac magis] *Σ Φ*
270 Quamquam *Δ*: Licet *Σ Φ*
271 <hactenus> dediti *Σ Φ*
275 ualentes *Σ Φ male*
283 in grauiori *O Φ*
287 petetis *Σ QYM*
288 et sic *Σ Φ*: Ergo *Δ contra auctoris usum (cf. tamen Introd. ad § 91.78)*

Before he could finish, they all roared their assent, ready to die rather than flee leaving their king alive on the field of battle.

170   Lucius Hiberius, discovering the trap set for him, abandoned his plan to flee and summoned up the courage to attack the Britons in the same valley. He assembled his chiefs and delivered the following speech:

'Venerable fathers, whose jurisdiction ought to embrace not only the eastern but also the western kingdoms, do not forget your ancestors, who, to overcome the enemies of the republic, did not shrink from shedding their blood, and left for their successors a model of brave service by fighting as if God could not countenance their death in battle. Thus they won many victories and avoided death, since no one was going to die unless it had been preordained by God's providence. So the republic grew stronger, as did their merit, and so all the honour, repute and generosity habitual to a noble man always flourished among them, making them and their descendants masters of the whole world. Wishing to awaken this spirit in you, I urge you to summon your ancestors' resolve and prove yourselves worthy of it by attacking our enemies in the valley where they lie in ambush, and by taking back from them what is yours. You should not think that I have retreated to this city to escape the Britons or their assault, but rather because I thought that they would make the mistake of following us, so that we could take them unawares and inflict heavy losses on them as they attacked piecemeal. Now, seeing that they have not done as we expected, let us too change our plans. Let us turn and deliver a bold attack. If they do not break immediately, let us stand together and beat off their first charge, then our triumph will be assured. Many battles demonstrate that the side that endures the first attack is usually the victor'.

With these and other arguments he ended his speech, whereupon they all unanimously cheered in approval, promising on oath to assist him, and hurried to arm themselves. When at last they were ready, they left Langres and marched to the valley where Arthur's troops were in position. There they formed twelve deep wedges

Adhuc autem ipso dicente, omnes uno clamore assentiunt, parati mortem 290
prius recipere quam uiuente ipso campum diffugiendo relinquere.

170   At Lucius Hiberius, comperiens insidias quae ei parabantur, noluit ut
affectauerat diffugere sed reuocata audatia ipsos in eandem uallem adire.
Denique duces suos conuocauit atque cum his uerbis ipsos allocutus est:

    'Patres uenerandi, quorum imperio et orientalia et occidentalia regna 295
subici deberent, ueterum uestrorum memores estote, qui ut aduersarios
rei publicae superarent non abhorrebant effundere sanguinem suum sed
exemplum probitatis et militiae posteris suis relinquentes ita decertabant
ac si in proelio Deus non prouidisset eos morituros. Triumphabant ergo
saepius et triumphando mortem euadebant, quia nulli alia mors erat 300
prouentura quam quae ex prouidentia Dei condescendebat. Augebatur
itaque res publica, augebatur eorundem probitas, et quod honestatis,
quod honoris, quod largitatis in generosis esse solebat in eis diutius
uigens ipsos et ipsorum posteros in dominium tocius orbis promouebat.
Id igitur in uobis excitare desiderans, hortor uos ut auitam bonitatem 305
reuocetis atque in eadem perstantes et inimicos uestros in ualle qua uobis
insidiantur petatis et quod uestrum est ab illis exigere contendatis. Ne
existimetis me iccirco infra ciuitatem hanc receptum esse ut uel eos
uel eorum congressum abhorruissem, immo arbitrans quod nos stulte
prosequerentur, prosequentibus uero ex inprouiso obuiaremus atque ipsos 310
segregatim irruentes magna strage infestaremus. Nunc autem, quoniam
aliter quam rati eramus fecerunt, et nos aliter faciamus. Petamus etenim
illos et audacter inuadamus. Vel si conualuerint, unanimiter resistamus
et primum impetum toleremus, et sic procul dubio triumphabimus. In
pluribus etenim decertationibus qui in primo congressu perstare potuit 315
cum uictoria saepissime abiuit'.

Vt his itaque et pluribus aliis finem dicendi fecit, omnes uno assensu
fauentes, socias quoque manus iure iurando promittentes, ad armandum
sese festinant. Armati tandem Lengrias egrediuntur atque praedictam
uallem adierunt, ubi Arturus cateruas suas statuerat. Porro et illi .xii. cuneata 320

---

290 dicente <talia> Φ
293-4 adire denique Δ: aditurus Σ Φ
294 [cum] Σ Φ
294 [ipsos] Σ Φ
300 [mors] Σ Φ, *fort. recte*
301 [quae] Σ Φ
305 aduitam Σ: (h)abitam Φ
306 [et] OCSE
306 nostros C(?)H U QGM
306 nobis CE
307 petatis et Δ: petentes Σ Φ
307 nostrum QYM
309 congressum eorum Σ Φ
310 persequerentur persequentibus C, *nescio an recte* (*cf.* § 178.46)
310 <et ut> prosequentibus [uero] Σ Φ
314 [et] primum<que> OHSE
320 <et> duodecim UAN

all on foot, each formed in the Roman manner and containing six thousand, six hundred and sixty-six soldiers. To each they assigned leaders to give orders to attack, or to defend while the others attacked; as commanders for the first column they appointed Lucius Catellus and Aliphatima king of Spain, for the second Hirtacius king of the Parthians and the senator Marius Lepidus, for the third Boccus king of the Medes and the senator Gaius Metellus, and for the fourth Sertorius king of Libya and the senator Quintus Milvius. These four units comprised the first line; behind them were four more, the first commanded by Serses king of the Ituraei, the second by Pandrasus king of Egypt, the third by Politetes duke of Bithynia and the fourth by Theucer duke of Phrygia; behind these were a further four, the first under the senator Quintus Carutius, the second under Laelius Hostiensis, the third under Sulpicius Subbuculus and the fourth under Mauricius Silvanus. Lucius himself ranged up and down the lines, giving encouragement and telling them how to conduct themselves. He ordered them to plant in the centre the standard which he had brought with him, an eagle of gold, with orders that it should serve as a rallying-point for any troops who became separated.

171   The Britons and Romans faced each other with spears raised for some time, until with a sudden blast of trumpets the column commanded by the king of Spain and Lucius Catellus boldly charged the troops who were under the king of Scotland and the duke of Cornwall, but failed to break them, as they countercharged in good order. The fierce Roman attack was also met by the forces commanded by Gerinus and Boso; the Romans fought back, but the latter delivered an unexpected cavalry charge, broke through and went on to attack another column, which was being led by the king of the Parthians against the troops of the Danish king, Aschillus. This brought on a general assault by both sides, and a huge battle developed as their ranks became mingled. The slaughter was terrible, as with their dying cries men from both armies beat their heads and spurs against the ground and coughed up their life-blood. It was the Britons who suffered the first losses, the butler Beduerus being killed and the steward Kaius mortally wounded. Beduerus had charged Boccus king of the Medes, but fell dead in the enemy ranks, impaled on the king's spear; the steward Kaius tried to avenge him, only to be surrounded by hordes of Medes and fatally wounded. Like the good soldier he was, Kaius would have cut his way out with his cavalry, killing and scattering the Medes and safely extracting himself and his men, had he not encountered the king of Libya's column,

agmina atque omnia pedestria fecerunt, quae Romano more ad modum cunei ordinata sex milia militum cum sexcentis .lxvi. singula omnia continebant. Sed et unicuique suos ductores dederunt, ut monitu eorum et inuaderent et ceteris irruentibus resisterent; uni etenim praefecerunt Lucium Catellum et Aliphatimam regem Hispaniae, alteri uero Hirtacium regem Parthorum et 325 Marium Lepidum senatorem, terciae Boccum regem Medorum et Gaium Metellum senatorem, quartae Sertorium regem Libiae et Quintum Miluium senatorem. Haec .iiii. agmina in prima acie statuta fuerunt; post ipsa uero alia quatuor a dorso, quorum uni Sersem regem Ituraeorum praeposuerunt, alteri uero Pandrasum regem Aegypti, terciae Politetem ducem Bithiniae, 330 quartae Theucrum ducem Frigiae; post haec quoque alia .iiii., et cuidam illorum dederunt Quintum Carutium senatorem, alii autem Laelium Hostiensem, terciae etiam Sulpicium Subbuculum, quartae Mauricium Siluanum. Ipse autem inter eos nunc hac nunc illac incedebat suggerendo, docendo qualiter sese haberent. In medio etiam auream aquilam quam 335 pro uexillo duxerat iussit firmiter poni et quoscumque casus segregasset submonuit ut ad eam reuerti conarentur.

171   Postquam tandem in aduersa parte hinc Britones illinc Romani erectis steterunt telis, confestim audito classicorum sonitu agmen illud cui rex Hispaniae et Lucius Catellus praeerat in cateruam illam quam rex Scotiae 340 et dux Cornubiae ducebant audacter irruit, sed illam stricte irruentem nequaquam disgregare potuit. Cui itaque saeuissime inuadenti occurrit caterua quam Gerinus et Boso regebant; et dum alia ut praedictum est resisteret, subito cursu equorum impetum in eadem fecit et penetrata illa obuiauit agmini quod rex Parthorum ducebat contra turmam Aschilli regis 345 Dacorum. Nec mora, concurrunt undique hinc et inde cateruae et sese mutuo penetrantes maximam pugnam lacessunt. Fit itaque miseranda caedes inter eos cum supremo clamore, et terram uertice et calcaneis pulsantes uitam in utraque parte cum sanguine eructant. Sed prius dampnum Britonibus illatum est, quia Beduerus pincerna peremptus fuit et Kaius dapifer 350 letaliter uulneratus. Nam dum Beduerus Bocco regi Medorum obuiaret, lancea eiusdem confossus inter hostiles cateruas peremptus corruit; Kaius autem dapifer, dum ipsum uindicare conaretur, infra Medorum turmas circumdatus mortiferum uulnus recepit. Qui tamen more boni militis cum ala quam ducebat uiam aperiens, caesis et dissipatis Medis, sese infra suos 355 integra caterua recepisset nisi in obuiam uenisset agmini regis Libiae,

322 singula omnia *Δ*: exercitum *(in* exercitum *K)* suum disponentes *Σ Φ (cf. 'Transm.' 105)*
327 quartum sertorium *OHS QYM*
328 <et> post ipsa [uero] *Σ Φ*
330 alii *Φ*
330-31 Frigiae ... Bithiniae *Φ*
339-40 rex Hispaniae *Δ Σ:* ex Hispania *Φ (*rex *add. Y,* Alifatima *M,* et *om. G)*
340 praeerant *E M*
341 districte *Σ*
344 eandem *OSE UD M*

which attacked and completely broke up his command. Retiring as best he could with a few survivors, Kaius retreated to Arthur's golden dragon with Beduerus' body. How the Normans groaned at seeing the torn and mangled corpse of their duke! How the men of Anjou grieved as they tended the many wounds of their count Kaius! But this was not the moment for lamentation since the bloody batttle-lines closing all around meant that they must defend themselves, and had no chance to indulge their sorrow.

172 Maddened by Beduerus' death, his nephew Hirelglas took three hundred men and, unexpectedly charging on horseback through the enemy ranks like a boar through a pack of hounds, made for the spot where he had seen the king of the Medes' standard, with not a thought for his own safety as long as he could avenge his uncle. When he got there, he killed the king, brought him back to his comrades and cut him to pieces beside the butler's body. Then with a great shout he urged the British troops, while their blood was still up, to attack the enemy, whose hearts were trembling with fear, and to press home continual charges, as they were better formed for close fighting and could keep inflicting severe losses on the foe. Heartened by his encouragement, they attacked on all sides and men of both armies fell. The Romans lost kings Aliphatima of Spain and Micipsa of Babylon and the senators Quintus Milvius and Marius Lepidus, as well as countless others. The Britons lost dukes Holdinus of Flanders and Leodegarius of Boulogne and three British earls, Cursalem of Chester, Gualauc of Salisbury and Urbgennius of Bath. The men they commanded were demoralised and fell back until they reached the ranks of the Armorican Britons, led by Hoelus and Gawain. Like a blazing fire, they charged the enemy, rallied the retreating soldiers and soon put their pursuers to flight. Taking up the pursuit themselves, they hacked at and killed the fleeing enemy, slaughtering them until they reached the emperor's troops. Seeing his comrades' plight, the emperor hurried to rescue them.

173 The Britons got the worse of the ensuing clash. Chinmarcocus earl of Tréguier and two thousand of his men were killed. Killed too were three eminent nobles, Richomarcus, Bloccouius and Iaguiuius of Bodloan, who, if they had been at the head of kingdoms, would have won undying renown for their

cuius irruptio illos quos ducebat omnino disgregauit. Vtcumque tamen cum paucis retro cedens, ad aureum diffugit draconem cum corpore Bedueri. O quanta lamenta Neustriensium dum corpus Bedueri sui ducis tot uulneribus dilaniatum aspicerent! O quantos etiam Andegauensium planctus dum Kaii 360 consulis sui uulnera pluribus modis tractarent! Sed non opus erat querela, quia undique sanguinolentae acies mutuo irruentes non permittebant eis spacium praedicti gemitus quin ipsos ad defendendum sese coegissent.

172 Hirelglas ergo nepos Bedueri, ultra modum ob mortem ipsius commotus, trecentos suorum associauit sibi et uelut aper infra turmam canum sic per 365 hostiles cateruas subito cursu equorum locum ubi uexillum Medorum regis aspexerat petiuit, parum excogitans quid sibi contingere posset dum auunculum suum uindicaret. Adeptus tandem locum quem affectauerat, praedictum regem peremit peremptumque ad socios suos deportauit, deportatum autem iuxta corpus pincernae omnino dilaniauit. Deinde 370 maximo clamore conciuium suorum turmas hortabatur in hostes irruere crebrisque irruptionibus infestare dum eis uirtus recenter feruebat, dum illis formidolosis pectus tremebat, dum cominus imminentes sapientius quam ceteri per cateruas dispositi essent atque crudelius dampnum ingerere saepius ualuissent. Inanimati igitur hortamine illius, impetum in hostes 375 undique fecerunt, quo maxima strages utrisque facta fuit. In parte namque Romanorum, exceptis innumerabilibus aliis, Aliphatima rex Hispaniae et Micipsa Babiloniensis, Quintus quoque Miluius et Marius Lepidus senatores corruerunt. Corruerunt etiam in parte Britonum Holdinus dux Rutenorum et Leodegarius Bolonensis, tres etiam consules Britanniae, Cursalem 380 Kaicestrensis, Gualauc Salesberiensis et Vrbgennius de Badone. Vnde turmae quas conducebant ultra modum debilitatae retro cesserunt donec uenerunt ad aciem Armoricanorum Britonum, quam Hoelus et Gualguainus regebant. Quae itaque uelut flamma ignescens impetum facit in hostes et reuocatis illis qui retro cesserant illos qui paulo ante insequebantur diffugere 385 coegit. Sed et usque insequentes nunc ipsos diffugientes prosternit, nunc interficit, nec stragem ingerere cessat donec ad turmam imperatoris uenit. Qui uisa calamitate sociorum properat ipsis succursum praestare.

173 Inito itaque congressu, debilitantur Britones. Chinmarcocus siquidem consul Trigeriae nec non et duo milia secum corruerunt. Corruerunt 390 etiam tres incliti proceres, Richomarcus et Bloccouius atque Iaguiuius de Bodloano, qui si principes fuissent regnorum, ob tantam probitatem quam

357 omni *QM:* omnes *YG*
359 Estrusiensium *UND Φ (cf. §§ 41.123, 176.468)*
359 [Bedueri] *Σ Φ*
360 [etiam] *Φ*
366-7 regis Medorum *D Φ*
370 [autem] *Φ*
371-2 <inanimando> hortabatur … crebris[que] … [infestare] *Σ Φ*
381 <et> Gualauc *H Y*
In §§ 173-99 nonnulla omittit O, quapropter nihil ex silentio concludendum

bravery. They charged with Hoelus and Gawain, and no foe they attacked escaped being cut down by their swords or lances. But when they reached the ranks of Lucius' men, they were surrounded by the enemy and dispatched along with Chinmarcocus and his two thousand soldiers. When they heard of these losses, Hoelus and Gawain, men whose like had never been born, pressed on more fiercely and separated to attack the emperor's column now at one point, now at another. Gawain burned with unflagging heroism and, eager for a chance to fight Lucius, charged like the boldest of knights, cutting down and killing the enemy. Elsewhere Hoelus was no less energetically encouraging his companions, striking the enemy and fearlessly receiving their blows, so that not a moment passed without stroke or counterstroke. It was not easy to say which of them outdid the other.

174   As Gawain hacked at the enemy, he found an opportunity at last to attack and fight the emperor. Lucius was in the prime of life, bold, strong and brave, and desired nothing better than to meet the warrior who could put his soldierly skills to the test. Facing Gawain, of whom he had heard so much, he was happy and proud to fight. They fought for some time, dealing stout blows and parrying them with their shields, each trying to finish the other. While the duel raged, the Romans suddenly rallied and, charging the Armoricans to rescue their emperor, cut at Gawain, Hoelus and their men and drove them back until they unexpectedly crashed into Arthur's troops. Hearing of the losses the Britons had just suffered, Arthur had rushed up with his legion and, drawing his mighty sword Caliburnus, was urging on his fellow-soldiers, shouting:

> 'What are you doing, men? Why are you letting these women get away unharmed? Let none of them escape with their lives. Think of your sword-hands, which have endured so many battles and subjected thirty kingdoms to my power. Think of your forefathers, whom the Romans, when they were mightier, forced to pay tribute. Think of your freedom, which these half-men, weaker than yourselves, wish to take away. Let not one escape alive, not one. What are you doing?'.

With cries such as these, he charged the enemy, bowling them over, cutting down any man who got in his way and killing him or his horse with a single blow.

habebant uentura aetas famam eorum celebraret. Nam dum praedictum
impetum cum Hoelo et Gualguaino facerent non euadebat hostis cui
imminebant quin ei uitam uel gladio uel lancea eripuissent. Sed postquam   395
infra aciem Lucii uentum fuit, undique a Romanis circumsaepti cum
praedicto consule et praedictis milibus conciderunt. Hoelus igitur et
Gualguainus, quibus meliores praeterita saecula non genuerant, comperta
strage suorum acriores institerunt et nunc hac nunc illac unus in una
parte alter in alia parte discurrentes cuneum imperatoris infestabant.   400
At Gualguainus, semper recenti uirtute exaestuans, nitebatur ut aditum
congrediendi cum Lucio haberet, nitendo ut audacissimus miles irruebat,
irruendo hostes prosternebat, prosternendo caedebat. Hoelus quoque non
inferior illo ex alia parte fulminabat, socios etiam suos hortabatur, inimicos
feriebat eorumque ictus haut timidus recipiebat, nec ulla hora deficiebat   405
quin saepissime percuteretur et percuteret. Non facile diffiniri poterat quis
eorum alterum excederet.

174   Porro Gualguainus caedendo turmas ut praedictum est inuenit tandem
aditum quem optabat et in imperatorem irruit et cum illo congressus est. At
Lucius, prima iuuentute florens, multum audatiae, multum uigoris, multum   410
probitatis habebat, nichilque maius desiderabat quam congredi cum milite
tali qui eum coegisset experiri quantum in militia ualuisset. Resistens itaque
Gualguaino, congressum eius inire laetatur et gloriatur, quia tantam famam
de eo audiuerat. Commisso diutius inter se proelio, dant ictus ualidos et
clipeos ictibus praetendendo uterque neci alterius imminere elaborat. Dum   415
autem acrius in hunc modum decertarent, ecce Romani, subito recuperantes,
impetum in Armoricanos faciunt et imperatori suo subuenientes Hoelum et
Gualguainum cum suis turmis caedendo pepulerunt donec in obuiam Arturo
et eiusdem agmini ex inprouiso uenerunt. Ipse etenim, audita suorum strage,
quae paulo ante eisdem dabatur, cum legione irruerat et abstracto Caliburno   420
gladio optimo celsa uoce atque his uerbis commilitones suos inanimabat,
inquiens:

'Quid facitis, uiri? Vt quid muliebres permittitis illaesos abire? Ne
abscedat ullus uiuus. Mementote dexterarum uestrarum, quae tot proeliis
exercitatae terdena regna potestati meae subdiderunt. Mementote   425
auorum uestrorum, quos Romani dum fortiores erant tributarios fecerunt.
Mementote libertatis uestrae, quam semiuiri isti et uobis debiliores
demere affectant. Ne abeat ullus uiuus, ne abeat. Quid facitis?'.

Haec et plura alia uociferando irruebat in hostes, prosternebat, caedebat,
et cuicumque obuiabat aut ipsum aut ipsius equum uno ictu interficiebat.   430

393 Nam *S:* Nam et *cett. (cf. Introd.)*
397 milibus *C Σ:* militibus *OHSE:* consulibus *Φ*
403 [hostes] *Σ Φ*
408 [caedendo] *Φ, deinde* est <infestans> *YM,* est <inuadens> *G*
413 mire *O G*
414 audierat *C YG*
416 recuper- *alibi transitiue*
421 [his] *Φ*

They fled from him like prey before a fierce lion, whose hunger-pangs drive it to devour whatever it can find. Their weapons could not prevent Caliburnus, wielded by the hand of so great a king, making them cough up their life-blood. He cut off the heads of two kings who were unlucky enough to meet him, Sertorius of Libya and Politetes of Bithynia, and dispatched them to hell. Seeing their king fighting so valiantly, the Britons took heart and all together assaulted the Romans, closing ranks as they advanced. While the infantry attacked in this way at one point, at another the cavalry were trying to fight their way in. Still the Romans fought back bitterly and, urged on by their celebrated emperor Lucius, attempted to inflict similar slaughter on the Britons. Both parties fought as bravely as if the battle had only just begun. On one side was Arthur, smiting the enemy time after time and stiffening British resistance, on the other Lucius Hiberius guided his men, leading them many times in famous exploits, striking ceaselessly and appearing everywhere among his troops to kill with spear or sword any foe he could reach. The slaughter on both sides was appalling, as at one moment the British gained the upper hand, and the Romans at the next.

175 So the battle raged until finally Morvid earl of Gloucester with the legion which, as I said, was stationed in the hills suddenly charged the enemy from behind and took them by surprise, breaking, scattering and slaughtering them. Many thousands of Romans fell. Then at last emperor Lucius was trapped in the melee and killed, struck down by an unknown lance. The Britons fought on until by dint of great effort they secured victory.

176 Fear drove some of the disorganised Romans to wander in the pathless woods, whilst others fled to cities, towns and other places of refuge. Pursuing energetically, the Britons subjected them to terrible slaughter, capturing and plundering them so that, to gain a little respite from death, the majority willingly stretched out their hands to be bound like women. So God had willed it, because in the past the early Romans had unjustly subjected the forefathers of the Britons to invasion, whereas now the Britons were trying to foil the Romans' plan to deprive them of their liberty and were refusing to pay the tribute they

Diffugiebant ergo ipsum uelut beluae ferocem leonem quem saeua fames instimulat ad deuorandum quicquid casus subuectat. Arma sua nichil eis proficiebant quin Caliburnus, dextra tam uirtuosi regis uibratus, cogeret ipsos animas eructare cum sanguine. Duos reges, Sertorium Libiae Bithiniaeque Politetem, infortunium ei obuios fecit, quos abscisis capitibus 435 ad Tartara direxit. Viso igitur rege suo in hunc modum decertare, Britones maiorem audatiam capessunt, Romanos unanimiter inuadunt, densata caterua incedunt. Et dum ex una parte pedestres hoc modo infestarent, equestres ex alia prosternere et penetrare conabantur. Resistunt tamen acriter Romani et monitu Lucii illustris regis uicem illatae cladis Britonibus 440 reddere elaborant. Tanta igitur ui in utraque parte pugnatur ac si tum primum recenter conuenirent. Hinc autem Arturus, saepius ac saepius ut praedictum est hostes percutiens, Britones ad perstandum hortabatur, illinc uero Lucius Hiberius Romanos suos et monebat et in praeclaras probitates multociens ducebat, nec ipse cessabat ferire sed in omnes partes turmas 445 suas circueundo quemcumque hostem casus offerebat uel lancea uel gladio perimebat. Fiebat itaque in utraque parte caedes abhorrenda, quia quandoque

175 Britones quandoque Romani uersa uice praeualebant. Postremo, dum talis decertatio inter eos fieret, ecce Moruid consul Claudiocestriae cum legione quam esse infra colles superius dixi subito cursu occurrit et hostes nichil 450 tale praemeditatos a dorso inuadit, inuadens penetrauit, penetrans dissipauit atque maximam stragem fecit. Tunc multa milia Romanorum conciderunt. Tunc tandem Lucius imperator, infra turmas occupatus, cuiusdam lancea confossus interiit. At Britones usque insistentes uictoriam licet maximo labore habuerunt. 455

176 Disgregati igitur Romani partim deuia et nemora cogente timore carpebant, partim ad ciuitates et ad oppida et ad quaeque tutissima loca diffugiebant. Quos Britones omni nisu insequendo miserabili caede afficiunt, capiunt, despoliant, ita quod maxima pars eorum ultro protendebat manus suas muliebriter uinciendas ut paxillum spacium uiuendi haberet. Quod 460 diuinae potentiae stabat loco, cum et ueteres eorum priscis temporibus auos istorum iniustis inquietationibus infestassent et isti tunc libertatem quam illi eisdem demere affectabant tueri instarent, abnegantes tributum quod

433 dextera *AKN G*
435 <ob> infortunium *Σ*
435 obuios fecit quos *Δ:* obuios *Σ:* obtulit quos *Φ (cf. 'Transm.' 92)*
437 (h)abundantiam *Σ YM*
441 tunc *E N Φ*
442 [ac saepius] *OC*
451 inuasit *QGM*
453 tandem *Δ:* etiam *Σ Φ*
457 [ad] ciuitates *OHS¹E UD*
457 [ad] oppida *H¹ N Φ*
460 uincendas *OCHS*
460 haberent *E UA¹ Φ*
462 inuisis *HSE*
462 nunc *Φ*

unfairly demanded. When the battle was finally won, Arthur commanded that the bodies of his nobles be separated from the corpses of the enemy, dressed in regal trappings and taken to the abbeys in the region for honourable burial. The Normans with great lamentation carried the body of the butler Beduerus to his city of Bayeux, which had been built by his ancestor, the first Beduerus. The body was buried with honour in a graveyard in the southern part of the city, next to its wall. The mortally wounded Cheudo was taken to the castle of Chinon, which he himself had built, and, when he died shortly afterwards from his injuries, he was buried as befitted a duke of Anjou at a convent of hermits in a wood not far from the town. Holdinus duke of the Flemings was taken to Flanders to receive burial at his city of Thérouanne. The remaining earls and nobles were carried to nearby abbeys as Arthur had instructed. He also took pity on his enemies, ordering the locals to bury them, and he sent Lucius' body to the senate together with a message that this was all the tribute that Britain needed to pay. He then wintered in the district and thereafter devoted himself to conquering the cities of Burgundy. With the coming of summer he decided to march on Rome, but just as he began to cross the Alps, he heard that his nephew Modred, to whose protection Britain had been entrusted, had treacherously usurped the crown, and that Queen Ganhumara had repudiated her former vows and united with him in sinful love.

BOOK ELEVEN

177 Geoffrey of Monmouth will not be silent even about this, most noble earl, but, just as he found it written in the British book and heard from Walter of Oxford, a man very familiar with many histories, he will tell, in his poor style, but briefly, of the battles the famous king fought against his nephew, when he returned to Britain after his victory. When the news of the disgraceful crime came to his ears, Arthur immediately put off the expedition he had intended to mount against the emperor Leo, dispatched Hoelus duke of the Armoricans with the French forces to maintain peace in their regions and returned hurriedly to Britain, accompanied only by the kings of the islands and their troops. That most foul traitor Modred had sent the Saxon leader Chelricus to Germany to collect there as many men as he could and sail back with them as quickly as possible. In return, Modred promised him

ab ipsis iniuste exigebatur. Habita denique uictoria illa, Arturus corpora procerum suorum ab hostilibus cadaueribus separari iubet, separata autem 465 regio more parari, parata uero ad comprouinciales abbatias deferri, ut ibidem honorifice sepelirentur. At Beduerus pincerna ad Baiocas ciuitatem suam, quam Beduerus primus et proauus suus aedificauerat, ab Neustriensibus cum maximis lamentis deportatur. Ibi in quodam cimiterio quod in australi parte ciuitatis erat iuxta murum honorifice positus fuit. Cheudo autem ad 470 Camum oppidum, quod ipse construxerat, grauiter uulneratus asportatur, et paulo post eodem uulnere defunctus in quodam nemore in coenobio heremitarum qui ibidem non longe ab oppido erant ut decuit Andegauensium ducem humatus fuit. Holdinus quoque dux Rutenorum, Flandrias delatus, in Terwana ciuitate sua sepultus est. Ceteri autem consules et proceres ut 475 praeceperat Arturus ad uicinas abbatias delati sunt. Hostes quoque suos miseratus, praecepit indigenis sepelire eos corpusque Lucii ad senatum deferre, mandans non debere aliud tributum ex Britannia reddi. Deinde post subsequentem hiemem in partibus illis moratus est et ciuitates Allobrogum subiugare uacauit. Adueniente uero aestate, dum Romam petere affectaret 480 et montes transcendere incepisset, nunciatur ei Modredum nepotem suum, cuius tutelae permiserat Britanniam, eiusdem diademate per tirannidem et proditionem insignitum esse reginamque Ganhumaram uiolato iure priorum nuptiarum eidem nefanda uenere copulatam fuisse.

LIBER XI

177 Ne hoc quidem, consul auguste, Galfridus Monemutensis tacebit, sed ut in praefato Britannico sermone inuenit et a Waltero Oxenefordensi, in multis historiis peritissimo uiro, audiuit, uili licet stilo, breuiter tamen propalabit, quae proelia inclitus ille rex post uictoriam istam in Britanniam reuersus cum nepote suo commiserit. Vt igitur infamia praenuntiati sceleris aures 5 ipsius attigit, continuo dilata inquietatione quam Leoni regi Romanorum ingerere affectauerat dimissoque Hoelo duce Armoricanorum cum exercitu Galliarum ut partes illas pacificaret, confestim cum insulanis tantummodo regibus eorumque exercitibus Britanniam remeauit. Praedictus autem sceleratissimus proditor ille Modredus Chelricum Saxonum ducem 10 Germaniam direxerat ut in illa quoscumque posset associaret sibi et associatis quibusque iterum citissimis uelis rediret. Spoponderat etiam se

468 Estrusiensibus (Estruen- *CG) C UND Φ:* Neustrusiensibus *A*
469 [cum] *OC*
469-70 [Ibi ... positus fuit] *Σ*
470 Cheudo *Δ Σ QG, hic primum sic nuncupatus:* Kaius *YM*
471 Cainum *41 (cf. Tatlock 97-8)*
479 sequentem *Σ*
1 Ne *76² (unde 92,71²):* De *CE:* Se *O¹:* Sed *O²:* Nec *HS(?) Σ Φ (cf. Introd.)*
6 dilatata *Δ Y¹N*
7 [-que] *Σ Φ*
9 eorum *A¹ Q:* et eorum *YM*
12 enim *Σ*

all the island from the river Humber to Scotland and as much of Kent as Hengest and Horsa had occupied in Vortigern's time. Chelricus had carried out his mission, returned with eight hundred ships full of armed pagans and now agreed formally to obey the traitor as if he were his king. Modred had also allied with himself the Scots, Picts, and Irish and all his uncle's sworn enemies. In total, both pagans and Christians, his forces numbered eighty thousand. Aided and abetted by this host, Modred opposed Arthur's landing at Richborough and in the ensuing fighting inflicted severe losses on the troops as they came ashore. King Auguselus of Scotland and the king's nephew Gawain were killed that day along with innumerable others. Auguselus was succeeded by Hiwenus, the son of his brother Urianus, who later distinguished himself through his many brave deeds in these battles. When they had at last got ashore with immense difficulty, they traded blows and put Modred and his army to flight. Thanks to their experience in years of warfare, they had wisely drawn up their battle-line with infantry and cavalry interspersed, so that when the infantry columns advanced to attack or defend, the mounted men immediately charged from the flank and made every effort to break the enemy; thus they forced them to flee. That night the traitor Modred gathered fugitives from all quarters and set off to Winchester. On hearing this, queen Ganhumara was quick to despair and, fleeing from York to Caerleon, took the veil in the church of Julius the Martyr, to live there in chastity among the nuns.

178 Arthur, yet more angry at the loss of so many hundreds of his soldiers, first buried the dead, then on the third day marched to Winchester and laid siege to the wretch who was taking refuge there. Modred, unwilling to give up, stiffened his companions' resolve, came out with his army and prepared to fight his uncle. Battle was joined with great slaughter on both sides, but eventually the tide turned against Modred and forced him into a shameful retreat. Scarcely caring who would bury his dead, he hurriedly took ship and fled to Cornwall. Arthur, greatly disheartened because Modred had escaped so often, pursued him there to the river Camblan, where his nephew was waiting. Modred, the boldest of men and always swift to attack, immediately drew up

ipsi hoc pacto daturum partem illam insulae quae a flumine Humbri usque ad Scotiam porrigebatur et quicquid in Cantia tempore Vortegirni Horsus et Hengistus possederant. At ille, peracto ipsius praecepto, octingentis nauibus 15 plenis armatis paganis applicuerat et foedere dato huic proditori quasi regi suo parebat. Associauerat quoque sibi Scotos, Pictos, Hibernenses, et quoscumque callebat habuisse suum auunculum odio. Erant autem omnes numero quasi octoginta milia tam paganorum quam Christianorum. Quorum auxilio fretus, quorum multitudine comitatus, Arturo in Rutupi 20 Portu applicanti in obuiam uenit et commisso proelio maximam stragem dedit applicantibus. Auguselus etenim rex Albaniae et Gualguainus nepos regis cum innumerabilibus aliis in die illa corruerunt. Successit autem Auguselo in regnum Hiwenus filius Vriani fratris sui, qui postea in decertationibus istis multis probitatibus praeclaruit. Postquam tandem 25 tametsi magno labore litora adepti fuerunt, mutuam reddendo cladem Modredum et exercitum eius propulerunt in fugam. Assiduis namque debellationibus usi, sapienter turmas suas disposuerant, quae partim pede partim equo distributae tali modo decertabant quod cum pedestre agmen ad inuadendum uel resistendum intenderet equestre ilico ab obliquo irruens 30 omni nisu hostes penetrare conaretur; unde eos ad diffugiendum coegerunt. Periurus ergo ille, reuocatis undique suis, in sequenti nocte Guintoniam ingressus est. Quod ut Ganhumarae reginae nunciatum est, confestim sibi desperans ab Eboraco ad Vrbem Legionum diffugit atque in templo Iulii martiris inter monachas eiusdem uittam suscepit et caste uiuere proposuit. 35

178   At Arturus, acriori ira accensus quoniam tot centena commilitonum suorum amiserat, in tercia die, datis prius sepulturae peremptis, ciuitatem adiuit atque infra receptum nebulonem obsedit. Qui tamen, coeptis suis desistere nolens sed ipsos qui ei adhaerebant pluribus modis inanimans, cum agminibus suis egreditur atque cum auunculo suo proeliari disponit. 40 Inito ergo certamine, facta est maxima caedes in utraque parte, quae tandem magis in partem ipsius illata coegit eum campum turpiter relinquere. Qui deinde, non multum curans quae sepelitio peremptis suis fieret, cito remige fugae euectus uersus Cornubiam iter arripuit. Arturus autem, interna anxietate cruciatus quoniam tociens euasisset, confestim 45 prosecutus est eum in praedictam patriam usque ad fluuium Camblan, ubi ille aduentum eius expectabat. Porro Modredus, ut erat omnium audacissimus et semper ad inuadendum celerrimus, confestim milites suos

27 in fugam propulerunt *(uerterunt K) OC K*
31 conaretur *K²:* conantur *CHSE Σ QYM:* conatur *O G (cf. Introd.)*
32 in sequenti, *non* insequenti *(cf. Introd.)*
33 [sibi] *Φ*
35 uitam *(uittam S,* habitum *E)* suscepit et *Δ Σ:* et uittam *(uitam QG)* suscepit *post* proposuit *Φ*
36 succensus *UAK*
40 disposuit *H QG*
42 [magis] *Σ*
44 *de* fugae *cf. Introd.*
46 persecutus *OH G, nescio an recte (cf. § 170.310)*

251

his men, preferring to conquer or die rather than to continue to flee. Of his old army there remained sixty thousand men, whom he formed in six bodies, each comprising six thousand, six hundred and sixty-six warriors; he assigned leaders to each, then assembled the remaining troops into a single body under his own command. Having made these dispositions, he encouraged every soldier, promising them the possessions of their enemies if they fought with success. Drawing up his own army opposite, Arthur formed it into nine columns of foot soldiers, each with a right and left wing, and appointed commanders for each, urging them to kill the disloyal thieves who, at the behest of a traitor, had come to Britain from foreign kingdoms to steal their titles. He said that the barbarians, disunited and from various lands, were weak and untrained warriors who could not face the bravery and military experience of the British, as long as they attacked boldly and fought valiantly. As the commanders on either side were addressing their troops, the two armies suddenly charged and collided, eager to exchange blows. It is a sad and difficult task to describe the slaughter that soon ensued among both parties, the groans of the dying, and the fury of the assailants. On both sides men dealt wounds or were wounded, killed or were killed. Most of the day passed in this way, until at last Arthur and a column of six thousand, six hundred and sixty-six men charged the force within which he knew Modred to be, using their swords to cut their way in and causing terrible carnage. The treacherous Modred and thousands of his men were killed; however, his death did not make the rest flee, rather they gathered from all corners of the battlefield to resist as boldly as they could. In the very bitter fighting that ensued, almost all the commanders on either side were killed, along with their soldiers. Among Modred's men, there fell the Saxons Chelricus, Elafius, Egbrictus and Bruningus; the Irishmen Gillapatric, Gillamor, Gillasel and Gillaruum; and also the Scots and the Picts with almost all their subjects; in Arthur's army, there died Odbrictus king of Norway, Aschillus king of Denmark, Cador Limenic and Cassibellaunus as well as thousands of their men, both British and the other nationalities which they had brought with them. The illustrious king Arthur too was mortally wounded; he was taken away to the island of Avallon to have his wounds tended and, in the year of Our Lord 542, handed over Britain's crown to his relative Constantinus, son of Cador duke of Cornwall.

179   After Constantinus had been crowned, the Saxons and Modred's two sons rose up against him and fought many battles, but without success, the first son fleeing to London, and the second to Winchester, both of which they tried to capture. At that time Daniel,

per cateruas distribuit, affectans prius uincere uel mori quam praedicto
modo diucius fugere. Remanserant ei adhuc ex praedicto numero sociorum 50
suorum .lx. milia, ex quibus fecit sex turmas et in unaquaque posuit sex
milia armatorum et sexcentos .lx.vi.; praeterea uero fecit unam turmam ex
ceteris qui superfuerant et unicuique aliarum ductoribus datis eam tutelae
suae permisit. His ita distributis, quemque eorum inanimabat, promittens
ceterorum possessiones eis si ad triumphandum perstarent. Arturus quoque 55
suum exercitum in aduersa parte statuit, quem per nouem diuisit agmina
pedestria cum dextro ac sinistro cornu quadrata, et unicuique praesidibus
commissis hortatur ut periuros et latrones interimant qui monitu proditoris
sui de externis regionibus in insulam aduecti suos eis honores demere
affectabant. Dicit etiam diuersos diuersorum regnorum barbaros inbelles 60
atque belli usus ignaros esse et nullatenus ipsis, uirtuosis uiris et pluribus
debellationibus usis, resistere posse si audacter inuadere et uiriliter decertare
affectarent. Ipsis itaque commilitones suos hinc et inde cohortantibus,
subito impetu concurrunt acies et commisso proelio crebros ictus innectere
elaborant. Fiunt ilico in utrisque partibus tantae strages, tanti morientium 65
gemitus, tanti inuadentium furores, quantos et dolorosum et laboriosum
est describere. Vndique etenim uulnerabant et uulnerabantur, perimebant et
perimebantur. Postquam autem multum diei in hunc modum duxerunt, irruit
tandem Arturus cum agmine uno, quo sex milia et sexcentos .lx.vi. posuerat,
in turmam illam ubi Modredum sciebat esse, et uiam gladiis aperiendo eam 70
penetrauit atque tristissimam caedem ingessit. Concidit namque proditor
ille nefandus et multa milia secum; nec tamen ob casum eius diffugiunt
ceteri sed ex omni campo confluentes quantum audacia dabatur resistere
conantur. Committitur ergo dirissima pugna inter eos, qua omnes fere duces
qui in ambis partibus affuerant cum suis cateruis corruerunt. Corruerunt 75
etenim in parte Modredi Chelricus, Elafius, Egbrictus, Bruningus Saxones;
Gillapatric, Gillamor, Gillasel, Gillaruum Hibernenses; Scoti etiam et Picti
cum omnibus fere quorum dominabantur; in parte autem Arturi Odbrictus
rex Norguegiae, Aschillus rex Daciae, Cador Limenic, Cassibellaunus, cum
multis milibus suorum tam Britonum quam ceterarum gentium quas secum 80
adduxerant. Sed et inclitus ille rex Arturus letaliter uulneratus est; qui illinc
ad sananda uulnera sua in insulam Auallonis euectus Constantino cognato
suo et filio Cadoris ducis Cornubiae diadema Britanniae concessit anno ab
incarnatione Domini .dxlii..

179   Illo igitur insignito, insurrexerunt Saxones et duo filii Modredi nec in eum 85
praeualere quiuerunt, sed post plurima proelia diffugiendo unus Lundonias,
alter uero Guintoniam ingressus eas optinere coeperunt. Tunc defunctus est

54 itaque *OHS UAK QY*
56 exercitum suum *K G*
67 <et> uulnerabant *Σ*
75 ambabus *Φ*
81 inclitus ille rex *HS UND YGM:* ille inclitus rex *C AK:* inclitus *O:* inclitus ille *E:* inclitus rex
ille *Q*

the most devout bishop of the church of Bangor, died, and Theonus, bishop of Gloucester, was promoted to become archbishop of London. At this time too David, archbishop of Caerleon, died in the city of Menevia in his abbey there, which he loved more than all the monasteries in his diocese because it had been founded by St Patrick, who had foretold David's birth. While he was staying there among his fellow-monks, David suffered a sudden illness, died and was buried in their church on the orders of king Malgo. His place as archbishop was taken by Kinocus, bishop of Llanbadarn, who was promoted to the see of Caerleon.

180   Constantinus pursued Modred's sons, subdued the Saxons and captured the two cities mentioned above. He butchered one of the sons in Winchester as the youth sought refuge before the altar in St Amphibalus' church, the other he eventually found in London, hidden by the altar in a monastery of certain brothers, and cruelly slew. Four years later he was struck down by the judgement of God and buried next to Uther Pendragon in the stone circle known in English as Stonehenge, which had been built with great skill not far from Salisbury.

181   Constantinus was succeeded by his nephew, Aurelius Conanus, a youth of great promise who ruled over the whole island, and who would have been worthy of the crown save for his fondness for civil strife. His uncle should have succeeded in his place, but Aurelius attacked and imprisoned him, killed his two sons and seized the throne, only to die three years later.

182   Aurelius Conanus was succeeded by Vortiporius, against whom the Saxons rebelled, bringing a great fleet of their countrymen from Germany; but he fought and overcame them and, after becoming monarch of the entire kingdom, in the end ruled his people well and in peace.

183   Vortiporius was succeeded by Malgo, probably the most handsome of all Britain's rulers; he drove out many tyrants, was a mighty warrior, more generous than the rest, and would have enjoyed the highest of reputations had he not made himself hateful to God by wallowing in the sin of sodomy. He too ruled the whole island as well as its six neighbours, Ireland, Iceland, Gotland, the Orkneys, Norway and Denmark, which he conquered in fierce battles.

sanctus Daniel Bangornensis ecclesiae religiosissimus antistes et Theonus
Gloucestrensis episcopus in archiepiscopum Lundoniarum erigitur. Tunc
obiit sanctissimus Vrbis Legionum archiepiscopus Dauid in Meneuia 90
ciuitate infra abbatiam suam, quam prae ceteris suae dioceseos monasteriis
dilexerat, quia beatus Patricius, qui natiuitatem eius prophetauerat, ipsam
fundauit. Dum enim ibi apud confratres suos moram faceret, subito languore
grauatus defunctus est et iubente Malgone rege in eadem ecclesia sepultus.
Pro eo ponitur in metropolitana sede Kinocus Lampaternensis ecclesiae 95
antistes et ad altiorem dignitatem promouetur.

180   At Constantinus insecutus est filios Modredi et Saxones potestati suae
subiugauit et praedictas ciuitates cepit. Et alterum iuuenem Guintoniae in
ecclesia sancti Amphibali diffugientem ante altare trucidauit, alium uero
Lundoniis in quorundam fratrum coenobio absconditum atque tandem 100
iuxta altare inuentum crudeli morte affecit. Exin quarto anno, sententia
Dei percussus, iuxta Vther Pendragon infra lapidum structuram sepultus
fuit quae haud longe a Salesberia mira arte composita Anglorum lingua
Stanheng nuncupatur.

181   Cui successit Aurelius Conanus, mirae probitatis iuuenis et ipsius 105
nepos, qui monarchiam tocius insulae tenens eiusdem diademate dignus
esset si non foret ciuilis belli amator. Auunculum etenim suum, qui
post Constantinum regnare debuit, inquietauit atque in carcerem posuit
eiusque duobus filiis peremptis optinuit regnum tertioque regni sui anno
defunctus est.   110

182   Cui successit Vortiporius, in quem insurrexerunt Saxones, conducentes
conciues suos ex Germania maximo nauigio; sed ipse proelium cum eis
iniuit et superauit et monarchiam tocius regni adeptus populum tandem
gubernauit cum diligentia et pace.

183   Cui successit Malgo, omnium fere ducum Britanniae pulcherrimus, 115
multorum tirannorum depulsor, robustus armis, largior ceteris, et ultra
modum probitate praeclarus nisi sodomitana peste uolutatus sese
Deo inuisum exhibuisset. Hic etiam totam insulam optinuit, et sex
comprouinciales occeani insulas, Hiberniam uidelicet atque Islandiam,
Godlandiam, Orcades, Norguegiam, Daciam, adiecit dirissimis proeliis 120
potestati suae.

---

88 Theonus *Φ (cf. § 186.160): om. Δ KND: lac. UA*
93 [enim] *CHSE Σ (*[dum ... sepultus] *O)*
94 <Venedotorum> rege *Φ*
97 filios Modredi et Saxones *Δ:* eos et Saxones *UND:* eum et Saxones *AK:* Saxones et eos *Φ*
101 uigesimo *Σ:* tertio *Φ*
101-2 sententia dei percussus *Δ Σ:* interfectus est a Conano et *Φ (cf. 'Transm.' 105)*
102 Vspanum Draconteum *UND (cf. § 143.1)*
107 suum *Δ Σ:* alium *Φ*
109 trigesimo- *Σ:* secundo- *Φ*
113 tandem *CHSE Σ:* -que suum *O:* .iiii. annis *QYG:* annis .iiii. *M (cf. 'Transm.' 105)*
114 cum diligentia et pace (cum pace et diligentia *Y*) gubernauit *O AK Y*
115 [ducum] *H¹ G*

184   Malgo was succeeded by Kareticus, a lover of civil war, hateful to God and the Britons; the Saxons learned of his weakness and went to Ireland to fetch Gormundus, the king of the Africans, who had landed there with a huge fleet and subdued its people. Thanks to the Saxons' treachery, Gormundus and a hundred and sixty thousand Africans crossed to Britain, which was being laid completely waste, on the one side by the faithless Saxons, and on the other by the continual civil wars waged by its own citizens. With the Saxons as his allies, Gormundus attacked king Kareticus and, after many battles, chased him from city to city, driving him in the end to Cirencester, where he besieged him. There Gormundus was joined by Isembardus, the nephew of the French king Lodewicus; he became Gormundus' sworn friend, renouncing Christianity out of affection for him, on condition that Gormundus would help him take the crown of France from his uncle, by whom he claimed to have been violently and unjustly exiled. Gormundus captured and burnt Cirencester, fought with Kareticus and pushed him across the Severn into Wales. Then, ravaging the fields, he heaped up against all the surrounding cities a fire which, once kindled, did not die down until it scorched almost the whole surface of the island from coast to coast, so that all the towns, along with their people and the priests of their churches, were laid in the dust by his relentless battering-rams, as blades flashed and flames crackled all around. The survivors, shocked by the

185   catastrophe, fled to any place of safety they could find. – Why, you slothful race, weighed down by your terrible sins, why with your continual thirst for civil war have you weakened yourself so much by internal strife? You once subjected far-off realms to your power, but are now unable to protect your land, wives and children from your foes, so that you resemble a vineyard once good, but now turned sour. Go on, wage your civil war, unmindful that in the gospel it says: 'every kingdom divided against itself shall be laid waste, and house fall on house.' Your kingdom is divided against itself, lust for civil strife and a cloud of envy has blunted your mind, your pride has prevented you from obeying a single king, and so your country has been laid waste before your eyes by most wicked barbarians, and its houses fall one upon another. Your descendants will regret it one day, when they see the cubs of the barbarian lioness take their towns, cities and other possessions, whilst they themselves will become miserable exiles who will scarcely if

186   ever regain their past glory. – When, as I have said, that ill-omened usurper and his countless thousands of Africans had laid waste almost the entire island, he gave the largest portion of it, called Loegria,

184   Cui successit Kareticus, amator ciuilium bellorum, inuisus Deo et
Britonibus, cuius inconstantiam comperientes Saxones iuerunt propter
Gormundum regem Affricanorum in Hiberniam, in quam maximis nauigiis
aduectus gentem patriae subiugauerat. Exin proditione eorum cum centum   125
sexaginta milibus Affricanorum ad Britanniam transfretauit, quam in una
parte mentitae fidei Saxones, in alia uero ciues patriae, ciuilia bella inter se
assidue agentes, penitus deuastabant. Inito igitur foedere cum Saxonibus
oppugnauit Kareticum regem et post plurima proelia fugauit eum a ciuitate
in ciuitatem donec eum trusit in Cirecestriam et obsedit. Vbi Isembardus   130
nepos Lodewici regis Francorum uenit ad eum et cum eo foedus amiciciae
iniuit et Christianitatem suam tali pacto et pro amore suo deseruit ut auxilio
suo regnum Galliae auunculo eripere ualuisset, a quo ut aiebat ui et iniuste
erat expulsus. Capta tandem praedicta ciuitate et succensa, commisit
proelium cum Karetico et fugauit eum ultra Sabrinam in Gualias. Mox,   135
depopulans agros, ignem cumulauit in finitimas quasque ciuitates, qui non
quieuit accensus donec cunctam paene superficiem insulae a mari usque
ad mare exussit ita ut cunctae coloniae crebris arietibus omnesque coloni
cum sacerdotibus ecclesiae mucronibus undique micantibus ac flammis
crepitantibus simul humi sternerentur. Diffugiebant ergo reliquiae, tantis   140
185 cladibus affectae, quocumque tutamen ipsis cedentibus patebat. – Quid,
ociosa gens pondere inmanium scelerum oppressa, quid semper ciuilia proelia
siciens tete domesticis in tantum debilitasti motibus, quae cum prius longe
posita regna potestati tuae subdidisses nunc uelut bona uinea degenerata in
amaritudinem uersa patriam, coniuges, liberos nequeas ab inimicis tueri?   145
Age ergo, age ciuile discidium, parum intelligens euangelicum illud 'omne
regnum in se ipsum diuisum desolabitur, et domus supra domum cadet'. Quia
ergo regnum tuum in se diuisum fuit, quia furor ciuilis discordiae et liuoris
fumus mentem tuam hebetauit, quia superbia tua uni regi oboedientiam ferre
non permisit, cernis iccirco patriam tuam ab impiissimis paganis desolatam,   150
domos etiam eiusdem supra domos ruentes, quod posteri tui in futurum
lugebunt. Videbunt etenim barbarae leaenae catulos oppida, ciuitates atque
ceteras eorundem possessiones optinere, ex quibus misere expulsi prioris
186 dignitatis statum uel numquam uel uix recuperabunt. – Postquam autem
ut praedictum est infaustus tyrannus cum innumerabilibus Affricanorum   155
milibus totam fere insulam uastauit, maiorem partem eius, quae Loegria

123 iuuerunt *HS¹*: miserunt *O*
129 a *Δ Σ*: de *Φ*
138 excussit *CH*
138 [-que] *C M*
140 sternerentur *KD*: sternerent *cett.*
141 patebant *Δ U QY*
142 odiosa *H K²*
143 te *O K*
143 quae *D G*: qui *cett.*
148 qui furor *CH*
152 barbarae *Σ*: barbariae *Δ Φ*
156 militibus *H Y*

to the Saxons, through whose treachery he had landed. The remnants of the Britons had retreated to Cornwall and Wales, the western parts of the kingdom, from where they continued to launch frequent damaging incursions. It was then that the archbishops of London and York, Theonus and Tadioceus, seeing that all the churches subject to them had been razed to the ground, fled to the safety of the Welsh forests along with all the priests who had survived the danger; with them they took the relics of the saints, fearful that the holy bones of so many ancient sages would be destroyed if they abandoned them in such peril by embracing their own imminent martyrdom. More priests sailed in a great fleet to Brittany, with the result that the churches of the two provinces of Loegria and Northumbria lost their entire congregations. But I shall relate their story elsewhere, when I translate the book about their exile.

187   Then for a long time the British lost the royal crown and control over the island; nor did they strive to recover it, but continually laid waste the area they still held, since it was ruled not by one king, but by three usurpers. Nor yet did the Saxons become masters of the island, as they too were subject to three kings and warred sometimes against each other and sometimes

188   against the Britons. At this time the blessed pope Gregory sent Augustine to Britain to preach God's word to the English, who, blinded by their pagan beliefs, had completely destroyed Christianity in the part of the island they occupied. It still flourished in the British part, never having wavered since it was introduced in pope Eleutherius' time. When Augustine landed, he found in their province seven bishoprics and an archbishopric, occupied by most holy incumbents, and many monasteries in which the Lord's flock observed the regular life. Amongst them was a most noble house in the city of Bangor, which had so many monks that, although it was divided into seven subunits, each with its own prior, none of them comprised less than three hundred monks, who all sustained themselves with their own labour. Their abbot, named Dinoot, was impressively well instructed in the liberal arts. To Augustine's request for the submission of the British bishops and his suggestion that they should share in his efforts to convert the English, Dinoot replied with various objections to the effect that they owed no obedience to him, since they had their own archbishop, nor did they preach to their enemies, since the Saxons persisted in depriving them of their country; and for that reason the British detested them, despising

uocabatur, praebuit Saxonibus, quorum proditione applicuerat. Secesserunt itaque Britonum reliquiae in occidentalibus regni partibus, Cornubiam uidelicet atque Gualias, unde crebras et ferales irruptiones incessanter hostibus fecerunt. Tunc igitur archipraesules Theonus Lundoniensis 160 et Tadioceus Eboracensis, cum omnes ecclesias sibi subditas usque ad humum destructas uidissent, cum omnibus ordinatis qui in tanto discrimine superfuerant diffugierunt ad tutamina nemorum in Gualiis cum reliquiis sanctorum, timentes ne barbarorum irruptione delerentur tot et tantorum ueterum sacra ossa si ipsa in imminenti periculo desererent et sese instanti 165 martyrio offerrent. Plures etiam Armoricanam Britanniam magno nauigio petiuerunt, ita ut tota ecclesia duarum prouinciarum, Loegriae uidelicet et Northamhimbriae, a conuentibus suis desolaretur. Sed haec alias referam, cum librum de exulatione eorum transtulero.

187   Amiserunt deinde Britones regni diadema multis temporibus et insulae 170 monarchiam nec pristinam dignitatem recuperare nitebantur; immo partem illam patriae quae eis adhuc remanserat non uni regi sed tribus tyrannis subditam ciuilibus proeliis saepissime uastabant. Sed nec Saxones diadema insulae adhuc adepti sunt, qui tribus etiam regibus subditi quandoque sibi 188 ipsi quandoque Britonibus inquietationem inferebant. Interea missus est 175 Augustinus a beato Gregorio papa in Britanniam ut Anglis uerbum Dei praedicaret, qui pagana superstitione caecati in illam insulae partem quam habebant totam deleuerant Christianitatem. In parte autem Britonum adhuc uigebat Christianitas, quae a tempore Eleutherii papae habita numquam inter eos defecerat. Postquam ergo uenit Augustinus, inuenit in eorum 180 prouincia .vii. episcopatus et archiepiscopatum religiosissimis praesulibus munitos et abbatias complures, in quibus grex Domini rectum ordinem tenebat. Inter ceteras erat in ciuitate Bangor quaedam nobilissima, in qua tantus fuisse fertur numerus monachorum ut cum in .vii. portiones esset cum praepositis sibi prioribus monasterium diuisum nulla harum portio minus 185 quam trecentos monachos haberet, qui omnes labore manuum suarum uiuebant. Abbas autem eorum Dinoot uocabatur, miro modo liberalibus artibus eruditus, qui Augustino petenti ab episcopis Britonum subiectionem et suadenti ut secum genti Anglorum communem euangelizandi laborem susciperent diuersis monstrauit argumentationibus ipsos ei nullam 190 subiectionem debere nec suam praedicationem inimicis suis impendere, cum et suum archipraesulem haberent et gens Saxonum patriam propriam eisdem auferre perstarent; unde eos summo habebant odio fidemque et

158 occidentales ... partes *G*
158-9 Cornubia ... Gualiis *Σ*
163 diffugerunt *OHS Σ G*
165 [in] *C AK*
167 durum *HS¹ Q¹ M*
169 exultatione *OE UA*: exultione *N*: exaltatione *D*
175 ingerebant *Φ*
184 fertur fuisse *Φ, Beda 2.2*
190 [monstrauit] *Φ*

189 their faith and beliefs and shunning them like dogs. Edelbertus, king of Kent, indignant that the Britons had refused to submit to Augustine and had rejected his preaching, incited Edelfridus, king of Northumbria, and the other Saxon subkings to collect a great army and go to the city of Bangor to kill Dinoot and the other priests who had slighted them. They obeyed, assembled a huge army and, entering the province of the British, came to Leicester, where Brochmail, its earl, awaited them. Countless monks and hermits had also gathered there from various British provinces, and particularly from Bangor, to pray for the salvation of their people. Edelfridus, the Northumbrian king, attacked Brochmail, who, resisting with inferior numbers, finally fled and abandoned the city, but only after inflicting heavy losses on the enemy. After the city was captured, Edelfridus learned the reason why the monks were there and ordered them to be slaughtered first, so that one thousand, two hundred of them were martyred that very day and won their place in the kingdom of heaven. Next the Saxon despot marched on Bangor. When they heard of his fury, British chiefs came from all sides, including Bledericus, duke of Cornwall, and Margadud and Caduanus, kings of the Demetae and Venedoti; a battle was fought, in which Edelfridus was wounded and put to flight and no fewer than ten thousand and sixty-six of his men were killed. On the British side there fell Bledericus, duke of Cornwall, who had been their overall commander.

190 All the British chiefs then assembled in the city of Leicester and agreed to make Caduan their king and to pursue Edelfridus across the Humber under his leadership. Once Caduan had received the royal crown, men flocked from all sides and crossed the river. On hearing this, Edelfridus gathered all the Saxon kings and marched on Caduan. Then, when their troops were drawn up for battle, their friends interceded and reconciled them, agreeing that Edelfridus should rule Britain north of the Humber and Caduan south of the river. They sealed the treaty with an exchange of hostages and oaths and became such good friends that they held all their possessions in common. Meanwhile it happened that Edelfridus remarried, having repudiated his first wife, whom he so hated that he banished her from Northumbria. She, with a baby in her womb, went to king Caduan, begging him to

religionem eorum pro nichilo habebant nec in aliquo Anglis magis quam
189 canibus communicabant. Edelbertus ergo rex Cantiorum, ut uidit Britones 195
dedignantes subiectionem Augustino facere et eosdem praedicationem suam
spernere, hoc grauissime ferens Edelfridum regem Northamhimbrorum
et ceteros regulos Saxonum instimulauit ut collecto grandi exercitu in
ciuitatem Bangor abbatem Dinoot et ceteros clericos qui eos despexerant
perditum irent. Adquiescentes igitur consilio eius, collegerunt mirabilem 200
exercitum et prouinciam Britonum petentes uenerunt Legecestriam, ubi
Brochmail consul urbis aduentum eorum expectabat. Venerant autem ad
eandem ciuitatem ex diuersis Britonum prouinciis innumerabiles monachi
et heremitae, et maxime de ciuitate Bangor, ut pro salute populi sui orarent.
Collectis igitur undique exercitibus, Edelfridus rex Northamhimbrorum 205
proelium iniuit cum Brochmail, qui pauciori numero militum resistens ad
ultimum relicta ciuitate sed prius maxima strage hostibus illata diffugit. At
Edelfridus ciuitate capta, cum intellexisset causam aduentus praedictorum
monachorum, iussit in eos primum arma uerti, et sic mille ducenti eorum
in ipsa die martirio decorati regni caelestis adepti sunt sedem. Deinde, cum 210
praedictus Saxonum tyrannus Bangornensium urbem peteret, audita ipsius
insania uenerunt undique obuiam illi duces Britonum, Bledericus uidelicet
dux Cornubiae et Margadud rex Demetarum, Caduanus Venedotorum, et
conserto proelio ipsum uulneratum in fugam propulerunt, sed et tantum
numerum exercitus eius peremerunt ita quod decem milia circiter et 215
sexaginta sex corruerunt. In parte etiam Britonum cecidit Bledericus dux
Cornubiae, qui ducatum in eisdem proeliis ceteris praestabat.
190   Exin conuenerunt omnes principes Britonum in ciuitate Legecestriae
communemque assensum habuerunt ut Caduanum facerent sibi regem
ipsoque duce Edelfridum ultra Humbrum sequerentur. Insignitoque illo 220
regni diademate, undique confluentes Humbrum praeterierunt. Cumque id
Edelfrido nuntiatum esset, associauit sibi omnes reges Saxonum obuiusque
Caduano perrexit. Deinde, cum cateruas suas in utraque parte statuerent,
uenerunt amici eorum talique pacto pacem inter eos fecerunt ut Edelfridus
trans Humbrum, Caduanus uero citra fluuium Britanniam possideret. Cum 225
autem conuentionem suam obsidibus cum iure iurando confirmassent,
orta est tanta amicitia inter illos ut omnia sua communia haberent. Interea
contigit ut expulsa propria coniuge Edelfridus aliam duceret expulsamque
tanto haberet odio ut eam ex regno Northamhimbrorum expelleret. Porro
illa, puerum in utero habens, regem Caduanum adiuit orans ut eius 230

195 canibus *Ω*: paganis *Beda 2.20*
196 eosdem *H N G*: eisdem *cett.*: eiusdem *48 omisso* suam*: fort. excidit aliquid*
199 desperant *OSE¹ UAK*: spreuerunt *G*
204 [sui] *Σ*
205 [igitur] *GM*
210 sedem adepti sunt *Φ*
218 [omnes] *Φ*
219 sibi facerent *O N Mᶦ*

***Periit in O §§ 190.224-193.289* eos fecerunt ... arrepto quoque**

intervene to reconcile her with her husband. Edelfridus would not agree, so she remained in Caduan's chamber until she gave birth to the child she was carrying. Shortly afterwards a son was also born to Caduan's queen, who had become pregnant at the same time. The boys were brought up as befitted their royal descent, Caduan's son being named Caduallo, the other Edwinus. When they had grown into young men, their parents sent them to Salomon, king of the Armorican Britons, to learn the codes of knighthood and courtly manners in his household. He received them well and they came to know him so intimately that no one of their age at court could be a closer friend to the king or talk with him more pleasantly. Moreover in battle they often attacked his enemies before he did, their fine deeds making their bravery renowned.

191   Later, after their parents died, they returned to Britain, and, succeeding to their thrones, became as firm friends as their fathers had been. Two years after that, Edwinus asked Caduallo's permission to wear a crown and hold regular ceremonies in Northumbria, just as by ancient custom Caduallo had been in the habit of doing south of the river. They held talks beside the river Duglas and, while their advisers were determining the best course, elsewhere by the river Caduallo was reclining in the lap of a nephew of his, called Brianus. While the respective representatives were exchanging views, Brianus wept and the tears he shed dripped onto the king's face and beard. Caduallo thought that rain was falling and raised his head, but when he saw the youth was weeping, he asked the reason for his sudden sadness. Brianus replied:

> 'I must weep constantly, I and the British people, who have been harried by barbarian attack since the time of Malgo and have never yet found a leader to restore their former glory. And now you allow what little honour they have left to be undermined, since Saxon newcomers, who have always betrayed us, are set to wear a crown in the kingdom they share with us. Moreover, emboldened by the royal title, they will gain greater repute in their native land and will soon be able to invite their fellow-countrymen to come and banish our people. Since they have always been traitors and never keep their word, I think we should not honour, but destroy them. When Vortigern first received them, they stayed here under a pretence of peace, allegedly to fight on the side of our people, but, once they were able to reveal their wickedness, they repaid good with evil,

interuentione marito suo resociaretur. Cumque id ab Edelfrido nullatenus impetrari potuisset, remansit illa in thalamo Caduani donec dies partus filium quem conceperat in mundum produxit. Natus est etiam paulo post Caduano regi filius ex regina sua; nam et illa eodem tempore grauida facta fuerat. Exin nutriti sunt pueri ut regium genus decebat; quorum alter, 235 uidelicet Caduani, Caduallo nuncupatur, alius uero Edwinus. Interea, cum progressior aetas ipsos in adolescentiam promouisset, miserunt eos parentes ad Salomonem regem Armoricanorum Britonum ut in domo sua documenta militiae ceterarumque curialium consuetudinum addiscerent. Excepti itaque diligenter ab eo, in familiaritatem ipsius accedere coeperunt ita ut 240 non esset alter aetatis eorum in curia qui posset cum rege aut esse secretius aut loqui iocundius. Denique frequenter ante illum in proeliis congressum cum hostibus faciebant uirtutemque suam praeclaris probitatibus famosam agebant.

191   Succedente tandem tempore defunctis parentibus in Britanniam 245 reuersi sunt susceptoque regni gubernaculo eam amicitiam quam prius patres illorum exercere coeperunt. Emenso deinde biennio, rogauit Caduallonem Edwinus ut sibi diadema habere liceret celebraretque statutas sollempnitates in partibus Northamhimbrorum quemadmodum ipse citra Humbrum antiquo more consueuerat. Cumque inde iuxta flumen Duglas 250 colloquium facere incepissent, disponentibus sapientioribus ut melius fieri poterat iacebat Caduallo in alia parte fluminis in gremio cuiusdam nepotis sui, quem Brianum appellabant. Ac dum legati hinc et inde mutua responsa deferrent, fleuit Brianus lacrimaeque ex oculis eius manantes ita ceciderunt ut faciem regis et barbam irrorarent. Qui imbrem cecidisse ratus erexit 255 uultum suum uidensque iuuenem in fletu solutum causam tam subitae maesticiae inquisiuit. Cui ille:

'Flendum michi est gentique Britonum perpetue, quae a tempore Malgonis barbarorum irruptione uexata nondum talem adepta est principem qui eam ad pristinam dignitatem reduceret. Adhuc etiam id tantillum 260 honoris quod ei remanebat te patiente minuitur, cum aduenae Saxones, qui semper proditores eius extiterunt, in uno cum illa regno diademate insigniri incipiant. Nomine etenim regis elati, famosiores per patriam ex qua uenerunt efficientur citiusque conciues suos inuitare poterunt, qui genus nostrum exterminare insistent. Consueuerunt namque proditionem 265 semper facere nec ulli firmam fidem tenere; unde a nobis opprimendos esse, non exaltandos censerem. Cum ipsos primo rex Vortegirnus retinuit, sub umbra pacis remanserunt quasi pro patria pugnaturi, sed cum nequitiam suam manifestare quiuerunt malum pro bono reddentes

247 eorum *H N YG*
248 Edwinus *hic M, ante* Caduallonem *N, ante* rogauit *male G: om. cett.*
256 fletum *Φ*
259 [talem] *Φ*
262 extiterant *Φ*
262 regni *Σ*
263 incipiant insigniri *Φ*

betraying Vortigern and slaughtering his subjects. Then they betrayed Aurelius Ambrosius, whom they poisoned at their feast, despite the solemn vows they had made. They also betrayed Arthur when they abandoned their obligations and fought on Modred's side against him. Finally they pretended to be loyal to king Kareticus, yet summoned against him Gormundus, king of the Africans, through whose intervention our countrymen lost their land and the king was ingloriously banished'.

192 On hearing this, Caduallo thought better of the proposed agreement and sent word to Edwinus that he had been quite unable to persuade his advisers to allow his proposal to be accepted, since they declared that it was contrary to the law and the tradition of their ancestors that an island under a single crown should be subject to two crowned heads. Edwinus angrily halted the talks and returned to Northumbria, saying that he would wear the regal crown without Caduallo's permission. When Caduallo was informed, he sent him messengers to the effect that, if Edwinus dared to crown himself in Britain, he would cut off his head, crown and all.

193 Hostilities thus began between them, and their men fought many engagements. The two kings clashed beyond the Humber and in the battle Caduallo was put to flight with the loss of many thousands of men, marched through Scotland and sailed to Ireland. The victorious Edwinus led his army through the provinces of the Britons, burning cities and putting town- and countrymen to the torture. While Edwinus was giving his cruelty free rein, Caduallo tried continually to return to Britain by sea, but was frustrated because, wherever he tried to land, Edwinus met him with his army and denied him entry. For a very skilled augur, named Pellitus, had joined him from Spain, and, thanks to his understanding of the flight of birds and the movement of the stars, warned Edwinus of all impending set-backs. Forewarned of Caduallo's return, Edwinus was able to meet him, sink his ships and, by drowning his companions, close every port to him. Caduallo, at a loss and despairing of return, eventually decided to visit Salomon, king of the Armorican Britons, to ask for his help and advice on how to get back to his kingdom. As Caduallo set sail for Brittany, a great storm suddenly blew up and scattered his companions' ships so that none remained together. The captain of the king's ship immediately became so frightened that he let go of the helm, trusting to chance. In fear for their lives, they were

prodiderunt eum populumque regni saeua clade affecerunt. Prodiderunt   270
deinde Aurelium Ambrosium, cui post horribilia sacramenta una cum
eo conuiuantes uenenum potare dederunt. Prodiderunt quoque Arturum
quando cum Modredo nepote suo, postposito iure quo obligati fuerant,
contra illum dimicuerunt. Postremo, Karetico regi fidem mentientes,
Gormundum Affricanorum regem super ipsum conduxerunt, cuius   275
inquietatione et patria ciuibus erepta est et praedictus rex indecenter
expulsus'.

192   Haec eo dicente, paenituit Caduallonem inceptae pactionis mandauitque
Edwino quod nullatenus a consiliariis suis impetrare poterat ut permisissent
eum peticioni illius acquiescere; aiebant enim contra ius ueterumque   280
traditionem esse insulam unius coronae duobus coronatis submitti debere.
Iratus igitur Edwinus, dimisso colloquio, secessit in Northamhimbriam,
dicens sese sine licentia Caduallonis regali diademate iniciandum. Quod
cum Cadualloni indicatum esset, nuntiauit ei per legatos se amputaturum
illi caput sub diademate si infra regnum Britanniae coronari praesumeret.   285

193   Orta igitur discordia inter eos, cum utrorumque homines sese plurimis
decertationibus inquietauissent, conuenerunt ambo ultra Humbrum
factoque congressu amisit Caduallo multa milia et in fugam uersus est,
arrepto quoque per Albaniam itinere Hiberniam insulam adiuit. At Edwinus,
ut triumpho potitus fuit, duxit exercitum suum per prouincias Britonum   290
combustisque ciuitatibus ciues et colonos pluribus tormentis affecit. Dum
autem saeuiciae suae indulgeret, conabatur Caduallo semper in patriam
nauigiis reuerti, nec poterat, quia quocumque portu applicare incipiebat
obuiabat illi Edwinus cum multitudine sua introitumque auferebat. Venerat
namque ad eum quidam sapientissimus augur ex Hispania uocabulo   295
Pellitus, qui uolatus uolucrum cursusque stellarum edoctus praedicebat
ei omnia infortunia quae accedebant. Vnde reditu Caduallonis notificato
obuiabat ei Edwinus nauesque suas illidebat ita ut submersis sociis eidem
omnem portum abnegaret. Nescius igitur Caduallo quid faceret, cum fere
in desperationem reuertendi incidisset, tandem apud se deliberat quod   300
Salomonem regem Armoricanorum Britonum adiret rogaretque illum
auxilium et consilium quo in regnum suum reuerti quiuisset. Cumque
uela uersus Armoricam dirigeret, ruunt ex inprouiso tempestates ualidae
disperguntque naues sociorum suorum ita ut in breui nulla cum altera
remaneret. Inuasit ilico timor nimius rectorem nauis regis, quam relicto   305
regimine dispositioni fortunae permisit. Vt igitur cum periculo mortis tota

---

274 dimicauerunt *N GM, sed cf. TLL 1197.42-8*
276 [rex] *Φ*
287 inquietassent *Φ*
289 arreptoque *H D*
294 ei *AKN M*
297 accidebant *N Φ*
298 obuiauit *H AKN G:* obuiabit *U*
303 dirigerent *Φ*
306 regimine *QGM:* remige (-ger *K) Δ Σ Y*

tossed hither and thither by contrary waves all night until at dawn they came to the island of Guernsey, where they landed with difficulty. Thereupon Caduallo was seized by such grief and anger at the loss of his comrades that he refused to eat and lay sick in his bed for three days and nights. On the fourth, he longed to eat game and called Brianus, to tell him of his desire. Brianus took his bow and quiver and began to roam the island to find a beast from which he could get meat. When he had traversed the whole island without finding what he wanted, he became very anxious at not being able to satisfy his lord's wants, fearing that Caduallo's illness might lead to his death if his appetite went unsatisfied. Falling back on a novel stratagem, he cut and removed a slice from his own thigh, which he roasted on a spit and presented to the king as venison. Caduallo, believing it to be the flesh of an animal, began to eat and refresh himself, full of wonder because he had never tasted meat so delicious. Once he had finished eating, he became more cheerful and at ease, and in three days was completely cured. When a favourable wind arose, they raised the mast, set the sails and crossed the sea to the city of Kidaleta. From there they went to king Salomon, who greeted them with kindness and due respect and, on learning the reason for their journey, promised to help them, saying:

194 'Excellent youths, it grieves us that the land of our forefathers has been overwhelmed by a barbarian race and you yourselves driven out with ignominy. Other peoples can protect their kingdoms, so we are surprised that your subjects have lost so fertile an island and cannot stand up to the English, whom we hold in contempt. When the people of this new Britain of mine lived with your subjects in your Britain, it was mistress of all the neighbouring realms, and there was no one who could conquer it except the Romans. And although they subjugated it for a time, the Romans were driven out shamefully, their governors lost and slain. But after my subjects came here, led by Maximianus and Conanus, the remaining Britons never again enjoyed the privilege of maintaining uninterrupted control of their land. Many of their leaders upheld the ancient prowess of their fathers, but more proved to be weaker heirs, who forgot it completely when their enemies attacked. Thus I am grieved by the weakness of your people, since we share the same origins and you are called British, just as we are, we who bravely protect this land you see from the attacks of all its neighbours'.

nocte inter obstantes undas nunc huc nunc illuc expulsa fuit, in sequentis diei aurora applicuerunt in quandam insulam quae Garnareia nuncupatur, ubi maximo labore nacti sunt tellurem. Occupauit continuo Caduallonem tantus dolor et ira ob amissionem sociorum suorum ita ut tribus diebus 310 et noctibus cibo uesci aspernaretur ac in lecto infirmatus iaceret. Quarta deinde instante die, cepit eum maxima cupiditas edendi ferinam carnem, uocatoque Briano indicauit quod concupiscebat. At ille sumpto arcu cum pharetra coepit ire per insulam ut si casus aliquam feram offerret escam illi ex ea acquireret. Cumque eam totam peragrasset nec id quod quaerebat 315 reperisset, maximis cruciatus est angustiis quia domini sui subuenire nequiret affectui; timebat enim ne mors infirmitatem ipsius subsequeretur si appetitum suum explere non ualuisset. Vsus igitur arte noua, scidit femur suum et abstraxit inde frustum carnis parataque ueru torruit illud et ad regem pro uenatione portauit. Mox ille, ferinam carnem esse existimans, coepit ea 320 uesci et sese reficere, admirans quod tantam dulcedinem in aliis carnibus non repperisset. Saciatus tandem hilarior factus est et leuior ita ut post tres dies totus sanus fieret. Incumbente deinde congruo uento, armamenta nauis parant erectoque uelo aequoreum iter aggrediuntur et in Kidaletam urbem applicant. Deinde, uenientes ad regem Salomonem, suscepti sunt ab illo 325 benigne et ut decebat uenerati, et cum causam aduentus eorum didicisset auxilium eis in hunc sermonem promisit:

194 'Dolendum nobis est, egregii iuuenes, patriam auorum nostrorum a barbara gente oppressam esse et uos ignominiose expulsos. Et cum ceteri homines regna sua tueri queant, mirum est populum uestrum 330 tam fecundam insulam amisisse nec genti Anglorum, quam nostrates pro uili habent, resistere posse. Cum gens huius meae Britanniae una cum uestratibus in uestra Britannia cohabitaret, dominabatur omnium prouincialium regnorum, nec fuit uspiam populus praeter Romanos qui eam subiugare quiuisset. Romani autem, licet eam ad tempus subditam 335 habuissent, amissis rectoribus suis ac interfectis cum dedecore expulsi abscesserunt. Sed postquam Maximiano et Conano ducibus ad hanc uenerunt prouinciam, residui qui remanserunt numquam eam deinceps habuerunt gratiam ut diadema regni continue haberent. Quamquam enim multi principes eorum antiquam patrum dignitatem seruarent, plures 340 tamen debiliores heredes succedebant, qui eam penitus inuadentibus hostibus amittebant. Vnde debilitatem populi uestri doleo, cum ex eodem genere simus et sic Britones nominemini sicut et gens regni nostri, quae patriam quam uidetis omnibus uicinis aduersatam uiriliter tuetur'.

---

307 in sequentis, *non* insequentis *(cf. Introd. ad § 177.32)*
311 aspernebatur *C¹*: aspernabatur *C² QYM*: asperneretur *G*
313 At *HS A Y*: Ast *OCE UKND QGM (cf. Introd. ad § 130.296)*
319 parataque *H K Y*
320 eam *H AK G*
328 nostrorum *Φ*: uestrorum *Δ Σ*
343 nominemini *scripsi*: nominemur *Δ Σ, unde mox* uestri qui ... tuemur *93, 113²*: nominentur *Φ* *(cf. Introd.)*
343 nostri *H N Φ*: uestri *OCSE UAKD*

195 When he had said this and much else, Caduallo, a little abashed, replied:

'To you, a king descended from regal ancestors, I give many thanks for the promise of aid in recovering my kingdom. But though you expressed surprise that my people have not preserved the prowess of their forebears since the Britons came to these lands, it is not surprising to me. It was the most worthy men of the whole kingdom that followed Maximianus and Conanus, leaving the unworthy to take their place. And as soon as they replaced them, the unworthy, puffed up beyond their station and growing proud through their excessive wealth, began to engage in immorality unheard of even among the pagans. And, as the historian Gildas bears witness, they harboured not just this sin, but all sins to which mankind is prey, and, above all, those which suppress all virtue, namely hatred of truth and those who maintain it, love of lies and those who weave them, preference for evil in the place of good, respect for wickedness in the place of kindness and the acceptance of Satan in the place of the angel of light. Kings were anointed not for the sake of God, but because they were crueller than the rest. Then, on false pretences, they were swiftly butchered by those who anointed them, and even crueller men anointed in their place. If any of them appeared milder and a little more open to the truth, the hatred and weapons of all men would be directed against him, as if he were betraying Britain. Things that were pleasing to God and those that were displeasing were all the same to them, if indeed those that were displeasing did not have more influence. Everything they did was unhealthy, as though they had received no medicine from the true Doctor of mankind. Nor was it only worldly men who acted in this way without discernment, but also the very flock of the Lord and its shepherds. It is not therefore surprising that these reprobates, hateful to the Lord because of such wickedness, should lose the country which they had so sullied. For God wished to take vengeance upon them by allowing a foreign people to come to banish them from their ancestral fields. Yet, God willing, it would be a worthy deed to restore our countrymen to their former glory, lest people criticise our nation because we were weak leaders who did not strive for that goal in our own time. Moreover, I seek your assistance all the more confidently because we share a common ancestor. Malgo, the great king of Britain, who was Arthur's fourth successor, had two sons, Ennianus and Run. Ennianus was the father of Belin, Belin of Iago, and Iago of Caduanus, my own sire. Run was driven out by Saxon incursions after his brother's death, came here and married his daughter to duke Hoelus, son of the great Hoelus who conquered lands with Arthur. Her son was Alanus, and his son was your father, Hoelus, whose name was feared throughout France while he was alive'.

196 Caduallo spent the winter with Salomon and it was agreed that Brianus should cross to Britain and somehow kill Edwinus' augur, to prevent him from predicting Caduallo's arrival as he usually did. Brianus landed at Southhampton,

195 Postquam his et aliis finem dicendi fecit, aliquantulum uerecundans 345
Caduallo in hunc modum respondit:

'Grates multimodas tibi ago, rex regibus attauis edite, quia auxilium
michi promittis ut regnum meum recuperem. Hoc autem quod dicebas,
mirum esse gentem meam non seruasse auorum dignitatem postquam
Britones ad has prouincias uenerunt, nequaquam admirandum censeo. 350
Nobiliores namque tocius regni praedictos duces secuti fuerunt et
ignobiles remanserunt, qui ipsorum potiti sunt honoribus. Qui cum uicem
nobilium optinere coepissent, extulerunt se ultra quam dignitas expetebat
et ob affluentiam diuitiarum superbi coeperunt tali et tantae fornicationi
indulgere qualis nec inter gentes audita est. Et ut Gildas historicus 355
testatur, non solum hoc uitium sed omnia quae humanae naturae accidere
solent et praecipue, quod tocius boni euertit statum, odium ueritatis cum
assertoribus suis amorque mendacii cum fabricatoribus suis, susceptio
mali pro bono, ueneratio nequitiae pro benignitate, exceptio Sathanae
pro angelo lucis. Vngebantur reges non propter Deum sed qui ceteris 360
crudeliores extarent, et paulo post ab unctoribus non pro ueri examinatione
trucidabantur, aliis electis trucioribus. Siquis uero eorum mitior et ueritati
aliquatenus propior uideretur, in hunc quasi Britanniae subuersorem
omnium odia telaque torquebantur. Denique omnia quae Deo placebant
et displicebant aequali lance inter eos penderent si non grauiora essent 365
displicentia. Itaque agebantur cuncta quae saluti contraria fuerant ac si
nichil medicinae a uero omnium medico largiretur. Et non solum hoc
saeculares uiri sed et ipse grex Domini eiusque pastores sine discretione
faciebant. Non igitur admirandum est degeneres tales Deo ob talia scelera
inuisos patriam illam amittere quam praedicto modo maculauerant. 370
Volebat enim Deus uindictam ex ipsis sumere dum externum populum
superuenire passus est qui eos patriis agris exterminarent. Dignum tamen
esset, si Deus permitteret, ciues pristinae dignitati restituere, ne generi
nostro opprobrium sit nos debiles fuisse rectores, qui tempore nostro
in id non desudauerimus. Idem etenim nobis attauus fuit, unde securius 375
auxilium tuum postulo. Malgo namque summus ille rex Britanniae, qui
post Arturum quartus regnauerat, duos generauit filios, quorum unus
Ennianus, alter uero Run uocabatur. Ennianus autem genuit Belin, Beli
Iagonem, Iago Caduanum patrem meum. Run uero, qui post obitum
fratris expulsus fuit inquietatione Saxonum, hanc prouinciam adiuit 380
deditque filiam suam Hoelo duci, filio magni Hoeli, qui cum Arturo
patrias subiugauerat. Ex illa natus est Alanus, ex Alano Hoelus pater
tuus, qui dum uixit toti Galliae non minimum inferebat timorem'.

196 Interea, hiemante eo apud Salomonem, inierunt consilium ut Brianus in
Britanniam transfretaret magumque Edwini regis aliquo modo perimeret, 385
ne solita arte aduentum Caduallonis indicaret. Cumque in portu Hamonis

345 aliquantum *HSE Σ*
354 superbire *K YM*
356-60 non solum ... angelo lucis *uerbo caret ut apud Gildam 21.3 (cf. N. Wright apud 'Transm.'*
101-2)
373-4 generi [nostro] *Φ*
383 timorem *GM: om. OCHS Q:* terrorem *hic O², ante* inferebat *E Σ*

used a pauper's clothes to disguise himself as a beggar and made himself a sharp iron staff to kill the augur if he could. Then he journeyed to York, where Edwinus was at that time. On arriving, Brianus joined the beggars who were waiting for alms at the king's door. As he paced to and fro, his sister came out of the palace, carrying in her hand a bowl to fetch water for the queen. Edwinus had carried her off from Worcester when he was ravaging the provinces of the British after Caduallo's flight. As she passed Brianus, he recognised her immediately and, bathed in tears, called her softly. The girl heard and turned her face in his direction, though she did not recognise him at first. But, on getting closer, she recognised her brother, and nearly fainted for fear that he might by some mischance be noticed and captured by his enemies. So, forgoing kisses and family talk, she told her brother, on the pretext of saying something else, about the situation of the court and the augur he was seeking, who chanced at that moment to be strolling among the beggars, while the alms were being given to them. As soon as Brianus knew the man's identity, he told his sister to leave the palace secretly the following night and to meet him outside the city by an old temple, in the enclosure of which he would be waiting. Then he mingled with the crowd of beggars, close to where Pellitus was assembling them. As soon as he had an opportunity to strike, he raised the staff I mentioned and struck the augur in the heart, killing him instantly. Then he dropped the weapon, hid among the others, quite undetected, and so, with God's help, set off for the prearranged rendezvous. But as night fell, his sister was unable to escape despite many attempts, because Edwinus, alarmed by Pellitus' murder, had placed guards around the palace, who checked hiding-places and so prevented her getting away. On discovering this, Brianus left that region and went to Exeter, where he summoned the Britons to tell them what he had done. Then he sent messengers to Caduallo, fortified the city and told all the British chiefs to take care to protect their towns and cities and await joyfully the arrival of Caduallo, who, with Salomon's assistance, would soon come to rescue them. When this news had spread throughout the whole island, Peanda, king of the Mercians, marched to Exeter with a great horde of Saxons and besieged Brianus there.

197   Meanwhile Caduallo had landed with ten thousand knights, given to him by king Salomon, and swiftly approached Peanda's siege-lines. As soon as they came in view, he divided his knights into four groups and hurried to attack the foe. As the armies met, Peanda was immediately captured and his troops slaughtered. Peanda could only save himself by submitting to Caduallo and giving him hostages, along with an undertaking to fight the Saxons with him. Having beaten Peanda, Caduallo assembled his nobles, who had been scattered for so long, and advanced to Northumbria against Edwinus, continually ravaging the countryside. Learning of this, Edwinus

applicuisset, finxit se infra uestimenta cuiusdam pauperis pauperem fecitque
sibi baculum ferreum et acutum quo magum interficeret si illum casus
obtulisset. Deinde perrexit Eboracum; nam tunc Edwinus in eadem urbe
manebat. Vt igitur illam ingressus est, associauit se pauperibus qui ante 390
ianuam regis elemosinam expectabant. Eunte autem eo et redeunte, egressa
est soror eius ex aula, habens peluim quandam in manu ut aquam reginae
asportaret. Illam rapuerat Edwinus ex urbe Wigornensium dum post fugam
Caduallonis per prouincias Britonum desaeuiret. Cum itaque ante Brianum
praeteriret, agnouit eam continuo et in fletum solutus demissa uoce uocauit. 395
Ad uocem ergo illius faciem puella uertens dubitauit primo quis ipse esset.
At ut propius accessit, agnito fratre paene in extasi collapsa est, timens ne
aliquo infortunio notificatus ab hostibus caperetur. Postpositis igitur osculis
et familiaribus uerbis, indicauit fratri breuiter quasi aliud loquens statum
curiae et magum quem quaerebat, qui forte tunc inter pauperes deambulabat 400
dum elemosina eisdem distribueretur. Porro Brianus, ut noticia uiri usus
est, praecepit sorori nocte sequenti ex thalamis furtim egredi et ad se extra
urbem iuxta quoddam uetus templum uenire, ubi ipse aduentum eius in
crepidinibus loci expectaret. Deinde intromisit se infra turbam pauperum in
parte illa ubi Pellitus ipsos collocabat. Nec mora, cum aditum percutiendi 405
habuisset, erexit burdonem quem supra dixi infixitque magum sub pectore
atque eodem ictu interfecit. Mox, proiecto baculo, delituit inter ceteros,
nulli astantium suspectus, et praefata latibula fauente Deo petiuit. At soror,
instante iam nocte, pluribus modis egredi conata est, nec ualuit, quia Edwinus
ob necem Pelliti exterritus uigiles circa curiam posuerat, qui quaeque abdita 410
explorantes egressum ei abnegabant. Cumque id comperisset Brianus,
recessit ex loco illo iuitque Exoniam, ubi conuocatis Britonibus ea quae
fecerat notificauit. Missis postmodum ad Caduallonem legatis, muniuit
urbem illam mandauitque uniuersis Britonum proceribus ut oppida sua et
ciuitates conseruare insisterent laetique aduentum Caduallonis expectarent, 415
qui in breui, auxilio Salomonis fretus, eis praesidio ueniret. Hoc itaque per
totam insulam diuulgato, Peanda rex Merciorum cum maxima multitudine
Saxonum uenit Exoniam Brianumque obsedit.

197   Interea applicuit Caduallo cum decem milibus militum quos ei rex
Salomon commiserat petiuitque celeriter obsidionem quam praedictus 420
dux tenebat. Vt autem cominus perspexit, diuisit milites suos in quatuor
turmas hostesque suos adire non distulit. Conserto deinde proelio, captus
est Peanda continuo et exercitus eius peremptus. Cumque ipse alium
aditum salutis non haberet, subdidit se Cadualloni deditque obsides,
promittens sese cum illo Saxones inquietaturum. Triumphato itaque illo, 425
conuocauit Caduallo proceres suos, multo tempore dilapsos, petiuitque
Northamhimbriam super Edwinum patriamque uastare non cessauit. Quod

387 [pauperem] *O AKN*
395 demissa *(di- HS)* uoce *CHS:* dimissa *OE:* dimissam *Σ:* eam uoce dimissa *Φ*
396 [ipse] *Σ*
400 [tunc] *O UAK*

assembled all the subkings of the English, met him on the plain of Hedfeld, and attacked the Britons. Battle was swiftly joined, and Edwinus and almost all his men were killed, as well as his son Offridus and Godboldus, king of the Orkneys, who had come as their ally.

198   The victorious Caduallo passed through all the provinces of the English, persecuting the Saxons so relentlessly that he spared neither women nor children; indeed he wanted to wipe out the whole English race from British soil, and subjected every one of them he could find to unheard-of tortures. Then he attacked Osricus, Edwinus' successor, and killed him, his two nephews, who were to succeed him, and also his ally Eadanus, king of the Irish.

199   Once they had been killed, Oswaldus became king of Northumbria; Caduallo next turned on him and pursued him from province to province all the way to the wall which the emperor Severus had once built between Britain and Scotland. Then he sent Peanda, king of the Mercians, and most of his army there to fight him. But one night while Oswaldus was besieged by Peanda in a place called Hevenfeld, or 'The field of heaven', he raised the Lord's cross there and instructed his companions to shout with their dying breaths:

> 'Let us all kneel and together entreat the one, true, almighty God to protect us from the haughty army of the British king and its wicked leader, Peanda. For he knows that we are waging a just war for the salvation of our race'.

They all did as he said and, advancing against the enemy at dawn, won the victory their faith deserved. This news made Caduallo burn with fierce rage, and he collected an army to pursue the holy king Oswald, whom Peanda attacked and killed in a battle fought at a place named Burne.

200   Now that Oswald and many thousands of his men were dead, he was succeeded as king of Northumbria by his brother Oswi. He, by giving many gifts of gold and silver to Caduallo, who now controlled the whole of Britain, was granted peace and became his subject. Oswi's son Alfridus and nephew Oidwald immediately rebelled against him, but finding that they were having little success, fled to Peanda, king of the Mercians, whom they begged to assemble an army and

cum Edwino relatum esset, associauit sibi omnes regulos Anglorum et in campo qui Hedfeld appellatur obuiam ueniens bellum cum Britonibus commisit. Illato ocius proelio, interficitur Edwinus et totus fere populus 430 quem habebat nec non et filius eius Offridus cum Godboldo rege Orcadum, qui eis in auxilium uenerat.

198   Habita igitur uictoria, Caduallo uniuersas Anglorum prouincias peruagando ita debachatus est in Saxones ut ne sexui quidem muliebri uel paruulorum aetati parceret; quin omne genus Anglorum ex finibus 435 Britanniae abradere uolens quoscumque reperiebat inauditis tormentis afficiebat. Deinde commisit proelium cum Osrico, qui Edwino successerat, atque interemit illum et duos nepotes eius, qui post ipsum regnare debuerant, sed et Eadanum regem Scotorum, qui eis auxiliari aduenerat.

199   His itaque interfectis, successit Oswaldus in regnum Northamhimbriae; 440 quem Caduallo post ceteros inquietatum a prouincia in prouinciam usque ad murum quem Seuerus imperator olim inter Britanniam Scotiamque construxerat fugauit. Postea misit Peandam regem Merciorum et maximam partem sui exercitus ad eundem locum ut cum eo bellum consereret. At Oswaldus, dum a praedicto Peanda in loco qui uocatur Heuenfeld, id est 445 caelestis campus, quadam nocte obsideretur, erexit ibidem crucem Domini et indixit commilitonibus suis ut supprema uoce in haec uerba clamarent:

'Flectamus genua omnes et Deum omnipotentem, unum ac uerum, in commune deprecemur ut nos ab exercitu superbo Britannici regis et eiusdem nefandi ducis Peandae defendat. Scit enim ipse quia iusta pro 450 salute gentis nostrae bella suscepimus'.

Fecerunt ergo omnes ut iusserat et sic incipiente diluculo in hostes progressi iuxta meritum suae fidei uictoria potiti sunt. Quod ut Cadualloni nuntiatum fuit, acri ira ignescens collegit exercitum suum et sanctum regem Oswaldum insecutus est, et collato proelio in loco qui Burne uocatur irruit in illum 455 Peanda atque interfecit.

200   Perempto igitur Oswaldo cum multis milibus suorum, successit ei in regnum Northamhimbrorum frater eius Oswi, qui multa donaria auri et argenti Cadualloni toti iam Britanniae imperanti donans pacem eius adeptus est et sese sibi submisit. Nec mora, insurrexerunt in eum Alfridus filius eius 460 et Oidwald filius fratris sui; sed cum perstare nequiuissent, diffugierunt ad Peandam regem Merciorum, ipsum implorantes ut collecto exercitu cum

434 nec *E YG*
438 post illum *Φ*
440 Northanhimbrorum *C:* Northanhimbr + *lac. U*
441 inquietauit *UAKN*
441 [a prouincia] *Φ*
442 in Britanniam *UAKD Y*
448 unum *Ω:* uiuum *34 cum Beda 3.2*
452 [ergo] *AK G*
459 pacemque *OM*
461 diffugierunt *H K G*

cross the Humber with them to deprive king Oswi of his crown. But Peanda, being reluctant to disrupt the peace which king Caduallo had established throughout the kingdom, hesitated to open hostilities without permission, until he heard whether Caduallo himself would attack king Oswi or give Peanda permission to fight him. One Whitsun, therefore, when king Caduallo, wearing the crown of Britain, was celebrating the holiday in London along with all the kings of the English—except only Oswi—and the leaders of the British, Peanda approached the king and asked him why Oswi alone was absent, when all the Saxon chiefs were there. When Caduallo replied that he was detained by illness, Peanda said that Oswi had sent to Germany for Saxons to take vengeance on them both for his brother Oswald. He added that Oswi had singlehandedly disturbed the peace of the kingdom, stirring up war between them by attacking his son Alfridus and Oidwald, his brother's son, and driving them from their homeland. Peanda then sought permission to kill Oswi or deprive him of his kingdom.

The king, in two minds, called aside his advisers and commanded them to voice their opinion of the matter. Various suggestions were made, and then Margadud, king of the Demetae, said:

> 'My lord, since it has been your intention to drive the entire English race from Britain's shores, why change your mind and permit them to live among us in peace? Come now, let them at least wage civil war against one another, and be exiled from our country after being weakened through slaughtering each other. There is no need to show loyalty to people who are always plotting to set cunning traps for those to whom they themselves owe loyalty. Ever since they first entered this land, the Saxons have always plotted to betray our race. Why should we be true to them? Do not hesitate to allow Peanda to attack Oswi, so that they will wipe each other out in civil war and disappear from our island'.

Caduallo was persuaded by these arguments, and others like them, to give Peanda permission to attack Oswi. Peanda assembled a huge army, crossed the Humber and began to harry the king mercilessly, laying waste the provinces of his realm. Finally Oswi was compelled to promise Peanda countless royal ornaments and gifts beyond number, if he would cease ravaging the country and return home, calling off the assault he had begun. When Peanda flatly refused his plea, the king enlisted God's help; even though he had the smaller army, Oswi joined battle at the river Vunued and won, killing Peanda and thirty of his commanders. After Peanda's death, he was succeeded as king, with Caduallo's blessing, by his son Wulfred, who allied himself with the Mercian leaders Eba and Edbert to rebel

eis trans Humbrum iret regi Oswi regnum suum auferre. At Peanda, timens
pacem infringere quam rex Caduallo per regnum Britanniae statuerat,
distulit sine licentia sua inquietationem incipere donec illum aliquo 465
modo incitaret ut uel ipse in Oswium regem insurgeret uel sibi copiam
congrediendi cum eo concederet. Quadam igitur sollempnitate Pentecostes,
cum rex Caduallo diadema Britanniae portando festum celebraret Lundoniis
et uniuersi Anglorum reges praeter Oswi solum nec non et Britonum duces
adessent, adiuit Peanda regem et quaesiuit ab eo cur Oswi solus aberat cum 470
ceteri Saxonum principes adessent. Cui cum Caduallo responderet ipsum
infirmitatis causa deesse, adiecit ipse dicens illum misisse propter Saxones
in Germaniam ut fratrem suum Oswaldum in ipsos utrosque uindicaret.
Adiecit etiam illum pacem regni infregisse, qui solus guerram inter eos
inceperat cum Alfridum filium suum et Oidwaldum fratris sui filium bellis 475
inquietatos a patria propria expulisset. Petiuit quoque licentiam ut illum uel
interficeret uel a regno fugaret.

Rex igitur, in diuersas meditationes inductus, familiares suos seuocauit
praecepitque conicere quid super tali re autumarent. Conicientibus eis
plura, Margadud rex Demetarum inter ceteros dixit: 480

'Domine mi, quoniam omne genus Anglorum te ex finibus Britanniae
expulsurum proposuisti, cur a proposito tuo diuertens ipsos inter nos in
pace manere pateris? Eia ergo, permitte saltem ut ipsi inter semet ipsos
ciuilem habeant discordiam et mutuis cladibus affecti a patria nostra
exterminentur. Non est enim fides illi seruanda qui semper insidiatur ut 485
eum cui eam debet uersutis laqueis capiat. Saxones ergo, ex quo primum
patriam nostram ingressi sunt, semper insidiantes gentem nostram
prodiderunt. Quam itaque fidem eis tenere debemus? Da ocius Peandae
licentiam ut in praedictum Oswium insurgat, ut sic ciuili discordia inter
illos exorta alter alterum perimens ab insula nostra deleatur'. 490

His igitur et pluribus aliis dictis motus Caduallo Peandae licentiam dedit
congrediendi cum Oswio. Qui deinde, collecto innumerabili exercitu,
praeteriuit Humbrum et prouincias eiusdem patriae uastando praedictum
regem acriter coepit inquietare. At Oswi ad ultimum, necessitate cogente,
promisit ei innumera regia ornamenta et maiora donaria quam credi potest 495
ut patriam suam uastare desineret et praetermissa inquietatione quam
inceperat domum rediret. Cumque ille precibus eius nullatenus assensum
praeberet, rex ille, ad diuinum respiciens auxilium, licet minorem habuisset
exercitum, iniuit tamen proelium cum illo iuxta flumen Vunued et Peanda
nec non et .xxx. ducibus peremptis uictoriam adeptus est. Interfecto igitur 500
Peanda, Vulfredus filius eiusdem, donante Caduallone, successit ei in
regnum; qui consociatis sibi Eba et Edberto Merciorum ducibus rebellauit

469 reges Anglorum *O Σ*
475 [suum] *Φ*
486 [debet] *Φ*
490 deleantur *E K Φ*
494 cogente *129, 57, et sic Beda 3.24 (cf. etiam § 176.456):* coactus *H M: om. cett.*

against Oswi, but eventually made peace with him on Caduallo's orders.

201   At last, after reigning for forty-eight years, Caduallo, the most noble and mighty king of the Britons, now old and ill, passed away on the seventeenth of November. The Britons embalmed his body with balsam and spices, and with great skill placed it in a bronze effigy, moulded to his size. This they placed, armed and mounted on an impressive bronze horse, high on London's western gate, as a memorial to his great victory and to intimidate the Saxons. Beneath it they also built a church dedicated to St Martin, in which to hold masses for the king and the faithful departed.

202   His son Cadualadrus, whom Bede calls Chedualla the Younger, inherited the kingdom, which, to begin with, he ruled well and peacefully. But twelve years after he was crowned, he fell ill, and civil strife arose among the British. His mother was Peanda's paternal sister, but by a different mother, belonging to the noble line of the Gewissei; after making peace with her brother Peanda, king Caduallo had taken her as his bride and had Cadualadrus by her.

203   When, as I was saying, Cadualadrus grew ill, the Britons fell prey to disunity and laid waste their rich land in contemptible strife. Another disaster followed, a most terrible and notorious famine, which so afflicted the foolish populace that in no region could be found the sustenance of any food, save for the consolation brought by the art of hunting. After the famine came a deadly plague, which killed more people than the living could bury. The wretched survivors, leaving the country in crowds, headed overseas, repeating with many a groan, beneath their swelling sails:

'You have given us up, God, like sheep to the slaughter, and scattered us among the pagans'.

King Cadualadrus, who was also voyaging to Armorica with a sorrowful fleet, added his own lament to theirs:

'Woe to us sinners for the terrible crimes with which we never ceased to offend God when we had time to repent. His mighty retribution is upon us, to uproot from our native soil us whom neither the Romans once nor later the Scots, the Picts or the deceitful treachery of the Saxons could drive out. In vain have we so often recovered our native land from them, since it was not God's will that we should reign there for ever. When the one true Judge saw that we would never renounce our sins

aduersum Oswi sed iubente tandem Caduallone pacem habuit cum illo.
201 Completis tandem .xlviii. annis, nobilissimus ille atque potentissimus
Caduallo rex Britonum, senio et infirmitate grauatus, .xv. kl. Decembris 505
ab hoc saeculo migrauit. Cuius corpus Britones, balsamo et aromatibus
conditum, in quadam aenea imagine, ad mensuram staturae suae fusa,
mira arte posuerunt. Imaginem autem illam super aeneum equum mirae
pulcritudinis armatam et super occidentalem portam Lundoniarum erectam
in signum praedictae uictoriae et in terrorem Saxonibus statuerunt. Sed et 510
ecclesiam subtus in honore sancti Martini aedificauerunt, in qua pro ipso et
fidelibus defunctis diuina celebrarentur obsequia.
202 Suscepit itaque regni gubernaculum Cadualadrus filius suus, quem Beda
Cheduallam Iuuenem uocat, et in initio uiriliter et pacifice tractauit. At
cum duodecim annos post sumptum diadema praeterisset, in infirmitatem 515
cecidit, et ciuile discidium inter Britones ortum est. Mater eius fuerat soror
Peandae patre tantum, matre uero diuersa, ex nobili genere Gewisseorum
edita; eam memoratus rex Caduallo post factam cum fratre concordiam in
societatem thori accepit et Cadualadrum ex illa progenuit.
203 Quo igitur ut dicere coeperam languente, discordia afficiuntur Britones 520
et opulentam patriam detestabili discidio destruunt. Accessit etiam aliud
infortunium, quia fames dira ac famosissima insipienti populo adhaesit
ita ut tocius cibi sustentaculo quaeque uacuaretur prouincia, excepto
uenatoriae artis solatio. Quam uero famem pestifera mortis lues consecuta
est, quae in breui tantam populi multitudinem strauit quantam non poterant 525
uiui humare. Vnde miserae reliquiae, patriam factis agminibus diffugientes,
transmarinas petebant regiones cum ululatu magno sub uelorum sinibus
hoc modo cantantes:

'Dedisti nos, Deus, tanquam oues escarum et in gentibus dispersisti nos'.

Ipse etiam rex Cadualadrus, cum nauigio miserabili Armoricam petens, 530
praedictum planctum hoc modo augebat:

'Vae nobis peccatoribus ob immania scelera nostra quibus Deum
offendere nullatenus diffugimus dum paenitentiae spacium habebamus.
Incumbit ergo illius potestatis ultio, quae nos ex natali solo exstirpat,
quos nec olim Romani nec deinde Scoti uel Picti nec uersutae proditionis 535
Saxones exterminare quiuerunt. Sed in uanum patriam super illos totiens
recuperauimus, cum non fuit Dei uoluntas ut in ea perpetue regnaremus.
Ipse uerus iudex, cum uidisset nos nullatenus a sceleribus nostris

503 aduersus *O KD QY*
514 [Iuuenem] *QY, sed cf. Bedam 4.15 'Ceadualla iuuenis strenuissimus'*
514 [in] *CHS D QY*
517 tantum *UK² Y:* tandem *CHSE AK¹ND QG:* eodem *O:* [tantum matre] *M (cf. 'Transm.' 106)*
517 [genere] *Σ*
518 edita *8, 42, 93, 142:* edita fuerat *Ω: antea <quae> ex 48 (cf. Introd.)*
529 [et] *CHS Φ*
535 proditiones *C QG*
536 Saxonum *C: om. S¹E QG: post* quiuerunt *M*

and that no one could drive our people from its kingdom, he sent his wrath to punish our foolishness, and now we abandon our home in droves. Come back, Romans, come back, Scots and Picts, come back, ravenous Saxons; see, Britain lies at your mercy, uninhabited because of God's anger, when you could never make it so. We have been driven out not by your bravery, but by the power of the highest King, against which we have never ceased to offend'.

204 Giving vent to these and other laments, Cadualadrus landed on the coast of Armorica and, accompanied by all the refugees, went to king Alanus, Salomon's nephew, who received him well. Britain, having lost its entire population, except a few whom death had spared in the regions of Wales, was hateful to the Britons for eleven years, and during the same period unwelcoming to the Saxons, who were also dying there without respite. Those Saxons who survived when the dreadful plague was over announced, as was their unfailing custom, to their fellow-countrymen in Germany that, if they came as immigrants, they could easily occupy the island, devoid as it was of its inhabitants. On receiving the news, that wicked people assmbled a vast crowd of men and women, landed in Northumbria and filled the empty tracts of land from Scotland to Cornwall. There were no natives to stop them, save a few remaining Britons living in the remote forests of Wales. This marked the end of British power in the island and the beginning of English rule.

205 A short time passed, in which the English grew stronger. Then Cadualadrus remembered his kingdom, now free of the plague, and sought Alanus' help to restore him to his former power. The king agreed, but as Cadualadrus was preparing a fleet, an angelic voice rang out, ordering him to give up the attempt. God did not want the Britons to rule over the island of Britain any longer, until the time came which Merlin had foretold to Arthur. The voice commanded Cadualadrus to go to pope Sergius in Rome, where, after doing penance, he would be numbered among the saints. It said that through his blessing the British people would one day recover the island, when the prescribed time came, but that this would not happen before the British removed Cadualadrus' body from Rome and brought it to Britain; only then would they recover their lost kingdom, after the discovery of the bodies of the other saints which had been hidden from the invading pagans. When the blessed man had heard this, he went immediately to king Alanus and reported what had been revealed to him.

cessare uelle ac neminem genus nostrum a regno expellere posse, uolens corripere stultos indignationem suam direxit, qua propriam nationem 540 cateruatim deserimus. Redite ergo Romani, redite Scoti et Picti, redite ambrones Saxones: ecce patet uobis Britannia, ira Dei deserta, quam uos desertam facere nequiuistis. Non nos fortitudo uestra expellit sed summi regis potentia, quam numquam offendere distulimus'.

204 Vt igitur inter hos et alios gemitus in Armoricano littore appulsus fuit, 545 uenit cum tota multitudine sua ad regem Alanum Salomonis nepotem et ab illo digne susceptus est. Britannia ergo, cunctis ciuibus, exceptis paucis quibus in Gualiarum partibus mors pepercerat, desolata, per .xi. annos Britonibus horrenda fuit, Saxonibus quoque eadem tempestate ingrata, qui in illa sine intermissione moriebantur. Quorum residui, cum tam feralis 550 lues cessauisset, continuum morem seruantes nuntiauerunt conciuibus suis in Germania insulam indigena gente carentem facile illis subdendam si in illam habitaturi uenirent. Quod cum ipsis indicatum fuisset, nefandus populus ille, collecta innumerabili multitudine uirorum et mulierum, applicuit in partibus Northamhimbriae et desolatas prouincias ab Albania 555 usque ad Cornubiam inhabitauit. Non enim aderat habitator qui prohiberet praeter pauperculas Britonum reliquias quae superfuerant, quae infra abdita nemorum in Gualiis commanebant. Ab illo tempore potestas Britonum in insula cessauit et Angli regnare coeperunt.

205 Deinde, cum aliquantulum temporis emensum esset et praedictus 560 populus roboratus fuisset, recordatus Cadualadrus regni sui iam a supradicta contagione purificati auxilium ab Alano petiuit ut pristinae potestati restitueretur. At cum id a rege impetrauisset, intonuit ei uox angelica dum classem pararet ut coeptis suis desisteret. Nolebat enim Deus Britones in insulam Britanniae diutius regnare antequam tempus illud uenisset 565 quod Merlinus Arturo prophetauerat. Praecepit etiam illi ut Romam ad Sergium papam iret, ubi peracta paenitentia inter beatos annumeraretur. Dicebat etiam populum Britonum per meritum suae fidei insulam in futuro adepturum postquam fatale tempus superueniret; nec id tamen prius futurum quam Britones, reliquiis eius potiti, illas ex Roma in Britanniam 570 asportarent; tunc demum, reuelatis etiam ceterorum sanctorum reliquiis quae propter paganorum inuasionem absconditae fuerant, amissum regnum recuperarent. Quod cum auribus beati uiri intimatum fuisset, accessit ilico ad Alanum regem et quod sibi reuelatum fuerat indicauit.

552 in Germaniam (in *om. G*, Germania *M²*) *H UKD Φ*
552 [gente] *Σ*
553 conuenirent *Φ*
553-4 nefandus populus ille *Δ Φ:* quaedam nobilissima regina Sexburgis nomine quae uidua fuerat *Σ*
556 [ad] *C Y¹*
562 <et> auxilium *HSE UA QYM*
563 [id] *Σ*
567 annumeretur *CSE UKD QY:* annumeratur *G*
573 [ilico] *Σ*

206   Alanus gathered various books of prophecies, uttered by the eagle which prophesied at Shaftesbury, by the Sibyl and by Merlin, and began to consult them all to see if what had been revealed to Cadualadrus was consistent with the written prophecies. When he found that they were in agreement, he advised Cadualadrus to obey what had been ordained by God, give up Britain and do what the angelic voice had told him; but he should send his son Ivor and nephew Yni to the island to rule the surviving Britons, so that the people descended from their ancient race should not lose their freedom because of barbarian invasion. Thereupon Cadualadrus for the sake of the Lord's eternal kingdom renounced the world, went to Rome and was confirmed by pope Sergius. He suddenly fell ill and on the twentieth of April in the year of our Lord 689 was freed from the prison of the flesh and entered the palace of the heavenly kingdom.

207   Ivor and Yni assembled a fleet, gathered as many men as they could and, having landed in Britain, subjected the English to savage incursions for sixty-nine years. All was in vain, however, since the once proud race had been so weakened by plague, famine and their habitual strife that they could not ward off their foes. As their culture ebbed, they were no longer called Britons, but Welsh, a name which owes its origin to their leader Gualo, or to queen Galaes or to their decline. The Saxons acted more wisely, living in peace and harmony, tilling the fields and rebuilding the cities and towns; thus, with British lordship overthrown, they came to rule all Loegria, led by Athelstan, who was the first of them to wear its crown. The Welsh, unworthy successors to the noble Britons, never again recovered mastery over the whole island, but, squabbling pettily amongst themselves and sometimes with the Saxons, kept constantly massacring

208 the foreigners or each other. The Welsh kings who succeeded one another from then on I leave as subject-matter to my contemporary, Caradoc of Llancarfan, and the Saxon kings to William of Malmesbury and Henry of Huntingdon; however, I forbid them to write about the kings of the Britons since they do not possess the book in British which Walter, archdeacon of Oxford, brought from Brittany, and whose truthful account of their history I have here been at pains in honour of those British rulers to translate into Latin.

206 Tunc Alanus, sumptis diuersis libris, et de prophetiis aquilae quae 575
Seftoniae prophetauit et de carminibus Sibillae ac Merlini, coepit scrutari
omnia ut uideret an reuelatio Cadualadri inscriptis oraculis concordaret.
Et cum nullam discrepantiam reperisset, suggessit Cadualadro ut diuinae
dispensationi pareret et Britannia postposita quod angelicus ei praeceperat
monitus perficeret, filium autem suum Iuor ac Yni nepotem suum ad 580
reliquias Britonum regendas in insulam dirigeret, ne gens antiquo genere
illorum edita libertatem barbarica irruptione amitteret. Tunc Cadualadrus,
abiectis mundialibus propter Dominum regnumque perpetuum, uenit
Romam et a Sergio papa confirmatus, inopino etiam languore correptus,
duodecima autem die kalendarum Maiarum anno ab incarnatione Domini 585
.dclxxxix. a contagione carnis solutus, caelestis regni aulam ingressus est.

207 Cum autem Iuor et Yni naues sibi collegissent, quos potuerunt
associauerunt sibi et applicuerunt in insulam atque .lxix. annis gentem
Anglorum saeuissima inquietatione affecerunt. Sed non multum profuit.
Supradicta namque mortalitas et fames atque consuetudinarium discidium 590
in tantum coegerat populum superbum degenerare quod hostes longius
arcere nequiuerant. Barbarie etiam irrepente, iam non uocabantur
Britones sed Gualenses, uocabulum siue a Gualone duce eorum siue a
Galaes regina siue a barbarie trahentes. At Saxones, sapientius agentes,
pacem etiam et concordiam inter se habentes, agros colentes, ciuitates et 595
oppida reaedificantes, et sic abiecto dominio Britonum iam toti Loegriae
imperauerant duce Adelstano, qui primus inter eos diadema portauit.
Degenerati autem a Britannica nobilitate Gualenses numquam postea
monarchiam insulae recuperauerunt; immo nunc sibi, interdum Saxonibus
ingrati consurgentes externas ac domesticas clades incessanter agebant. 600

208 Reges autem eorum qui ab illo tempore in Gualiis successerunt Karadoco
Lancarbanensi contemporaneo meo in materia scribendi permitto, reges
uero Saxonum Willelmo Malmesberiensi et Henrico Huntendonensi, quos
de regibus Britonum tacere iubeo, cum non habeant librum illum Britannici
sermonis quem Walterus Oxenefordensis archidiaconus ex Britannia 605
aduexit, quem de historia eorum ueraciter editum in honore praedictorum
principum hoc modo in Latinum sermonem transferre curaui.

---

577 *de inscriptis cf. Introd. ad § 177.32*
586 .dclxxix. Σ
588 .lxix. *HSE UAND YM:* .xlviii. *C:* .lxxi. *K:* .lxiiii. *Q:* .lxviii. *G*
594-7 At Saxones ... imperauerant *negligenter compositum (cf. Introd.)*

INDEX OF NAMES

Compound names, such as 'Gaius Iulius Caesar', are indexed under each, but the first or commonest element receives the main entry, the others just a cross-reference. It is debatable whether compound designations of places, such as 'columpnae Herculis', 'Portus Hamonis', 'Sabrinum mare', should be given a capital for each element and indexed accordingly; entries match the text, where complete consistency has not been attempted. * marks place names or components of place names, *O. T.* figures from the *Old Testament*; partly for the sake of distinguishing homonyms, kings and queens of Britain, or of Loegria if separately ruled, are numbered in order of succession from Brutus to Cadualadrus (the five anonymous rivals at the end of § 33 and the emperor Severus in § 74 are ignored).

Only the commoner or more substantial variants of spelling are given, and not always with full documentation. Forms that occur only as orthographical variants are put in brackets. Oblique cases are given where the nominative cannot safely be inferred. The *Vita Merlini*, cited for its forms of a few names, has a thin and poor transmission; for editions see n. 51 of the Introduction.

A. Thompson's translation (London 1718) is followed by 'An explication of the ancient names of countries, cities, rivers, mountains, etc., mentioned in this history'. For sources, forms, and etymologies, see especially A. E. Hutson, *British personal names in the* Historia regum Britanniae (Berkeley 1940); J. S. P. Tatlock, *The legendary history of Britain: Geoffrey of Monmouth's* Historia regum Britanniae *and its early vernacular versions* (Berkeley 1950); B. F. Roberts, 'The treatment of personal names in the early Welsh versions of *Historia Regum Britanniae*', *Bulletin of the Board of Celtic Studies* 25 (1972) 274-90.

Ascanius 6.48, 52, 55, 54.8

Aschil(lus) 156.346, 168.256, 171.345, 178.79

Asclepiodotus (*92nd king*) 76.69, 71, 77, 78, 91, 94, 77.98, 78.122

Assarach 27.99, 107

Assaracus 7.80, 86, 8.88, 89

(Astr-) *See* Estr-

*Auallonis (*gen. or indecl.*) 147.111, 178.82

Auguselus 152.202, 156.328 (Ag-*OHSUD*), 161.502 (Ag- *S*), 168.253, 177.22, 24

Augustinus 188.176, 180, 188, 189.196

*Augustudunum 166.111, 168.237, 169.277

Augustus Caesar 64.273

Augustus (*month*) 158.427, 162.533, 164.12

Aurelius Ambrosius (*104th king*) 72.432, 93.142, 144, 94.149, 95.176, 96.234, 97.244, 99.306, 118.15, 17, 22, 119.27, 34, 120.57, 72, 121.80, 86, 88, 122.103, 123.110, 115, 117, 120, 125, 128, 125.154, 168, 126.170, 179, 128.222, 129.239, 130.281, 286, 131.300, 132.312, 316, 322, 343, 133.365, 136.402, 142.611, 152.205, 191.271

Aurelius Conanus (*108th king*) 181.105

*Azara 17.321

Azarias (*O. T.*) 29.123

*Babilonia 163.6

Babiloniensis 172.378

*Bado 30.125, 115.143, 146.81, 156.338, 168.262, 172.381

*Baiocae 176.467

Baldulfus 143.23, 31 (*app.*), 147.130

*Bangor 188.183, 189.199, 204

Bangornenses 189.211

Bangornensis 179.88

*Barba 162.533, 164.30

Basclenses 46.249

Bassianus (*89th king*) 74.32, 33, 35, 37, 75.54, 55, 58

Beda 1.3, 202.513

Beduerus 155.301, 156.348, 157.380, 165.40, 46, 93, 166.195, 167.211, 168.259, 172.364, 176.467

Beduerus (*ancestor of the last*) 176.468

Beli (*22nd king*) 35.1 (-inus *G*), 160.495, -inus 35.6, 14, 36.39, 37.49, 60, 38.65, 71, 39.74, 40.92, 41.119, 125 (Beli *H*), 149, 42.157, 43.165, 175, 179, 184, 187, 44.216, 159.469

Beli (*great-grandfather of Caduallo*) 195.378 (2)

*Belinesgata 44.224 (Belnes- *Φ*)

Belinus = Beli

Bellinus 56.39 (Beli- *EG*)

*Bithinia 163.6, 170.330, 174.435

Bladud (*son of Ebraucus*) 27.98

Bladud (*tenth king*) 30.124, 31.134

Blangan 27.102

Bledericus 189.212

Bledgabred (*70th king*) 52.360

Ferreux 33.291, 294, 297

*Flandriae 176.474

Franci 31.175, 33.296, 42.158, 82.233, 84.311, 312, 184.131

Freia 98.282

Fridei 98.282

*Frigia 163.7, 170.331

Frollo (*usually* Flollo *Q* Fullo *Y* Follo *MG*) 155.252, 259, 264, 268, 275, 283, 284, 289 (2); *cf. Vita Merlini 1100* Froll-

Fulgenius (*57th king*) 52.358 (-gent- *O*)

Fulgenius (*rebel against Severus*) (Sul-, -gent-) 74.16, 22, 27, 29, 30, 75.56

Gabaonitae (*O. T.*) 126.182

Gabius 43.164, 200, 210

Gad (*O. T.*) 27.92

Gael 27.102

Gaius Iulius Caesar 22.496, 54.1, 55.18 (2), 23, 31, 56.33, 44, 48, 57, 58, 62, 65, 71, 57.80, 83, 58.86, 90, 91, 59.103, 104, 60.107, 113, 124, 61.165, 167, 62.193, 197, 200, 207, 224, 229, 231, 232, 238, 239, 63.247, 252, 253, 260, 262, 264, 64.269, 158.421, 159.457, 466

Gaius Metellus Cocta 163.9, 170.326

Gaius Quintilianus 166.125, 137, 139

*Galabroc 76.97

Galaes (*daughter of Ebraucus*) 27.103

Galaes (*queen*) 207.594

*Galahes (*gen. or indeclin.*) 116.186 -thes *β* -es *Y* -bes *OCSHMG*), 219 (Galaes *ζY* Galabes *O lac. C om. SE*), 128.224 (-bes *OCUNDQGM* -tes

SEAKH); *cf.* Galaes

Galerannus 3.23 (*app.*)

Galfridus 3.19 (Gau- *E*), 110.21 (Gal- *S* Gaul- *Q* Gau- *cett.*), 177.1 (Gau- *EUAKDG*)

Galli 20.417, 431, 435, 440, 446, 41.122, 42.159, 58.87, 60.129, 87.360, 365, 92.126, 155.281, 169.281; *see also* Senones

*Gallia 5.24, 18.385, 19.399, 27.103, 31.183, 185, 248, 250, 40.96, 54.2, 56.75, 84.318, 320, 322, 86.348, 355, 116.178, 180, 155.252, 298, 158.423, 159.475, 166.118, 119, 123, 184.133, 195.383

*Galliae 5.35, 18.384, 27.87, 31.211, 33.295, 41.153, 42.155, 63.264, 84.309, 85.339, 120.58, 155.251, 156.327, 350, 162.526, 177.8

Gallicanus 37.63, 40.93, 58.86, 112.41, 113.79, 115.115, 132.352, 133.369, 155.258

Gallicus 16.305

(Galluc) *See* Gualauc

Ganhumara 152.209 (Guen- *or* Gwen- *all*, -hwar- *OHSEUD* -hawar- *C* -heuar- *A* -hauer- *K* -iur- *N* -nwar- *Y* -uar- *G* -war- *QM*), 164.14 (Ganhumer- *S* Gwnhaur- *E* Guenheuar- *AK* Guenhuaur- *Y*), 176.483 (Wn- *E* Guen- *AKY* Guan- *N*, -humer- *HS* -hauer- *E* -heuer- *AK* - huaur- *Y* -hunar- *Q*), 177.33 (Gun- *O* Gwn- *E* Guen- *AKY*, -humer- *HS* - hauer- *E* -heuer- *AK* -huaur- *Y*); *much the same variants occur in Carad. Lancaruan., Vita Gildae 10 (M. G. H. Auct. Ant. XIII 109), namely* Guennuuar-, Guennimar-

*Garnareia 193.308

ARTHURIAN STUDIES

Lightning Source UK Ltd.
Milton Keynes UK
UKHW020150210722
406140UK00003B/208

9 781843 832065